The Handbook of Strategic Communication

Handbooks in Communication and Media

This series provides theoretically ambitious but accessible volumes devoted to the major fields and subfields within communication and media studies. Each volume provides experienced scholars and teachers with a convenient and comprehensive overview of the latest trends and critical directions, while grounding and orientating students with a broad range of specially commissioned chapters.

Published

The Handbook of Applied Communication Research, *edited by H. Dan O'Hair and Mary John O'Hair*

The Handbook of Public Sector Communication, *edited by Vilma Luoma-aho and Maria-Jose Canel*

The Handbook of European Communication History, *edited by Klaus Arnold, Paschal Preston, and Susanne Kinnebrock*

The Handbook of Magazine Studies, *edited by Miglena Sternadori and Tim Holmes*

The Handbook of Rhetoric and Organizations, *edited by Øyvind Ihlen and Robert L. Heath*

The Handbook of Communication Engagement, *edited by Kim A. Johnston and Maureen Taylor*

The Handbook of Financial Communication and Investor Relations, *edited by Alexander V. Laskin*

The Handbook of Global Media Research, *edited by Ingrid Volkmer*

The Handbook of Global Online Journalism, *edited by Eugenia Siapera and Andreas Veglis*

The Handbook of Media and Mass Communication Theory, *edited by Robert S. Fortner and P. Mark Fackler*

The Handbook of Psychology of Communication Technology, *edited by S. Shyam Sundar*

The Handbook of International Crisis Communication Research, *edited by Andreas Schwarz, Matthew W. Seeger, and Claudia Auer*

Forthcoming

The Handbook of Peer Production, *edited by Mathieu O'Neil, Christian Pentzold, and Sophie Toupin*

The Handbook of Listening, *edited by Deborah Worthington and Graham Bodie*

The Handbook of Strategic Communication

Edited by

Carl H. Botan
George Mason University Fairfax, VA, USA

WILEY Blackwell

This edition first published 2021

Registered Office
John Wiley & Sons, Inc., 111 River Street, Hoboken, NJ 07030, USA

Editorial Office
111 River Street, Hoboken, NJ 07030, USA

For details of our global editorial offices, customer services, and more information about Wiley products visit us at www.wiley.com.

Wiley also publishes its books in a variety of electronic formats and by print-on-demand. Some content that appears in standard print versions of this book may not be available in other formats.

Library of Congress Cataloging-in-Publication Data
Names: Botan, Carl H., editor.
Title: The handbook of strategic communication / edited by Carl H Botan.
Description: Hoboken, NJ : John Wiley & Sons, Inc., 2021. | Includes bibliographical references and index. | Contents: Introduction to strategic communication, the cocreational model and the book / Carl H. Botan -- Dialogic strategic communication : a key for effective, sustainable and ethical social conflict resolution in Guatemala / Karina J. Garcia-Ruano -- Strategic rhetoric, dialogue, and the long now : a case study for long-term thinking / Micheal L. Kent & Petra Theunissen -- Strategic communication in the Turkish public sector : through the lens of public relations / B. Pinar Ozdemir & Melike Aktas -- A cocreational approach to social mediated crisis communication : communicating health crisis strategies on social media / Yan Jin & Lucinda Austin -- The cocreational view of character assassination / Sergei Samoilenko -- Co-creational perspective on strategic communication in counterterrorism / Damion Waymer -- Communicating safety in Norwegian road tunnels : a co-creational perspective of strategic communication / Sverre Kjetil Rød & Daniel Nilsson -- Strategic communication in the military : an air force perspective / Ronaldo Martinez Jr., Katrina J. Cheeseman, Nicholas J. Mercurio & Cara A. Bousie -- Strategic communication in the defense industry : grand strategy, key publics, and tactics / Michael F. Doble & David P. MacNeil -- President Obama, the affordable care act and the challenges of strategic political communication / Steven J. Farnsworth -- Strategic communication for civil society and nation building : communication for social effectiveness / Maureen Taylor & Eric J. Sommerfeldt -- Crisis communication through the lens of strategic communication / W. Timothy Coombs -- Emergency preparedness and response for human generated disasters / Emily Helsel, Timothy Sellnow & Deanna D. Sellnow -- Emergency preparedness, response and strategic communication for natural disasters / Mathew W. Seeger, Khairul Islam & Henry S. Seege -- Overcoming the deficit model by applying the CAUSE model to climate change communication / Katherine Rowan, Allison Engblom, Julia Hathaway, Rebecca Boyd, Ian Voster, Erin Z. Anderson & Karen L. Akerloff -- Organizations and participation of environmental publics : a cocreational perspective case study / Janey G. Trowbridge -- Strategic communication in religious and belief communities : lessons from Holocaust re-education / Denise Edwards-Neff -- Gender in U.S. Strategic communication research and practice : confronting the master narrative / Linda Aldoory, Elizabeth L. Toth & Liang Ma -- Strategic communication campaigns in health / Satveer Kaur-Gill & Mohan J. Dutta -- Co-creating in wonderland : communication and patient-oriented healthcare in Russia / Alexandra Endaltseva, Nelli Bachurina & Maria Mordvinova -- Bridging tobacco control advocacy and public relations theories : can strategic social networks be an answer to challenges of new tobacco control? / Jungmi Jun, Changwon Cho & Joonkyoung Kim -- Research and evaluation in strategic communication / Yi Grace Ji, Zifei Chen, Zongchao Li & Don W. Stacks.
Identifiers: LCCN 2020047092 (print) | LCCN 2020047093 (ebook) | ISBN 9781118852149 (hardback) | ISBN 9781119735335 (paperback) | ISBN 9781118857038 (pdf) | ISBN 9781118857236 (epub) | ISBN 9781118857243 (mobi) | ISBN 9781118857205 (ebook)
Subjects: LCSH: Communication in organizations. | Conflict management. | Public relations.
Classification: LCC HD30.3 .H35775 2021 (print) | LCC HD30.3 (ebook) | DDC 658.4/5--dc23
LC record available at https://lccn.loc.gov/2020047092
LC ebook record available at https://lccn.loc.gov/2020047093

Cover image: © Arthimedes/Shutterstock
Cover design by Wiley

Set in 10/12pt ITC Galliard Std by Integra Software Services, Pondicherry, India
Printed and bound by CPI Group (UK) Ltd, Croydon, CR0 4YY

C043290_050421

Table of Contents

Introduction and Authors 1

1 Strategic Communication: Field, Concepts, and the Cocreational Model 6
Carl H. Botan

Part I Strategic Communication Around the World **15**

2 Dialogic Strategic Communication: A Key for Effective, Sustainable, and Ethical Social Conflict Management in Guatemala 17
Karina J. Garcia-Ruano

3 Strategic Rhetoric, Dialogue, and the Long Now: A Case Study of Long-Term Thinking 31
Michael L. Kent and Petra Theunissen

4 Strategic Communication in Turkish Public Sector: Through the Lens of Public Relations 45
B. Pınar Özdemir and Melike Aktaş

Other chapters addressing strategic communication around the world:
Chapters 6 & 8 (Part II), Chapter 12 (Part III), Chapter 18 (Part V), Chapter 21 (Part VI)

Part II Cocreational Perspective in Strategic Communication **59**

5 A Cocreational Approach to Social-Mediated Crisis Communication: Communicating Health Crises Strategically on Social Media 61
Yan Jin and Lucinda Austin

6 The Cocreational View of Character Assassination 76
Sergei A. Samoilenko

7 **Cocreational Perspectives on Strategic Communication in Counterterrorism** 91
Damion Waymer

8 **Communicating Safety in Norwegian Road Tunnels: A Cocreational Perspective of Strategic Communication** 102
Sverre Kjetil Rød and Daniel Nilsson

Other chapters addressing the cocreational perspective:
Chapter 1, Chapter 2 (Part I), Chapter 9 (Part III), Chapter 17 (Part V), Chapter 21 (Part VI)

Part III Strategic Communication in Business, Government, and Military 111

9 **Strategic Communication in the Military: An Air Force Perspective** 113
Ronaldo Martinez Jr., Katrina J. Cheesman, Nicholas J. Mercurio, and Cara A. Bousie

10 **Strategic Communication in the Defense Industry: Grand Strategy, Key Publics, and Tactics** 129
Michael F. Doble and David P. MacNeil

11 **President Obama, the Affordable Care Act, and the Challenges of Strategic Political Communication** 147
Stephen J. Farnsworth

12 **Strategic Communication for Civil Society and Nation Building: Communication for Societal Effectiveness** 165
Maureen Taylor and Erich J. Sommerfeldt

Other chapters addressing business, government, or military:
Chapter 4 (Part I), Chapters 6, 7, & 8 (Part II), Chapter 17 (Part V), Chapter 22 (Part VI)

Part IV Crisis and Emergency Strategic Communication 179

13 **Crisis Communication through the Lens of Strategic Communication** 181
W. Timothy Coombs

14 **Emergency Preparation and Response for Human-Generated Disasters** 194
Emily Helsel, Timothy L. Sellnow, and Deanna D. Sellnow

15 **Emergency Preparedness, Response, and Strategic Communication for Natural Disasters** 208
Matthew W. Seeger, Khairul Islam, and Henry S. Seeger

Other chapters addressing crisis and emergency communication:
Chapter 2 (Part I), Chapters 5 & 8 (Part II)

Part V Social, Climate, and Environmental Strategic Communication **223**

16 **Overcome the Deficit Model by Applying the CAUSE Model to Climate Change Communication** **225**
Katherine E. Rowan, Allison Engblom, Julia Hathaway, Rebecca Lloyd, Ian Vorster, Erin Z. Anderson, and Karen L. Akerlof

17 **Organizations and Participation of Environmental Publics: A Cocreational Perspective Case Study** **262**
Janey G. Trowbridge

18 **Strategic Communication in Religious and Belief Communities: Lessons from Holocaust Re-education** **273**
Denise Edwards-Neff

19 **Gender in US Strategic Communication Research and Practice: Confronting the Master Narratives** **292**
Linda Aldoory, Elizabeth L. Toth, and Liang Ma

Other chapters addressing social and environmental issues:
Chapter 2 (Part I), Chapter 7 (Part II), Chapter 22 (Part VI)

Part VI Strategic Communication and Health **307**

20 **Strategic Communication Campaigns in Health** **309**
Satveer Kaur-Gill and Mohan J. Dutta

21 **Cocreating in the Wonderland: Communication and Patient-Oriented Healthcare in Russia** **320**
Alexandra Endaltseva, Nelli Bachurina, and Maria Mordvinova

22 **Bridging Tobacco Control Advocacy and Strategic Communication Scholarship: Tackling the Tobacco Industry's Extrinsic Corporate Social Responsibility with Strategic Networking** **336**
Jungmi Jun, Chang-Won Choi, and Joonkyoung Kim

23 **Research and Evaluation in Strategic Communication** **360**
Yi Grace Ji, Zifei Fay Chen, Zongchao Cathy Li, and Don W. Stacks

Other chapters addressing strategic communication and health:
Chapter 5 (Part II), Chapters 11 & 12 (Part III), Chapter 14 (Part IV)

Index **374**

Introduction and Authors

Strategic communication (SC) is an increasingly popular term in business and higher education. In fact, it has become a widespread term used by millions. Unfortunately, this number includes many who do not understand what SC is and many more who consciously choose to use the term as a simple marketing gimmick to justify charging more for their services or products. This makes a volume such as this all the more important to explain and give examples of what SC really is, how it is practiced at the professional level, and how it is taught in leading universities in the United States and other countries.

Being strategic in communication means first researching both the groups of people we call publics and then our clients, as well as their sometimes very complex mutual relationships. Second, we develop and implement evidence-based communication plans for improving or modifying those relationships. Practiced at its best, SC employs both elements of social scientific research and experience/judgment. Thus, the best SC practitioners are those who learn to become comfortable with a mixture of both rigorous research and deep respect for experience and the "feel" of how groups and individuals think and behave. This, then, is the unifying thread of the book, valuing and using both rigorous research and a feel for the subjective humanistic aspects inherent in the relationships between organizations and their publics.

SC is practiced across many fields, few of which call it SC. Fields ranging from public health to selling dishwashing detergent, and from public relations to religious movements all use SC, often without calling it that. Among the myriad fields that practice SC, health communication and marketing communication should hold a special position in the eyes of many because of their advanced use of research and, in the case of the former, its advanced use of theories as well. Public relations should also hold a special place because of its breadth, its economic role, and its long history. Other subfields have earned special recognition in the eyes of SC practitioners because of their scope, social contributions, and the challenges they confront.

One effect of this scattering of labels for the practice has been the perpetuation of relatively isolated islands of social practice and research, each focused on its own uniqueness rather than on the more substantial communalities they share with other SC practices. The academic community may suffer even more from this balkanization than the practitioner community, in part because colleges and universities are subdivided into departments and schools that some have called silos. Because "operating dollars" typically get divided between these on the basis of how much enrollment they attract, each patrols its content and borders fairly assiduously. For

The Handbook of Strategic Communication, First Edition. Edited by Carl H. Botan.

example, business schools may be encouraged to teach marketing communication, while PR may be taught in communication or journalism. Of course, these are coarse generalizations that apply to many schools rather than necessarily any specific one.

The practitioner SC community may, or may not suffer from some of the same kinds of subdivision into units of turf. Professional communication firms often offer a mix of services to clients that cross many of the subdivisions colleges and universities use. There seems to be an emerging tendency in both academic and practitioner domains towards adopting the term strategic communication, however. Although in both cases it is often clear that the term is being used in quite different ways, or just to attempt to modernize or dress up what is being offered.

This kind of balkanization is counterproductive because knowledge and techniques developed for one SC campaign might well inform other kinds of SC campaign. This is particularly so when the publics involved are similar.

Government bodies often also steer away from terms like strategic communication or public relations in attempting to appear non-persuasive, ignoring the fact that they have a reason – a goal – for expending funds on a campaign. In pursuing this falsehood government agencies often take the further step of adopting a model of their relationship with publics that assumes the only thing publics need to hear about is the agency's expert knowledge, sometimes called the "best available science." Publics, however, may hear this as suggesting that government officials are attempting to be persuasive about only allowing them to get the kind of information that will lead them to reach decisions that conform to the government's wants and needs. The best SC campaigns, including public health campaigns, do not assume that the real problem is a public's lack of knowledge about what the client already knows; strategic homework is required to research what publics think they need, although in some cases – such as some weather emergencies – there is no time to do that research. This assumption that SC campaigns are necessary because of a lack of knowledge in publics and markets is called the "deficit model," and is the topic of Rowan et al.

Goals of the Book

This handbook has three main goals. First, and most importantly, the book seeks to identify examples of increasingly recognized areas of thought practice in SC by presenting the thinking of more than 50 leading practitioners and scholars in the field, many using case examples. Offering the views of scholars and practitioners from a wide range of SC specialties in one book may help make sharing strategic ideas and experiences between subfields easier by making it possible to see how very similar concepts may be used under different names in different fields. Identifying primarily as separate subfields has often made it difficult for similarities in practice between fields to be noticed. For example, the practitioner-based views of Rød and Nilsson may inform the academic views of Seeger, Islam, and Seeger, and vice versa.

No one benefits from multiple SC subfields thinking and acting as if what they do is somehow not SC because they use another term for it, thus partially isolating themselves from fellow practitioners and researchers. For example, it may be hard for those who call their planned communication campaigns health communication to learn from or share with those who call their planned campaigns "political communication," or marketing communication, or public relations. Likewise, those who call their planned campaigns environmental communication may find it hard to learn from, or share with, those who call their work religious communication, in part because they may well not think to check the other literature.

Second, this book also attempts to focus attention more on where the field of SC is going than where it has been. On what is pushing our boundaries rather than on what a lot has already been written about. For example, while Doble and MacNeil or June, Cho, and Kim do address aspects of the large core subfield of marketing communication, that subfield does not get a lot of attention in this handbook because there are currently about a dozen handbooks in print for marketing communication and its subset of advertising. See Botan (2018) for more about marketing communication and advertising and the former's contributions to the cocreational model in SC. Health communication, in contrast, only has two or three handbooks currently in print and a part is dedicated to it in this book.

Additionally, the growing role of social media is clearly an important topic that is mentioned in several chapters, but is the specific focus of Jin and Austin. The growth of social media is a good thing from the point of view of the cocreational model discussed by Jin and Austin, in part because it facilitates groups and individuals organizing themselves into publics. But social media has also become such a big part of virtually every kind of SC, at both the strategic and tactical levels, that I thought it better to simply allow each author to integrate it into their own work as they saw fit.

Third, since an understanding of key terms and concepts might help readers more clearly assess what the authors say, the first chapter briefly reviews the field, its key terms and concepts, and one new model of SC that informs many of the chapters herein. A more extended economic discussion of these three areas can be found in Botan (2018).

Organization and Structure of the Book

Structure

Organizing this book was an attempt to balance two, not quite incommensurable, goals. On the one hand is the clear understanding that SC is far too large and varied a field for any one book, even a handbook, to cover. Thus, chapters were recruited that tended to suggest where emerging issues, practices, and schools of thought may be leading SC in the coming decades, rather than offering a more retrospective analysis focusing on what we have been doing in the past decades.

Thus, the book's primary organization into six parts and 23 chapters is intended to reflect newly emerging or particularly fast-growing areas of interest by grouping chapters according to their primary topic. However, there are important instances of overlap between chapters, so in addition to the chapters in each main part there is also a short list in italics at the end of each part in the table of contents identifying other chapters in the book that address the main topic of that part to some degree.

Chapters and their Grouping

Following my introductory Chapter 1, Part I of the book involves chapters that focus mostly on what may be the most important trend in SC over the last quarter century, its growth and development into specialized forms around the world. This part includes chapters from Guatemala (Garcia-Ruano, Chapter 2) and Turkey (Özdemir and Aktas, Chapter 4), both of which address the unique experiences of other countries. Chapter 3 (Kent and Theunissen) might have fitted almost as well into some other parts of the book, but because of its emphasis on long-term thinking it may help address more of the long-term orientation often required in SC campaigns in developing countries.

Part II involves several chapters that explore the use of the cocreational model, which is becoming widespread. Chapter 6 (Samoilenko) and Chapter 8 (Rød and Nilsson) could both have gone into Part I, but fit best here because of their use of the cocreational model. Chapter 5 (Jin and Austin) could clearly fit into either Part VI on strategic communication for health communication or in Part IV on crisis and emergency communication, but mostly informs the role of a cocreational perspective. Chapter 7 (Waymer) is the book's only chapter that directly addresses counterterrorism in SC. Study and training in both terrorism and counterterrorism SC is growing exponentially, so not attracting more content addressing this area of concern is a shortage in this book.

The chapters in Part III discuss the role of strategic communication and business, the government, and the military. Chapter 9 (Martinez et al.) provides a military perspective on SC, drawing on the combined experience of four currently serving military officers. Chapter 10 (Doble and MacNeil) discusses SC from the perspective of a very large defense contractor, including the key role of various publics. In Chapter 11, Farnsworth (the author of numerous books and articles on political communication) discusses some of the challenges faced by the Affordable Care Act in the United States, so this chapter could also have fit well in Part VI. Finally, Chapter 12 (Taylor and Summerfeldt) addresses SC for nation building and civil society development. No less than seven chapters in other parts of the book would also have fitted well into this Part, and Chapter 12 could have fitted smoothly into Parts I or VI.

The chapters in Part IV cover crisis and emergency strategic communication. Chapter 13 (Coombs) differentiates between tactical level and strategic level responses to crisis. The distinction between tactical and strategic level communication is a key issue throughout this handbook, making this chapter relevant to much of the rest of the book. Chapter 14 (Helsel, Sellnow, and Sellnow) is particularly well timed given the recent COVID-19 pandemic and other contagions around the globe – providing a broad discussion of biosecurity. Chapter 15 (Seeger, Islam, and Seeger) addresses the role of SC in naturally occurring disasters. Like Coombs, these authors also differentiate between tactical and strategic level responses. Several other chapters could also have fitted into this part, particularly Chapters 2 and 8, both of which include discussions of how government bodies can or should respond to crises and emergencies, and Chapter 5, which is readily applicable to crises resulting from emergency situations because it explains much of the role of social media in such situations.

Part V addresses the very broad, and extremely rapidly growing area of Social climate and environmental strategic communication. Chapter 16 (Rowan et al.) challenges the widely adopted deficit model that is used as a default assumption in many, if not most, environmental, climate, and health campaigns. The authors call for replacing the deficit model with the cause model. Chapter 17 (Trowbridge), which would also have fitted into Part III as an example of government agency communication, or Part II because it seeks to apply the cocreational model. Chapter 18 (Edwards-Neff) examines the use of SC by and about religious and faith communities. The chapter discusses SC related to the Holocaust against Jewish communities, and draws on framing and other theories. Finally, Chapter 19 (Aldoory, Toth, and Ma) addresses arguably the broadest question regarding SC in the social context of gender. They argue for a "multifaceted perspective on gender and power" with which to better understand and thus use SC. They draw on multiple theoretic perspectives and a case example. Among related chapters, Chapter 2 also informs Part V because of its emphasis on social and environmental communication, and the same could be said for Chapter 22. Chapter 7 also informs this Part because it uses a cocreational perspective to explain the role of SC in both counterterrorism and terrorism efforts.

Part VI on strategic health communication takes on another very fast-growing fear area, even before the worldwide COVID-19 pandemic. Health communication is the third of the three big subfields of SC. Chapter 20 (Kaur-Gill and Dutta) kicks this Part off with a detailed breakdown of the parts of health communication campaigns focusing on the planning and execution of campaigns and, particularly, on formative campaign research and intervention strategies. Chapter 21 (Endaltseva, Bachurina, and Mordinova) discusses Russian health communication today, with an emphasis on the meaning-making strategies employed and the effects of mismatches between different sectors of health providers in Russia. Chapter 22 (June, Cho, and Kim) then examines how socially responsible the SC efforts of leading companies in the tobacco industry have been, particularly with respect to their pseudo-activism. Finally, Chapter 23 (Ji et al.) provides a wide-ranging discussion of research methods in SC, including explaining basic concepts such as measurement and data. This chapter could have fitted into other Parts of the book, but since health and marketing communication are arguably two subfields with the best record of consistently using research in campaign planning, this part is a reasonable home for the chapter even though it does not address health communication per se.

Reference

Botan, C. H. (2018). *Strategic communication theory and practice: The cocreational model.* Hoboken, NJ: Wiley-Blackwell.

1

Strategic Communication
Field, Concepts, and the Cocreational Model

Carl H. Botan
George Mason University

This chapter has three goals. First, it offers a very brief outline of the field of strategic communication (SC). Second, it introduces and defines key terms and concepts in SC. Third, it introduces the cocreational model that influences several later chapters. In doing so, this chapter draws on work previously published by the author in 2018, also with Wiley-Blackwell (Botan, 2018).

One challenge faced by any book about SC is that SC is practiced mostly in two kinds of organization. The first is organizations that have a primary purpose of conducting SC campaigns. The core work of an organization, what it exists to do, is sometimes called the "line function" of the organization. Examples include PR firms, advertising firms, and some government health communication agencies. "whose primary or line function is SC." For SC practitioners, the advantage of working in these firms is clear. Practitioners in this kind of organization work in an environment where the importance of SC work is highly valued when it comes to pay and promotions.

In contrast many, probably most, SC practitioners work in organizational cultures where something other than communication campaigns is the core function of the organization, its economic lifeblood. For example, they might work in a school system, digital provider, agriculture, or petroleums. In such cases, the practitioner is not at the center of the organization and is not the line function of the organization. Here SC may just be a support or staff function, as opposed to a line function. In these organizations, the value of SC work may not be fully understood and can be harder to measure than in organizations where SC is the line function. These practitioners may have to expend time and effort explaining what they do. Maybe more importantly, various kinds of SC work are often given different names. For example health and safety campaigns and HR benefits campaigns may be run out of different departments and under different names. So it can be hard to transfer ideas or employment between divisions of SC that conduct similar campaigns under very different names.

Strategic Communication Concepts and Terms

The term strategic communication may often be used mistakenly simply because it is a modern buzz term of the first rank. It is also sometimes intentionally used for puffery, or to make one's work product sound more important than it really is, thus allowing them to charge more than

The Handbook of Strategic Communication, First Edition. Edited by Carl H. Botan.

if the term "strategic" were not used. It can also be used in good conscience by someone working as part of an SC campaign, such as a large marketing campaign, who mistakenly assumes that if they are working on a large complex campaign it must be strategic.

There is no one simple test, no single line to cross, in creating or identifying a strategic versus non-strategic campaign. But there are some key concepts that can be used to differentiate strategic from non-strategic communication campaigns. The next part of this section discusses six key concepts: information, strategic information, strategic communication, grand strategy, strategy, and tactics. Then, the relationships between the latter three.

Information

Information has been defined in many ways, for example Buckland (1991) distinguishes between information as process, information as knowledge, and information as thing. However, the most useful definition for those in SC is probably the very common view that information is something that reduces uncertainty (Daft & Lengel, 1986; Grahramani, 2006; Shannon & Weaver, 1963/1998). For example, if someone comes to you and tells you something you already know that does not serve as information to you but if they tell you something you did not know that provides you with new information by reducing your degree of uncertainty about a fact or situation.

Strategic Information

One issue that remains is that not all information contributes to any one SC campaign because not all uncertainty reduction applies to any one SC campaign. The uncertainty most important in SC is that which directly addresses the strategic needs of a campaign, particularly that which reduces uncertainty about how the publics think and feel about a client and the relationship that the client shares with their publics. This information has strategic value to a campaign planner, so it can be called strategic information to differentiate it from facts or data about things that do not impact the relationship between a client and publics.

Strategic Communication

There are many kinds of communication, which again, not all of are strategic. Here the term strategic communication is reserved for campaigns with two minimum characteristics. First, research is conducted about the environment and the situation in which a campaign is to be carried out. This research has to assess, again at a minimum, the current opinions of the significant publics including an assessment of how the purpose, or goals, of a proposed campaign comport with the reality on the ground. Second, a plan is developed encompassing available resources, timing, sequencing of steps, and assignments that takes into account both the goals of the organization and the feelings, needs, and attitudes of the publics. This plan is the actual strategy. A third possible characteristic is some kind of evaluative process centered on assessing differences between the starting and ending views and plans of the relevant publics. This is not strictly necessary for SC to exist but it is for skills to grow, and changes in the publics and external influencers to be adjusted for. Such an evaluation often also constitutes at least part of the research phase for another future campaign. The actual definition of SC used in the 2018 book is that

> SC is the use of information flowing *into* the organization (research) to *plan* and carry out a communication campaign addressing the relationship between an organization and its publics. SC is research based and public centered rather than organization or message centered. (p. 8)

Further distinguishing between grand strategy, strategy, and tactics may help better explain the terms used here.

Grand Strategy

Grand strategy is the setting of policy, treaties, goals, and the like and is most easily seen in the case of a nation. Grand strategy is the domain of high government bodies that make treaties, set out policies, delineate goals, and apportion budgets. These act as directives for subordinate bodies such as the military and various ministries or departments. By analogy, in organizations where most SC campaigns are conducted, the policy level is the Board, CEO, President, or Executive Committee. These also set out policies, delineate goals, and apportion budgets, and set other parameters for SC campaigns that are conducted at the next level.

Strategy and Tactics

The literature on strategy is written from perspectives as different as business, military, religion, and politics, so it is not surprising that some authors might disagree on what strategy is. For example, although some have sought to draw a distinction between strategy and a plan (Mintzberg, 1994), many more tend to use the terms almost interchangeably. For most, a strategy is a plan, authorized by a decision at the policy level, the building of which takes into account at least current circumstances or conditions, a goal, and a set of steps for getting from the current situation to the goal. For example, Kay, McKiernan, and Faulkner (2003) state: "the definition of the objectives of the firm is the key to strategic formulation" (p. 28), which involves "information which a company can assemble about its environment and about itself" (p. 25).

As it is used in SC, we can define strategy as "the campaign level planning and decision making involving maneuvering and arranging resources and arguments to meet the needs of publics and organizational grand strategies" (Botan, 2018, p. 14). One could also think of strategy as a roadmap on which a plan for a trip can be laid out, while the actual driving is the tactic used to carry out that plan. Strategies are only a plan, an idea. It is the tactic that gives them substance. Thus, a strategy is not "better" or "higher" than the tactics because a plan is only an idea, without substance, unless given form and function through tactics.

Thus, tactics can be defined as "the specific activities and outputs through which strategies are implemented – the doing or technical aspects" (Botan, 2018, p. 14).

Relationship of Grand Strategy, Strategy, and Tactics

The relationship between grand strategy, strategy, and tactics is based on understanding level of analysis. Strategic communicators work at the level of the communication campaign. Grand strategy is a property of the higher policy level in relation to our campaign. Tactics are the actual implementation of the parts of a plan, so tactics are, in turn, subordinate to strategy. One's position in this relationship, so strategy is subordinate to grand strategy can alter what is seen as strategy or tactics. For example, a higher authority may assign an SC department to plan a campaign that is strategic-level work for the SC department but maybe just tactical-level work from the perspective of the higher authority. Put another way, the level of analysis can differ depending on one's position and role in a hierarchy but the level of analysis for SC itself does not vary, it remains at the campaign level.

Thus, strategy gets it guidance from the policy (grand strategy) level and strategy can have one or several subparts that can be thought of as sub-strategies. However, the only strategy or sub-strategies created should be necessary for addressing the policy in question. There should not be any of what I call "orphan strategies," sub-strategies that are not directly part of responding to the policy/grand strategy. Likewise, a strategy may require from one to several tactics to implement it. However, there should never be orphan tactics that do not directly implement one or more strategies.

Finally, we can think of authority as moving downward from the policy level to the strategic level, and finally to the tactical level. Each is subordinate to those above it. But we can also think of concreteness, or "reality," as flowing upward. Without actual tactics being applied both strategy and policy are just ideas, or wishes, without substance of their own.

Cocreational Model

Background

Botan and Taylor (2004) and Taylor and Botan (2006) introduced a model that they hoped would be the starting point for a change of assumptions and attitudes for many practitioners of SC. This cocreational model did not introduce new parts of the relationship with publics but was an attempt to depict what the present author had learned in the practitioner phase of his career that had changed his assumptions about the importance of some parts of that relationship. These authors sought to advocate a fundamentally different way of thinking about SC campaigns. In this sense, the cocreational model is close to serving as a normative theory in the way that Strough, Parker, and deBruin (2015) used the term when they said a normative theory is characterized by offering prescriptions or recommendations. Normative theories, they said, define "good decisions as one that most likely … provide the decision maker with [the] desired outcome" (p. 235).

Cocreational Scholarship

The cocreational school of thought was originally presented as a way to summarize the shift we thought we saw occurring in the literature over the last quarter century or so, saying "view[ing] publics as cocreators of meaning and communication is what makes it possible to agree to shared meanings, interpretations, and goals" (Botan & Taylor, 2004, p. 652). Publics, then, cocreate new meanings both individually and as publics by using their own knowledge and experience and the information they get from campaigns. The key aspect of this process of meaning cocreation is that the collective knowledge and experience of a public far outweighs the content of any one, or even many, SC messages in the meaning-making process in which publics engage. Indeed, as the line thicknesses in the modified cocreational model shown in Figure 1.1 suggest, except in rare circumstances, an SC campaign might best be thought of as accounting for no more than 10% or so of the outcome of that campaign – and often far less.

Marketing communication, in particular, has seen some of its followers embrace the idea of value cocreation. From this marketing perspective, value only comes into being when publics give a good or service value by buying it (Bhala, 2010; Edvardsson, Tronvoll, & Gruber, 2011; Prahalad & Ramaswamy, 2004a, 2004b, 2004c; Vargo, Maglio, & Akaka, 2008). These authors have used a publics centered view of value as the outcome of most interest in marketing by suggesting that whenever a product is brought to market, the producer is essentially asking if any public sees value in it. No takers means no value and those products may have to be written off. (The value other publics cocreate in other SC specialties, such as health communication, may be deciding to adopt new health behaviors rather than buying a product.)

Additionally, as I said in 2018:

> Health Communication has also contributed [to] cocreational work done, although much of it is marketing oriented. For example Nambisan and Nambisan's (2009) article, "Models of Consumer Value Cocreation in Health Care" is clearly marketing oriented as is McColl-Kennedy et al.'s article from 2012, "Healthcare Customer Value Cocreational in Practice Styles." Halkes' (2014) publicly available PowerPoint presentation is a little less marketing focused even though the author describes themselves as a consultant to pharmaceutical firms. There has also been non-marketing oriented work in Health Communication such as Elg et al. (2012) and Wallace et al.'s (2012) book *Cocreating Health: Evaluation of the First Phase*. Some works in the general field of communication (e.g., Stadler, 2013) also use the Corporation construct. (p. 42)

Thus, the cocreational view is far from new and has been used in various ways for some time. Indeed, scholarship in business management has used the term, and the concept, in the same way as it is used in this chapter for some time.

The cocreational view recognizes that there are many relationships of interest to public relations, some more important than others. But the relationship of central importance is the shared creation of meeting between members of the public. Further, the cocreational view sees what publics think and feel as the starting point for strategic planning in communication. Therefore, the cocreation view can also provide a scale by which to evaluate other theories in SC. The cocreational view asks how well a given theory opens a window into the social meaning-making process going on within publics, as well as between organizations in their publics. In this sense, the cocreational view can play the role of a meta-theory – a theory about how to evaluate other theories.

Cocreational Molecule

This final subsection of the chapter presents and explains a visual model of the procreational molecule (Figure 1.1). The molecule metaphor is used because others have used the idea to explain aspects of communication (e.g. Bradac, Mulac, & Thompson, 1995), and because many things with multiple parts or relationships can be a bit hard to understand as a whole unit without a visual depiction. Additionally, a molecule is the smallest way to depict a complex whole and all its constituent parts.

As I acknowledged in 2018, the elements of the cocreational molecule are not new, but what is new is the realization that (a) the publics are the main force in SC because theirs is the decision-making role and (b) the essence of strategy in SC is planning based on knowledge of the "lay of the land" – other forces in the environment and how these factors interact with each other and the resources, capabilities, and history of the planner (Botan, 2018, p. 47).

The molecule has three kinds of element. Circles represent behaviors of publics, while rectangles depict organizational behaviors, and lines represent the relationship between elements. The rectangle around boxes 2, 3, and 4 represents what the SC practitioner and client can control, or at least directly influence. Thus, the practitioner only controls, or directly influences, a part of the overall relationship. Suggesting otherwise to a client can be an ethical issue, and a client hoping an SC practitioner can do more than that is, at best, naive.

Circle 1 depicts a public before the organization begins to act. There is information, perhaps strategic information, available about both individual and group meanings, goals, beliefs, values, and views about the public's relationship with its environment, including the client. Note the three lines emanating from the public to the parts of an SC campaign that the publics can influence. The dashed line from circle 1 to box 2 indicates that research is often missing

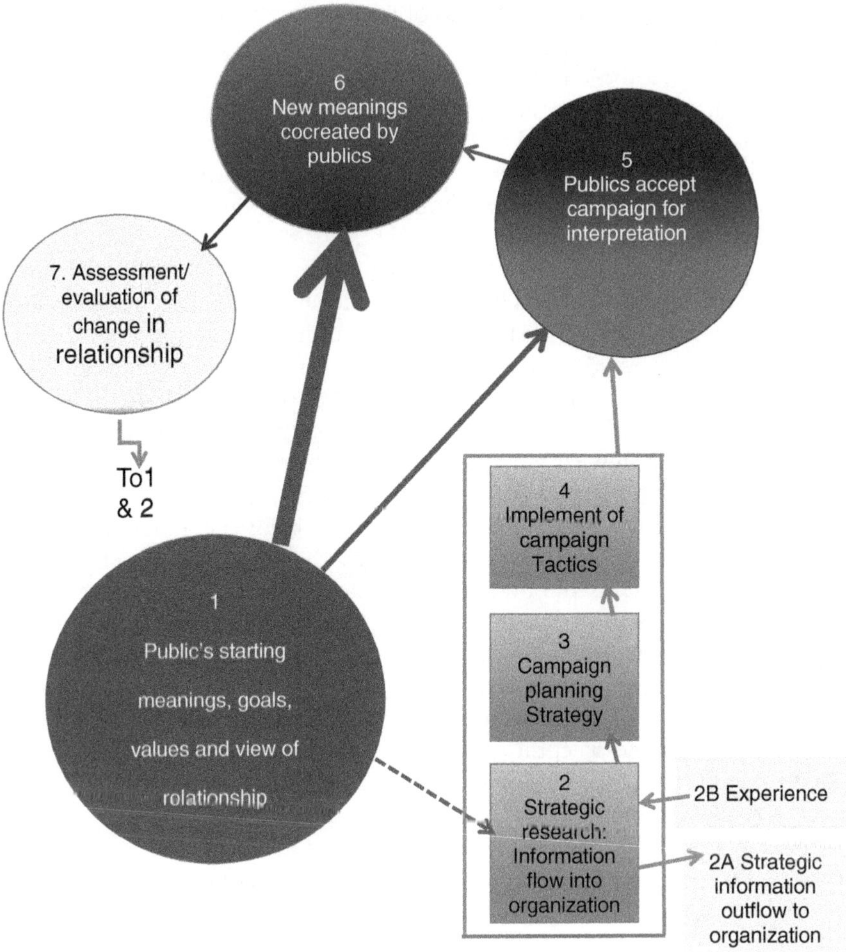

Figure 1.1 Cocreational molecule.

in campaigns, particularly those based on the deficit model (see Chapter 16) which privileges the knowledge of campaign sponsors and often lacks in publics centered strategy. Other times research may be limited to just experience from past campaigns or perfunctory research. Publics constantly evolve and change over time so even experience, which is of great value in SC, can become stale if not refreshed by new research periodically. To serve a strategic function, it is often wise for research to include some open-ended qualitative items in which publics have the opportunity to express what is on their mind, in addition to items designed to elicit information on things the researchers want to ask about.

The narrow arrow from box 4 to circle 5 depicts the sole point at which the practitioner can influence the meaning cocreation process of publics. The narrowness of this line compared to the three lines emanating from circle 1 *combined* roughly reflects how much influence an SC campaign has on the outcome compared to what publics bring to the final decision-making process. In this case, the practitioner influence is about 1/10 to 1/8 as strong as the influence publics bring to the relationship. These approximate arrow sizes were chosen to roughly reflect that the published literature reports on the actual success rate of several kinds of campaign (see Botan, 2018). The meanings publics share about their relationship to a campaign's content and sponsors before the campaign starts are typically the single best predictor of what the results of the campaign will be, regardless of how skilled the practitioner is or how much media coverage is earned or paid for.

This does not mean that the experience (box 2B) and insights of seasoned practitioners are unimportant. Again, experience is very important, in part because it often suggests some familiarity with how publics think and feel on a subject, possibly because experienced practitioners may have learned from both successes and mistakes earlier in their careers. Understanding how one or more publics are likely to feel about a particular campaign is part of the "art" of the SC that comes from experience.

Box 2A represents the sharing of strategic information gathered in the SC process with other elements of the organization, including the leadership responsible for overall organizational policy making, and is a kind of strategic information as discussed earlier in this chapter.

Campaign planning for box 3 is where the actual plan/strategy is developed. This, like any strategy, is essentially a new mini-theory about how best to get publics to attend to a campaign and then be influenced by it. The strategy includes "the logic of a campaign; *what* is to be said, *how* it will be said, in what *order*, to *whom*, and *when*" (Botan, 2018, p. 5). After all, it is still publics that decide whether these new mini-theories are adopted or rejected.

Box 4, campaign implementation, is the tactical component (i.e. units of work) in a campaign and is typically the only part of the campaign that publics experience and can also respond to. Thus, it represents the practitioner's sole bite at the apple. Some practitioners discussed above sometimes try to jump straight to this box because they believe they know what is best for these people, so content decisions only have to be based on their own expertise. This assumption is often partially responsible for unnecessarily poor success rates.

After publics see, or hear, campaign contents they issue their first verdict – whether they understand the campaign and accept it enough to invest time and effort into paying attention to it and understanding it (circle 5). Some campaigns fail to pass this first hurdle and, so they, have no – or virtually no – potential for success. Many publics today live and work in a dense fog of SC campaigns from commercial advertising, to guidance or directional messages, to the often breathless claims of political messages and social or religious campaigns. Thus, many members of publics use this first campaign hurdle to eliminate 90% or more of campaigns from their consideration; so understanding this stage is almost a necessary survival skill. SC campaigns in emergency situations may be able to adopt a "this is what you need to know from us" strategy in their campaigns, but they still have to pass the test of whether publics agree with them enough to attend to the campaign.

Actually deciding whether to accept the campaign (circle 6) is strictly the domain of publics. The SC practitioner already got their bite at the apple when they converted their strategy into tactics and presented their campaign. From then on, publics decide how well the campaign content, *and* the relationship implied in every campaign, fit with their own experience, values, and goals and, by mixing the contents of the campaign with what they brought to the relationship, create new meanings (using a mix of maybe 90% their own ideas, values, and experiences with maybe 10% campaign content). Of course, these decisions serve as a kind of campaign evaluation for publics and then constitute part of circles 5 and 6 for the next campaign from that campaign sponsor or on that topic. Thus, a poor choice of strategy, and therefore poor tactics, in one campaign prejudices a succeeding campaign's chances of success. Thus, as important as researching publics before determining strategies and tactics is, it is even more critical if the sponsor hopes to develop a relationship with that public or to revisit the topic with that same public. This is part of why campaign assessment by practitioners needs to include qualitative and quantitative elements, both for reporting to campaign sponsors and contributing to detailed planning for the next campaign. Note that while some very good practices, such as message testing, are useful in boxes 3 and 4, and may contribute to evaluation, of circle 5 they do not constitute a thorough evaluation in and of themselves.

References

Bhala, G. (2010). *Collaboration and cocreation: New platforms for marketing and innovation.* New York: Springer.

Botan, C. H. (2018). *Strategic communication theory and practice: The cocreational model.* Hoboken, NJ: Wiley-Blackwell.

Botan, C. H., & Taylor, M. (2004). Public relations: The state of the field. *Journal of Communication*, 54(4), 645–661.

Bradac, J. J., Mulac, A., & Thompson, S. A. (1995). Men's and women's use of intensifiers and hedges in problem-solving interaction: Molar and molecular analysis. *Research on Language and Social Interaction*, 28(2), 93–116.

Buckland, M. K. (1991). Information as a thing. *Journal of American Society for Information Services*, 42(5), 351–360.

Daft, R., & Lengel, R. (1986). Organizational information requirements, media richness and structural design. *Management Science*, 32, 554–571.

Edvardsson, B. E., Tronvoll, B., & Gruber, T. (2011). Expanding understanding of service exchange and value co-creation: A social construction approach. *Journal of the Academy of Management Science*, 39, 327–339.

Elg, M., Engström, J., Witell, L., & Poksinska, B. (2012). Co-creation and learning in health care service development. *Journal of Service Management*, 23(3), 328–343.

Grahramani, Z. (2006). Information theory. In *Encyclopedia of cognitive sciences*. New York: Wiley. doi: 10.1002/0470018860.s00643

Halkes, R. (May 2014). "Co-creation" and "experience co-creation" in health care: Introduction. Health Business Consult. Set of PowerPoints retrieved from http://www.slideshare.net/ARJHalk/cocreation-and-experience-cocreation-in-care

Kay, J., McKiernan, P., & Faulkner, D. (2003). The history of strategy and some thoughts about the future. In D. O. Faulkner and A. Campbell (Eds.), *The Oxford handbook of strategy. Volume 1: A strategy of overview and competitive strategy*. Oxford: Oxford University Press.

McColl-Kennedy, J. R., Vargo, S. L., Dagger, T. S., Sweeney, J. C., & van Kasteren, Y (2012, May 1). Health care customer value cocreation practice styles. *Journal of Service Research*. doi: 10.1177/1094670512442806

Mintzberg, H. (1994). The fall and rise of strategic planning. Harvard Business Review, Jan/Feb, 107–114.

Nambisan, P., & Nambisan, S. (2009). Models of consumer value cocreation in health care. *Health Care Management Review*, 34(4), 344–354.

Prahalad, C. K., & Ramaswamy, V. (2004a). Co-creation experiences: The next practice in value creation. *Journal of Interactive Marketing*, 18(3), 5–14.

Prahalad, C. K., & Ramaswamy, V. (2004b). *The future of competition: Co-creating unique value with customers*. Boston, MA: Harvard Business School Press.

Prahalad, C. K., & Ramaswamy, V. (2004c). Co-creating unique value with customers. *Strategy & Leadership*, 32(3), 4–9.

Shannon, C., & Weaver, W. (1963/1998). *The mathematical theory of communication*. Urbana, IL: University of Illinois Press.

Stadler, S. (2013). Speaker or listener or speaker and listener: Why intercultural interaction demands a dual role-relationship. *Language & Dialogue*, 3(2), 167–185.

Strough, J., Parker, A. M., & deBruin, W. (2015). Understanding life-span development changes in decision making competence. In T. Hess, J. Strough, & C. Lockenhoff (Eds.), *Aging and decision making: Empirical and applied perspectives* (pp. 235–257). New York: Academic Press.

Taylor, M., & Botan, C. (2006). Global public relations: Application of a cocreational approach. In M. Watson (Ed.), *Proceedings of the 9th International Public Relations Research Conference: Changing Roles and Functions in Public Relations* (pp. 484–491). Miami, FL: University of Miami Institute for Public Relations.

Vargo, S. L., Maglio, P. P., & Akaka, M. A. (2008). On value and value co-creation: A service systems and service logic perspective. *European Management Journal*, 26(3), 145–152.

Wallace, L. M., Turner, A., Kosmala-Anderson, J., Sharma, S., Jesuthasan, J., Bourne, C., & Realpe, A. (2012). *Co-creating health: Evaluation of the first phase*. London: The Health Foundation.

PART I

Strategic Communication Around the World

2

Dialogic Strategic Communication
A Key for Effective, Sustainable, and Ethical Social Conflict Management in Guatemala

Karina J. Garcia-Ruano
Universidad Rafael Landívar de Guatemala

Introduction

The contemporary communication industry emerged in the Guatemala region within a highly convulsive context, reflecting an interdependent relationship between democratic transition and social conflict at the end of the twentieth century. The demand for communication services grew in response to the new spaces that opened up for political dialogue and businesses with the advent of democracy in the mid-1980s. At the same time, more communication services were required to deal with social unrest and continuous conflicts among diverse social actors who had to remain silent during decades of repression and systematic censorship in the country (Garcia-Ruano, 2009). After three decades of democratic upsurge in Guatemala, there is ample evidence that (a) despite multiple efforts to effectively manage the social conflicts in the country, most of them have failed; and (b) although communication between confronting actors is not the only factor, it is one of the key factors to achieve the keenly awaited effectiveness in conflict management in this clashing environment.

Communication practitioners who have experienced the democratic transition in Guatemala acknowledge that the conflicting context of the country offers both opportunities and obstacles for the evolution of the profession. The censorship and political persecution that limited professional communication during dictatorships has almost completely disappeared. Traditional areas of strategic communication (SC) – such as public relations, formerly reduced to the superficial handling of press or publicity – have evolved to a more professional state that includes more strategic, comprehensive approaches to relationship management. Different from what happened during the years of war, actors involved in conflicts are now sitting together to address their problems and try to find solutions.

However, despite the general advances in professional communication in Central America, practitioners state that there is deadlock when it comes to contributing to the resolution of conflicts, especially in managing effective processes of dialogue, negotiation, and fulfillment of commitments (Garcia-Ruano, 2009). Even though the need for dialogue is acknowledged, the process gets blocked when it is required to move from the mere statement of needs and agreements to the fulfillment of commitments for the sustainable resolution of conflict.

Reports on social conflict in the region (United Nations Development Programme, 2013) have evidenced the ineffectiveness of the dialogues and negotiations at a local, national, or

The Handbook of Strategic Communication, First Edition. Edited by Carl H. Botan.

regional level, which hinders any communication effort. Paradoxically, despite the fact that the recent arrival of democracy has given voice to the different social actors, it seems that the dialogic interaction and the agreements on how to make progress in this transition are not achieved.

This chapter uses the example of the socioenvironmental conflict that emerged in Guatemala during the last two decades (2000–2018) to argue that SC, through a dialogic and participatory approach, could offer not only an effective but also a sustainable and ethical path to manage social conflict in unsteady environments. The first section of the chapter provides a country profile of Guatemala and describes the socioenvironmental conflict around the use of natural resources for industrial projects (e.g. mining, energy, agroindustry) that has confronted various actors (i.e. corporations, Mayan communities, government, nongovernmental organizations) at different levels (local, national, international) with regrettable consequences in the absence of a settlement (closure of investment projects, social leaders' repression and persecution, state of siege and deaths). The second section of the chapter discusses the role of SC for effective management of the socioenvironmental conflict in Guatemala and why the traditional approach that has been used by different actors has not been able to provide successful results. In the third section of the chapter, the author advocates for implementing alternative, dialogic communication approaches, such as development communication (Beltran, 2006; Gularte & Ozaeta, 2012) and the cocreational model (Botan, 2018) for effective, sustainable, and ethical management of the socioenvironmental conflict in Guatemala. Finally, the fourth section of the chapter draws some conclusions and discussion questions with the aim of continuing the conversation to strengthen the study and practice of dialogic SC in diverse clashing environments around the globe.

Guatemala: Old Problems, New Conflicts

Developing countries, characterized by fledgling democracies, low human development, and social exclusion, provide a breeding ground for social conflicts. Countries of the so-called Northern Triangle of Central America (the subregion formed by Guatemala, El Salvador, and Honduras) in a few decades have gone from scenarios of armed conflict that claimed hundreds of thousands of lives, to civil conflict that truncates opportunities to build up the well-being of millions of citizens. Armed conflicts arose during the 1950s to the 1980s, when the insurgency challenged the system, demanding better living conditions for a population affected by poverty and the repression of consecutive dictatorships. In 1986, the democratic transition began with the *Acuerdos de Esquipulas* (Esquipulas Accords) for the peace of Central America.

After 10 years of negotiations, the peace process in Central American evolved, but the conflict remained, although transformed. At the end of the 1990s, the Peace Accords were signed, marking the end of the war, and governments were democratically elected. However, the political agreements failed to eradicate social conflicts in the region. The undermined processes of recovery and reconciliation from the civil war increased the tense context of the unresolved poverty, inequality, and exclusion that had been its cause.

The democratic transition of the Central American countries evolved toward the twenty-first century, sheathed in social volatility. In the region, democratic pillars have been built through the strengthening of electoral processes, freedom of speech, and reduction of political persecution. At the same time, social discontent began to drain through protests, strikes, and popular demonstrations that could no longer be repressed with violence, as in the past decades.

The new forms of social conflict in Central America show that, although there are more citizen freedoms, the social commitments that emerged from the dialogues, negotiations, and political agreements of the peace process are still not fulfilled. In the last 20 years, the region has been the scene of an incessant profusion of conflicts mainly related to ineffective governance, inequality, corruption, and scarce presence of the state to provide basic services (Anon, 2017; United Nations Development Programme, 2013). In most cases, these conflicts become crises that have kept these countries in scenarios of instability, limiting opportunities for their citizens to prosper, which reproduces again and again the discontent and the already critical social conflictive situation.

The Socioenvironmental Conflict in Guatemala

The rise of the socioenvironmental conflict in Guatemala is part of the new wave of social conflicts that emerged as communities opposed industrial exploitation of natural resources and has rapidly grown as a nationwide governance issue in the last two decades. Taking advantage of the new open spaces for political participation in Guatemala with the return to democracy in the 1990s, after 50 years of civil war and dictatorships, communities, mainly Mayan groups in the Western highlands, started a movement against mining and other natural resources exploitation projects. One of the first and most publicized conflicts emerged in the early 2000s, when communities of the department of San Marcos (one of 22 subdivisions of the country, close to the border with Mexico) began mobilization against the Marlin mine, an open-pit mineral mine owned by Montana Exploradora, a subsidiary of Goldcorp Inc. This mining license was one of many resulting from the Mining Law amended in 1997, which included key changes to promote extractive industry investment, such as the reduction of mining royalties to 2% of profits.

Communities opposed the mine, arguing that the project: (1) contravened the right of indigenous people to prior consultation, full information, and free decision-making; (2) had adverse impacts on health and the environment, especially water, in their communities; (3) did not take into consideration the Mayan worldview on nature conservancy; and (4) did not bring sustained development opportunities for the communities (García-Ruano, 2013). Despite communities' opposition, the Marlin mine started operations, and this became the first of the numerous conflicts that not only failed to reach resolution but also led to greater polarization, riots, and even deaths in many communities. Between 2004 and 2016, there are reports of a dozen deaths associated with socioenvironmental conflicts in the country. A few examples of the most conflicted cases are San Juan Sacatepéquez–Cementos Progreso (2005–2014), Santa Cruz Barillas–Hidro Santa Cruz (2012), San Rafael Las Flores–Minera San Rafael (2013), Río La Pasión–Reforestadora Palma de Petén (2015), and Ixquisis–San Mateo Ixtatán Hidro San Mateo (2018), among many others.

From scarce public debate on the natural resources industry, the socioenvironmental issue became central for local governance across the country. In 2008, Mayan groups articulated the anti-mining movement under the *Consejo de Pueblos de Occidente* (Western People Council), CPO, which portrayed a united voice of Mayan communities against mining and natural resources exploitation. With the motto "for the defense of the territory, Mother Earth, collective rights, and good living," the CPO articulated local environmental mobilization and supported the more than 70 *consultas comunitarias* (community consultation processes, based on the International Labor Organization [ILO] 169 Convention), trying to influence policy and decision-making in the country. Gradually, other social and environmental organizations within and outside the country have also joined the movement (e.g. CALAS, Colectivo Madre Selva, OCMAL, REMA) and become a sounding board to generate more public opinion attention (García-Ruano, 2013).

Although the so-called anti-mining movement has become a milestone of social mobilization in the country, their demands have not been effectively responded to by companies or political decision-makers, making the conflict even more heated. In spite of the efforts of some of the opposing actors, the socioenvironmental conflict in Guatemala continues to grow. In 2016, more than 90 socioenvironmental conflicts were reported across the country (Anon, 2017), with communities opposing not only mining but also hydroelectric power and agro industry plants, and almost any kind of project involving local natural resources exploitation. Instead of helping to solve conflicts, it seems that communications between confronted actors intensify the tensions. In the face of the increasing conflicts, investing corporations have launched advertising and social responsibility campaigns, trying to show the economic and social benefits of their projects to deprived local communities. In some cases, these corporate communications reduce the crisis, but if the conflict is not deeply solved, it emerges in the future, most of the time stronger and more violent. Likewise, the government has not been able to either mediate or solve the conflicts effectively. Moreover, many government officials have been accused of backing corporations and worsening the crisis through repression and persecution of local leaders. Some government agencies have facilitated *mesas de diálogo* (dialogue committees) between parties in conflict, but none of them has reached effective and sustainable conflict resolution. The more communications fail, the less stakeholders trust each other, and the less effective they see dialogue as a means to solve conflict.

Thus, a case study of the socioenvironmental issue in Guatemala is relevant to test what has been the role of SC in solving – or not – growing conflict in this clashing society. The case is particularly interesting to analyze the role of SC models in a context different to the mainstream research conducted in developed countries and more mature democracies. The case is also relevant to inform environmental conflicts between peripheral communities and powerful transnational corporations, which have been occurring increasingly in several countries around the world with the advent of globalization and open-market economies.

Strategic Communication for Conflict Management in Guatemala

The description of the case of the socioenvironmental issue in Guatemala shows that the communication models used so far have not been successful at contributing to effective conflict management in the country. Thus, this section analyzes the reasons for this communication failure and what could be an alternative to effectively manage communications in conflicting settings.

The communication industry in Guatemala – particularly public relations – emerged in the last two decades, in response to the increasing demand for services associated with social conflict management, adapting traditional models from other countries with a longer trajectory in this field, mainly related to tactical communications, such as event planning, advertising, or materials production. However, practitioners have stated that the convulsing context of the country has increased demand for strategic services, to entail communication planning, implementation, and public relationships with a broader scope (Garcia-Ruano, 2009).

In the case of the socioenvironmental conflict in Guatemala, during the last decade, actors on different sides of the conflict assert that they have tried to approach the situation through strategic plans without having achieved totally successful results (Garcia-Ruano, Pacheco, & Suazo, 2013; Universidad Rafael Landívar, 2014). On the one hand, the majority of the companies involved in social conflicts (e.g. mining, hydroelectrics, palm oil industry) have a partial and/or traditional understanding of SC mainly focused on corporative reputation management, advertising, community relations, and corporate social responsibility (CSR). The messages have generally been oriented to show the positive impact of the projects in the communities, such as employment, and additional programs that provide basic services to the most marginalized populations, such as health centers, schools, sports centers, and training programs. Corporations have implemented CSR programs in order to reduce communities' opposition, supplying basic services in the absence of the state. Some of the companies also hire experts in community diagnosis and community relations, in order to assess social risk, map relevant stakeholders, and monitor companies' reputations.

In contrast, communities and social organizations also have a partial understanding of SC, mainly oriented to organize and mobilize support, seek relevant information, and protect themselves from political and criminal prosecution (García-Ruano, 2013). Their messages are addressed inward, within their own communities or organizations, to maintain the stamina of the movement and outward, to voice their demands and influence policy and decision-making. The government, both at local and national level, remains silent or unresponsive in most cases, until critical moments of the conflicts arise, then they take the role of mediator, through the *mesas de diálogo* (multi stakeholders round tables). A National Dialogue System and a Presidential Dialogue Commission were created in the early 2000s as means to open new spaces for policy discussion and conflict resolution. In spite of these government efforts, none of these dialogue exercises have achieved concrete or sustainable outcomes. The government has been the target of constant criticism for maintaining a biased position that benefits companies to then "return favors" as part of the corruption related to illicit electoral financing rooted in the Guatemalan political system. Even worse, the government sometimes plays the role of "restoring order" using repressive measures, which have reached the level of a declaration of state of siege (Hernández, 2012). The communication being used by government agencies usually stays at the tactical level, focusing on media relations, message production, and public image management. Messages are commonly oriented to holding communities and companies responsible for the conflict.

In general, communication practitioners from all sides of the socioenvironmental issue in Guatemala state that they perform communication actions for conflict management that they acknowledge as strategic. The actors identify progress in the way they manage communications, but they also see great limitations for achieving effective and sustainable conflict resolution over time. Growing frustration in solving socioenvironmental crises has also increased the distrust between actors and toward the use of a dialogue. Confronted actors are increasingly skeptical and reluctant to participate in more dialogue efforts (Universidad Rafael Landívar, 2014). Therefore, from the Guatemalan case, it can be inferred that applying SC for conflict management is not enough. It is rather critical to define the type of SC that can contribute to more effective conflict management in the country.

Why Strategic Communication for Conflict Resolution Has Failed in Guatemala

The case of socioenvironmental conflict in Guatemala shows that SC is valued for conflict management, but it is still necessary to identify an approach that responds to the particularities of the context to improve its effectiveness and sustainability. Increasing crises have led opposing participants to perceive the need for strategic handling, conceived as a planned, deep, and integrated approach to manage communication. This approach represents a step forward, compared to prior practices, overall, limited to scattered tactics of image management. Nevertheless, communication practitioners state that despite their efforts to approach communication strategically for conflict management, there are unbridgeable obstacles, mainly attributed to the context in which dialogue is developed in fledgling democracies (e.g. inequality, social exclusion, violence, etc.). Even though the SC approach helps as a first phase, to establish dialogue, the process remains stagnant during following phases of dialogue building, negotiation, and fulfillment of dialogue commitments.

In the phase of dialogue building, the study of the socioenvironmental conflict in Guatemala shows deficiencies in the strategic management of communication related to inequity of participation and available resources to generate communication actions. This inequity reflects the unequal context of the country that marginalizes large populations (e.g. indigenous, women, youth). The democratic transition has managed to banish the repression and exclusion resulting from colonialism, dictatorship, and internal war, but still, new political scenarios have not been achieved that consider the voices, necessities, and claims of the most disadvantaged. Mayan leaders of rural areas in the Western highlands of the country opposing mining or hydroelectric projects claim that the dialogues take place in locations and in ways that benefit corporations, disregarding the conditions of peasants. In order to participate in dialogue spaces, Mayan peasants lose their working day, walk long distances, and speak in a language different from their own. Furthermore, Mayan peasants state that neither the companies nor the government grant them access to trustworthy information about the projects and, rather than consulting and discussing the projects, they go to the communities with the decisions already taken (García-Ruano, 2013). These imbalanced conditions limit the potential of dialogue as communicative action to influence political decision-making and hinder the possibility of long-term commitment in social and political negotiations (Chang, Jacobson, & Zhang, 2013; Jacobson, 2003).

In a study of communication and socioenvironmental activism in Guatemala, Garcia-Ruano, Pacheco, and Suazo (2013) found that the asymmetry in communication resources to influence policies and decisions in the use of natural resources is both a disadvantage and an advantage for Mayan communities in the West of the country. While indigenous communities have limitations on accessing communication resources that lessen their ability to influence decision-makers, these shortcomings also strengthen ties of cooperation and social cohesion and thus, increase their mobilization capacity. When dialogue negotiations are unfavorable to them or the commitments are not fulfilled, the level of conflict with external actors increases, but social cohesion is strengthened and the stamina within groups is constantly reactivated. However, in the democratic process of Guatemala, with a weak culture of dialogue and high levels of inequality, decision-makers prefer to use their privileged position to impose their will instead of listening to dissident voices.

In the negotiation phase, the main limitations of dialogue are also linked to the inequity of conditions that affect the building phase, and result in deviation from communication toward measures of intimidation, censorship, and violence against opposing community members. Communities have pointed out that the content portrayed by companies in the negotiations is deceiving and confusing, and hides the disparity of benefits that the projects generate. Even though the projects generate local employment, the communities state that this is not enough in exchange for what companies earn from the resources of the territory.

In the same fashion, communities claim that companies first arrive without even presenting themselves and alter the natural environment and the social dynamics, and then, they expect communities to passively accept the project and relinquish all their demands. Communities define extractive industries as invasive and distrustful, and claim that they will not commit to any conflict resolution unless negotiations are carried out in more equidistant conditions (Universidad Rafael Landívar, 2014). The companies sometimes agree and, as a part of the negotiation, invest in CSR activities to avoid or mitigate conflicts, although they state that it should rather be the role of the state – which is inefficient at providing basic services, especially in the more rural populations where the projects operate.

The other limitation on negotiation is the deviation of the discussion from communication to aggressive and repressive actions that sharpen social crisis. Some SC actions for conflict resolution have achieved moving forward from the dialogue to the negotiation phase for some limited time. However, if the negotiation process wears out, communities often decide to take *medidas de hecho* (de facto measures) instead of continuing with the negotiations through communication. De facto measures can range from citizen protests to roadblocks, which often lead to more social unrest. The reaction of corporations is then to file arrest warrants against the community leaders, accusing them of violent acts. The negotiation radically changes its tone and content, and instead of discussing central issues of the original conflict, it deviates to negotiating the legal actions that were filed. In the last 10 years, human rights advocacy organizations have denounced increasing intimidation and criminalization of community leaders (Organización de Estados Americanos, 2018). Under these negotiation conditions, the communications turned out to be unviable.

The third phase of dialogue, directly associated with the previous two, is the communication process that is carried out for the agreement and fulfillment of commitments by confronted parties. As can be inferred, inequality patterns and intimidation measures also affect this stage, in addition to three other elements: community members report an unfavorable treatment that discourages them from fulfilling commitments; corporations report violence from the communities that breaks the intention of dialogue; and the government is ineffective to mediate and follow up the commitments between opposing actors. Communication falls under patterns of unequal and authoritarian relationships that have marked the history of the country. The wear and tear that opposing parties suffer during each specific process takes its toll at the moment of reaching an agreement. Then, when agreements are reached, they are rarely fulfilled. And this breach of agreements results in even more acute crises, and sometimes escalates at local, national, or even international level. This was the case of some of the most sharp conflicts (e.g. Marlin Mine in San Miguel Ixtahuacán, Hidro Santa Cruz in Barillas, and Cementos Progreso in San Juan Sacatepéquez), where negotiations resulted in roadblocks, violence, legal measures, and even deaths (Vidal, 2018).

The ineffectiveness of the communication as a conflict management mechanism harms trust. Community members often express their lack of credibility in corporations' communication when dialogue becomes just a show for publicity. They judge the communication efforts as superficial and instrumental, used only to argue legitimacy or, in the worse scenario, to target and intimidate community leaders. On the other hand, companies also point out that they have lost credibility in communication for conflict management because it is constantly being interrupted by the violent actions of the community (Universidad Rafael Landívar, 2014).

Even though there have been efforts to implement SC aimed at dialogue, this has been unsuccessful in the way that it has been implemented so far in the socioenvironmental issues of Guatemala.

Dialogue and Participation for Effective Strategic Communication

The socioenvironmental case of Guatemala described above shows that SC has not been effective in managing social conflict during the democratic transition in the country. A key obstacle seems to lie in the dialogue component of the conflict management process. However, a school of thought called "development communication" has emerged in Latin America that precisely describes forms of dialogic and participative communication to address social confrontations in the region. Since the 1960s, Freire (1970) and more recently Barranquero (2012) and Gumucio-Dagron (2011) placed dialogic relationships as a mechanism to address the blatant inequity, marginalization, and repression in the region. From different perspectives of social sciences, these thinkers saw communication as an ongoing process that must respect, listen to, and be open to the views, experiences, and context of others, especially those who are in a position of disadvantage. They propose participation as a means for defeating systemic oppression. Building genuine and sustainable dialogue strengthens collective problem-solving and social cohesion, and builds trust between interlocutors, especially in societies with divided and confronted populations.

In Guatemala, Gularte and Ozaeta (2012), using the same approach, advocated "other communication for other development" as an alternative to vertical, authoritarian, and marginalizing models prevalent in the country. They see communication as a key process to build relationships and share experiences between people who are otherwise isolated or confronted. According to the authors, the dialogic communication begins by listening to "the other" and continues in a process of mutual building. This type of communication is proposed as a catalyst to reverse the unequal and excluding structures and development models of the country, which have been the cause of pervasive division and social confrontation.

Similarly, García-Ruano (2010) proposed a paradigm shift in communication and public relations, toward a relational approach based on dialogue. Dialogue, equity, and mutual adaptation for relationship building would improve communication management. This alternative model would not only be more effective but also a more ethical approach, because relational, egalitarian relationships are a pending debt to many who have been historically marginalized in the country.

Cocreational Model for Effective Conflict Management in Clashing Environments

Based on the analysis of the case of socioenvironmental conflict in Guatemala and the postulates of the development communication advocated by Latin American scholars, this chapter argues that the cocreational model of SC (Botan, 2018) has high potential for the effective management of social conflict in unsteady contexts, such as Guatemala. The cocreational model is defined by Botan (2018) as a meta-theory of communication that "views publics as cocreators of meaning and communication as what makes it possible to agree to shared meanings, interpretations and goals" (p. 40). Echoing the development communication paradigm, the cocreational model poses three elements that may be useful when applying SC for conflict management in cases such as the socioenvironmental issues in Guatemala: (1) dialogic definition of SC; (2) central role of communication in organizations for change management; and (3) communication focused on publics.

Cocreational Definition of Strategic Communication

The cocreational definition of SC (dialogic, based on relations with the public/audiences) has high potential for effective management of social conflict, since it provides an alternative to the traditional definition (unidirectional, based on organization objectives) that has failed to manage the permanent tensions of unstable societies. The cocreational approach (Botan, 2018) defines SC as "the use of information flowing into the organization (research) to plan and carry out a communication campaign addressing the relationship between an organization and its publics" (p. 8). Coinciding with the development communication approach, the cocreational model provides an alternative to the traditional conception communication that identified sending messages as an initial step, and positioned listening upfront the communication process as the first phase of a two-way relationship. Thus, SC begins with research to know and understand publics and, based on that information, messages and campaigns are planned and conveyed. From the cocreational perspective, research is an omnipresent element through the communication process because it is used to diagnose, monitor, and evaluate the cocreation of meanings with publics.

Consequently, the cocreational definition of SC is relational in nature and focuses on the publics instead of relying solely on the organizational objectives, as promoted by the traditional approach. Like the development communication approach, the cocreational model promotes that meanings are developed with the publics, as an ongoing conversation. Thus, research provides inputs to the communication practitioner on how to initiate, maintain, and modify conversations with their public. This approach is different from traditional models in which organizations are only interested in investigating publics, aiming to influence them to achieve organizational goals.

The cocreational definition of SC is valuable for effective conflict management because, as the development communication approach, it is centered on the idea of listening to the interlocutor, which has been a constant demand from actors in conflicts. In the case of Guatemala, for example, with a history of recent civil war and with excluding socioeconomic structures, a new concept of communication that begins by trying to know and understand *the other* may help to establish the foundations of trust that are sometimes nonexistent and that are key to negotiations and commitments that arise from the dialogues. As described above, in multiple socioenvironmental conflicts, the Mayan communities ask corporations and government to be willing to listen and not just impose their decisions. Likewise, corporations have stated that de facto measures such as roadblocking sometimes used by communities are not effective because they interrupt the possibilities of dialogue. However, communities have pointed out that they use these pressure measures due to the unresponsiveness they perceive from companies and political decision-makers. If, instead of exclusion, communities perceive openness to listen to their needs, it is more likely that they will be willing to engage in dialogue. Although the cocreational approach can start from either side of the conflict, in cases such as Guatemala, communities expected that the first step would be taken by the companies, which are perceived as foreigners coming into the communities (Universidad Rafael Landívar, 2014). Prioritizing listening to publics can therefore be highly effective for building a more equitable conversation, increasing trust between the parties and making negotiation and commitment between the parties more feasible.

Core Role of Communication

The alternative definition of SC would be irrelevant if the role of such communication is secondary for the organization. The cocreational approach rightly proposes that communication is constitutive for organizations. On the one hand, the organizational decision to change to the cocreational approach should reflect an organizational worldview in which the role of publics and the relevance of listening and adapting to them is valued. On the other hand, this change implies that communication is at the center of that decision. Therefore, adopting a cocreational approach represents seeing communication beyond the traditional tactical role and working to raise it to the strategic level.

Resonant with some core postulates from systems theory and the open systems model (Cutlip et al., 2001), the cocreational model proposes constant monitoring and adaptation of the organization to its environment as key communication functions for playing a central and strategic role. Constant surveying and advising on the context helps for informed decision-making, which not only leads to more effective communication outcomes but also increases top managers' perception of the central and strategic role that communication plays in the organization (Grunig, 1992).

Despite the potential benefits for the organization, advocating for a core role of communication can be challenging in cases such as the socioenvironmental conflict in Guatemala, in particular from the companies' side, which has a more traditional approach, seeing communication as a tactical, instrumental function for achieving organization goals. Although some companies have started acknowledging the strategic role of communication, they usually design communication plans focused on advertising, CSR, and persuasive messages outcomes. These plans are more oriented to lowering immediate tensions than building long-term relationships with the opposing parties.

From the side of the communities, positioning the communication in a central role seems to be a less complex and even natural approach for advancing their mobilization goals. Limited socioeconomic conditions make communities realize the high value of communication for advancing their mobilization goals, in particular for social cohesion and advocacy. Resource scarcity may trigger momentum to develop communication networks that allow deprived populations to build networks through which they can share the few resources they have or look for alternative sources. The *consultas comunitarias* have shown how historically marginalized Mayan communities start getting organized using existing networks locally, but then expand these networks to other communities and allies within and across borders who usually provide them with moral support, experience, or communication resources. These communications result not only in an improved learning process, but also in stronger solidarity ties, enhancing interpersonal trust and group cohesion, which have proved key components of collective efficacy (Cartier, Castells, & Qiu, 2005).

Communities have developed SC despite their limitations in terms of access to information, cost of internet service, or illiteracy (both educational and digital). Many communities in resistance use digital platforms like Facebook, emails, YouTube, or short text messages (SMS) as a central part of their mobilization communications. These channels are complementary to physical social networks (i.e. community assemblies, community billboards), and both resonate with the relational and collective culture of most communities in Guatemala (García-Ruano, Pacheco, & Suazo, 2013). As part of what Castells (1996, 2007) defines as the network society, communities opposing extractive projects in Guatemala have empirically found communication to be a source of power and agency.

Publics at the Center

One of the key aspects of the cocreational approach that can strengthen the role of SC for social conflict management in countries such as Guatemala is the central role that is attributed to the public in a dialogic relation with the organization. This approach coincides with the constructivist communication model of the Latin American approach of development communication, in which communication begins by listening to the receivers – or publics –who in turn play a main role, as active interlocutors of an ongoing process (Gularte & Ozaeta, 2012). For contexts such as Guatemala, the cocreational proposal is almost revolutionary since it suggests that organizations change traditional closed, one-way models toward two-way models, open to listening, understanding, and adapting to the public. Although complex, this change has high potential to loosen halted dialogue processes since, as in the case of socioenvironmental conflicts in Guatemala, to be listened to and valued as an interlocutor represents one of the main demands of communities in resistance.

The cocreational conception of publics is particularly relevant for effective conflict management in contexts such as Guatemala in three areas of SC: design of messages and campaigns, issue management, and multicultural communication. As stated by Botan (2018), in the cocreational model, messages and campaigns are based on initial research and, therefore, listening to the publics. Messages and campaigns are designed, implemented, and evaluated to nurture an organization's relationship with the public. In the case of socioenvironmental conflicts in Guatemala, most of the messages used by the extractive companies follow one-way communication models, generally through advertising and marketing campaigns that barely take into consideration communities' points of view. Therefore, both messages and campaigns result in irrelevant and ineffective communication.

In some cases, as an effect of what Deutsch (2006) describes as the collaboration–competition effect of social conflict, communication even becomes the trigger for conflict, since messages can be offensive to the public if they exacerbate discriminatory stereotypes (e.g. "indigenous leaders are manipulated because they are easily influenced by others," "indigenous people are violent because they are not accustomed to talk"). Anthropological studies about the Guatemalan elites (Gedeón, 2016) have identified that some managers of big national corporations admit that they do not know much about the country's indigenous cultures. According to the analysis, this ignorance may lead corporate managers to fear and reject indigenous populations, which prevents dialogue and encourages conflict. A cocreational approach of meanings would assist organizations to identify these shortcomings and build new narratives aiming to solve conflicts by tearing down cultural myths about the indigenous cultures.

Issue management is an especially important area for conflict management because it represents the competing communication efforts (both from companies and mobilized groups) aimed at influencing public policies and political decisions. The cocreational approach (Botan, 2018) suggests three SC actions for issue management that can be useful in socioenvironmental conflicts such as those in Guatemala: issues defined and co-managed by the publics; issues based on organizational policies (grand strategy) that value dialogic relations; and issues addressed before reaching an advanced conflict phase. As described earlier, social environments characterized by social exclusion are at risk of reproducing such schemes in social conflict management. Communities and mobilized groups have frequently denounced lack of consultation and unequal dialogue conditions as part of a paternalistic, discriminatory, and marginalizing pattern of both corporations and government organizations, who claim that they have to make decisions for people who cannot do it for themselves given their underprivileged conditions (Garcia-Ruano, Pacheco, & Suazo, 2013; Universidad Rafael Landívar, 2014). Usually, conflicts worsen when marginalizing actions are constantly repeated and no effective resolving actions are taken promptly. Like development communication, the cocreational model could be useful in issue management since it advocates for inclusive processes, no matter what the condition of people, valuing their knowledge and aiming to understand their opinions and positions. As evidence of the cocreational model, the Guatemalan case shows that if the issues are not treated inclusively and at an early stage, they end up becoming a crisis and may be solved momentarily but can return to the active phase at any time.

The cocreational approach is valuable for conflict management in multicultural environments, as in Guatemala, since listening to the public avoids ethnocentric models, being open to diverse meanings and interpretations. In the case of Guatemala, socioenvironmental conflict is associated with the colonial structures of exclusion and repression of the Mayan population. Both the cocreational approach and communication for development provide useful tools to break these historical schemes, by suggesting organizational openness to include the voices of the publics and giving them the resources to make free and informed decisions. This proposal is resonant with the ILO 169 Convention, which reaffirms the right of native indigenous people to have free and informed decision-making in their territories. Therefore, the cocreational approach to SC contributes not only to the effective and sustainable management of conflicts but also to ethics, in observance of the rights inherent to different populations of the society, especially those traditionally excluded.

Conclusion: Toward a More Effective, Sustainable, and Ethical Communication

This chapter showed that SC should play a central role in managing socioenvironmental conflicts in Guatemala. However, the recent history of armed conflict and old structures of marginalization restrict both SC and conflict management. The armed war was left behind almost half a century ago, but the conflict remains. Democracy now allows Mayan communities to protest and complain against natural resource exploitation projects. Round-table discussions and negotiations are set up and communication campaigns are developed to solve the conflicts but commitments are not achieved, leading to ever-increasing crises.

Within this context, this chapter suggests that alternative models of SC should be used to disentangle social conflicts that have not been solved with traditional approaches used until now. Specifically, this chapter advocates for the use of the development communication and the cocreational models, which redefine communication in terms of dialogue built jointly by the organization and its. As an alternative to traditional management focused on achieving organizational goals, the dialogical approach is focused on publics, building and maintaining an attentive listening attitude to them, through constant research and cocreation of meanings.

Using dialogic models of strategic communication makes conflict management more effective, sustainable, and ethical. As shown in this chapter, placing publics at the center of the communication process makes them feel valued and included, which increases trust and strengthens dialogue and negotiations. Commitments based on stronger processes are also more durable and, therefore, sustainable over time. Although conflicts may reappear, the antecedents of effective dialogue and negotiation can be resumed, if needed, more expeditiously. Finally, opening spaces for more information, interaction, and equal participation strengthens the ethical parameters of communication, especially in societies hit by confrontation and marginalization.

The analysis of the socioenvironmental case in Guatemala shows that SC for social conflict management may lead to positive change, for both organizations and society. Societies' culture and dynamics are generally reflected in those of organizations (Sriramesh & Vercic, 2009), and this is also where social change can begin. It would be of great benefit for organizations to see SC as a catalyst for change, not only within themselves but also in their society. Organizations implementing dialogic communication models, promoting a culture of inclusion, listening, and cocreating meanings with their publics, not only manage conflict effectively, sustainably, and ethically, but also make a contribution to the governance and democratic strengthening of their society.

Discussion Questions

1. In the context where you work, which strategic communication practices reinforce traditional monologic models and which reinforce alternative dialogic models?
2. How could social network communication contribute to dialogic strategic communication for social conflict management in countries with incipient democracy and convulsive social context?
3. What could be the limitations to the application of dialogic approaches, such as the development communication or the cocreational model, in the context where you practice/want to practice strategic communication?
4. How can a communication practitioner promote the change from the monologic traditional paradigm to the alternative dialogic approach, especially in societies with marginalizing, closed, and discriminating systems?

References

Anon (2017). *Mapa de conflictividad social en Guatemala*. Guatemala: Procuraduría de los Derechos Humanos.

Barranquero, A. (2012). De la comunicación para el desarrollo a la justicia ecosocial y el buen vivir. (From development communication to ecosocial justice and wellbeing). *Cuadernos de información y comunicación*, 17, 63–78.

Beltran, L. R. (2006). La comunicación para el desarrollo en Latinoamérica: Un recuento de medio siglo. (Development communication in Latin America: A half-century review). *Anagramas: Rumbos y sentidos de la comunicación*, 4(8), 53–76.
Botan, C. H. (2018). *Strategic communication theory and practice: The cocreational model.* Hoboken, NJ: Wiley-Blackwell.
Cartier, C., Castells, M., & Qiu, J. L. (2005). The information have-less: Inequality, mobility, and translocal networks in Chinese cities. *Studies in Comparative International Development (SCID)*, 40(2), 9–34.
Castells, M. (1996). *The rise of the network society.* Malden, MA: Wiley-Blackwell.
Castells, M. (2007). Communication, power and counter-power in the network society. *International Journal of Communication*, 1, 238–266.
Chang, L., Jacobson, T. L., & Zhang, W. (2013). A communicative action approach to evaluating citizen support for a government's smoking policies. *Journal of Communication*, 63(6), 1153–1174.
Cutlip, S. M., Center, A. H., Broom, G. M., & Xifra, J. (2001). *Relaciones públicas eficaces.* Barcelona: Gestion.
Deutsch, M. (2006). Cooperation and competition. In M. Deutsch, P. T. Coleman, & E. C. Marcus (Eds.), *The handbook of conflict resolution: Theory and practice* (pp. 23–42). San Francisco, CA: Jossey-Bass.
Freire, P. (1970). *Pedagogy of the oppressed* (M. B. Ramos Trans.). New York: Continuum, 2007.
Garcia-Ruano, K. J. (2009). Public relations in Guatemala: Local features of a global profession. *Paper presented at the 12th International Public Relations Research Conference.*
Garcia-Ruano, K. J. (2010). Reinventar las relaciones públicas en Guatemala: El reto de una profesión para el diálogo. *Revista Comunicador*, 1(1–3).
García-Ruano, K. J. (2013). Communication networks for social mobilization in marginalized populations: The case of the antimining Mayan movement in Guatemala. Unpublished doctoral dissertation. Michigan State University, East Lansing, MI.
Garcia-Ruano, K. J., Pacheco, A., & Suazo, D. (2013). Latin America| the use of digital media for social mobilization in marginalized communities: The case of a Mayan socioenvironmental movement in Guatemala. *International Journal of Communication*, 7, 14.
Gedeón (2016). *Cómo pensamos las elites empresariales en Guatemala.* Retrieved on November 19, 2018 from http://gedeon.org.gt/es/blog/wp-content/uploads/2016/05/Gedeon-Estudio-elites-2016_8mb.pdf
Grunig, L. A. (1992). How public relations/communication departments should adapt to the structure and environment of an organization – and what they actually do. In J. E. Grunig (Ed.), *Excellence in public relations and communication management* (pp. 467–481). Hillsdale, NJ: Lawrence Erlbaum Associates.
Gularte, E., & Ozaeta, C. (2012). *Otra comunicación para otro desarrollo (Other communication for other development).* Guatemala: Centro de Comunicación para el Desarrollo.
Gumucio-Dagron, A. (2011). Comunicación para el cambio social: Clave del desarrollo participativo. *Signo y pensamiento*, 58, 26–39.
Hernández (2012). Un pueblo, un estado y… una empresa. Plaza Pública. Retrieved on November 11, 2018 from https://www.plazapublica.com.gt/content/un-pueblo-el-estado-y-una-empresa
Jacobson, T. L. (2003). Participatory communication for social change: The relevance of the theory of communicative action. *Annals of the International Communication Association*, 27(1), 87–123.
Organización de Estados Americanos (2018). *CIDH and OACNUDH condenan asesinatos de defensores indígenas y campesinos en Guatemala.* Retrieved on November 17, 2018 from http://www.oas.org/es/cidh/prensa/comunicados/2018/137.asp
Sriramesh, K., & Vercic, D. (2009). The relationship between culture and public relations. In *The global public relations handbook, revised and expanded edition* (pp. 91–106). New York: Routledge.
United Nations Development Programme (2013). *Understanding social conflict in Latin America.* Retrieved on November 13, 2018 from http://www.undp.org/content/dam/undp/library/crisis%20prevention/Understanding%20Social%20Conflict%20in%20Latin%20America%202013%20ENG.pdf

Universidad Rafael Landívar (2014). *Gestión social de proyectos hidroeléctricos en Guatemala*. (Social management of hydroelectric power projects in Guatemala). Retrieved on November 8, 2018 from https://www.url.edu.gt/PortalURL/Archivos/208/Archivos/Gesti%C3%B3n_e_%20 inclusi%C3%B3n_social_de_proyectos_hidroel%C3%A9ctricos_en_GuatemalaCOMPLETO.pdf

Vidal, J. (2018, August 19). How Guatemala is sliding into chaos in the fight for land and water. The Guardian. Retrieved on November 19, 2018 from https://www.theguardian.com/world/2018/aug/19/guatemala-fight-for-land-water-defenders-lmining-loging-eviction

3

Strategic Rhetoric, Dialogue, and the Long Now

A Case Study of Long-Term Thinking

Michael L. Kent[1] and Petra Theunissen[2]

[1]University of New South Wales and [2]Auckland University of Technology

Introduction

One of the central tenets of communication and rhetoric is that reality is *socially constructed*, and that how we talk about the world, combined with our personal experiences, subsequently shapes the world we live in. An abundance of empirical evidence exists to support this view, including cultivation research of the mass media called the "mean world syndrome" (cf. Gerbner, 1969; Gerbner & Gross, 1976). The mean world syndrome suggests that people who watch a lot of television, particularly news that reports primarily negative and stereotypical information (such as FOX news, SKY news, etc.), believe that the world is more dangerous than it actually is.

Ironically, violent crime in the US has been declining for decades, and yet, tens of millions of Americans still believe that the world is a more dangerous place now than in the past. Indeed, as the *New York Times* reports, although people believe crime is on the rise, the "F.B.I.'s count of violent crimes… has declined from a rate of 747 violent incidents per 100,000 people in 1993 to 387 incidents per 100,000 people in 2012" (Wolfers, 2014), an almost 50% decline in only a decade. So why do people not feel safer? The simple answer is because of communication (rhetoric) and a lack of genuine dialogue — topics that will be taken up in this chapter.

Simply put, rhetoric refers to the use of language to shape how people see the world, and because of its power to move people to action, rhetoric has been studied for thousands of years. Although rhetoric as a discipline and art form has been described variously by different scholars, most scholars and philosophers make note of the power of rhetoric to make the world a "better" place. Indeed, as Plato (1999) suggested thousands of years ago in the *Phaedrus*, "True rhetoric is like medicine, and the rhetorician has to consider the natures of men's souls as the physician considers the natures of their bodies" (e-text, NP). Aristotle (1991) subsequently argued that rhetoric was the art of persuasion and consisted of "discovering, in the specific instance, all the available means of persuasion." Rhetorical scholars, like Bryant (1953), have argued that rhetoric was a process of gradual adjustment, or a "process of adjusting ideas to people and people to ideas" (p. 407). Weaver (1953/1985) said rhetoric was "truth, plus its artful presentation" (p. 15), and Hart (1990) suggested, more pragmatically, that rhetoric was "the art of using language to help people to narrow their choices

The Handbook of Strategic Communication, First Edition. Edited by Carl H. Botan.

among specifiable, if not specified, policy options" (p. 4). However we define the term, rhetoric has been seen as a powerful tool, one that contemporary strategic communicators *should understand* but, regrettably, often do not.

The Power of Rhetoric and Dialogue

The "art of rhetoric," as it is often called, involves understanding an assortment of informative and persuasive techniques such as identification, ideology, metaphor, narrative and storytelling, framing, logical fallacies, and other rhetorical principles such as *ethos*, *pathos*, and *logos*. Although rhetoric is often associated with public or mass communication, rhetoric informs *all* strategic communication (SC) activities from social media postings, memos, letters, research reports, speeches, and advertisements, and should therefore form an unequivocal part of strategic public relations planning and teaching.

Unfortunately, the *word* "rhetoric" is often abused by people who know very little about the actual principles. Journalists say things like: "the rhetoric coming out of the Whitehouse is very contentious," or "the current negotiations appear to be little more than empty rhetoric with little substance." The pejorative use of the word rhetoric, however, should not detract from our appreciation of the power of the actual concepts described below. Rhetoric, quite simply, is the theory behind what goes into every moving and compelling message: written, spoken, or visual.

Dialogue is the second part of the rhetorical process described in this chapter. Dialogue comes into play when the focus of one's attention is not on the creation of external messages and informative or persuasive content, but the creation of long-term relationships. Understanding dialogic theory provides an additional perspective on how to strategically engage stakeholders and publics, and build organization–public relationships.

Ultimately, the goal of SC is embodied in the long-term concept of "strategy." As opposed to short-term, tactical planning and implementation of messages and activities aimed at achieving organization-centric goals — a phenomenon that has contributed to the institutionalization of expectations that public relations is merely "a messaging activity whose purpose is to make organizations look good in the media or to sell products" (Grunig, 2011, p. 12). In other words, instead of contributing to long-term strategic and sustainable relationships, public relations has been put to use for short-term advertising, marketing, and profit-making initiatives. Shifting our understanding of public relations strategy back to a long-term, future-oriented view of communication and organizational objectives, together with developing an appreciation for Long Now thinking, allows us to value both dialogue and rhetoric in achieving the relational goals of organizations, and shaping a society that functions to benefit *all* its members, not merely a few.

Rhetorical and Dialogic Principles

Rhetoric has a more than two millennia history, going back to ancient Greece and Rome, has been studied by thousands of scholars, and has been used by millions of speakers and writers to craft moving, informative, and persuasive messages. Dialogue, and the related concept of dialectic (using dialogue to discover truth), has equally ancient roots. Let us look briefly at the fundamental principles and challenges that underlie both theories before considering how they might be applied to Long Now thinking.

Rhetorical Theory

Rhetoric traces its history back to the ancient Greeks and Romans, to philosophers, sophists (private tutors), educators, politicians, and religious leaders. Indeed, for most of recorded history, the average person could not read or write; only the elites had access to what we might today call "higher education" (i.e. the medieval *trivium* and *quadrivium*, dating to ancient Greece), and thus the linguistic skills of rhetoric were known only to a handful of elites.

The early principles of rhetoric go back to the writings of Plato, Aristotle, Cicero, Quintillion, St. Augustine, Erasmus, and many others (Kennedy, 1980). Throughout its ancient history, the use of rhetoric varied. From being an instrument of philosophers in ancient Greek times, a political tool in ancient Roman times, to an instrument of religious truth and the church in St. Augustine's and later times.

Early rhetoric was largely focused on persuasion, but attention should be drawn to the five canonical elements of rhetoric identified by Aristotle in his book *Rhetoric*. The canon consisted of *invention*, or the finding and analysis of information; *disposition*, or the style and arrangement of messages; *elocution*, which essentially referred to the delivery and nonverbal aspects of a speech, gestures, language choices, etc.; *pronunciation*, or the use of and choice of proper grammar and language, voice use, etc.; and *memory*, or the ability to draw upon facts and information as needed, adapt to one's audience, and impromptu speaking.

Along with the canon or rhetoric, Aristotle described a number of other principles of rhetoric that had been known for some time: the importance of *ethos* (credibility: competence, integrity, and goodwill in a speaker or author), *pathos* (the use of emotion and ability to draw upon emotion in one's speeches or written messages), *logos* (the use of logical argument and clear structure in one's spoken or written messages), and concepts like *topoi* (or commonalities of arguments) and the importance of audience adaptation (cf. Aristotle, 1991; Kent, 2011b).

Beginning in about the early twentieth century, US and European scholars are credited with what might be called a renaissance of rhetorical studies, introducing and expanding concepts like *tropes* (figures of speech, metaphors, etc.) (Burke, 1969a; Kent, 2001), archetypes and symbolism (Osborn, 1967, 1977), ideological rhetoric (McGee, 1980; McGee & Martin, 1983), identification (Burke, 1969b), narrative (Fisher, 1978, 1984, 1985; Kent, 2015), framing (Hallahan, 1999), and logical fallacies (Kent, 2011b; Taylor & Kent, 2007), among other concepts.

One of the fundamental contemporary notions of the power of rhetoric is an understanding that how we *think* about the world is shaped by how we *talk* about it, how we *inhabit* the world, and how we *socially construct our reality*. In 1962, John F. Kennedy said we would send a man to the moon and by 1969 we had. Not simply because he said it, obviously, but because the *creation of the idea in the mind of the audience made it possible and acceptable*, thereby preparing audiences for what was to come. Simply put, the US went to the moon because of rhetoric, or as Bryant (1953) explained, through the "process of adjusting ideas to people and people to ideas" (p. 407).

The power of rhetoric to shape and change the world has been demonstrated time and time again over the last 200 years, with the abolition of slavery, suffrage for woman and people of color, institution of child labor laws, union movements, environmental movements, gay marriage, and hundreds of other "revolutionary" ideas and activist causes.

Indeed, organizations that do not take into account the power of rhetoric and the power of citizens and activists to change the world are short-lived. Excellent examples of this are the many organizations over the last decade that have publically taken racist, homophobic, or religiously intolerant stances and been driven out of business as word spread of their words and deeds. Both organizations and individuals play a role in shaping reality. The strategic communicator who understands this will be markedly more successful at getting their messages out to stakeholders.

Many of the key principles of effective rhetoric have already been incorporated into basic communication courses like public speaking and persuasion, but the subtler rhetorical concepts like understanding ideology, metaphors, archetypes, apologia (how to apologize effectively) (Benoit, 1995; Hearit, 2001; Kent & Boatwright, 2018; Ware & Linkugel, 1973), and narrative theory (Kent, 2015) require advanced training. Strategic communicators who are skilled in rhetoric understand how to direct messages to various publics, how to time messages for the maximum impact, and how to develop sophisticated, multipart messages that appeal to an assortment of stakeholders and publics. In short, rhetorical skills are what separate the most skilled communicators from everyone else.

Dialogic Theory

Classical dialogic theory can be traced back to the ideas of Socrates, Plato, and Aristotle. Indeed, Socrates (who wrote nothing down himself) is most famous through his student Plato and his "Socratic dialogues," where Socrates is portrayed interrogating various rhetorical concepts with his contemporaries through a series of questions (cf. *Gorgias*, *Phaedrus*, www.gutenberg.org). Similarly, Aristotle confronts many of the ideas of Socrates in his *Nicomachean ethics* (cf. Burger, 2008).

Modern dialogic theory — the "other" strategic instrument of the highly skilled communicator — emerged out of the post-WWI experiences of theorists and philosophers like Martin Buber's (1923/1970) wartime propaganda experiences, as well as 1960s and 1970s radicals, scholars, educators, and scientists like Carl Rogers (1957/1992), Paulo Freire (1970), R. D. Laing (1961/1969), Nel Noddings (1984), and Mikhail Bakhtin (1975/1991). Thus, broadly speaking, dialogic theory represents a body of communication principles going back to the early twentieth century and philosophical principles dating back thousands of years.

Dialogue was developed as a means of facilitating genuine interaction between two people, or among small groups of individuals (Buber, 1970/1923), and is therefore closely linked to *interpersonal communication;* unlike its brother, rhetoric, however, which is more closely tied to *public* or *mass communication.*

Dialogue begins with the assumption that various interpersonal communication features, such as *trust*, *risk*, *positive regard*, and *empathy*, are necessary in order for people to have a rewarding, honest, and meaningful interaction (cf. Johannesen, 1990). Dialogic theory itself comprises an assortment of principles and assumptions that revolve around relationship building and maintenance. A dialogic approach to communication is effectively designed to minimize or eliminate observable power dynamics, and ideally avoid exploitation of others. Dialogue, seen from this viewpoint, is *collaborative* and *genuine*, aimed at achieving a mutually satisfying relationship.

Features of Dialogue

The basic qualities of dialogue involve a combination of the following features: *mutuality*, which involves collaboration with others, and a spirit of joint equality; *propinquity*, which involves immediacy of presence or real-time interactions, an awareness of the temporal flow of relationships, and a recognition of the past, present, and potential future relationships that are possible with others, and engagement; *empathy*, which involves confirmation of others, supportiveness, and a communal orientation where the good of others matters as much, or more, than one's own good; *risk*, which involves vulnerability, being open to unanticipated experiences and consequences, a recognition of strange otherness, which involves the unconditional acceptance of the uniqueness of others; and *commitment*, which involves genuineness, commitment to maintaining an open and ongoing conversation, and commitment to interpretation or trying to make sense of what others say and how they feel (Kent & Taylor, 2002, pp. 25–29).

Not every two-way or interpersonal interaction is dialogic; nor is dialogue just talk, even very serious and polite talk. Thus, in order to make dialogue possible and to build it into the strategic plan as a means of developing and maintaining relationships, communicators must understand how the process works, that is to say, professional communicators need to have received some training in dialogue, and know the conditions for dialogue to take place and its role in strategic planning.

As a participant in dialogue, the communicator needs to be willing to take a risk when interacting with strangers; ultimately, there is no right or wrong in dialogue. Yet all dialogic interactions must contain within them the potential to be changed, or the possibility of being "wrong," but not in any sort of pejorative sense. True dialogue implies changing one's mind and learning new things that influence how one sees the world — consequences of a dialogic encounter with "strange otherness," empathy, engagement, and other dialogic principles.

In organizational management literature, dialogue is widely considered a tool for strategy development or consensus building (Romenti, Murtarelli, & Valentini, 2014), but dialogue is more than that. Dialogue is an attempt to make sense of the world and the uncertainty and ambiguity that surrounds us, just like campaign strategy does (cf. Carroll, 2015). Dialogue, therefore, *is* strategy.

As an instrument for SC, dialogue is indeed unique. Although dialogic communicators often use persuasion to try and explain their points to others (and skilled communicators use rhetorical strategies *whenever* they communicate with others), dialogue is in some aspects the opposite of persuasion.

Contained in many SC situations are what is referred to as "rhetorical situations" (Bitzer, 1968), which involve responding to the claims of others and an implicit desire to "win" by application of strategic and rhetorical communication principles. But with properly conducted dialogue, there should be no desire to "win." Indeed, coming away changed after an interaction with someone else is considered a success.

Trying to avoid being overtly persuasive does not mean that communicators in dialogic situations simply tell others what they *think* they want to hear. A better way to think about it is that in a dialogue, communicators avoid exercising power over others and try to allow all participants to share their views and make their own positions known. Through the neutral exchange of information and ideas, a better understanding of others emerges. However, dialogic participants are not "pushovers," who fail to advocate their own position in a compelling fashion. In fact, in dialogue, the interlocutors' beliefs, values, and attitudes *are* important.

However, what is *not* important is to persuade others of the superiority of one's own beliefs. Dialogue is not a polemic or campaigning situation. Dialogic encounters are not public settings where a communicator might be trying to influence a wider audience. Rather, dialogue is an interpersonal or small-group interaction; it is about understanding others, and co-creating reality. Helping people to understand our position and achieving joint understanding is central; convincing others to believe as we do is not. If your positions are valid and compelling, persuasion might take place, but we do not use dialogue as a venue to persuade others.

Stratēgia: "Peace" as a Viable Option

Too often, strategic thinking in business is obscured by a warlike mentality where the winner takes all, and where there is little room for dialogue. In war, strategy involves the use of fortified strength by carrying weapons of some sort "to achieve the military objectives and, by extension, the political purpose of the war" (Paret, 1986, p. 3). Rhetoric and dialogue often become such weapons of war, leading to crude and often inaccurate applications.

The term "strategy" found its way into the English language through the Greek *stratēgia*, meaning "generalship." The origin of strategy as the art of planning and directing military operations thus makes sense, and can contribute to the misunderstanding that strategy is necessarily about defeating an enemy. The strategist Carl von Clausewitz reputedly saw strategy as "the use of combat, or the threat of combat, for the purpose of war in which it takes place" (Paret, 1986, p. 3). Von Clausewitz (1976) wrote about war in its pure state as having the purpose to "*always* and *solely*" overcome the opposition and disarm the enemy (p. 90, authors' emphasis). If we approach public relations from a warlike that perspective, then the professional communicator's strategic function will always be to overcome an organization's opposition and emerge as the victor from whatever skirmish or battle that organization might have encountered. Such an approach cares little about organizational stakeholders and publics. The battle approach represents an outmoded view of organizations that are increasingly networked and situated in the public view. However, Von Clausewitz also points out that war, in its pure state, hardly ever exists. Often the parties at war are of unequal strength, and are unable to carry on a war. In such situations, *peace* is a viable alternative.

In practice, then, the inability, or unwillingness, to carry on a war can "be replaced by two other grounds for making peace: the first is the improbability of victory; the second is its unacceptable cost" (Von Clausewitz, 1976, p. 91). Recognizing that how we think about the world is socially constructed can have dramatic consequences. Humans are not required to see the world in only one way — often as the most powerful see it; each of us has a somewhat different view of the world based on our own circumstances and experiences. How we think about the world effectively creates the world that we live in.

If we imagine the potential costs of carrying on aggressive public relations strategies on behalf of organizations as being too high (cf. Kent & Lane, 2017; Kent & Taylor, 2016; Kent & Theunissen, 2016), and the strategies as having the potential to result in a society that is no longer free and open, where important stakeholders become alienated, where customers have become disillusioned, and where the organization's reputation has been tarnished, we would view our actions in a different light. Perhaps the time has come to apply a more peaceful and long-term strategy of relationship building, where aggressive confrontation is seen as an activity that wastes resources. Sun Tzu, another renowned scholar on warfare, observed that effective warfare is one that can be conducted and won with the minimum confrontation, risk, and loss (Huang & Rosenberg, 2011).

Although strategy is no longer merely restricted to military wars, its original connotation and objective — to win or, at the very least, achieve some sort of political advantage — remains integral to how many in businesses understand strategy and strategic thinking. In public relations, SC has evolved into an informational or persuasive objective rather than a military one (Smith, 2013), and the weapons of choice come in the form of *language*: written, spoken, and visual. If we think of language, and specifically rhetoric, as only enabling us to gain an advantage, then it would be easy to see why businesses would embrace rhetoric and shun dialogue. And yet, *both* have an important role to play in strategy and should be part of the strategic planning process to ensure a long-term view. Strategy, however, still remains notoriously difficult to describe, leading to a myriad of interpretations. As Murray and Grimsley (1994) argue:

> Straightforward definitions go fundamentally astray, for strategy is a process, a constant adaptation to shifting conditions and circumstances in a world where chance, uncertainty, and ambiguity dominate. Moreover, it is a world in which actions, intentions, and purposes of other participants remain shadowy and indistinct, taxing the wisdom and intuition of the canniest policymaker… While models and categories may assist analysis, they can offer no formulas for the successful framing of a strategy or conduct of war. (p. I)

Murray and Grimsley's description captures several aspects that are essential for us to understand when discussing the role and place of rhetoric and dialogue in strategic planning. Firstly, as mentioned earlier, we can draw similarities between dialogue and strategy. Just like dialogue is a product and a process (cf. Kent & Taylor, 2002), so too is strategy; with an outcome as uncertain as dialogue's (cf. Theunissen & Wan Noordin, 2012). Strategy is a sense-making activity, dealing with ambiguity and uncertainty, just like dialogue. While uncertainty implies that the result of whatever we do and plan is indeterminate, ambiguity can best be described as being present when a situation has "multiple possible meanings" or "no clear meaning at all" (Carroll, 2015, p. 59).

A lack of clarity poses a problem because ambiguity prevents us from asking the right questions because *we just don't know what to ask*, and a lack of clarity is not merely limited to the planning stage but is applicable to the strategic relationships that are formed between organizations and their stakeholders and/or publics. During the life of a relationship, whether strategic or not, information is required (Berko, Rosenfeld & Samovar, 1997). The information gathered allows us to ask questions, meet the objectives of that relationship, and is therefore needed to develop and maintain the relationship; *information* is the foundation for relational, and rational, decision-making. So, in essence, poor decisions that affect the organization's sustainability and long-term reputation are often the result of a lack of relevant information, or misguided assumptions about others.

Strategic thinkers engaging in dialogue not only need to deal with ever-increasing levels of ambiguity and uncertainty, they need to be able to organize and manage collective actions to ensure that effective decisions are made. To do this, they must understand the rhetoric of others' actions and the impact such actions have on their own practices. Strategies entail more than what can be captured in words (Gregory & Willis, 2013), and as Murray and Grimsley (1994) so eloquently highlighted, no model can accurately predict the process or outcome of the strategic plan because there are too many variables at play. Humans are irrational beings, and our actions and intentions do not always have the desired outcome.

Furthermore, change often happens faster than we can adapt to, and therefore, an aggressive approach to planning may not always provide us with appropriate solutions to the problem. Planning lulls professionals into a false sense of security that once we have clear goals and objectives, strategy will follow. "Being strategic" is a way of looking at the world that taxes the strategist's skills and knowledge. Finding examples of organizations that have chosen to focus on today's problem as "meeting the next quarter's profits" is not difficult. Ironically, while such decisions are short-term focused, the effects are often far-reaching and, at times, devastating.

Consider Volkswagen's emissions scandal. Having been caught in an emission control systems scandal that saw them paying a fine of $4.3 billion and pleading guilty on criminal misconduct charges (Volkswagen, 2017), Volkswagen is an example of having sacrificed their ethical beliefs and values of "positioning the Volkswagen Group as a global economic and environmental leader among automobile manufacturers" and deploying "intelligent innovations and technologies to become a world leader in customer satisfaction and quality," for an "8%… before tax… return on sales" (Volkswagen, 2014). Volkswagen sacrificed their 80-year-old reputation and organizational future for higher dividends in the present.

Although strategic thinking "is inevitably highly pragmatic" (Paret, 1986, p. 3), pragmatism should not be seen as a license to lose sight of the long-term goal or future-oriented thinking. In fact, strategy in public relations should be seen as a means to create a long-term vision of society (cf., Kent, 2011a). To be truly strategic and enact such a role, professionals need to overcome the short-term, operational focus of many organizations by working toward long-term goals in the vein of The Long Now. Strategy that incorporates the principles of rhetoric and dialogue, then, allows us to build a civil, fully functioning society by focusing on relationships and messages at multiple levels, and bringing back the ideas of relationships and responsibilities (Kent, 2011a).

Applying the Long Now: Toward a Fully Functioning Society

In 1993, computer designer and inventor Daniel Hillis proposed creating "a large (think Stonehenge) mechanical clock, powered by seasonal temperature changes. It ticks once a year, bongs once a century, and the cuckoo comes out every millennium" (Brand, 1999, p. 3). Hillis' clock idea eventually grew into a clock/library foundation (established in 1996) called *The Long Now*, which was designed to raise awareness about technology, capitalism, democracy, and long-term responsibility.

The Long Now (TLN) Foundation was established by a number of extraordinary professionals and academics:

- *Danny Hillis* (polymath, inventor, scientist, author, engineer, former Vice President for Research and Development at Walt Disney Imagineering, and a Disney Fellow).
- *Stewart Brand* (author, environmentalist, entrepreneur, creator of the Whole Earth Catalog, and cofounder of The WELL [Whole Earth'Lectronic Link], an online community established in 1985).
- *Keven Kelly* (author, publisher, and executive editor of *Wired Magazine* from its inception until 1999).
- *Douglas Carlston* (founder of Tawala Systems, and cofounder of Borderbund software).
- *Peter Schwartz* (chairman of Global Business Network, and author).
- *Brian Eno* (world-renowned musician, music performer, and artist).
- *Paul Saffo* (futurist, Stanford Professor, and spokesman for the Institute for the Future).
- *Mitchell Kapor* (founder of Lotus, and cofounder of the Electronic Frontier Foundation).
- *Esther Dyson* (a Harvard-educated author, journalist, businesswoman, philanthropist, entrepreneur, and creator and manager of *Release 1.0*, a computer industry newsletter, from 1983 to November 2006).

Of note are the diversity of skills and knowledge among the founders — consistent with the principles of The Long Now. The Long Now was not founded by a group of colleagues from the same organization and with the same professional skillset or those with "strong ties" (Granovetter, 1973), but by experts and intellectuals — and people of vision — from diverse backgrounds, beliefs, attitudes, values, and knowledge (http://longnow.org/people/board).

Network theorists have long known that people with diverse social and professional networks are capable of achieving *more* than people with fewer connections. Additionally, dialogic scholars understand the power of relationship building and genuine, transparent, interaction with others for understanding different worldviews and expanding our own cognitive perspectives (cf. Kent, Sommerfeldt, & Saffer, 2016).

Relationship skills are even more crucial in a world that is becoming increasingly complex with intricate issues to resolve. Unquestionably, one of the greatest challenges we face in this century is that the world has become hyper-complex, with large-scale systems, where change is moving at an ever-increasing pace — can we ever know enough, or ever have enough information (cf. Kent & Saffer, 2014; Malik, 2013) — and therefore we are prone to move continuously through a haze of uncertainty.

Our default response as human beings is to avoid, or at the very least limit, such ambiguity by engaging in collective actions (cf. Carroll, 2015). Collective action is exactly what TLN has done — they responded not by doing nothing, which Malik (2013) suggests is "one conceivable option" (p. 17), but by acting and being flexible in their strategic thinking. TLN therefore represents not just an ideal, but a *strategy in action*.

Principles of The Long Now

Of importance are TLN's principles that guide their actions. These principles, or the "Guidelines for a long-lived, long-valuable institution," include the following: "serving the long view, fostering responsibility, rewarding patience, minding mythic depth, allying with competition, taking no sides," and "leveraging longevity" (http://longnow.org/about). Essentially, as TLN explains:

> Civilization is revving itself into a pathologically short attention span. The trend might be coming from the acceleration of technology, the short-horizon perspective of market-driven economics, the next-election perspective of democracies, or the distractions of personal multi-tasking. All are on the increase. Some sort of balancing corrective to the short-sightedness is needed—some mechanism or myth which encourages the long view and the taking of long-term responsibility, where "long-term" is measured at least in centuries. (http://longnow.org/about)

In order to help foster long-term mechanisms, and long-term views, TLN initially formed around the millennial clock project, described above, and has subsequently grown into a community of more than 11,000 members who have an interest in helping foster long-term responsibility.

Since its inception, TLN has sponsored more than 200 talks by leaders in dozens of fields: Art, Business, Cities, Civilization, Climate Change, Culture, Economics, Evolution, the Environment, the Future, the Internet, Journalism, Law, Music, Public Policy, Religion, Terrorism, and so forth. Indeed, the diversity of lecture topics speaks to the ideological assumptions of TLN about the value of expert information, research, and informed reasoning. Problems are not solved by individual leaders who authoritatively urge people to do what they are told, but by complex thinkers rallying the best and the brightest in the world to find long-term solutions — and these solutions are not focused on the next quarter or even the next decade but span beyond our own lifetimes *far* into the future.

In keeping with its focus on the good of the future and long-term stewardship of the Earth and its inhabitants, TLN has also funded a number of long-view projects, including the following. (1) Purchasing a "two-mile-long swath of mountain land… covered by a forest of ancient bristlecone pine trees" (considered among the world's oldest living things, with some as old as 4,900 years) (http://longnow.org/clock/nevada). (2) The Rosetta Project, "a global collaboration of language specialists and native speakers working to build a publicly accessible digital library of human languages" (http://rosettaproject.org). (3) PanLex, an effort to make every word of every language of the world's 7,000 languages accessible to everyone. (4) The Long Bets, an effort to improve long-term thinking by encouraging people to find solutions to problems far into the future. (5) Revive&Restore, an effort to advance genomic technology and rescue and restore endangered and extinct species of plants and animals. (6) "The Interval," a bar, café, museum, and the home of TLN Foundation (http://theinterval.org/visit). And of course, the initial project, the 10,000-year clock.

As a US-based 501c3 nonprofit organization, the fact that TLN has accomplished all this in just over 25 years with nothing but donations and sponsorships is noteworthy, and speaks to the resonance of its long-term vision and in particular to its strategic approach. TLN draws upon the most pre-eminent and creative scholars and professionals in their respective fields. As Henry Ward Beecher, activist and social and political reformer, said more than a century ago, "When a nation's young men are conservative, its funeral-bell is already rung" (Drysdale, 1887, p. 70). Beecher's aphorism meshes well with the ideals of TLN, which involve understanding that one individual or group cannot know everything.

As suggested earlier, the rationale for TLN was a concern that "Civilization is revving itself into a pathologically short attention span." Strategic communication activities such as campaign planning, issues management, and crisis preparedness are activities that require a long view, and yet, focusing on the next quarter's profits obscures a long-term vision. Communication professionals often confuse *strategic* planning with *operational* and *tactical* planning, resulting in rushed decisions that focus on meeting the bottom line and "today's problem" (Kent, 2011a, p. 554) while neglecting to plan farther into the future.

The sooner that organizations and communication strategists begin to think farther down the road, the sooner they will be able to more effectively draw upon rhetorical and dialogic principles. TLN offers a blueprint for thinking about what the future holds: where rhetoric, persuasion, and dialogue are especially powerful tools that serve the interests of organizations, stakeholders, publics, *and* society, and, ideally, are not used to deceive or manipulate just to gain short-term advantage.

But the more important, and perhaps the most significant aspect of TLN, and the reason that it is featured here as our case study, is that the past success of TLN has been as a result of effective rhetoric and dialogue. Many of the founders of TLN, such as Stewart Brand, have a long history of understanding the importance of dialogue and rhetorical engagement (cf. Lane & Kent, 2018; Taylor & Kent, 2014), and value intellectual discussion.

TLN was an idea, then a metaphor, and finally a reality. But there is *nothing tangible* about the principles of TLN. In fact, TLN remains a metaphor and an idea, reified only through the efforts of a number of visionary professionals, and developed to foster long-lived and long-term thoughts and values. Rhetoric and dialogue have played a significant role in fostering and promoting TLN because of their ability to shape reality.

The Fully Functioning Society Theory (FFST) states that "public relations theory is best when it challenges and helps organizations be effective not only by what they do for themselves but also with the communities where they operate and on whose resources they depend" (Heath, 2013, p. 368). FFST separates *corporatas* from *communitas*, and emphasizes the value of the latter: "openness, trustworthiness, cooperation, aligned interests, compatible views/opinions/norms, and commitment inspired through cocreated meaning" (Heath, 2013, pp. 369–370).

A society such as the one envisioned here follows Long Now thinking, and is based on rhetorical and dialogic principles, recognizing the power of language (cf. Heath, 2013). To enact such a society, professionals need to understand the principles of dialogue and rhetoric, and embrace them in their message construction — not to unduly influence but to recognize the impact they have on constructing society, its values, and its long-term vision.

Essentially, a Long Now approach means that strategizing for business should have insight about the future of society, and therefore, public relations professionals must play a role in shaping the behavior of both organizations and publics and go beyond solely "negotiating" meaning that benefits organizations through enhancing or advocating the latter's position (of power) in society. Rather, organizations should aim to negotiate behavior that allows them to establish a democratic society where diversity is valued. Rhetoric must not only be used to craft messages for consumption but to engage decision-makers in thinking farther ahead, and dialogue must become part of this process.

As strategic planners for organizations, professionals must use all means at their disposal to gauge the (true) state of the environment by understanding rhetoric, dialogue, and the difference between operational and strategic planning. How can we know what human passions are, what values they hold, and what beliefs they follow, if we do not engage in dialogue? How can we develop an effective strategy when we do not know what moves people, or what makes people truly tick? As Kent (2011a) suggested:

> Ultimately, good decisions are made when organizations are open to feedback, people feel confident and safe in expressing their ideas (they should be encouraged to provide input), and decisions are made with the aim of making the best (long-term) decision and not just the most expedient. Good decisions are rhetorical, dialogic, and informed by research. (p. 555)

Conclusion

In its simplest form, for a plan to be truly a strategy, it must have a purpose, a planned sequence of actions, and a clearly identified, measurable goal. In Long Now thinking, this goal must be about creating a fully functioning society, one where sustainability and the welfare of future generations are key foci. To achieve this, we must become skilled in *both* dialogue and rhetoric.

Rhetoric allows us to engage all forms of message construction to communicate with and convince stakeholders, organizations, colleagues, media, and others of the importance of embracing the future and working toward a future that extends far beyond the next quarter. Having a convincing, strategic, future-oriented narrative is therefore important; this narrative must embrace the Long Now. Communicators must tell the story about the future and *communitas*, rather than *corporatas*, which means the focus must shift away from simply serving organizational interests, to serving society, to issues such as sustainability, the effects of global warming, and closing the increasing income gap, for example. Dialogue helps us to make sense of ambiguity, others' needs and desires, the meaning of their rhetorical actions, and build relationships that last. But, more importantly, dialogue and rhetoric are not merely tools; they are strategy. Applying these principles skillfully will allow professionals to be not just yeomen but generals who lead and construct organizational narratives in the vein of Long Now thinking.

Summary of Key Points

- Communication professionals confuse strategy with tactics, and strategic thinking with operational thinking, which narrows the focus to short-term profit-making objectives.
- In order to be truly strategic, the organizational focus needs to shift from meeting short-term goals to long-term, future-oriented thinking and society at large.
- Future-oriented or "Long Now" thinking implies focusing on constructing messages that address the community and society, such as sustainability and closing the wage gap. Long Now thinking moves beyond the next quarter or the next few years to future generations.
- The Long Now Foundation is an example of an organization that has embraced both dialogue and strategy, creating a vision that is rhetorical in nature but addresses the needs of the community. TLN embraces diversity to construct long-term solutions to current problems.
- Strategic dialogue aims to understand the community, their needs and wants, and reduce uncertainty. Dialogue is interpersonal in nature; aimed at minimizing obvious power differences and avoiding exploitation.
- Strategic rhetoric aims to construct messages that address organizational goals, and make organizational needs and desires a reality. Strategic rhetoric is public in nature and shapes the way people see the world.
- Both strategic rhetoric and dialogue are viable approaches to developing effective strategies. Effective communication professionals need to be trained in the use of both rhetoric and dialogue and understand their purpose and place in strategy.

URLs to Visit

Creative Commons: https://creativecommons.org
Electronic Frontier Foundation: www.eff.org
Project Gutenberg: http://www.gutenberg.org/about/

The Interval: http://theinterval.org/visit
The Long Now: http://longnow.org
The Rosetta Project: http://rosettaproject.org
Wikimedia Commons: https://commons.wikimedia.org/wiki/Commons:Welcome

References

Aristotle (1991). *Aristotle on rhetoric: A theory of civic discourse*, G. A. Kennedy (Trans.). New York: Oxford University Press.

Bakhtin, M. M. (1991/1975). *The dialogic imagination: Four essays.* Austin, TX: University of Austin Press.

Benoit, W. L. (1995). *Accounts, excuses, and apologies: A theory of image restoration strategies.* Albany, NY: State University of New York Press.

Berko, R. M., Rosenfeld, L. B., & Samovar, L. A. (1997). *Connecting. A culture-sensitive approach to interpersonal communication competency*, 2nd edn. Fort Worth, TX: Harcourt Brace & Co.

Bitzer, L. F. (1968). The rhetorical situation. *Philosophy & Rhetoric*, 1(1), 1–14.

Brand, S. (1999). *The clock of the long now: Time and responsibility.* New York: Basic Books.

Bryant, D. C. (1953). Rhetoric its function and scope. *Quarterly Journal of Speech*, 39, 401–424.

Buber, M. (1970/1923). *I and thou*, W. Kaufmann (Trans.). New York: Charles Scribner's Sons.

Burger, R. (2008). *Aristotle's dialogue with Socrates: On the Nicomachean ethics.* Chicago, IL: University of Chicago Press.

Burke, K. (1969a). *A grammar of motives.* Berkeley, CA: University of California Press.

Burke, K. (1969b). *A rhetoric of motives.* Berkeley, CA: University of California Press.

Carroll, J. S. (2015). Making sense of ambiguity and collaborative action. *Journal of Contingencies and Crisis Management*, 23(2), 59–65.

Drysdale, W. (1887). *Proverbs from Plymouth pulpit.* New York: D. Appleton & Co.

Fisher, W. R. (1978). Toward a logic of good reasons. *The Quarterly Journal of Speech*, 64, 376–384.

Fisher, W. R. (1984). Narration as a human communication paradigm: The case for public moral argument. *Communication Monographs*, 51, 1–21.

Fisher, W. R. (1985). The narrative paradigm: An elaboration. *Communication Monographs*, 52, 347–367.

Freire, P. (1970). *Pedagogy of the oppressed*, M. B. Ramos (Trans.). New York: Continuum.

Gerbner, G. (1969). Dimensions of violence in television drama. In R. K. Baker & S. J. Ball (Eds.), *Violence and the media: A staff report to the National Commission on the Causes and Prevention of Violence* (pp. 311–340). Washington, D.C.: U.S. Government Printing Office.

Gerbner, G., & Gross, L. (1976). Living with television: The violence profile. *Journal of Communication*, 26(2), 172–199.

Granovetter, M. S. (1973). The strength of weak ties. *American Journal of Sociology*, 78(6), 1360–1380.

Gregory, A., & Willis, P. (2013). *Strategic public relations leadership.* New York: Routledge.

Grunig, J. E. (2011). Public relations and strategic management: Institutionalizing organization–public relationships in contemporary society. *Central European Journal of Communication*, 1, 11–31.

Hallahan, K. (1999). Seven models of framing: Implications for public relations. *Journal of Public Relations Research*, 11(3), 205–242.

Hart, R. P. (1990). *Modern rhetorical criticism.* Glenview, IL: Scott, Foresman/Little, Brown, Higher Education.

Hearit, K. M. (2001). Corporate apologia: When an organization speaks in defense of itself. In R. L. Heath & G. Vasquez (Eds.), *Handbook of public relations* (pp. 501–511). Thousand Oaks, CA: Sage.

Heath, R. L. (2013). Fully functioning society theory. In R. L. Heath (Ed.), *Encyclopedia of public relations* (pp. 368–370). Los Angeles, CA: Sage.

Huang, C., & Rosenberg, A. D. (2011). *Women and the art of war. Sun Tzu's strategies for winning without confrontation.* Tokyo: Tuttle Publishing.

Johannesen, R. L. (1990). *Ethics in human communication*, 3rd edn. Prospect Heights, IL: Waveland.

Kennedy, G. (1980). *Classical rhetoric and its Christian and secular tradition from ancient to modern times.* Chapel Hill, NC: The University of North Carolina Press.

Kent, M. L. (2001). Managerial rhetoric and the metaphor of the World Wide Web. *Critical Studies in Media Communication*, 18(3), 359–375.

Kent, M. L. (2011a). Public relations rhetoric: Criticism, dialogue and the Long Now. *Management Communication Quarterly*, 25(3), 550–559.

Kent, M. L. (2011b). *Public relations writing: A rhetorical approach.* Boston, MA: Allyn & Bacon.

Kent, M. L. (2015). The power of storytelling in public relations: Understanding the 20 master plots. *Public Relation Review*, 41, 480–489.

Kent, M. L., & Boatwright, B. C. (2018). Ritualistic sacrifice in crisis communication: A case for eliminating scapegoating from the crisis/apologia lexicon. *Public Relations Review*, 44, 514–522.

Kent, M. L., & Lane, A. (2017). A rhizomatous metaphor for dialogic theory. *Public Relations Review*, 43(3), 568–578.

Kent, M. L., & Saffer, A. J. (2014). A Delphi study of the future of new technology research in public relations. *Public Relations Review*, 40(4), 568–576.

Kent, M. L., Sommerfeldt, E. J., & Saffer, A. J. (2016). Social networks, power, and public relations: *Tertius Iungens* as a cocreational approach to studying relationship networks. *Public Relation Review*, 42(1), 91–100.

Kent, M. L., & Taylor, M. (2002). Toward a dialogic theory of public relations. *Public Relations Review*, 28(1), 21–37.

Kent, M. L., & Taylor, M. (2016). From *homo economicus* to *homo dialogicus*: Rethinking social media use in CSR communication. *Public Relation Review*, 42(1), 60–67.

Kent, M. L., & Theunissen, P. (2016). Elegy for mediated dialogue: Shiva the Destroyer and reclaiming our first principles. *International Journal of Communication*, 10, 4040–4054.

Laing, R. D. (1961/1969). *Self and others.* New York: Pantheon Books.

Lane, A., & Kent, M. L. (2018). Engagement as dialogue, dialogue as engagement. In K. Johnston & M. Taylor (Eds.), *Handbook of engagement* (pp. 61–72). Hoboken, NJ: Wiley-Blackwell.

Malik, F. (2013). *Strategy. Navigating the complexity of the New World.* Frankfurt: Campus Verlag.

McGee, M. C. (1980). The "Ideograph": A link between rhetoric and ideology. *The Quarterly Journal of Speech*, 66, 1–16.

McGee, M. C., & Martin, M. A. (1983). Public knowledge and ideological argumentation. *Communication Monographs*, 50, 47–65.

Murray, W., & Grimsley, M. (1994). Introduction: On strategy. In W. Murray, M. Knox, & A. Bernstein (Eds.), *The making of strategy. Rulers, states, and war.* Cambridge: Cambridge University Press.

Noddings, N. (1984). *Caring: A feminine approach to ethics and moral education.* Berkeley, CA: University of California Press.

Osborn, M. (1967). Archetypal metaphor in rhetoric: The light–dark family. *Quarterly Journal of Speech*, LIII(2), 115–126.

Osborn, M. (1977). Evolution of the archetypal sea in rhetoric and poetic. *Quarterly Journal of Speech*, 63(4), 347–363.

Paret, P. (Ed.) (1986). *Makers of modern strategy from Machiavelli to the nuclear age.* Princeton, NJ: Princeton University Press.

Plato (Benjamin Jowett, Trans.) (1999) Gorgias. Project Guttenberg. Etext #1672. www.gutenberg.org/files/1636/1636-h/1636-h.htm.

Rogers, C. R. (1992/1957). The necessary and sufficient conditions of therapeutic personality change. *Journal of Consulting and Clinical Psychology*, 60, 827–832 (original work published 1956).

Romenti, S., Murtarelli, G., & Valentini, C. (2014). Organisations' conversations in social media: Applying dialogue strategies in times of crises. *Corporate Communications: An International Journal*, 19(1), 10–33.

Smith, R. D. (2013). *Strategic planning for public relations*, 4th edn. New York: Routledge.

Taylor, M., & Kent, M. L. (2007). Issue management and policy justification in Malaysia. In J. L. Courtright & P. M. Smudde (Eds.), *Power and public relations* (pp. 126–149). Cresskill, NJ: Hampton Press.

Taylor, M., & Kent, M. L. (2014). Dialogic engagement as a foundational concept in the practice of public relations. *Journal of Public Relations Research*, 26(5), 384–398.

Theunissen, P., & Wan Noordin, W. (2012). Revisiting the concept "dialogue" in public relations. *Public Relations Review*, 38(1), 5–13.
Volkswagen (2014). Group Strategy 2018. Retrieved on September 25, 2015 from http://www.volkswagenag.com/content/vwcorp/content/en/the_group/strategy.html
Volkswagen (2017, January 10). Volkswagen confirms $4.3bn payment of over diesel emissions. The Guardian. https://www.theguardian.com/business/2017/jan/10/volkswagen-confirms-43-billion-us-payment-over-diesel-emissions
Von Clausewitz, C. (1976). *On war*, M. Howard & P. Paret (Trans.). Princeton, NJ: Princeton University Press.
Ware, B. L., & Linkugel, W. A. (1973). They spoke in defense of themselves: On the generic criticism of apologia. *Quarterly Journal of Speech*, 59, 273–283.
Weaver, R. (1953/1985). *The ethics of rhetoric.* Hillsdale, NJ: Lawrence Erlbaum.
Wolfers, J. (2014, September 16). Pulse of the people: Perceptions haven't caught up to decline in crime. New York Times. www.nytimes.com/2014/09/17/upshot/perceptions-havent-caught-up-to-decline-in-crime.html?_r=0.

4

Strategic Communication in Turkish Public Sector

Through the Lens of Public Relations

B. Pınar Özdemir and Melike Aktaş
Ankara University

Due to its location at the intersection of the Middle East and Europe, the Turkish Republic, which was founded in 1923, has specific particularities and has both Eastern and Western characteristics. On the one hand, a strong Islamic tradition, which stems from the fact that Muslims comprise a large majority of the population, makes itself felt in every aspect of social life in Turkey. On the other hand, Turkey is a secular country, in which state and religious matters are separated, and it has a strong secular tradition. This particularity, which differentiates Turkey from many other Muslim countries, can be seen as one of the primary factors in Turkey's inclination toward the West. Modernization was the primary concern for the first administrators of the Republic, following the collapse of the Ottoman Empire. Despite the fact that modernization efforts were rooted in the last years of the Ottoman Empire, the alacrity of integration with the modern world affected the organization of the administrative structure of the Republic. The Turkish Republic inherited the governmental structure and bureaucracy of the Ottoman Empire and modernized the institutions that were founded in the Ottoman period. Strong state tradition, which came into being in the first years of the Republic when the private sector was not powerful, led state institutions to undertake several practices before the private sector. Public relations, which is the broadest subfield of strategic communication (SC), was one of these fields. Public institutions have been pioneering practitioners of public relations in Turkey. This study aims to analyze public relations in public administration in Turkey by focusing on approaches, regulations, and practices starting with the 1960s in three periods of 20 years. This study also aims to present an evaluation regarding the question of which of the three schools of thought in SC has been more dominant in public relations in public administration in Turkey.

The 1960s and 1970s: The Discovery of Public Relations in Public Administration

The establishment of public relations departments with specific duties, authority, and responsibilities in Turkish public administration dates back to the 1960s. Although public agencies already had press directorates or press offices before the 1960s, the operation of these

The Handbook of Strategic Communication, First Edition. Edited by Carl H. Botan.

departments was limited to monitoring the press and reporting relevant news to the administrators of the agency or institution they work for. Starting with the 1960s, there was a significant increase in the number of public relations departments in public agencies in affiliation with other departments with names like relations with the public, information and publicity, consultancy, administrative consultancy, publicity office, press consultancy, external relations, social relations, actuary, presentation, propaganda, public education, media, general secretary, and representation units.

The phenomenon of public relations, which first appeared as a subsection in translated books on public administration, gained shape following the second half of the 1950s, in line with the modern public communication framework (Gençtürk Hızal, Özdemir, & Aktaş Yamanoğlu, 2014). Public relations went through a period of institutionalization in the 1960s under the political, economic, and cultural atmosphere of the period. The modern public administration approach brought up the need for improved state–society relations and reorganized bureaucracy, allowing it to operate in an effective and efficient manner. Moreover, the relatively liberal character of the 1961 Constitution entrenched the right to association and expanded the parameter of citizens' participation in governance. Thus, the 1961 Constitution empowered citizens vis-à-vis public authority and provided a basis for practices of public relations in public administration. Finally, the need for the promotion and enforcement of the planned development approach, which put its stamp on the policies of the period, contributed to the recognition of the importance of public relations activities (Gençtürk Hızal, Özdemir, & Aktaş Yamanoğlu, 2014).

The State Planning Organization (SPT), which was established in 1960 for the promotion of planned development approach, has been one of the pioneering institutions that see public relations in public administration beyond press relations. The Press and Representation Department within the SPT published development plans and annual programs prepared by the SPT, distributed these publications, prepared informative materials, and organized seminars and other public activities for the promotion of the planned development approach (Aktaş Yamanoğlu, Gençtürk Hızal, & Özdemir, 2013).

The General Directorate for Family Planning, which was established in 1963, carried out a family planning campaign following its establishment. The Family Planning Campaign is accepted as the first planned public relations campaign in public administration in Turkey (Aktaş Yamanoğlu, Gençtürk Hızal, & Özdemir, 2013, p. 104). Lobbying efforts resulted in the adoption of a law on family planning by Parliament. Besides this, several planned public relations activities targeting press, health care workers, social service workers, and citizens were carried out. The campaign was remarkably successful as the population growth rate, mother–infant mortality rate, and rates of birth-related health problems diminished significantly in the years following the campaign.

The public relations approach in this period was shaped by the particular problems and needs of public administration. The divide between the rulers and the ruled, and the extreme complicatedness of the bureaucratic structure, were defined as primary obstacles for the improvement of public communication. The public relations approach brought struggle against these problems into the agenda. One such problem was the public sector's excessive complexity in official routines or procedures, resulting in delay or inaction in public services – also called "redtapism" (Merriam Webster, n.d.). The Struggle with Red-Tapism Program, which was also included in the government program in 1965, was a public relations campaign aimed at reorganizing the relations between citizens and the administration and simplifying the operations of state agencies on behalf of citizens. As the campaign did not yield effective results, the Struggle with Red Tapism Program stayed within the government programs for many years. The short-lived Administrative Information Center, which is accepted as the first central public relations department in public administration in Turkey, was established in 1967 for the promotion of the Struggle with Red Tapism Program. The Administrative Information

Center was established as a hot-line center tasked with responding to calls regarding the activities of public agencies and reducing complications in these activities. In contrast, the absence of dialogue between the center and other public agencies, lack of coordination, and the fact that a majority of the population did not have easy access to phones obstructed the operation of the center (Aktaş Yamanoğlu, Gençtürk Hızal, & Özdemir, 2013, p. 114).

Three reports – Central Government Organization Research Project (CGORP) (1963), An Analysis on the Provincial Organization of Central Administration (1966), and Reorganization of Administration-Principles and Recommendations (1971) – were prepared for restructuring public administration in line with administrative reforms (Aktaş Yamanoğlu, Gençtürk Hızal, & Özdemir, 2013, pp. 116–117). These reports provide significant insights for understanding the public relations approach in this period. The reports point to the functions of public relations in the improvement of the effectiveness of public administration and present recommendations regarding public relations organizations and activities (Aktaş Yamanoğlu, Gençtürk Hızal, & Özdemir, 2013, pp. 116–122). The emphasis of these reports on the improvement of connection with society and the development of methods for collecting feedback regarding public services signify that public relations was seen as an instrument for facilitating communication with society.

There were extensive recommendations related to public relations in the CGORP Report. In 1974, a study was carried out to evaluate the degree to which these recommendations were implemented (Dinçer & Ersoy, 1974). This study, entitled "Evaluation of the Degree of Implementation of CGORP Recommendations," found that the recommendations were either not properly understood by public agencies or implemented in a very limited fashion (Dinçer & Ersoy, 1974). According to Kazancı (1978), who analyzed the deficits of public relations practices in public administrations in the 1970s, focusing on the case of the Ministry of Public Works and Housing, factors that hindered public relations activities in public administration were insufficiencies in the structure and functioning of the administration and lack of public awareness. The main problems in public relations practices in public administration were the designation of public relations as optional activities left to the choice of administrators, the reluctance of administrators to familiarize themselves with the people and learn their expectations, the administrators' inclination toward limiting participation opportunities to a particular social strata – like political figures and businesspeople who can easily get in contact with the administration, and administrators' understanding of public relations as a means of affecting the people rather than initiating interaction (Kazancı, 1978, pp. 250–253).

The number of public relations departments in public administration rose in the 1970s. However, these departments did not function as operational units. Public relations in public administration during the 1960s and 1970s was limited to collecting petitions and complaints, facilitating appeal procedures, and informing the public. Public relations in public administration in this period lacked an integrative approach. Although extensive reports were prepared for the improvement of public relations activities, the lack of political will for the development of public relations in public administration, failure of centralization efforts, and limited resources of public relations departments inhibited effective implementation of public relations activities.

1980s to 1990s: Prevalence of Instrumental Communication in Public Administration

The 1980s was a decade of restructuring for Turkey. With the stabilization and structural adjustment programs put in motion on January 24, 1980, radical steps were taken for the mobilization of market forces for the effective distribution of resources and for the liberalization of the Turkish economy. Moreover, the political field was reshaped by the military coup of September 12, 1980.

Following the coup, the military junta banned the leaders of political parties represented in Parliament in the 1970s from politics for a period of 10 years. The media and universities were placed under strict control. In order to facilitate a return to democracy, the junta permitted the establishment of new political parties. Turgut Özal's Motherland Party, which was one of these parties established in the aftermath of the coup, managed to win the General Election in 1983. Turgut Özal promoted the new market policies, beginning with the first years of the Motherland Party's government (Dodd, 2012, pp. 57–59).

The implementation of these new market policies in Turkey, privatization efforts, restructuring of the market through de-regulation/re-regulation, and competition also affected public relations. In this process, the effects of market liberalization and the development of a consumer society in Turkey began to be felt in the field of SC in general and public relations in particular.

Following the 1980s, international corporations which increased their share in the Turkish market raised the demand for professional SC as their success depended on their ability to comprehend local particularities. Moreover, prestigious national firms, which competed with international corporations, began to look for a more professional approach to SC (Aktaş Yamanoğlu, Gençtürk Hızal, & Özdemir, 2014). In contrast, public relations in public administration could not gain the same momentum as the private sector. In terms of public relations in public administration, the instrumental approach continued to be the dominant trend in the 1980s and 1990s.

Despite the privatization policies of the Motherland Party government, the creation of new administrative agencies for circumventing the unwieldy bureaucracy contributed to the expansion of civil society in these years (Dodd, 2012, p. 59). At the same time, steps were taken for the restructuring the organization of public administration.

Two measures taken in this period are especially important for public relations. In 1984, public relations departments of different state agencies, established under various names, were designated as press and public relations offices with a legal regulation. "Press and Public Relations Offices" were defined as "optional" consultancy units in the regulation. This new regulation was a reflection of the public relations in public administration approach. The organization of public relations departments as units for the management of relations with the press, instead of units for improving relations with the public, indicates that the strategic understanding of public relations was not mature at the time (Aktaş Yamanoğlu, Gençtürk Hızal, & Özdemir, 2014, p. 126). Another striking point regarding this regulation is that, despite giving detailed information regarding the work description of other offices, the regulation did not specify the work description of the public relations offices. The lack of work description, which demonstrates the activities to be carried out within the framework of public relations in public administration, stemmed from the absence of comprehension, planning, and programming that would provide a basis for these practices and the inadequacy in understanding the strategic importance of public relations (Aktaş Yamanoğlu, Gençtürk Hızal, & Özdemir, 2014, p. 126).

Another interesting development in this period was the establishment of a public relations department under the Prime Ministry in 1984. With this regulation, the Prime Ministry Public Relations Department was given a rather limited field of responsibility. Although the department was authorized to evaluate the complaints of citizens, monitoring the media and providing consultancy services for citizens, there is no evidence of implementation in practice. A study conducted in 1994 to examine the functions of public relations in Turkish public administration showed that the public relations approach in Turkey was far away from being "strategical" (Acar, 1994). This study, which examined 176 public relations departments within different state agencies, all of which were responsible for state–society relations, showed how cautiously these departments carried out public relations activities. None of the departments which participated in this study had a work program. Participants in the study did not consider developing public relations strategies, conducting research for understanding the citizens and their expectations, developing public relations programs or campaigns as the responsibilities of public relations departments. The primary emphasis was put on the announcement of the activities of public agencies, and press relations were seen as the only instrument to present state policies and activities to the public.

The fundamental difference of the post-1980 period from the previous period is the use of television in the efforts of public relations in public administration. This development occurred in parallel with the increasing popularity of television in Turkish society. The state began to use TV advertisements for announcing various regulations and for triggering behavioral change among citizens. These TV ads were not part of a larger and more structured public relations program or campaign. They were rather short-term, tactical communication efforts, which aimed to direct citizens toward behaving in certain ways through striking and catchy slogans.

The most successful case of instrumental use of public relations was the public relations campaign for the promotion of receipt collection initiated by the Ministry of Finance. The Turkish Parliament introduced value-added tax to the Turkish economic system with Law No. 3065. Law No. 3065 was published as an Official Paper on November 2, 1984, and came into force on January 1, 1985. The collection of revenues from value-added tax mostly relies on documentation. Thus, directing citizens to collect receipts was an important challenge. While citizens did not have the habit of collecting receipts, sellers were reluctant to document sales because they could then keep the value-added tax in their pockets in the absence of documentation. Thus, the state was unable to collect value-added tax revenues. In order to overcome this problem, TRT – which was the only TV channel in Turkey at the time – began to broadcast TV ads to direct citizens to collect receipts. These TV ads were designed to appeal to different segments of the population, residing in cities and the countryside. In one of these ads, a famous folk singer was seen as a peasant demanding receipts while shopping in a small town near his village. In another ad, famous comedians portrayed a businessman and his secretary. The humorous language of these first TV ads – which aimed for awareness raising and persuasion – is remarkable, just the opposite of the top-down, didactic state approach.

From the 2000s Till Today: Toward Cocreational Communication

In 2002, the newly founded Justice and Development Party (JDP) led by Recep Tayyip Erdoğan, won the elections. The JDP has been the only political party to have the majority to form a single-party government since the 1990s. The JDP's rule has coincided with the consolidation of neoliberalism in Turkey. Since it came to power in 2002, the JDP has been an advocate of neoliberal paradigm in all spheres of life (Coşar & Yeğenoğlu, 2009, p. 38). The discourse of governance came to the fore in relation to the changing role of the state in economic and social fields.

The need for improved relations between the rulers and the ruled was also revealed in a study conducted by the Turkish Industry and Business Association (TIBA). This study presents data regarding the perception of the Turkish public administration by citizens (TIBA, 2002). It is interesting that this study, which is instructive for strategic public relations activities of the state, was conducted by a civil society organization instead of a public agency. The findings of this study show that the trust of citizens in public agencies is weak. The considered respectability of civil service officials is at a medium level. Four-fifths of citizens who participated in the study think that corruption in public agencies is very widespread. The study also shows that the primary source of information regarding public services is television.

The results of TIBA's research, which was focused on the perception of citizens, showed a disposition toward cocreational public relations at the time of the study. Three-quarters of participants agreed with the statement that the consideration of their views and suggestions would contribute to the functioning of public agencies. More than two-thirds of citizen participants agreed that information about the operations of public institutions should be accessible to everyone. However, more than half of participants also share the view that ordinary citizens should not have a say in the operations of public institutions with their current level of knowledge (TIBA, 2002). Based on this finding, it is possible to argue that citizens are more willing to engage with information services rather than participate in public operations. Other research conducted by Özdemir in 2006 shows that public officials are also not willing to enable such participation and do not believe that citizens can present their views, suggestions, or criticisms regarding public services (Özdemir, 2006).

It can be said that neoliberal transformation and the discourse of governance brought with it the need for reconsidering public relations in public administration and provided a basis for new practices. Since the 2000s, two baselines have guided the SC efforts of the state. One is the establishment of legal measures and new intermediary institutions in line with the governance approach. The other is the professionalization of campaigns conducted by public relations in public administration. It is known that these campaigns have been shaped through professional service procurements planned and carried out by ministries. Hereby in this process, the changes that took place in public administration public relations can be considered under two main headings: hearing the citizens and talking to them, and professionalization of public relations campaigns.

Hearing the Citizens and Talking to Them for Strategical Public Relations

The concept of governance came to the fore in the 1990s with the premise of bringing a more extensive approach than public administration by covering multiple actors and relations (Pierre & Peters, 2000, p. 1). While government focused on the distribution of goods and services, governance considers third parties as partners and aims to utilize their capacity and ability for solving problems (Salamon, 2002). Utilization of the capacity of agencies and citizens requires efficient familiarization with these actors. In this light, Tekeli argues that governance shifts the scale of responsibility regarding public management toward civil society rather than the state and relies upon the management of a multi-actor system through mutual interaction, called the "steering process" (Tekeli, 1999, pp. 239–248). Such an administrative approach, based on the premise of citizens' participation in governance, has the potential to transform the tactical communication approach of the state into a more strategic one. As publics are considered as primary decision-makers in SC between the state and citizens, their particular significance in state–society relations increases. Thus, identifying publics and ensuring their participation in governance becomes a requirement rather than an option. In order to initiate mutual interaction, which is a feature of an ideal steering process, the state is required to effectively understand its publics, especially its citizens. This is a precondition of interaction. The state can use information about expectations, demands, and requests of citizens at the first stage of a strategic public relations effort. Besides this, sharing information with actors is one of the primary instruments of the state for empowering and authorizing these actors and increasing their capacities. Thus, this new governance approach necessitates information sharing through an effective public relations scheme for any state that defines citizens as stakeholders.

The Prime Ministry Report entitled "Restructuration in Public Administration: Change in Management for Management of Change" (T.C. Başbakanlık, 2003) reveals the direction of restructuring in public administration and underlines the role attributed to public relations in this restructuring process. The report states that in line with the new global world order, the conceptualization and structure of public relations in Turkish public administration should evolve toward multi-directional actorship, have a participatory, governmental, and future-oriented approach that aims to prevent problems before they emerge, be results and target oriented, consider citizens as a target group, focus on primary functions without being overwhelmed by them, and undertake a facilitating role.

In the process following the publication of this report, a number of legal regulations and applications were introduced. These developments, which seek to improve citizen-oriented practices in public administration, are particularly important to understand the evolution of SC.

Right to Information Act

Law No. 4982 was adopted on October 9, 2003 (Bilgi Edinme Hakkı Kanunu, 2003). The regulation adopted on March 27, 2004 laid down the principles and procedures for the implementation of the law. The law states that: "Everyone has the right to information. Foreigners domiciled in Turkey and the foreign legal entities operating in Turkey can exercise the right in this law on the condition that the information they require is related to them or the field of their activities, and on the basis of the principle of reciprocity." According to the regulation, public agencies and institutions are responsible for sharing all kinds of documents and information with applicants, except for situations specified in the law, taking necessary administrative and technical measures in order to finalize information-sharing processes in an effective, fast, and accurate way. This law is related to public relations because it aims to function as an intermediary between the state and citizens, and it has the potential to function as an instrument which would inform the state and citizens about flaws in public services. At the same time, as citizens would gain the potential to criticize, change, and improve existing policies and public services in the light of information they receive, this would make the strategic use of public relations by the state possible.

The Prime Ministry Circular (2004/12) for the implementation of this law also reveals that the state gives particular importance to the potential of this law for providing a basis of interaction between the state and citizens and for facilitating interaction. In reference to the ensuring of the use of the right to petition and information, the circular states that: "Applicants who verbally submit their requests and claims to public agencies and institutions shall be served with tolerance and positive attitude. Applications shall be immediately reviewed, and utmost care shall be given for the solution of applicant's problems on-site" (Dilekçe ve Bilgi Edinme Hakkının Kullanılması, 2004). While this law brought about the recognition of the right to information, there are no regulations regarding the responsibility for providing information in Turkey. The Right to Information Act can be seen as a step to empower citizens in their relationship with public authority. Another similar arrangement is the Ethics Committee for Civil Servants.

Ethics Committee for Civil Servants and the Ombudsman Institution

The establishment of the Ethics Committee for Civil Servants in 2004 with Law No. 5176 on the Establishment of the Ethics Committee for Civil Servants and Amendment of Some Laws should be considered as a remarkable development for public relations. In 2005, the related regulation set forth the ethical codes of conduct for public officials and laid down the principles and procedures to regulate applications to the Ethical Board. As Sözen (2012, p. 170) states, "the overall aim was to increase public trust in public administration, to inform citizens as to what they are entitled to expect from public officials. The concerning Regulation identified the principles in the discharge of duties as justice, integrity, transparency and impartiality." This committee is important in terms of public relations because it aims to establish trust in public institutions and increase the respectability of public officials. The reorganization of the relations between public officials and citizens on behalf of citizens will balance the scales in relations.

Another institutional initiative that should be examined while elaborating on the public relations activities of the state is establishment of the Ombudsman Institution. Although there were some initial steps for the formation of the ombudsman, the law regarding the ombudsman was adopted in 2012 (Kamu Denetçiliği Kurumu Kanunu, 2012). The purpose of the institution is "to establish an independent and efficient complaint mechanism regarding the delivery of public services and investigate, research and make recommendations about the conformity of all kinds of actions, acts, attitudes and behaviours of the administration with law and fairness under the respect for human rights" (Ombudsman Institution, 2017). According to the law, the main responsibilities of the ombudsman are "to examine and investigate the complaints lodged to the institution, and submit recommendations to the administration accordingly; to draft the regulations concerning the implementation of this Law; to prepare annual reports; to prepare special reports on the matters requiring attention without waiting for the annual report; to make the reports public" (Ombudsman Institution, 2018). When the objective of the law and roles attributed to the Ombudsman Institution are taken into consideration, it can be said that the Ombudsman Institution was designed as an intermediary for the facilitation of state–society relations. This designation reveals itself in the primary objective of the ombudsman, which is stated as developing alternative methods for the solution of problems between individuals and public authority.

In addition to these institutions which aim to authorize citizens, the developments in communication and information technologies have proposed a number of new citizen-oriented applications and approaches. Within the framework of e-government, the e-Government Gateway and Prime Ministry and Presidency Communications Center are prominent among SC applications for the development of citizen participation.

e-Government Gateway

As a result of the efforts to facilitate government services and to make public services more efficient, e-government applications have been implemented by various ministries and metropolitan municipalities since the end of the 1990s. The opening of the e-government portal in 2008 can be seen as a new phase of e-government applications in Turkey. The e-Government Gateway is an internet portal that offers access to all public services from a single point. "The aim [of] the Portal is to offer public services to citizens, businesses, and government agencies in an efficient and effective manner through information technologies. The service ensures users to have easy access to services they need. With this service implemented, Government services in Turkey will be offered to the citizens in the easiest and most effective means possible, in a high quality, speedy, uninterrupted, and secure way" (e-Government Gateway, 2018). Through this portal, users can acquire information and access to main public services such as "citizenship, education, military obligation, social security, health, job and career, traffic, tourism, travel, culture art and sport, foreign citizens and law and regulations" (Üstüner & Yavuz, 2018, p. 828). According to the UN e-government metrics report in 2018, Turkey is among the most rapidly developing countries in e-government applications (UN, 2018).

Prime Ministry Communications Center (BİMER)

In 2006, the Prime Ministry issued a circular which underlines the importance of the concepts of governance and participation in governance in public administration literature. In the circular, it was stated that the establishment of a functional, fast, and effective system for the transmission of citizens' complaints, requests, views, and suggestions regarding administration is a fundamental necessity for the success of administration and for the functioning of democracy. Public relations activities of public agencies and institutions were reorganized in this light. The new regulation is also far from promoting citizens' participation in administration and facilitating systematic transmission of citizens' demands, requests, and suggestions to the administration. The new regulation foresees the use of a data-processing program along with the establishment of a nationwide phone line. It foresees immediate transfer of citizens' written and verbal appeals to the relevant public authorities, provision of responses as soon as possible, warning of relevant units in case of delays, conduct of all operations through an automation system, collection of statistical reports, and central monitoring. In the period following April 2018 when Turkey switched to a "presidential government system," the Presidency of the Republic of Turkey Directorate of Communications was established. The name of the Prime Ministry Communications Center (BİMER) was changed to Presidency Communications Center (CİMER) and it was put under the authority of the relevant directorate.

Presidency of the Republic of Turkey Directorate of Communications and Presidency Communications Center (CİMER)

This directorate, which has CİMER under its authority, is an important step – carrying the potential for advancing public administration public relations from tactical communication to SC in Turkey. The mission of the directorate is defined in broader terms, beyond analyzing citizen complaints: its vision is "to strengthen the brand of Turkey"; its task is defined as "the efforts to understand, explain, give meaning and value with national and international public opinion" (Presidency of The Republic of Turkey Directorate of Communications, 2018a). In accordance with its SC, the directorate has announced on its institutional website that it wants to create a communication context that includes not only questions and problem solving but also sharing of ideas and thoughts. An important feature that distinguishes the new system from the previous one is that the system is not limited to work as an intermediary to collect applications and send them to relevant institutions, it informs these institutions by carrying out reporting studies on the topics the applications are centered around and on the situations that carry a special importance for social benefit. 2,870,879 applications were submitted to CIMER in 2018. Compared to 2017, applications have increased about 7.5%. The number of answers given to these applications is 2,959,895 (Sabah, 2019).

Besides that, in order to ensure that citizens are able to share their suggestions and ideas directly with the relevant public institutions, the directorate initiated the project "I Have an Idea for My Country" in 2019. The aim of this project is to create a platform for gathering views on existing mechanisms, developing policies and mediating for the implementation of inspirational ideas (Presidency of The Republic of Turkey Directorate of Communications, 2018b). One of the most recent projects on the state's citizen-oriented communication efforts in Turkey is the Open Door Project implemented by the Ministry of the Interior.

Ministry of the Interior Open Door Project

The aim of the open door practices established within the governorships and district governorships is to ensure that citizens can communicate their demands and suggestions to expert personnel in person and solutions can be provided quickly. Improving the efficiency of communication between the state and citizens, increasing citizens' satisfaction, learning the demands of citizens, identifying and solving chronic problems are all aims of the project (T.C. İçişleri Bakanlığı, 2017). The most important feature that separates the project from CİMER is that although it is possible to make an electronic application, it is specifically based on face-to-face communication and rather than directing applicants to relevant units it tries to solve problems quickly at the application point. The project was initiated in 2017 by the Ministry of Interior and in mid-2018 there were Open Door Offices in 81 province and 48 district governorates. As of 2019, the aim is to establish new Open Door Offices in 112 district governorates.

Professionalization of Public Relations Campaigns in Public Administration

One of the primary changes in the SC efforts of the state in the 2000s was professionalization. The state began to procure services from professional communication firms for public relations campaigns in the early 2000s. Thus, communication campaigns conducted by public agencies began to have parallels with communication campaigns conducted by private firms. In contrast, the fact that public agencies only consider keeping budgets at the minimum level in service procurement decisions pushes creative and strategic dimensions of communication to the side.

The Ministry of Health has been one of the pioneer institutions conducting public relations campaigns with professional support. The Ministry periodically conducts public relations campaigns regarding public health issues. These campaigns include Vaccination Campaign, Hand-Washing Campaign, H1N1 Pandemic Public Information Campaign, Family Practice Information Campaign, and At Home Medical Care Promotion Campaign. The most systematic and extensive of campaigns conducted by the Ministry of Health has been the Campaign for the Prevention of the Use of Tobacco and Tobacco Products.

The Case of Communication Campaign for the Prevention of the Use of Tobacco and Tobacco Products

In 2004, Turkey signed the Tobacco Control Framework Convention, prepared by the WHO in 2003. The Law Amending the Law on Prevention of Hazards of Tobacco Products (Law No. 5727) came into force on January 19, 2008. This law substantially improved the legal framework of the struggle against tobacco. According to a survey conducted by Gallup in 2008 in 100 different countries, two-thirds of male participants and one-third of female participants from Turkey had smoked the day before they participated in the study (WHO, 2012). Thus, the need for an anti-tobacco communication campaign for the announcement of new legal measures and for informing the public regarding the harms of tobacco use was recognized and a campaign was put into action.

The anti-tobacco campaign of the Ministry of Health was planned and carried out in four stages. The first campaign – the Smoke-Free Air Zone Campaign – was conducted between May 14 and June 18, 2008 and aimed to provide public support for the law that abolished indoor smoking in public spaces. In order to appeal to an extensive public strata, the planners of the campaign enlisted the support of artists, communal leaders, athletes, and political leaders. The then Minister of Health Recep Akdağ became the primary advocate of the campaign. "Smoke-free air zone" and "guard your air" slogans were used in the media campaign, which aimed to inform the public and raise awareness. 25 TV and radio ads and five newspaper ads were published for this campaign, besides the use of billboards and banners, the distribution of leaflets, and 18 kinds of outdoor events (T.C. Sağlık Bakanlığı, 2012).

The campaign put out positive rather than negative messages and concepts, identifying passive smokers, children, youths, adults, tobacco addicts, the media, opinion leaders and role models, public agencies and institutions, and nongovernmental organizations (NGOs) as target groups. Different communication activities were carried out in line with the characteristics of these groups. Besides the active use of social media, a website (www.havanikoru.org.tr, "protect your air") was prepared for the campaign. Moreover, units and phone lines were established for informing the public and receiving their complaints and suggestions (T.C. Sağlık Bakanlığı, 2012).

The second campaign, which was conducted between June 18, 2009 and February 20, 2010, focused on passive smoking (T.C. Sağlık Bakanlığı, 2012). At this stage, positive attributes of clean and smoke-free air were underlined and harms of passive smoking were reflected in two TV ads. The campaign put specific emphasis on women's health and aimed to eliminate the positive perception of smoking among youths. The third campaign was conducted between November 2010 and November 2012 with the slogan "smoking is regret." At this stage, the target group was tobacco addicts. The harms of smoking were shown in TV and radio ads in a striking manner. The ads also gave information regarding assistance services for quitting smoking.

The fourth campaign began in November 2012. The slogan "your life, your choice" was used at this stage of the campaign, promoting the stories of those who quit smoking before suffering any serious medical problems (T.C. Sağlık Bakanlığı, 2015). At this stage, one of the objectives was directing non-smokers to stand behind their right to smoke-free air, which is protected by law, and raising awareness regarding the issue.

A "non-prohibitive and integrative approach" was adopted in the communication campaign for the prevention of the use of tobacco and tobacco products. During the campaign, various health organizations, public agencies, and NGOs acted in coordination. This coordination reinforced efforts to multiply the effects of the campaign. Several media strategies were used during the campaign. Besides radio and TV ads, newspaper and magazine ads, banners, posters, leaflets, and booklets were used. With a website and consultancy phone line, two-way communication was attempted. Ordinary citizens from various socioeconomic backgrounds who quit smoking advocated the campaign, along with opinion leaders. During the campaign, studies were conducted to examine the approaches, perceptions, and awareness levels of target groups. The studies also aimed to evaluate public support for campaign-related activities.

The Action Plan for National Tobacco Control Program 2015–2018 indicates that the utilization of SC activities in efforts to reduce demand for tobacco products will continue.

Conclusion

Despite the introduction of public relations in Turkey with a focus on public administration and well-intentioned efforts in the first period, particular specificities of public administration in Turkey and problems at the level of practice resulted in the development of a narrow approach to public relations. While public relations was seen as a fundamental instrument of public administration in the 1960s, public relations departments in the public sector remained inactive in the 1980s and 1990s. After the 2000s, public relations in the public sector gained operational ground as governance practices put forward a cocreational approach. Despite the adoption of new legal measures and the establishment of new mechanisms and institutions during the 2000s, there are serious deficits regarding the use of SC in public relations activities.

Even though the changes that occurred in public administration in the 2000s in Turkey have some deficiencies in implementation, it can be said that they created a basis for the understanding of "cocreational strategic communication." On this basis, public relations campaigns specialized in public administration have begun to be planned and implemented, and important strategic goals have been achieved through these campaigns. However, even if the established understanding of public relations in public administration is updated and modernized with some revisions, it is still hard to claim that SC has gained a cocreational dimension. The main obstacle for the adoption of cocreational SC is that the public relations understanding in the area of public administration is mainly based on information transfer, information sharing, and problem solving. In this context, the citizen-oriented approach consists of improving the ease, speed, and problem-solving capability of bureaucratic processes, rather than participatory governance with increased dialogue and interaction. As a result, it can be stated that SC in Turkish public administration has gained momentum in the cocreational direction by leaving the "instrumental approach" behind and with the current applications it is at a "somewhat cocreational" stage.

References

Acar, M. (1994). *Türk kamu yönetiminde halkla ilişkiler araştırması [Public relations research in Turkish public administration]*. Ankara: DPT Yayınları.

Aktaş Yamanoğlu, M., Gençtürk Hızal, G. S., & Özdemir, B. P. (2013). *Türkiye'de halkla ilişkiler tarihi: Kurumsallaşma yılları 1960–1980 [History of public relations in Turkey: Institutionalization years 1960–1980]*. Ankara: Deki.

Aktaş Yamanoğlu, M., Gençtürk Hızal, G. S., & Özdemir, B. P. (2014). Turkey. In T. Watson (Ed.), *Middle Eastern and African perspectives on the development of public relations* (pp. 121–137). London: Palgrave Pivot.

Bilgi Edinme Hakkı Kanunu (2003, October 24). *Official Gazette of TR*. http://www.resmigazete.gov.tr/eskiler/2003/10/20031024.htm#1

Sabah (2019). CİMER'e 2018 yılında 2 milyon 870 bin 879 başvuru (February, 18). Sabah. https://www.sabah.com.tr/gundem/2019/02/18/cimere-2018-yilinda-2-milyon-870 bin-879-basvuru.

Coşar, S., & Yeğenoğlu, M. (2009). The neoliberal restructuring of Turkey's social security system. *Monthly Review*, 60(11), 36–49.

Dilekçe ve Bilgi Edinme Hakkının Kullanılması (2004, January 24). *Official Gazette of TR*. http://www.resmigazete.gov.tr/eskiler/2004/01/20040124.htm#4

Dinçer, N. & Ersoy, T. (1974). *Merkezi hükümet teşkilatı araştırma projesi (MEHTAP) tavsiyelerinin uygulanma durumunu değerlendirme araştırması [Evaluation of the degree of implementation of CGORP recommendations]*. Ankara: TODAİE.

Dodd, C. H. (2012). The Republic of Turkey. In M. Heper & S. Sayarı (Eds.), *The Routledge handbook of modern Turkey*. New York: Routledge.

e-Government Gateway (2018). Retrieved March 11, 2019 from https://www.turkiye.gov.tr/non-citizens

Gençtürk Hızal, G. S., Özdemir, B. P., & Aktaş Yamanoğlu, M. (2014). Tracking public relations history in 1960s' Turkey: The prevalence and reflections of development discourse. *Public Relations Review*, 40(4), 632–638.

Kamu Denetçiliği Kurumu Kanunu (2012, June 29). *Official Gazette of TR*. http://www.resmigazete.gov.tr/eskiler/2012/06/20120629-2.htm

Kazancı, M. (1978). *Halkla ilişkiler açısından yönetim ve yönetilenler [Public administration and citizens in terms of public relations]*. Ankara: AÜ SBF Yayını.

Merriam Webster (n.d.). Red-tapeism. In Merriam Webster online. https://www.merriam-webster.com/dictionary/red-tapeism

Ombudsman Institution (2017). About us. Retrieved April 21, 2019 from https://www.ombudsman.gov.tr/English/about-us/index.html

Ombudsman Institution (2018). Law on the ombudsman. Retrieved April 21, 2019 from https://www.ombudsman.gov.tr/contents/files/Law%20no_%206328-revised-03-08-2018.pdf

Özdemir, B. P. (2006). *Küreselleşme ve halkla ilişkiler: Küreselleşmenin Türk halkla ilişkiler sektörü üzerine etkileri [Globalization and public relations: The effects of globalization on Turkish public relations sector]*. Ankara: İmaj Yayınları.

Pierre, J., & Peters, B. G. (2000). *Governance, politics and the state*. Hong Kong: Macmillan.

Presidency of The Republic of Turkey Directorate of Communications (2018a). About DoC. Retrieved April 21, 2019 from https://www.iletisim.gov.tr/english/kurum-hakkinda

Presidency of The Republic of Turkey Directorate of Communications (2018b). 2019'da Ülkem İçin Bir Fikrim Var. Retrieved April 21, 2019 from https://www.iletisim.gov.tr/english/kurum-hakkinda

Salamon, L. M. (2002). *The tools of government – a guide to the new governance*. New York: Oxford University Press.

Sözen, S. (2012). Recent administrative reforms in Turkey: A preliminary assessment. *International Journal of Business and Social Science*, 3(9), 168–173. 10.30845/ijbss.

T.C. Başbakanlık (2003, October). Değişimin yönetimi i'çin yönetimde değişim [Restructuration in public administration: Change in management for management of change]. Retrieved March 12, 2019 from http://www.sp.gov.tr/upload/xSpKutuphane/files/ewRtIDegisimin_Yonetimi_icin_Yonetimde_Degisim_2003_pdf

T.C. İçişleri Bakanlığı (2017, October 15). Açık Kapı Projesi (Milletin Kapısı). Retrieved February 20, 2019 from https://www.icisleri.gov.tr/acik-kapi-projesi-19-01-2018

T.C. Sağlık Bakanlığı (2012, June 27). Kampanya Hakkında. Retrieved March 25, 2019 from https://sggm.saglik.gov.tr/TR,4003/kampanya-hakkinda.html

T.C. Sağlık Bakanlığı (2015, January 27). Kampanya Hakkında. Retrieved March 25, 2019 from https://sggm.saglik.gov.tr/TR,4062/ilgili-gorseller–spot-filmler-.html

Tekeli, İ. (1999). *Modernite aşılırken siyaset [Politics while overcoming modernity]*. Ankara: İmge Kitapevi.

TIBA (2002). *Kamu Reformu Araştırması [Research on public reform]*. İstanbul: TÜSİAD Yayınları.

UN (2018). eGovernment survey 2018. Retrieved March 30, 2019 from https://publicadministration.un.org/egovkb/Portals/egovkb/Documents/un/2018-Survey/E-GovernmentSurvey2018_FINALforweb.pdf

Üstüner, Y., & Yavuz, N. (2018). Turkey's public administration today: An overview and appraisal. *International Journal of Public Administration*, 41(10), 820–831.

WHO (2012). Turkey's transformation. *Bulletin of the World Health Organization*, 90(6), 408–409.

PART II

Cocreational Perspective in Strategic Communication

5

A Cocreational Approach to Social-Mediated Crisis Communication
Communicating Health Crises Strategically on Social Media

Yan Jin and Lucinda Austin
University of Georgia and University of North Carolina at Chapel Hill

Introduction

Crisis communication is a research and practice area, underneath the overarching framework of strategic communication (SC). Crisis communication research has traditionally focused on how organizations can respond to crises more reflectively. A more audience-oriented approach to crisis communication has recently emerged in the discipline, which echoes the paradigm shift in SC called for by Botan and Taylor (2004), moving from functional approaches to more cocreational approaches, with genuine interest and concrete emphasis on how publics create and share meaningful messages on issues. To further understand publics in the increasingly complex media landscape, the social-mediated crisis communication (SMCC) model is proposed to fully understand publics in times of crisis situations, including influential social media creators who cocreate messages and meanings of these messages on social media, social media followers, and social media inactives (Liu et al., 2012b). The SMCC model provides insight into how social media changes the way publics communicate with each other and interact with organizations, resulting in how organizations and publics cocreate meaning about crises through the social-mediated relationships they share and manifest on- and offline. Among the three primary publics, ***influential social media creators*** are defined as individuals who perceive the importance of crises and talk about crises online. By doing so, these social media creators exert direct influence on ***social media followers*** online and indirectly on ***social media inactives*** offline or via traditional interpersonal channels (Austin, Liu, & Jin, 2012; Jin & Liu, 2010; Liu et al., 2012a).

Jin, Pang, and Cameron (2007) advocated for crisis communication research to take a publics-based approach, which centers strategic decision-making and crisis messaging design on primary publics in a given crisis situation. According to the proposed characteristics, primary publics: (1) are most affected by the crisis; (2) have shared common interests, and destiny, in seeing the crisis resolved; and (3) have long-term interests in the organization's reputation and operation.

A shift to a publics-based approach to crisis communication is likely to facilitate voices outside of organizations to be not only heard but also play an essential role in shaping and forming crisis communication strategies before, during, and after crises. This will ultimately guide how organizations and others respond more effectively and efficiently, particularly in SMCC

The Handbook of Strategic Communication, First Edition. Edited by Carl H. Botan.

when publics are especially active information creators, seekers, and sharers, as the SMCC model has outlined (Liu et al., 2012a). More research is needed that not only describes and predicts publics' crisis communication behaviors, but also understands publics' core values. Also essential is examination of how publics' perspectives and values can be authentically cocreated with organizations, as well as with publics, so that crisis information can reflect what publics think and feel and be effectively communicated via traditional and social media channels.

Grounded in a cocreational approach (Botan & Taylor, 2004) and the SMCC model framework, this chapter focuses on how organizations can practice cocreational crisis communication through social media. A set of cocreational SMCC indicators are identified from the literature on cocreational frameworks, dialogic communication, the SMCC model, and crisis emotion theories. A recent public health crisis case – the 2014 Ebola outbreak crisis and how three major health organizations communicated crisis information with publics using Twitter and Instagram (Guidry et al., 2017) – is summarized and evaluated according to cocreational indicators to illustrate how a cocreational approach to SMCC could be applied to SC practice.

Literature Review and Theoretical Framework

Strategic Communication and Crisis Communication Research

As mentioned earlier, crisis communication is a communication area under the umbrella of SC. Over the past two decades, several theories or theoretical frameworks have emerged as predominant approaches to crisis communication research. The majority of crisis communication studies have focused on organizational perspectives, viewing crises as threats to the operation or reputation of an organization; through this perspective, the primary function of crisis communication is to respond to problems effectively in order to minimize damages and protect the assets (including reputation and image) of an organization. Advocating for such a shift to publics-based approaches to crisis communication, Jin, Pang, and Cameron (2012) proposed that effective crisis communication needs to match with primary publics' crisis emotions (e.g. anger, sadness, fright, and anxiety), their coping preferences (i.e. cognitive coping versus conative coping), and their preferred level of organizational engagement in handling and responding to the crisis situation.

As a practice area of SC, crisis communication focuses on how to shape appropriate strategies in response to a crisis, which is critical for organizations and crisis managers. Lukaszweski (1997) argued that the strategic management of message response in crisis communication is a "fundamental communication principle" (p. 8). Ray (1999) posited that strategies establish and enact "control (at least in its appearance) in the face of high uncertainty" (p. 19). The goal of crisis communication, defined as the "ongoing dialogue between the organization and its publics" prior to, during, and after a crisis (Fearn-Banks, 2002, p. 2), is to restore organizational normalcy and influence public perception, as well as to regain reputation and repair image by way of maneuvering appropriate crisis communication strategies. Designing effective and ethical SC messages to communicate with publics about a crisis in order to minimize damages to an organization's image has been described as "management at its zenith" (Stocker, 1997, p. 203). It is clear, however, that crisis communication has yet to integrate fully a cocreational view, which goes beyond shaping crisis response strategies to include publics in final decision-making about the meaning of the crisis information and whether organizational crisis responses are appropriate or not.

Image Repair Theory and Situational Crisis Communication Theory

Arguably, the two dominant theories on crisis strategies are Benoit's (e.g. 1995, 1997, 2003) image repair strategies and Coombs' (e.g. 1995, 1998) crisis response strategies. Both are designed to understand what strategies are relevant to use under what circumstances, often stemming from a situation-based response to a crisis. According to Benoit and Brinson (1994), image repair theory is appropriate to be used when the situation leads to a loss of face, which usually occurs when the accused is believed to have committed an offensive act by its salient audience (Benoit, 2003). Coombs' (1998) strategies are positioned according to the crisis situation and the organization's locus of control: when the organization is deemed by the publics to have strong organizational responsibility for the crisis, more accommodative strategies such as full apology are recommended for use; when the organization has low perceived responsibility for the crisis, more defensive strategies such as attack and denial are recommended.

From Organization-Focused to Publics-Based Approaches to Crisis Communication

Strategies, according to Massey (2001), are "message repertoires that are designed to repair the organization's image by influencing stakeholder perceptions" (p. 155). Ray (1999) argued that strategies would either deny the crisis exists, provide "partial, inaccurate or delayed information," or maintain an open communication channel with constituents (p. 20). Candor and openness, where possible, is a hallmark of excellent crisis communication (Greer & Moreland, 2003). Effective and authentic crisis communication practice demands a full understanding of not only the crisis situation and organizational stances and positioning, but also the needs, wants, and feelings of publics affected by a crisis. This demand provides impetus for a shift from organization-response-centric crisis communication models to more publics-based approaches to crisis communication research and practice (Jin, Pang, & Cameron, 2007, 2012).

In light of such a paradigm shift, questions regarding (1) to what extent publics are involved in crisis information production and dissemination and (2) how their values are embedded and reflected in organizational crisis responses become increasingly critical in evaluating crisis communication effectiveness. By definition, publics are a "group of people who face a common issue" (Gonzalez-Herrero & Pratt, 1996, p. 84). In a crisis, publics are defined differently, according to their importance in resolving the situation, their functional roles, and their long-term influences. For instance, according to Lukaszweski (1997), four key publics the organization must communicate with are: (1) those most directly affected – the victims; (2) employees, who may bear the brunt of the wrath of the publics; (3) those indirectly affected, like families and relatives; and (4) news media and other channels of external communication. Priorities must be made to communicate with media and other channels as soon as possible. However, this definition seems to exclude investors and stockholders as key publics in organizational crisis communication, who often develop and share meanings with organizations that are different from the management of the organization. In addition, from a cocreational perspective, key publics in crisis communication include all individuals and groups who develop similar meanings about a crisis before and after its occurrence, whose active role helps define a crisis situation itself. In the same vein of a cocreational view, when confronted by the same crisis, while publics regard it as an issue they have to deal with, an organization affected by it tends to approach the situation as a managerial problem that threatens the organization's operation or reputation. Such a misalignment of interpreting a crisis between publics and organizations contributes to organizations confusing management problems with issues publics have with the organizations, which often leads to a mismatch between how organizations decide to solve business problems and what organizational responses publics expect regarding issue resolutions.

One of the hallmarks of the cocreational model of SC lies in the central role publics play in making communication decisions and creating meanings and values in communication activities. The definition of publics, however, varies depending on where theoretical perspectives stand in relation to organization-centric versus audience-centric approaches. From an organization-centric approach to crisis communication, publics are primarily examined in terms of their functional roles (Dougherty, 1992): (1) *enabling publics*, including shareholders, boards of directors, and regulatory agencies, have the power and authority to control the organization's resources; (2) *functional publics* mainly consist of an organization's consumers; (3) *normative publics* are formed because of shared values, such as political or interest groups; and (4) *diffused publics* are those who are not members of a formal organization, yet are powerful groups. In line with this functional view of publics in crisis communication, Ulmer (2001) categorized publics in terms of their long-term influences on an organization's well-being, regarding the *primary publics* as (1) the community in which the organization works and (2) the employees, while the *secondary publics* mainly consists of customers and media. However, this definition does not reflect the need for organizations to not only respond to crises but also genuinely interact with publics and cocreate meaningful understanding and problem-solving decisions with publics. Social media has presented new opportunities for engaging with publics and, with them, the urgency for understanding the needs, wants, and values of primary publics has increased in this complex media environment, which provides interconnected communication channels and platforms for publics to interact with each other and organizations before, during, and after crises.

Social-Mediated Crisis Communication Model

The SMCC model is an emerging framework describing the current landscape for crisis communication. It is one of the first theoretical frameworks to explain the relationship between an organization, key publics, social media, traditional media, and offline word-of-mouth communication before, during, and after crises (Liu et al., 2012a, 2012b). On the one hand, the SMCC model positions an organization in the center of the crisis information flow, which reflects the traditional functional approach to crisis communication by recommending crisis communication responses on- and offline according to the characteristics of a crisis-stricken organization and the situation. On the other hand, this framework maps out and places high priority on the meaning-making role of primary publics who create and share crisis information, thus emphasizing the importance in crisis communication decision-making of integrating publics, including news media and on- and offline publics, in a changing multiple-media environment (see Figure 5.1).

Specifically, the SMCC model consists of two parts (Liu et al., 2012a): the ways publics seek and distribute crisis information based on a variety of factors and how the organization experiencing a crisis can effectively respond to primary publics. The ultimate goal of the framework, primarily focusing on the organization, is to offer recommended organizational message strategies for crisis response utilizing social media, traditional media, and word-of-mouth (WOM) communication, which vary according to different publics' levels of blame attributed to the organization, along with their negative crisis-related emotions, existing relationship with the organization, and perceptions of whether the organization has had a history of similar crises.

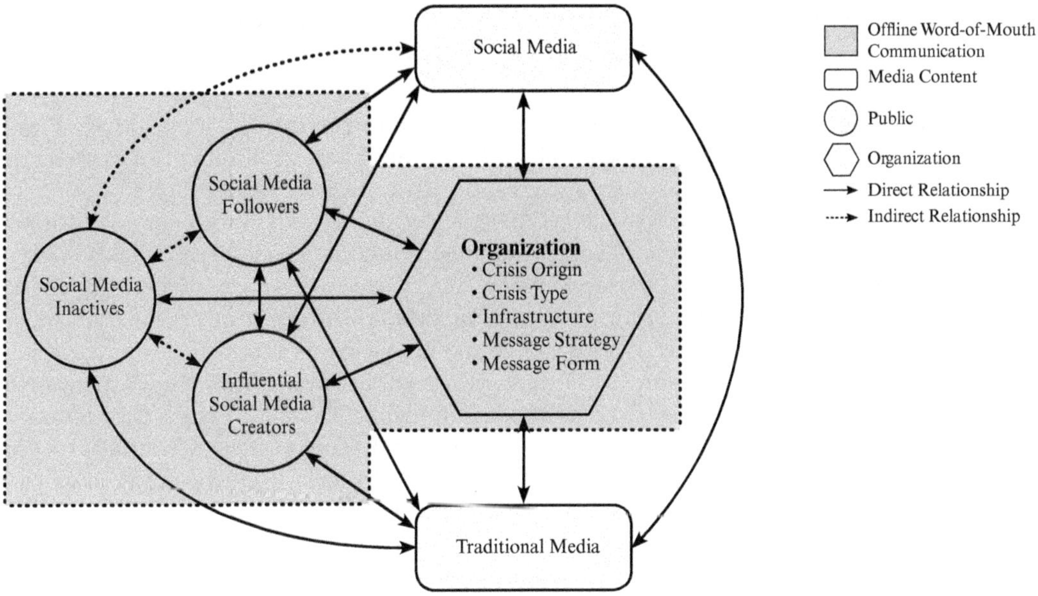

Figure 5.1 Social-mediated crisis communication model (Liu et al., 2012b).

In order to make insightful recommendations for organizations, understanding primary publics' crisis information creation, distribution, and consumption patterns is pivotal (Liu et al., 2012a). The three types of primary publics identified by the SMCC model, as indicated earlier, are: (1) *influential social media content creators*, who communicate about the crisis via social media; (2) *social media followers*, who communicate about the crisis by posting *creators'* crisis information online and otherwise communicating the content to others both on- and offline; and (3) *social media inactives*, who communicate about the crisis by garnering information from traditional media and conveying it via WOM with both the social media content creators and followers, and who may in turn communicate this content on- and offline. While social media creators and followers may seek or share crisis information primarily from or with their social peers, other publics, organizations, and news media outlets online, social inactives may engage in such activities offline and/or via traditional interpersonal communication channels such as making a phone call, texting, and emailing.

Thus far, empirical testing of the SMCC model has mostly focused on how information form (i.e. channel or medium), source, message characteristics, and context impact publics' cognitive, affective, and intended communicative/behavioral responses (Austin, Liu, & Jin, 2012; Jin & Liu, 2010; Jin, Liu, & Austin, 2014; Liu, Austin, & Jin, 2011, 2013; Liu, Fraustino, & Jin, 2015, 2016). No particular form or source consistently outperforms the others in terms of generating positive responses for organizations in crises. One of the much-needed SMCC research areas is to delve deeper into the understanding of online influencers, before, during, and after crises (Jin & Liu, 2010; Liu et al., 2012a, 2012a). Research is recommended to move beyond monitoring and measuring publics' responses to issues, crisis information, and organizational strategies, to also gauge publics' interpretations of crisis situations, assess publics' trust in and use of various information sources in crisis situations as a function of different crisis types versus their trust in and use of the same sources in non-crisis situations, evaluate publics' emotions embedded in their sense-making processes, and explore how crisis information and organizational messages can be developed and refined through integrating and collaborating with publics in managing crises. A cocreational approach thus sheds light on this possibility and future directions of theory development and practice refinement in SMCC.

A Cocreational Approach to Social-Mediated Crisis Communication

The SMCC model provides several implications in light of the cocreational model of SC. First, as indicated by the two-headed arrows, publics cocreate meanings within themselves through their communicative relationships with organizations and other message sources or content creators. Second, publics use social media to develop new and broader meanings both within themselves and between themselves and organizations, as indicated by the two-headed arrows interconnecting these key players on- and offline. Third, the two-way arrow between social media inactives and the traditional media indicates that those who are inactive on social media turn to traditional media and press their agenda to traditional media as well. This mutual influence between traditional media and social media is crucial, because if individuals are inactive on social media and also inactive with respect to traditional media about a crisis, then they are not considered primary publics in relation to the issue and problem the crisis brings to the primary publics and organizations affected. Fourth, social media inactives depicted in the SMCC also have a direct relationship with organizations via offline communications and traditional communication channels. They obtain crisis information and create meanings about such information via interactions with traditional media and direct relationships with the organization.

As indicated earlier, Botan and Taylor (2004) observed two main research themes in SC research: a functional perspective and a cocreational perspective. While a functional perspective views publics and communication mainly as a way to help achieve an organization's goals, a cocreational perspective "sees publics as cocreators of meaning and communication as what makes it possible to agree to shared meanings, interpretations, and goals" (p. 652). Based on this definition, existing crisis communication theories and frameworks are predominantly based on the functional perspective. Recent theoretical development, such as the SMCC model, points to the need for crisis communication to shift more toward a cocreational perspective, viewing publics in crises as cocreators of the meanings of crisis information, which should reflect the shared meanings, interpretations, and goals of an organization and its primary publics.

In suggesting future directions in social media for SC practitioners and scholars, Kent (2010) argued that effective organization–publics communication on social media needs to have the capacity for practitioners to communicate with individuals as valued and trusted companions. Kent (2013) further proposed that in order to use social media for relationship building, practitioners need to: (1) develop social media spaces that allow organizational members to communicate with individuals; (2) allow organizational members and publics to freely interact and collaborate; (3) make the identity of participants public and verifiable; (4) provide clear rules for social media participation; (5) seek out and invite experts to participate; and (6) nurture and encourage divergent voices to participate.

Although such a cocreational perspective has been adopted in SC research and tested in organization–stakeholder relationship studies, it has not yet been incorporated and tested in crisis communication research. Questions remain in terms of, for example, (1) whether and to what degree crisis managers should follow dialogic communication principles to engage publics on sensitive topics with legal and regulatory risks and (2) whether and how an organization and its publics can work together to cocreate effective and ethical crisis information when social listening and real-time interactions and engagement are made possible by the digital revolution. In addition, according to Jin, Pang, and Cameron's (2012) argument on the importance of crisis emotions in publics-based crisis communication models, organizations need to engage publics with crisis emotions as appropriate, which could be positive (e.g. hope) or negative (e.g. anger), or a balance of both.

Therefore, this chapter argues that – in order to integrate a cocreational SC perspective with the SMCC model – refinement of the SMCC model needs to take cocreational indicators into consideration, starting with the following indicators stemming from cocreational definitions and dialogic communication principles in social media:

- Organization–public shared meanings, interpretations, and goals of communication are reflected in organizational crisis information.
- Organization develops social media spaces that allow organizational members to communicate with publics.
- Organization supports members to interact and collaborate with publics, when feasible and capable.
- Organization seeks out and invites experts, who are members of the publics themselves and share the same meanings with fellow individuals about the issue confronting the publics, to participate in discussing and disseminating crisis information.
- Organization nurtures and encourages divergent voices to participate in discussing and disseminating crisis information.
- Organization facilitates publics' coping with crisis emotions by providing timely and accurate crisis information as well as options for them to make joint decisions about protective actions and implement these actions together with the organization.

Communicating Infectious Disease Outbreak Crises on Social Media

Health crisis communication is an emerging field of SC, which intersects with both crisis and health communication. There has been a rather small body of research on SC in health situations (Akpabio, 2008; Bowen & Heath, 2007; Kiwanuka-Tondo, Hamilton, & Jameson, 2009; Lee, 2014). Even more scarce is SC research on health crisis communication, such as health pandemics or outbreak situations, which are uniquely challenged by "limited and unverified information, high uncertainties, and a distinctly urgent need for effective communication, interventions, and community cooperation in a race against time to contain a deadly virus" and pose "severe challenges to conventional conceptualizations of communication campaigns" (Lee, 2014, p. 295).

Among public health crises, infectious disease outbreaks (IDOs), whether ongoing (e.g. HIV/AIDS) or sporadic (e.g. SARS), can imperil the physical health of millions of people, adversely influence the social fabric of affected communities, and burden economies (Morens & Fauci, 2013). As Vijaykumar, Jin, and Nowak (2015) argued, efficient and effective communications are critical to the performance of IDO preparedness, response, and recovery programs, given the sudden occurrence, unpredictable nature of spread and reach, and the public sentiments of uncertainty surrounding prevention and treatment of IDOs.

Crisis information about IDOs can now spread instantaneously from an individual through online social networks, to millions of individuals globally. Social media platforms thus are creating new challenges and opportunities for communications during crises such as pandemics: while social media provide new opportunities for health organizations to engage in real-time dialogue and limit the lag in information flow from traditional media to and among individuals, they are also prone to the spread of rumors and misinformation when the accuracy of the information is not vetted by credible sources.

The role of social media in health emergency communication, particularly the 2009 H1N1 pandemic – the first pandemic in the social media era (Chew & Eysenbach, 2010) – has been studied (e.g. Freberg, Palenchar, & Veil, 2013; Liu & Kim, 2011; Signorini, Segre, & Polgreen, 2011) from a crisis communication perspective. More importantly, traditional media and health organizations have evolved to the point where they, too, use social media to create multimedia stories and presentations, graphics, interactive websites, and applications to obtain information for stories (Vijaykumar, Jin, & Nowak, 2015).

Therefore, a case example, based on Guidry et al.'s (2017) study of Ebola on Instagram and Twitter, is described later to illustrate how a cocreational approach can be taken in a crisis situation. Specifically, this case example aims to (1) address the question of how organizations can best utilize social media in order to influence crisis information flow among primary publics from the on- to the offline world and (2) facilitate the process of designing and implementing cocreational crisis communication messages in the new era of social media. The depiction of social media strategies and tools used by major public health organizations during the 2014 Ebola outbreak crisis helps illustrate a cocreational approach to the SMCC model.

Case Application: Ebola Outbreak Crisis and Social Media

Background

The recent Ebola outbreak in West Africa was one of the most severe IDOs in history. Public health and nonprofit health organizations struggled to address publics' concerns as well as the need for accurate information regarding the IDO as a global public health threat. After the arrival of the first Ebola patient in the US, tens of thousands of messages using the hashtag #Ebola were published on both Twitter and Instagram, showcasing both the importance of SMCC to society and community well-being, as well as the need for effective, cocreational SC practices by public health and nonprofit health organizations.

The Ebola outbreak in West Africa was officially declared on March 22, 2014, and by the end of 2014 more than 21,000 individuals had been infected and more than 8,300 had lost their lives. Along with this infectious disease pandemic, a pandemic of fear had surfaced, especially on social media platforms. By then, little was known about how public health organizations addressed this IDO on social media. In the case selected for this chapter, Guidry et al. (2017) analyzed how the Centers for Disease Control and Prevention (CDC), World Health Organization (WHO), and Doctors Without Borders addressed the Ebola outbreak crisis on Twitter and Instagram.

Key findings reported include that Instagram appeared to be a helpful tool to engage publics in time of a global IDO crisis, such as the Ebola outbreak (Guidry et al., 2017). Using more positive/solution-based messages was deemed by publics as crucial in communicating about the IDO. In order to engage publics in IDO communication, use of images and reassuring publics while informing them of the necessary details of how health organizations were dealing with this IDO outbreak were found to be the most effective and reflective of the expectations of publics from a cocreational perspective. These findings shed light on how large health organizations facing IDO communication challenges utilized social media to engage external publics. Whether and how cocreational each of the health organizations was in their Ebola communication practice was assessed according to the cocreational indicators identified earlier in the chapter.

Case Overview

Health Organizations

The three health organizations selected by Guidry et al. (2017) were: the CDC, the WHO, and Médecins Sans Frontières (MSF, also known as Doctors without Borders). CDC is one of the national public health institutes of the US. WHO is the coordinating health authority within the UN. MSF is an international humanitarian aid organization that provides emergency medical care to millions of people caught in crises and catastrophic events in more than 70 countries worldwide.

According to Guidry et al. (2017), all three organizations were involved in fighting the Ebola outbreak, but their efforts were hampered by limited budgets and decisions that were questioned and criticized by various publics. These challenges make it even more important for public health organizations to reach their primary publics where they are looking for crisis information and to provide them with consistent, clear, and accurate messaging (Guidry et al., 2017).

Twitter and Instagram

Different social media platforms differ greatly in their conventions and characteristics. In Guidry et al.'s (2017) study, researchers chose to focus on the microblogging platform Twitter and the photo- and video-sharing platform Instagram, because they are among the most popular social media platforms, while being significantly different from each other. For instance, Twitter, at the time of the Ebola outbreak, imposed a 140-character limit on its tweets, thereby forcing the user to be concise. Instagram instead is focused on photos and videos with the text/caption taking a secondary role. In addition, Instagram is an entirely mobile platform. While posted photos and videos can be viewed on a desktop or laptop computer, Instagram content, at the time of the Ebola outbreak, could only be posted via a smartphone or tablet.

In the context of IDO communication, Twitter has been used during an infectious disease pandemic. For instance, during the 2009 H1N1 outbreak, Twitter was one of the most popular public information sources according to Freberg, Palenchar, and Veil (2013). Instagram did not exist during the H1N1 outbreak, but has since overtaken Twitter for user popularity in the US and provides the contrast of a visual-focused service versus Twitter's 140 characters. The CDC, WHO, and MSF all are active on both Twitter and Instagram, educating publics about Ebola and answering publics' questions.

Case Analysis

In their study, Guidry et al. (2017) conducted a content analysis of how these three health organizations utilized Twitter and Instagram in Ebola communications to their external publics, examining any differences between the different platforms and about public engagement with these posts. Researchers collected the following social media data and conducted data coding following protocols:

- 779 Twitter posts (tweets) sent by the CDC (@CDCgov), WHO (@WHO), and Doctors without Borders (@MSF) between September and December 2014 were randomly selected from a larger sample of tweets.
- All (107) Instagram posts by the three organizations between September and December 2014 were selected based on coding protocols developed for tweets and Instagram posts relating to the topic of Ebola.
- The collected tweets and Instagram posts were coded for the timeframe of the post, the handle of the user who posted, whether and how many times a post was shared, whether and how many times a post was favorited/liked, whether a post received comments and number of comments, and whether the post included a hyperlink and to what type of website it linked. Additional analysis was conducted on both tweets and Instagram posts for Ebola-related risk perception variables.

Cocreational Assessment

Using the cocreational indicators identified earlier in the SMCC context, CDC, WHO, and MSF's Ebola crisis communication on Twitter and Instagram are evaluated in this chapter (see Table 5.1), based on Guidry et al.'s (2017) content analysis results and key findings.

The key findings include the following. First, across the three health organizations, the visual social media platform Instagram emerged as a prominent tool to engage publics when health risk issues such as an Ebola outbreak were discussed, according to Guidry et al. (2017), which in this case elicited more engagement than Twitter as evidenced in the number of retweets and likes. Second, the three organizations differed in how they used Twitter to engage their publics in Ebola crisis information dissemination: MSF used mentions more on Twitter; CDC used the reply function more than both WHO and MSF did. Third, all three health organizations, on both Twitter and Instagram, sent out more positive and solution-based tweets and Instagram posts than neutral or negative tweets or Instagram posts when it came to communicating about the Ebola outbreak crisis.

Guidry et al.'s (2017) study also found that among the three health organizations, MSF was particularly strong in communicating about the Ebola crisis with publics on Instagram. Specifically, even though MSF posted less than the CDC and WHO, MSF mentioned what was likely the most severe characteristic of Ebola (i.e. its deadly nature) more frequently. In

Table 5.1 Cocreational assessment of Ebola crisis communication by health organizations.

Ebola crisis communication	*Crisis information forms*	
Cocreational indicators[a]	*Tweets*	*Instagram posts*
Sharing meanings, interpretations, goals of communication with publics	CDC: √√ WHO: √ MSF: √√	CDC: √ WHO: √ MSF: √√√
Developing social media spaces to allow organization–publics communication	CDC: √√ WHO: √ MSF: √√	CDC: √ WHO: √ MSF: √√√
Interacting and collaborating with publics	CDC: √√ WHO: MSF: √	CDC: √ WHO: √√ MSF: √√√
Experts participating in discussion and information dissemination	CDC: √√ WHO: √ MSF: √	CDC: √ WHO: √√ MSF: √√√
Encouraging divergent voices in discussion and information dissemination	CDC: √√ WHO: MSF: √	CDC: √ WHO: √√ MSF: √√√
Facilitating publics' coping with crisis emotions	CDC: √ WHO: √ MSF: √	CDC: √ WHO: √ MSF: √

Note: √ = mild engagement and interaction with publics; √√ = moderate engagement and interaction with publics; √√√ = high engagement and interaction with publics.

[a]Cocreational indicators are measured in the form of organization–publics engagement and interaction activities on social media channels, as evidenced in "retweeting" or "liking" a post or "replying" to a post in the comments section, etc.

addition to referring to its own credibility and trustworthiness as a health organization, MSF's posts portrayed its internal publics, such as staff members, and how they worked with external publics like Ebola patients and other agencies. According to the SC continuum (Botan, 2018) ranging from non-cocreational to highly cocreational, although all three health organizations' Ebola communications via Twitter and Instagram appeared to be on the right side of the continuum (between somewhat cocreational and highly creational), MSF's SMCC efforts seemed to be nearer the highly cocreational end of the continuum than CDC's and WHO's communication approaches. Specifically, MSF focused more on engaging publics with Ebola crisis information by using visual social media such as Instagram more effectively. First, organization–publics shared meanings, interpretations, and goals of crisis communication seemed to be reflected in the crisis information sent by MSF. Second, the Instagram space MSF utilized for its Ebola crisis communication allowed members and other agencies to interact fully with publics. Third, MSF included divergent voices, ranging from internal and external experts to patients, to participate in discussing Ebola crisis information. Fourth, MSF facilitated publics' coping with negative emotions, such as fear, anxiety, and frustration, by providing timely and accurate information as well as disseminating instructions on taking proper protective actions.

As Guidry et al. (2017) reported, when it comes to Twitter-based crisis communication, CDC engaged publics on Twitter at the highest level, as evidenced in the form of Twitter engagement and the depth of interactions its members utilized in Ebola crisis communication. CDC used the reply function, which is one of the strongest communication tools available to a social media manager, more than both MSF and WHO did. By replying more frequently, CDC interacted with publics, raising health issues and other concerns in a timely manner. In addition, while WHO focused on one-way information dissemination, CDC and MSF appeared to not only produce and distribute crisis information generated by the organization, but also actively seek and share verified information from more divergent voices and other trusted sources via Twitter (Guidry et al., 2017).

When it came to engaging publics with appropriate crisis emotions, Guidry et al.'s (2017) findings indicated that all three health organizations were strategic in aligning the emotional tone (e.g. fear, anxiety, frustration) of the Ebola crisis information with the emotional coping needs of the publics on Twitter and Instagram. For instance, all three organizations sent out more positive and solution-based tweets and Instagram posts than neutral or negative ones across the two social media platforms. As Guidry et al. (2017) concluded:

> Given the negative sentiments associated with Ebola as a health crisis and criticism health organizations received in their communication activities, the CDC, WHO, and MSF seemed to have mindfully taken the control of the tone and direction of their information production and distribution, with a strong focus on positivity and instruction, capitalized on their established credibility as trustworthy health information authorities. (p. 12)

Summary

This chapter proposed taking a cocreational approach to SMCC theory development and practice. By identifying cocreational SMCC indicators, this chapter provides a checklist on assessing how cocreational an organization's crisis communication is when it comes to interacting with and engaging publics on social media and reflecting publics' values, interpretations, and emotional needs in crisis information production and dissemination. Applying the cocreational framework and key aspects of the SMCC model (Liu et al., 2012a) to understand the case of how three major health organizations communicated about the 2014 Ebola outbreak crisis (Guidry et al., 2017), this chapter points out the possibility for organizations to engage publics cocreationally and the opportunities social media, especially visual social media, provide for organizations and publics.

Insights for Theory Development

The cocreational approach can be further integrated into all key aspects of the SMCC model. First, organizations in crises need to make strategic decisions on which crisis information form(s) to utilize, based on the preferences of influential social media followers and inactives and the features and characteristics of both traditional and social media platforms. Second, to be more highly cocreational, organizations need to not only tailor crisis information content according to publics' informational, emotional, and behavioral needs, but also act as active social media followers who constantly identify, verify, and share credible information created by other sources, including some of those publics themselves. The divergent voices provided by an organization and real-time interactions facilitated by organizations will help publics lower the uncertainty of crisis issues and cope with crisis situations more effectively. Third, organizations may further create a space for the voices of publics to be truly cocreational. Such a space, created for dialogues and opportunities that enable organizational members to interact more with publics and facilitate publics to process crisis information in order to reach their own conclusions, allows organizations to cocreate information and messages that are genuinely derived from shared values and understandings between organizations and publics.

Insights for Strategic Communication Practitioners

Social media and the SMCC model provide a platform opportunity and theoretical guidance to engage publics effectively in communicating during crisis situations. Genuine, ethical, and effective crisis engagement on social media calls for cocreational approaches from both the organization and its publics when it comes to crisis information generation and sharing. Organizations not only create crisis information and response strategies by incorporating and reflecting the values of their publics, they also value and acknowledge the critical role of crisis information created and disseminated by their publics. In addition to constantly monitoring crisis information created and shared by influential publics, organizations can establish a partnership with these influencers, when proper and feasible, to cocreate crisis messages, using social media platforms that are appropriate to the crisis situation and the expectations of the publics in need of crisis information and emotional support. Visual elements, such as photos and infographics created by an organization or publics, or even cocreated by the organization and its publics, should be included to facilitate information supply and provide publics with easy-to-follow action plans in dealing with a crisis together.

A cocreational approach to crisis communication is not without its limitations or challenges, however. Opening a space for dialogues between organizations and publics to cocreate messages may take time and unavoidably create more space for rumor generation and spread, which might lead to legal, regulatory, or ethical issues. With accurate and timely information listed as perhaps the most important considerations for organizations communicating with journalists in crisis coverage (Austin & Jin, 2015), establishing a cocreational approach may incur some initial risk including evoking higher emotions spread by publics such as anger, fear, sadness, and anxiety (Jin, Pang, & Cameron, 2007). Future research needs to tackle these challenges and advance SMCC effectiveness cocreationally.

Discussion Questions

1. What makes cocreational approaches to crisis communication possible and feasible, from an SC practitioner's point of view?
2. Confronted with an escalating crisis on social media eliciting strong negative emotions from primary publics, how would you recommend top management try to cocreate crisis information with publics? What concrete procedures and steps might you suggest to bring publics on board to share their values and interpretations of the crisis situation?
3. Do different crisis emotions, positive or negative, expressed by publics posit different opportunities or challenges in implementing cocreational approaches to communicating about organizational crises? How might different crisis emotions impact taking a cocreational approach to SC?
4. Are certain types of crises (e.g. man-made versus natural disaster) or crisis topics (e.g. health versus litigation) more naturally aligned with cocreational approaches? If so, which ones and why?
5. What unique cocreational opportunities do visual social media platforms (e.g. Instagram, Pinterest, Snapchat) provide for organizations and influential publics in the SMCC process?

Further Reading

Austin, L., & Jin, Y. (2016). Social media and crisis communication: Explicating the social-mediated crisis communication model. In A. Dudo & L. A. Kahlor (Eds.), *Strategic communication: New agendas in communication* (pp. 163–186). New York: Routledge.

Kim, I., & Dutta, M. (2009). Studying crisis communication from the subaltern studies framework: Grassroots activism in the wake of Hurricane Katrina. *Journal of Public Relations Research*, 21, 142–164.

Overton-de Klerk, N., & Verwey, S. (2013). Towards an emerging paradigm of strategic communication: Core driving forces. *Communication: South African Journal for Communication Theory and Research*, 39(3), 362–382.

References

Akpabio, E. (2008). Management of "Killer" Indomie scare and impact on consumer confidence: A case study. *International Journal of Strategic Communication*, 2(4), 244–252.

Austin, L. L., & Jin, Y. (2015). Approaching ethical crisis communication with accuracy and sensitivity: Exploring common ground and gaps between journalism and public relations. *Public Relations Journal*, 9(1). http://www.prsa.org/Intelligence/PRJournal/Documents/2015v09n01AustinJin.pdf

Austin, L., Liu, B. F., & Jin, Y. (2012). How audiences seek out crisis information: Exploring the social-mediated crisis communication model. *Journal of Applied Communication Research*, 40, 188–207.

Benoit, W. L. (1995). *Accounts, excuses, and apologies: A theory of image restoration discourse*. Albany, NY: State University of New York.

Benoit, W. L. (1997). Image repair discourse and crisis communication. *Public Relations Review*, 23, 177–186.

Benoit, W. L. (2003). Image restoration discourse and crisis communication. In D. P. Millar & R. L. Heath (Eds.), *Responding to crisis: A rhetorical approach to crisis communication* (pp. 263–280). Mahwah, NJ: Lawrence Erlbaum.

Benoit, W. L., & Brinson, S. L. (1994). AT&T: Apologies are not enough. *Communication Quarterly*, 42(1), 75–88.

Botan, C. H. (2018). *Strategic communication theory and practice: The cocreational model*. Malden, MA: Wiley-Blackwell.

Botan, C. H., & Taylor, M. (2004). Public relations: State of the field. *Journal of Communication*, 54, 645–661.

Bowen, S. A., & Heath, R. L. (2007). Narratives of the SARS epidemic and ethical implications for public health crises. *International Journal of Strategic Communication*, 1(2), 73–91.

Chew, C., & Eysenbach, G. (2010). Pandemics in the age of Twitter: Content analysis of Tweets during the 2009 H1N1 outbreak. *PloS One*, 5(11), e14118.

Coombs, W. T. (1995). Choosing the right words: The development of guidelines for the selection of the "appropriate" crisis-response strategies. *Management Communication Quarterly*, 8(4), 447–476.

Coombs, W. T. (1998). An analytic framework for crisis situations: Better responses from a better understanding of the situation. *Journal of Public Relations Research*, 10, 177–191.

Dougherty, D. (1992). *Crisis communications: What every executive needs to know*. New York: Walker.

Fearn-Banks, K. (2002). *Crisis communications: A casebook approach*. Mahwah, NJ: Lawrence Erlbaum.

Freberg, K., Palenchar, M. J., & Veil, S. R. (2013). Managing and sharing H1N1 crisis information using social media bookmarking services. *Public Relations Review*, 39, 178–184.

Gonzalez-Herrero, A., & Pratt, C. B. (1996). An integrated symmetrical model for crisis communications management. *Journal of Public Relations Research*, 8, 79–105.

Greer, C. F., & Moreland, K. D. (2003). United Airlines' and American Airlines' online crisis communication following the September 11 terrorist attacks. *Public Relations Review*, 29, 427–441.

Guidry, J., Jin, Y., Orr, C., Messner, M., & Meganck, S. (2017). Ebola on Instagram and Twitter: How health organizations address the health crisis in their social media engagement. *Public Relations Review*, 43(3), 477–486.

Jin, Y., & Liu, B. F. (2010). The blog-mediated crisis communication model: Recommendations for responding to influential external blogs. *Journal of Public Relations Research*, 22, 429–455.

Jin, Y., Liu, B. F., & Austin, L. (2014). Examining the role of social media in effective crisis management: The effects of crisis origin, information form, and source on publics' crisis responses. *Communication Research*, 41(1), 74–94.

Jin, Y., Pang, A., & Cameron, G. T. (2007). Integrated crisis mapping: Towards a publics-based, emotion-driven conceptualization in crisis communication. *Sphera Publica*, 7, 81–96.

Jin, Y., Pang, A., & Cameron, G. T. (2012). Toward a publics-driven, emotion-based conceptualization in crisis communication: Unearthing dominant emotions in multi-staged testing of the Integrated Crisis Mapping (ICM) model. *Journal of Public Relations Research*, 24, 266–298.

Kent, M. L. (2010). Directions in social media for professionals and scholars. In R. Heath (Ed.), *The Sage handbook of public relations* (pp. 643–656). Thousand Oaks, CA: Sage.

Kent, M. L. (2013). Using social media dialogically: Public relations role in reviving democracy. *Public Relations Review*, 24, 321–334.

Kiwanuka-Tondo, J., Hamilton, M., & Jameson, J. K. (2009). AIDS communication campaigns in Uganda: Organizational factors and campaign planning as predictors of successful campaign execution. *International Journal of Strategic Communication*, 3(3), 165–182.

Lee, S. T. (2014). Predictors of H1N1 influenza pandemic news coverage: Explicating the relationship between framing and news release selection. *International Journal of Strategic Communication*, 8(4), 294–310.

Liu, B. F., Austin, L. L., & Jin, Y. (2011). How publics respond to crisis communication strategies: The interplay of information form and source. *Public Relations Review*, 37, 345–353.

Liu, B. F., Jin, Y., & Austin, L. L. (2013). The tendency to tell: Understanding publics' communicative responses to crisis information form and source. *Journal of Public Relations Research*, 25, 51–67.

Liu, B. F., Fraustino, J. D., & Jin, Y. (2015). How disaster information form, source, type, and prior disaster exposure affect public outcomes: Jumping on the social media bandwagon? *Journal of Applied Communication Research*, 43, 44–65.

Liu, B. F., Fraustino, J. D., & Jin, Y. (2016). Social media use during disasters: How information form and source influence intended behavioral responses. *Communication Research*, 43(5), 626–646.

Liu, B. F., Jin, Y., Austin, L. L., & Janoske, M. (2012a). The social-mediated crisis communication model: Guidelines for effective crisis management in a changing media landscape. In S. Duhé (Ed.), *New media in public relations* (2nd edn, pp. 257–266). New York: Peter Lang.

Liu, B. F., Jin, Y., Briones, R., & Kuch, B. (2012b). Managing turbulence in the Blogosphere: Evaluating the blog-mediated crisis communication model with the American Red Cross. *Journal of Public Relations Research*, 24, 353–370.

Liu, B. F., & Kim, S.-H. (2011). How organizations framed the 2009 H1N1 pandemic via social and traditional media: Implications for US health communicators. *Public Relations Review*, 37, 233–244.

Lukaszweski, J. E. (1997). Establishing individual and corporate crisis communication standards: The principles and tools. *Public Relations Quarterly*, 42(3), 7–15.

Massey, J. E. (2001). Managing organizational legitimacy: Communication strategies for organizations in crisis. *The Journal of Business Communication*, 38(2), 153–182.

Morens, D. M., & Fauci, A. S. (2013). Emerging infectious diseases: Threats to human health and global stability. *PLoS Pathog*, 9(7), e1003467.

Ray, S. J. (1999). *Strategic communication in crisis management*. Westport, CT: Quorum.

Signorini, A., Segre, A. M., & Polgreen, P. M. (2011). The use of Twitter to track levels of disease activity and public concern in the US during the influenza A H1N1 pandemic. *PloS One*, 6(5), e19467.

Stocker, K. P. (1997). A strategic approach to crisis management. In C. L. Caywood (Ed.), *The handbook of strategic public relations and integrated communications* (pp. 189–204). New York: McGraw-Hill.

Ulmer, R. R. (2001). Effective crisis management through established stakeholder relationships. *Management Communication Quarterly*, 14(4), 590–615.

Vijaykumar, S., Jin, Y., & Nowak, G. J. (2015). Social media and the virality of risk: The risk amplification through media spread (RAMS) model. *Journal of Homeland Security and Emergency Management*, 12(3), 653–677.

6

The Cocreational View of Character Assassination

Sergei A. Samoilenko
George Mason University

Introduction

Character assassination (CA) refers to the strategic effort to discredit an individual or group target via subversive communication (Samoilenko et al., 2020). CA is a natural social process and the rhetoric of character attack, or subversive rhetoric, represents one of four motivations for human communication (Fisher, 1970). The anti-ethos rhetoric is considered instrumental to goal achievement and prevails in politicized and adversarial contexts. The use of ***ad hominem*** attacks is an acceptable rhetorical device during open debate in liberal democracies (Walton, 1999). Benoit (2017) considers a persuasive attack on character to be useful when it exposes wrongdoing, informs voters, or influences consumer buying decisions.

CA is a relatively new topic in communication studies. Communication research has addressed the effects of negative advertising, character attacks during political conflicts, and the importance of strong personality traits during corporate crises (Ma et al., 2019; Samoilenko et al., 2017; Seiffert-Brockmann, Einwiller, & Stranzl, 2018). Traditionally, CA is studied through the lenses of rhetorical and psychological theories (Benoit, 2017; Shiraev, 2014). These schools of thought see CA mainly from the functional perspective – as a means to an end, a tool in the hands of a powerful attacker. These perspectives do not always acknowledge the transactional complexity of CA activities, including the reality that multiple actors may engage simultaneously in attack and defense. They often disregard the target's agency and ignore opportunities for mutual influence. Moreover, these approaches fail to explain how and why interdependent actors' strategies of attack and defense are produced in social interactions within groups and institutions.

This chapter introduces CA to the body of literature on strategic communication (SC). CA campaigns are inherently strategic because they are produced by understanding various publics and their attitudes toward CA events. The cocreational perspective highlights the key role of various publics in the production of CA campaigns. It permits us to make sense of the relational complexity of CA events that are jointly produced by interdependent publics. This chapter argues that participatory internet media have changed the perception of CA as a tool in the hands of power structures. Moreover, social media have enabled subversive actors to implement strategic campaigns, even in authoritarian political systems. This argument is supported through a discussion of political activist Alexei Navalny's SC campaigns, which use ***kompromat***, or compromising materials, against the Russian political establishment. The chapter concludes by providing directions for future research.

The Handbook of Strategic Communication, First Edition. Edited by Carl H. Botan.

Embracing a Shift Toward the Sociocultural Paradigm

As noted earlier, the traditional approaches to CA research are instrumental for tracing the cause–effect relationships between attackers and targets. However, they add little to our understanding of the sociocultural context in which CA actions take place. Hence, a paradigmatic shift toward the sociocultural view is a logical step toward capturing the complexity of CA as a communication phenomenon.

The sociocultural tradition of communication posits that social reality is created by people exercising their agency in relation to others in the context of a particular group, network, or culture (Craig, 1999). It supports the constitutive view of communication, or the notion that the symbolic means of language do not simply reflect but also produce and shape all sorts of social phenomena. On this view, meaning is not inherent in objects; it is created and negotiated in interactions between interdependent actors through commonly shared and understood symbols and interpretations. Communication has the power to attach labels, shape positive or negative attitudes, and thus create individual and group identities. Our social identities are socially constructed: they are ascribed to us by the way others talk about us and are then legitimized via public opinion (Hecht, 1993).

This approach sees CA as both the process of communication (e.g. a smear campaign) and the outcome of this process, such as a damaged reputation. Importantly, a character attack is a persuasive attack that has the potential to affect public opinion and produce damaged identities (Benoit, 2017; Nelson, 2001). This distinctive mark (e.g. stigma) is "a kind of curse … which attempts to imprison its victim in an accusation which also depicts his destiny" (Bourdieu, 1991, p. 121). Notable CA campaigns leave their mark on history. The term "monkey business," for example, became part of the American cultural lexicon after being coined to describe the 1987 Gary Hart scandal (Bai, 2014). This idea corresponds to Goffman's (1963) assessment that a discredited attribute is not a thing in itself; rather, it constitutes a language of relationships.

The sociocultural approach to CA emphasizes the relational nature of communication, seen as a process of ongoing mutual orientations. According to Nicotera (1997), every relationship is a type of social structuring created by communication patterns. People and their messages cannot be understood in isolation from the history of their relationships with others. Hence, any communication is an intersubjective and purposive activity embedded in group interactions. This corresponds with views in contemporary rhetoric that people are so motivated to communicate with one another in order to create identification or shared identity that they become consubstantial (German, 2009). For Burke (1969), consubstantiality is a way of acting together and sharing stylistic identifications and symbolic meanings, which persuade and create a sense of acceptance that is defined by a common context despite social divisions and hierarchies. People identify with each other when they agree on symbolic meanings, especially connotative meanings that trigger positive and negative values and emotions.

All social behaviors are part of a continuum that spans from interpersonal to intergroup interactions in groups, institutions, and networks. It is impossible to discuss communication in isolation from the "social groups and context in which these individuals are placed" (Tajfel, 1981, p. 45). Relational communication in social groups involves various forms of strategic self-presentation and impression management techniques. This *facework* allows social actors to create the impressions of credibility and legitimacy required for interacting with other members (Cupach & Metts, 1994; Goffman, 1959).

The construction of these impressions inevitably entails the display of character. This is public image, the impression of honesty and personal integrity that meets the accepted standards of appropriate social interaction or aligns with the role that a person is supposed to be playing at a given point in time (Walton, 1998). The outcome of these efforts is the public evaluation of reputation, or "the sum of the images" in which various audiences in different situations view a person or an organization (Fombrun, 1996). Essentially, facework and image restoration are critical elements of habitus, a structuring mechanism that generates learned dispositions, stratagems and skills for survival, and struggles for social power (Bourdieu, 1984). Effective reputation management helps build overall symbolic and social capital, a network of "institutionalized relationships of mutual acquaintance and recognition" (Bourdieu & Wacquant, 1992, p. 119). The mastery of life-saving stratagems also involves the management of various face-threatening acts and communication transgressions, including accusations, criticism, or *ad hominem* attacks.

Social actors engage in relationships with each other not only for identification purposes, but also in order to obtain, distribute, or protect asymmetrically distributed resources in social systems (Bourdieu, 1984). These strategic actions may eventually involve some form of power relations. These types of relations depend on practical knowledge of contextual rules, social competence, and the achievement of a rationally held consensus with other group members in a specific social environment. Both individual and contextual factors help to determine whether these relations will be characterized by cooperation or by competition.

CA practices are intrinsic to any social process that involves competition or conflict (Sande et al., 1989; Sherif et al., 1961). Since reputation is a crucial but also easily depleted asset, strategic actors often resort to character attacks in their polemics to invalidate arguments or create a precedent for the public revaluation of someone's moral standing (Benoit, 2017; Walton, 1998). The use of strategic character attacks is emblematic of the political field, where it is used by contenders to destroy an opponent psychologically, to deplete the resources of another party, or to reduce opponents' chances of gaining public support (Shiraev, 2014).

Strategic CA campaigns produce CA events (scandals, reputational crises, etc.) that have the capacity to discredit individuals and organizations by reducing their credibility to a degree that is unacceptable to a specific public. Most subversive campaigns attempt to trigger a highly mediated event linked to a character-based issue or a highly contested social conflict (e.g. the #MeToo movement). The goal is to make mediated events resonate with multiple publics and their communities and to spark public outrage that eventually brings about a crisis of legitimacy for the target of the attack.[1] The effectiveness of CA campaigns is determined by a number of factors, including the types of authoritative resources (social position, expertise, reputation, etc.) available to the attacker and the target, respectively (Giddens, 1984). Omnipotent actors, such as totalitarian states, have unlimited resources and instruments for CA campaigns at their disposal (Samoilenko & Karnysheva, 2020; Yang, 2020).

The patterns of interaction between the attacker and the target during a CA event produce conditions that allow various publics, including the media and online communities, to intervene and cocreate the course of CA campaigns. This point will be developed further in the next section.

The Cocreational Perspective of Strategic Character Assassination

The cocreational perspective sees SC as planned campaigns that are based on studying and understanding the needs and wants of various publics rather than simply focusing on message production (Botan, 2018). The importance of being publics-centered is therefore fundamental to the cocreational model. This meta-theoretic view of SC will be elaborated upon next.

[1] There are also clandestine strategic CA campaigns that involve covert actions, such as spreading rumors and conspiracy theories. These campaigns are discussed in Samoilenko (2017).

The Cocreational Model of Strategic Communication

Under the cocreational model, a public is understood to be an "interpretative community engaged in an ongoing process of developing a shared understanding of its relationship with a group or organization that can differ substantially from that of the organization" (Botan, 2018, p. 59). An interpretive community does not simply decode messages but rather creates subjective knowledge structures by identifying "the objects upon which its members can then agree" (Fish, 1980, p. 338). Publics have agency, or the capacity to make free choices, act independently, and self-consciously produce social change. They decide which campaigns and messages to attend to and whether a relationship with a message sender is in their best interest. For example, a public may choose not to support a SC campaign because they disagree with its values or one of its core messages.

Next, the members of a public are involved in an ongoing process of developing and sharing meanings. This assumption supports the perception of cultural groups and online communities in late modernity as constantly developing and transforming across time, space, and traditional norms and attitudes (Bauman, 2000; Beck, Giddens, & Lash, 1994). Finally, a public may have a different view and understanding of social processes (e.g. emergencies, crises, corporate wrongdoings) than traditional groups and institutions because of local knowledge or broader experience.

Importantly, the notion of a public is linked to the concept of the public sphere. The public sphere is a space where citizens come together to deliberate over state affairs and is a key concept of civic communication in liberal democracies (Habermas, 1962). The quality of this public forum is crucial because the stronger the public sphere, the more it can counter the state's abuse of power. For example, in an open, democratic society, the ability to launch or respond to CA campaigns is diffused more widely among various actors and moderated by the active public sphere, as evidenced by dynamic interactivity, political participation, and the pluralism of voices.

In societies where the public sphere is marginal and power is distributed unevenly, dominant elites take advantage of formal and informal means of coercion, including CA, to put pressure on dissenting voices and enforce compliance. Public opinion influences the progress and outcome of public events, including those produced by CA campaigns. In authoritarian societies, CA practices become integrated into social structures and later routinized through everyday narratives, resulting in sustained norms. As a product of structuration, CA often becomes a normalized sanctioning mechanism and an additional form of cultural violence (Galtung, 1990; Giddens, 1984).

Another important line of research suggests that in pluralistic and diverse societies, multiple publics jointly construct permeable boundaries of relationships (Asen & Brouwer, 2001). Such societies allow for plural public spheres, not all of which have the same amount of power and influence. This mainly depends on the limits and characteristics of the particular social field in which power resources are assigned to hierarchical positions in a network of relationships between actors (Bourdieu, 1984).

Despite economic or structural limitations, even under-resourced and marginalized publics have the ability to cocreate public issues, intervene in ongoing events, and produce new social arrangements. Giddens (1984) argues that "knowledgeable actors" see power resources as the transformative capacity of human agency. Hence, they are able to take over the resources created by dominant structures – including CA strategies and tactics – and use them to produce desired social change. CA's transformative capacity is illustrated by subversive campaigns.

Subversive Campaigns as a Cocreational Practice

Subversive campaigns are campaigns that attempt to weaken or destroy an ideological order. They can be carried out by activist publics, competing ideological groups, or motivated individuals. Fisher (1970) refers to subversive rhetoric as "an anti-ethos rhetoric" intended "to undermine the credibility of some person, idea, or institution" (p. 138). Essentially, these are CA campaigns that seek to challenge power structures. Subversion can be associated with mild forms of resistance and non-conformity, including strategies and tactics intended to appropriate mainstream cultural materials and reorganize their meaning (Williams, 2011). For example, in January 2019, fake editions of *The Washington Post* were handed out by members of the culture-jamming activist group the Yes Men at several Washington, D.C. locations (Heil & Farhi, 2019). The group's co-founder, Jacques Servin, told the real *Post* that the fake paper was meant to be a newspaper from the future providing ideas for how to impeach President Trump that would serve as a roadmap for other subversive actors.

Botan (2006, 2018) argues that SC should be designed and implemented at three levels: grand strategy, strategy, and tactics. He advises communicators to envision an enduring and complex relationship with various publics as a key element of strategic planning. This corresponds to Habermas' (1987) argument that the normative ethics of strategic action cannot be justified purely by appealing to a purposive rationality that is based on the realization of specific ends by known means. Instead, it should be oriented toward achieving a rationally held consensus via discursive or communicative action. This involves participating in ongoing public discourses and persuading the various audiences that make up public opinion. This cannot be achieved without investing time in learning about the current beliefs, attitudes, and emotions of all publics, especially those who make it easier for campaign producers to attain goals. In short, contemporary SC campaigns strive for co-orientation, or the common orientation of campaign planners and various publics toward mutual interest and understanding (McLeod & Chaffee, 1973; Newcomb, 1953). Ultimately, the producers of subversive SC campaigns have the same goal.

Strategic subversive campaigns appeal to invested and motivated stakeholders that have a legitimate interest in a particular public figure or organization. This is particularly evident in crisis situations when the targets of attacks are surrounded by active investors who capitalize on the collapse of the target's reputation. As Dezenhall (2014) puts it, "your crisis is someone else's meal ticket." These invested stakeholders (the media, bloggers, activists, competitors, etc.) also seek to develop CA events that often cause strong public reactions.

A strategic attacker needs to persuade various publics to revisit their prior consensus on the perceived character of an individual under attack. This sometimes involves logical evidence-based appeals that justify why such a re-evaluation and re-interpretation of character is necessary. The image of character is thus a subjective knowledge structure (Boulding, 1973). It is discussed and agreed upon by different interpretive communities. Various publics then decide whether to ignore or attend to an allegation and share their opinion concerning an issue raised by the attacker. Hence, it is the publics that have the upper hand and the final say. The target's reputation is damaged only when public opinion issues its verdict, regardless of the truth and relevance of the attacker's allegations.

A strong reason for subversive actors' embrace of a proactive dialogic approach is the development of mobile internet and social networking. Social media have increased the opportunities for subversive campaigners to engage in meaningful participation with various networked communities. According to Botan (2018), "...social media have a natural fit with the cocreational paradigm [...] and are thus best understood [...] from that perspective as opposed to the older instrumental-functional perspective..." (p. 174). Social media campaigns are essentially strategic because any online activity is always situational, constructed for the public, and presumes the expectation of multiple "imagined audiences" (Marwick & boyd, 2011; Robinson, 2007).

Subversive digital campaigns thus embrace the cocreational perspective in the sense that they challenge traditional power structures and promote various communication agendas. I will next discuss the mechanics of subversive internet campaigns in more detail.

Cocreation as the Foundation of Subversive Internet Campaigns

Social media have expanded the opportunities for participative engagement and provided new tools for cocreational SC campaigns. As Jenkins, Ford, and Green (2013) point out, "the shifting relations between media producers and their audiences are transforming the concept of meaningful participation" (p. 153). Social networking sites enable individuals to create "shared awareness" (Shirky, 2008) and engage other networked individuals in various political and social causes.

Globalized networks and new information technologies have increased networking opportunities and made social actors across the world more interdependent. According to Dutton (2009), the development of networked individuals has increased the ability of ordinary people to participate in and have an impact on the online public sphere. In 2016, the concept of (dis) empowered citizens, excluded by elites and empowered by social media, was reported as one of today's main global risks (World Economic Forum, 2016). Importantly, one networked individual has the power to create a networked institution. This is an online platform that provides "space to share information, generate online discussion and enable new forms of collective action that achieve common goals" (Machleder & Asmolov, 2011, p. iv). Networked institutions can set and promote their own agenda that competes against agendas and frames promoted by other estates. Their legitimacy is based on the trust inherent in community. This trust is often personalized and built around a charismatic person who functions as both a social hub and an influencer.

The role of networked institutions becomes critical in times of uncertainty and low trust in many traditional authorities, including political institutions and the mass media (Gallup, 2016). For example, during the 2016 US presidential election, low levels of trust in mainstream media made people look for alternative sources to trust. This partially explains the surge in popularity of niche and peer-influenced media as the most used source of news and information (Edelman, 2016).

The niche media cater to people with similar political beliefs and facilitate connections among them. Multiple networked and "gated" communities are public spaces for ordinary citizens to emphasize their ingroup identity and express their dissatisfaction with the political situation. These communities often become breeding grounds for subversive campaigns. According to Gerbaudo (2012), social media are responsible for the construction of a choreography of assembly, or the process of the "symbolic construction of public space which facilitates and guides the physical assembling of a highly dispersed and individualized constituency" (p. 5). In other words, the habitus of political attitudes and skills acquired online may later translate into real-life street protests and social movements.

Activist and social movement campaigns represent active subversive campaigns taking place on social media. For example, the "#MeToo" hashtag, originally created on Twitter to denounce misogynic behavior and sexual harassment, became a global movement (Carlsen et al., 2018). Scholars have addressed the impact of activist and nonprofit campaigns on corporate image and reputation (Lievonen, Luoma-aho, & Bowden, 2019; Manheim, 2000). The type of negative engagement produced by these campaigns is damaging due to their speed, anonymity, and malice.

Social media have made it easier for special interest groups and activists to produce subversive smear campaigns through communities of concern that emerge as bottom-up grassroots initiatives. Coombs and Holladay (2020) classify CA campaigns targeting corporations according to two types of attacker's goals. The first category includes angry stakeholders that are seeking revenge and purposely trying to damage an organization's reputation. Some active revenge-seekers and trolls are also motivated by the prospect of political, financial, and ideological gain or a desire to impress their peers (Bishop, 2014). Griffin (2014) refers to some non-governmental organization groups as "shouters," known for anti-corporate agendas devoted to agitating, campaigning, and exposing corporate wrongdoings to the global community. The power of these groups and nonprofit organizations stems from their perceived status as "independent" and "more ordinary" – and thus more trustworthy – than for-profit or government actors.

The second category involves activist stakeholders that seek to change organizational practices. Their CA efforts often result in paracrises and may lead to decreased revenues, boycotts of products and services, image problems, or other forms of harm to an organization's valuable assets (Coombs & Holladay, 2007, 2015). These campaigns follow similar patterns in both corporate and political contexts. Political activists belong to the second type of invested stakeholders. They present a serious threat to individual targets and organizations because they intend to cause long-term reputational damage.

Moreover, subversive campaigns that produce CA events now develop almost instantaneously and in an unpredictable manner due to high connectivity and a greater number of individual and collective contributors (Samoilenko, 2020). This reality reduces the effectiveness of traditional crisis management strategies and prevents organizations from controlling for multiple risks. As noted by Coombs and Holladay (2020), stakeholders can even push management to change problematic behavior by threatening to harm the corporate image of their company.

Today, smartphones and mobile applications enable campaigns to deploy subversive tactics in real time. Newsjacking, for instance, can be used to inject their own messages into breaking news to hijack and reframe a topic in favor of other issues (Meerman Scott, 2012). In addition, subversive actors use satire and ridicule to deconstruct and undermine the power of dominant meanings and symbols (Boyd, 2012). Ridicule is a backdrop for CA in political discourse and a breeding ground for intemperate or unjustified personal attacks (Lichter & Farnsworth, 2020). The popularity of memes in internet culture represents the cocreational nature of participative discourse, as memes subvert traditional media messages and replace them with new meanings (Huntington, 2013). Memes challenge and deconstruct dominant symbols by trivializing and adding new layers of meaning to them. Some memes become weaponized during subversive campaigns. According to Seiffert-Brockmann, Einwiller, and Stranzl (2018), memes prove especially dangerous because they are uploaded via anonymous accounts, tend to become viral and quickly spread throughout decentralized networks, and are constantly changing through remixing and mimicry.

CA is traditionally perceived as a power resource of governments and corporations (Klicperová-Baker, 2014; Proctor, 1995). However, subversive actors see it as the transformative capacity to challenge power structures via SC campaigns. With the rise of participative media, this is no longer possible solely in liberal democracies with a high level of public participation and civic engagement. It also affects authoritarian societies where the state has traditionally had a monopoly on CA.

To illustrate this point, this chapter examines how Russian political activists cocreate subversive campaigns with their supporters by crowdsourcing compromising materials to put pressure on state officials. Russia is emblematic of a country with a highly developed internet ecosystem and a long tradition of CA campaigns.

Kompromat as a Power Resource of Russian Politics

The Dual Nature of Kompromat

In the Soviet Union, CA traditionally accompanied state-run propaganda campaigns that were intended to settle scores with ideological rivals and ostracize political dissidents (Samoilenko & Karnysheva, 2020). *Kompromat* is a CA method that has been inherited from Soviet times and still represents a common CA method in many post-Soviet countries. It refers to "discrediting information that can be collected, stored, traded, or used strategically across all domains…" (Ledeneva, 2006, p. 58). Following the collapse of the USSR, kompromat transitioned into the private sector and politics.

Frequently labeled as an "illiberal democracy" by Western pundits, today's Russia is no longer a totalitarian Stalinist society. Nor is it a typical authoritarian regime, as it still leaves some space for civic actors. Malle (2013) defines Russia as a corporatist state in which a stable political consensus is assured by arrangements and agreements between power groups representing oligarchs, government officials, and security structures. At the same time, this corporatist state model rests on the so-called "power vertical," which allows for fast and unchallenged top-down decision-making. This involves the application of CA strategies and tactics as a means of informal governance (Ledeneva, 2013). Spreading rumors about opposition leaders, for example, is an informal strategy intended to prevent individual actors from acting in a manner that may affect the interests of a political system. In fact, the entire state media system can be set into motion in order to deliver selective cheap shots on critics or launch heavy artillery – namely, propaganda campaigns targeting political adversaries (Samoilenko & Laruelle, 2020).

In the 1990s, kompromat took the form of electoral wars. The dubious legality of many early business practices in Russia, such as the chaotic privatization of the early 1990s, meant that compromising materials could be found on almost any active businessmen or politician. Kompromat is a multi-purpose device that can be employed to create negative publicity, blackmail, mute critics, or ensure loyalty. According to Mesquita (2018), Russian central and regional tax and law enforcement agencies hold "frozen files" to be used against government officials and private entrepreneurs where necessary; these files can be overlooked as long as loyalty is maintained. The Russian legal system is selectively lenient with regard to kompromat. Under Russian law, journalists are not obliged to reveal their sources, except when ordered by court, which serves to amplify the number of compromising materials and fakes in the media. Taking this one step further, a notorious website, kompromat.ru, was launched in 1999 to offer anyone, for a small fee, a space to publish defamatory content. (Targets had to pay more to make the compromising materials disappear.)

Kompromat and other CA practices are used extensively in internet propaganda campaigns run by pro-government actors (Mesquita, 2018; Simons & Samoilenko, 2017). Asmolov (2018) examines the notion of participatory propaganda as a new set of propaganda strategies emerging on social networks in Ukraine and Russia. These strategies seek to set a particular political agenda and persuade users to change their opinions. They also aim to destroy digital social capital by dividing friends, breaking social networks, and cutting individuals off from their social networks.

However, the Russian state no longer has a monopoly on CA. It is now available as a power resource to non-systemic actors. These changes were made possible by the widespread popularity of internet media and the rise of activism during Dmitri Medvedev's presidency (2008–2012). The Russian internet's new status as an alternative to state-controlled media enabled activists to mobilize their personal resources for a variety of social causes (Asmolov, 2013). The watchdog function of Russian social networks proved especially efficient during grassroots campaigns against discriminatory practices on the part of the state and corporations that would otherwise have gone uninvestigated.

In December 2011, Russia saw massive protests against the ballot-rigging of the legislative election results. The protests were organized by the non-systemic opposition and drew over 100,000 people to the streets in 39 cities (Elder, 2011). One of the protest leaders was Alexei Navalny, a lawyer, politician, and online activist who gained prominence as a critic of government corruption.

Kompromat as a Wild Card of Navalny's Campaigns

Alexei Navalny is a non-traditional politician. He is a cross between a video blogger, an investigative journalist, and a social justice activist. Combating corruption in the Russian government is the key theme of Navalny's video reports. He appeals to viewers with both high and low issue involvement (Petty & Cacioppo, 1986) and offers strong arguments based on thorough fact-checking that appeal to the logic of the high-involvement audience. For viewers with low involvement, his reports feature drone footage of politicians' expensive mansions and luxurious lifestyles. Navalny fits the description of a populist in that he seeks the total reform of the political regime rather than narrow, negotiated policy concessions from the state (Laclau, 2005). Navalny's narratives exploit common stereotypes of the unjust Russian political system and its dishonest politicians. His populist techniques include "us versus them" rhetoric, emotional appeals, simplified interpretations of politics, a focus on the negative, distrust of government agencies, and many more (Lassila, 2016; Magun, 2014).

Navalny's reports feature compromising materials that reveal the wrongdoings of state officials. His investigative reports combine evidence in the form of open-source legal documents and videos with viral content. He presents kompromat through the prism of critical watchdog journalism according to the click-bait logic of social media. His materials repeatedly promote catchy nicknames and labels for politicians from the presidential party, United Russia, such as "crooks and thieves." There are multiple references to popular memes and funny viral videos. Sometimes, Navalny campaigns use venomous innuendos that appeal to conspiracy thinkers. For instance, in his most popular anti-corruption investigation "He is Not Dimon to You," published on March 2, 2017, Navalny warned his audience that then-Prime Minister and United Russia Party Chairman Dmitry Medvedev's highly sophisticated corruption schemes demonstrated that he was not a bumbling fool (Tamkin, 2017). In his attack on Medvedev, Navalny claimed to reveal the politician's true colors as a corrupt businessman who represented a serious threat to Russia's modernization.

Navalny's subversive campaigns follow the collaboration and crowdsourcing model. This is a sourcing practice in which campaign managers obtain information or services from a large group of internet users by dividing work among participants to achieve a final result. The politician became famous for his anti-corruption platform RosPil, an example of both civic activism and personal political branding. The idea was that average Russian citizens would expose the financial violations and budget schemes of government officials by submitting anonymous online reports. The site has been active, with hundreds of recommendations and links posted on major social networks. In the event that there is evidence of corruption, RosPil lawyers file a lawsuit and submit a complaint to the relevant government agency.

Navalny's campaigns often hijack popular news headlines in order to refocus the central storyline and bring public attention to issues promoted by the political activist. In January 2014, the Russian news agency RIA Novosti asked their Twitter followers to use the hashtag **#считаемвместе** ("let's count together") and upload photos to count down the days until the kickoff of the 2014 Olympic Games in Sochi. Navalny's activists started using the official RIA Novosti hashtag by linking it to his site, which invited visitors to count the event's unreasonable expenditures together. Shortly after this, RIA Novosti stopped promoting the photo contest and had to change its hashtag.

Navalny's subversive campaigns seek to achieve two main goals. They intend to delegitimize the Russian political system and also cocreate shared meanings of current political and social issues with their primary publics, mostly the Russian youth, middle class, and intellectuals. These campaigns provide such "interpretive communities" with a public space to engage in public dialogue and deliberation; a networking institution for dealing with serious issues and informal practices in Russia. Importantly, Navalny's strategic campaigns are aligned with his grand strategy and are linked to his policies on corruption and economic reform, as declared during his 2018 presidential campaign. The cocreational nature of Navalny's campaigns is best illustrated by the following case.

The "Rybkagate" Case

In February 2018, Navalny's team published a YouTube video showing then-Russian Deputy Prime Minister Sergei Prikhodko talking to aluminum magnate Oleg Deripaska on a yacht in Norway. The report was mainly based on escort service worker Nastya Rybka's Instagram photos and video footage, as well as her book on how to bed oligarchs. Following the story in Rybka's tell-all book, Navalny's team tracked the movements of the oligarch's yacht through Norwegian waters. A fictitious character resembling the Russian deputy minister was allegedly on board the boat. Rybka's video showed two men discussing international affairs, explaining to the escort why relations between Russia and the US had gone bad. They discussed former US Assistant Secretary of State for European and Eurasian Affairs Victoria Nuland. In 2018, the Russian oligarch was frequently mentioned in the Western media in relation to Paul Manafort, a former campaign chief of Donald Trump who was involved in the Special Counsel investigation of Russia's interference in the 2016 US presidential election (Reuters, 2018). The investigative video was posted a few weeks after the release of the "Kremlin Report," which outlined new sanctions for Russia (Department of the Treasury, 2018). Navalny's video speculated that the meeting between the oligarch and the prime minister was a missing link of coordination between the Kremlin and Donald Trump's presidential campaign.

Following the release of Navalny's report, internet service providers in Russia blocked access to his website. A court ordered Instagram to remove Rybka's posts and demanded that Google delete or block access to her videos and photos on YouTube. In January 2019, Nastya Rybka was extradited from Thailand back to Russia and arrested at the airport upon arrival (Troianovski, 2018).

The report created an embarrassing situation for the Kremlin before the upcoming Russian presidential election. The story presented the deputy prime minister as a negligent official who would discuss matters of national interest in the presence of a sex worker with a smartphone. The story also created unwanted publicity for the Russian oligarch in the US media and drew the attention of Western policymakers. Two months later, the US Treasury Department announced sanctions on Deripaska as well as dozens of other Russian tycoons and companies with ties to the Russian state. According to data from Bloomberg, Deripaska saw his net worth drop by 64% in 2018 (Mohsin, 2018).

Navalny's strategic CA campaign capitalized on the heightened media interest in Robert Mueller's investigation into Russian interference in the 2016 US election. It sought to cocreate the narrative of Russian meddling by appealing to various active publics, including the international media, the Democratic establishment in Washington, and other invested stakeholders looking for new evidence of Russia's illegal actions.

By exposing a top Kremlin official and an oligarch, Navalny reinforced his public image as the key opposition leader fighting corruption. The "Rybkagate" story gained prominence because of its relevance, absurdity, and potential for viral effect. Navalny's report was fully compatible with the commercial logic of internet media: it was a negative, sensationalized click-bait story. An exposé of corruption was circulated online via memes and jokes. The case study demonstrates that contemporary CA campaigns are no longer controlled by their producers but are shaped and transformed by various publics. The visibility, connectivity, and transparency of the internet media amplified the damage produced by this CA campaign by causing unintended collateral damage.

Key Takeaways and Future Research

This chapter offers a fresh perspective on CA as a strategic effort embedded in power relations within social groups and institutions. It underscores the importance of the cocreational view, which explains the socially constructed nature of contemporary CA campaigns. The following takeaways can be derived from this discussion.

CA is fundamentally strategic. CA planned campaigns are based on understanding members of different interpretive communities and finding ways to build relations with them. Strategic CA campaigns seek to persuade various publics to side with an attacker and reach agreement on the target's moral profile. Attackers strive to occupy a moral high ground and exert influence on public opinion. If they succeed, the target's character is tainted and becomes a new subjective knowledge structure.

CA campaigns are jointly produced in interactions between members of different interdependent publics. During an attack, publics play the leading role in deciding the outcome of CA campaigns. They shape the public image of the target by reinterpreting its social value and agreeing on its new shared meaning. CA is thus the power resource of both dominant and subversive actors. The latter see CA as a transformative capacity to challenge power structures and spark change.

The participatory culture of internet media has translated cocreational theory into practice. Internet technologies streamline the production and implementation of cocreated subversive campaigns. Activist and social movement campaigns represent popular forms of online subversion. Social networking sites provide strategic actors with resources to realize subversive campaigns in both liberal democracies and authoritarian societies. The case of Russian political activist Alexei Navalny demonstrates the power of subversive campaigns in an authoritarian society with a developed internet ecosystem.

This discussion of CA as SC through the lens of cocreational theory illuminates multiple directions for further scholarly investigations of this surprisingly overlooked topic. Future research should address several issues that have not been studied in depth in this chapter.

First, the early utopian vision of internet media as a purely democratic space (Shirky, 2008) has been challenged by critical scholars (Morozov, 2011), who predict the exploitation of participatory media by governments and corporations for spin and information control. As research demonstrates, social networking sites have become highly susceptible to ideological and corporate propaganda (Keller et al., 2020; Simons & Samoilenko, 2017). State and corporate actors have learned to manipulate online communities via participatory propaganda and *astroturf* (i.e. fake grassroots) campaigns promoting their policies and products. Scholars should investigate the growing manipulation of participatory media by hegemonic actors as a premise for the new widespread use of CA for coercion and domination.

Second, the chapter uses the case of Alexei Navalny to show the power of subversive campaigns in authoritarian societies with a developed internet ecosystem. However, it does not explain whether these effects will persist in the face of ongoing state efforts to shape and control the development of the public sphere. These state activities include tightening censorship of internet media, suppressing inconvenient narratives with pro-government propaganda, and normalizing peer pressure on dissent through fake-grassroots campaigns. More empirical research is needed to measure the effects of authoritarian manipulation of the internet.

Finally, this chapter describes CA as a form of power relations among strategic actors that either reproduces or transforms the boundaries of social systems. However, it is not clear what happens when power struggles lead to unresolved social conflicts becoming locked in "hamster wheel" situations and recurrent cycles of structural divergence (Nicotera & Mahon, 2013). These scenarios abound in authoritarian democracies in which institutions of power openly rely on informal means of governance (e.g. kompromat) rather than totalitarian repressive measures. In the Russian context, this often occurs when grassroots activities clash with astroturf campaigns that are outsourced to moral entrepreneurs, promoting state policies, jingoism, and sanctions for dissent. As activism and social developments are impeded, unresolved conflicts are perpetuated by new cycles of CA. Future research studying the sociocultural effects of CA should address these and other considerations.

References

Asen, R., & Brouwer, D. C. (2001). *Counterpublics and the state.* New York: SUNY Press.

Asmolov, G. (2018). The disconnective power of disinformation campaigns. *Journal of International Affairs, 71*(1.5), 69–76.

Asmolov, G. (2013). Natural disasters and alternative modes of governance: The role of social networks and crowdsourcing platforms in Russia. In S. Livingston & G. Walter-Drop (Eds.), *Bits and atoms: Information and communication technology in areas of limited statehood* (pp. 98–114). New York: Oxford University Press.

Bai, M. (2014). *All the truth is out: The week politics went tabloid.* New York: Vintage Books.

Bauman, Z. (2000). *Liquid modernity.* Cambridge: Polity Press.

Beck, U., Giddens, A., & Lash, S. (1994). *Reflexive modernization. Politics, tradition and aesthetics in the modern social order.* Palo Alto, CA: Stanford University Press.

Benoit, W. L. (2017). Criticism of actions and character: Strategies for persuasive attack. *Extended Relevant Rhetoric, 8.* https://bit.ly/2Y0rqvC

Bishop, J. (2014). Representations of "trolls" in mass media communication: A review of media-texts and moral panics relating to "internet trolling". *International Journal of Web-Based Communities, 10*(1), 7–24.

Botan, C. H. (2006). Grand strategy, strategy and tactics in public relations. In C. H. Botan & V. Hazleton (Eds.), *Public relations theory II* (pp. 223–247). Mahwah, NJ: Lawrence Erlbaum.

Botan, C. H. (2018). *Strategic communication: Theory and practice.* Hoboken, NJ: Wiley-Blackwell.

Boulding, K. E. (1973). *The image: Knowledge in life and society.* Ann Arbor, MI: University of Michigan Press.

Bourdieu, P. (1984). *Distinction: A social critique of the judgement of taste.* London: Routledge.

Bourdieu, P. (1991). *Language and symbolic power.* Cambridge: Polity Press.

Bourdieu, P., & Wacquant, L. J. D. (1992). *An invitation to reflexive sociology.* Chicago, IL: University of Chicago Press.

Boyd, A. (2012). *Beautiful trouble: A toolbox for revolution.* New York: OR Books.

Burke, K. D. (1969). *A rhetoric of motives.* Berkeley, CA: University of California Press.

Carlsen, A., Salam, M., Miller, C. C., Lu, D., Ngu, A., Patel, J. K., & Wichter, Z. (2018, October 29). MeToo brought down 201 powerful men. Nearly half of their replacements are women. *New York Times.* https://nyti.ms/2PQj4Q7

Coombs, W. T., & Holladay, S. J. (2007). The negative communication dynamic: Exploring the impact of stakeholder effect on behavioral intentions. *Journal of Communication Management, 11*(4), 300–312.

Coombs, W. T., & Holladay, S. (2015). CSR as crisis risk: Expanding how we conceptualize the relationship. *Corporate Communications: An International Journal, 20*(2), 144–162.

Coombs, T., & Holladay, S. (2020). Corporate character assassination and crisis communication. In S. A. Samoilenko, M. Icks, J. Keohane, & E. Shiraev (Eds.), *Routledge handbook of character assassination* (pp. 225–235). New York: Routledge.

Craig, R. T. (1999). Communication theory as a field. *Communication Theory, 9*(2), 119–161.

Cupach, W. R., & Metts, S. (1994). *Facework.* Thousand Oaks, CA: Sage.

Department of the Treasury (2018, January 29). *Report to Congress pursuant to Section 241 of the countering America's adversaries through Sanctions Act of 2017 [CAATSA] regarding senior foreign political figures and oligarchs in the Russian Federation and Russian parastatal entities.* https://bit.ly/35RkmTj

Dezenhall, E. (2014). *Glass jaw.* New York: Twelve.

Dutton, W. H. (2009). The fifth estate emerging through the network of networks. *Prometheus, 27*(1), 1–15.

Edelman (2016). *2016 Edelman Trust Barometer.* https://www.edelman.com/research/2016-edelman-trust-barometer

Elder, M. (2011, December 6). Russian police and troops clash with protesters in Moscow. *The Guardian.* https://bit.ly/2P2Zd2w

Fish, S. (1980). *Is there a text in this class? The authority of interpretive communities.* Cambridge, MA: Harvard University Press.

Fisher, W. R. (1970). A motive view of communication. *Quarterly Journal of Speech, 56*(2), 131–139.

Fombrun, C. J. (1996). *Reputation. Realizing value from the corporate brand.* Boston, MA: Harvard Business School Press.

Gallup (2016, September 14). *Americans' trust in mass media sinks to new low.* https://bit.ly/35zASty

Galtung, J. (1990). Cultural violence. *Journal of Peace Research, 27*(3), 291–305.

Gerbaudo, P. (2012). *Tweets and the streets: Social media and contemporary activism.* London: Pluto Press.

German, K. M. (2009). Identification. In S. W. Littlejohn & K. A. Foss (Eds.), *Encyclopedia of communication theory* (pp. 491–492). Thousand Oaks, CA: Sage.

Giddens, A. (1984). *The constitution of society: Outline of the theory of structuration.* Berkeley, CA: University of California Press.

Goffman, E. (1959). *The presentation of self in everyday life.* New York: Doubleday.

Goffman, E. (1963). *Stigma: Notes on the management of spoiled identity.* Englewood Cliffs, NJ: Prentice Hall.

Griffin, A. (2014). *Crisis, issues, and reputation management: A handbook for PR and communicators professionals.* London: Kogan Page.

Habermas, J. (1962). *Strukturwandel der Offentlichkeit. Untersuchungen zu einer Kategorie der burgerlichen Gesellschaft* [The structural transformation of the public sphere: An inquiry into a category of bourgeois society]. Berlin: Neuwied.

Habermas, J. (1987). *The theory of communicative action. Vol. 2. System and lifeworld: A critique of functionalist reason.* Boston, MA: Beacon Press.

Hecht, M. L. (1993). 2002 – A research odyssey: Toward the development of a communication theory of identity. *Communication Monographs, 60*, 76–82.

Heil, E., & Farhi, P. (2019, January 17). Fake editions of *The Washington Post* handed out at multiple locations in D.C. *The Washington Post.* https://wapo.st/2J8t3yH

Huntington, H. E. (2013). Subversive memes: Internet memes as a form of visual rhetoric. *AoIR Selected Papers of Internet Research, 3.* https://doi.org/10.5210/spir.v3i0.8886

Jenkins, H., Ford, S., & Green, J. (2013). *Spreadable media: Creating value and meaning in a networked culture.* New York: New York University Press.

Keller, F. B., Schoch, D., Stier, S., & Yang, J. H. (2020). Political astroturfing on Twitter: How to coordinate a disinformation campaign. *Political Communication, 37*(2), 256–280.

Klicperová-Baker, M. (2014). A character assassination attempt: The case of Václav Havel. In E. Shiraev & M. Icks (Eds.), *Character assassination throughout the ages* (pp. 253–269). New York: Palgrave Macmillan.

Laclau, E. (2005). *On populist reason.* London: Verso.

Lassila, J. (2016). Aleksei Naval'nyi and populist re-ordering of Putin's stability. *Europe-Asia Studies, 68*(1), 118–137.

Ledeneva, A. (2006). *How Russia really works. The informal practices that shaped post-Soviet politics and business.* Ithaca, NY: Cornell University Press.

Ledeneva, A. (2013). *Can Russia modernise? Systema, power networks and informal governance.* Cambridge, UK: Cambridge University Press.

Lichter, S. R., & Farnsworth, S. (2020). Late night TV humor and the culture of ridicule. In S. A. Samoilenko, M. Icks, J. Keohane, & E. Shiraev (Eds.), *Routledge handbook of character assassination* (pp. 352–365). New York: Routledge.

Lievonen, M., Luoma-aho, V., & Bowden, J. (2019). Negative engagement. In A. Johnston & M. Taylor (Eds.), *The handbook of communication engagement* (pp. 529–547). Hoboken, NJ: Wiley-Blackwell.

Ma, T., Atkin, D., Snyder, L. B., & Van Lear, A. (2019). Negative advertising effects on presidential support ratings during the 2012 election: A hierarchical linear modeling and serial dependency study. *Mass Communication and Society, 22*(2), 196–221.

Machleder, J., & Asmolov, G. (2011). Social change and the Russian network society: Redefining development priorities in new information environments. *Internews.* https://bit.ly/31uDqmL

Magun, A. (2014). The Russian protest movement of 2011–2012: A new middle-class populism. *Stasis, 2*(1), 160–191.

Malle, S. (2013). Economic modernisation and diversification in Russia. Constraints and challenges. *Journal of Eurasian Studies, 4*(1), 78–99.

Manheim, J. B. (2000). *The death of a thousand cuts: Corporate campaigns and the attack on the corporation.* New York: Routledge.

Marwick, A. E., & boyd, d. (2011). I tweet honestly, I tweet passionately: Twitter users, context collapse, and the imagined audience. *New Media & Society, 13*(1), 114–133.

McLeod, J., & Chaffee, S. (1973). Coorientation and interpersonal perception. *American Behavioral Scientist, 16*, 469–499.

Meerman Scott, D. (2012). *Newsjacking: How to inject your ideas into a breaking news story and generate tons of media coverage.* Hoboken, NJ: Wiley-Blackwell.

Mesquita, M. (2018). Kompromat. In A. Ledeneva (Ed.), *The global encyclopaedia of informality* (Vol. 2, pp. 435–438). London: UCL Press.

Mohsin, S. (2018, August 21). Deripaska's pain shows Trump is tough on Putin, Treasury says. *Bloomberg.* https://bloom.bg/2VVrzgC

Morozov, E. (2011). *The net delusion: The dark side of internet freedom.* New York: Public Affairs.

Nelson, H. L. (2001). *Damaged identities, narrative repair.* Ithaca, NY: Cornell University Press.

Newcomb, T. M. (1953). An approach to the study of communicative acts. *Psychology Review, 60*(6), 393–404.

Nicotera, A. M. (1997). Managing conflict communication in groups. In L. R. Frey & J. K. Barge (Eds.), *Managing group life: Communicating in decision-making groups* (pp. 104–130). Boston, MA: Houghton Mifflin.

Nicotera, A. M., & Mahon, M. M. (2013). Between rocks and hard places: Exploring the impact of structurational divergence in the nursing workplace. *Management Communication Quarterly, 27*(1), 90–120.

Petty, R. E., & Cacioppo, J. T. (1986). The elaboration likelihood model of persuasion. *Advances in Experimental Social Psychology, 19*, 123–205.

Proctor, R. N. (1995). *Cancer wars: How politics shapes what we know and don't know about cancer.* New York, NY: Basic Books.

Reuters (2018, June 27). *Manafort had $10 million loan from Russian oligarch: Court filing.* https://reut.rs/2Mrquas

Robinson, L. (2007). The cyberself: The self-ing project goes online, symbolic interaction in the digital age. *New Media & Society, 9*(1), 93–110.

Samoilenko, S. A. (2017). Strategic deception in the age of "truthiness." In I. Chiluwa (Ed.), *Deception and deceptive communication: Motivations, recognition techniques and behavioral control* (pp. 129–168). New York: Nova Science.

Samoilenko, S. A. (2020). Character assassination in the context of mediated complexity. In K. Sriramesh & D. Verčič (Eds.), *The global public relations handbook: Theory, research, and practice* (pp. 268–282). New York: Routledge.

Samoilenko, S. A., Erzikova, E., Davydov, S., & Laskin, A. (2017). Different media, same messages: Character assassination in the television news during the 2014 Ukrainian crisis. *International Communication Research Journal, 52*(2), 31–55.

Samoilenko, S. A., Icks, M., Keohane, J., & Shiraev, E. (Eds.). (2020). *Routledge handbook of character assassination and reputation management.* New York, NY: Routledge.

Samoilenko, S. A., & Karnysheva, M. (2020). Character assassination as modus operandi of Soviet propaganda. In P. Baines, N. O'Shaughnessy, & N. Snow (Eds.), *The SAGE handbook of propaganda* (pp. 189–204). Thousand Oaks, CA: Sage.

Samoilenko, S. A., & Laruelle, M. (2020). Character assassination as strategic communication in EU–Russia relations. In E. Pashentsev (Ed.), *Strategic communication in EU–Russia relations: Tensions, challenges and opportunities* (pp. 135–160). New York: Palgrave Macmillan.

Sande, G. N., Goethals, G. R., Ferrari, L., & Worth, L. T. (1989). Value-guided attributions: Maintaining the moral self-image and the diabolical enemy-image. *Journal of Social Issues, 45*(2), 91–118.

Seiffert-Brockmann, J., Einwiller, S., & Stranzl, J. (2018). Character assassination of CEOs in crises. Questioning CEOs' character and values in corporate crises. *European Journal of Communication, 33*(4), 413–429.

Sherif, M., Harvey, O. J., White, B. J., Hood, W. R., & Sherif, C. W. (1961). *Intergroup conflict and cooperation: The robbers cave experiment.* Norman, OK: University of Oklahoma Book Exchange.

Shiraev, E. (2014). Character assassination: How political psychologists can assist historians. In M. Icks & E. Shiraev (Eds.), *Character assassination throughout the ages* (pp. 15–36). New York: Palgrave Macmillan.

Shirky, C. (2008). *Here comes everybody: The power of organizing without organizations.* London: Penguin.

Simons, G., & Samoilenko, S. A. (2017). The effects of social media in the context of public sphere insularity in Russia. In F. Roumate & A. La Rosa (Eds.), *Civil society and democracy in the age of social media.* (pp. 189–223) Marrakech: Institut International de la Recherche Scientifique.

Tajfel, H. (1981). *Human groups and social categories: Studies in social psychology.* Cambridge: Cambridge University Press.

Tamkin, E. (2017, March 2). Navalny's anti-corruption fund accuses Medvedev of secret massive estate. *Foreign Policy.* https://bit.ly/32yr4vo

Troianovski, A. (2018, February 27). A self-described sex expert says she will spill information on Trump and Russia to get out of a Thai jail. *The Washington Post.* https://wapo.st/2JmYl5l

Walton, D. N. (1998). *Ad hominem arguments.* Tuscaloosa, AL: University of Alabama Press.

Walton, D. (1999). Ethotic arguments and fallacies: The credibility function in multi-agent dialogue systems. *Pragmatics and Cognition, 7*, 177–203.

Williams, J. P. (2011). *Subcultural theory: Traditions and concepts.* Cambridge: Polity Press.

World Economic Forum (2016). *The Global Risk Report 2016.* http://www3.weforum.org/docs/GRR/WEF_GRR16.pdf

Yang, Z. (2020). Character assassination and the contemporary anti-corruption campaign in the Chinese military. In S. A. Samoilenko, M. Icks, J. Keohane, & E. Shiraev (Eds.), *Routledge handbook of character assassination and reputation management* (pp. 117–130). New York, NY: Routledge.

7

Cocreational Perspectives on Strategic Communication in Counterterrorism

Damion Waymer
University of Alabama

Organizations tend to fund strategic communication (SC) campaigns to achieve desired organizational ends. From a cocreational perspective, strategic communicators should not approach campaigns as functionalists in search of the magic bullet that they can use to get publics to behave according to strategic communicators' predetermined goals, objectives, and desires. Rather, these communicators should glean firsthand insights from the publics they intend to reach via campaigns. While an attractive approach in theory, the cocreational approach is not without its challenges and critics in theory and practice. As Botan (2018) has noted, one obvious criticism of the cocreational view of campaigns and their evaluation is that the cocreational view does not focus on the reason for most communication campaigns; most campaigns are orchestrated to achieve some limited short-term goal, which is another way of saying they focus on tactical rather than strategic goals.

This is especially true in the case of counterterrorism – whereby law enforcement, intelligence agencies, governments, and businesses develop strategies to neutralize terrorist threats. This reduces the role of communication on the sponsoring side to simple, tactical, one-way publicity, while ceding the strategic use of communication to terrorist organizations. If those organizations are astute enough to seize this strategic gift, which many are, a communication mismatch is created in which those seeking to do harm are free to make strategic appeals to emotions and to the cultural, political, or religious beliefs of listening publics through media events and the internet. At the same time, those opposing such terrorist practices are self-restricted to merely expressing what is on their own minds in the short term.

Terrorism often creates fear and panic among the masses, and it involves an organization using intentional violence as a means of leveraging fear to achieve financial, ideological, political, or religious aims. Counterterrorism is an organization's systematic efforts to combat and prevent terrorism. Organizations' antiterrorism efforts often incorporate military tactics, techniques, and strategy. In these counterterrorism scenarios, there does not appear to be room for perspective-taking and cocreational strategies. Take, for example, the familiar adage several Western countries abide by: no negotiation with terrorists. At its core, that confrontational posture demonstrates strength, not weakness, and hierarchy, not equal status, to terrorists. Given this justifiably adversarial discursive posture of Western counterterrorism efforts, how can strategic communicators use cocreational approaches in developing and understanding

The Handbook of Strategic Communication, First Edition. Edited by Carl H. Botan.

counterterrorism campaigns? Consider that the term "counterterrorism" or "antiterrorism" by definition is establishment-centered: one organization has deemed the actions of another organization as terrorism – actions that they must stop and/or counter.

In this chapter, I problematize the term counterterrorism via a cocreational lens. AsHeath and Waymer (2014b) have noted, "[to] truly understand, one must explore the links among terrorism and various discourses; terrorism can never be completely understood from the establishment perspective" (p. 230).

Using the National Consortium for the Study of Terrorism and Responses to Terrorism (START) as one rhetorical approach to counterterrorism, this chapter explores how engaging community partners, building community resilience, and understanding the human consequences and causes of terrorism are deemed examples of cocreational theory in action – a shift from most prevailing counterterrorism strategies and tactics. In essence, this chapter compares START, which uses a rhetorically sensitive and more cocreational approach to counterterrorism, to the more common non-rhetorically sensitive approaches to counterterrorism.

I also challenge researchers and practitioners interested in terrorism/counterterrorism alike to consider and use cocreational perspectives in campaign design and implementation whenever possible.

The War Metaphor

Much of the counterterrorism discourse present today is similar to the language found in the mission statement of the US Department of State counterterrorism division: the Bureau of Counterterrorism and Countering Violent Extremism. The organization's mission is "to promote US national security by taking a leading role in developing coordinated strategies and approaches to defeat terrorism abroad and securing the counterterrorism cooperation of international partners" (Bureau of Counterterrorism and Countering Violent Extremism, n.d.).

The mission appears to have face validity in terms of being cocreational. Keywords in the mission include "coordinated strategies and approaches," "securing … counterterrorism cooperation," and "international partners." However, upon closer examination the mission is selectively cocreational. The mission is to "promote US national security" by cocreating meaning and partnerships with "international allies" yet the intent is clear: "to *defeat* terrorism abroad." Based on this written mission statement, one can assume that those deemed terrorists are not involved in the discussion and resolution of the problems. Only the US and its allies are involved in discussion and resolution. Rather, terrorists – *they* – are deemed the problem, and *they* and their tactics must be defeated. War metaphor language (see Lakoff & Johnson, 1980) frames and is central to this mission statement: "developing coordinated strategies to defeat terrorism."

A metaphor is a figure of speech that takes one thing (often referred to as the source domain) and equates it to or overlaps it with another thing (often referred to as the target domain) for rhetorical effect. Scholars in SC disciplines have studied metaphors and their implication on SC outcomes in general (see Waymer, 2018) and the use of the war metaphor specifically (see Boyd, 2003).

To demonstrate the power of metaphor, I present the following example. In my analysis of the use of metaphor, I highlight how metaphors can create hegemonic blind spots that serve as a source of marginalization and alienation (Waymer, 2012). In this particular example, city officials, by labeling a neighborhood as blighted, empower the city government and developers to undertake land saving, urban renewal, and gentrification efforts that completely disregard the interests of residents, and even the residents themselves who already reside in the neighborhood. By definition, blight is a plant malady that manifests itself in the form of discoloration and dark spots on a plant. The dark spots, the blight, must be removed from the plant (the city) to save it from ruin. It is not farfetched in this example to see how some city officials might attribute some black and brown community residents as the cause of the blight or the blight themselves.

Drawing on Boyd's (2003) work on war metaphor, I posit the following example to elucidate the point that the war metaphor can also be limiting and insensitive. A *US football game/contest is war*, for example, is a metaphor. In 2003, during the ascent of the war in Afghanistan, former football player Kellen Winslow was attacked in the media for a post-game rant whereby he claimed to be a soldier while expressing immense frustration that opposing players were trying to injure him on the field of play: "It's war … They're out there to kill you, so I'm out there to kill them. I'm a soldier" (Associated Press, 2013, para 5). While not his intent, Winslow was reminded swiftly of his misappropriation of the war metaphor and was compelled or pressured into apology (Associated Press, 2013). Comparing football contests to war demonstrates the fierceness and high stakes of the sport. While football games are competitive, have winners and losers, and are contested battles, in the trenches, where one team's goal is to enter the opposing team's territory and red zone for the score, US football is still a game. Rarely are there life and death consequences – arguably the highest stake – on the line in these contests.

To see a scholarly example of war metaphor analysis, consider Boyd's (2003) corporate organizational rhetoric research article that uses metaphor to analyze the merger of two large energy companies. In this analysis, he pointed out how the organization being acquired invoked a war metaphor to describe the insurgence of the unwanted acquiring organization. Boyd examined the case of an unlikely winner in a corporate dispute over control of Indiana's PSI Resources. Moreover, he offered questions and conclusions about the efficacy, consequences, and ethics of the war metaphor as a weapon of corporate persuasion, especially since this metaphor is inherently polarizing by nature. Viewing terrorists as the enemy evokes the war metaphor and cements the relationship between state actors and terrorists as adversarial and antagonistic.

The US War on Terror: Actual and Metaphorical

Zhang's (2007) anti-terrorism, public relations, and public diplomacy research found that the major metaphors the US government created to define the post-September 11 terror attacks on the country "share the archetypal metaphor of 'democracy vs. tyranny' and 'freedom vs. oppression'" (p. 31). More than a decade after Zhang's research was published, the war against terrorism discourse remains prevalent in US society. In a press statement released on May 1, 2018, the US announced that it was launching operations to liberate the final strongholds of the ISIS in Syria (US Department of State, 2018). According to that official statement: "The fighting will be difficult, but we and our partners will prevail. We will defend United States, Coalition, and partner forces if attacked. The days of ISIS controlling territory and terrorizing the people of Syria are coming to an end" (para 1). This statement appears to indicate that the fight against global terrorism is ending. However, critics and politicians have noted, unfortunately, that the longest running war (the global war on terrorism) in US history undoubtedly will continue because the US is fighting the wrong battle (Berman & Thompson, 2018; Cardin, 2017; Zimmerman, 2018).

According to Zimmerman (2018), the US is not winning the war on terrorism because Islamic State and al Qaeda constitute a small portion of the true threat: a "global movement, unified by an ideology – Salafi jihadism – that exists outside of al Qaeda or the Islamic State. The tenets of this militaristic theology justify and demand the use of violence to bring about a narrow vision of Islam" (para 3). Furthermore, the guiding principles of Salafi jihadism enable this movement to act as a self-organizing entity, "which means that winning against extremist groups alone is a losing battle" (para 4). Senator Ben Cardin (2017) of Maryland reflects the sentiment when he argues that military solutions alone will not resolve the conflicts that are present in these regions. Therefore, whether metaphorical or actual, several believe that war and attempting to defeat terrorism are a failed approach.

As Zimmerman (2018) has lamented: "What US policymakers never seem to learn is that when it comes to global terrorism, the mission is not yet accomplished … While the United States was fighting the Islamic State, other groups clearly benefited" (para 2). Al Qaeda is attempting to infiltrate Iraqi Sunni insurgents once again. Furthermore, "The US intelligence community is already warning of a continued Sunni insurgency in Iraq, which would permit the rise of yet another extremist group in Iraq" (Zimmerman, 2018, para 2). Additionally, foreign intelligence experts are currently saying that "the Bin Laden network controls more territory than at any time in its history, and has positioned itself as a long-term threat to the West. The Taliban, too, is resurgent in Afghanistan" (Berman & Thompson, 2018, para 3). Additionally, on the continent of Africa, groups such as "Nigeria's Boko Haram and Ethiopia's al-Shabaab continue to threaten the continental peace, despite the best efforts of local authorities" (para 3). Hence, the actual war against terror needs to be coupled with diplomacy strategies to be successful.

Simply stated, the US must focus its counterterrorism strategy on "removing the conditions that enable the growth of the Salafi jihadist movement," and the country should adjusts its emphasis on "militarily defeating specific groups and on seeking to counter the ideology to helping make Sunni communities more secure. As the experiences in Afghanistan, Iraq, Yemen, and elsewhere prove, military defeats of Salafi jihadist groups are only temporary" (Zimmerman, 2018, para 6).

These groups, including the Islamic State and al Qaeda, have not grown in number and strength because their ideology suddenly appealed to the masses. Instead, these groups have strengthened and expanded because following the chaos in the wake of the Arab Spring, local Sunni populations were forced into offering their support for Salafi jihadist groups in exchange for security and protection against a greater threat – "whether that threat was a general rise in crime, instability in Libya, invading forces in Yemen, some combination thereof in Mali, or, most poignantly, the Bashar al-Assad regime in Syria" (Zimmerman, 2018, para 5). Additionally, these groups offered Sunni populations goods and services that met their basic communal needs, and then followed up by introducing local populations to the Salafi jihadist ideology (Zimmerman, 2018). As scholars have noted, similar circumstances allow gangs to recruit new members into criminal activity or potential members to seek out gang membership: meet recruits' basic needs and then introduce them to the good associated with gang life and membership (Alleyne & Wood, 2012; Farmer & Hairston, 2013; Sonterblum, 2018). The US must take a similar, understanding and meeting needs-based approach to the communities they are trying to rid of terrorism in order to be successful in these efforts.

As several have noted, the US cannot win its war against terrorism by relying upon US military or other partnered military forces alone; rather, these military actions must be coupled with broader diplomatic efforts designed to "return security to Sunni communities and to thus open up a space to compete with the Salafi jihadist movement. American diplomats need to develop relationships with key stakeholders in order to understand their positions and negotiate conflict resolutions" (Zimmerman, 2018, para 11). These efforts, "when properly applied to foster legitimate local governance or used as leverage to shape regime behavior" can play a pivotal role in countering the Salafi jihadist movement (para 11) and can provide US diplomats with "a better understanding of local dynamics and foster relations with substate actors and local power brokers" (para 7). This sort of SC approach is foundational to nation building, diplomacy, and constructing a civil society (Taylor, 2000). Viewing terrorism via a cocreational lens allows counterterrorism personnel to see terrorism as a microcosm of the human condition. Thus, counterterrorism efforts will differ vastly when viewed cocreationally as opposed to when key administrators frame and view terrorism as a war against enemy combatants (terrorists) that they must win militaristically at all costs.

In short, framing is powerful (Entman, 1993), especially when it pertains to the negative framing of societal ills such as terrorism or crime (Waymer, 2009). By invoking war metaphor language, labeling and framing a group as terrorists, an organization discursively positions the group as other, as villainous, as worthy of eradication. The next section explores in greater depth how terrorism is framed and the implications of various frames.

Terrorism, Like Beauty, Is in the Eye of the Beholder: Framing of Terrorism

Heath and Waymer (2014a) assert that following 9/11, "terrorism has become defined as violent attack(s) perpetrated against civilian populations, for the most part, for the purpose of sociopolitically motivated intimidation and issue advancement" (p. 210). While many view terrorism pejoratively and want to stomp out terrorism because it is inherently evil (see Sinclair & Antonius, 2012 for a discussion), terrorism – as Hoffman (2006) has noted – has not always had a negative connotation. In fact, terrorism is often not empty acts of violence and mayhem; rather, terrorism is often a SC act carried out by terrorists. Despite this fact, in contemporary times, the war against terror is both a war of military tactical force and alliances as well as a literary war of framing. It is the latter that I discuss in detail later.

As mentioned earlier, framing is powerful (Entman, 1993), and frames "represent powerful mechanisms" that shape and influence public policy issues and their outcomes (Knight, 1999, p. 383). Not all government attempts to frame violent actions, such as bombings, as terrorism are successful (Canel, 2012). Canel's (2012) analysis demonstrates how the Spanish government's use and framing of the war metaphor failed when that metaphorical framing of terrorism did not resonate with key publics following the 2004 Madrid bombing attacks. While this is a rare example of a failed governmental framing of terrorism, what terrorism scholars find is that if "you can pin the label 'terrorist' on your opponent, you have gone a long way toward winning the public relations aspect of any conflict. Even terrorists don't like the label" (Richardson, 2006, p. 4).

Important considerations, however, are as follows. Who gets to determine who is a terrorist? What actions constitute terrorism? What counts as terrorism, does it change over time? To shed light on these considerations, consider the words of Richardson (2006):

> It is often claimed, and not without reason that history is written by winners so that a victorious terrorist becomes a statesman and a failed terrorist remains a terrorist. Terrorists with whom I have spoken invariably invoke Nelson Mandela and Menachem Begin as evidence that someone considered a terrorist today can be considered a statesman tomorrow. (p. 10)

Thus, as several scholars have noted (Best, McLaren, & Nocella, 2007; Canel, 2012; Heath & Waymer, 2014a, 2014b; Richardson, 2006; Somerville & Purcell, 2011), terrorism can never be completely understood from the establishment perspective.

The fact that terrorism can never be completely understood from the establishment perspective is due to one of several negative aspects of framing. Stated simply, one negative aspect of framing is that usually the power to frame successfully requires social and economic capital and due to disparities in necessary social and economic resources, not all groups have access to the news media and public platforms as a political resource (Ryan, Carragee, & Meinhofer, 2001), though social media is increasing access for terrorists and other non-dominant groups to promote and frame their causes (Rothenberger, 2012). In a similar vein, the establishment is often treated as an official source on terrorism matters and as a result often "promote[s] elite social discourses as the public discourse or the common sense of society" (Tucker, 1998, p. 143). Hence, while there might be more than one frame operating within the discourse about terrorism per se, "a dominant frame usually is fixed within the discourse to become the preferred reading of an issue, event or character" (Tucker, 1998, p. 144) – usually the establishment perspective. Thus, the lack of resources available to terrorists and other non-dominant groups symbolizes a lasting problem "in efforts to advance their definitions of political issues ... [whereas] considerable resources available to those who hold institutional power contribute to their sponsorship of frames and to their ability to have these frames influence public discourse" (Ryan, Carragee, & Meinhofer, 2001, p. 179).

This negative aspect of framing, that is social and economic capital disparity, is one reason why non-dominant groups and terrorists alike often use outlaw discourse as a key component of their SC strategy. Scholars (see Boyd & VanSlette, 2009) argue that as a form of outlaw discourse, terrorism is "necessary and even invited in some cases when the standards of argument are not flexible enough to accommodate dissent and may leave no other place for dissent other than outside the previously established norms and logics of argumentation" (p. 334). Overly optimistic thinking might suggest that terrorism can be supplanted by non-violent protest and that wars on terrorism are not inherently ironic (Best, McLaren, & Nocella, 2007). Yet, these state-centered actions might trigger more violence from the disempowered groups "who want to effect change, and to do so quickly, but lack the numbers to prevail in a democratic system or to launch a viable military campaign" (Richardson, 2006, p. 11).

Therefore, critics of contemporary, more common, non-rhetorically sensitive approaches to counterterrorism argue that the key to counterterrorism SC lies in engaging with dialectical communication with those labeled as terrorists. For example, an analysis of the 2007 Taliban Korean hostage case – where Taliban militants kidnapped South Korean church volunteers in the southern Ghazni Province of Afghanistan (Kim, 2008) – found that negotiating with terrorists works best if those organizations or persons dealing with the terrorists use a "constant dialectical process of firmness and softness" (p. 268). As an important aside, rhetorically, dealing with terrorists connotes a different orientation and framing than stomping out or eradicating terrorism. Kim (2008) adds that officials negotiating with terrorists "should be adamant about the principle, but at the same time seek alternative options to turn the current debacle into a route for possible agreements. Without these bilateral tensions, terrorists never change their original terms" (p. 268).

So while there is no such thing as a relationship being completely cocreational or completely non-creational (just degrees in between) to counter terrorism strategically, organizations should strive to be dialectical – that is to be as cocreational as possible. As Richardson (2006) states: understanding terrorists through the lens of the nature of the goals that they seek is "essential in understanding how terrorists terminate their campaigns and how they can most effectively be countered" (p. 11). START is one such organization that appears to have taken this rhetorically sensitive approach.

In the section that follows, I view START as one rhetorical approach to counterterrorism and then explore how START's strategies of engaging community partners, building community resilience, and understanding the human consequences and causes of terrorism can be considered examples of praxis – that is, applied cocreational theoretical approaches to counterterrorism

START: One Rhetorical Approach to Counterterrorism

Established in 2005 as a US Department of Homeland Security (DHS) Center of Excellence, the DHS charged START to use "state-of-the-art theories, methods, and data from the social and behavioral sciences to improve the understanding of the origins, dynamics, and social and psychological impacts of terrorism" (START, n.d.a, para 8). START was funded by an initial

$12 million grant from the DHS to complete projects in the research areas of terrorist group formation and recruitment, terrorist group persistence and dynamics, and societal responses to terrorist threats and attacks.

According to its website, START "is a university-based research and education center comprised of an international network of scholars committed to the scientific study of the causes and human consequences of terrorism in the United States and around the world" (START, n.d.a, para 1). What is interesting about START, I argue, is that it is taking a rhetorically sensitive and more cocreational approach to counterterrorism than the more common non-rhetorically sensitive approaches to counterterrorism. For example, START, in an attempt to address the root causes of terrorism and to train US government agencies on the nuances and tactics that terrorist groups use, recently "taught Department of Homeland Security investigators how extremist groups around the world use rhetoric to radicalize people" (Hodjat, 2018, para 16). In a similar vein, in December 2018 START officials traveled to Tirana, Albania, to conduct a forum for the Bureau of Diplomatic Security's Antiterrorism Assistance program (Goff, 2018). START leadership, via this training forum, highlighted "governmental approaches for disrupting the foreign terrorist fighter lifecycle and responding to a threat," and they shared "best practices and lessons learned from the international community and the US Department of State with senior leadership from the criminal justice community within Albania" (Goff, 2018, para 2).

According to START (n.d.a) it is an organization that is committed to the conducting, finding, and development of terrorism-related knowledge: "START supports the research efforts of leading social scientists at more than 50 academic and research institutions, each of whom is conducting original investigations into fundamental questions about terrorism" (para 2). For example, START features the research of scholars, such as Thomas Guarrieri, who are using data analytics to conduct research that will aid public policymakers and counterterrorism practitioners in the field to develop more effective counterterrorism strategies (Moses, 2017). Guarrieri stated, "There are so many puzzling, unanswered questions about extremist violence. I hope the research we're doing at START can help mitigate this threat" (Moses, 2017, para 5). From a rhetorical standpoint, consider the positioning of Guarrieri's statement. If terrorism is just empty violence with the intent to do harm, then what fundamental questions would exist that are worthy of such robust academic scholarship and attention? The START director and many of the START researchers believe that terrorism is a complex issue to be managed, in part because terrorist organizations are not all alike and in fact differ vastly. As such, counterterrorism efforts need far more nuanced strategy if they are to be successful:

> When most people think of terrorist groups an image comes to mind of some well-organized and highly-publicized entity like the Islamic State or al Shabaab. In reality, it's hard to generalize about terrorist groups. On one extreme are individuals who have no recognized links to a terrorist organization – so-called lone wolves. On the other end of the spectrum are highly organized groups that persist over time, have a well-defined chain of command and a stable leadership. In between are loosely connected small groups as well as shadowy networks – for example, Neo Nazis or radical Islamists. All of these disparate entities are typically in a state of flux. Change is constant; stability rare … It is one thing to respond to a well-organized group, with clear leadership, a chain of command and an identifiable membership. But responses are much more complicated when there is no central organization, no identifiable leader or only an ill-defined group of individuals with varying connections and commitments undergoing constant change. (LaFree, 2017)

LaFree's comments strongly suggest that a one-size-fits-all, terrorists-as-enemy-to-be-eradicated-through-force, approach to counterterrorism is limited at best and most likely will not yield the desired results. Rather, studying, understanding, and addressing the motivations of terrorists and their current and potential supporters – that is, being more dialectical and more rhetorically cocreational – might be a more fruitful counterterrorism strategy.

From a rhetorical vantage point, if one compares the mission and vision statement of START to the mission statement of the Bureau of Counterterrorism and Countering Violent Extremism, one sees a stark difference in how terrorism is framed and how it is to be countered. START's mission is "To advance science-based knowledge about the human causes and consequences of terrorism and serve as a leading resource for homeland security policymakers and practitioners" (START, n.d.b, para 1). Some might argue that START's language does not draw upon the war metaphor because the organization has no physical weaponry at its disposal to fight terrorism. While this position is valid, START at its core is an organization committed to understanding terrorism as a manifestation and by-product of the human condition. START seeks to help address the underlying causes of terrorism, not defeat it. According to its vision statement, START provides "homeland security policy-makers and practitioners with the highest quality, data-driven research findings on the human causes and consequences of terrorism in an effort to ensure that homeland security policies and operations reflect these understandings about human behaviors" (START, n.d.b, para 2).

In essence, START sees itself as an educational hub on terrorism. For example, START offers internships and funding opportunities to undergraduate and graduate students conducting terrorism research, and START provides educational materials including teaching tools and data sets that can be used in secondary and post-secondary schools in an attempt to "deepen students' understanding of the dynamics of terrorism" (START, n.d.a, para 5). Yet, START's educational reach is far beyond secondary and post-secondary entities. Various journalists, bloggers, and media outlets use data from START in their reports, analysis, and commentary; for example, Dalal (2017) uses START data, charts, and graphs to make a compelling argument about how the US media (such as the *New York Times*) fuels citizens' fears of terrorism by overcovering and overtelling terrorism stories. In short, "START is committed to the widespread dissemination of its research findings not only to homeland security professionals through tailored research, education and training efforts, but also to students of all levels and to the general public" (START, n.d.a, para 5). In this vein, START is the quintessential embodiment of cocreational approaches to terrorism – as the organization attempts to truly understand the perspective of terrorist organizations and then share those findings broadly, so others can be informed.

As such, consider some of the following fundamental questions about terrorism that START researchers posit and examine:

- What is the nature of terrorism in the world today? How has terrorist activity evolved over time? How does terrorism vary across geographies? And what do these trends indicate about likely future terrorism?
- Under what conditions does an individual or a group turn to terrorism to pursue its goals? What is the nature of the radicalization process?
- How does terrorism end? What are the processes of deradicalization and disengagement from terrorism for groups and individuals?
- What actions can governments take to counter the threat of terrorism?
- What impact does terrorism and the threat of terrorism have on communities, and how can societies enhance their resilience to minimize the potential impacts of future attacks? (START, n.d.a, para 2).

Hence, many of the questions that its researchers study do not address "defeating" terrorism at all. Instead, the focus is on "deradicalizing" terrorism because, as Heath and Waymer (2014b) have noted, terrorism is not a new phenomenon. Thus, a useful approach might be "to continue the analysis of terrorism to sort out what of it might be constructive as opposed to its mere destruction" (p. 228).

Conclusion

Whether we are talking about counterterrorism or SC in general, a common refrain persists: unqualified "strategists" are assigned to SC writ large. The real question is, why is this so? As indicated earlier, the war metaphor and militaristic approach to counterterrorism has proven to be mostly ineffective, yet people who adhere vehemently to that stance are the ones in power positions to implement the counterterrorism campaign. In a similar vein, in organizations where a supervisor states that research is not necessary because the only strategy he or she will allow as the supervisor is "getting the story out" is in the power position; the practitioner who has SC training but has no authority to develop or implement a SC plan is reduced to an almost exclusively tactical role. In these instances, organizations might continue to not achieve their campaign goals because they do not understand their publics and what motivates them; yet in the same breath they will speak against research and not empower the people to conduct the research necessary to lead to successful campaign outcomes.

Now more than ever, practitioners need to be guided by cocreational approaches as they engage their work, and design and implement SC campaigns. There are several valid critiques of the cocreational model, not least of which is that the cocreational model elevates research ing and better understanding our publics to a central and vital role in SC. Elevating publics, including terrorists, to this indispensable role is often challenged by critics who have a simplistic view of SC, who espouse the belief that SC is only about "getting our story out," "getting our point across," or "achieving our desired end by the simplest means." Adhering to this narrow mindset, organizational leaders often claim that there is no budget and no time for, or no budget nor time to waste, on conducting research to better understand publics – despite the fact that such research might lead to better campaign design and implementation. Botan (2018), in his book *Strategic communication theory and practice*, addresses the claims and limitations of the espoused "lacking time and budget" argument. In a spirit that aligns with Botan's (2018) work, I argue that it is rather refreshing to see an entity like START prioritizing the research in its strategic counterterrorism efforts, a much-needed deviation from conventional wisdom and practice in both counterterrorism and SC efforts.

I reiterate, now more than ever, practitioners need to be guided by cocreational approaches as they engage their work, and design and implement SC campaigns. The rhetorical analysis above of START and its approach to counterterrorism highlights this point very well. The US has been fighting a war on terrorism for more than 17 years (Cardin, 2017), and critics have gone so far as to say that we are fighting the "wrong war"; critics make a compelling argument by highlighting how support for terrorist organizations has grown, despite the US military success against "terrorist" groups.

The key idea behind the cocreational view is not at all revolutionary to the way scholars and lay persons alike speak and think; however, the cocreational view is revolutionary to the way public relations and the rest of SC are actually practiced. The cocreational view foregrounds this principle: the meanings publics cocreate in their relationships with us, and each other (thus the "co") may be influenced in small part by the things practitioners say and do in our campaigns; however, their meaning is much more determined in majority by their own experiences, values, culture, judgments, etc. Thus, what we might very well know but seldom practice in public relations and SC is that the better we come to understand our publics, the more successful all parties involved will be. Thus, the key publics in counterterrorism SC are the potential members and supporters/funders of terrorist groups, and if one is to counter terrorism successfully, those are the groups we must understand better and to whom we must adapt our counterterror efforts.

References

Alleyne, E., & Wood, J. L. (2012). Gang membership: The psychological evidence. In F.-A. Esbensen & C. L. Maxson (Eds.), *Youth gangs in international perspective* (pp. 151–168). New York: Springer.

Associated Press (2013, November 10). Winslow 'regrets' making comments. Retrieved from http://www.espn.com/college-football/news/story?id=1657901

Berman, I., & Thompson, C. (2018, July 26). Fight against terror entering a new phase, still just as vital. USA Today. Retrieved from https://www.usatoday.com/story/opinion/2018/07/26/donald-trump-war-terror-islamic-state-syria-iraq-europe-column/828886002

Best, S., McLaren, P., & Nocella, A. J. (2007). Revolutionary peacemaking: Using a critical pedagogy approach for peacemaking with "terrorists". *Journal for Critical Education Policy Studies*, 5(2), 1–18.

Botan, C. H. (2018). *Strategic communication theory and practice*. Hoboken, NJ: Wiley.

Boyd, J. (2003). A quest for Cinergy: The war metaphor and the construction of identity. *Communication Studies*, 54, 249–264.

Boyd, J., & VanSlette, S. H. (2009). Outlaw discourse as postmodern public relations. In R. L. Heath, E. L. Toth, & D. Waymer (Eds.), *Rhetorical and critical approaches to public relations II* (pp. 328–342). New York: Routledge.

Bureau of Counterterrorism and Countering Violent Extremism (n.d.). Retrieved from https://www.state.gov/j/ct

Canel, M.-J. (2012). Communicating strategically in the face of terrorism: The Spanish government's response to the 2004 Madrid bombing attacks. *Public Relations Review*, 38, 214–222.

Cardin, B. (2017, August 22). Sen. Ben Cardin: Don't send more U.S. troops. USA Today. Retrieved from https://www.usatoday.com/story/opinion/2017/08/22/dont-send-american-troops-afghanistan-ben-cardin-editorials-debates/104862768

Dalal, N. (2017, January 12). How media fuels our fear of terrorism. Priceonomics. Retrieved from https://priceonomics.com/our-fixation-on-terrorism

Entman, R. (1993). Framing: Toward clarification of a fractured paradigm. *Journal of Communication*, 43, 41–58.

Farmer, A. Y., & Hairston, J. T. (2013). Predictors of gang membership: Variations across grade levels. *Journal of Social Service Research*, 39(4), 530–544.

Goff, B. (2018, December 14). START team offers counterterrorism training to Albanian officials. Retrieved fromhttps://www.start.umd.edu/news/start-team-offers-counterterrorism-training-albanian-officials

Heath, R. L., & Waymer, D. (2014a). John Brown, public relations, terrorism, and social capital: "His Truth Goes Marching On". *Public Relations Inquiry*, 3, 209–226. 10.1177/2046147X14539697.

Heath, R. L., & Waymer, D. (2014b). Terrorism: Social capital, social construction, and constructive society? *Public Relations Inquiry*, 3, 227–244. 10.1177/2046147X14529683.

Hodjat, A. (2018, November 8). Students are calling on UMD to divest from its contract with ICE: The university provides ICE officials with counterterrorism training. The Diamondback. Retrieved from http://www.dbknews.com/2018/11/08/umd-ice-contract-undocumented-immigration-zero-tolerance-deportation-trump-training-money

Hoffman, B. (2006). *Inside terrorism*. New York: Columbia University Press.

Kim, Y. (2008). Negotiating with terrorists: The iterated game of the Taliban Korean hostage case. *Public Relations Review*, 34, 263–268.

Knight, M. G. (1999). Getting past the impasse: Framing as a tool for public relations. *Public Relations Review*, 25, 381–398.

LaFree, G. (2017, May 22). Six reasons why stopping terrorism is so challenging. Retrieved from https://www.start.umd.edu/news/six-reasons-why-stopping-terrorism-so-challenging

Lakoff, G., & Johnson, M. (1980). *Metaphors we live by*. Chicago, IL: University of Chicago Press.

Moses, Z. (2017, November 9). Combatting terrorism with data analytics: Q&A with Thomas Guarrieri. Retrieved from https://www.start.umd.edu/news/combatting-terrorism-data-analytics

Richardson, L. (2006). *What terrorists want: Understanding the enemy, containing the threat*. New York: Random House.

Rothenberger, J. (2012). Terrorist groups: Using internet and social media for disseminating ideas. New tools for promoting political change. *Journal of Communication & Public Relations*, XIV, 7–23.

Ryan, C., Carragee, K. M., & Meinhofer, W. (2001). Theory into practice: Framing, the news media, and collective action. *Journal of Broadcasting & Electronic Media*, 45, 175–182.

Sinclair, S. J., & Antonius, D. (2012). *The psychology of terrorism fears*. New York: Oxford University Press.

Somerville, I., & Purcell, A. (2011). A history of republican public relations in Northern Ireland from "Bloody Sunday" to the "Good Friday Agreement". *Journal of Communication Management*, 15, 192–209.

Sonterblum, L. (2018). Gang involvement as a means to satisfy basic needs. Retrieved from https://steinhardt.nyu.edu/appsych/opus/issues/2016/spring/sonterblum

START (n.d.a) About START. Retrieved from http://www.start.umd.edu/about/about-start

START (n.d.b). Mission and vision. Retrieved from http://www.start.umd.edu/about/mission-and-vision

Taylor, M. (2000). Media relations in Bosnia: A role for public relations in building civil society. *Public Relations Review*, 26, 1–14.

Tucker, L. R. (1998). The framing of Calvin Klein: A frame analysis of media discourse about the August 1995 Calvin Klein Jeans advertising campaign. *Critical Studies in Mass Communication*, 15, 141–157.

US Department of State (2018, May 1). Launching of operations to liberate final ISIS strongholds in Syria. Retrieved from https://www.state.gov/r/pa/prs/ps/2018/05/281355.htm

Waymer, D. (2009). Walking in fear: An autoethnographic account of media framing of inner-city crime. *Journal of Communication Inquiry*, 33, 169–184.

Waymer, D. (2012). A city divided: Understanding "class issues" in government public relations. In D. Waymer (Ed.), *Culture, social class, and race in public relations: Perspectives and applications* (pp. 31–44). Lanham, MD: Lexington Books.

Waymer, D. (2018). Spades, shovels, and backhoes: Unearthing metaphors in organizational rhetoric. In Ø. Ihlen & R. L. Heath (Eds.), *The handbook of organizational rhetoric and communication* (pp. 245–256). Malden, MA: Wiley-Blackwell.

Zhang, J. (2007). Beyond anti-terrorism: Metaphors as message strategy of post-September-11 U.S. public diplomacy. *Public Relations Review*, 33, 31–39.

Zimmerman, K. (2018, May 11). The never-ending war on terror: Why the U. S. keeps fighting the wrong battle. Foreign Affairs. Retrieved from https://www.foreignaffairs.com/articles/2018-05-11/never-ending-war-terror

8

Communicating Safety in Norwegian Road Tunnels

A Cocreational Perspective of Strategic Communication

Sverre Kjetil Rød[1] and Daniel Nilsson[2]
Norwegian Public Roads Administration[1] and University of Canterbury[2]

Norway has more than 1,100 open road tunnels, among them the world's longest subsea (292 m deep, 14.4 km long) tunnel and the world's longest tunnel (24.5 km). The first tunnels were built already in the 1960s. Ninety of the tunnels are one-tube tunnels with bidirectional traffic, of which 33 are subsea. In many of the tunnels, especially the subsea tunnels, there is a steep gradient resulting in an increased risk of heavy goods vehicle fires due to engine and brake failures (Njaa, 2019). The uniqueness of these old Norwegian tunnels is their one-tube construction with no rescue chambers (i.e. relatively limited means of escape in emergencies). This means that traffic from both directions goes through the same tube. For instance, in case of a fire and without rescue chambers inside the tunnel, tunnel occupants need to evacuate to the outside environment as fast as possible to not be overcome by fire smoke. Needless to say, this is a demanding process for a diverse population of occupants where time is critical. On the contrary, in a tunnel with two tubes, which is the standard in many countries today, evacuation is a lot easier since tunnel occupants can evacuate into the unaffected tube through evacuation cross-passages. These cross-passages can be placed every couple of hundred meters, creating a large number of possible evacuation routes throughout the tunnel.

The guideline for safety in road tunnels is the non-publicized self-rescue principle; the driver and passengers must evacuate unassisted by foot or by car when an emergency occurs (i.e. before the fire brigade arrives). The same unspoken principle rules when evacuating out of any public building. The owner of the Norwegian tunnels – the Norwegian Public Roads Administration (NPRA) – has only to a limited extent distributed information about the fire risks in tunnels. As such, information about what to do in emergencies (self-rescue) in tunnels has been scarce – until December 2019, when the NPRA launched a national PR campaign for the first time. The campaign consisted of six different videos with instructions on what to do in emergencies, reaching out to the youngest drivers, adult drivers, and truck drivers, by utilizing social media, such as Instagram, Snapchat, and Facebook. The videos will also be used in connection with drivers' education.

Evacuation from a road tunnel can be a very difficult and traumatic experience for those concerned. This is evident after reading the testimonies in the accident investigation reports after the fires in the Oslofjord Tunnel in 2011 (AIBN, 2013) and in the Gudvanga Tunnel in 2013 and 2015 (AIBN, 2015, 2016). The main problems of tunnel occupants were caused by the fact that they had to evacuate through dense smoke, which in turn is partially explained by

The Handbook of Strategic Communication, First Edition. Edited by Carl H. Botan.

the fact that evacuation was initiated relatively late. An early start to evacuation in the case of fire is necessary in order not to be injured, which means that the tunnel and the surrounding infrastructure must be designed to meet this need.

This chapter provides a review of the factors that may influence the ability of tunnel occupants to evacuate more effectively during fire emergencies in tunnels, and the predictors, including risk communication, that may influence the occupant's perception of safety while driving through tunnels. In addition, included is an introduction to how tunnel occupants behave during a tunnel fire evacuation. This knowledge is important to fully understand the need for specific instructions when an accident in a tunnel has occurred. Since the NPRA has limited the information related to risk and self rescue in tunnels over the years, this chapter will discuss and recommend ways of making tunnels safer by communicating strategically, guided by the cocreational perspective. The aim of the chapter is to demonstrate how a cocreational method of collaboration between authorities and publics at risk of future fire emergencies in tunnels may contribute to make the Norwegian road tunnels safer.

Introduction

The tunnels that are relevant in this context are one-tube, long (more than 3 km), and steep (slopes more than 5%) with bidirectional traffic. The reason for this delimitation is that these tunnels are common in the Norwegian road network and are also those perceived as being associated with the highest level of risk. Long bidirectional tunnels with steep gradients pose a special problem for evacuation. The conditions mean that some people will inevitably be exposed to smoke and evacuation will be both prolonged in time and constitute a heavy workload for people who have to evacuate the uphill slope.

Human behavior is described based on established theories of observed activities in the case of a fire and essentially based on the behavior sequence theory of Canter, Breaux, and Sime (1980). Other theories are included to explain why certain behaviors can be observed and how technical installations can be designed to meet the information needs of tunnel users. Basically, many future improvements are related to an early detection of fire and ensuring that motorists are informed about what has happened and what they are expected to do. With this information, self rescue activities may be successful. Included in the term "information" is also the type of information that is gained before the accident by, for example, education or information campaigns. Tunnel occupants must deal with the situation themselves, with the possible assistance of staff from a road traffic center (VTS). Assistance by other early responders can typically not be assumed.

Risk Communication

The principal rationale for risk communication before, during, and after natural hazards is to initiate and direct protective action and insure public safety. Government agencies and experts tend to engage in one-way dissemination of information (McComas, 2003, p. 166); they often fail to recognize risk communication as a dialogue and to acknowledge that people perceive and interpret risks differently. Risk managers have rarely focused on how people with different personal and contextual characteristics process risk communication and relate to adverse events.

Most research on risk has traditionally taken the form of risk analysis and considered the probabilities and consequences of hazards, as communicated by experts to initiate preventative behavior. To a lesser extent, the focus has been on how risk communication is perceived and processed, and how sociocultural and emotional aspects and relationships among publics may influence how they respond to the risks. Kasperson et al. (1988) argue, via the social amplification of risk framework, that the perception of risk may intensify or attenuate, depending on each individual's interpretation of the threat. Affect may have a stronger impact on the publics' probability assessments than logic and facts. According to Slovic et al. (2004), there are two fundamental systems by which humans understand risk. The *analytical* system which uses probability calculus, formal logic, and risk assessment, and the *experiential* system which uses intuition and is fast, mostly automatic, and not characterized by conscious awareness. "The experiential system encodes reality in images, metaphors, and narratives to which affective feelings have become attached" (Slovic et al., 2004, p. 316).

The National Research Council made an effort to revitalize the concept of risk communication in 1989 by coining it as a "democratic dialogue"; implying an interactive process of information exchange expressing multiple concerns, opinions, or reactions to risk messages (Sellnow et al., 2009). Because risk is manifested socially, it may also prove useful for risk communicators to address people's needs at both the rational and the emotional levels. The next paragraphs will describe how strategic communication (SC) guided by a cocreational approach may help communicators balance the delicate complexity of meeting the needs of potential tunnel users and communicating strategically.

A Cocreational Perspective on Communication

Botan and Taylor (2004) distinguish between a functional and cocreational perspective of communication. The cocreational perspective emphasizes the relationship between an organization and its multiple publics – "sharing meanings, interpretations and goals" (Botan & Taylor, 2004). Only when an issue is defined by the publics, is it possible for an organization to decide what needs to be done strategically to reach predetermined objectives.

The cocreational perspective is based on the tenets of sense-making theory and co-orientation theory to explain publics' use of information, for example in making sense of and responding to emergency situations. According to Botan and Penchalapadu (2009) and Hodgson (2007), the goal of sense-making is to find rational explanations to chaotic situations in an attempt to reduce uncertainty and complexity so that the situation makes more sense. Indeed, when drivers are stuck in a traffic jam in a tunnel it would be useful to know the basics of what to do. Should they wait for information or start evacuating right away? To understand better how the cocreational perspective relates to preventative action in evacuation situations, it may be useful to explore the relationship between consensus and two-way communication.

Communication Fulfilling the Needs of Whom?

According to Scheff (1967), co-orientation is a relationship-focused construct that deals with consensus – the kind of shared sense-making needed to respond to emergencies. In one of its early forms, Papa, Auwal, and Singhal (1995) said: "Scheff's (1967) simplified co-orientation model focuses only on accuracy and agreement. According to this model, an organization with knowledge of a certain topic presents the information to publics lacking such knowledge. Upon receiving this new information, the publics reach a certain level of accuracy (or understanding) and agreement with respect to what they have learned. Co-orientation occurs when two parties reach a state of mutual accuracy and mutual agreement with respect to the presented information" (p. 193).

Both sense-making and co-orientation theories suggest that two-way communication mechanisms are in place so that risk communicators can not only understand what information publics need to reduce their uncertainty and make sense of the situation, but also ensure there is enough co-orientation between officials and publics to facilitate effective response actions. As described by Taylor and Botan (2004), the cocreational perspective implies that publics and organizations may become partners in the meaning-making process of perceiving and managing a risk situation together. At this early stage in an imminent risk situation, most strategic options are available, for example customizing messages aiming to initiate risk-reducing preventative behavior, which may be achieved by informing about tunnel safety.

In a functional perspective, specific activities and outputs, as tactics, are implemented in accordance with the selected strategy. The publics and PR campaigns are seen as tools to achieve specific goals, for example what to do in emergency situations in tunnels.

The government agency disseminates information to the publics with the intention to enhance its image. At the risk of oversimplifying, we can view the functional perspective as tactical communication, disseminating information solely for the purpose of fulfilling the needs of the organization conducting the campaign. The cocreational perspective, in contrast, utilizes the relationship between an organization and its publics as a source of both strategic and tactical information.

Communication Facilitating Evacuation

So, how can the cocreational perspective of communication be applied strategically when the objective is to enhance tunnel safety? First, a basis for communication is the existence of two parties exchanging information in a dialogue. In the case described in this chapter, before 2019 there was limited communication between the publics and the NPRA, because the NPRA hesitated to share information about issues related to evacuation (self-rescue) in tunnels. This is most likely in order to avoid fear among potential tunnel users, which could be due to a belief that this fear might lead to inappropriate behavior. However, numerous studies demonstrate that publics who receive relevant information about evacuation beforehand and during an emergency evacuate more effectively than others (Auboyer, Andersen, & Wybo, 2007; Boer, 2002, 2005; Kinateder et al., 2012, 2013; Martens, 2006; van Wijngaarden, Bronkhorst, & Boer, 2005). A study from Norway (Vatsvåg, 2016) confirms that knowledge about safety behavior and equipment in tunnels, along with trust in authorities, had a positive influence on publics' perception of safety when driving through tunnels. Typically men, young drivers (18–28 years old), those who haven't experienced any accidents in tunnels, and those who drive often through tunnels feel safer than others. These studies emphasize the need to understand how people behave when evacuating in emergencies.

Human Behavior in Fire Emergencies

A useful model for describing human behavior in case of fire emergencies in road tunnels is the explanatory timeline model (Frantzich, Nilsson, & Rød, 2016). This model is based on the RSET model (Proulx, 2008) traditionally used for fire safety engineering analyses, but takes the perspective of the tunnel occupant (Figure 8.1). It is therefore a useful theory for identifying the information needs of different tunnel occupant groups in case of evacuation.

According to the explanatory timeline model, the evacuation process starts already before the incident has occurred. During this preliminary phase, potential tunnel occupants can be informed about fire risks in road tunnels, which cues to look out for, and what actions to take

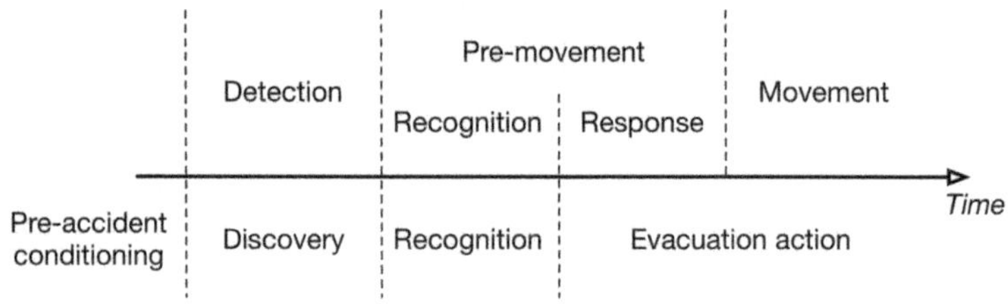

Figure 8.1 The RSET model (top) and the explanatory timeline model (bottom).

in case of a fire (e.g. information about the self-rescue principle). The idea is that this type of pre-accident conditioning of potential tunnel users can reduce the time subsequently required for evacuation.

Once inside the tunnel, the explanatory timeline model claims that occupants need to go through the process of ***discovery***, ***recognition***, and ***evacuation action***. During the discovery phase, tunnel occupants are unaware that a fire has occurred. The phase ends when occupants receive the first cue that something is out of the ordinary (e.g. they see smoke, hear an alarm, etc.). The length of the discovery phase relies heavily on the detection and notification technologies in the tunnel. In many Norwegian tunnels, however, there is a lack of technology for detection and notification, which means that the discovery phase often ends when occupants see fire, smoke, or stopped vehicles.

During the recognition phase, occupants try to make sense of the received cues in order to adequately understand the situation. It has been shown that the interpretation phase can be reduced by providing ample means of notification (Proulx & Sime, 1991), but it is argued that appropriate information before an incident (e.g. training) would also have a positive influence. If tunnel occupants are aware of the meaning of different cues, they are arguably also more prepared to quickly interpret the situation as an emergency. Research also suggests that one of the most important cues in tunnel emergencies is the behavior of other tunnel occupants (Boer, 2002; Nilsson, Johansson, & Franzich, 2009) – that is, social influence. For example, seeing someone leave their vehicle and evacuate on foot is seen as a very strong indicator that the situation is serious.

Finally, during the evacuation action phase the tunnel occupants act in order to reduce the consequences of fire. This can involve movement toward a safe location (e.g. emergency exit or rescue chamber) or an attempt to address the threat directly (e.g. extinguish the fire). It has been shown that evacuation systems can be valuable for tunnel occupants during the evacuation action phase (Boer, 2002; Fridolf & Franzich, 2015; Nilsson & Frantzich, 2009), but knowledge about evacuation procedures in road tunnels could arguably improve the effectiveness of existing evacuation systems. The main difference between the RSET model and the explanatory timeline model is the time spent in pre-movement: according to Frantich, Nilsson, and Rød (2016), tunnel occupants spend almost 60% of the total evacuation time (from detection of fire to arrival at assembly point) interpreting what to do before starting to evacuate. The explanatory timeline model cuts down this prolonged time by enhancing risk communication (pre-accident conditioning) – informing publics what to do in emergencies in tunnels.

The explanatory timeline model is consistent with experiences from several evacuation experiments in road tunnels (Boer, 2002; Nilsson & Frantzich, 2009). Experiments have thus far mainly been performed in two-tube tunnels for European contexts, which means that knowledge about perception and human behavior in Norwegian one-tube tunnels is still scarce. The main difference between evacuating in one-tube and two-tube tunnels relates to evacuation options: whereas you can leave the car behind and evacuate (i.e. walk) into the other tube in a two-tube tunnel, the only alternative in a one-tube tunnel is to evacuate out of the tunnel.

An essential first step toward a successful communication strategy between operator and tunnel occupants is an understanding of the process tunnel occupants go through in a fire emergency situation. The explanatory timeline model offers a simplified representation of the decision process (i.e. the phases a tunnel occupant needs to go through in case of a tunnel fire evacuation). In each phase, specific information is needed to minimize the time required. However, the information provided must be based on the perspective of the tunnel occupants, which is virtually impossible to foresee unless occupants are directly involved in the development phase (e.g. take part in experiments or otherwise advise/inform operators about their needs). Communication strategies would therefore greatly benefit from a cocreational approach based on studying human behavior beforehand, and thus understanding the needs of tunnel occupants when stuck in a smoke-filled tunnel.

Worry and the Willingness to Evacuate

Research on worry has demonstrated positive correlations with problem-solving or dealing with the risk: those who worry are more willing to evacuate than others (Davey, 1993; Davey et al., 1992; Miceli, Sotgiu, & Settanni, 2008; Rød, Botan, & Holen, 2012). According to MacGregor (1991), worry may create useful mental scenarios or images preparing people to meet future events.

Sattler et al. (2000) suggested that there is a relationship between disaster experience and disaster preparedness. Therefore, it is arguable that publics who live in areas with road tunnels are more likely to adhere to evacuation warnings than those who have never been exposed to such risks (Drabek & Boggs, 1968; Sattler, Kaiser, & Hittner, 2000). Numerous studies have documented correlations between people's trust in the government and their willingness to comply with official evacuation orders (Burton and Silver, 2006; Granatt, 2004; West, 2001; West & Orr, 2007). The more people trust government officials and evacuation orders, the more willing they are to comply (West & Orr, 2007).

A study by Vatsvåg (2016) demonstrated that knowledge about safety behavior and equipment during evacuation in tunnels leads to increased perceived safety, in line with earlier research (Boer, 2002). Another predictor – trust in experts – leads to an adequate level of worry, which again correlates positively with regard to the willingness to evacuate.

Socially Necessary Information

If publics are to engage in the social process of meaning cocreation and make free and informed choices, socially necessary information (adequate and accurate) must be provided to them by organizations holding that information (Botan, 2018). According to Botan (2018), responsible organizations must openly provide publics with socially necessary information and engage them in the decision-making process. But, as stated by Botan (2018, p. 92):

> Conversely, when an organization or politician decides to withhold part of the facts from their publics they may be deciding against social responsibility and are consciously denying their publics agency. This is most blatant when the decision to withhold is based on the claim that such withholding is for the public's own good, because publics are thought not to be calm, skilled or knowledgeable enough to be trusted with the information. These excuses for withholding socially necessary information tend to reduce publics to a dependent status through information control.

Panic is regarded as a myth in evacuation situations. Researchers (Fahy, Proulx, & Aiman, 2009; Sime, 1980) have studied the phenomenon of panic and found that panic in terms of irrational behavior is rarely seen in fires. Research has shown that more and clearer information about an incident leads to a faster response without triggering any behavior that could be labeled as "panic" (Proulx & Sime, 1991). Hence, there should be no effort to reduce information based on fear of panic.

Discussion

This chapter suggests that the NPRA would be wise to prioritize the objective of strengthening the bond (i.e. trust) between themselves and publics by continuing to provide the publics' with knowledge about tunnel safety, and in particular issues related to the tacit self-rescue principle. In this way, the publics will receive socially necessary information, being able to interpret the meaning of it individually and/or engage in a social process of meaning cocreation (i.e. creating and sharing the meaning of imminent risk situations in tunnels and making free and informed choices). Most likely, by receiving relevant risk information beforehand, publics will have sufficient information to make the right choices when stuck in a tunnel or when the tunnel is filled with smoke. But the only way to know this for sure is to study human behavior in evacuation scenarios, whether this is in virtual-reality settings or real life. Engaging proactively in dialogue and reaching consensus about preventative behavior and evacuation equipment and procedures may ensure that communication from then on will create cocreation, and be strategically useful for both the NPRA and the publics.

Tactics used by the NPRA may be continuing to launch national PR campaigns, addressing the issues related to tunnel safety, emphasizing preventative behavior (i.e. evacuating by foot or vehicle), and utilizing equipment/installations inside the tunnel, to facilitate evacuation. According to research, knowing what to do beforehand when there is a traffic jam inside a tunnel would contribute to make the publics capable of evacuating more effectively – not causing fear or "panic" as discussed in this chapter.

Although driver education has not been explored in this chapter, it has been implicit in the discussions of cocreating meanings before tunnel accidents occur. In this context, it is necessary that tunnel safety becomes an integral part of car and truck drivers' education. Research shows that most accidents in steep downgrade are caused by heavy goods vehicles losing braking power or engines becoming overheated. Therefore, drivers of trucks and tourist buses (i.e. professional drivers) should be well educated on tunnel safety issues, representing a major concern for the NPRA. Professional drivers, if appropriately educated, could also be taught to quickly recognize and respond to initial fire cues, and through the process of social interaction in the tunnel also influence other motorists and passengers to evacuate promptly. Education of professional drivers on tunnel fire safety is a strategy that has been used in Sweden for many years, since it was recognized that there would most likely always be a bus or truck driver inside a tunnel in case of fire.

Modern technology used for education purposes – such as serious games for safety education, virtual reality, and augmented reality – have proven useful in making evacuation in tunnels more efficient (Chittaro, 2016; Kinateder et al., 2013; Li & Tay, 2014). These technologies could therefore be further explored as part of a communication and education strategy.

A cocreational perspective on communication would suggest that the NPRA builds strong relations with its key publics, like truck drivers' unions and driving schools, in addition to the publics in general. When reaching consensus about the need to enhance education about tunnel safety, the NPRA would lay the foundation for SC. After the consensus, specific activities – like tailoring a PR campaign to women (who tend to feel less safe than men in tunnels) – can be implemented. Successful SC should be based on the relationship with the publics in the meaning-making process of perceiving and managing risk situations. By applying such a cocreational perspective, the NPRA would be better able to communicate strategically with versatile publics driving through road tunnels.

References

AIBN (Accident Investigation Board Norway, 2013). https://www.aibn.no/Road-Traffic/Reports/2013-05

AIBN (Accident Investigation Board Norway, 2015). https://www.aibn.no/Road-Traffic/Published-reports/2015-02-eng

AIBN (Accident Investigation Board Norway, 2016). https://www.aibn.no/Road-Traffic/Published-reports/2016-03-eng

Auboyer, A., Andersen, V., & Wybo, J. L. (2007). State-of-the-art road tunnel safety. *International Journal of Emergency Management*, 4(4). doi: 10.1504/IJEM.2007.015733

Boer, L. C. (2002). Gedrag van automobilisten bij evacuatie van een tunnel [*Behaviour by motorists on evacuation of a tunnel*]. Report TM-02-C034. Amsterdam: TNO.

Botan, C. (2018). *Strategic communication theory and practice: The cocreational model.* Hoboken, NJ: Wiley-Blackwell.

Botan, C., & Penchalapadu, P. (2009). Using sense-making and co-orientation to rank strategic public communication in State Emergency Operations Plans (EOPs). *International Journal of Strategic Communication*, 3(3), 199–216. doi: 10.1080/15531180902984216

Botan, C. H., & Taylor, M. (2004). Public relations: State of the field. *Journal of Communication*, 54, 645–661

Burton, P. W., & Silver, B. D. (2006). The credibility of disaster evacuation warnings: The effects of issue framing and trust in government. Retrieved from http://35.8.71.4/Documents/SOSSRelated/Burton_Silver_APSA2006_Final_Paper.pdf

Canter, D., Breaux, J., & Sime, J. (1980). Domestic, multiple occupancy, and hospital fires. In D. Canter (Ed.), *Fires and human behaviour* (1st edn). New York: Wiley.

Chittaro, L. (2016). Designing serious games for safety education: Learn to brace vs. traditional pictorials for aircraft passengers. *IEEE Transactions on Visualization and Computer Graphics*, 22(5), 1527–1539.

Davey, G. C. L. (1993). A comparison of three worry questionnaires. *Behaviour Research and Therapy*, 31, 51–56.

Davey, G. C. L., Hampton, J., Farrell, J., & Davidson, S. (1992). Some characteristics of worrying: Evidence for worrying and anxiety as separate constructs. *Personality and Individual Differences*, 13, 133–147.

Drabek, T. E., & Boggs, K. (1968). Families in disaster: Reactions and relatives. *Journal of Marriage and the Family*, 30, 443–451.

Fahy, R., Proulx, G., & Aiman, L. (2009). 'Panic' and human behaviour in fire. In *Proceedings of the 4th International Symposium*, Robinson College, Cambridge, pp. 387–398.

Frantzich, H., Nilsson, D., & Rød, K. (2016). *Utrymning och tekniska installationer i vägtunnlar med dubbelriktad trafik*. Lund: Brandteknik, LTH.

Fridolf, K., & Frantzich, H. (2015). *Test av vägledande system i en tunnel – Slutrapport*. Report 3189. Lund: Department of Fire Safety Engineering, Lund University.

Granatt, M. (2004). On trust: Using public information and warning partnerships to support the community response to an emergency. *Journal of Communication Management*, 8(4), 354–365.

Hodgson, R. W. (2007). Emotions and sense-making in disturbance: Community adaptation to dangerous environments. *Human Ecology Review*, 14(20), 233–242.

Kasperson, R. E., Renn, O., Slovic, P., Brown, H. S., Emel, J., Goble, R., Kasperson, J. X., & Ratick, S. (1988). The social amplification of risk: A conceptual framework. *Risk Analysis*, 8(2), 177–187.

Kinateder, M., Müller, M., Mühlberger, A., & Pauli, P. (2012). Social influence in a virtual tunnel fire – Influence of passive virtual bystanders, human behaviour in fire 2012. In *Proceedings of Human Behaviour in Fire Conference* (art. 506e516). Gosport: Interscience Communications Ltd.

Kinateder, M., Pauli, P., Müller, M., Krieger, J., Heimbecher, F., Rönnau, I., Bergerhausen, U., Vollmann, G., Vogt, P., & Mühlberger, A. (2013). Human behaviour in severe tunnel accidents: Effects of information and behavioural training. *Transportation Research Part F: Traffic Psychology and Behaviour*, 17, 20–32. http://dx.doi.org/10.1016/j.trf.2012.09.001

Li, Q., & Tay, R. (2014). Improving drivers' knowledge of road rules using digital games. *Accident Analysis and Prevention*, 65, 8–10.

MacGregor, D. (1991). Worry over technological activities and life concerns. *Risk Analysis*, 11(2), 315–324.

Martens, M. H. (2006). Human behaviour in tunnel accidents: Users, operators and rescue teams. In Proceedings of the Second International Symposium on Safe and Reliable Tunnels, Lausanne.

McComas, K. A. (2003). Citizen satisfaction with public meetings used for risk communication. *Journal of Applied Communication Research*, 31(2), 164–184.

Miceli, R., Sotgiu, I., & Settanni, M. (2008). Disaster preparedness and perception of flood risk: A study in an alpine valley in Italy. *Journal of Environmental Psychology*, 28, 164–173.

Nilsson, J., & Frantzich, H. (2009). Evacuation experiment in a road tunnel: A study of human behaviour and technical installations. *Fire Safety Journal*, 44(4), 458–468. http://dx.doi.org/10.1016/j.firesaf.2008.09.009

Njaa, A. (2019). Modelling fire occurrences in heavy goods vehicles in Norwegian road tunnels. Master's thesis, University of Stavanger.

Papa, M. J., Auwal, M. A., & Singhal, A. (1995). Dialectic of control and emancipation in organizing for social change: A multitheoretic study of the Grameen Bank in Bangladesh. *Communication Theory*, 5(3), 189–223.

Proulx, G. (2008). Evacuation time. In P. J. DiNenno (Ed.), *The SFPE handbook of fire protection engineering* (4th edn, pp. 3-355–3-372). Quincy: National Fire Protection Association.

Proulx, G., & Sime, J. (1991). To prevent 'panic' in an underground emergency: Why not tell people the truth? In *Fire Safety Science – Proceedings of the 3rd International Symposium*, Edinburgh, pp. 843–852.

Rød, S. K., Botan, C., & Holen, A. (2012). Risk communication and worried publics in an imminent rockslide and tsunami situation. *Journal of Risk Research*, 15(6), 645–654. doi: 10.1080:13669877.211.652650

Sattler, D. N., Kaiser, C. F., & Hittner, J. B. (2000). Disaster preparedness: Relationships among prior experience, personal characteristics, and distress. *Journal of Applied Social Psychology*, 30(7), 1396–1420.

Scheff, T. J. (1967). Toward a sociological model of consensus. *American Sociological Review*, 32(1), 32–46.

Sellnow, T. L., Ulmer, R. R., Seeger, M. W., & Littlefield, R. S. (2009). *Effective risk communication: A message-centered approach*. New York: Springer Science.

Sime, J. D. (1980). The concept of 'panic'. In D. Canter (Ed.), *Fires and human behavior*. Chichester: Wiley.

Slovic, P., Finucane, M. L., Peters, E., & MacGregor, D. G. (2004). Risk as analysis and risk as feelings: Some thoughts about affect, reason, risk, and rationality. *Risk Analysis*, 24(2), 311–322.

van Wijngaarden, S. J., Bronkhorst, A. W., & Boer, L. C. (2005). Auditory evacuation beacons. *Journal of the Audio Engineering Society*, 53, 44–53.

Vatsvåg, N. (2016). En undersøkelse av ulike faktorers betydning I forhold til opplevd trygghet ved tunnelkjøring – en studie basert på fokusgruppeintervju og en spørreundersøkelse blant norske trafikanter. Master's thesis, University of Stavanger.

West, D. (2001). *The rise and fall of the media establishment*. Boston, MA: Bedford/St. Martin's Press.

West, D. M., & Orr, M. (2007). Race, gender, and communications in natural disasters. *Policy Studies Journal*, 35(4), 569–586.

PART III

Strategic Communication in Business, Government, and Military

9

Strategic Communication in the Military

An Air Force Perspective

Ronaldo Martinez Jr., Katrina J. Cheesman, Nicholas J. Mercurio, and Cara A. Bousie

George Mason University

Within the US government, the Department of Defense (DoD) and the subordinate military service branches constitute the largest department in the executive branch, with more than 2.8 million active duty, guard, reserve, and civilian personnel stationed throughout more than 150 countries (Defense Manpower Data Center, 2018; United States Office of Personnel Management, 2018). The military forces within the US serve as one of the four instruments of national power, which also include diplomacy, information, and economy (Farlin, 2014). As the world evolves, the role of the military in relation to the instruments of power changes. The technological superiority, size of the US military forces, and ability to operate in any of the six domains in which warfare occurs (land, sea, air, space, cyber, and information), provides stability to our nation, partners, and allies while discouraging potential adversaries from attack (Farlin, 2014).

Strategic communication (SC) is an important aspect of successful operations across all domains of warfare, as well as just below the level of warfare – the deterrent and coercive nature of the military instrument requires communication to potential adversaries. Everything the US joint military force does sends a message – whether it is dropping a 500-pound bomb on a terrorist training camp in Afghanistan or deploying a tank battalion to the border of Russia and Estonia for a last-minute military exercise. These actions, particularly when publicized, communicate messages to many different publics, and those publics will create their own meanings of those actions; the intended message sent is not always the message that was understood (Joint Doctrine Note 2-13, 2013).

Because the US military is globally present and often used (and perceived) as a geopolitical instrument of power, the US dedicates vast financial and personnel resources to it. In a democracy, there is a requirement for accountability, wherein political and military leaders assure the taxpayer their investment in national defense is organized, funded, and employed as openly and transparently as possible. Specifically, the US government, including the DoD, "has an obligation to inform our citizens about the nature of its activities" (Joint Doctrine Note 2-13, 2013, p. 17) while simultaneously communicating with international publics and adversaries (Joint Doctrine Note 2-13, 2013).

In this chapter, we define and assess SC from a military perspective, drawing on many years of practitioner experience and theoretical understanding. The chapter will broadly address military SC, but we do so using case study examples and vignettes from our USAF careers.

The Handbook of Strategic Communication, First Edition. Edited by Carl H. Botan.

While the USAF operates as a separate branch within the Defense Department, complete with unique policies, guidance, and practices, there are many similarities with the other branches of the Armed Forces regarding how the USAF engages in SC activities.

The chapter begins by establishing a working definition of SC from a theoretical and military perspective. Then, we illuminate the grand strategy guiding USAF SC. Third, we address USAF planning and execution of USAF SC. Finally, we draw on three case studies in military SC that illustrate the role and application of theory in practice – or the lack thereof.

Defining Strategic Communication

Strategic communication (SC) is a term that is used by many organizations and practitioners, but one which possesses a variety of meanings. Thus, we draw heavily on Botan's work "to unify the understanding and practice of strategic communication across all the subfields" of communication practitioners (Botan, 2018, p. 3). In this body of work, SC is defined as "the use of information flowing into the organization (research) to plan and carry out a communication campaign addressing the relationship between an organization and its publics and is based on research and centered on publics rather than the organization or a message" (Botan, p. 8).

SC is a singular practice made up of two distinct parts: strategic information and planned SC campaigns (Botan, 2018). Botan describes the first part, strategic information, as "information that can be used to describe, explain or predict the relationships between an organization and its publics" (p. 7). Strategic information is foundational to the second part, SC campaign planning.

Therefore, SC begins with information inflow, that is the understanding of publics, and not internal organizational desires. This understanding of the public is gained through deliberate research to understand their "starting meanings, goals, values, and view of the relationship" with the organization (Botan, 2018, p. 48). Botan calls this strategic research, and it helps organizations to understand the public's culture, relationships, history of past campaigns, goals, and values. It also allows planners to understand the frames from which publics will derive their meanings and make decisions. This is known as a cocreational process whereby publics and organizations create meaning together for given messages (Botan).

The information inflow from the strategic research provides SC campaign planners a clear view of the public's landscape and enables these planners to best align their organization's goals in this landscape with information outflow. There are a few key terms that must be understood which explain how an organization identifies these goals. They are grand strategy, strategy, and tactics.

Information outflow is guided by the organization's **grand strategy**, which is defined as "policy level decisions an organization makes about goals, alignments, ethics and relationships with publics and other forces in its environment" (Botan, 2018, p. 13). This grand strategy is the foundation upon which all SC campaigns are built. **Strategy** is defined as "campaign-level planning and decision-making involving maneuvering and arranging resources and arguments to carry out organization grand strategies" (Botan, 2018, p. 14). Thus, strategy used for a SC campaign is constrained by and must directly support and align with the organization's grand strategy. Finally, **tactics** are "specific activities and outputs through which strategies are implemented – the doing or the technical aspect of public relations" (Botan, 2018, p. 14).

The Military Approach to Strategic Communication

While there are certainly some similarities between this definition of SC and the US military's doctrinal definition, it contrasts in some key areas. First, military SC focuses on creating and strengthening outcomes favorable to national interests, policies, and objectives "by understanding and engaging key audiences through the use of coordinated programs, plans, themes, messages, and products synchronized" with the rest of the instruments of national power (The Joint Chiefs of Staff, 2014, p. II-5). The process drives communication from internal organizational goals instead of from strategic information, research, and relationships with publics. Second, a joint doctrine identifies SC as achieved by "understanding and engaging key audiences through the use of coordinated programs, plans, themes, messages and products," viewing the publics as information-receivers instead of meaning-makers. Third, it is a whole-of-government approach to coordinate and synchronize communication of national strategy – something driven by internal inter-agency processes, not by leveraging and aligning relationships with publics. In short, the US government defines SC as starting first with desired outcomes, which are not informed by strategic information from key publics. This tension between both definitions is key to understanding why the US military communicates the way it does, which we explore in various case studies.

In an institution as large and complex as the DoD, SC can be a difficult task to undertake, particularly because on a daily basis there are numerous, simultaneous operations and activities taking place around the world, each of which require planning and coordination to carefully align intended messages in the publics' mind with the grand strategy of the US. While global organizations address complex geopolitical decisions and engagements, the DoD is different as decisions often carry the gravity of potential warfare. As we are USAF officers, the next few paragraphs will lay out the grand strategy used at this level for SC.

Military Grand Strategy

The grand strategy within the USAF is reliant on decisions made by echelons that exist above the service, within the hierarchy of the US government. Everything the military does is guided by a grand strategy issued by the President of the United States, acting in his role as Commander-in-Chief of the US military. The current mechanism for issuing this strategy is the President's National Security Strategy (NSS), although some experts argue that the US lacks a comprehensive grand strategy at all (Lissner, 2017) – or one that puts national security in the context of other vital interests such as economic health (Howard, 1979; Krepinevich, 2010) and citizens' welfare (Brooks & Wohlforth, 2019; Light, 2002; McCormack, 2017). Some debate the sources of US grand strategy, arguing that it is driven by its powerful global statehood (Ikenberry & Mearsheimer, 2001; Kupchan, Kapstein, & Mastanduno, 2000; Waltz, 1993; Wohlforth, 1999) or domestic factors (Dueck, 2005). Additionally, some deny the Presidency impacts grand strategy due to the power shifts inherent to democracy, but that grand strategy is driven by foreign policy elites, creating a stable base in primacy of the US on the global stage (Porter, 2018). For the intent of this handbook, the NSS is the closest thing that approximates a US grand strategy, particularly as it codifies the current priorities of the nation (Pilon, 2016; Quinn & University of Birmingham, 2018). In essence, the NSS is a broad document that provides the President's strategic vector for how the nation will protect its vital interests while ensuring the long-term wellbeing of the nation (Farlin, 2014). The stated purpose of the NSS is to synergistically "protect the American people, the homeland, and the American way of life," to "promote American prosperity," to "preserve peace through strength," and to "advance American influence" (Trump, 2017).

While the NSS provides the President's grand strategy for all four instruments of power, the US Secretary of Defense issues their own strategy, known as the National Defense Strategy (NDS), to further refine how the military power of the nation will be used. This serves as the DoD's grand strategy and guides how the department will ensure the President's NSS will be achieved by defining the strategic environment within which the DoD must operate, as well as setting specific, strategic defense objectives for the nation (Mattis, 2018). The NDS also establishes a strategic approach to how the department will achieve the strategic objectives. The NDS provides the grand strategy from the department's most senior civilian leader. However, because of the political nature of senior government officials serving in their posts as Presidential appointees, the uniformed perspective must also be represented, and that comes in the form of the Chairman of the Joint Chief of Staff's (CJCS's) National Military Strategy (NMS). Under the Goldwater-Nichols Department of Defense Reorganization Act of 1986 (Public Law 99-433), the CJCS has a statutory obligation to present to the President, the Secretary of Defense, and Congress an unbiased, apolitical military grand strategy. The NMS provides military strategic guidance in support of the NDS and NSS, but may present different perspectives or considerations from both. The NMS also describes the military perspective of the strategic environment and establishes strategic military-specific objectives to support the NDS and the NSS.

It is from these guiding grand strategies that the Secretary of the Air Force (SecAF), the top civilian who leads the department, and the Chief of Staff of the Air Force (CSAF), the services top military officer, establish their own, service-specific grand strategies. SC within the USAF must further the objectives set by each echelon of leadership from the President down to the SecAF. The SecAF and CSAF determine the USAF's vision, lines of effort, strategic plans, and doctrine in support of these national strategies to achieve the national security objectives of the current Presidential administration. These written documents serve as ***institutional messages*** that function as a launchpad for internal and external SC activities (Lammers, 2011).

Air Force Strategic Communication: Planning and Practice

To understand how SC occurs within the USAF, it is important to first understand how the CJCS, the highest-ranking military officer in the US, views the use of SC campaigns for the joint force. In Joint Doctrine Note 2-13 (2013), the CJCS defines SC as a process by which communication planners "consider the national communication goals, and strategic objectives in the planning process to engage specific audiences and coordinate joint force actions ... to achieve unity of effort" (p. v). This definition differs from the one derived from Botan, in that rather than starting with the publics, this view starts with organizational objectives, which will be evident in the case studies presented later in this chapter. The normal military approach is to use instrumental communication, an outcome-oriented approach whereby a message with a predetermined meaning is transmitted and which views communication as merely a means to an end (Chandler & Munday, 2016), rather than a cocreational approach. The joint forces communication focuses on "the behavior of publics that can have an impact on mission success" (Joint Doctrine Note 2-13, 2013, p. I-12). However, for some specific, priority topics of interest to each service, there are dedicated attempts at engaging in SC campaigns.

The Chairman provides each service, including the USAF, four basic SC goals. Improve US credibility and legitimacy, weaken an adversary's credibility and legitimacy, convince a selected audience to take specific actions that support US or international objectives, and cause a competitor or adversary to take, or not take, specific actions. It also enables the alignment of multiple lines of operation, including how we implement policy, how and where we move our forces, and public affairs efforts.

In order to achieve these goals, the SecAF and the CSAF build their own grand strategy, identifying specific lines of effort upon which the SC campaigns are built. These lines of effort enable the USAF to meet the mandates of the NDS, and are separate and distinct from the primary efforts of the Army, the Navy, and even the Office of the DoD. This grand strategy is the foundation upon which the planning cycle for SC campaigns are built. The planning cycles for these lines of effort make up the core of SC within the USAF.

As the planning cycle for each line of effort begins, the first step is for the USAF's top two leaders to provide planners with their strategic intent on how these efforts will enable the service's ability to meet the NDS. As part of that intent, they provide planners a clear desired end state, with specific, measurable outcomes. This first step of planning is critical, as planners base all subsequent efforts in the SC processes guided by the stated intent and working toward making that end state a reality.

Next, planners move onto the research phase of the campaign planning process. This begins with planners describing the current state of the environment surrounding the topic of the strategic line of effort. This includes identifying key stakeholders and publics, followed by a careful examination of their existing opinions or beliefs about the topic of the line of effort. Planners use the strengths, weaknesses, opportunities, and threats (SWOT) analysis model to define the campaign environment. SWOT analysis is a tool that strategic planners use which allows them to analyze their own organization's strengths and weaknesses, while also examining the external environment to identify important opportunities and threats (Gurel & Tat, 2017). The results of the SWOT analysis inform how USAF SC planners will begin formulating the long-term engagement strategy for their specific line of effort. Planners create interim objectives that help them measure successes and serve as milestones for the campaign as it progresses.

Planners next develop key themes and messages that will be used throughout the campaign, and are presented to the SecAF and the CSAF for their review and approval. These themes and messages will be repeated by multiple USAF leaders in a variety of planned engagements during the tactical stages of the campaign, thus the senior USAF leaders ensure these messages align with their grand strategy. Of note, this usually lacks an assessment and research of the publics' perspective and openness to messaging, which limits the cocreational aspect of narrative-building. However, once approval for these messages and themes is received, planners take the information from the SWOT analysis and begin tactical planning, whereby they formulate engagement strategies targeting specific publics and look for communication engagement opportunities. For each opportunity, planners will develop tactical objectives and identify public-specific end states. Planners will also look at the timing and location of these events to ensure they take place at times when press coverage can be maximized and in locations where the engagement will attract media attention. At this point, the plans are turned over to action officers to execute the specific engagements.

After each key engagement, USAF planners conduct multiple assessments, that range in scope from surface-level examination to detailed, in-depth assessments. Regardless of the assessment that is chosen, planners base their analysis on the strategic intent, desired outcomes, and end state approved by the SecAF and the CSAF. Their research attempts to ascertain whether that engagement contributed to achieving the intent and end state, and if so, how well or how much it contributed. For each assessment, planners undertake quantitative assessments to derive measures of performance and couple those results with qualitative assessments to provide measures of effectiveness. When conducting assessments, planners will use quantitative and qualitative measures to assess how well an engagement met the desired objectives and the extent to which that engagement contributed to the intent of the strategic line of effort. A report is written and given back to planners to inform the next round of engagement planning. Measures of performance, outputs, can be one-dimensional. For example, if the targeted public for an event was 25 defense journalists, the goal for planners would be to have each journalist publish an article about the event. If, however, only 15 journalists published a story, the planners would assess a 60% effectiveness rate for that objective. However, this metric alone falls short in illuminating any meanings created within the 15 articles. Thus, qualitative measures must be employed to determine if the publics created and reported similar meanings to those the SC planners intended. This is done through sentiment analysis, where planners look at how messages are presented and if that message was supportive, neutral, or contrary to the intended meaning.

Strategic Communication Case Studies

Now that we have discussed the SC planning and assessment processes, we will present and analyze three military case studies. First, we will cover a geopolitical SC case study involving Russia and the illegal seizure of the Ukranian landmass known as Crimea. Second, we will explore a case study about SC as it relates to ensuring space security. Finally, we will discuss a case study on the repeal of the "Don't Ask, Don't Tell" (DADT) policy about penalizing homosexuality within the US military.

The Modern Iron Curtain: A Case Study in Geopolitical Strategic Communication

On February 23, 2014, Russian President Vladimir Putin summoned his security service chiefs for a 2-day meeting on seizing the Ukrainian landmass known as Crimea (AFP, 2015). This meeting was held shortly after Ukraine's Maiden Revolution and its President Victor Yanukovych's flight from Kiev, in which Ukrainians peacefully ousted the pro-Russian government.

On February 27, masked soldiers, without insignia but with Russian fatigues and Russian weapons, took the Parliament in Simferopol, Crimea. These "little green men" also seized key infrastructure (Pifer, 2014), including the Simferopol International Airport and most military bases in Crimea. On March 1, US President Barack Obama warned against Russian military intervention, saying "there would be costs." Russia, however, said reports were "not always true" and that they were "acting within the framework of our agreement" at military bases within Ukraine (Carter, Formanek, & Magney, 2014).

By March 16, a pro-Russian government was installed and validated via a referendum by local populations in Crimea. With guarded polling places, and no third-party presence, the new Crimean government claimed 97% voted to join Russia as a federal subject, with a similarly high turnout rate. The same day the Crimean Council declared themselves independent of Ukraine, Russia recognized the Republic of Crimea.

US and European allies condemned the "invasion" of Crimea and recognized Ukrainian sovereignty in the region. By March, the European Union (EU) and the US applied visa and financial sanctions, and increased military presence in the "satellite countries" like Poland and Lithuania. By April, pro-Russian separatists and the Ukrainian government were at war in eastern Ukraine – a province called Donbass – over its self-proclaimed independence. While Russia denied supplying the separatists with materials and weapons in Donbass, Ukraine states otherwise.

Today, the conflict in Donbass continues, with more than 13,000 people dead and 2 million displaced since its start. Putin, whose popularity in Russia was boosted by the relatively peaceful takeover of Crimea, allegedly views Donbass as a key wedge between Ukraine and North Atlantic Treaty Organization (NATO) members (Pifer, 2014). The US and the EU still have economic sanctions in place, and still don't recognize the referendum resulting in Crimea's annexation.

Through the lens of a cocreational model, the invasion of Crimea is a case study of SC – in which military, diplomatic, and economic communication are entangled inextricably, and the meaning is created by various publics. Like many parts of the US government, the US military does not communicate alone, but instead in concert (or in contest) with other organizations. Nor does it communicate to one audience, but instead multiple publics simultaneously.

As the US media reported on the economic sanctions and political rhetoric that proved ineffective in restraining Russia, the US military was ordered to send a message to its allies and its adversaries. European Command (EUCOM), along with its subsidiary service commands – like US Air Forces in Europe, US Europe Army, and US Naval Forces Europe – were positioned to communicate with presence.

On March 3, 15 days before Russia claimed Crimea as a federal state, the DoD put a hold on all military exercises with Russia. Two days later, it announced an uptick in training with key countries bordering Russia and a vastly augmented air policing mission with NATO in the Baltics. The DoD was clear on why: to deter further Russian aggression, and to assure the Eastern European and Baltic allies.

Within days, the US presence in Eastern Europe had already been bolstered significantly and framed as a "reinforced commitment" with "unscheduled training" or "increased rotations" (EUCOM, 2014).

Three hundred thousand Meals, Ready-to-Eat were delivered to Ukraine. 22 F-16 Fighting Falcons and three C-130J Super Hercules landed in Poland. A naval destroyer arrived in the Black Sea to train with Romanian and Bulgarian forces. Ten F-15C Eagles flew over Europe to Lithuania. A company-sized contingent of US Army paratroopers deployed to Estonia, Latvia, Lithuania, and Poland.

Bureaucracy both helped and hindered the communication processes: across the Eastern European breadth of radio towers, TV signals, and internet chat, the US pushed its message of a strong NATO alliance. US Embassy staffs and foreign military partners translated and shared articles, brought in local media, and then reported on the local populations' interpretation of its coverage. This level of local engagement could have fed some US military meaning, and slightly reframed how the US communicated in the following months. However, the local media reports were used as a litmus test of the success of US messages – did they repeat our words, embrace our meaning? At the ground level, where public affairs specialists were embedded in the units, a constant stream of imagery and interviews flowed to partner nations, embassies, and governments to project a vision of power and strength.

Yet this information flow was carefully curated and controlled by a centralized approving authority. While strategic success was dependent upon the tactical public affairs specialists' successes, the bureaucracy also limited that success. The communication methods, manner, and messages were prescriptive. Every image, video, article, and social media post was approved through a lengthy chain of command, limiting timeliness and centralizing communication. Messages did not morph as the situation grew more dire in Ukraine, nor did they change based on location: if you were in Lithuania, your messages aligned with those in Estonia and Poland. The vision of communication was that of the antiquated sender–receiver model, without a full recognition of how meaning was created at every interaction in the information environment (IE).

Interestingly, while this concrete centralized messaging method remained static, the local populations were dynamic. Local language within the satellite countries was often much stronger than the US government, which found itself restrained in the face of conflict. The presence, the US government believed, was communicating enough. From the US government, there was little direct acknowledgment of Russian aggression within externally expressed language – strong rhetoric was limited to senior leaders like Secretaries of Defense and State and the US President. However, local media outlets in Eastern Europe would often bolster the rhetoric as direct deterrence and speculate if the US presence was more permanent than mere training. Presidents of countries like Poland would openly state a desire for permanent basing, with Congressional support for more military presence (Belkin, Mix, & Woehrel, 2014). To some partners, the US was doing enough to curb their neighboring bully from threatening their way of life but could do more. When locals from Lithuania or Poland encountered US personnel in their cities and towns, they'd often shake hands and ask if they could stay for good (Cheesman, 2019). To the local populations of Eastern Europeans, the presence was largely enough – for now. For military communication practitioners in the field, there was a striking disparity between cocreational interactions at the lowest levels and the strategic messaging development, which was born from defined NDS objectives, political and diplomatic goals, and known intelligence on Russian intent and projected behavior (Bartles & McDermott, 2014).

To assess if the SC efforts were successful is difficult. Did they deter further aggression, or was Putin's plan to only take Crimea? Did they bolster Eastern Europeans' trust in the US, and show Russia as an authoritarian expansionist and not a cultural protector? Or did Russia's actions deter potential partners of NATO, and road-test a military capability and power grab? Finally, did the West's continued assumptions in its communication practices limit the ability to achieve strategic objectives, or strengthen its unity of voice?

What we know is that today, the region of Donbass is still violently pulled between two geopolitical entities espousing divergent world views: Western Europe and Russia. Yet Russia has not annexed Donbass, as it did Crimea, while it remains in the shadows of the fight. The US continues to train with – and communicate both locally and globally with – its partners in the Warsaw Pact countries and beyond. One of Russia's strongest issues was the West's encroachment upon its borders – and none symbolizes this alliance better than the NATO.

In March 2014, 47% of Ukrainians were against joining NATO (Unian, 2014). In December 2016, 71% were for joining NATO ... despite Russia's strong opposition to the threat of NATO at its borders (Interfax, 2016). While this Ukrainian poll may be skewed by a shortage of surveying in pro-Russian conflict areas, it may also represent the cocreational reality of communication. In spite of the bureaucratic, centralized nature of the US government, it may be the amplification of the dynamic, daily interactions between US military service members and their partners that drove the success. Regardless of what the US actively pushed through its official channels, meaning was not made and managed within the centralized constructs. The narrative took on a life of its own within the partners and allies at the old Iron Curtain's edge. To them, the US was a partner in the fight against a Russian takeover of culture and country, thereby framing US military presence as a key part of that meaning-making.

In this, SC built a barrier of cocreated meaning – the US protection and threat were as real as all publics made it. For our allies, they believed protection from Russia was real, and spoke boldly against their bully. And for our adversaries, the threat from the US was real enough. While Putin may have doubted the reality of a US–Russia military conflict, he saw that his small neighbors had big friends with big guns. With a wall of literal American steel at Russia's borders, today's Iron Curtain may very well be a cocreated one of power and protection.

"The Battle Above": A Case Study in Strategic Communication for Space

Everything the joint force does communicates a message. Whether it is holding a press conference to outline the President's Budget request, dropping leaflets to influence adversary forces prior to battle, carrying out kinetic strikes through precision-guided munitions, or sailing a Carrier Strike Group through the South China Sea during a Freedom of Navigation operation, each activity must be integrated and synchronized to avoid the appearance of a "say–do gap" (Mullen, 2009). It is imperative that activities and messages align because in today's operational environment typified by global, nonlinear networks, tactical actions can reverberate with strategic consequences. This operational environment is punctuated by the great power competition between the US, Russia, and China and nowhere is the competition more intense – and the rules less defined – than in the ubiquitous domains of space and cyberspace. In the IE that permeates these two domains, the public affairs apparatus of the military figures prominently in strategic success because in an uncertain or emerging domain, framing an issue, program, or operation before an adversary will determine the direction of the follow-on narrative and dictate that the adversary employs a reactionary course-of-action calculus.

In 2014, the USAF faced a problem – the space domain which afforded the ultimate high ground and had, through the integration of space effects across the range of military operations, yielded a tremendous strategic advantage ever since Operation Desert Storm was no longer under an American hegemony. It was now considered contested, degraded, and operationally limited (Bell & Rogers, 2014). By that time, the Russians and Chinese had developed a spectrum of counterspace capabilities from reversible jamming, to direct-energy weapons, to ground-launched and co-orbital anti-satellite technology (Chow, 2017). In addition, both countries had demonstrated the ability to perform complex on-orbit maneuvers, and each had developed doctrine to use US superiority in – and reliance on – space integration against it by escalating a terrestrial conflict to the space domain (Chow, 2017). In testimony delivered to the House Armed Services Committee, Subcommittee on Strategic Forces (HASC-SF) on March 25, 2015, then-Lt. Gen. John Raymond, USAF, at the time commander of the Joint Functional Component Command for Space, stated that space was "no longer the relative sanctuary it once was … We are quickly approaching the point where every satellite and every orbit can be threatened and the strategic, operational and tactical advantages derived from space are no longer a given" (Raymond, 2015, p. 6).

This statement was a carefully orchestrated shift in narrative that accompanied a strategic recalibration of the US National Security Space Strategy. It was followed almost exactly 1 month later by the airing of a rare, two-part CBS News *60 Minutes* report on space entitled "The Battle Above," a first-of-its-kind public affairs operation for the DoD (see SpaceNews, 2015). This media engagement was completely out of character for the national security space enterprise, as the public affairs planners would discover when repeatedly told how the Sensitive Compartmented Information Facilities – even when sanitized of the classified information they usually held – were designed to keep cameras and recording equipment out. Many reacted to its unexpected nature and the information revealed during the segment, including everyday Americans who up until that point had no idea how much their daily lives were dependent upon space capabilities. Key members of Congress had tuned in, and the influential HASC would, approximately 1 month after the air date, authorize $5 billion additional in Future Years Defense Program funding for space capabilities (Clark, 2015). Finally, Russian and Chinese officials also took notice of the change in US rhetoric, although the extent to which this occurred cannot be discerned through non-classified means. This was, of course, all by design.

While the actual content of the communication plan created for this media engagement is marked For Official Use Only, we are able to share the central organizing ideas that shaped its production and implementation. The plan was a collaborative effort between three primary agencies: Headquarters Air Force Space Command Public Affairs (AFSPC/PA), Joint Functional Component Command for Space Public Affairs (JFCC Space/PA), and US Strategic Command Public Affairs (USSTRATCOM/PA). Serving in a coordinating role were the Secretary of the Air Force Public Affairs (SAF/PA) and the Office of the Secretary of Defense Public Affairs (OSD/PA). Rounding out the coordination were representatives from the Legislative Liaison offices at AFSPC, USSTRATCOM, and OSD, as well as space policy and legal experts from the same agencies. Coordination also occurred outside of the DoD, to include the National Security Council (NSC) and Department of State. Due to the uniqueness of this proposed media engagement, and the signaling to allies and potential adversaries that was inherent in this manner of high-profile news-making, a whole-of-government approach was critical. The resulting plan was nested within NSC space policy guidance and the USSTRATCOM campaign plan, by which the space forces provided by AFSPC – and operationally commanded by JFCC Space – were governed. The communications end state stipulated in the plan centered around both a knowledge-based and an attitude-based objective; the aim was that Congress and the American people, after viewing the *60 Minutes* piece, would understand, and support additional funding for, the national security space enterprise.

As the plan was implemented and public affairs professionals at each echelon of command negotiated with the CBS News producers at *60 Minutes*, deliberate choices were made regarding the visuals that would be offered to the cameras and the topics that would, and would not – due to classification levels, be discussed. An important visual was that of a GPS satellite in the final stages of production, as well as a visit within the GPS constellation control center, with the desired effect being the American public discovering that the space capabilities provided by the USAF are crucial not only to the American way of war, they are essential to the modern way of life. There were also pointed messages delivered during the broadcast by two USAF general officers directed at near-peer competitors in Russia and China. Then-Lt. Gen. Raymond related a story about Object E, which was initially categorized as debris resulting from a Russian space launch (a normal occurrence) and was being tracked by the USAF – just as they do with all 23,000 man-made objects in orbit. However, after several weeks the debris began to maneuver, indicating that it was actually an unregistered Russian satellite. Additionally, Gen. John Hyten, then-Commander of AFSPC, acknowledged Chinese counterspace activities, asserting that the US was watching and would not be surprised, especially in the value geosynchronous orbital regime. When correspondent David Martin asked if he would use force in self-defense of vital US space capabilities, Gen. Hyten replied, "That's why we have a military. You know, I'm not NASA" (SpaceNews, 2015). The intent behind these targeted messages was signaling, with the desired outcome of a change in the decision calculus of Russian and Chinese defense officials. The US wanted its near-peer competitors to see what it was willing to discuss openly in the media and then begin extrapolating, perhaps worrying about the intelligence US defense officials might possess at classified levels and contemplating contingency planning or even policy shifts as a result. While more an instrumental approach than cocreational, attention was paid to how messages would potentially be received and interpreted by foreign publics. Again, the efficacy of this communication strategy cannot be determined through unclassified means, but at a minimum it is clear that this coordinated, whole-of-government media engagement significantly altered the US national security space narrative, informing key publics in Congress and the American people (according to DoD media analysis conducted at the time, more than 12 million Americans viewed the piece and Rep. Mike Rogers, then-Chairman of the HASC-SF, described it as a "wake-up call"; C. J. Dorian, personal communication, April 30, 2015), and ostensibly influencing potential adversaries contemplating ways to deny, disrupt, or degrade US access to critical space capabilities.

Repealing "Don't Ask, Don't Tell": A Case Study on Communicating Culture Change

So far, the preceding case studies have included deliberate and tangible military operations on land and in space, complete with clear objectives and outcomes. This final scenario will examine how the military communicated and implemented culture change through the creation and then repeal of Don't Ask, Don't Tell – a DoD policy that lifted the outright ban on military service for gay members but simultaneously restricted open dialogue about sexual orientation. The President, DoD, and individual service branch strategy surrounding this hypersensitive policy change displayed clear characteristics of cocreational theory, specifically the focus on understanding multiple publics and their needs. However, ensuring adequate communication flow of the policy repeal, its meaning, and expectations to personnel around the globe presented a multifaceted challenge – communicating to and through intangible cultures and sub-cultures created over many generations.

The DoD and its services, as direct reflections of the American public, have evolved to align with the ever-changing culture and beliefs of the US. In fact, policy, programs, and offices exist to safeguard their commitment to equality, but this hasn't always been the case. Conversely, and it's well known now, policies once existed specifically rejecting or minimizing people based on race, gender, and sexual orientation. Specifically related to sexual orientation, early written policies date back to The Articles of War – pre-colonial regulations governing the military – and show themselves again in the 1950s military law revamp known as the Uniformed Code of Military Justice; this laid out the military justice system and governs military service members to this day. Similar to times in history when social backlash occurred as US policy did not support race and gender equality, service members defended against the rule for sexual orientation inequality, especially those charged and/or discharged from military service based on homosexuality or homosexual acts. But the DoD and other US leaders maintained their stance and directive, asserting that homosexuals were incompatible with military service, homosexuals impaired military missions, and such members adversely affected discipline, good order, and morale (Evans, 2002). All of these claims were embodied for public consumption during relevant Congressional testimony, when the President spoke about gays in the military, and each time a homosexual service member was discharged from the military based solely on sexual orientation.

Fast-forwarding from the 1950s to the early 1990s, the social narrative about equality had morphed greatly from personal whispers to overt dialogue in politics, households, and amongst national leaders, including one notable figurehead of Dick Cheney, then Secretary of Defense – the highest military affairs and national security position. Cheney made headlines when he openly shunned ideas that homosexuals posed any risk to national security during a House testimony hearing. His bold statements dismissed a decades-long policy and were widely discussed by members of the media, military leaders, and Congressional representatives. Through a communication lens, Cheney fully capitalized on his position of power and organic political audience to create a pivot point communicating necessary change. While he was not the only voice in US leadership to bridge social sentiment, this was a clear example of grand strategy in the making – the military's most senior leader taking the ideas of the public and making them his own to influence change. In the same timeframe, a Presidential election season peppered with a call for greater equality came and went.

After running a successful election campaign including human rights promises to LGBT Americans, newly elected President Clinton banned the former policy against gay and lesbian personnel from military service early in his tenure (Belkin, 2003). In its place, Clinton partially followed through on his pledge to end discrimination based on sexual orientation by announcing the service member-focused policy originally called "Don't Ask, Don't Tell, Don't Pursue" ... shortened to "Don't Ask, Don't Tell" (DADT). Despite disagreement and resistance, senior Pentagon staff agreed to eliminate application questions to do with sexual orientation and re-address equal rights for all service members, and Congress signed the latest NDAA into law supporting the new policy in November 1993 (Burrelli, 2011).

While some of the nation's leaders seemingly rejoiced in the win for equality, sentiment was not matched by many, especially throughout the LGBT community in and out of the military because the law's ambiguous language appeared in many ways a repackaging of the previous ban on homosexuals – stating in many more words that homosexuality is an unacceptable risk to morale, order, and discipline ... but now we just won't ask or talk about it (Burrelli, 2011). While the new proposed policy superficially looked and sounded like our most senior US officials wanted equality for all, the intended audience perception was not at all the same.

At the time, government officials claimed allegiance to both ends of the policy's spectrum – for and against. All the while the court of public opinion, media outlets, and individuals in the military held their own opinions toward equality and DADT. In a 2010 CNN report, retired CJCS General Colin Powell inferred that the Defense policy referencing homosexuals' military service was outdated – that "attitudes and circumstances have changed ..." and he supported a new approach to the policy. His statement is another single exclamation point strategically influencing change through deliberately timed and placed communication. His support and that of grass roots programs, human rights activism, and other publics' discourse championing human rights and equality ushered in continued talks of DADT.

Insert President Barack Obama and DoD studies pointing directly to the repeal of DADT. Not only did the sitting President campaign and win election to office on a promise to overturn DADT, quantitative and qualitative data sets existed now showing a low risk associated with lifting a ban on open LGBT service (Rostker et al., 2010). Though later than expected,

Obama formally repealed DADT when he signed the repeal into law just before Christmas 2010. His directive quickly reverberated throughout military channels, despite the Senate clash, collecting enough votes to pass the repeal.

Unfortunately, researchers and scholars estimated that over 100,000 service men and women across the USAF, Army, Navy, and Marine Corps had been discharged because of their sexual orientation (Evans, 2002). But data and stats really moved the needle in this case; the repeal leaned heavily on researched facts indicating the right move. In relation to communication strategy, leaders who sought to get rid of DADT had greater context and reasoning for the repeal than leaders who created DADT and previous iterations that banned homosexuals from military service. However, the number of publics in this case were many! It was critical for those navigating the narrative to intentionally chart implementation strategy and tactics.

Despite polarized debate on the topic, once instituted, senior military leaders handled the repeal swiftly. The Joint Chiefs of Staff released an implementation plan outlining a path to socialize and integrate the repeal; it included data from current active duty and reserve military members and their perception of the repeal – over 90% of those surveyed said the impact of a homosexual's presence was positive or neutral (Parco & Levy, 2013). Former SecDef Robert Gates (acting SecDef during the repeal process) told Senate leaders during a 2010 hearing, "the question before us is not whether the military [is] prepared to make change, but how we best prepare for it … we have received our orders from the commander in chief, and we are moving out accordingly." Communication from the senior DoD aligned seamlessly with the President's.

With much work to do, individual branches of the military were still required to fully transition from old policy standards and behavior. Formal regulation updates reflecting the repeal took place throughout 2011, and all the while each branch received an onslaught of media queries. The communication plan was well orchestrated from the Pentagon out to field units. Public affairs spokespersons across the globe operated with approved language and guidance – navigating touchy questions and unresolved issues with the same intent across services.

Along with external facing communication, services also needed to ensure intent was clear inside the DoD. One approach branches took to ensure compliance was requiring all members complete training to educate personnel on repeal directives and information about equality for all, regardless of sexual orientation. However, dictating policy, sharing guidance, and forwarding computer-based training can only take a message so far. This cultural shift was bound to be a cumbersome change as there were countless third- and fourth-order questions to navigate. Examples include: What happens to those kicked out under the original policy during the DADT repeal process … are they allowed in now? What about showers … do I have to share a bay with a homosexual? What happens to service members who do not agree with the policy change? Can homosexuals get married in military churches … what if a chaplain's religious beliefs do not allow marrying a same-sex couple? Each of these smaller, less impactful questions might seem pointless, but queries like these and others all play a big role in fully instituting change through communication. The questions point to what each public finds important. So, while all of these questions may not have been in public affairs spokesperson guidance, they offer a clear path to the next iteration of cocreated strategy.

The government and DOD represent policies and structures dedicated to equality and diversity now more than ever. Strategically speaking, functioning with these kinds of guidelines attracts diversity and, more importantly, communicates a high level of senior leaders' commitment to transparency and respect for difference. The repeal of DADT will always stand as a memorable example of social evolution and culture change within vast, intertwined institutions.

Other questions to consider include: What will our next human rights issue look like within the context of national security strategy? How did the US and military leaders overcome issues related to allowing black Americans and women to serve? Who is responsible for grand strategy in politics? Does your grand strategy push change outside of your organization or implement what others are doing? What role do grassroots activists play in a communication plan? What is communicated when leaders do not communicate at all?

Conclusion

When the tenets of US joint military doctrine discussed earlier are juxtaposed with the case studies mentioned, it seems that the answer to the question "How does the US military perform strategic communication?" is technically, it does not, but not for lack of trying. What the US military refers to as SC is really integrated communication that, unfortunately, regularly employs an instrumental approach. While there is often a herculean effort in pursuit of the meta-rhetorical alignment – consistency between what is communicated by activities, policies, messages, images, and inactions – of the whole-of-government strategy, the dearth of cross-cultural competency, influence of perceptual biases amongst planners and SC practitioners, and short time horizons of most operations that precludes extensive research often relegates the resulting integrated communication to instrumental execution.

Nowhere is the lack of a cocreational approach to SC more glaring than in US counter-violent extremist organization (VEO) strategy. Specifically, the failure to adequately understand and address the discursive nature of the current VEO threat has hampered US policy. Given its inherently abstract and communicative nature, terrorism must be viewed as a tactic – a sophisticated rhetorical act implemented through a campaign – and not an ideology. This stance would correct the definitional drift that has plagued US foreign policy and national security strategy since the 9/11 terrorist attacks, one characterized by a false equivalency between terrorism and radical Islamism and subsequent creation of a "false analogy" to secular ideologies like Communism and Fascism that produced the specious term "Islamofascism" (Boyle, 2008, pp. 193–196). Although intellectually convenient, this superficial image of VEOs maintained by the US foreign policy executive, one that combines anti-Western sentiment, Arab nationalism, and jihadist groups under the banner of Islamic radicalism and is subsequently filtered through the lens of predetermined historical correlation, ultimately "commits American policy-makers to the cardinal sin of war-fighting: not understanding the enemy as it understands itself" (Boyle, 2008, p. 198). Also, in framing the US-led, counter-VEO activities as a response to an ideology and not a tactic – terrorism – American policymakers have inadvertently reinforced the crusader image and fed the idea of cosmic struggle, now focused more sharply than ever against an American tormentor (Kaldor, 2004, p. 173).

Future joint force activity and planning will have to contend with national security challenges situated primarily on three threat vectors: greater power competition, within which we bin grayzone conflict and hybrid warfare; irregular warfare (IW); and counter-terrorism. Grayzone conflict "is characterized by intense political, economic, informational, and military competition more fervent in nature than normal steady-state diplomacy, yet short of conventional war" (Votel et al., 2016, p. 102). Along the same spectrum, hybrid warfare is best understood as a manifestation of the ever-changing character of war, wherein adversaries seek to offset US conventional superiority by combining military and non-military capabilities and blurring normative distinctions in modes of warfare to produce pockets of asymmetric advantage that may be exploited for gain (Monaghan, 2019).

Both grayzone conflict and its intensified outgrowth into hybrid warfare stipulate a reduced role for conventional military power. Similarly, as "IW is [defined as] violent struggle among state and non-state actors for legitimacy and influence over the relevant population," the focus in planning resides in securing a political solution, so the military maintains a supporting role (Coons & Harned, 2009, p. 98). Finally, terrorism "communicates a political message …

[wherein] the victims or objects of terrorist attack have little intrinsic value to the terrorist group but represent a larger human audience whose reaction the terrorists seek" (Crenshaw, 1981, p. 379). Said another way, terrorism is abstract; the attack itself is not the objective and the victims, except in instances of political assassination, are not the targets. A failure to adequately understand and address the discursive aspects of not just terrorism, but the totality of the current threat has limited the joint force's effectiveness in the range of military operations. Moving forward, activities to establish, maintain, or enhance influence within target publics, and to secure access, maneuver, and effects across domains to dominate the perceptual terrain of an adversary, must be the primary focus of joint planning and operations.

In instituting a joint planning focus on influence and perception, "greater attention must be paid to the political, social, economic, and cultural context of the operation because those conditions have a serious impact on how military actions work and how those actions are perceived" (Gregor, 2010, p. 111). SC is of paramount importance in this endeavor, particularly the construction and perpetuation of an alternative narrative as opposed to attempts to counter, disrupt, undermine, and discredit the prevailing adversary narrative (Votel et al., 2016). Accordingly, information operations should not remain a support function, nor should planning for effects in the IE remain confined to information-related capabilities (Thompson & Paul, 2018). Additionally, a new planning framework – such as the situation, objective, perception, story, means, feedback, and termination approach – should be considered (Szerdy, 2015). In this approach, the story describes "the marketing campaign for the operation and supports the internal, local, and international audiences," and represents the necessary focus on managing perceptions and securing influence through an alternative narrative (Szerdy, 2015). To be successful, planners must avoid the instrumental modality that typically characterizes integrated communications and instead consider the contextual factors that influence how a target public cocreates and encodes meaning from overt signals and implicit communication. Instead, the planning goal must become ensuring the meta-rhetorical alignment of a whole-of-government response executed through a publics-centered, cocreational approach so as to maximize the potential for influence. Ultimately, by focusing on influence rather than merely defeat of an adversary, the joint force can avoid the pitfalls of "the 'tactization' of strategy" (Thompson & Paul, 2018, p. 10).

References

AFP (2015, March 8). Putin describes secret operation to seize Crimea. Retrieved from https://news.yahoo.com/putin-describes-secret-operation-seize-crimea-212858356.html

Bartles, C., & McDermott, R. (2014). Russia's military operation in Crimea. *Problems of Post-Communism*, 61(6), 46–63. doi: 10.2753/PPC1075-8216610604

Belkin, A. (2003). Don't ask, don't tell: Is the gay ban based on military necessity? *Parameters*, 40(4). Retrieved from https://press.armywarcollege.edu/parameters/vol40/iss4/3

Belkin, P., Mix, D. E., & Woehrel, S. (2014, July 31). NATO: Response to the crisis in Ukraine and security concerns in Central and Eastern Europe. Congressional Report. Retrieved from https://fas.org/sgp/crs/row/R43478.pdf

Bell, C. B. M., & Rogers, T. (2014). Space resilience and the contested, degraded, and operationally limited environment: The gaps in tactical space operations. *Air and Space Power Journal*, 28(6), 130–147.

Botan, C. (2018). *Strategic communication theory and practice: The cocreational model.* Hoboken, NJ: Wiley-Blackwell.

Boyle, M. J. (2008). The war on terror in American grand strategy. *International Affairs*, 84(2), 191–209.

Brooks, S. G., & Wohlforth, W. C. (2019, August 14). The once and future superpower. Retrieved from https://www.foreignaffairs.com/articles/united-states/2016-04-13/once-and-future-superpower

Burrelli, D. F. (2011). "Don't Ask, Don't Tell": The law and military policy on same-sex behavior. Darby, PA: Diane Publishing.

Carter, C., Formanek, I., & Magnet, D. (2014, March 01). Obama warns Russia: There will be costs for intervention in Ukraine. Retrieved from https://www.cnn.com/2014/02/28/world/europe/ukraine-politics/index.html

Chandler, D., & Munday, R. (2016). *A dictionary of media and communication*. Oxford: Oxford University Press.

Cheesman, K. C. (2019). Personal records.

Chow, B. G. (2017). Stalkers in space: Defeating the threat. *Strategic Studies Quarterly*, 11(2), 82–116.

Clark, C. (2015, April 22). US commits $5B in NEW $$ to countering space threats; HASC protects it. Retrieved fromhttps://breakingdefense.com/2015/04/us-commits-5b-in-new-to-countering-space-threats-china-russia

Coons, K., & Harned, G. (2009). Irregular warfare is warfare. *Joint Force Quarterly*, 52(1), 97–103.

Crenshaw, M. (1981). The causes of terrorism. *Comparative Politics*, 13(4), 379–399.

Defense Manpower Data Center (2018). *Number of military and DoD appropriated fund (APF) civilian personnel permanently assigned*. Washington, DC: United States Department of Defense.

Dueck, C. (2005). Realism, culture and grand strategy: Explaining America's peculiar path to world power. *Security Studies*, 14(2), 195–231. doi: 10.1080/09636410500232891

Evans, R. L. (2002). US military policies concerning homosexuals: Development, implementation, and outcomes. *Law & Sexuality: Review of Lesbian, Gay, Bisexual, and Transgender Legal Issues*, 11, 113.

Farlin, J. (2014). *Instruments of national power: How America earned independence*. Carlisle Barracks, PA: United States Army War College. Retrieved from https://publications.armywarcollege.edu/pubs/87.pdf

Gregor, W. (2010). Military planning systems and stability operation. *Prism*, 3(1), 99–114.

Gurel, E., & Tat, M. (2017). SWOT analysis: A theoretical review. *The Journal of International Social Research*, 10(51), 994–1006.

Howard, M. (1979). The forgotten dimensions of strategy. *Foreign Affairs*, 57(5), 975. doi: 10.2307/20040266

Ikenberry, G. J., & Mearsheimer, J. J. (2001). The tragedy of great power politics. *Foreign Affairs*, 80(6), 173. doi: 10.2307/20050342

Interfax-Ukraine (2016, December 28). Most Ukrainians favor joining NATO. Retrieved from https://en.interfax.com.ua/news/general/393739.html

Joint Doctrine Note 2-13 (2013). *Commander's communication synchronization*. Washington, DC: Joint Chiefs of Staff.

Kaldor, M. (2004). Nationalism and globalisation. *Nations and Nationalism*, 10(1–2), 161–177.

Krepinevich, A. F. (2010). *National security strategy in an era of growing challenges*. Washington, DC: Center for Strategic and Budgetary Assessments.

Kupchan, C. A., Kapstein, E. B., & Mastanduno, M. (2000). Unipolar politics: Realism and state strategies after the Cold War. *Foreign Affairs*, 79(2), 158. doi: 10.2307/20049663

Lammers, J. C. (2011). How institutions communicate: Institutional messages, institutional logics, and organizational communication. *Management Communication Quarterly*, 25(1), 154–184. doi: 10.1177/0893318910389280

Light, J. S. (2002). Urban security from warfare to welfare. *International Journal of Urban and Regional Research*, 26(3), 607–613. doi: 10.1111/1468-2427.00403

Lissner, R. F. (2017, December 19). The national security strategy is not a strategy. Retrieved from www.foreignaffairs.com/articles/united-states/2017-12-19/national-security-strategy-not-strategy

Mattis, J. N. (2018). *Summary of the 2018 national defense strategy of the United States of America: Sharpening the American military's competitive edge*. Washington, DC: Office of the Secretary of Defense.

McCormack, K. (2017). Governing 'ungoverned' space: Humanitarianism, citizenship, and the civilian sphere in the territorialising practices of the US national security complex. *Critical Military Studies*, 4(2), 161–180. doi: 10.1080/23337486.2017.1371375

Monaghan, S. (2019). Countering hybrid warfare: So what for the future joint force? *Prism*, 8(2), 85. doi: 10.2307/26803232

Mullen, M. G. (2009, August 28). Strategic communication: Getting back to basics. Retrieved from https://foreignpolicy.com/2009/08/28/strategic-communication-getting-back-to-basics

Parco, J. E., & Levy, D. A. (2013). The rise and fall of DADT. *Journal of Homosexuality*, 60(2-3), 147–151.

Pifer, S. (2014). Watch out for little green men. Retrieved from https://www.brookings.edu/opinions/watch-out-for-little-green-men

Pilon, J. G. (2016). *The art of peace engaging a complex world.* Somerset, NJ: Transaction Publishers.

Porter, P. (2018). Why America's grand strategy has not changed: Power, habit, and the U.S. foreign policy establishment. *International Security*, 42(4), 9–46. doi: 10.1162/isec_a_00311

Quinn, A., & University of Birmingham (2018). Obama's national security strategy: Predicting US policy in the context of changing worldviews. Retrieved from https://www.chathamhouse.org/publication/obamas-national-security-strategy-predicting-us-policy-context-changing-worldviews

Raymond, L. G. J. (2015) *Subcommittee on Strategic Forces hearing on fiscal year 2016 budget request for national security space.* HASC Publication No. 114–30. Washington, DC: House of Representatives Committee on Armed Services.

Rostker, B. D., Hosek, S. D., Winkler, J. D., Asch, B. J., Asch, S. M., Baxter, C., ... Collins, R. L. (2010). *Sexual orientation and US military personnel policy: An update of RAND's 1993 study.* Santa Monica, CA: RAND Corporation.

SpaceNews (2015). Transcript of "60 Minutes" Air Force space command segment. Retrieved from https://spacenews.com/transcript-of-60-minutes-air-force-space-command-segment

Szerdy, J. (2015). Filling the gap: A strategy to harmonize joint and interagency planning. *InterAgency Journal*, 6(1), 52–66.

The Joint Chiefs of Staff (2014). *Information Operations.* Joint Publication 3-13. Retrieved from https://www.jcs.mil/Portals/36/Documents/Doctrine/pubs/jp3_13.pdf

Thompson, S. K., & Paul, C. E. (2018). Paradigm change: Operational art and the information joint function. *Joint Force Quarterly*, 89(2), 8–14.

Trump, D. J. (2017). *National security strategy of the United States of America.* Washington, DC: The White House.

U.S. European Command (2014). Press release [no longer available on website].

Unian (2014, March 22). Most Ukrainians happy to deal with the EU, but are not ready for NATO membership. Retrieved from https://www.unian.ua/society/899494-bilshist-ukrajintsiv-radi-ugodi-z-es-ale-ne-gotovi-do-chlenstva-v-nato-opituvannya.html#ad-image–0

United States Office of Personnel Management (2018). *Sizing up the executive branch: Fiscal year 2017.* Washington, DC: United States Office of Personnel Management.

Votel, J. L., Cleveland, C. T., Connett, C. T., & Irwin, W. (2016). Unconventional warfare in the gray zone. *Joint Force Quarterly*, 80(1), 101–109.

Waltz, K. N. (1993). The emerging structure of international politics. *International Security*, 18(2), 44. doi: 10.2307/2539097

Wohlforth, W. C. (1999). The stability of a unipolar world. *International Security*, 24(1), 5–41. doi: 10.1162/016228899560031

10

Strategic Communication in the Defense Industry
Grand Strategy, Key Publics, and Tactics

Michael F. Doble and David P. MacNeil
George Mason University

Introduction

The defense industry is uniquely situated in US corporate life. Its main mission is to research, create, and maintain the technologies that keep the US ahead of fledgling superpowers (historically Russia and now China). So dominant is the US in this sector that in recent years American firms have accounted for over half of all military exports worldwide, and 41 American companies have been responsible for 63% of the arms sales made by the world's top 100 defense firms (Neuman, 2010).

The industry comprises a wide variety of firms with management structures, which are, as with all such companies, beholden to shareholders, but at the same time those companies exist in a symbiotic relationship with many agencies of the US government, primarily with the military. The defense industry relies upon Congress to appropriate funds for weapons systems and the military to approve of those systems for operational use and to monitor the procurement process from start to finish. This close interrelationship, which the former Supreme Allied Commander in Europe and two-time President, Dwight Eisenhower, characterized as the "military–industrial complex" (Eisenhower, 1961), has ramifications for both the strategies and tactics pursued by defense firms.

These key relationships determine the key publics for defense firms, their strategic goals, and the tactics they use to reach these publics. In this chapter we will first examine two case studies of military equipment, the Lockheed Martin F-35 Joint Strike Fighter and the Bell-Boeing CV-22, which exemplify some of the issues that arise when the defense industry attempts to communicate about its products. We will then look at the role that strategic communication (SC) plays in business strategy, focusing on the need for the SC function to support the broader business goals of the organization, along with a description of the acquisition process unique to the defense industry. Then, to better understand the way in which communication strategies and tactics contribute to the overarching goals of defense firms, we will discuss organizational grand strategies and which are most applicable in this context. Next, we will define more clearly what SC in the defense industry is and is not. After that we will explore the key publics of interest to defense companies, from Congress and the military to others of varying degrees of importance. Finally, we will conclude with about ethical considerations for strategic communicators and the consequences of not engaging in ethical practices.

The Handbook of Strategic Communication, First Edition. Edited by Carl H. Botan.

Case Study I: The Lockheed Martin F-35 Joint Strike Fighter

Some programs are so large and visible that they attract attention, both good and bad, from the public. The largest defense program in history, the F-35 Joint Strike Fighter, whose total acquisition cost is valued by the Government Accountability Office (GAO) at just under $400 billion (Government Accountability Office, 2015), is a good perhaps the best example of such a program. The prime contractor for the aircraft is Lockheed Martin, with other major defense firms, such as Northrop Grumman, Pratt & Whitney, and the British-owned firm, BAE Systems, as subcontractors. Eight other countries were brought in as partners for the project, making any attempt by the Pentagon or Congress to cancel the program problematic for US relations internationally. As a result, the driving force behind a program this big is that it is deemed by many to be "too big to kill" (Miller, Capaccio, & Ivory, 2013), a phrase reminiscent of the banks deemed "too big to fail" during the financial crisis of 2007–2008. In 2020, the GAO determined that, from 2012 to 2019, the total acquisition costs of the program had increased over $32 billion, while the costs to sustain the program would be $1.2 trillion, meaning the total cost of the program during its life cycle would be $1.6 trillion (GAO, 2020). Indeed, the cost could climb even higher, as the path to its launch has already been strewn with schedule delays and disappointing test results. "I don't think we anticipated the number of issues that were going to arise out of testing, be it issues with the frame, the fuselage, the engines or the integrating of the software or the weapons systems," said Jerry Hendrix, senior fellow at the Center for New American Security (Cohen, 2015).

In the defense industry, companies will invest heavily in SC to win a program and then throttle back spending after the win to a sustained "keep sold" level. With the F-35, the cadence of communication has continued unabated after the win. For the win phase, there was a huge budget for outreach of all kinds. For example, Lockheed Martin used almost every possible outreach tactic to engage almost every conceivable stakeholder group. These tactics included grassroots outreach, advocacy by third parties, extensive media engagement, influence by clergy, and gathering support from state and local elected representatives and many other groups traditionally not part of a SC program within the aerospace and defense industry. Lockheed claimed that the program would employ 1,200 subcontractors and parts suppliers, supporting 129,000 jobs in the early years (Lockheed Martin, n.d.) and as many as 260,000 when full production begins (Chandrasekaran, 2013). One think-tank study, while arguing that Lockheed is substantially overstating the number of jobs the program will create, nonetheless predicts that all but four US states will have jobs related to the F-35 created in them, though only five (Texas, California, Florida, Connecticut, and New Hampshire) will account for over 70% (Hartung, 2014). By dispersing the F-35 jobs throughout the country, Lockheed was able to garner immense political support for the project nationwide, making it better able to influence key stakeholders in Congress on behalf of the project.

As an example of the type of political effort the F-35 generated in the US, a campaign called "Luke Forward" was created by the city of Glendale, Arizona, and surrounding localities to lobby Washington to base F-35s at Luke Air Force Base in Glendale (Luke AFB to receive three additional F-35 squadrons, 2013). One of the chairs of the campaign boasted that 21,000 citizens were involved in supporting the decision, while 10,000 attended public hearings or contacted the Air Force to encourage the choice of Luke, with the result that the Air Force decided to eventually base six squadrons of the fighter in Arizona (Associated Press, 2010; Fighter Country, 2013). Then, to convince the government of Canada to purchase the plane, Lockheed Martin employed Billie Flynn, a veteran Canadian Air Force pilot who flew combat missions in Kosovo and piloted 70 different aircraft, to tout the advantages the fighter will bring to future engagements (CTV News, 2013; Milewski, 2013). Likewise, many partner-countries of the project also received contracts to build major components of the jet, ensuring that any attempts to derail it would have international repercussions.

Stakeholder Criticism

But while Lockheed's campaign was successful in getting the F-35 program approved and developed. However, it was not able to shield the company and its partners from relentlessly critical government, media, and stakeholder criticism. First, a report by the GAO (Government Accountability Office, 2015) notes that in developing it, the contractor relied heavily upon concurrency (i.e. significant overlap between the development, testing, and production phases). Thus, if problems were found, say, during the testing phase, production had likely already begun, and so both the government and the contractor had a vested interest in making sure that production continued in order to drive down costs over the long term. Second, numerous design flaws were discovered in the aircraft during testing, resulting in the grounding of many planes while the problems were resolved. Third, costs continued to balloon, from projected acquisition costs of $233 billion when the program began in 2001 to $391 billion in 2015, an increase of 68% (adjusted for inflation; Government Accountability Office, 2015). As one Washington-based watchdog group noted:

> The F-35 is an example of how large weapons programs can plow ahead amid questions about their strategic necessity and their failure to arrive on time and on budget. It's got a lot of political protection. In that environment, very, very few members of Congress are willing to say this is an unaffordable dog and we need to get rid of it. (Miller, Capaccio, & Ivory, 2013)

Other complaints come from technical experts. One longtime critic of the F-35 is Pierre Sprey, who spent 20 years in the Pentagon helping develop two planes due to be replaced by the F-35, the A-10 Warthog and the F-16 fighter (Ricks, 2006). In an interview with a Russian media outlet, Sprey claimed that the effectiveness of Lockheed Martin in moving the program forward, despite the technical problems that have arisen with it, is due to the company's marketing prowess, which he terms "political engineering:" (RT.com, 2014)

> As of January 2021, more than 600 of the F-35 program's potential 3,200 aircraft already have been delivered, and the fighter is in use by the military in nine nations, including the U.S. Air Force and Marine Corps. Yet the Department of Defense has yet to make the decision to go to full-rate production because of continuing concerns.

Case Study II: The Bell-Boeing CV-22 and the Mosque

A famous case of a poorly conceived SC initiative occurred in 2005 with an advertisement for a CV-22 Osprey. The Osprey, jointly manufactured by Bell Helicopter Textron and Boeing, is an aircraft possessing the vertical takeoff and landing capability of a helicopter, along with the ability to fly at airplane-like ranges and speeds. One ad for it showed soldiers rappelling off the aircraft above a mosque (Rahman, 2005), with a headline that read: "It descends from the heavens. Ironically it unleashes hell." The Council on American–Islamic Relations (CAIR) objected strongly to the ad (CAIR, 2005), and an official at Boeing said that the ad had not been vetted through the normal channels at Boeing after it had been created by the advertising firm. Both of the contractors also stated that they had contacted the *National Journal*, the publication in which the ad appeared, to have it pulled before publication, but staff at the *National Journal* claimed that a clerical error had caused the ad to be published anyway. The ad was criticized by the advertising industry (10 follies, 2005) and all three organizations – Bell, Boeing, and the *National Journal* – issued apologies (Williamson, 2005). The timing of this crisis was especially unfortunate for Bell and Boeing. Not only were the companies hoping to sell their products to Islamic countries (Bernton, 2005), they had also sought to encourage positive media coverage after the Osprey suffered a series of crashes and other setbacks during development. The program has been successful in recent years, and the 400th Osprey was delivered to the U.S. Air Force in late 2020. The Pentagon expects this aircraft to be in service through the 2050s.

Strategic Communication and Business Strategy

The essence of successful SC in the corporate world is to understand its relationship to the business strategy of the organization. A corporation will cease to exist if it does not make money for shareholders, and so all business functions must ultimately serve to make the company profitable. Too often communication departments can languish on the outskirts of a company's staff when they are not perceived to be contributing to the firm's larger strategic business goals. Thus, those responsible for SC must do more than devise and execute clever campaigns. A campaign may win awards from the public relations industry but still not be seen as valuable by business leaders if it does not effectively support business strategy. Rather, strategic communicators must understand the need for metrics by which to measure the success of their campaigns, metrics that relate less to the campaigns themselves than the extent to which those campaigns help the company reach its business goals. For example, if a campaign results in 10 million media impressions but fails to communicate the right message to the right public, it will not be perceived as helpful to the business as a whole, no matter how creatively the campaign was designed.

Contributing to Business Outcomes

In the defense industry, strategic communicators are not "paid by the pound" for their efforts; rather, they are held accountable for their contribution to the desired business outcomes of the company. Being able to measure and show business-relevant results to senior leaders is the key to receiving sustained budget and organizational support for the communication function. Thus, the continued success of communicators depends upon their ability to gain a deeper understanding of the goals of the organization and their role in helping the leadership attain those goals. A useful heuristic in this regard is the acrostic CAMERA:

Connect to strategic organizational goals
Appropriate channels for each public
Match needs of key stakeholders/publics
Execute targeted communication strategies
Results obtained
Actions by publics

However, the defense industry presents particular challenges for the strategic communicator. Communicating in this business-to-government vertical means understanding the disciplined framework in which the government identifies needs for weapon systems, runs competitions for the right to build them, and then chooses the manufacturer or manufacturers for each. This is a "long lead-time" industry, with requirements identified years in advance of an actual competition and with many additional years to get concepts from the drawing board to a finished product. Littlefield (2008) argues that one significant problem with the acquisition process is that the Department of Defense DOD) does a poor job of communicating its projected technological needs to industry, so that defense firms are left to guess what its most important client will need and when. He quotes one former Secretary of the Navy, who noted that most DoD personnel lack an understanding of how industry operates, the role of competition in corporate planning, or the impact of investor opinion upon decision-making. The result is that large amounts of either taxpayer funds or stockholder investments are wasted, in addition to the loss of defense capability that occurs.

The Defense Acquisition Process

To understand the role that SC plays in the defense industry, it is important to have a basic understanding of how the military acquires its weapon systems. The Defense Acquisition System (Department of Defense, Defense Acquisition University, n.d.) has been designed to be a predictable, event-based process. As indicated in Figure 10.1, it proceeds through a series of well-defined phases. Each phase is punctuated with a series of decision points, milestone reviews, and preliminary design reviews, each of which must be passed successfully before the next major phase may proceed.

Once selected to provide a product or service to the US government, a company is monitored by government program managers, committees in Congress, government watchdog groups, and the media to see whether it achieves its intermediate and final goals. It is therefore necessary for the senior leadership of a company to determine how communication can and should influence the decision-making of the government customer and other publics, even before products are developed.

Strategic Communication and Market-Shaping

True SC starts with "market-shaping," when decision-makers are considering what future military needs will be. For example, as the government is either establishing requirements or in the process of selecting a company to make a product, companies will advertise their overall capabilities, demonstrating technological prowess in a broad mission area. They provide enough information on their websites, through advertising, and in social and traditional media to show that their solution is worthy, but not enough information to reveal what specific recommendations they will offer in a formal proposal. They will often enlist third parties to extoll the virtues of their solution and/or validate the need for the program or product in question.

Furthermore, throughout the development and production process, the importance of key publics may vary from phase to phase (e.g., the publics a company targets as system requirements are being developed). A good example is that of the US Air Force Long Range Strike

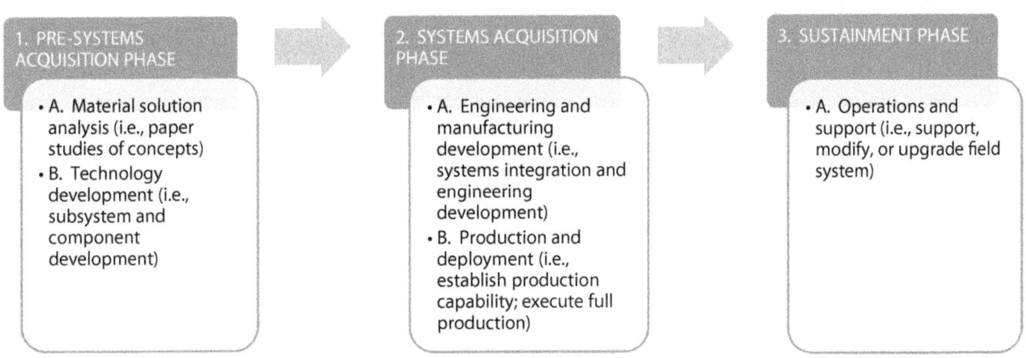

Figure 10.1 The Defense Acquisition System process. Source: https://www.dau.mil/tools/Lists/DAUTools

Bomber (LRS-B) competition, which began in 2014 (Gulick, 2014). The major competitors positioned their offerings in the media, at trade shows, and online before a decision was made (i.e., they used the traditional defense-industry channels to target key government influencers during the decision-making process). However, Northrop Grumman, one of the competing prime contractors, then produced an ad showcasing its expertise in building cutting-edge aircraft, including a covered-up version of what was presumably the company's prototype of the LRS-B. Unusually, the ad was originally released on YouTube, the popular video site, in early 2015 and was shown about a week later during the broadcast of one of the world's most watched sporting events, the Super Bowl (Cenciotti, 2015) in order to reach the broadest possible array of audiences. The Pentagon chose Northrup Grumman to build the aircraft later that year, but work was halted almost immediately when the rival Boeing-Lockheed team protested against the $80 billion award (Hillis, 2015). In early 2016 the GAO ended the dispute by ruling that Boeing and Lockheed had no grounds on which to challenge the decision (Seligman, 2016). The aircraft has been designated the B-21 Raider and will be in service in the early 2030s.

While requirements for a system are being developed, formal and informal meetings are held with customers face-to-face and at trade shows and similar public forums to help the company explain its business philosophy and the technical solutions it is offering. But requirements are mostly written in Washington, D.C., so communicating effectively within the Beltway is key to influencing most decisions. Once the requirements are created and approved and the acquisition process begins, however, there are many possible government organizations charged with selecting the company to build and deliver military equipment. These organizations can be in far-flung, little-known places such as Dahlgren, Virginia, home to the Naval Surface Warfare Center, which is responsible for some missile defense, railgun technology, and directed energy weapons.

Time-phasing is also critical in this industry and creates challenges to conventional communication planning and thinking. In business-to-consumer and business-to-business communication, the publics, while not static, tend to be more stable than those in the defense industry. Publics for the defense industry are a changing mosaic of influencers and agendas that the skilled strategic communicator must microtarget every step of the way. Thus, matching and timing communication strategies and tactics to appropriate publics is a major challenge for defense companies.

Grand Strategy

Botan discusses the importance of grand strategy in an organization. "Grand strategy," he says, "is the policy-level decisions an organization makes about goals, alignments, ethics, and relationships with publics and other forces in its environment" (Botan, 2006, p. 225). Thus, an automobile manufacturer may have a grand strategy of building several different models to compete in multiple automobile categories, and the marketing division for each model must devise a campaign that respects the limits imposed on them by the corporate grand strategy. For example, the marketing staff of a mid-market car cannot direct its efforts toward the target audience for a luxury brand. Botan also defines four different types of grand strategy. An organization with an *intransigent* grand strategy resists change, looks at its publics as merely instrumental in meeting the needs of the organization, and sees little or no need to adapt to others or collaborate with them. An organization, though, with a *resistant* grand strategy will, as the name implies, attempt to resist change, but it will adapt to new conditions when necessary. It is likewise wary of its publics, but it will enter into dialogue with them when the situation demands it.

However, it is the last two types of grand strategy that are most relevant to the defense industry, since it encompasses elements of both of them. An organization pursuing a *collaborative* or *partnership* grand strategy views itself as separate from but interdependent with its environment, a situation that well describes defense firms. Certainly, they remain independent corporations, but they depend upon government contracts to maintain themselves in business, while at the same time government entities, and the various military and intelligence organizations in particular, depend on the firms to provide them with weapons and other equipment necessary to the fulfillment of their missions. In this model publics are looked at as legitimate stakeholders in the achievement of the organization's goals, and defense contractors would agree that members of Congress, senior military officers, and operators responsible for actually using their products all have a vested interest in the outcome of their work. Similarly, such publics help define relevant issues in this model: legislators do so by their willingness to fund various projects, while the military does so by requesting particular products in order to achieve their mission objectives.

At the same time, the defense industry reflects elements of the final type of grand strategy, the *cocreational*. In his earlier writings, Botan had labeled this grand strategy the *integrated*, but in either formulation what he highlights is the deep and interpenetrating nature of the relationship between the entities involved. Because of the unique relationships that defense firms have with various agencies of the US government, those relationships could be understood to go beyond the merely collaborative to be closely integrated into that environment. Thus, while firms work with members of the military in developing and testing weapons systems, it is also true that many retired and former military personnel find homes in contracting companies, allowing a cultural symbiosis to occur. Similarly, retired members of Congress, as well as former members of the military, often join defense firm boards, where they continue to influence decisions in the industry. Others join lobbying firms in order to influence decision-making in Washington among current legislators on behalf of defense-industry clients. Since those providing law-making and contractual oversight to these firms are also their customers, decisions about which products to make are made only in consultation with the customers. In this case it may be said, in Botan's language, that the organizations and their environment cocreate their meanings (i.e. what threats need to be addressed) and their decisions (i.e. what specific capabilities must be produced in order to meet those threats) (Botan & Hazleton, 2006; Botan & Taylor, 2004).

The Role of Strategic Communication in the Defense Industry

Guerrero-Castro (2013) defines SC in relation to national defense as follows:

> … [S]trategic communication is not marketing, advertising, public relations, journalism, psychology, sociology, social communication, visual communication, anthropology nor any other area related to these. However, strategic communication should fulfill the role of selecting, leading, integrating, coordinating, activating, and executing the resources of these disciplines in order to support the national objectives and permanent interests of a nation-state. (Guerrero-Castro, 2013, p. 49)

Thus, SC is *not* public relations, marketing, or any of the other fields he mentions. Rather, the role of SC in this context is to (a) support the national objectives and permanent interests of the nation-state and (b) select and integrate elements from a variety of related disciplines in order to achieve those goals. While the author is referring specifically to SC in the context of national defense understood in political and military terms, his explication is valuable in understanding SC's role in the defense industry as well, since defense firms may also be understood as critical elements of the ability of a nation-state to protect itself and its interests. Thus, what strategic communicators in defense firms do is work with their political and military partners to select and integrate marketing, public relations, journalism, and other elements into campaigns that will allow them to help achieve the national objectives (as determined by the political leadership) and permanent interests of the country.

Key Publics

There is a constellation of key publics (often referred to as "audiences" or "stakeholders" within the industry) that defense companies must address throughout the product development process, and these can be understood as a core (i.e. Congress) surrounded by concentric rings, reflecting their relative influence in the process. Both the companies and the various publics work together out of mutual self-interest. Within the highly regulated business-to-government defense industry, the communication challenges are more narrowly focused than either the government itself or mass-market, consumer-facing industries. There are special challenges in identifying, targeting, engaging, and evaluating the effectiveness of communicating with key audiences.

While our primary concern here is with external publics, it is worth noting the role that internal publics play in a firm's SC efforts. Technology today, because of its ubiquity and rapidity, has blurred the distinction between internal and external publics, since information released in one forum tends to find its way to others. The speed with which internal communications find their way out to external audiences and external information permeates an employee population is unprecedented. As a result, some organizations have merged their internal and external staffs together to create consistent messaging to all their publics; while consistent messaging is not new, more recently there has been an urgency to implement it in order to prevent crises inside or outside the organization. Of course, these organizations recognize the continued, if increasingly blurred, distinction between internal and external publics, but they also realize that they must adopt a new strategy to be effective in a vastly different communication and media environment.

The act of communicating in the industry is less like a shotgun blast and more like a laser beam, since it is usually narrowly focused on particular, highly influential publics. Indeed, a target public may not be the same as the critical (i.e. decision-making) public, as is the case in public diplomacy, when a government *targets* the citizens or business leaders of a country in order to influence the *critical* public of the political class. A similar phenomenon occurs in Washington, D.C., when a defense contractor saturates a Metro station with ads in order to put pressure on, for example, the decision-makers in the Pentagon. The desired effect is that the ads are seen not only by decision-makers, but also by publics who influence the decision-makers. The military procurement hierarchy is a complex system of decision-makers, influencers, and the checks and balances of one of the biggest bureaucracies in the world.

Moreover, the key publics change throughout the phases of product development, competitive purchasing, and sustaining (or "keeping sold," in the vernacular of the industry – maintaining and upgrading the systems). The list of publics remains the same, but the focus on each one changes during the course of the different phases. To the surprise of many outside the industry, defense firms are not exclusively focused on the Executive Branch of the government, as represented by the Pentagon. Figure 10.2 represents the concentric circles that constitute the key publics of the defense industry, including Congress at the core, surrounded by the "rings" of the military services, other government officials, other domestic influencers, and international and adjacent markets.

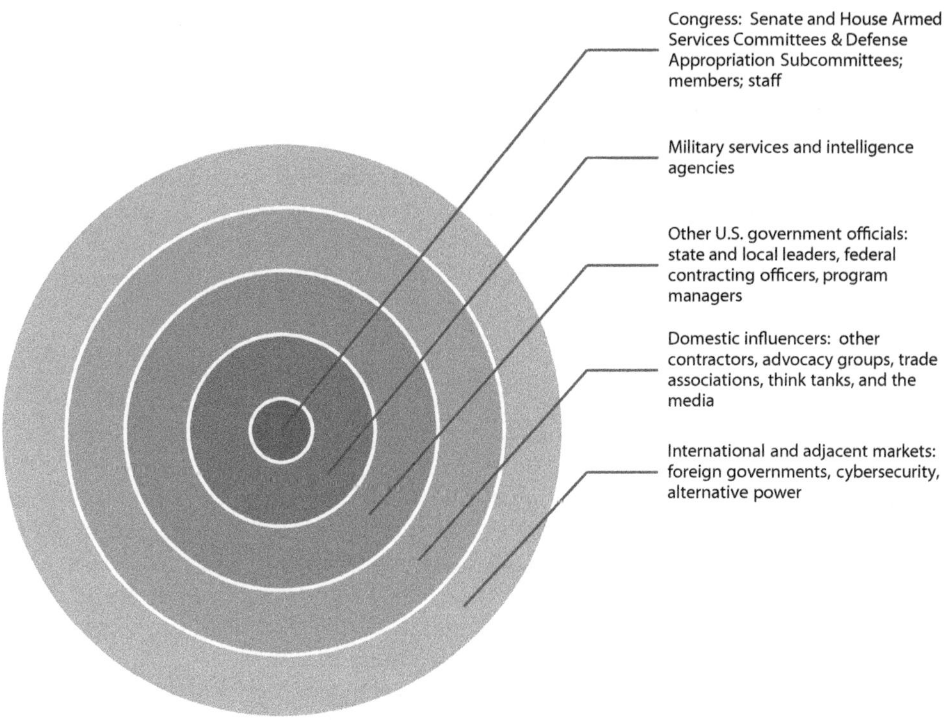

Figure 10.2 Key publics of the defense industry, with the most important closer to the core.

The Core: Congress

The role of Congress in the defense process is at once critical and complicated, and so the way that contractors communicate with that institution are similarly complicated. Since Congress funds defense projects, its approval of a weapon system is crucial for the financial sustainability of defense firms. The role of those responsible for SC in such a firm is to work to ensure that particular projects are given funding in the latest budget and that a persuasive case for such projects is made in the public hearings that Congress calls. In such a situation, relationship-building with key influencers in Congress is vital to obtaining or increasing funding for programs and systems. For example, when Northrup Corporation (before its acquisition of Grumman Aerospace) was urging Congress to support its B-2 Stealth bomber in 1991, a key ally was Senator Sam Nunn (D-Georgia), then Chairman of the Senate Armed Services Committee. Nunn was a powerful champion of the aircraft and someone other members of Congress feared to cross on the issue for a variety of reasons (e.g. they wanted his help in getting re-elected; they sought to preserve their working relationship with him in Congress; or they wished to protect defense contracts in their own states) (Isaacs, 1991).

These influencers, however, consist not only of the individual senators and representatives who will vote on bills, but above all high-ranking members of the Senate and House Armed Services Committees, which provide oversight to both the Pentagon and defense contractors, and the corresponding Appropriations Committees, which pass appropriations bills and therefore control government expenditures. Furthermore, in order to influence members of Congress, it is necessary to build strong relationships with both their personal and committee staffs, upon whom members rely in order to determine which way to vote on important pieces of legislation.

One particularly helpful communication tactic with respect to Congress is for companies to plan industry days on Capitol Hill. These are popular and effective means of creating visibility for issues and getting the attention of key members and staffs. Major defense firms bring representatives of smaller companies that produce parts for the larger weapon systems to Congress and introduce them to those members who represent the districts where those companies are located. It becomes clear to members that curtailing a particular system would have a negative impact upon employment back home and therefore their prospect of re-election.

However, any approach to members of Congress requires careful pre-planning. This process involves identification of issues, both positive and negative, of interest to:

- the company
- relevant members of Congress
- key committee and personal staffers
- key influencers in home state/districts

Dealing with Congress also requires a thorough understanding of the local economic impact of programs and systems. Especially helpful is stressing the economic impact of work done back home, not only of jobs, but the economic activity in the area that exists because people are able to pay for housing, retail products, restaurants, and similar things. A good communication plan should emphasize the role of, say, corporate philanthropy in the state or district as well. Materials used in such presentations should be short and succinct, featuring bullets and infographics rather than dense text. Members of Congress and their staffs are busy, and so materials should provide a maximum amount of information in a minimum amount of time.

The First Ring: The Military Services and Other Government Agencies

The primary clients of defense firms are, unsurprisingly, the various branches of the military: the Army, Navy, Air Force, Marines, Special Operations Command, and associated agencies, such as the Defense Advanced Research Projects Agency. Those in the field provide feedback about weapons systems, what they believe is working well and what is not. Senior officers are responsible for determining what systems are likely to be needed in the years ahead, and with those projections defense contractors are able to begin their product development cycle. To facilitate greater understanding between those responsible for product acquisition in the military and employees of defense contractors, the DOD sponsors industry days, just as defense firms do with Congress (Secretary of Defense, 2007). However, it is vital that those engaged in SC in the defense industry be aware of the organizational needs of those with whom they work in the Pentagon. For instance, the military commands must convince the regulatory and legislative bodies that watch over them that their programs and operations are well managed and within budgetary, procedural, and ethical guidelines. Also, both the military services and the defense industry are interested in keeping the importance of military equipment salient to the media, Congress as a whole, and especially members serving on key committees. For example, with the Pentagon spending so much money on the F-35 Joint Strike Fighter, it began placing fewer orders for other aircraft. As a result, Boeing, which began production of the F/A-18 Super Hornet fighter jet for the Navy and foreign militaries in 1995, lobbied Washington to purchase more of the jets and so keep its plant in St. Louis open (Cameron & Wall, 2014). In early 2015, the Navy requested of Congress the right to purchase 12 more F/A-18s, and all four Congressional defense committees agreed (Cavas, 2015; DiMascio, 2015). As a result, Boeing estimated that its production line for the fighter would continue at least an extra year, possibly longer with foreign orders.

Similarly, when a defense program is in budgetary and/or schedule crisis, both those in the government and those in the defense industry have a mutually helpful role to play: officials seek to appear as if they are in control of the situation and demanding adequate performance by the company, while the company, in turn, seeks to appear responsive and competent to fix the problem. Even so, there is always a tension between the two groups that must be managed both in private and in public, but both parties understand that it is in their mutual interest to change their behavior appropriately during crises. As Larkin and Larkin (1994) observe, if communication is to change behavior, it must be grounded in the desires and interests of the receivers. Culture changes only after the new behaviors produce benefits for a period of time and people can see the connection between the new actions and the improvement (Kotter, 1996). In the case of the federal sector, this means that those in defense firms must address the needs of not only the customers who make the decisions about buying their products, but the end users of the products as well, since their satisfaction will be taken into account when further purchases are made in the future.

Of course, the purpose of all defense industry programs is to provide to branches of the military the tools they need to fulfill their missions. It is the responsibility of the service chiefs of each branch of the military, acting together and under the leadership of the Chairman of the Joint Chiefs, to ensure that soldiers, sailors, airmen, and Marines are properly trained and equipped. While the chiefs establish requirements, it is the staff of the Secretary of Defense that oversees the development and testing of equipment by defense contractors, such as by ensuring that systems meet the requirements set down by the military, monitoring production and testing, and eventually overseeing the fielding of the equipment. It is imperative that those involved in SC in defense firms familiarize themselves with both the system development process and the vernacular which the military uses, because an effective communication strategy can influence outcomes from the time the requirements are formed to their eventual use by the various services. Indeed, defense firms do extensive research on problems faced by those on the front lines and in formulating the requirements and building the equipment that will allow them to solve those problems.

Furthermore, the defense industry is faced with the reality that any product failure will receive widespread attention, since it is expected that those products will perform flawlessly when they are needed. A good strategic communicator therefore plans for both the success and failure of systems as they are being developed and during their actual use in combat. A fundamental principle of crisis communication is to prepare for the nightmare scenario and be ready to address failure with the same confidence with which one addresses success. In addition, members of the military cannot endorse a particular company or its products formally, but if the products have been used in combat or over an impressive number of years, those facts can find their way into a company's outreach materials. Not surprisingly, such materials often feature content that emphasizes the support that the company is offering to the warfighters who will be using particular combat systems.

In addition to the military, other categories of government clients include agencies within the intelligence community, such as the Central Intelligence Agency, the National Security Agency, the Defense Intelligence Agency (which, of course, is also part of the military), and the National Reconnaissance Office. The "three-letter agencies," as the intelligence community is often called, provide challenges to the strategic communicator. The old line that "I can't talk about that – it's classified" is frequently invoked during many discussions of the work done for them. The task of the strategic communicator is to find ways of appropriately discussing broad capabilities and presenting the company's message to key decision-makers without causing risk to the agency and its contracting companies. Other agencies that do frequent business with defense firms include the Department of Homeland Security, the State Department, NASA, the National Oceanographic and Atmospheric Administration, and the Federal Aeronautics Administration. (See Figure 10.3 for some of the most important government clients of the defense industry.)

Figure 10.3 Primary US government clients of the defense industry.

The Second Ring: Other US Government Officials

Outside of Congress and the military services, however, there are a number of other government officials with whom it is imperative to build good relationships. For example, state and local elected officials are also in a position to influence budgets and funding for some projects within their jurisdictions, and so engaging them is vital to get their cooperation and support for federal appropriations.

Likewise, strategic communicators have an important role to play in the development of documents in response to government requests for proposals, such as ensuring that the transmittal letter and executive summary are written clearly and succinctly. Moreover, while proposals are primarily the responsibility of contracting officers and program managers, it is necessary for a company to have a plan to target government contracting officers and decision-makers to influence the final result. Sometimes such engagement is done behind the scenes, but when an approach to a problem is not proprietary, it is frequently done publicly. Tactically, this can mean something as simple as taking out an advertisement in a key publication that says, "Our solution for the ABC missile does X, Y, and Z," taking the wording directly from the proposal. It can also entail, however, a much more elaborate campaign, involving media pitching, briefings, social media posts, product demonstrations, and bylined articles by third parties extolling the virtues of the product and approach. What determines the extent of the campaign is whether one's customer tolerates high-profile communications or not.

Another determinant of the kind of campaign that is run is the location of the particular defense program. Many are run out of smaller military installations, well outside the orbit of the Washington Beltway, and influencing those within a smaller media market is often easier, since there is less competition for messaging compared to the cacophony in advertising that exists in and around Washington. In all cases it is necessary to identify the command with responsibility for the program, who the ultimate decision-makers are, and where they are located in order to properly allocate campaign resources.

The Third Ring: Other Domestic Influencers and the Media

Additionally, there are a host of other groups that have influence over the interaction between a defense company and various elements of government and which therefore need to be considered as a SC plan is put into place. Among these are other defense companies with which one's own is working on a project (in the role of either prime contractor or subcontractor); advocacy groups; trade associations; think tanks; and the troops on the ground who will be the end-users of the weapon systems that are procured. Often such groups are vital in gaining support for a firm's products and services, and therefore it is necessary to adopt a strategy of microtargeting to ensure that they are engaged adequately.

Media organizations constitute a special category of such domestic influencers. Members of the media may be considered a public for any strategic communicator, but they are always intermediate (hence the term "media") and never ultimate targets, since the goal of a communication strategy or tactic is to reach other key publics through them. However, it is important for anyone trying to communicate the position of a defense company to understand the various media venues by which its messages may be conveyed. For example, in the media ecosystem there are several tiers of publications relevant to the defense industry. First are media specifically focused on the defense trade, such as *Defense News* (https://www.defensenews.com); its sister publications, including *Military Times* (https://www.militarytimes.com); and journals dedicated to each of the four service branches – *Defense One* (https://www.defenseone.com), *Breaking Defense* (https://breakingdefense.com), and *Inside Washington Publishers* (https://iwpnews.com) – which are all quick to run stories relevant to the field with minimal urging from communication staff.

Next are the technical publications that have a broader aperture than those focused strictly on defense issues. For example, *Aviation Week* (https://aviationweek.com) is populated with some of the most technologically literate writers in the business. For this reason, experts preparing for interviews with the journal are advised, with only slight exaggeration, that the reporters they will be meeting know as much about the technology as they do. *Aviation Week* and its affiliated publications showcase detailed, carefully researched stories that are accurate and capture both the technological and programmatic issues of the issue under discussion.

A third level includes the more mainstream publications, from medium-sized dailies to the top-tier outlets such as Bloomberg (https://www.bloomberg.com), Reuters (https://www.reuters.com), Associated Press (https://ap.org), *The Washington Post* (https://www.washingtonpost.com/regional), *The New York Times* (https://www.nytimes.com), *The Boston Globe* (https://www.bostonglobe.com), *The Los Angeles Times* (https://www.latimes.com), CNN (https://www.cnn.com), MSNBC, Fox News, and the networks. It takes more news (e.g. the involvement of large sums of money, controversy, system failure, deaths, and/or destruction) to capture the attention of these publications. However, while mainstream news outlets will always pay attention to bad news, the size and reach of these organizations makes it vital for those responsible for communication efforts to nurture relationships with them and ensure they have access to timely information. Moreover, websites such as The Daily Beast (https://www.thedailybeast.com), The Huffington Post (https://www.huffingtonpost.com), and the online organs of all the major news organizations are always looking for content to fill their pages 24 hours a day. Likewise, those responsible for SC in the defense industry must be focused on Twitter and other social media channels, keeping in mind that some will come and go and others will be narrowly focused on a specific audience.

Especially relevant to the dissemination of news about the defense industry are the former senior military officials who appear as experts on various cable news programs to explain military operations, both by the US and other actors, throughout the world, as well as researchers at think tanks who compose reports about defense issues. In some cases, former military officials are truly independent sources of information, seeking to offer the public the benefit of their technical expertise. Sometimes, however, such experts may be directly or indirectly part of an integrated communication plan developed by a defense company, helping to support the point of view of the business by which they are employed, and it is frequently impossible to know in which category any particular expert belongs. Similarly, researchers at think tanks appear on television as highly credible sources of information. Each of their institutions also has a particular overarching philosophy and examines issues with various degrees of partisanship. Companies in the defense industry will often commission studies from the top-tier think tanks which are released with the cachet of that institution's name, but which actually reflect the perspective of the defense firm. A good SC practice for those in the industry is to follow defense experts at think tanks on social media and keep them informed about the firm's programs and technological developments.

The Outer Ring: International and Adjacent Markets

The defense industry not only sells to the US domestic market, but also engages in extensive commerce with foreign governments and establishes alliances with foreign defense firms. These relationships are governed by strict national and international legal arrangements, but there is also a wide array of cultural codes that govern such relationships in every country that must be taken into account by those responsible for communicating the company's message. Butler (2010), in his survey of UK defense companies, found that while their managers value honesty and clarity in business communication, executives from other cultures, such as the Arabs and French, adhere to a code of etiquette in which junior members of a team do not contradict a superior, even if the latter says something that is poorly formulated or technically wrong. In such instances, clarity and honesty can sometimes be difficult to achieve, and the relationship suffers. Hence, it is vital that a defense firm forge close relationships with legal experts and business leaders in whatever market it is seeking to operate, since a public misstep could jeopardize a business deal or cause difficulties between governments that could be disastrous.

For instance, it is not enough to simply translate documents intended for an American audience into another language, since technical terms and industry jargon often do not translate well and require staff with native proficiency in the relevant language to carefully vet them before anything is released in another country. In fact, the whole approach a company takes when entering into a foreign market, both the strategies and the tactics, may be completely different than those for the same products or services sold in the US market. For example, advertising plays a major role in US commerce, while there are few culturally appropriate opportunities to advertise in many international markets. All strategies and tactics need to be run through a cultural filter, preferably with the input of local communication experts, before launching a communication campaign outside the US. There is immense risk in simply taking the US business template and superimposing it in an international market. As the example of the Bell-Boeing ad demonstrates, something published for distribution in the US can quickly be picked up on the internet and social media and result in international repercussions. Furthermore, in many parts of the world, such as the Middle East, there are few, if any, opportunities to advertise defense and aerospace products. Alternative channels do exist, such as government-supported think-tank publications and some quasi-government publications which might take either advertising or bylined articles, but those efforts must be carefully vetted with in-country experts immersed in the language and culture of the country.

In addition to selling to foreign governments, there is a growing trend for US defense companies to either adapt their technologies for other uses or move toward high-technology markets with little or no direct connection to the defense industry, such as alternative power generation, clean water technologies, or commercial aspects of cybersecurity. Targeting these markets requires, as in the case of international markets, a rethinking of all aspects of a company's SC efforts, including strategies, tactics, publics, and channels. Even the media which cover the adjacent markets are different from the ones that cover the traditional defense markets.

Ethical Considerations

Because of the intense scrutiny that defense firms receive from the government, the media, and the public, most have elaborate safeguards to ensure high levels of ethical compliance on the part of their employees. There have been examples of companies cutting corners in their production and supply chains, while at the same time boasting about the quality and dependability of their products. Such incidents create a credibility gap between the company's messages about its products and reality, not only damaging its reputation but also causing the imposition of monetary sanctions by the government and even being banned from future government contracts if the offense is particularly heinous. A further punishment can be inflicted by Wall Street if an offense affects a company's ability to provide predictable financial results. The ethical responsibility of professional strategic communicators concerns both the content of the campaigns they run (i.e., that the messages are truthful in all respects) and also the reasonably predictable results of those campaigns. Many companies in the industry belong to the International Forum on Business Ethical Conduct (https://ifbec.info), an organization created by the member companies of the Aerospace Industries Association of America and the Aerospace and Defense Industries Association of Europe in 2010 and which has developed a set of Global Principles of Business Ethics to guide its members' activities.

Conclusion

We have examined the role that SC plays in the defense industry, beginning with two case studies: the F-35 Joint Strike Fighter, supported by a multi-faceted and effective communication strategy, and the Bell-Boeing CV-22 Osprey, whose public relations image was damaged by the deployment of an ill-considered advertisement. We then explored how SC aligns with the business strategy of defense firms and the ways in which it represents a fusion of Botan's collaborative/partnership and cocreational grand strategies. Finally, we discussed the role of the various key publics which are critical to the success of defense firms, concluding with a few words about the importance of ethics in the SC function.

There are a few central lessons to be drawn from this discussion. First, as illustrated by the efforts Lockheed Martin made to promote the F-35, a successful SC campaign must employ as many channels and tactics as necessary to achieve the desired results, often requiring out-of-the-box thinking. Second, cultural sensitivity is vital when attempting to sell to international customers: the debacle of the Osprey ad is an example of what occurs when communication professionals fail to take cultural norms into account in the messages they create. Third, it is too easy for communicators to focus on strategies and tactics but ignore the way their plans must fit into a company's grand strategy, helping the company as a whole achieve its business goals. Lastly, the relative importance of each of a defense company's key publics must be accurately assessed, so that Congress and the military must always be placed above the other groups, which then will be prioritized depending upon the focus of the particular campaign.

Furthermore, these lessons may be applied, *mutatis mutandis*, to other kinds of SC campaigns. For example, it is as necessary for strategic communicators in a supermarket chain or entertainment company to be clear about the firm's grand strategy and how their work fits into it as it is for communicators in defense firms. Likewise, cultural sensitivity is important when devising any SC plan, not just for international campaigns but also when targeting various key publics of a domestic campaign. Finally, clearly understanding one's key publics and which are most important when trying to sell a product or communicate a message is necessary in order to properly focus the organization's resources and time.

Discussion Questions

1. The F-35 Joint Strike Fighter program has suffered from withering criticism about its cost and effectiveness in combat. However, such a large program certainly produces benefits for the many companies working on it, their employees, and their states. Do you think that Lockheed Martin's public relations campaign in defense of the program has been a justifiable investment? Are there any tactics that the company has used that you believe are not justifiable? If so, why? If not, why not?
2. The size and strength of the US defense industry suggests that its SC efforts have been largely successful. What elements of these efforts do you believe are most effective in achieving both national and corporate goals? Which should be modified or ended to make them more effective or ethical?
3. Does the defense industry focus too much on one particular key public? If so, which one, and why? If not, why not? Is there a public that the industry should be paying more attention to than it does? If so, which one and why? If not, why do you believe that the defense industry has correctly identified and targeted its key publics?
4. Given that the US military has been fighting wars for a long time in the Middle East (the Gulf War, as well as the wars in Iraq and Afghanistan) that have both targeted and supported many Arabs and Muslims, what precisely was the problem with the Osprey ad that Boeing, Bell, and the *National Journal* all felt the need to condemn? Was it the portrayal of a culture (e.g., Arab culture), a religion (i.e., Islam), the site (i.e., a mosque), or all of these? Would a similar ad targeting Russians during the Cold War have been seen as offensive? Why or why not?
5. Do you agree that the defense industry represents both a collaborative/partnership type of grand strategy and an integrated one? Are there elements of the industry–government relationship that do not fit into these two categories? Explain your answer.

References

10 follies. (2005, December 19). *Advertising Age*, 4.

Associated Press. (2010, July 29). Luke preferred at F-35 site. *YourWestValley.com*. Sun City, AZ. Retrieved from https://www.yourwestvalley.com/glendale/article_473efd22-9b47-11df-b811-001cc4c03286.html

Bernton, H. (2005, October 1). *Magazine ad "unleashes hell" for Boeing and Bell.* Seattle, WA: Seattle Times.

Botan, C. (2006). Grand strategy, strategy, and tactics in public relations. In C. Botan & V. Hazleton (Eds.), *Public relations theory II* (pp. 223–247). Mahwah, NJ: Lawrence Erlbaum Associates.

Botan, C., & Hazleton, V. (2006). Public relations in a new age. In C. Botan & V. Hazleton (Eds.), *Public relations theory II* (pp. 1–18). Mahwah, NJ: Lawrence Erlbaum Associates.

Botan, C. H., & Taylor, M. (2004). Public relations: State of the field. *Journal of Communication*, 54(4), 645–661.

Butler, C. J. (2010). Internal and lateral communication in strategic alliance decision making. *Management Decision*, 48(5), 698–712. doi: 10.1108/00251741011043885

CAIR: Boeing, Bell, National Journal apologize for "mosque attack" ad. (2005, September 30). *PR Newswire*.

Cameron, D., & Wall, R. (2014, September 19). Fighter jet may vanish from Boeing's horizon. *Wall Street Journal*, p. B1.

Cavas, C. P. (2015, March 15). World events, F-35 delays drive Hornet push. *Defense News*. Retrieved from https://www.defensenews.com/story/defense/naval/naval-aviation/2015/03/12/navy-carriers-aircraft-fighters-strike-fighters-f-18-fa-18-super-hornet-boeing-f-35-joint-strike-fighter-jsf/70243170

Cenciotti, D. (2015, February 2). Northrop Grumman's Super Bowl ad teased a new top-secret stealth bomber. *Business Insider*. Retrieved from https://www.businessinsider.com/david-cenciotti-northrop-grummans-stealth-bomber-teaser-ad-2015-2

Chandrasekaran, R. (2013, March 9). F-35's ability to evade budget cuts illustrates challenge of paring defense spending. *The Washington Post*. Washington, D.C. Retrieved from https://www.washingtonpost.com/world/national-security/f-35s-ability-to-evade-budget-cuts-illustrates-challenge-of-paring-defense-spending/2013/03/09/42a6085a-8776-11e2-98a3-b3db6b9ac586_story.html

Cohen, Z. (2015, July 16). The F-35: Is the world's most expensive weapons program worth it? Retrieved February 16, 2016, from https://www.cnn.com/2015/07/16/politics/f-35-jsf-operational-costs

CTV News. (2013, April 8). Lockheed kicks off cross-country PR blitz for F-35. Retrieved November 14, 2015, from https://www.ctvnews.ca/canada/lockheed-kicks-off-cross-country-pr-blitz-for-f-35-1.1229858

DiMascio, J. (2015, June 16). Boeing bullish on F/A18 sales, F15 upgrades. *Aviation Week*. Retrieved from https://aviationweek.com/paris-air-show-2015/boeing-bullish-fa-18-sales-f-15-upgrades

Eisenhower, D. D. (1961, January 17). Farewell Address. Retrieved from https://www.eisenhower.archives.gov/research/online_documents/farewell_address/Reading_Copy.pdf

Fighter Country. (2013, June 27). Luke AFB to receive three additional F-35 squadrons. Retrieved November 14, 2015, from https://fightercountry.org/luke-forward/luke-afb-to-receive-three-additional-f-35-squadrons/76349

Government Accountability Office. (2015). *F-35 Joint Strike Fighter: Assessment needed to address affordability challenges* (Report to Congressional Committees No. GAO-15-364). Washington, D.C. Retrieved from https://www.gao.gov/assets/670/669619.pdf

Guerrero-Castro, C. E. (2013). Strategic communication for security & national defense: Proposal for an interdisciplinary approach. *Connections: The Quarterly Journal*, 12(2). Retrieved from https://connections-qj.org/article/strategic-communication-security-national-defense-proposal-interdisciplinary-approach

Gulick, E. (2014, July 12). AF moves forward with future bomber. Retrieved December 5, 2015, from https://www.af.mil/News/ArticleDisplay/tabid/223/Article/486167/af-moves-forward-with-future-bomber.aspx

Hartung, W. D. (2014). *Promising the sky: Pork barrel politics and the F-35 combat aircraft* (International Policy Report). Washington, D.C.: Center for International Policy. Retrieved from https://www.ciponline.org/images/uploads/publications/Hartung_IPR_0114_F-35_Promising_the_Sky_Updated.pdf

Hillis, A. (2015, November 6). Boeing, Lockheed protest LRS-B, claim competition was botched. *Aviation Week & Space Technology*.

Isaacs, J. (1991). Northrup bungles B-2 PR package. *Bulletin of the Atomic Scientists*, 47(5), 3.

Kotter, J. P. (1996). *Leading change*. Boston, MA: Harvard Business School Press.

Larkin, T. J., & Larkin, S. (1994). *Communicating change: How to win employee support for new business directions*. New York: McGraw Hill.

Littlefield, S. (2008). Bridging the DoD–industry communications gap: Improving strategic knowledge sharing. *Defense AT&L*, 37(3), 18–21.

Lockheed Martin. (n.d.). F-35 fast facts (graphic). Retrieved November 14, 2015, from https://www.f35.com/assets/uploads/documents/F-35-Fast-Facts-Infographic-Horiz.jpg

Luke AFB to receive three additional F-35 squadrons. (2013, June 27). Retrieved November 14, 2015, from https://fightercountry.org/luke-forward/luke-afb-to-receive-three-additional-f-35-squadrons/76349

Milewski, T. (2013, April 8). Lockheed Martin launches Canadian PR campaign for F-35. Retrieved November 14, 2015, from https://www.cbc.ca/news/politics/lockheed-martin-launches-canadian-pr-campaign-for-f-35-1.1324551

Miller, K., Capaccio, T., & Ivory, D. (2013, February 22). Flawed F-35 too big to kill as Lockheed hooks 45 states. Retrieved November 14, 2015, from https://www.bloomberg.com/news/articles/2013-02-22/flawed-f-35-fighter-too-big-to-kill-as-lockheed-hooks-45-states

Neuman, S. G. (2010). Power, influence, and hierarchy: Defense industries in a unipolar world. *Defence and Peace Economics*, 21(1), 105–134. doi: 10.1080/10242690903105398

Rahman, M. A. (2005). Bell, Boeing and TM Advertising blame others for their tasteless ad. *Washington Report on Middle East Affairs*, 24(9), 58–59.

Ricks, T. E. (2006, May 16). What ever happened to … Pierre Sprey? *The Washington Post*. Washington, D.C. Retrieved from https://www.washingtonpost.com/wp-dyn/content/article/2006/05/15/AR2006051501518.html

RT.com. (2014, December 7). Every F-35 a country buys from Lockheed Martin damages its defense. Retrieved November 14, 2015, from https://www.rt.com/op-edge/212115-lockheed-f-35-marketing-clout

Secretary of Defense. (2007). *Defense acquisition transformation: Report to Congress. John Warner Defense Reauthorization Act. Fiscal year 2007, section 804*. Washington, D.C.: Department of Defense. Retrieved from https://archive.defense.gov/pubs/pdfs/804JulFinalReport_to_Congress.pdf

Seligman, L. (2016, February 16). GAO denies Boeing's protest of bomber contract; Northrop gets back to work. Retrieved February 16, 2016, from https://www.defensenews.com/story/breaking-news/2016/02/16/gao-denies-boeings-protest-long-range-strike-bomber-contract/80433300

Williamson, R. (2005, September 30). Bell, Boeing won't defend mosque ad. *Adweek*.

11

President Obama, the Affordable Care Act, and the Challenges of Strategic Political Communication

Stephen J. Farnsworth
University of Mary Washington

Case Study: Enacting the Affordable Care Act

In terms of health care outcomes, Americans have long lagged far behind other democracies at comparable levels of economic development. American babies are less likely to live past infancy (Organization for Economic Cooperation and Development, 2017a), and adult Americans die years earlier than their counterparts in Japan, Canada, South Korea, and the nations of western Europe (Organization for Economic Cooperation and Development, 2017b). In exchange for those worse health care outcomes, Americans spend far more than other nations at comparable levels of economic development (Organization for Economic Cooperation and Development, 2017c).

Improving health care in the United States has long been a domestic policy priority, with debates over health care reform initiatives going back more than half a century (Skocpol, 1997). More recently, Bill Clinton sought to pass a comprehensive health care bill, but doubts over its workability and concerns over its cost led to abandonment of the bill by the Democrats and to Democratic defeats in the 1994 midterm elections (Sinclair, 2000). While George W. Bush shied away from comprehensive health care reform packages, he did secure passage of a significant expansion of Medicare via a prescription drug benefit program (Foreman, 2008). As a presidential candidate in 2008, Barack Obama repeatedly emphasized that he would focus on health care reform if elected (Abramson, Aldrich, & Rhode, 2010; Kenski, Hardy, & Jamieson, 2010). Once elected, Obama took office facing profound partisan divides that deepened during the Bill Clinton and George W. Bush presidencies (Campbell, 2016; Farnsworth & Lichter, 2006; Fiorina, 2008; Sabato, Stencel, & Lichter, 2000).

The political challenges of profound partisan divides, together with long-running public concerns about the potential uncertainties of changes to a new health care system, created a very difficult environment for moving beyond the status quo. This chapter examines President Obama's SC efforts to try to build public support for and enrollment in his health care reform program.

Political circumstances were not entirely unfavorable. Obama won a large Electoral College victory in 2008, and those elections secured relatively large Democratic congressional majorities. Even so, Obama's health care reform plan moved slowly on Capitol Hill. At first, more pressing matters – particularly the economic crisis that developed during the last years of

The Handbook of Strategic Communication, First Edition. Edited by Carl H. Botan.

George W. Bush's presidency – commanded Washington's attention. In addition, Obama himself devoted significant energies during his first months in office to rebuilding international relationships that he viewed as having been damaged during the Bush years and to scaling back US military involvement in the Middle East (Farnsworth, Lichter, & Schatz, 2013; Sinclair, 2012; Singh, 2012).

When he turned to the health care debate, Obama offered general policy preferences and bill-drafting assistance, but left much of the heavy lifting to Capitol Hill (Sinclair, 2011). Public criticism of the reform plan increased as it was being prepared. A rising anti-government movement dubbed itself the Tea Party and spread its criticisms of Obama and his health care bill through social media and through many contentious congressional district meetings that focused on health care reform (Skocpol & Williamson, 2012). Powerful anti-reform themes, like the false claim that the bill contained provisions for government "death panels," emerged on social media and received considerable attention from more traditional media as well (Hopper, 2017). In terms of the legislation itself, the administration preferred to engage with policy specifics only in the final stages, believing that members who took leading roles in drafting the bill would be more personally invested than if they were moving a White House bill (Sinclair, 2011). Passage of the Affordable Care Act (ACA) proved to be a legislative marathon as well, with back-and-forth struggles between the Democratic House and Senate majorities, made doubly difficult when the Democrats lost their 60-seat majority following a Republican victory in a Senate special election in Massachusetts in early 2010 (Hulse & Palmer, 2009; Sinclair, 2011).

Communication Struggles After ACA Became Law

Once President Obama signed the ACA, another round of presidential political communication struggles began. Republicans lawmakers, who gained control of the House after the 2010 midterm elections, challenged the president over many aspects of the legislation, as did Republican activists who employed pro-Republican news outlets and social media to make their case to the public. Opponents of the law first sought to have the federal courts declare the measure unconstitutional, and when that failed, critics sought to undermine it by reducing the law's scope and effectiveness through additional court action (Busch, 2016). Several states under at least partial Republican legislative control refused to expand eligibility for Medicaid, which was part of the reform package. By choosing not to do so, those states limited the ability of millions of Americans to obtain affordable insurance coverage and undermined the reform program itself (Snell, 2016).

Opposition to the ACA following its enactment moved forward on more communication-oriented tracks as well. As the new plans rolled out, Republicans frequently repeated Obama's ill-fated promise, "If you like your insurance, you can keep it," a comment named the "Lie of the Year" by Politifact in 2013 (Busch, 2016). (Of course, Sarah Palin's claim that the bill contained "death panels" was the organization's 2009 "Lie of the Year"; Hopper, 2017.) Republicans were convinced that the legislation would continue to drag down Democrats, including the president himself, and therefore sought to rebrand the measure as "Obamacare." In response, the president himself embraced the term, arguing that the eventual success of the health care reform plan would be net plus for his public opinion ratings (Ceaser, Busch, & Pitney, 2015).

But arguably the biggest problem that the ACA faced during its early implementation was not the litigation, not the angry Tea Party movement, and not Republican legislative opposition in Washington and in many state capitals. Rather it was the misfire of the health care registration website itself. People trying to enroll in the insurance program via healthcare.gov faced frozen computer screens, painfully long waits, and other obstacles that made it difficult for people to buy a policy (Busch, 2016). Obama sought to increase enrollment in the health exchanges via an appearance on *Between Two Ferns*, an online comedy program hosted by Zach Galifianakis, and that effort did drive more people – particularly young people – to the government's health insurance website shortly before an enrollment deadline (Azari, 2014; Blake, 2014). But, as the saying goes, one does not get a second chance to make a first impression.

Ironically, the best salesmen for Obamacare turned out to be President Trump and US House Speaker Paul Ryan. In early 2017, as Republicans began their efforts to repeal and replace the ACA, public support for the controversial health care plan surged and Republicans in Congress abandoned – at least temporarily – the "repeal and replace" promise (Hohmann, 2017).

Presidential Communication Advantages and Limitations

At least since the rise of television, American politics has centered on the White House. Presidential power of course is limited by the Constitution, but presidential communication advantages are legion. Reporters pay far more attention to the White House than to Capitol Hill, giving presidents' far greater ability to shape the policy discourse than members of Congress (Farnsworth & Lichter, 2006). With unparalleled access to information – particularly that relating to international concerns – presidents can learn about many things sooner and more comprehensively than can other political actors. That gives the White House powerful strategic communication advantages in many instances, particularly cases relating to foreign and military policy, where information may not be readily available away from US government sources. In addition, any administration contains a cadre of top officials ready to buttress presidential claims about a given policy matter (Farnsworth, 2009). Citizens usually view presidents less negatively than the legislative branch, and so increasingly presidents seek to use their various communication advantages by "going public" to shape public opinion in ways designed to force greater acquiescence – if not agreement – from Congress (Kernell, 2007). Presidents also engage in a global "road show" to sell themselves and their policies to the nation and world (Farnsworth et al., 2013; Heith, 2013). While they may not always be successful in moving public opinion through these presidential marketing efforts, presidents nevertheless frequently employ public strategies in their attempts to shape public discourse and policymaking (Edwards, 2003).

But presidential framing advantages have their limits, particularly for domestic policy matters. Members of Congress and other political actors have the ability to try to shape the discourse in a different direction than that favored by the White House, but their ability to shape the discourse in a way contrary to the president on high salience matters is a challenge (Entman, 2004). Overall, presidential efforts to frame a given event in a certain way depend on some level of agreement with other political actors, including legislators, reporters, and the public. If the claim is not widely seen as credible – for example, if a president were to claim that an uptick in unemployment is comparable to 9/11 – it will be debunked rapidly through a political, media, and cultural feedback loop where more credible messages would dominate (Entman, 2004).

Because few citizens pay close attention to the particulars of public policy matters, much presidential marketing shapes the public views of the president, who could be thought of as the "spinner in chief" of the modern media environment (Farnsworth, 2009). Likewise, running for president has become an intensely personal affair, as candidates sell themselves in the media first on the basis of who they are and then, if they become viable candidates, their issue positions may receive more attention. Indeed, part of the reason for Obama's electoral success in 2008 stems from his campaign's effective use of YouTube videos and online peer-to-peer communication efforts (Kellner, 2010). All this public visibility comes with problems for modern presidents though, as increasing public expectations of the chief executive often trigger eventual citizen disappointment with a president who can only do so much in a system of separate institutions and overlapping powers (Jones, 1995; Lowi, 1985).

In the highly partisan contemporary media environment, White House teams frequently attempt to use a variety of media outlets, including social media, to enlist public support to give the president advantage in convincing Congress to back the White House. This strategy involves two steps: presidents sell themselves and their policies to the public; then the citizens who receive these media messages encourage lawmakers to support the president's policy agenda (Kernell, 2007). Although the results of the going-public strategy are mixed at best, presidents devote enormous energies to selling themselves and their policy preferences to the public (Edwards, 2004). Perhaps they are optimistic that they possess skills that previous presidents lacked. Regardless, one can only make so much progress trying to sell the public on policy specifics, which are only marginally interesting to many citizens and therefore of little concern to reporters trying to satisfy public demand for news. As a result, presidents try to manage the news and shape policy by trying to control – or at least influence – their public portrayals.

Presidential Marketing and New Media

Modern social media environments – including YouTube, Facebook, and Twitter – allow presidents and their critics to make their cases in a variety of venues. They also allow citizens to participate in the conversation in a variety of ways, by reposting political content, commenting upon it, or even offering reformatting of presidential content through mash-ups, GIFs, and memes (Scacco & Coe, 2016; Stuckey, 2010). In an environment that features both government–media–public and peer-to-peer communication, "presidential framing resilience" explains a president's continuing, but arguably diminished, SC advantages in today's malleable media environment (Hopper, 2017).

Obama's social media efforts involved reaching out in a number of ways and on a number of media venues. Obama reached a distinctly less politically obsessed audience on ESPN, where he routinely offered his college basketball tournament picks during "March Madness" (Scacco & Coe, 2016). The White House website during Obama's tenure likewise offered opportunities for citizens to obtain email updates and provided clickable opportunities to engage and otherwise participate in ongoing administration political activities. The White House Twitter feed also emphasized direct interaction with the White House and with Obama through popular hash tags like #whchat and #whtweetup (Scacco & Coe, 2016). While these efforts did not always focus on selling a particular policy, like health care, a presidential administration employs social media outreach in the hopes of making citizens more likely to support the president generally, as well as regarding specific policy priorities (Farnsworth, 2009; Heith, 2013).

There were also specific efforts to employ social media in support of the ACA. The Obama team asked the president's supporters to reclaim the word Obamacare, encouraging the president's Twitter followers to tweet what they liked about the new law (Hopper, 2017). But there are limits to efforts to reframe a term that was already being used extensively by the president's critics. Despite the Obama team's best efforts to use the word Obamacare in a more positive way, media coverage that used the word still tended to be more negative than positive (Hopper, 2017).

Looking at the Person, Not the Policy: Framing Presidential Character

Modern mass media have given the American public the opportunity to gain a sense of who the president is as a person and what the president intends to do by way of public policy. Despite the far greater amount of information now available in these two areas of interest, both sets of impressions can be flawed. Presidents – and presidential candidates before that – aggressively seek to manage all aspects of how they are presented to the public. Successful campaigns and effective modern presidencies employ massive SC operations to ensure the president is presented as likable and working diligently to supply the public with popular policy outcomes. These media management efforts frequently involve selective revelations and nondisclosures on a large scale.

Defining character is a difficult business. US politicians, particularly presidential candidates, generally need to be likable to win an election (Barber, 1992; Brooks, 2006). Americans have a fondness for presidents who are like them, who have – or at least appear to have – the common touch (Brooks, 2006). In US presidential politics, character routinely trumps experience. People want to like their president, perhaps because television and internet news makes the chief executive a regular fixture in the nation's living rooms. Reporters, particularly those working in television, find it easier and more interesting to write about character than issues. With this heavy emphasis on character in both traditional and new media, many presidential candidates have lost to more personable opponents (Barber, 1992; Ceaser & Busch, 1993, 2001, 2005; Ceaser et al., 2009, 2015). Social media likewise contains a heavy diet of emotional discourse when it comes to presidential candidates and presidents (Scacco & Coe, 2016).

For Obama, whose election in November 2008 was heralded as a transformative event like few presidencies of the past half century, the expectations were extraordinarily if not impossibly high (Campbell, 2009; Ceaser et al., 2009; Conley, 2009; Harris & Martin, 2009). Even before he became president, Obama was the political equivalent of a global rock star. A 2008 Berlin rally drew hundreds of thousands of adoring Europeans. In the United States, Obama filled stadiums and arenas across the country. His inauguration in January 2009 brought one of the largest crowds ever to the Washington Mall. Throughout the campaign, the Obama team appreciated the importance of new media for presenting presidential character, connecting with younger voters, and their parents, via Facebook and YouTube (Goldfarb, 2007; Owen, 2009). In particular, the campaign emphasized the candidate's youth and optimism, and the general campaign mantra of "change" allowed people to see in the candidate the change they wished to see (Ceaser et al., 2009).

In a time of social media mash-ups, YouTube videos, and the like, presidents have to be a good deal more inventive to reach citizens than was the case during the days when tens of millions of Americans tuned in to watch the evening news. To reach audiences that may have little interest in politics, presidents have to be informal and "not only to make a joke but in some cases to be in on the joke" (Scacco & Coe, 2016).

In this mixed media environment, presidents tend to emphasize the personal and the informal, such as when President Obama sought to increase health care enrollment by joining late night comic Jimmy Fallon to "slow jam the news," wielding a selfie stick to a *BuzzFeed* video, and trading insults with Zach Galifianakis on *Between Two Ferns* (Scacco & Coe, 2016). There are limits to what these sorts of efforts can accomplish. When the website crashed, the administration mishandled the problems by trying to frame the startup as "just glitches" and argued that the president's staff, not the president, was responsible for the screw-ups (Hopper, 2017). This communication misstep provided critics with further ammunition to claim that the ACA was unworkable (Hopper, 2017).

Obama's critics also sought to frame the president's character negatively as a way of undermining his ability to shape policy, mainly by arguing that the new president was an elitist – and maybe not even an American. From the start of his presidential campaign, Obama consistently faced suspicions, fueled by conservative media and conservative activists, that he wasn't really born in America as he claims, and that he was a Muslim, not a Christian (cf. Kurtz, 2007a, 2007b). During a private California fundraiser, a secretly recorded tape revealed Obama's dismissive view of ordinary Americans who were "clinging to guns and religion" during hard times (Owen, 2009).

Counter-narratives Regarding Obama's Character

Another use of social media to emphasize the character of Obama in a negative way can be seen through the rise to celebrity of "Joe the Plumber" during the 2008 campaign. Republicans regularly presented him as the everyman objecting to Obama's plans to raise taxes on small businesses (Kellner, 2009). The conservative effort to shape the Obama narrative generated considerable attention during the campaign, even though Joe made too little money to be subject to Obama's proposed tax increase, nor was he a plumber, nor was his first name Joe (Kellner, 2009). But, as the polls below show, the argument that Obama was not an ordinary American was a major concern of many citizens during his presidency.

Republicans sought to portray the ACA website crash as "Obama's Katrina," but the analogy was not well received on social media. A sample of Twitter users using the term during the crisis rejected the comparison by a more than two-to-one margin (Hopper, 2017). The comparison was notably less likely to be rejected in media reports at the time, with a plurality of reports saying that linking these two matters was legitimate (Hopper, 2017).

President Obama, the Affordable Care Act, and Public Opinion

Presidents fear the public will view them as out of touch, so administrations swing into action when there is concern that the public may think that a president does not understand the public's problems (Farnsworth, 2009, 2015). But health care, a long-running policy challenge, lacked the immediacy of the 2008 economic crisis, the 9/11 terrorist attacks, or Hurricane Katrina. Obama first addressed the immediate concerns of the economic crisis, and subsequently focused on the health care reform package that was passed in early 2010.

Table 11.1 offers approval ratings for President Obama from late 2008, when he was president elect, through mid-2014, after the health care plan's implementation was underway. Apart from the very enthusiastic support he received at the start of his term, the Gallup surveys showed Obama's ratings in a relatively narrow range around 50%, usually a few points above and sometimes a bit below. The sharpest drop in Obama's ratings came during the summer of 2009, when the Tea Party movement attacked the health care bill in the media and at congressional town halls around the country. His approval dipped around the time of the 2010 midterm elections, when Republicans took control of the House, but quickly rebounded. It peaked again around the time Obama was re-elected in November 2012, and fell again in late 2013. The relatively narrow range of approval ratings serve as a useful reminder of the challenges presidents face when they try to go public on policy items: public appeals generally have little impact overall (cf. Edwards, 2003) or policy frustrations may undermine public approval of a president, as was the case for Obama and health care (Jacobson, 2011).

Apart from times of crisis, Americans worry about governmental overreach. As the support for health care reform coalesced, so too did its opposition. The president's Tea Party critics tapped into a traditional American skepticism of big government that would serve the movement well as the 2010 midterms approached.

Public Opinion After Passage of the Affordable Care Act

Next, we take a closer look at public opinion shortly before the 2010 midterm elections, a high point in political discussion of the health care law that had been passed earlier that year. As shown in Table 11.2, the public did not view the Obama presidency or the policy actions

Table 11.1 Public opinion and presidential approval.

"We would like to get your overall opinion of some people in the news. As I read each name, please say if you have a favorable or unfavorable opinion … Barack Obama"

	Favorable	*Unfavorable*	*No opinion*
2014 Jun 5–8	47	52	1
2014 Apr 24–30	51	48	2
2014 Mar 22–23	50	46	4
2014 Feb 6–9	52	46	1
2013 Dec 5–8	48	50	3
2013 Oct 3–6	49	49	2
2013 Sep 15–16	53	43	4
2013 Jul 10–14	52	45	3
2013 Jun 1–4	54	45	1
2013 Apr 11–14	55	43	2
2012 Nov 15–18	58	40	2
2012 Nov 9–12	58	41	1
2012 Nov 1–2	55	42	3
2012 Sep 24–27	55	44	1
2012 Aug 20–22	53	46	1
2012 Jul 19–22	53	45	2
2012 Jul 9–12	54	43	3
2012 May 10–13	52	46	2
2012 Feb 16–19	50	48	2
2011 Dec 15–18	55	44	1
2011 Apr 20–23	52	46	2
2011 Mar 25–27	54	43	3
2011 Jan 14–16	53	45	2
2010 Nov 4–7	49	48	3
2010 Oct 14–17	47	50	3
2010 Jul 8–11	52	44	4
2010 May 24–25	54	43	3
2010 Mar 26–28	52	48	1
2009 Dec 11–13	56	42	2
2009 Oct 16–19	55	42	3
2009 Oct 1–4	56	40	4
2009 Jul 10–12	66	33	1
2009 May 29–31	67	32	1
2009 Mar 27–29	69	28	3
2009 Jan 9–11	78	18	5
2008 April 18–20	60	34	6
2008 March 14–16	62	33	6

Source: Jones (2014). Results are based on telephone interviews conducted June 5–8, 2014, with a random sample of 1,027 adults, aged 18 or more, living in all 50 US states and the District of Columbia. Comparable Gallup surveys used to provide earlier results.

Table 11.2 Obama and the Democrats versus the Republicans, October 2010.

Do you approve or disapprove of the way (ITEM) are/is doing their/his job?

	Approve	*Disapprove*	*No opinion*
Barack Obama	50	47	3
Congress	24	73	3
Democrats in Congress	36	61	3
Republicans in Congress	30	67	3

Which political party, the (Democrats) or the (Republicans), do you trust to do a better job handling (ITEM)?

	Democrats	*Republicans*	*Both (vol.)*	*Neither (vol.)*	*No opinion*
a. The economy	44	37	4	14	2
b. Health care	46	38	1	12	3
c. Immigration issues	37	37	3	17	6
d. The situation in Afghanistan	39	34	4	19	4
e. The federal budget deficit		39	40	2	18
f. Taxes	39	40	2	19	1
g. Helping the middle class	50	34	2	11	2

[Half sample asked items a–c; other half asked items d–f, full sample g.]

Do you think the money the federal government has spent on the economic stimulus has been mostly (well spent) or mostly (wasted)?

	Well spent	*Wasted*	*No opinion*
10/3/10	29	68	4

Given what you know about them, would you say you support or oppose the changes to the health care system that have been enacted by (Congress) and (the Obama administration)? [Congress/Obama order is rotated.]

	Support	*Oppose*	*No opinion*
10/3/10	47	48	5
3/26/10	46	50	4

Source: Balz and Cohen (2010). This *Washington Post* ABC News Poll was conducted by TNS of Horsham, PA by telephone, September 30–October 3, 2010. It is based on a random national sample of 1,002 adults using both conventional and cellular phones. The results from the full survey have a margin of sampling error of ±3 percentage points.

of Obama and the Democrats all that unfavorably going into the 2010 midterm elections. The president's overall job approval rating stood at 50% in October 2010, roughly where presidents usually are at that mid-point of their first term (cf. Balz & Cohen, 2010). In addition, he remained far more popular than Congress.

On specific issue areas, the Democrats also did pretty well. More voters favored the Democrats over the Republicans on a host of issues, including the key issues of the economy and health care and particularly helping the middle class. The Republicans, for their part, had slight public opinion advantages relating to the federal budget deficit and to tax policy. The public was deeply divided over the health care bill, which had passed several months earlier but had yet to go into effect.

Obama's decision to leave many of the details of the health care bill to Congress may have been smart politics – Clinton tried and failed to pass a health care bill in 1994 the administration designed – but it didn't enhance Obama's leadership credentials. Efforts by endangered Congressional Democrats to campaign at some distance from the president – and the bill – made it difficult for Obama to trumpet its accomplishments. In addition, the uncertain pace of economic recovery has not given the administration much to talk about along those lines either. "It could have been worse," is not a message that generates voter enthusiasm or sympathetic news coverage.

The GOP's newly energized congressional leadership said after the 2010 elections that they planned to try to repeal the new law (Murray & Bacon, 2010). Like many midterm elections, 2010 was the battle over intensity, and there Republicans had the advantage.

Public opinion regarding the health care plan was pretty consistently negative during the health care rollout and beyond. As shown in Table 11.3, support for the ACA never topped 50% during Obama's second term. Most of the surveys showed support for the measure in the lower 40s, and sometimes under 40% support. The high level of consistency in the public's views regarding the law once again demonstrates how hard it is even for a president, who possesses a greater ability to be heard on policy issues than any other political actor, to generate significant change in public opinion.

Obama and the Marketing of Presidential Character

National public opinion surveys by Gallup during Obama's first 6 years showed generally high approval of the president's character. As shown in Table 11.4, evaluations of Obama as a person were consistently high during his months as a presidential candidate and as a new president. Three months into his presidency, more than two-thirds of Americans believed that Obama "understands the problems Americans face in the daily lives" and considered him "a strong and decisive leader." Solid majorities also believed that Obama "shares your values" and "can manage the government effectively."

All four of these categories were notably lower 1 year later, around the time the ACA was signed into law. While solid majorities continued to believe that Obama understood the problems of ordinary people and considered him decisive, only roughly half thought he could manage the government effectively or shared the public's values. By 2014, when citizens were getting some sense of how the ACA would work in practice, personal evaluations of Obama's temperament and competence were even lower.

One key factor that distinguished the Obama media strategy from those of Bush and Clinton is a greater hesitancy to try to dominate the discourse in the mass media (cf. Farnsworth, 2009). Despite the powerful advantages a president has in the shaping of

Table 11.3 Public opinion regarding the Affordable Care Act.

"Do you generally approve or disapprove of the 2010 Affordable Care Act, signed into law by President Obama that restructured the US health care system?"

	Approve	*Disapprove*	*No opinion*
2016 Nov 9–13	42	53	5
2016 Aug 30–31	44	51	5
2016 May 6–8	47	49	4
2015 Nov 4–8	44	52	4
2015 Jul 1–5	47	48	5
2015 Apr 1–4	41	53	6
2014 Nov 6–9	37	56	6
2014 Oct 1–2	41	53	6
2014 May 21–25	43	51	5
2014 Apr 7–8	43	54	3
2014 Feb 28–Mar 2	40	55	5
2014 Jan 31–Feb 1	41	51	9
2014 Jan 3–4	38	54	8
2013 Dec 11–12	41	51	8
2013 Nov 23–24	40	54	6
2013 Nov 7–10	40	55	4
2013 Oct 26–28	44	47	9
2013 Oct 18–20	45	50	6
2013 Aug 17–18	41	49	11
2013 Jun 20–24	44	52	4
2012 Nov 15–18	48	45	7

Source: Brands and Newport (2016). Results are based on telephone interviews conducted November 9–13, 2016, with a random sample of 1,019 adults, aged 18 or more, living in all 50 US states and the District of Columbia. For results based on this sample of national adults, the margin of sampling error is ±4 percentage points at the 95% confidence level. Comparable Gallup surveys used to provide earlier results.

Table 11.4 Public opinion regarding President Obama's character.

"Thinking about the following characteristics and qualities, please say whether you think each applies or doesn't apply to Barack Obama. How about – [random order]?"

"Is a strong and decisive leader"	*Applies*	*Doesn't*	*No opinion*
2014 Jun 5–8	45	53	2
2013 Nov 7–10	47	51	2
2013 Sep 5–8	53	46	1
2013 Jun 20–24	53	47	*
2012 Jun 7–10	53	47	1
2011 Mar 25–27	52	47	1
2010 Mar 26–28	60	39	1
2009 Sep 11–13	66	33	2

(Continued)

Table 11.4 (Continued)

2009 Jul 17–19	67	31	2
2009 Apr 20–21	73	25	2
2008 Oct 10–12	61	37	2
2008 Apr 18–20	55	39	6
2008 Mar 14–16	56	37	7
"Understands the problems Americans face in their daily lives"	*Applies*	*Doesn't*	*No opinion*
2014 Jun 5–8	48	50	2
2013 Nov 7–10	54	45	1
2013 Sep 5–8	56	43	1
2013 Jun 20–24	56	42	1
2012 Jun 7–10	58	41	1
2011 Mar 25–27	57	42	1
2010 Mar 26–28	56	43	1
2009 Sep 11–13	64	36	*
2009 Jul 17–19	66	33	1
2009 Apr 20–21	72	27	1
2008 Oct 10–12	73	26	1
2008 Apr 18–20	63	34	3
2008 Mar 14–16	67	30	3
2014 Jun 5–8	34	65	1
2013 Nov 7–10	38	60	1
2013 Sep 5–8	38	59	3
2013 Jun 20–24	38	60	2
2012 Jun 7–10	40	59	2
2011 Mar 25–27	36	60	4
2008 Oct 10–12	51	46	3
2008 Apr 18–20	40	53	7
2008 Mar 14–16	41	53	6

"Is honest and trustworthy"	*Applies*	*Doesn't*	*No opinion*
2014 Jun 5–8	47	51	2
2013 Nov 7–10	50	47	3
2013 Sep 5–8	55	42	3
2013 Jun 20–24	55	44	1
2012 Jun 7–10	60	38	2
2011 Mar 25–27	61	36	3
2008 Apr 18–20	60	32	8
2008 Mar 14–16	63	29	7

(Continued)

Table 11.4 (Continued)

"Can manage the government effectively"	*Applies*	*Doesn't*	*No opinion*
2014 Jun 5–8	39	60	2
2013 Nov 7–10	42	57	2
2013 Sep 5–8	47	52	2
2013 Jun 20–24	44	54	2
2012 Jun 7–10	45	54	1
2010 Mar 26–28	49	49	2
2009 Sep 11–13	55	43	2
2009 Jul 17–19	59	39	2
2009 Apr 20–21	66	29	5
2008 Oct 10–12	55	41	4
2008 Apr 18–20	48	45	6
2008 Mar 14–16	48	45	7
"Shares your values"	*Applies*	*Doesn't*	*No opinion*
2014 Jun 5–8	43	56	2
2013 Jun 20–24	48	50	1
2012 Jun 7–10	53	46	1
2011 Mar 25–27	51	47	2
2010 Mar 26–28	48	50	2
2009 Sep 11–13	52	46	2
2009 Jul 17–19	55	43	2
2009 Apr 20–21	60	37	2
2008 Oct 10–12	58	40	2
2008 Apr 18–20	51	44	5
2008 Mar 14–16	51	44	5

*Less than 0.5%.

Source: Jones (2014). Results are based on telephone interviews conducted June 5–8, 2014 with a random sample of 1,027 adults, aged 18 or more, living in all 50 US states and the District of Columbia. Comparable Gallup surveys used to provide earlier results.

domestic news content, Obama's team tended to be relatively deferential in policy matters, leaving the many health care legislative details to Capitol Hill and giving Congress considerable authority to shape the economic stimulus package and regulatory reform for the banking industry.

This same diffidence was also sometimes seen in debates over Obama's personality. Nowhere are the consequences of failing to drive the narrative of one's own identity clearer than in the large numbers of Americans who wondered whether the 44th president was a Christian.

Obama's identity as a practicing Christian was made clear during one of the major religious issues of the 2008 campaign, the controversy over the sermons of Obama's outspoken pastor, Rev. Jeremiah Wright (Denton, 2009). But the president's critics were able to reshape the narrative for many, particularly online (Kellner, 2009). Conservative blogs were key early voices in spreading the myth that Obama was not a Christian a couple of years before the 2008 election, and the claim was subsequently picked up by Fox News (Chadwick, 2013). While mainstream media quickly debunked the claims and Obama's supporters fought back online with contrary evidence, the continuing conversation about this matter on social media and elsewhere kept Obama's religious status from being resolved in the minds of many voters (Chadwick, 2013; Kellner, 2009; Kenski et al., 2010).

The conviction among some voters that Obama was a Muslim did not disappear after he won the 2008 election. As shown in Table 11.5, only 34% of Americans were convinced in August 2009 that Obama was a Christian, down 14 percentage points from a March 2009 survey. While less than one in five Americans believed at that time that Obama was a Muslim, a surprising 43% said they did not know Obama's religion. The declining percentages of people saying that Obama was a Christian was seen, even among supportive groups, as increased numbers of even Democrats and African-Americans saying that they were uncertain about Obama's religious preference.

Obama could have done more to combat this perception, which was not helpful to his public approval. (Although the US Constitution prohibits the establishment of any religious qualification for public office, the US population is largely Christian and every president in American history has been a Christian.) Had he chosen to do so, the president could have spoken more about his Christian faith during his many public statements and made more public appearances with his family in churches on Sundays to resolve this important lingering public doubt

Table 11.5 Many uncertain about Obama's religion.

	Obama is a Christian		*Obama is a Muslim*		*Don't know*	
	Aug 2010	*Change from 3/09*	*Aug 2010*	*Change from 3/09*	*Aug 2010*	*Change from 3/09*
Total	34	–14	18	+07	43	+09
White	35	–15	21	+10	40	+08
Black	43	–13	07	+01	46	+10
Republican	27	–20	31	+14	39	+11
Independent	34	–11	18	+08	44	+06
Democrat	46	–09	10	+03	41	+09
White Evangelical	27	–12	29	+09	42	+09
White Mainline Protestant	36	–15	22	+12	40	+08
White Catholic	32	–19	18	+08	46	+10
Unaffiliated	38	–09	13	+07	44	+07

Source: Pew (2010). "Growing Number of Americans Say Obama is a Muslim," released August 19, 2010. The survey was conducted among a random national sample of 3,003 adults contacted by telephone between July 21 and August 5, 2010. Sample includes people contacted via landline and cellular telephone. The results from the full survey have a margin of sampling error of ±2.5 percentage points.

about his character. (Although biblical teachings suggest one should pray in private and not make too public a demonstration of one's religious devotion, practical political realities in the United States suggest otherwise.)

Discussion

As we consider presidential marketing of the ACA, one must note above all the difficulty of trying to move public opinion in such a difficult – and emotionally laden – policy area. Few policy areas generate as much public anxiety as health care, since one never knows when one will be sick and what treatments insurance will cover for future illness. Economic uncertainties like those around the time of Obama's election heighten concerns in other ways: even people who have good health insurance today might lose their jobs and therefore their health insurance for themselves and their families in the days ahead. Further, critics of the plan could also underscore concerns among the well insured that the quality of their health care would deteriorate if the current system of doctors and hospitals suddenly had to take on large numbers of people who would start consuming larger amounts of medical services because they obtained health insurance (Hopper, 2017). For all these reasons, uncertainty over health care changes represents a massive barrier to legislative success.

Obama's more diffident media style had its advantages in an era when character counts in terms of presidential communication. His approach seemed particularly well suited to those likely to be checking out *Between Two Ferns*, the late-night comics, and other places where the policy content of discourse is not emphasized. Likewise, the invitations to participate in Twitter events promoting Obamacare and other administration priorities offered opportunities for the president to use new media in ways to advance his standing. Policymaking, which generally contains greater uncertainty than the status quo, requires a high level of confidence in the policymaker to secure support for change. Obama's popularity was enough to secure legislative support for passage, though with very mixed public support for the idea during rollout.

In other words, the ACA case study is also a story of how effective social media opportunities exist for a president's opponents. Obama's critics were successful, at least among a significant number of voters, in convincing a significant number of citizens that Obama was not one of them, and that he might not even be a Christian. Likewise, conservative attacks on alleged incompetence by liberals when it comes to health care policy management helped set the stage for high levels of criticism of Obamacare once the website failed to launch promptly and effectively.

The evidence here suggests the contemporary social media environment can provide a president's critics with new and effective tools to generate and sustain doubts about a president and his policies. Even so, it is important to appreciate that this case study also demonstrates presidents do have some "resilience" in shaping discussion of this policy matter (cf. Hopper, 2017). After all, Obama did succeed in getting Congress to pass a health care bill – something that President Clinton could not accomplish – and he kept his presidential approval numbers considerably higher than his predecessor (Farnsworth, 2015), despite a highly problematic rollout of the new health insurance program and continuing Republican efforts to undermine the policy initiative.

In these highly partisan times (cf. Campbell, 2016), some voters seem primed to believe the best about the president they support and the worst of the other party's elected officials. So rather than looking at the ACA as an example of how a president continues to win media battles or how a president's opponents have new tools to oppose the White House, one should note how difficult it is to change policy in a political environment marked by high levels of partisanship and in a media environment marked by decentralized news that increasingly moves away from policy substance and toward more personalized matters.

Summary

While presidents do face more SC challenges than most people in politics or in public life, the communication problems they face – and the ways they address them – are not unique to the Oval Office. This case study of Obamacare implementation offers three important lessons for strategic communicators at all levels who are dealing with the presentation of public policy issues.

The first, and most important, lesson is to **control what you can**. One of the biggest struggles during the implementation of the new health care law was the fact that the government's own enrollment website did not work. Clearly far greater investment in preparation would have helped increase the number of people signing up for the new law right away, as well as helping convince some skeptical citizens that the health care plan was well designed. In these times of wide-ranging social media, many issues are not going to be framed solely by one's own narrative. It is important to plan ahead and avoid crucial mistakes in those areas where one has maximum opportunity to do so.

Obama's decision to **employ a targeted mass media strategy** to maximize policy success was one of the key positive examples for other SC campaigns. The president's decision to appear on certain media outlets like *Between Two Ferns* represented a very effective way to aim a communication message directly at a portion of the uninsured population likely to be using a particular slice of social media: young adults who have jobs that do not come with health insurance. Other Obama media efforts also helped create a positive image of Obama's character, allowing the president to reach people who might not be following traditional news closely. Obama's "March Madness" college basketball post-season picks on ESPN, hyped by the White House on social media, is an effective example of how one can help build support – or at least reduce opposition – to a president by reaching news consumers where they are in today's very decentralized media environment. As public opinion data show, Obama's approval ratings remained quite stable throughout much of his presidency, a sharp contrast from the downward approval spiral of many other recent presidents (Farnsworth, 2009, 2015).

Finally, the Obamacare marketing case study reminds strategic communicators of the wisdom of trying to **help sell the policy by selling the salesperson**. For many people, the intricate details of a policy debate are not scintillating reading or viewing. People are often more interested in something other than a bill's subchapters, as Obama realized when he decided to go on ESPN and *Funny or Die*. Likewise, showing up on late-night television to "slow jam" the news is another example of how to try to connect with people who are not necessarily political junkies. Such efforts may not be dignified, but dignified might not move the merchandise these days. Policy organizations have more opportunity to select the public face of an issue than the White House does, and find someone who seems trustworthy and personable and who is also comfortable appearing on social media. The person doing the presenting may do as much if not more for a cause than providing reporters with sophisticated arguments and fact-sheets, as the ACA implementation process demonstrated.

Acknowledgements

Acknowledgements to Emma Valinski for research assistance, to Laura Sudulich for helpful comments, and to the Center for Leadership and Media Studies at the University of Mary Washington for financial assistance. An earlier version of this chapter was presented at the 2017 Annual Meeting of the Western Political Science Association. All errors remain the author's responsibility.

References

Abramson, P., Aldrich, J. H., & Rhode, D. W. (2010). *Change and continuity in the 2008 elections.* Washington, D.C.: CQ Press.

Azari, J. (2014). How Obama's 'Between Two Ferns' appearance compares to FDR's fireside chats. Washington Post, March 12. https://www.washingtonpost.com/news/monkey-cage/wp/2014/03/12/how-obamas-between-two-ferns-appearance-compares-to-fdrs-fireside-chats/?utm_term=.c2b494db7791

Balz, D., & Cohen, J. (2010). Democrats gain in poll, but GOP still leads as midterm elections near. Washington Post, October 5.

Barber, J. D. (1992). *Presidential character: Predicting performance in the White House.* Englewood Cliffs, NJ: Prentice-Hall.

Blake, A. (2014). White House: Obama's 'between two ferns' cameo driving traffic to HealthCare.gov. Washington Post, March 11. https://www.washingtonpost.com/news/post-politics/wp/2014/03/11/white-house-obamas-between-two-ferns-cameo-driving-traffic-to-healthcare-gov/?utm_term=.c3cfd70ea2dc

Brands, R., & Newport, F. (2016). Most Americans want changes to Affordable Care Act. Gallup.com. http://www.gallup.com/poll/198158/americans-changes-affordable-care-act.aspx?g_source=Affordable+care+act&g_medium=search&g_campaign=tiles

Brooks, S. (2006). *As others see us: The causes and consequences of foreign perceptions of America.* Peterborough, Ont.: Broadview.

Busch, A. (2016). The limits of governmental accomplishment. In S. E. Schier (Ed.), *Debating the Obama presidency* (pp. 195–220). Lanham, MD: Rowman & Littlefield.

Campbell, D. E. (2009). Public opinion and the 2008 presidential election. In J. M. Box-Steffensmeier & S. E. Schier (Eds.), *The American elections of 2008* (pp. 99–116). Lanham, MD.: Rowman & Littlefield.

Campbell, J. E. (2016). *Polarized: making sense of a divided America.* Princeton, NJ: Princeton University Press.

Ceaser, J., & Busch, A. (1993). *Upside down and inside out: The 1992 elections and American politics.* Lanham, MD: Rowman & Littlefield.

Ceaser, J., & Busch, A. (2001). *The perfect tie: The true story of the 2000 presidential election.* Lanham, MD: Rowman & Littlefield.

Ceaser, J., & Busch, A. (2005). *Red over blue.* Lanham, MD: Rowman & Littlefield.

Ceaser, J., Busch, A., & Pitney, J. J., Jr. (2009). *Epic journey: The 2008 elections and American politics.* Lanham, MD: Rowman & Littlefield.

Ceaser, J., Busch, A., & Pitney, J. J., Jr. (2015). *After hope and change: The 2012 elections and American politics (post 2014 election update).* Lanham, MD: Rowman & Littlefield.

Chadwick, A. (2013). *The hybrid media system.* Oxford: Oxford University Press.

Conley, P. (2009). A mandate for change? Decisive victory in a time of crisis. In W. J. Crotty (Ed.), *Winning the presidency, 2008* (pp. 169–184). Boulder, CO: Paradigm.

Denton, R. E. (2009). Identity politics and the 2008 presidential campaign. In R. E. Denton (Ed.), *The 2008 presidential campaign: A communication perspective* (pp. 99–126). Lanham, MD: Rowman & Littlefield.

Edwards, G. C., III. (2003). *On deaf ears: The limits of the bully pulpit.* New Haven, CT: Yale University Press.

Edwards, G. C., III. (2004). Riding high in the polls: George W. Bush and public opinion. In C. Campbell & B. A. Rockman (Eds.), *The George W. Bush presidency: Appraisals and prospects* (pp. 16–45). Washington, D.C.: CQ Press.

Entman, R. M. (2004). *Projections of power: Framing news, public opinion, and U.S. foreign policy.* Chicago, IL: University of Chicago Press.

Farnsworth, S. J. (2009). *Spinner in chief: How presidents sell their policies and themselves.* Boulder, CO: Paradigm.

Farnsworth, S. J. (2015). Studying the presidency after 9/11: Re-considering presidential character in domestic and international contexts. 9/11 and the Academy Conference, Emory & Henry College, Emory, VA.

Farnsworth, S. J., & Lichter, S. R. (2006). *The mediated presidency: Television news and presidential governance*. Lanham, MD: Rowman & Littlefield.

Farnsworth, S. J., Lichter, S. R., & Schatz, R. (2013). *The global president: International media and the U.S. government*. Lanham, MD: Rowman & Littlefield.

Fiorina, M. P. (2008). A divider, not a uniter – but did it have to be? In C. Campbell, B. A. Rockman, & A. Rudalevige (Eds.), *The Bush legacy* (pp. 92–111). Washington, D.C.: CQ Press.

Foreman, C. H., Jr. (2008). The braking of the president: Shifting context and the Bush domestic agenda. In C. Campbell, B. A. Rockman, & A. Rudalevige (Eds.), *The Bush legacy* (pp. 265–287). Washington, D.C.: CQ Press.

Goldfarb, Z. (2007). Mobilized online, thousands gather to hear Obama. Washington Post, February 3.

Harris, J. F., & Martin, J. (2009). The George W. Bush and Bill Clinton legacies in the 2008 elections. In J. M. Box-Steffensmeier & S. E. Schier (Eds.), *The American elections of 2008* (pp. 1–8). Lanham, MD: Rowman & Littlfield.

Heith, D. (2013). *The presidential road show: Public leadership in an era of party polarization and media fragmentation*. Boulder, CO: Paradigm.

Hohmann, J. (2017). The Daily 202: Threat of repeal making it easier for Democrats to finally sell Obamacare. Washington Post, February 9. https://www.washingtonpost.com/news/powerpost/paloma/daily-202/2017/02/09/daily-202-threat-of-repeal-making-it-easier-for-democrats-to-finally-sell-obamacare/589bcddae9b69b1406c75c9f/?utm_term=.f9a5d7a8b180

Hopper, J. L. (2017). *Presidential framing in 21st century news media*. New York: Routledge.

Hulse, C., & Palmer, A. (2009). Sweeping health care plan passes the house. New York Times, November 8.

Jacobson, G. C. (2011). Legislative success and political failure: The public reaction to Obama's early presidency. *Presidential Studies Quarterly*, 41, 220–244.

Jones, C. O. (1995). *Separate but equal branches: Congress and the presidency*. Chatham, NJ: Chatham House.

Jones, J. M. (2014). Americans' ratings of president Obama's image at new lows. Gallup.com. http://www.gallup.com/poll/171473/americans-ratings-president-obama-image-new-lows.aspx?g_source=Obama+honest+trustworthy&g_medium=search&g_campaign=tiles

Kellner, D. (2009). Barack Obama and the celebrity spectacle. *International Journal of Communication*, 3, 715–741.

Kellner, D. (2010). Celebrity diplomacy, spectacle, and Barack Obama. *Celebrity Studies*, 1, 121–123.

Kenski, K., Hardy, B. W., & Jamieson, K. H. (2010). *The Obama victory: How media, money and message shaped the 2008 election*. New York: Oxford University Press.

Kernell, S. (2007). *Going public: New strategies of presidential leadership* (4th edn). Washington, D.C.: CQ Press.

Kurtz, H. (2007a). Campaign allegation a source of vexation. Washington Post, January 22.

Kurtz, H. (2007b). Headmaster disputes claim that Obama attended Islamic school. Washington Post, January 23.

Lowi, T. J. (1985). *The personal president: Power invested, promise unfulfilled*. Ithaca, NY: Cornell University Press.

Murray, S., & Bacon, P., Jr. (2010). GOP deciding which direction to go with new authority after midterm victory. Washington Post, November 5.

Organization for Economic Cooperation and Development. (2017a). Life expectancy at birth (indicator). doi: 10.1787/27e0fc9d-en

Organization for Economic Cooperation and Development. (2017b). Infant mortality rates (indicator). doi: 10.1787/83dea506-en

Organization for Economic Cooperation and Development. (2017c). Health spending (indicator). doi: 10.1787/8643de7e-en

Owen, D. (2009). The campaign and the media. In J. M. Box-Steffensmeier & S. E. Schier (Eds.), *The American elections of 2008* (pp. 9–31). Lanham, MD: Rowman & Littlefield.

Pew Research Center for the People and the Press. (2010). Growing number of Americans say Obama is a Muslim. Release date August 19.

Sabato, L., Stencel, M., & Lichter, S. R. (2000). *Peepshow: Media and politics in the age of scandal*. Lanham, MD: Rowman & Littlefield.

Scacco, J. M., & Coe, K. (2016). The ubiquitous presidency: Toward a new paradigm for studying presidential communication. *International Journal of Communication*, 10, 2014–2037.
Sinclair, B. (2000). The president as legislative leader. In C. Campbell & B. A. Rockman (Eds.), *The Clinton legacy* (pp. 70–95). New York: Chatham House.
Sinclair, B. (2011). Congressional leadership in Obama's first two years. In J. Thurber (Ed.), *Obama in office* (pp. 89–106). Boulder, CO: Paradigm.
Sinclair, B. (2012). Doing big things: Obama and the 111th congress. In B. A. Rockman, A. Rudalevige, & C. Campbell (Eds.), *The Obama presidency: Appraisals and prospects* (pp. 198–222). Washington, D.C.: Sage/CQ Press.
Singh, R. S. (2012). Continuity and change in Obama's foreign policy. In B. A. Rockman, A. Rudalevige, & C. Campbell (Eds.), *The Obama presidency: Appraisals and prospects* (pp. 268–294). Washington, D.C.: Sage/CQ Press.
Skocpol, T. (1997). *Boomerang: Health care reform and the turn against government.* New York: Norton.
Skocpol, T., & Williamson, V. (2012). *The Tea Party and the remaking of Republican conservatism.* Oxford: Oxford University Press.
Snell, K. (2016). Budget scorekeeper: Obamacare costs rising as more enroll in Medicaid. Washington Post, March 24. https://www.washingtonpost.com/news/powerpost/wp/2016/03/24/budget-scorekeepers-obamacare-costs-rising-as-more-enroll-in-medicaid/?utm_term=.787d18da5f0e
Stuckey, M. E. (2010). Rethinking the rhetorical presidency and presidential rhetoric. *The Review of Communication*, 10, 38–52.

12

Strategic Communication for Civil Society and Nation Building
Communication for Societal Effectiveness

Maureen Taylor and Erich J. Sommerfeldt
University of Technology Sydneym and University of Maryland

Introduction

Strategic communication (SC) is traditionally thought of as an organizational communication function aimed at enhancing organizational effectiveness. Indeed, the history of the discipline – which includes the sub-areas of public relations, advertising, marketing, and others – shows that SC is primarily used as a means to facilitate organizationally desired ends. This, in and of itself, is not necessarily problematic, as organizations have the right to assert their views within the public sphere of debate and to persuade others to accept that view. An alternative perspective – possibly even a paradigm – of SC is one wherein the function is seen as not just making organizations more effective, but making communities and societies more effective. How can SC be used to accomplish such lofty ends? Often, this occurs when communication is used to build and buttress a civil society – the foundation of a strong citizenry informed by robust public debate. Strategic communication makes societies more effective when it works toward building the structures and norms that facilitate healthy, trusting, and strong relationships between individuals, groups, institutions, communities, and governments.

Everyone wants to live in a society where people and organizations trust each other and work together for a common good. The field of SC can make important contributions to this ideal. Indeed, Taylor and Kent (2006) suggested that if SC can be used to (re)build corporate reputation, then it can also be used to help build and rebuild communities and nations. This line of research argues that SC is not only used by corporate forces, but by governments, activists, and non-governmental organizations (NGOs) for aims outside those traditionally ascribed to SC in service to Western, neo-liberal economies. By studying public relations in the context of these organizations, we may get a more accurate and well-rounded view of what SC is and how it impacts society.

Civil society campaigns provide a useful lens to understand SC because they do more than just using communication to sell a product or service. Campaigns that promote a civil society are selling ideas, actions, and relationships that can help build a nation or make a community a better place to live. Many civil society campaigns have worked toward this end. Herein, we will overview the SC campaigns within the country of Liberia, as mass media and face-to-face communication campaigns touch nearly every aspect of life in that nation – including health, economics, gender empowerment, education, and ethnic relationships. The SC initiatives put

The Handbook of Strategic Communication, First Edition. Edited by Carl H. Botan.

in place by civil society actors in the early 2000s were put to the test in 2013–2014 when Ebola threatened Liberia. We briefly discuss the case of Liberia and civil society campaigns to address the Ebola threat before returning to our explanation of civil society and the role of SC within it.

The Ebola Crisis in Liberia: A Dire Need for Strategic Communication

Liberia is a small West African country founded in 1847 by freed American slaves. Liberia developed its economy through natural resource concessions. Many thought the nation to have great potential in the 1960s and 1970s, when its population had an equivalent standard of living to that of Hungary. However, rampant corruption and a violent civil war from 1989 to 1997 forced millions to flee. When the Liberian civil war ended, Ellen Sirleaf Johnson was elected in 2006 as the first female president of the nation. When citizens gradually began to return to Liberia, nearly every part of the society needed rebuilding. Communication was one of the available resources for rebuilding the Liberian nation.

Following long periods of turmoil, distrust, and violence, multiple actors, communication channels, and strategies are required to rebuild a nation's civil society. As we will explain in more detail later, civil society is conditioned on the participation of several kinds of social and organizational actors, such as local and international NGOs, and their use of communication channels to promote pro-social messages. Civil society campaigns in Liberia used traditional mass communication tactics such as billboards, television, and radio to start building and rebuilding trust in social institutions and to build a Liberian national identity. Additionally, civil society groups such as religious organizations, youth groups, and women's empowerment groups spread face-to-face messages that motivated people to act in ways that promoted a freer and fairer society. Finally, there were external organizations such as the United Nations, European Union, and United States Agency for International Development (USAID) that also contributed communication resources for building a civil society in Liberia.

Media is a particularly important player in ensuring the spread of civil society messaging. Whereas much has been made of late of the potential for digital communication to disseminate messages and build civil society in the more developed Global "North," the primary mass media in Liberia – and many other countries in the Global South – is community radio. The geographic composition of Liberia, poor roads, and diverse language communities make community radio the best means for getting information to people. Community radio serves community (not financial) interests, and stations are always looking for free content to broadcast. The radio stations are also open to playing public service announcements (PSAs) that bring in small donations.

Secondary mass media for civil society SC in Liberia included billboards, bus shelters, and television public service announcements. These channels often hosted pro-social messages that are part of larger communication campaigns. For example, one of the key campaigns in Liberia is for people and businesses to pay taxes to meet their obligations to society. The Liberian government needs a tax base to fund education, health, infrastructure, and other national development initiatives. Yet many Liberians go to extreme lengths not to pay taxes. Billboards often remind Liberians to "pay your taxes to Mama Liberia."

Since 2004, millions of dollars of foreign assistance and training have created a civil society network of organizations across the 15 counties of Liberia. The organizations worked on various communication campaigns around social and political issues. The civil society communication network in Liberia was put to the test by events that occurred in Guinea in December 2013, when a 2-year-old child died from Ebola. Borders in West Africa are porous, with people moving easily between countries. In March 2014, Ebola appeared in rural Lofa County, in the northwest corner of Liberia that borders Guinea. The disease spread through Lofa in May, as the failures in both the health system and the government's capacity to treat those affected by the virus exacerbated the situation. By early August, the first cases of Ebola appeared in the capital of Monrovia as people from rural areas, hoping to escape the disease outbreak, brought it with them and infected family and friends.

Community radio stations quickly mobilized to communicate accurate information campaigns about real health risks and government policies regarding Ebola, and to rally community action. The capacity of the community radio stations that had been built (and rebuilt) over 15 years meant that Liberians living in rural counties had the information they needed to safeguard their families. Campaigns focused on health messages, and local and national media reported about the disease. The campaigns addressed myths and misconceptions of Ebola. Community radio stations broadcast campaign messages in local languages to help their community address the health crisis.

The Ebola response was not just a victory that demonstrated the capacity of the media in Liberia. The epidemic also worked to illustrate the competence of local civil society groups to disseminate information about the virus, and more importantly de-escalate tensions between the people, the police, the military, and the government. Liberian civil society groups played an important role in both the health of communities and the sustainment of peace. Many groups that had worked on pro-social civil society topics – such as election monitoring, gender empowerment, and community peace initiatives – from 2004 to 2013 instead mobilized their resources to talk about Ebola prevention and treatment.

Indeed, most interesting was the near seamless shift civil society groups took from their usual issues of interest to focusing on Ebola prevention and education. Civil society groups like the YMCA, the National Women's Commission of Liberia, and Business Start Up Center Monrovia became key players in disseminating information – in some cases training members in Ebola facts and prevention methods (Beekman et al., 2015). They mobilized and moved into vulnerable communities to communicate Ebola messages. YMCA peer mentors implemented a nationwide prevention and response strategy for on-going Ebola outbreaks. Teams worked to increase awareness about the spread and dangers of Ebola, particularly targeting youth and adolescents in the concerned communities through training of staff and volunteers, radio programming, and other outreach activities. The volunteers engaged both urban and rural communities, urging them to be more proactive in their response to preventing the spread of Ebola. At the civil society level, groups facilitated outreach and community engagement activities to help diffuse tensions in the community. They helped facilitate town hall meetings and public forums. Thus, while civil society organizations are often thought of as issue-based and the organizational manifestation of publics' issues of interest, the Liberia case shows that such organizations, at their core, are dedicated to sustaining the public good. The SC supported and enhanced community effectiveness in the Ebola crisis.

The preceding discussion on Liberian civil society included many terms that need to be defined and explained. The next section provides the background to the concepts used in the Liberia Ebola crisis case study and goes deeper into how SC builds civil society and nations.

What Is Civil Society?

Every day many people across the world receive pro-social messages that seek to persuade them to stop smoking, wear seatbelts, vaccinate children, or get more exercise. These pro-social messages may be, on the face of it, health communication campaigns aimed at bettering citizens' wellbeing, but they are also SC campaigns for enhancing civil society. Civil society describes a set of relationships in society that allow for enlightened, productive, and responsible decision-making (Castells, 2008). Communication through trusted channels and trusting relationships is the means through which meaning is cocreated and decisions are made (Botan & Taylor, 2005).

Civil society SC campaigns vary by nation, with some nations developing wide-reaching communication campaigns addressing a myriad of topics. Strategic communication can be used to co-orient relationships and facilitate dialogue (Kent & Taylor, 1998) between the public and government officials. To that end, researchers have studied the role SC functions like public relations can play in cocreating the relationships that help to establish a civil society, build public trust, and enact social capital (Doerfel & Taylor, 2004, 2017; Sommerfeldt & Taylor, 2011; Taylor, 2000a, 2000b, 2009, 2011; Taylor & Doerfel, 2003, 2011). Indeed, modern SC techniques have extraordinary influence on civil society and resulting public debates (Sommerfeldt, 2013). To best understand the role of SC in civil society, we should first examine its historic roots.

Historic Roots

Some of the earliest manifestations of civil society occurred in ancient times. Gerald Hauser (1998) traced the notion of civil society through the Greek and Roman civilizations. In these early societies, the concept of civil society created the conditions for a practice of debating different ideas related to public concerns. Philosophers and sophists embraced a rhetorical approach to decision-making in the public sphere. Two thousand years later, the concept of civil society re-emerged as Enlightenment philosophers such as Hobbes and Locke wrote about the concept of "responsibility" to others in a society. They argued that the state (government) should serve the citizens and that the different groups in society should be responsible to each other. Aristotle, Hobbes, and Locke, in turn, influenced Georg Hegel. In the *Philosophy of right*, Hegel (1974) prescribed the foundation for a government and public that work together to achieve societal goals. Italian philosopher Antonio Gramsci wrote extensively of civil society in the *Prison notebooks* (Gramsci, 1971) and Habermas addressed civil society in his *The theory of communicative action* (Habermas, 1981).

Civil society has been treated as a political process. Ernest Gellner (1994), Joshua Barber (2004), and Robert Putnam (2000) have written extensively about public participation in social groups, and how this participation (or lack thereof) influences policy decisions and ultimately many aspects of social life. From an SC and organizational perspective, civil society can be understood as "the network of associations independent of the state whose members, through social interactions that balance conflict and consensus, seek to regulate themselves in ways consistent with a valuation of difference" (Hauser, 1998, p. 277). The interactants in a civil society include "private and public associations and organizations, all forms of cooperative social relationships that create bonds of trust, public opinion, legal rights and institutions and political parties" (Alexander, 1998, p. 3). When these civil society actors put SC to use, they show their position and power in mediating between the interests of the state and those of the people.

Strategic communication practice of all types – mass, digital, interpersonal, and public relations – contributes to our understanding of civil society. At the heart of most scholarly discussions on civil society is the convergence of information, media, activism, rhetoric, networks, and deliberative decision-making. While the concept is multifaceted, and capable of being studied in different ways, we suggest that civil society can best be understood by looking at the ways in which meaning is cocreated. Meaning is cocreated when individuals and organizations seek to participate in the public sphere. Meaning is cocreated through media organizations that carry messages, and meaning-making occurs through today's social media tools that link actors and ideas around social and political issues. Who are these actors? The next section identifies the civil society participants.

Civil Society Participants

Taylor (2010) identified seven partners in civil society. Each partner makes unique contributions to civil society and has key roles to play.

Partner 1. Individuals, the first partner, become members of publics when they cocreate meaning, identify problems, and work toward the resolution of those problems (Botan & Soto, 1998; Taylor & Botan, 1997). Empowered and engaged individuals are the foundation of civil society. Civil society occurs when an informed and empowered public is willing and able to participate in local, regional, and national decision-making. Most often, this participation is channeled through defined social and civic groups with other like-minded individuals – though forging relationships with others different than oneself is vital to a robust civil society (cf. Sommerfeldt, 2013). Civil societies provide a safe space for individuals when they participate in the public sphere. Safe spaces can include public forums such as town halls, public meetings, and deliberative bodies. Today, there are also online spaces for participation. Individuals make their positions heard by using SC to identify problems and offer solutions to others, including people, organizations, groups, and institutions. Members of active publics engage other individuals and often use traditional media, and now social media, to extend the reach of their rhetoric.

Partner 2. Societal institutions – such as religious organizations, professional groups (associations of doctors, lawyers, and educators), universities, unions, and political parties – are the next level of partners in civil society. Institutions are comprised of individuals who join together for a common goal or objective. Citizens can articulate their needs and priorities through institutions. Legitimate institutions, such as those that have public and government acceptance, have the power to speak and act on issues in public decision-making forums. For instance, religious groups, unions, and other societal groups have a role in civil society because they are respected. Their positions on issues of the day are valued. In a civil society, institutions operate across all sectors of the society, including health, education, political, cultural, and economic sectors. Institutions are also influential when they join with other organizations in society to work together on issues. Indeed, networks of civil society groups and institutions are powerful players in affecting policy change (Sommerfeldt & Yang, 2017).

Partner 3. NGOs or the non-profit organizations (NPOs) that work on behalf of issues are also valued partners. These voluntary associations are not part of formal governmental or institutional structures. NGOs and NPOs are organized groups of individuals, some small and others quite large. NGOs are valuable in civil society because they often work to create social capital. Social capital is that which creates "trust in a society or in certain parts of it" (Fukuyama, 1995, p. 26). Trust in others – as well as trust in institutions – is essential to a strong civil society, for without trust there can be no meaningful communication. Moreover, NGOs and NPOs create public goods that benefit those who do not contribute to an activity. Consider parks or libraries – people can use them even if they did not build them or contribute to them. NGOs and non-profits fill in gaps in services and opportunities that weaker or negligent national governments are not able to fill (Fukuyama, 2001).

Partner 4. The scale of civil society is both local and global. Thus, a fourth type of partner in civil society includes the international organizations (INGOs) that provide financial and human resources to help facilitate development in many parts of the world. These international organizations fund local groups who work to achieve their own societal goals. INGOs are especially important during the initial stages of civil society building, because they work directly with indigenous organizations and provide important training and activating of local civil society leaders. INGOs such as Oxfam, Save the Children, Ford Foundation, and International Labor Organization (ILO) and others provide services and support to individuals, groups, and communities across the world. Like NGOs and NPOs, INGOs also create community-level social capital – the social support that makes participation in public debate possible.

Partner 5. Small, medium, and large businesses also have a role to play in the development and sustainment of civil society. The business community seeks to build economic capital – the more tangible cousin of social capital. Sometimes these two types of capital are at odds with one another, as businesses often seek to minimize external threats and maximize profits. Business members of a society have opinions on issues such as regulation, licensing, access to natural resources, price controls, immigration laws, and legal reform. Their voices must also be included in civil discussions. However, too much influence from businesses or corporations on decision-making may inhibit civil society development. Indeed, philosophers like Habermas (1991) lamented the influence of business and its SC efforts within civil society, and claimed that mass communication by business had co-opted the ability of publics to determine their own best interests.

Partner 6. A sixth partner features the offices of government. Local, regional, and national government officials shape what civil society will look like. In a healthy democracy, elected government leaders must answer to all partners in civil society. Elected leaders, and members of the unelected bureaucracy that support the day-to-day operations of government, need to be accountable to the aforementioned partners. Government leaders need to carefully monitor public opinion and be willing to adapt to changing public needs. In a civil society, government understands important issues and resolves them in a manner that benefits members of the society.

Partner 7. The media serve as a cross-cutting partner in civil society. Mass media and digital media facilitate the dissemination of information across civil society. People need factual information to make informed decisions. Media organizations often perform the agenda-setting function, informing the public on the most pressing issues of the day. They cover topics of interest, as well as being opinion leaders on key topics. The media also serve as watchdogs to ensure that government officials, businesses, and other groups are held accountable for their actions. In a nation where there has been violence and distrust in government and in others, the media can work to persuade individuals to trust one another, their representative institutions, democratic processes, and government.

Civil society occurs at the intersection of the interests of these seven partners. The various partners in civil society rarely work together all at once on one issue. They do not have to always engage with each other. Some issues will only involve a few partners. In a civil society, each actor does not have to agree on all things at all times. The acceptance of different opinions on a topic is a central tenet of civil society and healthy public debate. Civil societies endure because they are created, recreated, and changed in iterative communication processes. Each time citizens or organizations publicly discuss a policy, law, or cultural values, and the resulting decision is made in a transparent way, the resolution strengthens the society. Disagreements should not weaken civil society. Instead, civil society emerges from these points of difference as the "evolution of cooperation and trust among citizens" (Hadenius & Uggla, 1996, p. 1622). Civil society is a communicative process grounded in the communicative process among trusting relationships. Civil society is enacted and changed by SC. The next section explores the role of SC in civil society.

The Role of Strategic Communication in Civil Society

Civil society theory embodies cocreational assumptions about SC but also accepts that functional practices of SC are inherent in a fully functioning society. Some social theorists, like Habermas, critiqued those who work in the SC fields of public relations or corporate communication. These critics argue that public relations or corporate communication serve elite interests and that the professional communicator's actions only serve business goals, not society-driven goals. Yet, today, so many different kinds of organizations engage in SC that there is a large marketplace of ideas, positions, and solutions. As Hauser correctly noted, "whether civil society embraces and lives in truth is fundamentally dependent on whether or not its members are informed and attentive to the truth" (p. 30). In other words, people must have information and they must be interested and able to pursue what they believe to be right. Civil society is a process grounded in rhetoric that is premised on at least five conditions.

Discussions About Contested Issues

In a civil society, individuals and groups are safe to make statements and counter statements about their views. As they advocate for or against some issue, they can position their ideas within societally accepted values, beliefs, or experiences or they may choose to challenge long-held beliefs and practices. Individuals have to have enough trust in others and in institutions to take stands so that they can make their views known. This is civil society at the relational level.

Trusted Communication Channels Carry Statements to Broader Audiences

Independent communication channels, not owned by the government or corporate interests, provide an amplifier effect for participants in civil society. Independently funded channels are often more trusted than government-owned or advertising-based channels (Botan & Taylor, 2005). Channels for communication include print, electronic (radio and television), billboards, pamphlets, web, or social media. This part of civil society is currently at risk, as many governments are eavesdropping on citizens' phone calls and reading computer messages. Hacking by governments (foreign or domestic) or activists also suggests that open, transparent, communication is at risk.

Openness to Arguments

Civil society requires that there are other members in the society that are open to listening to the messages and considering the arguments made by others. Open-mindedness and venues to talk about issues are required in a civil society. Ancient Rome had the forum and rural America had the town hall. Today, social media platforms such as Twitter create virtual spaces for people to listen to other's ideas. Yet, these platforms also provide bullies, demagogues, and haters the "space" to spread their messages.

Civil Society is Dependent on Relationships

Relationships or linkages between organizations and individuals are essential to cope with social change, help with problem solving, and accomplishing shared goals or tasks. Relationship building is a key component of making civil society work (Sommerfeldt, 2013; Taylor, 2000a, 2000b). Taylor (2009) defined civil society as "the process of interactions that lead to relationships, build trust and create social capital" (p. 77). From this perspective, quality relationships among civil organizations with similar goals is paramount to the efficacy of civil society. Indeed, Hadenius and Uggla (1996) posited that civil society only manifests itself when groups are arranged in reasonably fixed social networks, and characterized by relationships of trust, affinity, and cooperation. When such bonds of established civil cooperation are lacking, they surmised, society becomes but a mass of unconnected, atomized individuals incapable of accomplishing shared objectives. As an example, Renshaw (1994) observed that a lack of collaborative relationships among civil organizations contributed to a failing of Philippine civil society.

Systems for Acting on the Statements and Counter Statements

There must be some societal processes or systems that enable people to pursue calls for action. In some nations, there are political systems that allow individuals, groups, and organizations to make their ideas into laws. People must have the capacity to organize, bond with others, and use SC processes to influence the formation of – or changes to – policy (Sommerfeldt & Yang, 2017). In other nations, the political system may be closed, so those who want to create change may have to work through institutions such as schools, unions, cultural or religious groups. The capacity of a system to process input from citizens is a key part of civil society. Indeed, a system's capacity to manage citizen input influences the type and amount of trust citizens have in that system.

Civil Society and Trust

As explained above, civil society is a relational phenomenon. For any quality relationship to exist, there must be an underlying sense of trust between two actors. Therefore, any discussion of civil society and SC would be incomplete without a thorough examination of trust and its role in building and maintaining relationships. Without trust in others, in the media, and in social institutions, the conditions for an ideal civil society cannot be met. Trust may therefore be the single most important consideration for civil society. The (re)building of trust is thus often the first task of strategic communicators seeking to reconstitute civil society and nations. Indeed, the vast and complicated civil society literature can be roughly described as falling into three more or less distinct groups: (1) relationships among people; (2) relationships among organizations themselves; and (3) relationships among people, organizations, and the state. Trust is at the heart of building and maintaining all of the relationship forms that play a vital role in civil society.

But what is trust, and how can trust be built or maintained in these relationships? In interpersonal relationships, trust is often abstractly described as whether or not a person can be "relied on" (e.g. Rotter, 1980). Trust is also consistently included as a part of organization–public relationships (e.g. Huang, 2001; Ledingham & Bruning, 1998). Hon and Grunig (1999) defined trust as "one party's level of confidence in and willingness to open oneself to the other party" (p. 3). They suggested that integrity, dependability, and competence are the primary dimensions of trust in organization–public relations. A public's trust in an organization is a precondition of a positive, successful, and mutually beneficial relationship, which has made trust a central concern of the relational paradigm of SC research.

When we perceive trust as comprised of concepts like reliability, integrity, dependability, and confidence in others, it is easy to accept Fukuyama's (2001) claim that trust is the basis of social order, and that "communities depend on mutual trust and will not arise spontaneously without it" (p. 70). Some have gone so far as to assert that trust is a precondition of any form of social behavior – as Botan and Taylor (2004) argued, "every social interaction, from crossing a street to using an elevator, purchasing products, or exchanging services, is based on an implicit assumption of trust in others" (p. 687). Their observation suggests that trust involves a certain degree of risk and uncertainty. Risks in a trusting society are deemed more acceptable based on the premise that others – people, organizations, and even governments – will not let us down. Thus, trust is a social norm essential to reciprocity and social support. Consequently, a group that has high levels of trust is able to accomplish much more than a comparable group without such trust.

Two general variations of trust are important to consider when discussing civil society. The first is known as *particularized trust* (Uslaner, 1999). Particularized trust is exhibited in groups, communities, or even societies where trust is abundant among one's in-group (whether that is families, ethnic groups, or other collectives), but hesitantly extended to those outside the in-group. Conversely, ***generalized trust*** is manifested in the ability to build relationships with individuals and groups outside one's in-group (Uslaner, 1999). Many studies have employed the measure of generalized trust in the World Values Survey: "generally speaking, would you say that most people can be trusted?" The higher the percentage who responds "yes," the higher a nation's generalized trust is thought to be (Sommerfeldt & Taylor, 2011). The consequences of generalized trust to a society are numerous: people who trust others more are less likely to lie, less likely to cheat or steal, and more likely to respect the rights of others (Rotter, 1980). Without a generalized trust in others, there are lower levels of civic engagement (Putnam, 2000). Sommerfeldt (2013) therefore argued that public relations should work to encourage a transition from particularized to generalized trust, as a more general trust in others is essential for people to take an active role in their community and establish organizations and networks that are capable of participating in public debates, and thereby a democratic society.

Indeed, societies with poorly functioning social institutions, such as weak government and politicized media, are more likely to have lower levels of generalized trust. Increased generalized social trust in people, government, and public officials is, conversely, linked to participation, civic engagement, and better-functioning democracies. Despite the enhanced role in criticizing governments that comes with increased trust (and thereby civil society), levels of social trust appear to help stabilize governments (Rossteutscher, 2008). The relationship is a reciprocal one: trust in government can help to generate trust in people.

Conversely, lower levels of generalized trust reduce levels of civic participation that might affect democratization. Iglic (2003) has written that a lack of trust in Eastern European societies was a significant obstacle to mass democratic resistance of authoritarian and communist regimes. (Re)establishing generalized trust is therefore of particular importance to civil society initiatives in environments undergoing dramatic social change and in emerging democracies and economies (Rose, 1994). In the transitional democracies and economies of Eastern Europe and the former Soviet Bloc, trust in government, social institutions, and even the media suffered for decades due to the perceived inefficiency and blatant corruption of the socialist economic system (Uslaner & Badescu, 2003). To compensate for lower levels of generalized trust, people in those nations developed strong personal networks of particularized trust (Rose, Mishler, & Haerpfer, 1998). Because of this, several SC studies have suggested that the real work of communication in these transitional states is that of (re)building trust in government, institutions, and the media (e.g. Kent, Taylor, & Turcilo, 2006; Taylor, 2000a, 2000b).

While trust in media may be eroded or lessened in transitional states with a long history of media bribery and no transparency, as noted above, media is nonetheless a crucial civil society partner and a potential vehicle through which public relations can help build generalized trust in society and in government. Media has the capacity to integrate society and increase levels of political knowledge and competence (Sommerfeldt, 2013). However, while media can enlighten and engage publics, it can also induce fear, apathy, isolation, and political ignorance (Putnam, 2000). Indeed, in countries without high levels of generalized social trust people do not accept messages filtered through the media. That said, the ideal role for media in environments characterized by long periods of distrust in government and in others is to help restore the ability of individuals to trust one another, their representative institutions, democratic processes, and government (Rose, 1994). Trust is at the heart of social capital and civil society.

Social Capital and Civil Society

While sporadically mentioned in the preceding sections, no thorough discussion of civil society would be complete without consideration of social capital. Social capital has become a subject of increasing popularity in SC research. The notion of social capital holds great normative promise, but how it can be practically assessed is a matter of some debate. Many have equated social capital with generalized trust – or at least as a precondition for social capital. Fukuyama wrote, “social capital is a capability that arises from the prevalence of trust in a society or in certain parts of it” (Fukuyama, 1995, p. 26). Coleman (1988) saw trust as a form of social capital, resulting from positive relations. Regardless of the specific relationship trust takes with social capital, generalized trust is commonly employed as a component or an indicator of social capital (cf. Fukuyama, 1995).

Others have suggested a communitarian or institutional perspective that equates social capital with the sheer number of voluntary associations, clubs, or civil groups such as NGOs (Grootaert & van Bastelaer, 2002). The institutional view suggests the existence of formal legal, political, and nonprofit organizations in the environment are the main determinants of the ability of social groups to act. Wiktorowicz (2002) described NGOs as the institutional manifestation of civil society due to their efficacy in facilitating “political transformation and the consolidation of democracy” (p. 79). The mere presence of NGOs reflects the levels of social capital in a civil society because they often emerge from informal associations that were organized to respond to collective problems.

However, Sommerfeldt and Taylor (2011) cautioned that the existence of civil society groups aimed at improving social conditions might not be sufficient for social capital to occur. Renshaw (1994) has argued that civil society is, above all else, a relational construct. In her view, civil society is defined by the relationships that exist among the actors that comprise civil society, and only when these actors are joined together can they become a force for development and democratization. In a similar vein, Hadenius and Uggla (1996) understood civil society as groups arranged in networks engaged in cooperative behavior aimed at accomplishing common objectives. As such, relationships among civil society actors provide the social capital for such groups to pursue and enact desired positive outcomes. NGOs must be embedded in cooperative relationship networks with other social actors. Their networks of association and support must be well developed, so that they may accomplish their work with less physical capital. Most forms of work are more easily accomplished with the support of others. Simply put, NGOs should be engaged in networks of cooperation to deal with problems too large or complex for a single organization to accomplish alone (Sommerfeldt, 2013; Taylor & Doerfel, 2003).

By building trust in institutions and governments, bringing together people from diverse backgrounds, and promoting civic engagement and public dialogue, SC can contribute to social capital formation within a community (Sommerfeldt, 2013). Social capital therefore emphasizes the long-term effects of positive community relationships and the role organizations can play in making societies a better place in which to live. Social capital is an outcome of societal effectiveness and it has an iterative role in that social capital begets more social capital.

Toward a Fully Functioning Society

An understanding of the fundamental tenets of civil society can help organizations to participate more ethically in the public sphere, grow social capital, and contribute to their communities. Scholars and practitioners of SC should proceed from the assumption that reality is socially constructed and that individuals, groups, organizations, and institutions cocreate meaning through their actions, statements, and counter-statements (Heath, 2006). In so doing, organizations can help to build not only a civil society, but one that is fully functional.

Civil society is a fundamentally optimistic concept that describes how communication and relationships contribute to a robust and healthy society. A civil society is a place where individuals, groups, and organizations engage in interactions that balance conflict and consensus. The concept of civil society is premised on communication and relationships, as civil society activities of debate, deliberation, advocacy, risk management, and public relations strive for a balance between publics, organizations, institutions, and government interests. It is never completed and it is in everyone's best interest to keep the iterative process of civil society alive through SC.

Heath (2006) conceptualized fully functioning society theory (FFST) to argue that public relations as SC can add value to community if it helps foster a fully functioning society. Heath identified eight premises that articulate a societal role for organizational rhetoric and public relations in making a community a better place to live. The premises can be summarized around management functions, conceptualizations of community as conflicting and conjoined interests and expectations, relationships as symmetry: *communitas* versus corporatas, organizational communication, responsible advocacy, and narrative and other forms of rhetoric leading to enlightened choice (pp. 99–110).

FFST identifies the premises of how rhetoric and SC can help to make society a better place to live. Heath's (2006) image of a fully functioning society makes an implicit claim that the relationships among organizations and groups create a social capital that makes the community stronger and better able to meet the needs of its members. Social capital is an outcome of organizational orientations, organizational capacity to respond to positions advocated by publics, and the collective advocacy (through rhetoric and public relations) of different actors to advance choice to the benefit of the community. Public relations is the enactment of organizational rhetoric and together they help to create organizational and social capital.

The central thesis of FFST is that public relations communication, in the form of SC, has larger roles to play in society than merely media relations. Make no mistake: the media have a role to play in FFST, as Heath (2006) described the media as incubators of *communitas*. *Communitas* is a concept where individuals and organizations recognize they are bound and act for the good of the community. Within the normative theory, Heath posited that the media could highlight the boundedness of a community and scrutinize the behavior of individuals and organizations not acting in favor of larger community.

Scholars furthering FFST have presented an applied description of the media's role. Taylor and Doerfel (2003) and Taylor (2010) found the quality of interpersonal relations, media relations, and interorganizational relations in a civil society network influences the dissemination of information. Sommerfeldt (2013) recognized that gaining media coverage is challenging in the current communication environment and asserted public relations as an "essential tool" (p. 4). For Sommerfeldt, public relations' expertise in publicity tactics can provide a voice to organizations and groups that normally receive infrequent media coverage. Bringing together the rhetorical and media relations aspects of public relations, Taylor (2011) wrote: "The media (print, electronic, digital, and social) extend rhetorical and public relations efforts by holding up the arguments and actions of organization rhetors to public scrutiny" (p. 437). The goal of SC is to build relationships whereby factual information is shared with the public, not propaganda or spin. The media share the information and create a venue for discussion.

FFST has emerged as an organizing framework in the public relations literature because it has provided an organizational and societal-level picture of how public relations can help sustain a society (cf. Taylor, 2011). When organizations work to add certainty, reduce confusion, and wield their power responsibly, SC can make societies better places in which to live. When organizations communicatively engage publics from a relationship-building perspective, wherein the goals of the community are favored over the individual needs of the organizations, SC can make societies better places in which to live. And when organizations work to foster enlightened choice, SC can make societies more fully functional and better places in which to live.

Conclusion

This chapter has explained how SC works in civil society and nation building. The use of communication to enhance societal effectiveness is needed across all nations and communities. The Ebola health crisis showed how different civil society partners – INGOs, NGOs, media, citizens, and institutions – worked together to communicate information that saved lives. The social capital that had been created for social, economic, and political development from 2004 to 2013 was leveraged during the crisis. What we see emerging from the Ebola crisis is what Heath termed a fully functioning society.

While the Ebola outbreak in Liberia was a public health crisis of the highest order, the crisis, no doubt, would have been much worse without the existence of a robust civil society network ready and willing to combat the spread of the disease. The individuals and organizations in the Ebola response forged partnerships, utilized media, and reached out to the population to educate and empower Liberian citizens. This is civil society at its best, making the worst of times a little less horrible.

References

Alexander, J. (1998). *Real civil societies: Dilemmas of institutionalization.* Thousand Oaks, CA: Sage.

Barber, B. R. (2004). *A place for us: How to make society civil and democracy strong.* New York: Macmillan.

Beekman, G., Bulte, E., Peters, B., & Voors, M. (2015). Civil society organizations in Liberia and Sierra Leone during the Ebola epidemic: A cross-section of changes and responses. Wageningen University: Development Economics Group. Retrieved from https://www.partos.nl/documents/CSOs%20in%20Liberia%20and%20Sierra%20Leone%20during%20the%20Ebola%20Epidemic.pdf

Botan, C. H., & Soto, F. (1998). A semiotic approach to the internal functioning of publics: Implications for strategic communication and public relations. *Public Relations Review*, 24, 21–44.

Botan, C. H., & Taylor, M. (2004). Public relations: The state of the field. *Journal of Communication*, 54(4), 645–661.

Botan, C. H., & Taylor, M. (2005). The role of trust in channels of strategic communication for building civil society. *Journal of Communication*, 55(4), 685–702.

Castells, M. (2008). The new public sphere: Global civil society, communication networks, and global governance. *The Annals of the American Academy of Political and Social Science*, 616(1), 78–93.

Coleman, J. S. (1988). Social capital in the creation of human capital. *American Journal of Sociology*, 94, S95–S120.

Doerfel, M. L., & Taylor, M. (2004). Network dynamics of interorganizational cooperation: The Croatian civil society movement. *Communication Monographs*, 71(4), 373–394.

Doerfel, M. L., & Taylor, M. (2017). The story of collective action: The emergence of ideological leaders, collective action network leaders, and cross-sector network partners in civil society. *Journal of Communication*, 67, 921–943.

Fukuyama, F. (1995). *Trust.* London: Penguin.

Fukuyama, F. (2001). Social capital, civil society and development. *Third World Quarterly*, 22(1), 7–20.

Gellner, E. (1994). *Encounters with nationalism.* New York: Blackwell.

Gramsci, A. (1971). *Prison notebooks* H. Henderson (Trans.). London: Zwan.

Grootaert, C., & van Bastelaer, T. (2002). Conclusion: Measuring impact and drawing policy implications. In C. Grootaert & T. van Bastelaer (Eds.), *The role of social capital in development* (pp. 341–350). Cambridge: Cambridge University Press.

Habermas, J. (1981). *The theory of communicative action* T. McCarthy (Trans.). Boston, MA: Beacon Press.

Habermas, J. (1991). *The structural transformation of the public sphere: An inquiry into a category of bourgeois society.* Cambridge, MA: MIT Press.

Hadenius, A., & Uggla, F. (1996). Making civil society work, promoting democratic development: What can states and donors do? *World Development*, 24(10), 1621–1639.

Hauser, G. (1998). Civil society and the public sphere. *Philosophy and Rhetoric*, 31, 19–40.
Heath, R. L. (2006). Onward into more fog: Thoughts on public relations' research directions. *Journal of Public Relations Research*, 18, 93–114.
Hegel, G. (1974). *The philosophy of right* T. M. Knox (Trans.. Oxford: Clarendon Press.
Hon, L. C., & Grunig, J. E. (1999). *Measuring relationships in public relations.* Gainesville, FL: Institute for Public Relations.
Huang, Y. H. (2001). OPRA: A cross-cultural, multiple-item scale for measuring organization–public relationships. *Journal of Public Relations Research*, 13(1), 61–90.
Iglic, H. (2003). Trust networks and democratic transition: Yugoslavia in the mid-1980s. In G. Badescu & E. Uslaner (Eds.), *Social capital and the transition to democracy* (pp. 24–41). London: Routledge.
Kent, M. L., & Taylor, M. (1998). Building dialogic relationships through the World Wide Web. *Public Relations Review*, 24(3), 321–334.
Kent, M. L., Taylor, M., & Turcilo, L. (2006). Marketing and public relations by newly privatized organizations in Eastern Europe. *Public Relations Review*, 32(1), 10–17.
Ledingham, J. A., & Bruning, S. D. (1998). Relationship management in public relations: Dimensions of an organization–public relationship. *Public Relations Review*, 24, 55–65.
Putnam, R. D. (2000). *Bowling alone: The collapse and revival of American community.* New York: Simon & Schuster.
Renshaw, L. (1994). *Strengthening civil society: Issues for a funding agency.* New York: Oxfam America.
Rose, R. (1994). Postcommunism and the problem of trust. *Journal of Democracy*, 5(3), 18–30.
Rose, R., Mishler, W., & Haerpfer, C. (1998). *Democracy and its alternatives: Understanding post-communist societies.* Baltimore, MD: Johns Hopkins University Press.
Rossteutscher, S. (2008). Social capital and civic engagement: A comparative perspective. In D. Castiglione, J. W. Van Deth, & G. Wolleb (Eds.), *The handbook of social capital* (pp. 208–240). Oxford: Oxford University Press.
Rotter, J. B. (1980). Interpersonal trust, trustworthiness, and gullibility. *American Psychologist*, 35(1), 1–7.
Sommerfeldt, E. J. (2013). The civility of social capital: Public relations in the public sphere, civil society, and democracy. *Public Relations Review*, 39(4), 280–289.
Sommerfeldt, E. J., & Taylor, M. (2011). A social capital approach to improving public relations efficacy: Diagnosing internal constraints on external communication. *Public Relations Review*, 37(3), 197–206.
Sommerfeldt, E. J., & Yang, A. (2017). Relationship networks as strategic issues management: An issue-stage framework of social movement organization network strategies. *Public Relations Review*, 43(4), 829–839.
Taylor, M. (2000a). Media relations in Bosnia: A role for public relations in building civil society. *Public Relations Review*, 26, 1–14.
Taylor, M. (2000b). Toward a public relations approach to nation building. *Journal of Public Relations Research*, 12(2), 179–210.
Taylor, M. (2009). Public relations and media relationships in global contexts: Resisting the temptation of protocol journalism. *Public Relations Review*, 35, 23–30.
Taylor, M. (2010). Public relations in the enactment of civil society. In R. L. Heath (Ed.), *Handbook of public relations II* (pp. 5–12). Thousand Oaks, CA: Sage.
Taylor, M. (2011). Building social capital through rhetoric and public relations. *Management Communication Quarterly*, 25, 436–454.
Taylor, M., & Botan, C. H. (1997). Public relations campaigns for national development in the Pacific Rim: The case of public education in Malaysia. *Australian Journal of Communication*, 24, 115–130.
Taylor, M., & Doerfel, M. L. (2003). Building inter-organizational relationships that build nations. *Human Communication Research*, 29(2), 153–181.
Taylor, M., & Doerfel, M. L. (2011). The Croatian civil society movement: Implications, recommendations, and expectations for donors and NGOs. *Voluntas: The International Journal of Voluntary Associations*, 22, 311–334.
Taylor, M., & Kent, M. L. (2006). Nation-building: Public relations theory and practice. In V. Hazelton & C. H. Botan (Eds.), *Public relations theory II* (pp. 341–360). Hillsdale, NJ: Lawrence Erlbaum Associates.

Uslaner, E. M. (1999). Democracy and social capital. In M. Warren (Ed.), *Democracy and trust* (pp. 121–150). Cambridge: Cambridge University Press.

Uslaner, E. M., & Badescu, G. (Eds.). (2003). *Social capital and the transition to democracy*. London: Routledge.

Wiktorowicz, Q. (2002). The political limits to nongovernmental organizations in Jordan. *World Development*, 30(1), 77–93.

PART IV

Crisis and Emergency Strategic Communication

13

Crisis Communication through the Lens of Strategic Communication

W. Timothy Coombs
Texas A&M University

Like many applied fields, organizational crisis communication began life with a tactical focus. The earliest published works devoted to crisis communication were lists of "Dos" and "Don'ts" based upon experiences of professionals with crises. For instance, one early piece of advice was to respond quickly to a crisis (Mitchell, 1986). This tactical orientation is only natural given professionals had to cope with crises long before researchers appeared to help develop guidance for crisis communication. Eventually descriptive theories, such as corporate apologia and image restoration theory, emerged from research to help capture and understand crisis communication. This was followed by prescriptive crisis communication theories, such as situational crisis communication theory (SCCT), that provided more precise guidance based upon cause and effect relationships between crisis factors, crisis communication, and crisis outcomes.

SCCT is an example of how crisis communication can be strategic communication. Strategic communication extends beyond pursuing the objectives of the organization to understanding the concerns and reactions of stakeholders as part of the communication process. While the descriptive theories of crisis communication have a strong organizational focus, it is a misunderstanding that SCCT shares those same traits simply because SCCT draws upon those early writings to develop a list of crisis response strategies. The reality is that SCCT places as much or greater emphasis on stakeholders than on the organization in terms of crisis communication. SCCT defines crises as occurring when stakeholders experience a violation of their expectations and crisis communication can only be effective when stakeholders accept the crisis accounts offered by the organization (Coombs, 2019; Fediuk, Pace, & Botero, 2010). SCCT does view crisis communication as an interaction between the organization and the stakeholder. I will return to this point later in the chapter.

The most significant development affecting crisis communication over the past decade has been the increased use of digital communication by stakeholders. These various digital platforms, with a heavy emphasis on social media, provided new means for stakeholders to express themselves. Moreover, the digital platforms provided many risks and opportunities for crisis communication (Coombs & Holladay, 2016; Liu, Austin, & Jin, 2011). As with the genesis of the field, crisis communication again took a tactical turn with the emergence of digital communication. This turn was due in part to the need for professionals to utilize these digital platforms when engaging in crisis communication and crisis management. Practice often

The Handbook of Strategic Communication, First Edition. Edited by Carl H. Botan.

precedes applied research in problem-solving, resulting in the initial tactical emphasis. Even researchers became seduced by the tactical aspect of digital platforms. But once again, strategy did reassert itself as professionals and researchers began to integrate digital platforms into crisis communication thinking. The focus of this chapter is the movement of crisis communication from tactical to strategic communication. A chronological approach is used to illuminate the development of crisis communication into a form of strategic communication and the initial regressive effects of integrating digital platforms into crisis communication.

The Early Crisis Communication Articles

The term "organizational crisis communication" was used purposefully in the first sentence of this chapter. The term "crisis" is a broad research umbrella that encompasses an array of crisis domains. By crisis domains I mean distinct areas of crisis studies that share some similarities but have critical differences that prevent us directly applying research findings from one domain to another. There are at least four crisis domains: disaster, public health, political, and organizational. This chapter is dedicated to organizational crisis communication. Furthermore, I am focusing on organizational crises that are operational in nature – meaning they disrupt the organizational routine and create victims and potential victims (Coombs, 2019). This is to differentiate it from social media crises and even reputational crises (Sohn & Lariscy, 2014). Social media and reputational crises tend to be the public management of crisis risks (paracrises; Coombs & Holladay, 2012b) rather than traditional crises that are operational.

You can spend time trying to find the earliest mentions of "crisis" in articles. This is largely a waste of time, because crisis can mean so many different things, hence can appear in many publications. But isolated mentions of crisis do not constitute a field. A field emerges when there is a consistent appearance of crisis and crisis communication in print. In the US, the late 1980s is when crisis communication began to consistently appear in print (Coombs, 2014). The early crisis communication articles were in professional rather than research journals. These articles offered advice on crisis communication based upon the authors' own experiences with crises. The end result was crisis communication being largely a tactical practice populated with advice on what to do and what not to do in a crisis.

Initial Practitioner Writings

Consistency began to emerge in the writings, creating a common set of tactical advice that aimed to be quick, consistent, and open. Being quick meant an organization should respond fast to a crisis. But speed is relative. The recommendation of an hour emerged based upon the emergency medicine notion of the golden hour. If an emergency physician can stabilize a patient in the first hour, the chance of survival increases significantly. Bear in mind that the hour response was pure speculation – coming from medicine not crisis experience. Being consistent means the organization should not be changing information or providing contradictory information. The key here is to be confident in information before sharing it with stakeholders. There can be a tension between speed and consistency. Being open means an organization should share crisis information that is relevant to its stakeholders. "Relevant" is another imprecise term, but experts seem to agree that any information which affects the safety and wellbeing of stakeholders should be shared with those stakeholders (Coombs, 2019). Other pieces of advice included never speculate and avoid saying "no comment." If you speculate, you could be wrong, meaning you are either incompetent or were lying. No comment gives the impression the organization has something to hide and is trying to stonewall stakeholders. These last two pieces of advice reflect the emphasis on media training for spokespersons that is pervasive in these early writings.

While most of the professional advice was proven correct by later research, the heart of these writings was informed speculation that is tactical. The advice reflects ways for the organization to enhance its response, with little consideration given to the analysis of situational factors or stakeholder concerns. For instance, much of the attention in media training was on getting out the organization's message rather than answering questions or providing information to meet stakeholder needs. We have tactical advice born of experience but a serious lack of cause and effect evidence to develop a richer evidence-based crisis communication approach that would be driven by strategy rather than emphasize tactics. An evidence-based approach combines the best evidence (preference given to causal evidence) with professional experience to develop a strategic intervention to solve a problem (Latham, 2011). The late 1980s and early 1990s witnessed the emergence of research-based crisis communication publications.

Rhetoric Influences Emerging Crisis Communication Theory

The early crisis communication frameworks had strong roots in rhetoric. Corporate apologia was the first framework to be applied in crisis communication. Dionisopolous and Vibbert (1988) developed corporate apologia by extending the application of the apologia genre of self-defense developed for political communication and individuals to corporate discourse. Hearit (1994, 2006) would go on to refine and extend corporate apologia for application to organizational crises. Hearit (1994) saw crises as threats to social legitimacy and corporate apologia as a means of rebuilding social legitimacy. Hearit's work integrated the concept of dissociation into corporate apologia, creating new response options. A dissociation breaks a concepts into two parts. Hearit developed three dissociations based upon the work of Olbrects-Tyteca: (1) opinion/knowledge, people think something bad has happened but facts prove otherwise; (2) individual/group, a few employees – not the organization as a whole – is responsible for the crisis; and (3) act/essence, the organization did something wrong but the action is not representative of the organization (Hearit, 1994).

Benoit (1995) believed apologia was too limiting and expanded his review of rhetoric, adding account acceptance to create a more comprehensive list of what he termed image repair strategies (IRT). Image repair is a broad theory that can be used anytime an image (reputation) is threatened. IRT holds that communication is goal-oriented and one of those goals is protecting reputations. IRT has five primary strategies and a number of substrategies (Benoit, 1995). Table 13.1 is a summary of the IRT as developed by Benoit. IRT has been applied not only to organizations, but to politicians and celebrities (Benoit, 1997; Benoit & Brinson, 1999).

The point here is not to provide detailed discussions of these early applications of theory to crisis communication, but to provide a flavor for the nature of these theories and relate that to strategic communication. These two early theories are heavily rhetorical and descriptive, rather than prescriptive, and utilize qualitative research methods. The theories are frameworks that can be applied to crisis cases to determine what crisis responses were utilized. The researchers then examine other evidence to determine the success or failure of the crisis communication efforts. The crisis response strategies indicate the general objectives pursued by the crisis managers. There is more concern about the sender and less concern about the concerns and needs of stakeholders. For instance, both approaches often argue that crisis managers can try to impose the organization's definition of the crisis on the situation rather than accepting how stakeholders define the crisis. However, there is some concern with the audience in the theories, but that concern is overshadowed by the perceived sender orientation. While there is a focus on strategies used in crisis communication, these two early theories do not capture how this volume conceptualizes strategic communication.

Table 13.1 Image restoration strategies.

Denial
Simple denial: managers argue the organization is not involved with the crisis
Shift the blame: managers claim another actor is responsible for the crisis
Evading responsibility
Provocation: managers argue they are reacting to the actions of other actors
Defeasibility: managers argue they lacked information or control over events
Accidental: managers argue there are times when bad things happen
Good intention: managers argue they meant well but things turned out badly
Reduce offensiveness
Bolstering: managers praise those who have helped during the crisis and/or remind stakeholders of past good works
Minimizing offensiveness of the act: managers argue the situation is not as bad as it seems
Differentiation: managers compare their crisis to other, more serious, crises
Transcendence: managers attempt to place the crisis in a new and more favorable context
Attack the accuser: managers attack those actors claiming the crisis exists
Compensation: managers offer goods, service, or money to those harmed by the crisis
Corrective action: managers take steps to prevent a repeat of the crisis and/or take action to repair the damage done by the crisis
Mortification: managers accept responsibility for the crisis and express remorse for it

Crisis Communication Theory and Cognition

SCCT was developed contemporaneously with IRT in the mid-1990s. Though using strategies articulated in IRT, SCCT is a cognitive-based theory drawing heavily from Wiener's (1986) treatment of attribution theory. Moreover, SCCT is a prescriptive theory that makes recommendations about the crisis response strategies that should be used based upon an assessment of situational factors in the crisis. The central variable in SCCT is crisis responsibility, or how much attribution for the crisis stakeholders attribute to the organization. SCCT holds that the stakeholders drive the interpretation of the crisis.

Thus far, SCCT has established crisis type, crisis history, and prior reputation as factors that affect crisis attributions stakeholders attribute to an organization in crisis. SCCT groups crises into three types, based upon attributions of crisis responsibility: (1) victim, minimal attributions of crisis responsibility; (2) accidental, weak attributions of crisis responsibility; and (3) preventable, strong attributions of crisis responsibility (Coombs & Holladay, 1996). Past crises (crisis history) and a negative prior reputation will increase attributions of crisis responsibility (Coombs, 2004; Coombs & Holladay, 2006; Eaddy & Jin, 2018). SCCT prescriptions posit that organizations should use more accommodative strategies as crisis responsibility increases. Accommodative strategies prioritize the concerns of the victims or potential victims of a crisis and include apology and compensation. For instance, denial and scapegoating are defensive, apology and compensation are accommodative, while excuse and justification fall between the two endpoints (Coombs, 2007).

SCCT and the Ethical Base Response

What is often overlooked in SCCT is the ethical base response, the basic message an organization should use first when a crisis creates victims or potential victims. Crisis responses can be broadly grouped into instructing information, adjusting information, and reputation management (Sturges, 1994). Instructing information seeks to protect people physically from a crisis. Examples of instructing information include orders to evacuate and product recall notifications. Adjusting information seeks to help people cope psychologically with a crisis. Examples of adjusting information include expressions of regret or sympathy and corrective action to prevent a repeat of the crisis. The ethical base response is composed of both instructing and adjusting information. Unless a crisis is perceived as creating strong attributions of crisis responsibility, the ethical base response is an optimal strategy. An optimal strategy is one that addresses stakeholder concerns and protects organizational assets. When attributions or crisis responsibility are high, SCCT recommends adding compensation and/or apology to the ethical base response. SCCT treats bolstering as a secondary strategy and can be used to support any crisis response (Coombs, 2007; Park, 2017). Table 13.2 is the short version of the prescriptions SCCT offers for crisis communication.

SCCT and Account Acceptance

Another overlooked factor in SCCT is the criticality of account acceptance. Account acceptance is the degree to which people accept the crisis response. The ethical base response, accommodative strategies, and bolstering all work by introducing positive information about the organization in crisis that should help to offset the negative information generated by the crisis. The ethical base response is contrary to the views of some writers who characterize crisis communication as efforts to control perceptions of crisis responsibility or to avoid responsibility. If stakeholders do not accept the crisis response (account acceptance), we should not expect the crisis response to have the desired effect of protecting organizational assets – such as organizational reputation, purchase intention, and negative word-of-mouth (Fediuk et al., 2010). Again, the stakeholders are an important consideration when considering the effects of crisis communication. Any experiment that seeks to study the effects of crisis response strategies should assess account acceptance. If account acceptance is low, the crisis response is unlikely to produce the anticipated and desired effect (Fediuk et al., 2010). Crisis managers must be aware of and respect the potential of stakeholders to reject their crisis response strategies.

Table 13.2 Prescriptive recommendations from SCCT.

1. Any time a crisis creates victims or potential victims, the first response should be the ethical base response (instructing and adjusting information).
2. When managing a preventable crisis, managers should add an apology and/or compensation to the ethical base response.
3. When an accidental crisis involves either a history of crises or a negative prior reputation, managers should add an apology and/or compensation to the ethical base response.
4. Bolstering is a supplemental strategy that can be added to any crisis response.

In addition to the nature of the crisis response strategy, the timing of the crisis communication is important. Drawing from law, crisis communication researchers have identified the concept of stealing thunder (Arpan & Pompper, 2003). Stealing thunder occurs when an organization is the first source to disclose the existence of a crisis. Thunder is not stolen when the news media or some other source is the first to inform stakeholders about a crisis (Claeys, 2017; Claeys & Cauberghe, 2010). A hypothetical example is useful to illustrate stealing thunder. Say an organization has just finished investigating charges that top managers had been discriminatory in advancement decisions. The investigation finds that indeed there had been such discrimination. If the organization is the first source to announce the problem, that would be stealing thunder. If a news report gets information about the findings and reports those findings before any statement by the organization, thunder has not been stolen. Stealing thunder is recommended because the data from various studies consistently show an organization suffers less reputational damage when it steals thunder versus when the organization does not steal thunder. More precisely, in the exact same crisis, there is less damage when the organization is the first to report the crisis than when another source is the first to disclose the crisis (Claeys, 2017). Stealing thunder does offer support for the early practitioner advice to respond quickly to a crisis, and there are theoretical reasons for how and why stealing thunder affects stakeholders' perceptions about the organization in crisis.

Private-Facing Aspects Crisis Communication

These early theories applied to crisis communication all focus on the crisis response, which is the public-facing aspect of crisis communication. For a more complete view of crisis communication, we need to consider the private-facing aspects that involve preparation and monitoring. Preparation are the actions taken before a crisis occurs. Important communication tasks are pre-drafting messages and scanning. Organizations can anticipate the most likely crises that will occur. To enhance the speed of the response, crisis teams pre-draft messages before those crises. The pre-drafted messages are holding statements that anticipate the informational concerns of stakeholders in a particular crisis. The crisis team drafts a message that will have blanks for specific information about a crisis. For instance, if the release of a toxic chemical is a possible crisis, the pre-drafted messages leave blanks for the time and location of the release, areas affected by the release, and the exact chemical or chemicals released. Standard information would include what to do if exposed to the chemical and links to additional resources. The pre-drafted messages will identify specific target stakeholders to be reached, along with the identification of channels through which to disseminate the message. Scanning is searching the environment for crisis warning signs – indicators that specific crisis risks seem to be manifesting. The crisis team is also looking for signals that indicate stakeholders are beginning to define a situation as a crisis.

Monitoring occurs after a crisis emerges and involves tracking how people are reacting to the crisis and to the organization's crisis communication efforts. People's reactions to a crisis indicate how people are framing the crisis – what type of crisis stakeholders believe the organization is managing. One reason crisis communication fails is because managers are using a crisis frame that is inconsistent with the stakeholder crisis frame – the crisis team is managing the wrong crisis type. Monitoring reactions to the crisis response strategies will indicate if stakeholders are accepting or rejecting the crisis response. A negative stakeholder reaction would indicate a need to revise the crisis response. Consider how Amazon's initial response to its removing books from Kindles was received negatively. Amazon used the feedback to create a new response that stakeholders received more positively (Coombs & Holladay, 2012a).

It is helpful here to restate I am examining research that focuses on organizational crises (not disasters, political, or public health crises) and operational crises rather than paracrises (Coombs & Holladay, 2012b). These distinctions are important because there are differences in guidance between these various crisis domains. The crisis communication writings, both academic and professional, have coalesced around a set of guidance for crisis communicators. That guidance recommends responses that demonstrate concern for victims, value being the first to disclose the existence of a crisis when possible, a need to scan for risk, the value of pre-drafting messages, and a need to monitor stakeholder reactions to crisis responses. Together, this guidance reflects how crisis communication has become strategic and evolved beyond its tactical roots, epitomized by a concern about response speed.

Crisis Communication in the Digital Age

As access to and usage of digital communication has increased, new demands have been placed upon crisis communication. Digital naturals, those who are comfortable using various digital platforms (Young & Åkerström, 2016), now populate the stakeholder groups organizations must face during a crisis (Coombs & Holladay, 2016). Oddly, the emergence of digital communication, often captured under the heading of social media, caused a regression in the crisis communication research relative to strategic communication. I would argue that crisis communication regressed because it became more concerned with tactics (i.e. digital communication platforms and speed), forcing strategy to a background concern. This regression might have been natural given that once more the practice was encountering problems with crisis communication that researchers had yet to explain. Regardless of the reason, there was some regression, moving crisis communication away from being strategic communication. This section will discuss the regression, note some important exceptions to the regression, and identify the return to a more strategic focus in crisis communication writings that reflect the earlier establishment of crisis communication as a form of strategic communication.

The regression is illustrated with a focus on channels and an obsession with response speed – two tactical concerns. A clear manifestation of this phenomenon was coining the phrase "social media crisis." From the start, the term social media crisis was poorly defined, simply being viewed as a negative event that transpired or was amplified in social media (Brynley-Jones, .n.d). Too many situations were being labeled as "crises" with this lens. Crises are reserved for important considerations that require organizational focus and resources (Billings, Milburn, & Schaalman, 1980). For instance, incidents are easy to handle by a few people in the organization, while a crisis requires assembling the crisis team to address the concern. A careful look at what was being identified as social media crises showed that these were actually customer relations problems rather than crises. Even some of the early proponents of the term social media crisis, such as crisis consultant and writer Melissa Agnes, later moved away from the term because it was problematic. The focus on social media crises created confusion, diluted the crisis communication research by including non-crisis events, and placed the focus on the channel – often with little regard for strategy.

Initial Emphasis on Speed

A strong theme that emerges from the professional writings about digital communication and crisis communication is speed. Here are some sample statements about the growing importance of speed in crisis communication driven by digital communication:

> The rapid speed of information dissemination has led to a reduced window of response time for organizations. The significance of response time is stressed in research findings and testimonials of professionals highlighting that a failure to provide a quick response leaves organizations susceptible to attack. (Kara, 2019, p. 2)

> In this age of connectivity and the always-on digital world, reputation has never been more vulnerable. In a matter of 15 minutes or fewer, a company can go from riding high to an all-time low. (Elliott, 2018, p. 1)

> Activation speed is one of the vital components of crisis management planning. And with every passing year, quick activation becomes even more important. (Britton, 2017, p. 2)

> The proliferation of digital technology has quickened the pace of emerging crises. When a crisis breaks, it unfolds incredibly fast. (Britton, 2017, p. 3)

Some professionals even claimed digital channels made everything we know about crisis communication obsolete, but those were mostly claims made by consultants seeking to solicit clients. Woods (2014) sums up the speed point by noting the pace of crisis communication has been sped up by social media. What we find is a return to the tactical advice of speed found in the very early professional writings about crisis communication. This is one indication of how digital communication created a regression in crisis communication away from strategic communication.

Obsession with Channels: From Background to Foreground

The obsession with channels refers to the way researchers and professionals wanted to tie crisis communication to social media. In the crisis communication research, the channel (more precisely platform) became a focal point with limited effort to connect it with strategy. The channel obsession is epitomized by the crisis research of Shultz and coworkers (Schultz, Utz, & Göritz, 2011; Utz, Schultz, & Glocka, 2013). The research was driven by the belief that there could be a channel effect for how people react to crisis communication. Granted, there is a background sense of strategy, but the emphasis is clearly on the tactical aspect of channel. There is a strong bond between tactics and strategy, but researchers and professionals can vary in terms of which one is emphasized. The focus on channel is clear in how the data from the experiments are interpreted. In the two studies, there is no attempt to control for the source of the message, just the channel. The source is important because of stealing thunder. Each of the two articles generated by this research argued the effects found in the study were due to a channel effect (Schultz, Utz, & Göritz, 2011; Utz, Schultz, & Glocka, 2013).

When a message comes from the social media feed of the organization in crisis, the effect could be source (stealing thunder) and not channel. By not controlling for source, a plausible alternative hypothesis that is given scant attention in these articles is the effects that were found were not created by the channel but by the source. Research conducted later by other researchers did control for source. When source was controlled, the channel effect disappeared. The researchers concluded that at least in the types of crises tested in their experiment, stealing thunder was a more viable explanation for the differences than channel effect (Coombs, Holladay, & Claeys, 2016). The problem of interpreting the results as channel (tactical) is not a minor point because later crisis researchers followed this channel effect – often assuming it is there because of this earlier research – and sought to use a questionable channel effect as a rationale for their studies. Again, these later studies are more tactical because the focus is on channel coupled with some thought to its effect on stakeholders, while lacking the more encompassing view of crisis communication as strategic communication (e.g. Roshan, Warren, & Carr, 2016).

Another illustration of the obsession with channels would be literature reviews that claim to demonstrate how social media has changed crisis communication. Cheng has produced two separate reviews that seek to show the intersection of crisis communication and social media and how social media has reshaped crisis communication (Cheng, 2018; Cheng & Cameron, 2017). Both reviews produce questionable results due to the obsession (foregrounding) of channel. The focus on digital channels in the selection of the literature caused the researchers to overlook the critical role of the crisis domain and crisis types. First, disaster and public health crises are mixed with organizational crises. These crisis domains have very important differences, the key difference being that people are much more motivated to find information during disasters and public health crises than your typical organizational crisis. The disaster research especially has been highly attuned to how people use digital channels during disaster events (e.g. Guan & Chen, 2014). But this is a different dynamic from organizational crises. Second, crisis types have proven to have a significant effect on crisis response selection and effectiveness (Coombs, 2007; Coombs & Tachkova, 2019).

By foregrounding the channels, these reviews miss the subtle but important influence of crisis domain and crisis types. The end result is the reader should question the conclusions about how social media has changed crisis communication, especially organizational crisis communication. Being precise about the domain of a review is a critical element in scoping studies, reviews that seek to map a domain, and generate insights and gaps from the review (Arksey & O'Malley, 2005). By emphasizing channel over crisis domain, the studies become flawed because it is unclear which crisis domain has been affected by social media and how precisely social media has affected that domain. It is a mistake to assume any of the conclusions from these two scoping efforts can be applied to organizational crisis communication. The point is that the emphasis on channel (primarily a tactical concern in crisis communication at this point) has caused a regression in yields of scoping studies related to crisis communication because the critical factor of crisis domain (a strategic concern because different crisis domains create unique communicative dynamics with stakeholders) and crisis types gets ignored. There can still be value in the data being generated, but at the very least the studies must be separated by crisis domain and reassessed.

Retaining a Strategic Focus for Crisis Communication in the Digital World

Not all crisis communication research fell into the channel of obsession and regressed toward tactical concerns. There are a number of researchers who integrated digital communication into crisis communication, thinking often with a focus on organizational crisis communication. This section features one study as a prototype for retaining a strategic focus by backgrounding channel and another that pushed forward theorizing about how digital communication locates within crisis communication.

Van Zoonen and van der Meer (2015) is the prototypical study for backgrounding digital communication in organizational crisis communication research. They conducted an experiment where Twitter was the background by being the channel used to deliver a crisis message. The point was not to determine a channel effect, but to explore crisis communication that transpires within a digital platform. The focal point of the research was on the strategic connection between the crisis response strategy and the source of the organizational response. The source was the key point and involved the source being either the organization in crisis or an employee of the organization. The experiment examined the effect of the source of the effects on various crisis response strategies. The outcomes included evaluations of source credibility, content credibility, and organization reputation (three important assessments stakeholders make related to crisis communication). The study found employees created more favorable post-crisis reputations due to source and content credibility. The study adds strategic value to crisis communication by articulating the effects of source and perceptions of credibility on how stakeholders react to crisis response strategies (van Zoonen & van der Meer, 2015).

The notable example of crisis communication theory building using digital channels is the social-mediated crisis communication model (SMCC) (e.g. Austin, Liu, & Jin, 2012). SMCC seeks to integrate digital channels into crisis communication thinking. The digital channel becomes one variable among many in efforts to enhance our understanding of crisis communication as strategic communication. The initial SMCC research centered on information seeking by stakeholders during a crisis and how people use social media (crisis information and sources) during a crisis. SMCC also created an agenda for future research, integrating what the initial research on information seeking discovered with other crisis communication factors including crisis response strategies, organizational infrastructure, and crisis type (Austin, Liu, & Jin, 2012). SMCC is a balanced approach to crisis communication that seeks to integrate social media into crisis communication and not simply obsess about channel. SMCC reflects the developed view of strategic communication presented in this book. You can refer to Chapter 5 for more information about SMCC.

Return to Guidance

More recently, both academic and professional writings on guidance related to crisis communication and digital channels reflect the earlier guidance generated from crisis communication research that appeared at the end of the second section of this chapter. We find an emphasis on concern for victims (Eriksson, 2018; Segal, 2018), the value of stealing thunder (Eriksson, 2018; Segal, 2018), the importance of scanning for risks (Eriksson, 2018; Segal, 2018), the importance of pre-drafted messages (Segal, 2018), and the need to monitor stakeholder reactions to crisis responses (Eriksson, 2018; Segal, 2018). New recommendations related to digital communication and crisis communication include the need for social media policies and making social media part of the mix of channels used to communicate the crisis response (Coombs, 2019; Eriksson, 2018). The guidance reflects the various ways digital communication has affected crisis communication. Once more we see that crisis communication extends beyond just the crisis response to a richer understanding of the broader crisis communication context, reflecting how crisis communication is a form of strategic communication.

Conclusion

Crisis communication as a field of practice and study first emerged with a strong tactical focus involving quick responses and advice on how to avoid common communicative mistakes – such as never speculate. Over time, crisis communication developed a more strategic focus. Researchers and professionals began to think of crisis communication as a way to achieve specific outcomes, including protecting stakeholder wellbeing, preserving reputational assets, and bolstering purchase intentions. However, the focus was not solely sender-oriented, as many critics would imply. Much of crisis communication theory, such as SCCT and SSMC, is deeply rooted in an understanding of stakeholders. Stakeholders help to establish when an organization is in crisis and determine the effectiveness or ineffectiveness of crisis response strategies. Crisis response strategies only produce the desired outcomes if stakeholders accept the account being offered by the organization. Crisis communication is treated as a cocreation process.

Reputation, a key outcome in crisis communication, is a stakeholder-driven concept. Reputations reside within and are assessed by stakeholders. Moreover, the effectiveness of any crisis response has to start with the organization addressing the physical and psychological needs of the crisis victims (Coombs, 2007). Theories, such as SCCT, depend on crisis communicators taking the perspective of stakeholders when assessing the nature of the situation, how to respond to the crisis, and assessing the effects of the crisis response efforts. Crisis communication only works when crisis communicators listen to stakeholders and anticipate their concerns.

Initially, crisis communication's movement toward becoming more fully a type of strategic communication experienced a backslide with the emergence of digital communication and digital naturals. Both professionals and many researchers become obsessed with "the channel" and the digital world's demand for speed. The result was a limited return to the tactical focus of the early crisis communication research. Luckily not all crisis communication researchers were seduced by channels. Researchers began to understand that digital channels had to be integrated with existing crisis knowledge to generate new strategic insights. Digital channels become **one of** – rather than **the** – variables in crisis communication. The original core guidance that was emerging pre-digital channels was updated and revised to include the new digital platforms. The crisis communication guidance rests heavily upon understanding stakeholders during a crisis and communicating in a way that recognizes and addresses their concerns.

Crisis communication research and practice is organizational-centric because it was created to help people in organizations to manage crises. This is natural because when an organization is in crisis, stakeholders expect the organization to manage that crisis situation. Crisis communication is constructed from the view that organizations manage crises. This does not deny there can be multiple voices that try to influence the crisis situation, as articulated by the rhetorical arena theory (Frandsen & Johansen, 2017). Rather, crisis communication theory recognizes managers of an organization have a responsibility to manage the crises associated with their organizations. This does not mean that crisis communication serves only – or even primarily – the interests of the organization. A crisis response that fails to consider how stakeholders view the crisis, how they are reacting to crisis messaging, and/or fails to recognize and to address the needs of victims (stakeholders) is likely to fail. Most organizational crisis communication theory recognizes effective crisis communication, efforts that do protect stakeholders and organizational assets, are a result of making stakeholder needs the top priority in the crisis, and making sure the crisis communication efforts are perceived as meeting those needs. In other words, most crisis communication theory is now aligning itself with strategic communication.

References

Arksey, H., & O'Malley, L. (2005). Scoping studies: Towards a methodological framework. *International Journal of Social Research Methodology*, 8(1), 19–32.

Arpan, L. M., & Pompper, D. (2003). Stormy weather: Testing "stealing thunder" as a crisis communication strategy to improve communication flow between organizations and journalists. *Public Relations Review*, 29, 291–308.

Austin, L., Liu, B. F., & Jin, Y. (2012). How audiences seek out crisis information: Exploring the social-mediated crisis communication model. *Journal of Applied Communication Research*, 40(2), 188–207.

Benoit, W. L. (1995). *Accounts, excuses, and apologies: A theory of image restoration*. Albany, NY: State University of New York Press.
Benoit, W. L. (1997). Hugh Grant's image restoration discourse: An actor apologizes. *Communication Quarterly*, 45(3), 251–267.
Benoit, W. L., & Brinson, S. L. (1999). Queen Elizabeth's image repair discourse: Insensitive royal or compassionate queen? *Public Relations Review*, 25(2), 145–156.
Billings, R. S., Milburn, T. W., & Schaalman, M. L. (1980). A model of crisis perception: A theoretical and empirical analysis. *Administrative Science Quarterly*, 25(2), 300–316.
Britton, C. (2017). The importance of activation speed in crisis management planning. Retrieved from www.rockdovesolutions.com/blog/the-importance-of-activation-speed-in-crisis-management-planning
Brynley-Jones, L. (n.d.). 6 examples of social media crises: What can we learn? Retrieved from https://oursocialtimes.com/6-examples-of-social-media-crises-what-can-we-learn
Cheng, Y. (2018). How social media is changing crisis communication strategies: Evidence from the updated literature. *Journal of Contingencies and Crisis Management*, 26(1), 58–68.
Cheng, Y., & Cameron, G. (2017). The status of social mediated crisis communication (SMCC) research: An analysis of published articles in 2002–2014. In L. Austin & Y. Jin (Eds.), *Social media and crisis communication* (pp. 9–20). New York: Routledge.
Claeys, A. S. (2017). Better safe than sorry: Why organizations in crisis should never hesitate to steal thunder. *Business Horizons*, 60(3), 305–311.
Claeys, A. S., & Cauberghe, V. (2010). Crisis response and crisis timing strategies: Two sides of the same coin. *Public Relations Review*, 38, 83–88.
Coombs, W. T. (2004). Impact of past crises on current crisis communications: Insights from situational crisis communication theory. *Journal of Business Communication*, 41, 265–289.
Coombs, W. T. (2007). Protecting organization reputations during a crisis: The development and application of a situational crisis communication theory. *Corporate Reputation Review*, 10(3), 163–176. doi: 10.1057/palgrave.crr.1550049.
Coombs, W. T. (2014). Editor's introduction: Crisis communication – a field emerges. In W. T. Coombs (Ed.), *Crisis communication* (pp. xxv–xivi). Thousand Oaks, CA: Sage.
Coombs, W. T. (2019). *Ongoing crisis communication: Planning, managing, and responding* (5th edn). Thousand Oaks, CA: Sage.
Coombs, W. T., & Holladay, S. J. (1996). Communication and attributions in a crisis: An experimental study of crisis communication. *Journal of Public Relations Research*, 8, 279–295.
Coombs, W. T., & Holladay, S. J. (2006). Halo or reputational capital: Reputation and crisis management. *Journal of Communication Management*, 10, 123–137.
Coombs, W. T., & Holladay, S. J. (2012a). Amazon.com's Orwellian nightmare: Exploring apology in an online environment. *Journal of Communication Management*, 16, 280–295.
Coombs, W. T., & Holladay, J. S. (2012b). The paracrisis: The challenges created by publicly managing crisis prevention. *Public Relations Review*, 38(3), 408–415.
Coombs, W. T., & Holladay, S. J. (2016). Digital naturals and crisis communication: Significant shifts in focus. In W. T. Coombs, J. Falkheimer, M. Heide, & P. Young (Eds.), *Strategic communication, social media and democracy: The challenge of the digital naturals* (pp. 54–62). New York: Routledge.
Coombs, W. T., & Tachkova, E. R. (2019). Scansis as a unique crisis type: Theoretical and practical implications. *Journal of Communication Management*, 23(1), 72-88. doi: 10.1108/JCOM-08-2018-0078
Coombs, W. T., Holladay, S. J., & Claeys, A. S. (2016). Debunking the myth of denial's effectiveness in crisis communication: Context matters. *Journal of Communication Management*, 20(4), 381–395.
Dionisopolous, G. N., & Vibbert, S. L. (1988). CBS vs. Mobil Oil: Charges of creative bookkeeping. In H. R. Ryan (Ed.), *Oratorical encounters: Selected studies and sources of 20th century political accusation and apologies* (pp. 214–252). Westport, CT: Greenwood.
Eaddy, L. L., & Jin, Y. (2018). Crisis history tellers matter: The effects of crisis history and crisis information source on publics' cognitive and affective responses to organizational crisis. *Corporate Communications: An International Journal*, 23(2), 226–241.
Elliott, K. (2018). The speed of crisis in the digital age: Creating a modern crisis-preparedness plan. Retrieved from www.prnewsonline.com/speed-of-crisis-in-digital-age

Eriksson, M. (2018). Lessons for crisis communication on social media: A systematic review of what research tells the practice. *International Journal of Strategic Communication*, 12(5), 526–551.

Fediuk, T., Pace, K. M., & Botero, I. C. (2010). Crisis-response effectiveness: Methodological considerations for advancement in empirical investigation into response impact. In W. T. Coombs & S. J. Holladay (Eds.), *Handbook of crisis communication* (pp. 221–242). Malden, MA: Wiley-Blackwell.

Frandsen, F., & Johansen, W. (2017). *Organizational crisis communication*. Los Angeles, CA: Sage.

Guan, X., & Chen, C. (2014). Using social media data to understand and assess disasters. *Natural Hazards*, 74(2), 837–850.

Hearit, K. M. (1994). Apologies and public relations crises at Chrysler, Toshiba, and Volvo. *Public Relations Review*, 20, 113–125.

Hearit, K. M. (2006). *Crisis management by apology: Corporate response to allegations of wrongdoing*. Mahwah, NJ: Lawrence Erlbaum.

Kara, A. S. (2019). *Crisis communication in the digital age: Manage of rampage*. Newcastle-upon-Tyne: Cambridge Scholars Publishing.

Latham, G. P. (2011). *Becoming the evidence-based manager: Making the science of management work for you*. Boston, MA: Davis-Black.

Liu, B. F., Austin, L., & Jin, Y. (2011). How publics respond to crisis communication strategies: The interplay of information form and source. *Public Relations Review*, 37(4), 345–353.

Mitchell, T. H. (1986). Coping with a corporate crisis. *Canadian Business Review*, 13, 17–20.

Park, H. (2017). Exploring effective crisis response strategies. *Public Relations Review*, 43(1), 190–192.

Roshan, M., Warren, M., & Carr, R. (2016). Understanding the use of social media by organisations for crisis communication. *Computers in Human Behavior*, 63, 350–361.

Schultz, F., Utz, S., & Göritz, A. (2011). Is the medium the message? Perceptions of and reactions to crisis communication via twitter, blogs and traditional media. *Public Relations Review*, 37(1), 20–27.

Segal, S. (2018). Social media crisis management: 5 principles you need to apply. Retrieved from www.oktopost.com/blog/social-media-crisis-management

Sohn, Y. J., & Lariscy, R. W. (2014). Understanding reputational crisis: Definition, properties, and consequences. *Journal of Public Relations Research*, 26(1), 23–43.

Sturges, D. L. (1994). Communicating through crisis: A strategy for organizational survival. *Management Communication Quarterly*, 7, 297–316.

Utz, S., Schultz, F., & Glocka, S. (2013). Crisis communication online: How medium, crisis type and emotions affected public reactions in the Fukushima Daiichi nuclear disaster. *Public Relations Review*, 39(1), 40–46.

van Zoonen, W., & van der Meer, T. (2015). The importance of source and credibility perception in times of crisis: Crisis communication in a socially mediated era. *Journal of Public Relations Research*, 27(5), 371–388.

Weiner, B. (1986). *An attributional theory of motivation and emotion*. New York: Springer Verlag.

Woods, M. K. (2014). Breaking news at the speed of social media. Retrieved from http://platformmagazine.org/2014/11/07/breaking-news-at-the-speed-of-social-media

Young, P., & Åkerström, M. (2016). Meet the digital naturals. In W. T. Coombs, J. Falkheimer, M. Heide, & P. Young (Eds.), *Strategic communication, social media and democracy: The challenge of the digital naturals* (pp. 1–10). New York: Routledge.

14

Emergency Preparation and Response for Human-Generated Disasters

Emily Helsel, Timothy L. Sellnow, and Deanna D. Sellnow
University of Central Florida

Viewing biosecurity measures in the midst of an animal disease outbreak offers several insights into strategic communication (SC). First, biosecurity requires a collaborative effort from all members within an industry. The protective actions of biosecurity are only as strong as its weakest link. If some producers choose not to follow biosecurity measures, they will likely increase both their risk of contracting the disease and the risk of their neighbors as well. Similarly, a stakeholder in the industry – such as a feed distributer who delivers products from farm to farm – can intensify the spread of the disease if strict biosecurity practices are not followed. Managing crises during animal disease outbreaks therefore requires compelling SC to build commitment and collaboration among all relevant publics. This analysis adds to our understanding of SC during such periods of high consequence.

Emergency Preparation and Response for Human-Generated Disasters

In their natural form, animal diseases typically have limited impact on humans. If, however, the animal disease thrives in agricultural animals, the impact on the animals and the potential for spread to humans is greatly intensified. For purposes of efficiency, farms often group large numbers of animals in close proximity. Consequently, a disease can spread rapidly once it is introduced to a herd or flock. Biosecurity is the agriculture industry's strategic process to prevent the spread of harmful diseases. From a biosecurity perspective, however, many aspects of animal disease outbreaks are human-driven (National Pork Board, 2018). In other words, diseases spread slowly if viral infections are limited to animals spreading disease in the wild. Human interaction with animals on farms, particularly involving those who visit multiple farms or interact socially with other farmers, can increase the speed with which many animal diseases spread. The bad news is that many viruses can live for days on the clothing of individuals, on the tires of vehicles, or in the trailers of those who haul animals, thereby spreading the disease miles away from the original source in hours or days. The good news is that, through SC, biosecurity warnings and directives can alter human actions in a manner that allows them to stop the spread of disastrous diseases. This chapter views Indiana's response to the recent HPAI crisis as a form of SC. The objective of this communication was to help producers take

The Handbook of Strategic Communication, First Edition. Edited by Carl H. Botan.

appropriate biosecurity actions to protect their livelihood. These actions are focused largely on the human-driven aspects of the outbreak.

HPAI, also known informally as bird flu, poses a major risk to the poultry industry worldwide (Highly Pathogen Avian Influenza, 2017). The Centers for Disease and Control and Prevention (CDC) explain that this virus can infect a variety of birds, including turkeys, ducks, geese, guinea fowl, and others. Most troubling for the poultry industry is the fact that the disease is extremely contagious within domesticated flocks and, without effective biosecurity measures, HPAI spreads easily from birds in the wild to captive birds (Information on Avian Influenza, 2017). HPAI infection spreads through saliva, nasal secretion, and the feces of infected birds. A major issue for poultry farms is that, at most poultry production facilities, birds are contained in close quarters, giving the disease a higher potential to spread rapidly. The disease also has an extremely high mortality rate (Highly Pathogen Avian Influenza, 2017).

On rare occasions, HPAI can affect humans as well. The virus has mutated into three strands that have the ability to infect humans (Information on Avian Influenza, 2017). The severity in these human cases has ranged from mild to fatal. Human infection is uncommon, but has the capability to occur when people have close and prolonged contact with infected birds or the feces of infected birds. Unlike COVID-19, no cases of human-to-human transmission have been reported to date, which would ultimately also cause a global pandemic (Yang et al., 2007). At this time, biosecurity is the best known means for preventing and containing an outbreak of HPAI.

The United States has struggled with HPAI outbreaks recently. After devastating outbreaks of HPAI in Iowa, where 32 million birds were lost, and Minnesota, where 9 million birds died or were euthanized from 2014 to 2015 (Johnson, Seeger, & Marsh, 2016), the destructive disease resurfaced in early 2016 in Dubois County, Indiana (2016 HPAI Information, 2016). Though HPAI was not new to the United States (there had been previous outbreaks in 1924, 1983, and 2004), the disease was still taken extremely seriously and deemed a crisis situation (Highly Pathogen Avian Influenza, 2017). The rapid spread of HPAI in the previous outbreak in 2014–2015 made poultry producers hyperaware of the situation and the need to manage it. Responding to the Indiana outbreak was the responsibility of the Board of Animal Health (BOAH) with assistance from the US Department of Agriculture Veterinary Services (USDA-VS), United States Department of Agriculture (USDA), Indiana Department of Homeland Security (DHS), and other agencies (Indiana State Board of Animal Health, 2016, January 15). Together, this group of specialists helped take control of the situation and respond to the threat of HPAI with excellent internal and external communication and a hands-on approach. The group of specialists created a steady flow of communication about how to contain and eliminate HPAI. Ultimately, with the lessons learned from the previous outbreak in 2015, the Indiana outbreak was quickly contained and only approximately 414,000 birds died (Indiana State Board of Animal Health, 2016, May 2). The Indiana State Veterinarian, Bret D. Marsh, DVM, explained that "our teams in the field had to scale-up, overnight. But we did it, and completed the task, in 38 days" (Indiana State Board of Animal Health, 2016, May 2, p. 1).

This chapter follows with an explanation of how SC is linked to the protective actions needed during crisis situations. We then provide a template for strategically introducing protective actions to relevant publics during crises. This template is then applied to the Indiana HPAI crisis, and the resulting series of conclusions and implications are discussed.

Crisis Communication as Strategic Action

By way of its emphasis on purposefully advancing an organization's mission through "deliberate communication practice," we see SC as closely aligned with crisis communication (Hallahan et al., 2007, p. 4). Broadly speaking, "an organizational crisis is a specific, ***unexpected***, and

nonroutine event or series of events that create high levels of ***uncertainty*** and simultaneously present an organization with both ***opportunities*** for and ***threats*** to its ***high-priority goals***" (Ulmer, Sellnow, & Seeger, 2019, p. 7). In crisis situations then, SC "involves the strategic application of communication to limit the harm a crisis inflicts on an organization and its stakeholders" (Coombs & Holladay, 2015). This perspective of SC has been applied to a wide range of crises spanning reputation, health, and terrorism (Benoit, 2015; Rossmann, 2015; Rothenburger, 2015).

A Productive Bias Toward Action

Dewey's (2013/1938, 2016/1927) pragmatic perspective on communication serves to clarify the link SC provides between the organization and its stakeholders during crises. A primary objective of SC is the quest to better understand the relationship "between public communication and public action" (Bentele & Nothhaft, 2015, p. 71). Dewey (2013/1938) argues that the uncertainty and related problems caused by indeterminate situations are a catalyst for public inquiry. Inquiry in the form of public communication can potentially convert an "indeterminate problematic situation into a determinate resolved one" (p. 252). When faced with such problems and the uncertainty caused by them, people seek out and act to engage in innovative solutions (Grunig, 1966). Self (2010) reasons that, for Dewey, public discourse is a form of action. From this perspective, "publics are (networks or) relationships of action assembled to solve problems" (p. 80). Crises, due to their inherent threat, surprise, and short response time (Hermann, 1963), are indeterminant situations that, by reason, require the level of action-based discourse Grunig and Self see as central to Dewey's view on the public sphere. These actions, in crisis situations, manifest "supportive behaviors" that "serve to benefit the organization and its stakeholders in some way" (Coombs & Holladay, 2015, p. 499).

Action as emergent. Actions manifested through public engagement, however, must be adaptable based on indeterminant factors of the crisis situations (Gilpin & Murphy, 2008). Recent research suggests that the volatility of crises demands flexibility in such actions (Raupp, 2015). In fact, from a SC perspective, the often prescribed "rigid focus on planning and control, can be destructive" (Eriksson, 2015, p. 510). In place of such inflexibility, Holtzhausen and Zerfass (2015) extend Mintzberg's (1990) depiction of emergence by arguing that the concept of emergence dismisses an emphasis on control and asks communicators to instead "embrace the messiness, risk taking and chaos of communication practice" (p. 9). For Holtzhausen and Zerfass, emergent communication is "dependent on the participation of many people including external stakeholders to provide true richness" to the communication process (p. 9). Ultimately, this inclusive process leads to behavioral outcomes or actions that address specific problems. Dewey agreed with this notion of nimble impermanence for prescribed actions in response to problems. Self (2015) explains that Dewey's "vision presented organizations as shifting networks of discourse" through which problems are defined, solutions are debated, and recommended actions are continuously assessed through shared experiences of those who are impacted by the success or failure of those solutions (p. 88).

Emergent action as participative communication. Torp (2015) describes a shift in our understanding of organizational communication that he labels "the strategic turn" (p. 44). The strategic turn, Torp explains, "entails that informal communication within and outside the organization are included" in our understanding of effective management (p. 45). Strategic communication eschews a linear view of communication in favor of a participative process involving multiple stakeholders. Rather than seeing publics as audiences, those ascribing to a contemporary strategic view of communication see publics as cocreators of meaning (Caldiero, 2016). Kent and Theunissen (2016) argue that this cocreation extends from mere dialogue to actually engaging an organization and its publics. Done effectively, Kent and Theunissen contend that engaging publics in dialogue can ultimately result in "long lasting relationships nurtured, sought, and undertaken with humility and understanding that the purpose of the conversation is not to get one's way, but to truly understand and gain deeper knowledge" (p. 4042). This strategic turn, then, is consistent with Dewey's (2016/1927) call for inclusivity in public discourse to address problems.

Creating an Action-Based Message: The IDEA Model

The IDEA model was conceived by Sellnow and Sellnow (2019) to aid spokespersons in crafting effective strategic instructional messages during times of risk and crisis. IDEA is an acronym that stands for internalization (I), distribution (D), explanation (E), and action (A). Previous research has demonstrated that effective crisis communication spokespersons address all four elements in their messages. The model is grounded in Dewey's (1938) experiential learning theory, which posits that authentic learning only occurs when ideas are embraced via knowing plus doing plus reflecting. Important to note is the fact that, unlike other theoretical notions of learning, Dewey prioritizes doing as essential in the process.

The IDEA model has been tested across risk and crisis types, including but not limited to natural disasters, food contamination outbreaks, and health pandemics (e.g. Sellnow et al., 2017, 2019a, 2019b; Sellnow-Richmond et al., 2018; Sellnow & Sellnow, 2019). To address internalization, spokespersons must motivate listeners to attend to the message by highlighting its relevance to and potential impact on them. This can be achieved via personal narratives from those already impacted by the crisis, as well as by highlighting timeliness to act and proximity of the event. Distribution has to do with determining which channel or channels will best reach the target populations, as well as which sources are most credible for influencing diverse populations and stakeholder groups. For example, some populations may use smartphone apps, others the television or radio, and still others face-to face communication with those whom they respect. Explanation is achieved via accurate science and information that is translated in ways that make it comprehensible to disparate publics. Many scientists and specialists err by explaining in too much detail and using too much technical jargon. The details do not matter if the people being addressed do not understand the scientific jargon. Finally, action has to do with providing specific action steps regarding what to do or not to do for self-protection and to mitigate harm. In the case of HPAI, this means specific steps about how to practice good biosecurity. Central to this construct is the need to be nimble in terms of adapting appropriate action steps to fit the evolving crisis. For example, appropriate action steps prior to an HPAI outbreak may include specific biosecurity steps such as shower in/shower out, maintaining a distinct line of separation between the farm, the animals, and various people entering and exiting the farm. However, as the crisis emerges into a pandemic, more specific measures may also need to be adopted to stop the outbreak from spreading.

Best practices research also reveals that the best IDEA model messages are created collaboratively among communities of practice (Sellnow et al., 2017). Essentially, communities of practice are comprised of diverse representatives from an industry. For example, in the case of earthquake early warning (EEW), these networks are comprised of seismologists, emergency managers, risk communication specialists, and earth scientists. In the case of HPAI and other animal pandemics, a community of practice may consist of agricultural extension agents, veterinarians, farmers, feed lot handlers, and risk communication specialists (Sellnow, Sellnow, & Martin, 2019).

Ultimately, the IDEA model is a simple-to-understand and easy-to-use framework for crisis spokespersons across communities of practice to collaboratively create and distribute effective messages across disparate populations that may be at risk. Such participatory collaboration is essential to the success of adapting these messages as a crisis emerges and evolves.

Explaining the HPAI Crisis Through the Lens of the IDEA Model

The Indiana outbreak of HPAI is an exemplar of effective strategic crisis communication. As with all crisis situations, communication played a central role in alerting publics to the crisis and establishing an action plan. In this section, we apply the IDEA model to the Indiana HPAI crisis, paying close attention to the participatory communication and emergence of recommended actions.

Data for Analysis

Our case study is based on interviews conducted with three individuals who were prominent in creating the strategic crisis communication response to the Indiana HPAI outbreak. We chose to base our analysis on interviews in order to move beyond simply observing what was said to more strategically listen to the creators of the messages as they talked about the strategic process through which they determined what to say, when to say it, and why. The individuals we interviewed were recommended by agricultural biosecurity experts who were familiar with the Indiana outbreak. Our interview questions followed the IDEA model. As such, our interviewees were asked to describe the communication strategies they employed to motivate their publics to internalize the risk of HPAI, to intelligibly explain the nature of the disease, and to call for specific protective action steps. Interviewees were also asked to describe their strategies for distributing the message. Our interviewees include:

- A Purdue Extension disaster communication specialist.
- A communication specialist with the Indiana State Board of Animal Health.
- A veterinarian focusing on avian health and field operations for the Indiana State Board of Animal Health.

Each of these interviewees participated in critical decision-making about the information shared during the outbreak. Each interview lasted between 30 and 60 minutes. The interviews were transcribed and analyzed thematically by the authors. To provide context for our analysis, our database also includes the press releases shared by the Indiana State Board of Animal Health.

Internalization

Recall that internalization is achieved when receivers are motivated to attend to the message because they realize its relevance. We observed three primary themes focused on internalization during the HPAI crisis: collaboration #1, local focus #2, and targeted messaging #3. In the following paragraphs, we describe each of these themes and provide examples from the interview transcripts.

Collaboration. Effective SC via internalization may be achieved by moving beyond merely transmitting messages to passive audiences to, instead, strategically including them in the discussion about finding and implementing potential solutions. The BOAH took the lead in forming a response team comprised of a diverse group of specialists to address the HPAI crisis. Initially, a joint information center (JIC) was created to coordinate communication. As Participant 1 explained:

> Right away, I called our counterparts at the Indiana Department of Homeland Security and we decided to activate the joint information center right off the bat and that was part of our plan. In

> Indiana, we have a really strong relationship with our DHS folks. Here at the state level, we train with them especially at the public affairs level. I've gotten loaned to them in tornado incidents and work it. That process was very seamless. So, from a communications standpoint we did that. (Participant 1)

Participant 1 clarified that the JIC included "top hitters" from both the DHS and the USDA. Participant 1 further explained that county emergency managers in the zone impacted by the crisis, Purdue University's Extension agents, and representatives from Indiana's Department of Agriculture were also included in the collaborative communication structure. Overall, Participant 1 described the group's philosophy by saying, "we tried to look at it more as a partnership" (Participant 1).

Food industry personnel from states receiving products from Indiana's poultry industry comprised another important collaborator in the communication process. Participant 2 explained that maintaining the "trust" of these industry partners was an essential part of the response:

> We also were communicating with our other states, because we had an egg processing facility that was within the quarantine zone and so, communicating with our counterparts in other states saying we have a testing protocol that we are not letting out of this control zone. (Participant 2)

This effort to keep stakeholders outside of Indiana was part of a general effort to be as open and transparent as possible in sharing information.

Local focus. Although the response team included state, local, and federal officials, the interviewees emphasized the importance of maintaining a local emphasis in the crisis communication process. The federal government was also directly involved in the communication process, however, Participant 2 explained that Indiana representatives maintained leadership of the JIC:

> We were the lead agency. Our local homeland security followed us. We really led the charge and did it our way. The USDA was there to shadow and offer assistance. At no point did we hand the keys to the car over to the USDA. We were running it all from Indiana. (Participant 2)

Participant 1 clarified that the biosecurity specialists coming to Indiana from agencies outside the state were welcomed for their expertise, but "they don't know the local people" (Participant 1). Participant 1 argued that local residents understood the importance of the poultry industry to their neighbors and the local economy. This fact was evident in the number of volunteers who participated in the response effort: "so everyone cooperated and the community pitched in like crazy, because poultry is so important to that community" (Participant 1).

Participant 1 also indicated that taking a local focus provided the added advantage of expediency and commended BOAH for acting locally rather than waiting for the USDA to arrive. S/he explained, Minnesota and Iowa compounded their situation by waiting because "the USDA isn't going to get there immediately. You might think they would, but they won't. With all animal diseases, there is an exponential increase in the infestation if you wait to treat it" (Participant 1).

Targeted messaging. Participant 2 explained that they had access to detailed records, which afforded them the ability to identify which farms were within an affected area and warn them immediately:

> We can come up with a map and get variables very, very quickly with a few key strokes if we need to make staffing needs, what farms are at risk and pulling up farm information, so we can get notifications sent out quickly to say you are now in a circle. Your birds are under quarantine; you now have to get permits to move product or birds. (Participant 2)

Indiana's State Poultry Association was also helpful in targeting the message. Participant 3 said, "we actually worked with our state poultry association who is a gathering of state representatives. We used them as a conduit to get in contact with the companies and the right people in the companies" (Participant 3).

The message was not, however, restricted to the infected area. Participant 2 noted that producers in the surrounding areas were also involved in the response effort:

> Another audience we had to deal with was producers, the growers, in the poultry setting. While this was very focused in one county, we had a lot of production in other parts of the state and getting them to understand that they need to step up biosecurity and be more alert in what is happening in their barn and knowing when and how to report and work with their flock veterinarian. (Participant 2)

Participant 1 agreed with this assessment by claiming that "we communicated to the farmers outside of the quarantine. Inside the quarantine, those corporations are so big. They had their own response team. Like I said, they cooperated with the Indiana Board of Health" (Participant 1).

In all phases of the outbreak, the response team "communicated quite regularly with the industry" (Participant 2). Participant 3 observed that emphasizing the threat of HPAI was aided by the vivid examples of recent outbreaks in Minnesota and Iowa. S/he explained that the team emphasized how quickly the disease spread due to migratory fowl in those states:

> As far as the buy in, I think that when you have an Iowa and Minnesota occurring, you know what it appears to be from the outside looking in. There are two factors. One: it appears not to be in your control. I think that's a huge motivating factor. And two, I think that the especially the larger poultry companies completely understand that while we have all these rules and regulations for interstate movement, those wild birds in poultry really don't know state lines. (Participant 3)

In part, the industry's willingness to internalize the message was also influenced by the high level of trust they shared with the response team. Participant 3 explained the value of trust built up before the crisis played in helping the producers internalize the threat:

> We also, I would say, have a poultry community. We like to joke that most of our job is trying to keep up with them and what they expect from us. We are very fortunate to have a very open and honest relationship with them and have very candid conversations that get down to the core of what needs to be discussed, so that neither one of us can be caught off guard during an incident. (Participant 3)

In short, the open and honest relationship shared by the response team and the industry helped both parties recognize and commit to responding strategically to the crisis.

Distribution

Distribution is achieved when messages are communicated via a variety of credible sources through myriad communication channels. The response team communicated with its publics using a variety of channels. In addition to the direct interaction among industry and response team members mentioned above, traditional media, new media, Purdue Extension, door-to-door visits, and conference calls were also involved in distributing the information during the crisis. Analysis of the interview data produced four key themes regarding distribution: traditional media #1, new media #2, door-to-door #3, and conference calls #4.

Traditional media. Participant 1 observed that the traditional media outlets in Indiana were supportive during the crisis:

> Indiana media are really friendly. They trust Purdue, they trust the board of animal health, so we don't get pressing issues that you would in New York or California with the news media. The USDA did the release and BOAH supplemented the information. And with the website I sent you all the news releases are recorded there. (Participant 1)

Participant 2 indicated further that the response team remained attentive to the traditional media throughout the crisis, claiming that "we were just trying to make sure that we responded to all the media calls as soon as we could, like within a few hours if possible" (Participant 2).

Participant 2 praised the Purdue Extension team and how they "worked with extension a lot. They pushed things out" (Participant 2).

New media. Participant 2 also highlighted the role of social media in distributing messages from the response team and other agencies. More specifically, they established a Facebook presence and capitalized on the gov.delivery system:

> The CDC uses it, the FA uses it, the entire state of Indiana uses it. It helps with setting up with email subscriptions and now people can opt in for text updates. So, now people don't have to just have email. So, we pushed a lot of information out that way. It was the first big event where we used that system so actively to push information out. (Participant 2)

The use of new media represented an attempt by the response team to take advantage of new opportunities to quickly distribute information.

Door-to-door. Participant 1 described a face-to-face effort to share information. S/he explained:

> The other good thing that BOAH did, they had veterinarians go door to door every. Every door got knocked on in the quarantine zone and I can't give you a number, but they found more than 1,000 backyard flocks and all the backyard flocks tested negative. They didn't have it. (Participant 1)

This door-to-door initiative helped the response team and owners of small flocks understand that the disease was not spreading among backyard flocks.

Conference calls. Conference calls were also used regularly to distribute information. Participant 3 explained:

> We started notifying producers and hosted a conference call with the industry right away trying to make them aware and of course, like I said, we have about a dozen companies we can really target and get the key individuals on a phone pretty quickly. So, we started hosting calls initially daily and some days more than one. Just to keep them apprised of what was happening. We were drawing the circles and created a testing protocol. (Participant 3)

Conference calls provided a consistent and widely accessible means of sharing information throughout the crisis.

Explanation

In terms of conveying an accurate message intelligibly, it is important first to note that the HPAI message was not new. The fact that members of Indiana's poultry industry had recently observed two serious outbreaks in nearby states meant that many in the industry already understood the disease and the urgent need for strict adherence to biosecurity standards. Two themes emerged in the interviews: capitalizing on previous experience #1 and human risk #2.

Capitalizing on previous experience. Learning from previous experience was both formal and vicarious. Participant 3 explained that Indiana had an extensive biosecurity training program in place prior to the outbreak: "in our planning and preparedness we have been working a lot with the commercial poultry industry and looking to the prevention, but also what business continuity looks like for them" (Participant 3). Ironically, one such training session was underway when the disease outbreak was diagnosed. Participant 2 explained that individuals who served as part of the response team were conducting formal biosecurity training at one of the sites the day the disease was diagnosed there. As s/he explained, "They were doing an education session with them that day that their veterinarian called and said they have positives coming back" (Participant 2). Participant 3 actually participated in this training event and described it in relation to the timing of the outbreak:

> As soon as we pulled into the parking lot, we got the initial word that we had samples preliminary positive for high pathogen avian influenza. So, that was one of the companies we were going to go train, was actually one of the three companies impacted by our animal health emergency. So, the timing was kind of peculiar. (Participant 3)

The interviewees emphasized that having this formal training process in place was an important advantage for explaining the dangers of HPAI.

Vicarious learning also played an informative role in explaining the nature of HPAI. Participant 1 explained:

> We were fortunate it happened in Minnesota the year before, because a lot of lessons were learned ... They had to put down about 54 million birds in Iowa and Minnesota, we only had to put down 500,000. (Participant 1)

The interviewees expressed the value of applying these lessons learned from Minnesota and Iowa by both their response team and producers.

Human risk. For consumers, farm workers, and responders in the impacted region, the response team perceived the need to explain this strain of HPAI posed little or no danger to humans. Participant 2 recognized that consumers were initially apprehensive about eating products such as eggs during the outbreak. Thus, s/he mentioned the importance of "reiterating that food safety message, because I think a lot of people were nervous about it ... like buying eggs" (Participant 2). Participant 1 agreed, indicating that the messages focused on no risk to humans were effective. S/he said the essence of the message was "that this is not a human health threat. You can get pink eye from it if you handle it, but no consumer health threat. People were very cooperative" (Participant 1).

Participant 3 agreed that the strain of HPAI in Indiana did not pose a human health risk. However, s/he expounded upon the importance of testing and clear communication about any human risk, particularly for those in direct contact with infected birds, whenever such outbreaks occur:

> Usually, we can tell from the early beginning if it is highly adapted to humans or not. We can say minimal, high risk, low risk, whatever. But understanding that and having a message for the general public and a message for responders is different, the message for the public driving down the street saying there is no risk to humans is probably very accurate, but to say there is minimal risks to someone who is responding, who is in the barns with AI, with birds in front of them, even if they have their repository protection, there is still more of a risk. (Participant 3)

Regardless of how confident the response team was that this strain of HPAI was not a risk to humans, they wisely took the precautions needed to verify the safety of consumers and those in direct contact with infected flocks.

Action

Actions recommended by the Indiana response team emphasized the need for producers to report any unusual appearance of their birds. The team also emphasized the need for heightened biosecurity on both infected and uninfected farms. Heightened biosecurity focused on disease recognition and reporting #1, a clear line of separation #2, and general preparedness #3.

Disease recognition and reporting. Participant 3 expounded on the significance reporting played in managing the outbreak:

> Our constant message to small flock producers was ADR. Ain't Doing Right. If you see your flock ain't doing right, for any reason, let someone know. Let a regulatory official know and we are more than happy to, it is our job, to give you a call, we will walk through that process with you. If there truly is a concern, we will get it sampled. You know I think that communication is, so, you don't want the constituents to feel like they are burdening us to do our job. Even if it is one bird, five birds, ten birds, it doesn't matter. It is our job and we care. (Participant 3)

Participant 2 agreed, emphasizing how the reporting process was a central feature for all bird owners in the response team's ongoing crisis communication. "If your bird appears sick, call the healthy bird hotline for the hobby flock sector, as well. Those were really the main ones" (Participant 2).

With HPAI in the region, Participant 3 further clarified that any unusual bird losses warranted reporting:

> One, keep a close eye on your birds. Two, understand the critical signs of highly pathogenic avian influenza. Generally speaking, that is really easy. Ok, if you can't explain a death, let us know. If you can't explain it, it doesn't make sense and you are unsure and it died, let us know. (Participant 3)

The response team simplified and expedited the reporting process by establishing a hotline that linked callers to a veterinarian.

Line of separation. As is the case with all biosecurity threats, producers were asked to fortify the line of separation between their farms and anyone or anything outside their farms. For example, anyone coming onto the farm needed to go through a sanitizing process before setting foot inside one of the barns or pens. Any equipment coming onto the farm or moving among barns or pens also had to be sanitized. Participant 2 summarized this process, saying "we had to do some major communication and communicate the importance of changing corporate policies. Truck washes, footbaths and those types of things" (Participant 2). Participant 1 said they advised people to avoid contaminated areas, saying "now, what we told them is to not go into the control zone or the quarantine zone, because once you go in, you have to stay there or disinfect or whatever" (Participant 1).

To help enforce the line of separation, the response team placed a ban on bird movement. Participant 3 described the ban this way: "During that time is when we put on the bird ban, so the preventing of any comingling events, bird swapping, exhibition events for the small flock producers" (Participant 3).

The ban on bird movement was not without controversy. Participant 2 illuminated a level of frustration experienced by small flock owners and young people in agriculture programs such as 4-H and FFA: S/he said, “we had 92 counties that go to the state fair here and we had a lot of folks upset. A lot of kids that were like ‘oh, I wanted to show my birds,’ and that type of thing. So that was irritating stepping up biosecurity” (Participant 2).

Preparedness. The response team also asked producers to take actions to prepare themselves financially for the possibility of being infected. Producers needed to register their farms and complete the necessary preparation and required paperwork to be eligible for federal financial assistance if their farms were infected and their flock had to be euthanized. Participant 3 explained that getting this certification in advance gave producers a distinct advantage. S/he clarified, “You can get it during the incident, but it takes longer and you don’t need to be waiting for that. For a large corporation, talk to your local farm agency with your local USDA, because most of them already have one” (Participant 3). Participant 2 explained that this and other action-related messages were well received because of the earlier outbreaks in other states: “So, that played to our benefit in the long run because the commercial industry was very keyed up and very interested in what can we do to avoid what’s happening in Iowa” (Participant 2).

Conclusions and Implications

The HPAI outbreak in Indiana posed an immediate threat to the mission of the region’s poultry industry. When the crisis began, the outcome was, in Dewey’s (2013/1938) terms, an indeterminate situation in need of resolution. When the first birds were diagnosed, Indiana’s poultry producers could not have known whether the crisis would spread as it had in Iowa and Minnesota or be contained as it eventually was in Indiana.

The response team’s internalization messages set the stage for an effective response. Leaders of Indiana’s BOAH configured a diverse response team, allowing for participative communication from a range of stakeholders impacted by the crisis. This process of inclusion served two productive purposes. Specifically, those publics included in the communication process were much more likely to internalize the messages the response team generated because: (a) they had access to the most current information and (b) they had a say in the content of the messages. Interviewees characterized this aspect of internalization as keeping a local focus. Collaborating across a diverse community of practice was key to the success of internalization across disparate publics. Other organizations facing crises could benefit from enacting similar internalization strategies. Inviting representatives from the publics impacted by the crisis creates an opportunity to engage in participatory communication that, in turn, increases the likelihood that participants will internalize the risk.

Internalization is also aided by a clear understanding of who is at greatest risk and why. The interviewees mentioned that pre-existing relationships and planning resulted in the creation of a detailed mapping system regarding where the flocks were located and who managed them. Thus, they were able to determine whom to contact once they identified a high-risk zone in the state. Pre-crisis planning of this nature would likely assist other industries in their efforts to inspire internalization during crisis events. Thus, the capacity for mapping and network formation is a strategy worth exploring for industry groups in their crisis planning.

Indiana’s capacity for distributing their crisis message is impressive in three ways. First, the team capitalized on the trust it had built with traditional media representatives well before the crisis began. Second, the team blended both new media and traditional media for sharing their message. In doing so, they used the most promising technology provided both by government agencies and a popular social media platform. Third, the team had the capacity and empathy needed to engage in door-to-door communication, as well as to invite anyone with concerns to call a hotline where they could speak directly with a veterinarian about the event.

The door-to-door visits and the hotline bolstered the capacity of the response team to engage in participatory communication. The conversations allowed bird owners to both ask questions and share information about their flocks. Accordingly, this strategy created the opportunity for dialogue as suggested by Kent and Theunissen (2016). The interviewees explained that this flow of information coming to them from producers helped the response team maintain a map of all infected areas and share tailored messages appropriate for individual farms. Other industries who have the capacity for interacting with their publics would benefit from initiating similar forms of dialogue.

Sadly, producers in Minnesota and Iowa suffered tremendous losses during their recent HPAI outbreaks. These outbreaks, however, did create two opportunities for the Indiana HPAI response team as they provided explanations about the outbreak. First, Indiana producers were keenly aware of what had happened in the previous outbreaks. Producers knew how quickly the disease could spread and how dangerous it was. Thus, they had learned vicariously about the nature of the disease from watching what happened in nearby states. Second, Indiana had a proactive training program in place that had already established a high level of knowledge about HPAI. Post-crisis learning and pre-crisis planning combined to aid the Indiana response team in their explanation efforts. Both of these strategies are considered best practice in crisis communication and can readily be employed by other industries.

The actions emphasized by the Indiana HPAI response team were a balance between a standard biosecurity protocol and reporting of unusual bird behavior. The standard biosecurity protocol involved heightened security. These strategies were consistent with the training many of the farms had already completed. The continuous reporting process encouraged by the response team allowed both the producers and the response team to engage in emergent behaviors. The response team could quickly adapt their mapping and response strategies based on this continuous influx of information. As such, the team remained emergent in its planning, communication, and distribution of response strategies. This adaptation allowed them to avoid the pitfalls of rigid response structures. Other industries would benefit from considering such nimble reporting and adaptive response strategies.

Summary

The Indiana HPAI response team created a SC process that included high levels of participation among publics and emergent flexibility based on continuous tracking of the disease. These qualities afforded the response team with the means to maintain a local adaptability in their communication, while accepting the input of outside agencies and learning lessons from earlier outbreaks. In the end, Indiana's outbreak caused far less damage than those in Minnesota and Iowa. Other biological factors likely played a role in limiting the spread of the disease, but the SC offered by the response team likely played a major role in diminishing the human-driven aspects of HPAI's spread in Indiana. Thus, the SC process employed by the Indiana response team serves as an exemplar for effective SC during crises.

References

2016 HPAI Information. (2016, January). Indianapolis, IN: Indiana State Board of Animal Health. Retrieved from https://www.in.gov/boah/2745.htm

Benoit, W. L. (2015). Image repair theory in the context of strategic communication. In D. Holtzhausen & A. Zerfass (Eds.), *The Routledge handbook of strategic communication* (pp. 303–311). New York: Routledge.

Bentele, G., & Nothhaft, H. (2015). Strategic communication and the public sphere from a European perspective. In D. Holtzhausen & A. Zerfass (Eds.), *The Routledge handbook of strategic communication* (pp. 53–73). New York: Routledge.

Caldiero, C. (2016). *Public relations in a postmodern world*. New York: Peter Lang.

Coombs, W. T., & Holladay, S. J. (2015). Strategic intent and crisis communication: The emergence of a field. In D. Holtzhausen & A. Zerfass (Eds.), *The Routledge handbook of strategic communication* (pp. 497–507). New York: Routledge.

Dewey, J. (1938). *Experience and education*. New York: Simon & Schuster.

Dewey, J. (2013). *Logic: The theory of inquiry*. Redditch: Read Books. (Original work published in 1938).

Dewey, J. (2016). The public and its problems. In M. L. Rogers (Ed.), *The public and its problems: An essay in political inquiry* (pp. 144–170). Athens, OH: Ohio University Press. (Original work published 1927).

Eriksson, M. (2015). Crisis communication and improvisation in a digital age. In D. Holtzhausen & A. Zerfass (Eds.), *The Routledge handbook of strategic communication* (pp. 34–52). New York: Routledge.

Gilpin, D. R., & Murphy, P. J. (2008). *Crisis management in a complex world*. Oxford: Oxford University Press.

Grunig, J. E. (1966). The role of information in economic decision making. *Journalism Monographs*, 3.

Hallahan, K., Holtzhausen, D., Van Ruler, B., Vercic, D., & Sriramesh, K. (2007). Defining strategic communication. *International Journal of Strategic Communication*, 1(1), 3–35.

Hermann, C. F. (1963). Some consequences of crisis which limit the viability of organizations. *Administrative Science Quarterly*, 8(1), 61–82.

Highly Pathogen Avian Influenza. (2017, August). Washington, D.C.: United States Department of Agriculture. Retrieved from https://www.aphis.usda.gov/aphis/ourfocus/animalhealth/emergency-management/fadprep-hpai

Holtzhausen, D., & Zerfass, A. (2015). Strategic communication: Opportunities and challenges of the research area. In D. Holtzhausen & A. Zerfass (Eds.), *The Routledge handbook of strategic communication* (pp. 3–17). New York: Routledge.

Indiana State Board of Animal Health. (2016, January 15). Animal health advisory: High-Path Avian Influenza: Preparedness, surveillance and reporting [Press release]. Retrieved from https://www.in.gov/boah/files/HPAI_Surveillane_AHAdvy-1-15-16.pdf

Indiana State Board of Animal Health. (2016, May 2). Final Indiana Avian Influenza quarantine lifted; State achieves AI-Free [Press release]. Retrieved from http://www.choicesmagazine.org/UserFiles/file/cmsarticle_505.pdf https://www.in.gov/boah/files/HPAI_Final_Quarantine_Released_b_PR_5-2-16.pdf

Johnson, K. K., Seeger, R. M., & Marsh, T. L. (2016). Local economies and highly pathogenic avian influenza. *Choices*, 31(2), 1–9. Retrieved from https://www.researchgate.net/publication/303049138_Local_Economies_and_Highly_Pathogenic_Avian_Influenza

Kent, M. L., & Theunissen, P. (2016). Elegy for mediated dialogue: Shiva the destroyer and reclaiming our first principles. *International Journal of Communication*, 10, 4040–4054.

Mintzberg, H. (1990). The design school: Reconsidering the basic premises of strategic management. *Strategic Management Journal*, 11(3), 171–195.

National Pork Board. (2018, November 7). German African Swine Fever expert: It's a human-driven disease. Farm Journal's PORK. Retrieved from https://www.porkbusiness.com/article/german-african-swine-fever-expert-its-human-driven-disease

Rakow, L. F. (2018). Public relations and the eclipse of the public. In Ø. Ihlen & M. Fredriksson (Eds.), *Public relations and social theory: Key figures, concepts and developments* (pp. 315–333). New York: Routledge.

Raupp, J. (2015). Strategizing risk communication. In D. Holtzhausen & A. Zerfass (Eds.), *The Routledge handbook of strategic communication* (pp. 520–532). New York: Routledge.

Rossmann, C. (2015). Strategic health communication: Theory- and evidence-based campaign development. In D. Holtzhausen & A. Zerfass (Eds.), *The Routledge handbook of strategic communication* (pp. 409–424). New York: Routledge.

Rothenberger, L. (2015). Terrorism as strategic communication. In D. Holtzhausen & A. Zerfass (Eds.), *The Routledge handbook of strategic communication* (pp. 481–496). New York: Routledge.

Self, C. C. (2010). Hegel, Habermas, and community: The public in the new media era. *International Journal of Strategic Communication*, 4(2), 78–92.

Self, C. C. (2015). Dewey, the public sphere, from a European perspective. In D. Holtzhausen & Zerfass (Eds.), *The Routledge handbook of strategic communication* (pp. 74–92). New York: Routledge.

Sellnow, D. D., & Sellnow, T. L. (2019). The IDEA model for effective instructional risk and crisis communication by emergency managers and other key spokespersons. *Journal of Emergency Management*, 17(1), 67–78. doi: 10.5055/jem.2019.0399

Sellnow, D. D., Iverson, J. O., & Sellnow, T. L. (2017). The evolution of the operational earthquake forecasting (OEF) community of practice: The L'Aquila communication crisis as a triggering event for organizational renewal. *Journal of Applied Communication Research*, 45(2), 121–139.

Sellnow, D. D., Sellnow, T. L., & Martin, J. M. (2019). Strategic message convergence in communicating biosecurity: The case of the 2013 porcine epidemic diarrhea virus. *Communication Reports*, 32(3), 125–136.

Sellnow, D. D., Lane, D. R., Sellnow, T. L., & Littlefield, R. (2017). The IDEA model as a best practice for effective instructional risk and crisis communication. *Communication Studies*, 68, 552–567.

Sellnow, D. D., Johannson, B., Sellnow, T. L., & Lane, D. R. (2019a). Toward a global understanding of the effects of the IDEA model for designing instructional risk and crisis messages: A food contamination experiment in Sweden. *Journal of Contingencies and Crisis Management*, 27(2), 102–115.

Sellnow, D. D., Jones, L. M., Sellnow, T. L., Spence, P., Lane, D. R., & Haarstad, N. (2019b). The IDEA model as a conceptual framework for designing earthquake early warning (EEW) messages distributed via mobile phone apps. In J. Santos-Reyes (Ed.), *Earthquakes – Impact, Community Vulnerability and Resilience*. London: InTechOpen. Advanced online publication. doi: 10.5772/intechopen.85557

Sellnow-Richmond, D. D., George, A., & Sellnow, D. D. (2018). An IDEA model analysis of instructional risk communication messages in the time of Ebola. *Journal of International Crisis and Risk Communication Research*, 1(1), 135–159.

Torp, S. M. (2015). The strategic turn in communication science: On the history and role of strategy in communication science from ancient Greece. In D. Holtzhausen & A. Zerfass (Eds.), *The Routledge handbook of strategic communication* (pp. 34–52). New York: Routledge.

Ulmer, R. R., Sellnow, T. L., & Seeger, M. W. (2019). *Effective crisis communication: Moving from crisis to opportunity*. Sage: Thousand Oaks, CA.

Yang, Y., Halloran, M. E., Sugimoto, J. D., & Longini, I. M. (2007). Detecting human-to-human transmission of Avian Influenza A. *Emerging Infectious Diseases*, 13(9), 1348–1353. doi: 10.3201/eid1309.07-0111

15

Emergency Preparedness, Response, and Strategic Communication for Natural Disasters

Matthew W. Seeger[1], Khairul Islam[1], and Henry S. Seeger[2]

[1]Wayne State University, [2]Purdue University

Introduction

Natural disasters, such as hurricanes, floods, tornadoes, and earthquakes, create significant disruption and harm to public health and property. According to McFarlane and Norris (2006), disaster is "a potentially traumatic event that is collectively experienced, has an acute onset, and is time delineated; disasters may be attributed to natural, technological or human causes" (p. 4). Natural disasters are the function of some general hazards that threaten a community or region and typically activate a community-based response to limit harm and manage any damage (see Perry, 2007). A natural disaster typically will have broad community and regional impact and will require significant resources and coordination for both emergency preparation and disaster response.

Perry and Lindell (2003) provide a foundational definition for emergency preparedness, stating that the term "refers to the readiness of a political jurisdiction to react constructively to threats from the environment in a way that minimizes the negative consequences of impact for the health and safety of individuals and the integrity and functioning of physical structures and systems" (p. 338).

While this perspective favors the readiness of political jurisdictions and the state to react, other perspectives may also include meso-level organizations, groups, and communities. Emergency preparedness typically involves a process of anticipating and reducing risks, identifying necessary resources and capacities, clarifying roles and responsibilities, encoding plans in written form, and testing plans through training and exercises. While emergency preparedness is often seen as synonymous with a written plan, emergency preparedness is increasingly regarded as a negotiated process leading to the enhancement of a group, organization, or community's capacity to respond to an emergency situation. This capacity, along with changes in structures and procedures, is strongly related to the concept of resilience (Norris et al., 2008).

Emergency response in its most basic form consists of strategies used by a body to manage the impacts of an emergency, and can be understood in terms of a spectrum from emergent self-organization to formalized preset response systems. Emergent self-organization may take place among communities affected by an emergency as they attempt to make sense of the event and manage immediate needs and risks (Comfort, 2007; Seeger, 2002). At the other end of the spectrum are highly formalized and bureaucratic response systems, such as the

The Handbook of Strategic Communication, First Edition. Edited by Carl H. Botan.

National Incident Management System (NIMS), which includes preset structures, procedures, roles, rules, and operating systems (Federal Emergency Management Agency, 2015). While response strategies are highly variable and contingent upon the circumstances of the events, they can be classified into risk avoidance behaviors, disaster preparedness behaviors, and personal protection such as shelter in place, or relocation and evacuation. Both emergency preparedness and response rely on a variety of communication activities, including the development and distribution of risk messages, warnings, and recommendations for action.

This chapter explores current conceptualizations of natural disasters as the intersection of naturally occurring phenomena and human-built environments. Disaster and emergency management are sets of planned and formalized preparation and response processes and structures, as well as a set of adaptive and emergent processes and behaviors. These structures include a variety of communication activities, processes, and systems typically framed as tactics in support of other emergency management functions.

In this chapter we first describe and define disasters and disaster management. These are well-developed domains of study and practice in a variety of fields, including sociology. Communication functions in crisis are discussed both as tactics in support of emergency management and as strategic components. We argue that emergency preparedness and response require a set of specialized forms of strategic communication (SC) across the disaster lifecycle and that effectiveness of preparedness and response can be enhanced through an SC orientation.

Disasters Versus Natural Disasters

Disasters, both so-called natural and those that are clearly human caused, have powerful and often physical impact. Communication is inherent to the onset, management, and aftermath of disasters. They are events or series of events that can be designated in time and space and which have impacts on society, impacts which drive responses and changes to manage these impacts (Fritz, 1961). Most investigations of disaster focus on the physical impacts of a disaster, as well as emergent social problems caused by the unplanned and disruptive nature of the disaster (Kreps, 1984, p. 311). Disasters generally occur suddenly and can cause significant harm to people and infrastructure. Disasters necessitate actions by individuals, groups, organizations, and communities in order to mitigate the impacts. Quarantelli (2005) argued that disaster is rooted in two fundamental ideas. First, disasters are social phenomena as opposed to simply naturally occurring forces. Natural forces, wild fires, hurricanes, floods, or earth quakes are sources of damage, while the disaster is the impact on human goals, social systems, and processes. Second, a disaster involves the established social structure and associated changes, such as disruption, disorder, and bifurcation to that structure. The established order, patterns of routine behaviors and interactions, economic processes, transportations as well as communications are often disrupted and thrown into confusion and in some cases, chaos.

A natural disaster is a disastrous event with "atmospheric, geological, and hydrological origins (e.g., droughts, earthquakes, floods, hurricanes, landslides) that can cause fatalities, property damage and social environmental disruption" (Xu et al., 2016, p. 39). These events have both social and physical impacts and can pose significant harm toward society. The World Health Organization (WHO) defines a natural disaster as:

> an act of nature of such magnitude as to create a catastrophic situation in which the day-to-day patterns of life are suddenly disrupted and people are plunged into helplessness and suffering, and, as a result, need food, clothing, shelter, medical and nursing care and other necessities of life, and protection against unfavourable environmental factors and conditions. (Assar, 1971, p. 14)

These events (floods, wildfires, hurricanes, tornadoes) are not solely natural, and involve the interaction of natural phenomena with human-built systems (dams, levees, buildings, roads, bridges, and housing developments). The impact of naturally occurring events on human-built systems, goals, values, and needs creates the requirements for a disaster (Seeger & Sellnow, 2016). Human activities often interact with naturally occurring phenomena to increase the probability of a disaster, and human systems often exacerbate the harm caused by natural disasters. Modern food production practices have increased the prevalence and impact of some zoonotic diseases, such as H1N1, colloquially known as bird flu. The building of levees to control rivers has contributed to increased risks of flooding in some areas. Fire suppression in forests has paradoxically enhanced the likelihood of catastrophic wild fires. Most dramatically, human-caused climate change can be expected to significantly increase the prevalence of floods and droughts, superstorms, heat waves, wild fires, and emerging infectious diseases, among other disasters (Van Aalst, 2006). The US Geological Survey notes:

> With increasing global surface temperatures the possibility of more droughts and increased intensity of storms will likely occur. As more water vapor is evaporated into the atmosphere it becomes fuel for more powerful storms to develop. More heat in the atmosphere and warmer ocean surface temperatures can lead to increased wind speeds in tropical storms. Rising sea levels expose higher locations not usually subjected to the power of the sea and to the erosive forces of waves and currents. (US Geological Survey, 2019)

The impact of human-caused climate change on the prevalence and severity of disasters illustrates that human and natural systems are tightly coupled. Tight coupling occurs when there is "no slack or buffer between two items" (Perrow, 1984, p. 90). As a consequence, changes in a system impact other systems, sometimes in very direct ways, and these interactions are often underlying factors in disasters.

The US Federal Emergency Management Agency (FEMA) identifies 32 types of disaster. Of these, 15 are events that would be considered natural disasters (see Table 15.1).

Floods are the most common disasters, while historically, the worst crises have been earthquakes and infectious disease pandemics (Seeger & Sellnow, 2016). The 1918–1919 influenza, or Spanish flu, infected an estimated 500 million people worldwide and may have caused

Table 15.1 Disaster events identified as natural by FEMA

Avalanche
Drought
Earthquakes
Extreme heat
Floods
Hurricanes
Landslides and debris flow
Pandemic
Severe weather
Snowstorms and extreme cold
Thunderstorms and lightning
Tornadoes
Tsunamis
Volcanoes
Wildfires

as many as 20 million deaths. The 1976 Tangshan China earthquake was the most destructive of the twentieth century, with official death tolls of 255,000 and another 150,000 injured. The 1931 floods of the Yangtze–Huai rivers in China claimed (by some estimates) up to 3.5 million lives.

Many observers suggest that crises are occurring with greater frequency and causing more harm than they have in the past (Perrow, 1984; Seeger, Sellnow, & Ulmer, 2003). The WHO estimates that annually, natural disasters kill around 90,000 people and affect close to 160 million people worldwide. Crises can also precipitate rapid change in policies, populations, and understanding of risks. Recent examples, including the 2018–2019 Ebola pandemic in Central Africa, the 2018 Camp Fire in Northern California, Hurricane Maria in Puerto Rico, and the 2004 Indian Ocean tsunami, illustrate the rapid changes that happen following a crisis. The events of 9/11 not only precipitated a fundamental rethinking of US federal policy regarding security but also created the most comprehensive reorganization of the US federal government to occur in decades. Hurricane Maria devastated the island of Puerto Rico, claimed 3,000 lives, and prompted a massive migration of residents from the island to the US mainland. Hurricane Katrina also created a major demographic shift in New Orleans and prompted new understandings of risk and the role of governments in response to disasters. The 2004 tsunami claimed as many as 230,000 lives in 14 countries, wiped away entire communities, and created widespread economic and environmental damage. This event also called attention to the risks associated with tsunamis and development in coastal areas. The Camp Fire in 2018 was the worst wildfire in California in over 100 years, resulting in the loss of 85 lives and costing over $1.5 billion in damages, leading to a strong public push for changes in development and building policies.

These and similar disasters are significant in terms of the extent of interaction between human and natural systems as well as their massive scope and impact, necessitating the term *mega-crisis*. Mega-crises are events that "defy boundaries, limits, neat demarcations, patterned connections and linear consequences" (Helsloot et al., 2012, p. 5). Mega-crises create especially significant threats and harm, overwhelm the capacity to respond and manage, and have both short and long-term consequences. Mega-crises also illustrate the fallacy of the "traditional dichotomy between natural and man-made disasters" by demonstrating the complex interactions between human-caused and natural phenomena (Helsloot et al., 2012, p. 5).

The level of harm, risk, and frequency of disaster events creates an imperative for thoughtful, intentional, and strategic responses. These responses are typically framed as disaster or emergency management and include a variety of organizational processes, coordination, logistics, planning, and communication.

Disaster and Emergency Management

Social processes, structures, and techniques have been developed to help avoid disasters when possible and mitigate harm when not. These processes are typically referred to as disaster management or emergency management. The International Federation of Red Cross and Red Crescent Societies (n.d.) defines disaster management as "the organization and management of resources and responsibilities for dealing with all humanitarian aspects of emergencies, in particular preparedness, response, and recovery in order to lessen the impact of disasters."

FEMA defines emergency management as "the managerial function charged with creating the framework within which communities reduce vulnerability to hazards and cope with disasters" (Federal Emergency Management Agency, n.d.-a) and uses a four-phase approach to emergency management (see Figure 15.1). These phases of mitigation, preparedness, response,

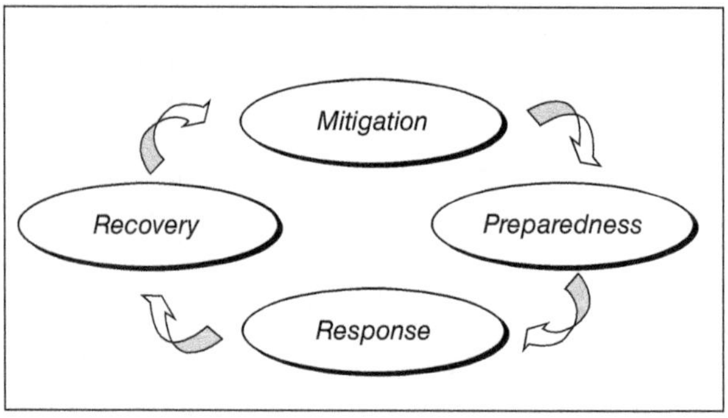

Figure 15.1 Four phases of emergency management: FEMA.

and recovery activities broadly track the development of a disaster over time. Mitigation is a set of strategies designed to prevent future emergencies and/or minimize their effects through proactive behaviors, such as buying flood insurance or building water diversion structures. Preparedness involves planning for an event by developing response tactics, such as evacuation plans, stockpiling food, water, and other resources. The response phase involves the implementation of a preparedness plan in order to save lives, reduce harm, and limit property damage in an emergency situation. Recovery involves activities after the emergency has subsided, oriented toward returning to a more stable status quo (Federal Emergency Management Agency, n.d.-b).

Emergency management in the United States is a highly structured governmental activity that is coordinated between the local, state, national, and international levels. Disasters are typically tied to a specific geographic location, and as a result local municipal, county, or tribal authorities usually provide the initial response. When those capacities are exceeded, state resources are deployed. Federal resources are deployed when state resources are no longer seen as adequate (Federal Emergency Management Agency, n.d.-c). Events may also become internationalized if they extend beyond national borders or if they exceed the capacity of an individual country. In these cases, international organizations such as the WHO may become involved. In addition, private nonprofit organizations such as the Red Cross, as well as faith-based relief organizations, may provide important response capacity. Finally, organizations often emerge naturally in response to a disaster to fulfill needs that are not being met by existing organizations (Dynes, 1970). These may be informational, logistic, resource, or humanitarian needs. Volunteer civilian groups often develop during floods, for example, to assist in evacuations. The numbers and diversity of public, government, nonprofit, private, and emergent organizations involved in catastrophic disasters require effective inter-organizational and multimodal communication and coordination (Kapucu, Arslan, & Demiroz, 2010). Coordination is the most common challenge in emergency response.

Disaster management is a highly structured set of activities, most often overseen by government agencies and governed by regulations, policies, procedures, and conventions. These agencies include police, fire, and emergency response personnel at the local, state, and federal level who coordinate and structure their activities through the National Incident Management System (NIMS). NIMS is a standardized approach and organizational structure designed to facilitate coordinated management and response to an emergency situation. This approach was initially developed by the Department of Homeland Security in 2004 as a solution to the confused and uncoordinated response to the attacks of September 11. NIMS offers a uniform set of processes, procedures, and functions for emergency responders so that operations can be easily coordinated (Perry, 2003).

Quarantelli (1988) emphasizes that the processes of emergency planning and emergency management are distinct but related activities. The process of planning is related to preparedness. This process involves developing and writing the emergency plan, including conducting vulnerability assessments, and determining who will manage which potential risks, harms, and impacts. Planning also requires a review of demands made by stakeholder agencies and groups, inventories of community resources available to meet those demands, the development of strategies for response, and the creation of capacity to execute those strategies. Personnel, equipment, and supplies are used to meet the requirements of response.

Communication Functions of Emergency Management

Communication processes are integral to each stage of the disaster and emergency management process, but are most often framed as a support function. Emergency management frameworks, such as NIMS, tend to view communication as a tactical activity in support of other functions, such as operations, coordination, and public information. Comfort (2007) notes that at its most basic, "communication in emergency management practice has focused on the interoperability of mechanical devices, such as radios, hand-held data devices, cell phones, and landline and satellite telephone networks" (p. 94). In other cases, communication tends to be framed within the narrow context of warning messages and systems, such as warning sirens for tornadoes or fires. Many of these views are grounded in a relatively simplistic action framework of communication, which presents senders as homogeneous and passive, and assumes messages that are sent are received, interpreted, and acted on as intended.

Arguably, however, the management of a disaster or emergency is itself a set of coordinated communication activities that follow from a larger strategy and that occur over time throughout the development of a crisis lifecycle. For example, Reynolds and Seeger (2005) identify a variety of communication activities across the five stages of crisis development (see Table 15.2). These stages include pre-crisis, initial event, maintenance, resolution, and evaluation. The activities they identify include both traditional risk communication tactics, such as promoting public understanding of risks, seeking to change risky behaviors, and promoting preparedness, as well as traditional crisis communication activities, such as issuing specific warnings and recommendations, reducing uncertainty, and providing updates on response activities. They also suggest that communication functions in the initial monitoring identification of risks before a crisis erupts and in encoding and distributing lessons that may be learned from a crisis.

This view of communication in emergency preparedness and response is more comprehensive and strategic than traditional perspectives, as it allows for communication to extend throughout the crisis lifecycle. The communication processes are also additive and build upon one another across the crisis lifecycle. This perspective also allows for communication to strategically influence coordination.

Seeger and Sellnow (2016) offer an even more extensive and strategic set of communication processes associated with disaster and emergency management (see Table 15.3). They emphasize both the epistemic and constitutive views of communication, with communication the process whereby risks are known and understood and communication the process whereby groups and communities organize in response to those risks.

The functional framework incorporates a variety of other crisis and risk communication frame-works to build and support a larger strategic approach to communication. For example, issue management (Heath & Palenchar, 2008), sensemaking (Weick, 1988), and boundary spanning (Tushman & Scanlan, 1981) are part of the larger scanning function. Image repair

Table 15.2 Communication functions.

I. Pre-crisis (risk messages; warnings; preparations)

Communication and education campaigns targeted at both the public and the response community to facilitate:

- Monitoring and recognition of emerging risks.
- General public understanding of risk.
- Public preparation for the possibility of an adverse event.
- Changes in behavior to reduce the likelihood of harm (self-efficacy).
- Specific warning messages regarding some imminent threats.
- Alliances and cooperation with agencies, organizations, and groups.
- Development of consensual recommendations by experts and first responders.
- Message development and testing for subsequent stages.

II. Initial event (uncertainty reduction; self-efficacy; reassurance)

Rapid communication to the general public and to affected groups seeking to establish:

- Empathy, reassurance, and reduction in emotional turmoil.
- Designated crisis/agency spokespersons and formal channels and methods of communication.
- General and broad-based understanding of the crisis circumstances, consequences, and anticipated outcomes based on available information.
- Reduction of crisis-related uncertainty.
- Specific understanding of emergency management and medical community responses.
- Understanding of self-efficacy and personal response activities (how/where to get more information).

III. Maintenance (ongoing uncertainty reduction; self-efficacy; reassurance)

Communication to the general public and to affected groups seeking to facilitate:

- More accurate public understanding of ongoing risks.
- Understanding of background factors and issues.
- Broad-based support and cooperation with response and recovery efforts.
- Feedback from affected public and correction of any misunderstandings/rumors.
- Ongoing explanation and reiteration of self-efficacy and personal response activities (how/where to get more information) begun in Stage II.
- Informed decision-making by the public based on understanding of risks/benefits.

IV. Resolution (updates regarding resolution; discussions about cause and new risks/new understandings of risk)

Public communication and campaigns directed toward the general public and affected groups seeking to:

- Inform and persuade about ongoing clean-up, remediation, recovery, and rebuilding efforts.
- Facilitate broad-based, honest, and open discussion and resolution of issues regarding cause, blame, responsibility, and adequacy of response.
- Improve/create public understanding of new risks and new understandings of risk as well as new risk avoidance behaviors and response procedures.
- Promote the activities and capabilities of agencies and organizations to reinforce positive corporate identity and image.

V. Evaluation (discussions of adequacy of response; consensus about lessons and new understandings of risk)

Communication directed toward agencies and the response community to:

- Evaluate and assess responses, including communication effectiveness.
- Document, formalize, and communicate lessons learned.

Table 15.2 (*Cont*)

• Determine specific actions to improve crisis communication and crisis response capability.
• Create linkages to pre-crisis activities (Stage I).

Source: Reynolds and Seeger (2005, pp. 52–53).

Table 15.3 Functions of crisis communication

Environmental scanning and spanning	(Monitoring and maintaining external relationships: collecting information, building relationships with external stakeholders) Sensemaking of information Issue management Spanning agency, organization, and community boundaries Risk communication
Crisis response	(Planning for and managing crises) Uncertainty reduction, providing information and interpretations, warnings, evacuations notices, product recalls Coordination with key stakeholders and response agencies Information dissemination Promoting strategic ambiguity
Crisis resolution	(Restructuring, repairing, and maintaining relationships after a crisis) Defensive messages Explanatory messages Image restoration Renewal Grieving and memorializing
Organizational learning	(Emerging from a crisis with enhanced knowledge, relationships, and capacity) Dialogue Networks and relationships Understanding and norms

Source: Seeger and Sellnow (2016).

(Benoit, 2014), situated crisis responses (Coombs, 2014), and the discourse of renewal (Seeger et al., 2005) are all positioned within the larger function of crisis resolution and are part of the strategic management of the organization's reputation. Comfort (2007) calls for a reframing of the basic function of emergency management. She argues that traditionally, emergency management serves three functions, the three Cs of communication, coordination, and control. Communication involves the sharing of information so as to create a common understanding of an event, and is necessary to achieve coordinated actions among agencies and groups. Control is most effective when a centralized authority both transmit orders, yet is open to receiving feedback regarding emerging conditions. In the case of the government response to Hurricane Katrina, communication, coordination, and control all functioned as planned, but the emergency management system was unable to enact emergent and innovative responses to the dynamic situation.

Comfort further reframes crisis management as a dynamic inter-organizational system that incorporates a variety of response agencies and organizations. This system is characterized by four primary decision points: "(1) detection of risk, (2) recognition and interpretation of risk for the immediate context, (3) communication of risk to multiple organizations in a wider region, and (4) self-organization and mobilization of a collective, community response system to reduce risk and respond to danger" (p. 189).

Cognition, according to Comfort, involves the ability to recognize and act upon emerging risks and – acting upon them through emergent and adaptive responses – unites these activities. This involves interpreting cues, assessing feedback, and enacting emergent responses (Comfort, 2007).

While most authors agree that communication plays an important role in the response to natural disasters, this role is most often relegated to a set of tactics in support of other emergency management functions. More comprehensive frameworks, such as those of Reynolds and Seeger, Sellnow and Seeger, and notably Comfort, point to a much broader strategic role for communication across the lifecycle of a crisis and integrated into larger processes of organizing. Sellnow and Seeger (2019), for example, suggested that communication about disasters is a form of SC in that it seeks to reconcile the goals of organizations and the public. Coombs (2014) argued that "crisis communication should be strategic; efforts should be designed to improve the situation." This includes meeting the needs of diverse stakeholders, individuals, agencies, and organizations.

Strategic Communication

Increasingly, the range of communicative activities used to achieve organizational goals are described as SC. Organizations of all forms communicate in strategic ways in pursuit of their mission, including government agencies, profit-making organizations, non-government organizations, and emergent organizations (Hallahan et al., 2007). Organizational communication activities flow from and contribute to the organizations' purposes, goals, missions, and stakeholders. Strategic communication has been conceptualized to include a wide variety of communication activities, such as marketing, management, public relations, political and technical communication (Holtzhausen, 2008). Hallahan et al. (2007, p. 7) argued that SC is by definition purposeful in that it focuses on "how the organization itself presents and promotes itself through the intentional activities of its leaders, employees, and communication practitioners." Zerfass and Huck (2007) argued that SC "expands the traditional set of institutionalized communication measures in order to manage meaning in all kinds of interactions with internal and external stakeholders" (p. 107). Public relations often involves the development of a larger strategic plan which draws on organizational knowledge and resources to develop communication strategies which then inform the development of tactics (Smudde, 2011).

Strategic Communication in Disaster Management

An SC approach to disaster management involves an integrated set of purposeful activities to achieve preparedness, management, and response goals across the life cycle of a disaster. These goals often include the development of a consensus in terms of the risks and response needs related to an event, the development of resilient organizations and institutions, and the capacity to see these events in complex and even positive ways and to integrate stakeholders as full participants.

Consensual understanding of risks, risk awareness, and normative responses regarding natural disasters is a central goal of strategic disaster management. These factors support a set of behavioral outcomes leading to increased preparedness during pre-crisis. Risk awareness and associated behavioral changes are often the target of communication campaigns, such as those developed by the Ready.Gov website. These campaigns promote awareness, planning, and the development of competencies in first aid and emergency responses for an array of human-caused and natural disasters.

Although ubiquitous and heavily funded by state and federal governments, historically, preparedness campaigns have limited impact in terms of behavioral change (Adame & Miller, 2015). A variety of explanations have been offered for this phenomenon, including public beliefs that the government will provide protection from disaster, a lack of perceived vulnerability, the diversity of audiences and communities, and a general lack of perceived agency (Paton & Johnston, 2001). Moreover, publics are often presented as victims of a crisis without power over circumstances. An SC approach to creating consensual understanding of risks, risk awareness, and normative responses requires a more nuanced, sustained, comprehensive, and processed approach. This requires understanding and accommodating existing beliefs, perceptions, and experiences and recognizing cultural and regional differences in risk experiences. Two-way symmetric exchanges between risk and crisis stakeholders is necessary to a larger strategic approach. In addition, these efforts must acknowledge the heterogeneous nature of audiences, victims, and stakeholders, as well as the tendency of individuals to seek additional information and consensual validation of risk messages from multiple sources, including their own support networks. Finally, addressing agency and self- and community efficacy is necessary to a strategy supporting preparedness (see Mileti & O'Brien, 1992; Mileti & Peek, 2000; Perry, Lindell, & Tierney, 2001).

Resilience

Along with strategically presenting and promoting risk awareness and preparedness, an additional function of SC involves promoting resilience for organizations, agencies, and communities. Resilience has become a popular concept in emergency management because it integrates both preparedness and response and because of the emphasis on localized capacity. Ayyub (2014) argues that resilience is "the ability to prepare for and adapt to changing conditions and withstand and recover rapidly from disruptions" (p. 4). Buzzanell (2010) suggests that "resilience is developed, sustained, and grown through discourse, interaction, and material consideration" and "includes: (a) crafting normalcy, (b) affirming identity anchors, (c) maintaining and using communication networks, (d) putting alternative logics to work, and (e) downplaying negative feelings" (p. 1).

Organizational, agency, and community resilience involves systemic attributes that accommodate risks, avoid crises, cope with disruption, bounce back, pull through, or adapt to the disruption of a crisis (see Boin & McConnell, 2007; Kendra & Wachtendorf, 2018). Characteristics of a resilient system include capacity, skill, availability of resources (as well as the speed with which they can be deployed), and level of training and preparation (including both width and depth and level of integration). In addition, communicative connections between systems allowing for coordination and cooperation are factors in resilience. Norris et al. (2008) offers a concept of community resilience that emphasizes adaptability as an ongoing process rather than stability as a system attribute (p. 130). Resilience is marked by the ability of a community or organization to effectively adapt and change as opposed to the ability of a community to merely resist and withstand a disruption.

An SC approach to resilience included building competencies and connections within and between organizations and agencies. Houston et al. (2015) synthesize four categories of SC processes that are related to community resilience literature: “community competence, community narratives, disaster and risk processes, and community and economic development” (p. 276). Community competence involves a set of interrelated activities including disaster planning, risk mitigation, critical reflection, problem-solving, and empowerment of members. Narratives are important processes for encoding and transmitting lessons, experiences, beliefs, and values related to disasters and responses (Seeger & Sellnow, 2016).

Disaster and risk processes include the dissemination and exchange of disaster and risk information in forms that can be used in education, discussions, preparedness activities, and planning. Finally, SC processes that support government and community economic development are related to resilience. This includes building economic opportunities and addressing inequities.

Impacts

A third goal related to natural disaster preparedness and responses concerns the ways in which the impacts of these events are understood. Most often, a natural disaster is framed as a destructive and negative event that must be overcome so that the community or organization may return to its pre-disaster state. There is a growing recognition that a disaster may also have positive impacts and that a communication strategy of renewal may help activate positive outcomes. The concept of post-traumatic growth, for example, acknowledges that positive changes can occur as an outcome of challenging situations. This may include “an increased appreciation for life in general, more meaningful interpersonal relationships, an increased sense of personal strength, changed priorities, and a richer existential and spiritual life” (Tedeschi & Calhoun, 2004). Organizational scholars have also described a discourse of renewal that can sometimes replace the often contentious arguments about blame and responsibility and efforts to strategically repair images. Renewal emphasizes the opportunities for change that exist following a significant disruption, capitalizing on shared values and visions of the future, and relying on leadership to articulate those values and visions (Ulmer, Seeger, & Sellnow, 2007).

An SC orientation is required to help manifest the positive elements and opportunities that follow a natural disaster. This includes activities designed to frame the event in terms of shared community and organizational values, efforts to promote unified action, and narratives that emphasize the potentially positive outcomes. Values such as community, family, and faith are important to contextualize a traumatic event such as a natural disaster. These events often activate a sense of common threat and common purpose that can be leveraged for support. Narratives about rebuilding that emphasize lessons learned and future opportunities can also be part of a larger SC program.

An SC approach to disasters preparedness and management can connect a variety of communication tactics into a coherent program that serves larger goals. This approach may be especially important in preparedness and management, where communication has a wide variety of disparate functions across the lifecycle of an event. Connecting pre-crisis risk mitigation and preparedness messages to post-crisis recovery, learning, and renewal, for example, may be enhanced under an SC framework. The three larger goals – the development of a consensual understanding of natural disaster risks and normative responses, the development of resilient organizations and institutions, and the capacity to see these events in complex and positive ways – can provide coherence to communication activities.

Conclusion

This chapter presented a conceptualization of natural disasters as the intersection of naturally occurring phenomena and human factors. Disaster and emergency management involve structured formalized response processes, procedures, capacities, and organizational structures, as well as a set of improvised emergent processes and behaviors. These depend on a variety of communication activities and tactics. Most often, these communication activities have been framed as a larger strategic process across the lifecycle of a disaster. Both preparedness and response may be enhanced by an SC orientation. This includes development of a consensual understanding of the risks of natural disaster, integrated response plans, the development of resilient organizations and institutions, the capacity to see these events in positive ways, and the involvement of stakeholders as partners in preparedness and response.

References

Adame, B. J., & Miller, C. H. (2015). Vested interest, disaster preparedness, and strategic campaign message design. *Health Communication*, 30(3), 271–281.

Assar, M. (1971). *Guide to sanitation in natural disasters.* Geneva: World Health Organization. Retrieved from https://apps.who.int/iris/bitstream/handle/10665/41031/10678_eng.pdf;jsessionid=04EDA74E878D55634C7DE8C30C169543?sequence=1

Ayyub, B. M. (2014). Systems resilience for multihazard environments: Definition, metrics, and valuation for decision making. *Risk Analysis*, 34(2), 340–355.

Benoit, W. L. (2014). *Accounts, excuses, and apologies: Image repair theory and research.* New York: SUNY Press.

Boin, A., & McConnell, A. (2007). Preparing for critical infrastructure breakdowns: The limits of crisis management and need for resilience. *Journal of Contingencies and Crisis Management*, 15(1), 50–59.

Buzzanell, P. M. (2010). Resilience: Talking, resisting, and imagining new normalcies into being. *Journal of Communication*, 60(1), 1–14.

Comfort, L. K. (2007). Crisis management in hindsight: Cognition, communication, coordination, and control. *Public Administration Review*, 67(s1), 189–197.

Coombs, W. T. (2014). *Ongoing crisis communication: Planning, managing, and responding.* Thousand Oaks, CA: Sage.

Dynes, R. R. (1970). Organizational involvement and changes in community structure in disaster. *American Behavioral Scientist*, 13(3), 430–439.

Federal Emergency Management Agency (2015). National incident management system (NIMS). Retrieved from https://www.fema.gov/national-incident-management-system

Federal Emergency Management Agency (n.d-a).The four phases of emergency management. Retrieved from https://training.fema.gov/emiweb/downloads/is111_unit%204.pdf

Federal Emergency Management Agency (n.d-b). Emergency management: Definition, vision, mission, principles. Retrieved from https://training.fema.gov/hiedu/docs/emprinciples/0907_176%20em%20principles12x18v2f%20johnson%20(w-o%20draft).pdf

Federal Emergency Management Agency (n.d.-c). Disaster sequence. Retrieved from https://training.fema.gov/emiweb/downloads/is208sdmunit3.pdf

Fritz, C. E. (1961). Disasters. In R. K. Merton & R. A. Nisbet (Eds.), *Contemporary social problems.* (pp. 651–694). New York: Harcourt.

Hallahan, K., Holtzhausen, D., Van Ruler, B., Verčič, D., & Sriramesh, K. (2007). Defining strategic communication. *International Journal of Strategic Communication*, 1(1), 3–35.

Heath, R. L., & Palenchar, M. J. (2008). *Strategic issues management: Organizations and public policy challenges.* Los Angeles, CA: Sage.

Helsloot, I., Boin, A., Jacobs, B., & Comfort, L. K. (Eds.). (2012). *Mega-crises: Understanding the prospects, nature, characteristics, and the effects of cataclysmic events.* , IL: Charles C. Thomas.

Holtzhausen, D. (2008). Strategic communication. *The International Encyclopedia of Communication.* doi: 10.1002/9781405186407.

Houston, J. B., Spialek, M. L., Cox, J., Greenwood, M. M., & First, J. (2015). The centrality of communication and media in fostering community resilience: A framework for assessment and intervention. *American Behavioral Scientist*, 59(2), 270–283.

International Federation of Red Cross and Red Crescent Societies (n.d.). About disaster management. Retrieved from https://www.ifrc.org/en/what-we-do/disaster-management/about-disaster-management

Kapucu, N., Arslan, T., & Demiroz, F. (2010). Collaborative emergency management and national emergency management network. *Disaster Prevention and Management: An International Journal*, 19(4), 452–468.

Kendra, J. M., & Wachtendorf, T. (2007). Community innovation and disasters In H. Rodriguez, E. L. Quarantelli, R. R. Dynes (Eds.), *Handbook of disaster research* (pp. 316–334). New York: Springer.

Kreps, G. A. (1984). Sociological inquiry and disaster research. *Annual Review of Sociology*, 10, 309–330.

McFarlane, A. C., & Norris, F. H. (2006). Definitions and concepts in disaster research. In F. H. Norris, S. Galea, M. J. Friedman, P. J. Watson (Eds.), *Methods for disaster mental health research* (pp. 3–19). New York: The Guilford Press.

Mileti, D. S., & O'Brien, P. W. (1992). Warnings during disaster: Normalizing communicated risk. *Social Problems*, 39(1), 40–57.

Mileti, D. S., & Peek, L. (2000). The social psychology of public response to warnings of a nuclear power plant accident. *Journal of Hazardous Materials*, 75, 181–194.

Norris, F. H., Stevens, S. P., Pfefferbaum, B., Wyche, K. F., & Pfefferbaum, R. L. (2008). Community resilience as a metaphor, theory, set of capacities, and strategy for disaster readiness. *American Journal of Community Psychology*, 41(1–2), 127–150.

Paton, D., & Johnston, D. (2001). Disasters and communities: Vulnerability, resilience and preparedness. *Disaster Prevention and Management: An International Journal*, 10(4), 270–277.

Perrow, C. (1984). *Normal accidents: Living with high-risk technologies.* New York: Basic Books.

Perry, R. W. (2003). Incident management systems in disaster management. *Disaster Prevention and Management*, 12(5), 405–412.

Perry, R. W. (2007). What is a disaster? In H. Rodriguez, E. L. Quarantelli, R. R. Dynes (Eds.), *Handbook of disaster research* (pp. 1–15). New York, NY: Springer.

Perry, R. W., & Lindell, M. K. (2003). Preparedness for emergency response: Guidelines for the emergency planning process. *Disasters*, 27(4), 336–350.

Perry, R. W., Lindell, M. K., & Tierney, K. J. (Eds.). (2001). *Facing the unexpected: Disaster preparedness and response in the United States.* Washington, D.C.: Joseph Henry Press.

Quarantelli, E. L. (1988). Disaster crisis management: A summary of research findings. *Journal of Management Studies*, 25(4), 373–385.

Quarantelli, E. L. (Ed.). (2005). *What is a disaster?: A dozen perspectives on the question.* London: Routledge.

Reynolds, B., & Seeger, M. W. (2005). Crisis and emergency risk communication as an integrative model. *Journal of Health Communication*, 10(1), 43–55.

Seeger, M., & Sellnow, T. L. (2016). *Narratives of crisis: Telling stories of ruin and renewal.* Stanford, CA: Stanford University Press.

Seeger, M. W. (2002). Chaos and crisis: Propositions for a general theory of crisis communication. *Public Relations Review*, 28(4), 329–337.

Seeger, M. W., Sellnow, T. L., & Ulmer, R. R. (2003). *Communication and organizational crisis.* Westport, CT: Greenwood Publishing Group.

Seeger, M. W., Ulmer, R. R., Novak, J. M., & Sellnow, T. (2005). Post-crisis discourse and organizational change, failure and renewal. *Journal of Organizational Change Management*, 18(1), 78–95.

Sellnow, T. L., & Seeger, M. W. (2019). Crisis/emergency communication and security. In *The handbook of communication and security* (pp. 41–54). Routledge.

Smudde, P. (2011). Public relations as dramatistic organizing: A case study bridging theory and practice. *Psychological Inquiry, 15*(1), 1–18.

Taylor, B. C., & Bean, H. (Eds.). (2019). *The handbook of communication and security.* Routledge.

Tedeschi, R. G., & Calhoun, L. G. (2004). " Posttraumatic growth: Conceptual foundations and empirical evidence". *Psychological Inquiry, 15*(1), 1–18.
Tushman, M. L., & Scanlan, T. J. (1981). Characteristics and external orientations of boundary spanning individuals. *Academy of Management Journal*, 24(1), 83–98.
US Geological Survey (2019). How can climate change affect natural disasters? Retrieved from https://www.usgs.gov/faqs/how-can-climate-change-affect-natural-disasters-1?qt-news_science_products=0#qt-news_science_products
Ulmer, R. R., Seeger, M. W., & Sellnow, T. L. (2007). Post-crisis communication and renewal: Expanding the parameters of post-crisis discourse. *Public Relations Review*, 33(2), 130–134.
Van Aalst, M. K. (2006). The impacts of climate change on the risk of natural disasters. *Disasters*, 30(1), 5–18.
Weick, K. E. (1988). Enacted sensemaking in crisis situations [1]. *Journal of Management Studies*, 25(4), 305–317.
Xu, J., Wang, Z., Shen, F., Ouyang, C., & Tu, Y. (2016). Natural disasters and social conflict: A systematic literature review. *International Journal of Disaster Risk Reduction*, 17, 38–48.
Zerfass, A., & Huck, S. (2007). Innovation, communication, and leadership: New developments in strategic communication. *International Journal of Strategic Communication*, 1(2), 107–122.

PART V

Social, Climate, and Environmental Strategic Communication

16

Overcome the Deficit Model by Applying the CAUSE Model to Climate Change Communication

Katherine E. Rowan[1], Allison Engblom[1], Julia Hathaway[1], Rebecca Lloyd[1], Ian Vorster[2], Erin Z. Anderson[1], and Karen L. Akerlof[1]

[1]George Mason University, [2]Dragonfly Environmental Communications

Each spring, our university holds a "School Environmental Action Showcase." Youth from regional elementary, middle, and high schools showcase their semester-long projects. Projects include aerating soil around schools to allow rain to be cleaned on its journey through rocks and soil. This step helps clean water reach rivers, rather than filling them with polluted water running over built surfaces. One might assume this event is formal and stuffy. Perhaps it includes formal talks by elementary school youth? Perhaps professors discuss the regional watershed and threats to the environment? There are many such didactic moments, but the event is also experiential and emotional. Youth meet a falconer, touch worms building soil, and the senior scientist who created this event begins it by leading attendees in song to Woody Guthrie's "This Land Is Your Land." The objective is to inspire learning and love for our land.[1]

We open this chapter with this anecdote to preface our thesis: communicating about the environment, and especially climate change, is tough, and it requires research and reflection about communication objectives. Guided by Besley and associates' research on communication training for scientists (e.g. Besley, Dudo, & Storksdieck, 2015) as well as Carl Botan's work on strategic communication (Botan, 2018), we argue that scientists need guidance on the sorts of communication objectives (or specific, short-term goals) they should pursue, especially when communicating a challenging topic such as climate change. When with family and friends, should they plan to listen mostly when conversing about climate change? Communicate respect? Be warm and welcoming? Support decision-making? Explain key terms and workable options? Each option *might* be the right choice in a particular situation. This chapter offers research-backed analysis to guide scientists in making *strategic and ethical* choices about their climate change communication in a range of contexts, formal and informal. We see reflection and planning for science communication as highly ethical and strategic, far more ethical and sensible than *not* thinking about one's audience and their concerns. Well planned communication is needed, given the challenges climate change creates.

---

[1] Information about the Student Environmental Action Showcase, held during spring at George Mason University in Northern Virginia, is available at https://www.novaoutside.org/events/school-environmental-action-showcase/. The authors would like to thank Drs. Cindy Smith, R. Chris Jones, and Mr. Kurt Moser of NoVA Outside, an alliance of environmental educators, for their leadership on this event and the cause of environmental education.

The Handbook of Strategic Communication, First Edition. Edited by Carl H. Botan.

Why Communicating Climate Change Is Essential and Difficult

Climate change is dangerous. The average global temperature is increasing due to the growing concentration of heat-trapping gases in the atmosphere. These gases are emitted through transportation, heating, cooling, and many other human activities (Forster et al., 2007; Myhre et al., 2013). This rising global temperature has an array of harmful environmental effects, including increased flooding and risk of extreme weather, changes in frequency and scope of insect-borne diseases, and an increased number of dangerous high-temperature days (Intergovernmental Panel on Climate Change, 2014; National Research Council, 2011; Smith et al., 2014; Wong et al., 2014).

The health of the abiotic environment and that of humans, animals, and plants are integrally connected: a negative impact on one eventually affects the others. For example, in humans, extreme heat leads to increases in heart disease, stroke, and chronic diseases of the lower respiratory tract (Martiello & Giacchi, 2010). Extreme heat hurts plant growth as well. According to Porter et al. (2014), a warming climate will reduce wheat, rice, and maize crop yields. Schlaepfer et al. (2017) conclude that climate change may cause land masses that currently experience temperate climates to become subtropical drylands. This change would affect budding and birth for plants and animals. Further, these effects could lead to increases in human diseases such as dengue and malaria, and cause cool season crops such as wheat and potatoes to no longer be viable in areas where they currently abound.

Economic impacts from climate change can be staggering. Unmitigated warming is expected to reshape the global economy by reducing average global incomes by roughly 23% by 2100 (Burke, Hsiang, & Miguel, 2015). On a regional level, the economic analyses for specific regions and activities are sobering. For example, in the Great Lakes region of the US, anglers spend about $9.3 billion annually fishing within the Great Lakes and surrounding bodies of water (Anderson, 2016; Ficke, Myrick, & Hansen, 2007). If Midwestern US fish populations decline due to warmer waters, state economies could suffer.

Despite these dangers, climate change is not a frequent topic of conversation in the US, nor is it one on which accurate information is widely shared. Though a majority of Americans (58%) now understand that global warming is mostly human-caused, three in ten still say, wrongly, that the rate of climate change currently experienced is caused mostly by natural changes in the environment (Leiserowitz et al., 2017). Many do not realize theirs is the majority view on this issue, and perhaps because they lack this awareness, they are reluctant to talk about it. Only about one in three discuss global warming or climate change with family and friends (Leiserowitz et al., 2019).

To communicate about climate change and its harms, all parties need some understanding of climate change science and an informed sense of *how* and *when* to discuss this issue. A frequent way of communicating about climate change – is to proceed intuitively. Unfortunately, research suggests that this approach to science communication is not sufficient. To explain why intuition is not sufficient, this chapter first analyzes several frequent approaches to communicating climate science. We identify their appeal, strengths, and limitations. We then argue for an alternative, this chapter discusses the strengths and limitations the CAUSE model of strategic science communication. In so doing, this chapter casts *science communication as strategic communication*, which can be made more effective when communicators *research* – through listening and more formal means – their audiences' concerns, identify communication *objectives* possible in a variety of situations, and develop good reasons *for prioritizing one or two objectives over others*, such as earning trust or being likeable, over defending science or correcting inaccuracies. Each of these objectives may be important. Scientists need support determining what situations warrant which choices.

This chapter's view of science communication as strategic communication is consistent with Botan's (2018) definition of communication strategy as "campaign-level planning and decision-making involving maneuvering and arranging resources and arguments to meet the needs of publics and organizational grand strategies" (p. 14). The following discussion distinguishes unplanned communication from insincere communication, and argues that climate change requires *collective action by communities and nations*, the sort of action that does not occur without carefully researched and planned campaigns, not solely the sincere efforts of individuals.

The Deficit Model of Science Communication

One challenge for anyone attempting to discuss climate change is that these efforts may be guided by default assumptions; assumptions described by what is called the deficit model of science communication. The deficit model conceptualizes communication *solely* as information transfer from experts to lay persons (Bucchi, 2008). This model assumes, first, that non-scientists are often hostile toward science because they lack sufficient or accurate information. Second, it assumes that providing lay people with this information will automatically result in positive attitudes toward science or scientifically informed analyses of hazards. Thus, according to the model, while non-scientists may be ignorant, they are also persuadable as long as they are provided a set of relevant facts (Trench, 2008).

The technical model

Somewhat similar to the deficit model is the technical model of risk communication. This model derives from risk analysis, a field that emerged after World War II (e.g. Rowan, 1994a). The technical model of risk communication says that dangers resulting from emissions, manufacturing, or plant operations are misunderstood by the public principally because lay audiences *lack knowledge of these phenomena* (e.g. Fiorino, 1989). Supporting the technical model are studies by Slovic and others (e.g. Slovic, Fischhoff, & Lichtenstein, 1985) showing physical hazards are perceived differently in part because of lack of knowledge. For example, Slovic, Fischhoff, and Lichtenstein (1985) demonstrated that people were more concerned about nuclear power than bicycle accidents, even though bicycles are more likely to be associated with fatalities than the operation of nuclear power plants. For example, bicycle and motor vehicle collisions caused 818 fatalities in 2015 (Pedestrian & Bicycle Information Center, n.d.), but in that year, in the US, there were no fatalities associated with nuclear power. One problem, however, with this analysis – as discussed by Slovic, Fiorino, and others – is that rates of death, injury, and illness are *not* the only concerns stakeholders have: bicycles are relatively simple, familiar, and controllable machines. They are unlikely to cause large-scale destruction. In contrast, nuclear power plants are complex, less familiar than bikes, and require considerable expertise to manage safely.

Disadvantages of the Deficit and Technical Models

There are additional, serious criticisms of the deficit and technical views of science and risk communication. First, these models are at odds with research showing that exposure to scientific knowledge has limited impacts on attitudes and behavior (e.g. Sturgis & Allum, 2004). Instead, a variety of factors, including worldviews and values, shape people's views concerning scientific issues (Akerlof et al., 2016; Bauer, Allum, & Miller, 2007; Kahan, 2012). For example, Kahan et al. (2012) found that people with the highest levels of science knowledge and reasoning are *not*, in fact, the most concerned about climate change. Rather, they are the most *divided* on climate change, with some questioning whether this set of processes is occurring, if humans are contributing, and whether the effects of climate change are serious and immediate. Kahan and colleagues showed that, when asked questions about the science of climate change, individuals who are knowledgeable about science often answered correctly. However, when asked whether they *believe* in climate change, their answers varied depending in part on their worldviews (Kahan, Jenkins-Smith, & Braman, 2011; Kahan et al., 2012). This pattern of findings suggests that worldviews (or political orientations) affect responses to discussions of climate change more than science knowledge.

Second, the deficit and technical models place no value on relevant lay knowledge and do not encourage lay stakeholders to participate in learning about or managing risks. This is a serious problem. If the only information needed to manage climate change impacts such as flooding were scientific analyses, then perhaps technical information would be sufficient for effective communication. But like many challenges, climate change requires analysis of community values and resources as well as scientific information. A policy, for example, to protect a coastal community from flooding and dangerous storms needs to be evaluated for its effectiveness and cost (Akerlof et al., 2016; Bucchi, 2008; Fishkin & Luskin, 2005). The deficit and technical models fail to articulate how issues such as the cost and other stakeholder concerns will be explored.

A third set of problems with the deficit and technical models lie in their implicit analysis of relationships and communication. Regarding relationships, these models are silent. That is, they assume that for unspecified reasons and in unspecified contexts, stakeholders will simply want to learn science from scientists. Research suggests this is unlikely. Numerous studies show that people are more apt to be influenced by experts whom they perceive as likeable and concerned about their welfare, as well as competent (e.g. Anderson et al., 2013; Fiske & Dupree, 2014). In essence, the deficit and technical models of science communication apply a "one-size-fits-all" approach to dealing with challenges in science communication. According to these models, *every* challenge stems from a deficiency in knowledge; therefore, efforts to overcome challenges should be aimed at increasing stakeholders' knowledge of science rather than encouraging scientists to learn about local concerns and practices. A related concern is that these models are not informed by research on the *range of contexts* in which people may encounter or seek information about scientific topics such as climate change. For example, the National Academy of Science 2009 consensus report (National Research Council, 2009) describes both formal contexts – such as school, work, regulatory, legislative, and judicial settings – where science learning is required, and informal contexts, where voluntary learning occurs as people converse, read, cook, hike, fish, enjoy television, play educational games, visit museums, or explore science topics on the internet. Appreciation of the full range of contexts, both formal and informal, where climate science might be shared can assist scientists and professional communicators in thinking about the social hierarchies, relationships, and options likely to affect or shape policies informed by science. This information can assist as well in selecting situationally appropriate communication objectives.

Audience-Centered, Democratic, and Dialogic Models

A second approach to theorizing science communication may be found in "audience-centered," democratic, or dialogic models. Instead of exploring what lay stakeholders do not know about science, research in science communication documents the extent to which *scientists understand specified lay stakeholders' interests, values, and concerns* (Dudo & Besley, 2016; National Academies of Science, Engineering, and Medicine, 2017). This audience-centered turn in science communication research is showcased in the Sackler Colloquia, a set of high-level academic meetings sponsored by the National Academies of Science, Engineering, and Medicine (NASEM) (Sackler Colloquia Home, n.d.). The 2017 NASEM report suggests researchers study science communication from a "systems perspective," to identify the systems or "ecological niches" that support stakeholders and scientists in productive interaction.

This current focus on scientists' understanding of specified lay stakeholders' views and concerns is similar in some ways to the "democratic" model of risk communication promoted by Fiorino (1989), Bradbury (1989), and others (Bradbury et al., 2009). According to Fiorino and Bradbury, the key concern in science and risk communication is justice – not education. That is, physical hazards often disproportionately harm some groups more than others, particularly those in low socio-economic conditions. Research in public participation (Akerlof et al., 2016: Besley, 2010; Fishkin & Luskin, 2005) identifies practices such as deliberative polling and deliberative meetings designed to enhance both knowledge and justice in such contexts. Another scholarly tradition emphasizing the importance of audiences or stakeholders is that of Botan and associates (e.g. Botan & Hazleton, 2010; Botan & Taylor, 2004; Kent & Taylor, 2002). These scholars maintain that the core relationships for any organization are those between it and its core stakeholder groups, *not* the relationships between the organization and news media outlets, which receive considerable scholarly and practitioner attention. For Botan and colleagues, working toward dialogue and respect between stakeholders and organizations is what makes public relations among organizations and their stakeholders ethical and effective.

Encouraging Inquiry About Audiences and Situations: The CAUSE Model of Strategic Science Communication

Unlike the deficit model of science communication, the audience-centered, democratic, and deliberative approaches to public participation and science communication are informed by extensive research. One limitation to audience-centered and dialogic models, though, is that they often assume achieving justice is the only goal essential in science and risk communication. We argue that both the deficit/technical view that education must be prioritized and the audience-centered/dialogic view that justice must be prioritized are both limited. Instead, scientists need a map or taxonomy of the full range of situations in which they might share climate science. To choose communication objectives carefully, and to make progress on a planet-wide problem like climate change, they need a conceptual tool that alerts them to likely tensions and options for learning about audiences' concerns as well as research-backed steps to assist audiences.

Theoretical context

The CAUSE model of strategic science communication was developed as a refinement of the technical and democratic approaches to "risk communication"; that is, communication about physical hazards (Rowan, 1991, 1994a; Rowan et al., 2009). Somewhat like the technical model, it assumes that education is an essential goal in science communication, but that this goal is shared by *all parties*, not solely scientists. Like the audience-centered, democratic, and dialogic models, it also says that pursuing matters of justice or satisfaction with policy is essential in science communication. But, the CAUSE model critiques the technical/deficit and audience-centered/democratic approaches by noting that they tend to focus on a *single* set of challenges or goals, either education or justice, instead of building an analysis of the range of communication goals humans pursue in formal and informal science communication contexts and the ways in which these goals can be shaped into measurable objectives.

The CAUSE model first uses Kinneavy's (1969, 1971) theory of the aims of discourse to identify contexts in which science or scientific information might be shared. In sharp contrast to those who argue that there is only one goal in communication, persuasion – that is, gaining agreement or change in behavior – Kinneavy argues that it is illuminating to instead consider *four* fundamental communication goals. He uses classic analyses of communication such as Shannon and Weaver (1949) to identify these fundamental goals or aims. For Kinneavy, consideration of encoders or sources suggests "self-expressive" discourse (e.g. diaries, journals, rants); consideration of audience suggests persuasion (e.g. ads, editorials, deliberative speech); thinking about discourse designed to represent some slice of reality evokes scientific studies, textbooks, and news stories which he calls "reference discourse." In reference discourse, the principal aim is to illuminate some aspect of the natural or social world, not agreement. Lastly, reflecting about channels suggests literary discourse. Instances of literary discourse include language designed for play, enjoyment, or edification (jokes, cartoons, drama, novels, and song, such as "This Land is Your Land"). For Kinneavy, seeing each of these discursive forms or contexts solely as "persuasion" obscures the differing expectations communicators bring to these contexts.When there are important differences, he argues, in our expectations for the discourse of self-expression and as compared to the discourse required for a scientific study. These differences are blurred, not clarified, by classifying all discourse as persuasion. Kinneavy (1969, 1971) next identifies sub-types in each major aim, and illustrates ways to use his theory as a basis for analyzing and evaluating communication effectiveness in each. This analysis provides a more differentiated framework for considering the full range of formal and informal contexts where science might be shared than does the notion that all communication is explained through the single goal of persuasion, where persuasion involves changing attitudes and behavior.

CAUSE next draws on Bitzer's (1968) notion that there are identifiable rhetorical or communication situations and that communicators must consider the social expectations and tensions in these situations to be effective. Bitzer argues that communication or rhetorical situations develop because some "imperfection" is detected in a social context, an imperfection, defect, or obstacle (p. 6), which, Bitzer writes, is marked by urgency. A classic example of a communication situation is that of a funeral. Those attending detect the principal "imperfection" as the loss of the deceased person. To grieve that loss, they want to comfort themselves, their family, and friends. A guest at a funeral who insisted on discussing the recently departed person's smoking, and the fact that cigarette butts are harmful to the environment, would probably not be successful in her goal of persuasion. She would be viewed as inconsiderate and unfeeling because of her failure to appreciate that the funeral's purpose is to honor the deceased and comfort those grieving, not to wage an environmental campaign.

Inspired by Kinneavy's and Bitzer's analyses, we argue that science communication about dangers, such as climate change, can arise in a variety of communication contexts, formal and informal. Rather than assuming that educating the uninformed is the only important objective in any science communication context, the letters in CAUSE can encourage curiosity and research concerning possible tensions scientists may face. First, because climate change is principally discussed by scientists, and only one in three Americans report conversing about climate change in interpersonal communication settings (Leiserowitz et al., 2019), we can expect, based on research concerning speaker credibility (e.g. O'Keefe, 2002), that audiences will question the character, motives, and competence of those who discuss climate science. These tensions are indexed by the "C" in CAUSE, which stands for lack of *confidence* in communicators. For example, a community may distrust climate change communicators who are not native to their region, doubting these individuals truly care about the community's well-being or, noting – hypothetically – a lack of competence because of the communicator's limited familiarity with relevant local expertise such as the fish native to their region or the local flood patterns.

Second, because climate change messages may or may not receive the attention of specified sets of lay stakeholders, a second set of tensions is linked to challenges involved in creating attention or *awareness* of a message, particularly steps such as making messages detectable through the senses (e.g. sight, sound, touch) and emotionally compelling (e.g. Heath & Heath, 2007). Additionally, there are challenges in locating the right channels, settings, or experiential "niches" where messages about climate change are most apt to be detected by specified groups. These tensions are indexed by the letter "A" in CAUSE, which stands for *awareness*.

Third, because science is often complex, stakeholders need to ***understand*** the aspects of reality it explains, such as the difference between weather and climate, or the ways in which heat-trapping gases can harm plants, animals, humans, and machinery. This goal is indicated by the U in CAUSE. People are more apt to understand complexities if they have opportunities to learn through materials that address key confusions (Rowan, 1988, 2003) and in the context of emotionally supportive relationships (National Research Council, 2009).

Fourth, the letters "S" and "E" in CAUSE are both suggested by considering audiences or stakeholders. The S stands for the challenges associated with ***supporting stakeholders' decision-making***. Should one advocate for a certain policy or support stakeholders in understanding the strengths and limitations of several policy options (Pielke, 2007)? For example, communities may wrestle over whether sea-level rise requires drastic steps such as banning development along coasts or more moderate ones such as encouraging establishment of coastal parks. The S in CAUSE examines research on steps that help stakeholders analyze proposed policies.

Fifth, even when satisfaction exists with decisions about the nature of some problem and the best solutions, enduring behavioral change or actual "***enactment***" of change is not inevitable. People may be convinced they need to change their personal use of air conditioning to reduce heat-trapping gases, but struggle to keep thermostats set at slightly uncomfortable levels. Helpfully, there are bodies of research on strategies that assist people in moving from agreement to enactment and in making a behavioral change enduring (e.g. Foxall et al., 2006; Maibach, Steg, & Anable, 2009). Further, because climate change is a global problem, research on how to bring about support for collective, not solely individual, action is needed. Research by Bain et al. (2016) finds that emphasizing economic or health "co-benefits" associated with policies that address climate change enhances support for collective actions such as voting. Guided by this work, the "E" in CAUSE stands for research on effective *enactment* or *establishment* of behavioral change by individuals and communities.

None of these tensions and challenges are easily tackled, though research suggests that creating awareness of some topic may be the easiest to accomplish (e.g. Janiszewski & Meyvis, 2001). The following analysis illustrates ways in which to use CAUSE strategically to research audience perspectives on climate change and to select measurable communication objectives and strategies. We argue that using CAUSE to listen to and analyze audiences' concerns and values prior to selecting communication objectives and messages is the ethical way of approaching climate change communication. To assume that unplanned communication – or a lack of research on what others want to know – is somehow more ethical than researched and planned communication is to confuse representing one's feelings honestly (a worthy objective) with failing to think or care about an audience's needs (an ineffective approach to science communication).

The C in CAUSE: Lack of Confidence in Communicators

People often find unrequested advice irritating (MacGeorge et al., 2004). Unrequested advice may suggest the advice-recipient is not managing some danger effectively, threatening that audience's perceptions of their competence. Therefore, those sharing scientific information about the alarming rate at which the Earth's average temperature is increasing may be viewed with mixed feelings: people may feel concerned, but also motivated to question the accuracy of this information and the communicator's motives for sharing it.

Along with the annoyance or ambivalence with which unrequested advice on danger management may be viewed, there are additional factors that make sharing scientific research about climate change challenging. First, as noted earlier, the topic of climate change has become politicized (Kahan, 2015; Kahan et al., 2012). That is, the phrase "climate change" – or its functional equivalent, "global warming" – has become a trigger term, one that cues many stakeholders to align themselves as either proponents or opponents, rather than listening carefully to messages about this topic. Interestingly, Kahan (2015) maintains that an adversarial context can be created simply by uttering words such as "climate change" or "vaccination." For some, these words signal that people with an interest in such topics have little interest in *their* group's needs and values, which harms a scientist's credibility.

Still another reason that scientists and science communicators sharing information about climate science may be viewed with suspicion is that the science underlying climate change is often complex. For example, from groundwater depletion and post-glacial rebound climate change is causing sea-level rise world-wide, but a host of factors lead some regions to feel its effects sooner and more severely than others (https://climate.nasa.gov/blog/3002/sea-level-101-part-two-all-sea-level-is-local/; Holgate & Woodworth, 2004). This complexity makes coastal management challenging. It also increases uncertainty, leading some to feel scientific concerns about climate change and sea level rise are suspect.

Steps for Earning Confidence

FOCUS ON LISTENING TO ALL PARTIES

Work by Besley (2014) and Dudo and Besley (2016) emphasizes the importance of *scientists learning about lay stakeholders' values and concerns* and contributing days or weeks each year to communication about science. Besley (2015) found that among university faculty who are members of the American Association for the Advancement of Science, one of the world's largest general science organizations, roughly half reported spending at least one day in a recent year in online interaction about science with adults who are not university students. Eleven percent in that survey reported spending more than ten days in the prior year engaged in public communication concerning science. This included interaction on websites, blogs, or social media. While it is commendable that scientists already spend some amount of time possibly listening to lay stakeholders and sharing scientific information with them, incentivizing more such behavior seems warranted. Enjoyable contexts for sharing science (e.g., science talks at pubs or museums) encourage listening.

CREATE FACE-TO-FACE CONTEXTS FOR DELIBERATION

A more direct way to earn confidence by listening to stakeholders is to do so in face-to-face discussion concerning policies to address climate change and its regional impacts. Currently, knowledge among scientists about dialogue and deliberative meetings designed for interaction with lay stakeholders is relatively low. As noted by Besley, Dudo, and Storksdieck (2015), the Pew Research Center (see Poff, Brinson, & Day, 2002) found that only 24% [of scientists] had heard about meetings where scientists and the general public discuss controversial issues related to research. Nevertheless, when scientists do learn about these types of events, some participate. For example, Fishkin and Luskin (2005) developed methods for "deliberative" surveys and "deliberative" meetings. That is, rather than solely asking stakeholders their top-of-mind views concerning options for energy use or flood management in their region, deliberative surveys and deliberative meetings create conditions for stakeholders to learn and converse about such topics. To accomplish these goals, Fishkin and others use random sampling to invite a range of stakeholders in a specific region to day-long sessions where topics such as energy options or flood management are discussed and policy options considered. Often a report is written summarizing the discussion, and sent to local officials. It may be that deliberative meetings are an ideal context for what Botan (2018) calls the "cocreation of meaning" by publics and organizations. For example, in one case, a Texas utility learned that its customers initially thought only of cost when asked about which sources of power they preferred for their region. After a random sample of customers participated in a deliberative meeting about energy options, a meeting sponsored by the utility, they reported that in addition to cost, these consumers now considered other factors such as the reliability and environmental impact of energy sources when asked which energy sources (e.g. nuclear, wind, solar, gas, coal) should be encouraged in their area (Lehr et al., 2003).

ADDRESS QUESTIONS STAKEHOLDERS RAISE

A third approach to earning lay stakeholders' confidence is to learn what questions *they most want answered*, acknowledge those questions, and, when possible, provide answers. Leiserowitz et al. (2011) surveyed US residents to learn their knowledge and views concerning global warming. Participants were asked: "If you could ask an expert one question about global warming, what would you ask?" (p. 10). Respondents were divided based on their level of concern about global warming or climate change, as well as their knowledge of this topic. Roughly 45% were "alarmed" or "concerned." The question the alarmed and concerned most wanted to ask was: "What can the US do to reduce global warming?" Thirty-five percent were either "cautious" or "disengaged." That is, this group knew the least about global warming and were the least emotionally involved with this issue. Their key question was: "What harm will global warming cause?" The final group was the "doubtful" and "dismissive." These stakeholders are more informed about global warming than the cautious and disengaged, but focused on counter-arguing. Their key question was: "How do you know global warming is occurring?" (Maibach et al., 2011). Maibach and associates say that to earn confidence, scientists should respond to specific lay stakeholders' concerns, rather than providing information of most interest to the scientist.

LOCATE TRUSTED OPINION LEADERS

Maibach and associates also use opinion leader interventions to communicate about climate change science; this approach is built on the notion that locating an already trusted messenger – opinion leaders for a set of stakeholders – and ensuring that these opinion leaders share key messages establishes liking for the messenger *and* his or her message (e.g. O'Keefe, 2002; Rogers, 2003). In one line of work, Maibach and associates study TV meteorologists educating viewers about climate change and its impacts. A September 2012 analysis found that television meteorologists are among the most trusted sources of information on the issue, with 60% of Americans saying they trust television meteorologists, a belief topped only by respondents' trust in climate scientists (76%) and other kinds of scientists [67%] (Leiserowitz et al., 2012). A study by Anderson et al. (2013) found that viewers who *liked* a TV meteorologist *learned more* from an educational video about climate change presented by the meteorologist than did those who did not view the meteorologist positively. As Anderson et al. (2013) noted, this finding is consistent with research showing associations between credibility of sources and message reception. Further, working with trusted messengers encourages two-way communication because discourse occurs in the "ecological niche" of each set of lay stakeholders. As Moser and Dilling (2011) note, with outreach to opinion leaders, business leaders can communicate with their associates about climate change, religious leaders can discuss climate change with congregants, and teenagers can discuss climate change with their peers. Of course, working with trusted messengers incurs responsibility to ensure that information shared is accurate and useful for stakeholders' decision-making. Pidgeon and Fischhoff (2011), as well as others (e.g. Zhao et al., 2014), have shown that working in multi-disciplinary teams on science communication that include scientists, communication scholars, practitioners, and stakeholders assists in ensuring that trusted messengers are sharing accurate and helpful information.

MAKE THE INHERENT "MONITOR-ABILITY" OF SCIENTIFIC METHODS CLEAR AND AVAILABLE TO STAKEHOLDERS

The essence of science is to avoid making assertions without evidence and instead to test claims, explain methods used to arrive at findings, and make methods clear to peer reviewers in "blind" review processes where neither the investigator nor the reviewers know one another. Lay stakeholders may experience neither the methods of science nor its review processes. What they learn most about are scientific results (National Research Council, 2009). But there are ways to involve lay stakeholders in the methods of science. Bailey et al. (1998) analyzed the effectiveness of the *Investigate* exhibit at the Boston Museum of Science at getting visitors to ask questions, problem solve, and form conclusions. *Investigate* provided visitors with 30 open-ended experiments and activities. For example, at one station visitors could build parts of small solar-powered cars and test them on a track, while another station asked visitors to explore the insulating properties of paper and plastic cups using probes to measure temperature differences. Through following and observing 93 visitor groups in the *Investigate* exhibit and by conducting 76 exit interviews and 38 post-visit phone interviews, Bailey et al. (1998) discovered, with high confidence, that the exhibit prompted visitors to ask questions, form hypotheses, problem solve, form conclusions, and share their findings with friends, family, and strangers around them. The post-visit interviews, conducted three months later, confirmed that even after their visit, people recalled the steps they took in solving experiments, the conclusions they created, and had discussed what they had done with others.

ENCOURAGE LAY STAKEHOLDERS TO HAVE CONFIDENCE IN THEIR OWN ABILITIES TO ENJOY AND CONTRIBUTE TO SCIENCE

A sixth method of earning confidence in scientists communicating climate change is, perhaps surprisingly, to encourage feelings of confidence among stakeholders in themselves, and specifically in their abilities to enjoy and even conduct science. Citizen science projects do just that: they invite citizens to work with scientists on research. Examples of citizen science projects that encourage citizen involvement are the Christmas Bird Count and the Breeding Bird Survey. Annually, volunteers conduct bird counts during Christmas in efforts to help the Audubon Society, US Geological Survey and Canadian Wildlife Service to determine the current state of bird populations in North America (Audubon, 2017; Sauer & Butcher, 2014). These citizen reports helped aid the 2007 discovery that, over the past 40 years, 20 common bird species have reduced in population size by 68%, which was reported in the *New York Times* (Silvertown, 2009). Activities where stakeholders and citizens work with one another are likely to encourage feelings of confidence in one another's character and competence, making such projects ones in which confidence may be earned in an array of messengers.

Hypotheses on Earning Confidence

To research ways in which to earn confidence in those communicating the science of climate change, we suggest these hypotheses:

- H1: Scientists and government officials who prioritize listening to others above educating others will be perceived as more credible than those who prioritize educating.
- H2: Scientists and government officials who are accessible by phone, email, and in person will be perceived as more credible than those who are less accessible.
- H3: Scientists who are transparent about methods used for research will be perceived as more credible than those who do not describe their methods.
- H4: Prominent lay stakeholders such as pastors, business leaders, community members, fishers, and farmers are more likely to be viewed as credible sources of environmental information by members of their own communities than are those community members perceived as outsiders.
- H5: Local government officials will be more credible discussing science underlying local environmental challenges and policies for addressing these challenges if they encourage engagement with stakeholders through deliberative meetings or online comment prior to initiating approval processes than if these meetings or online comment opportunities do not occur.
- H6: Local planning commissions will be more trusted if they include members of specified lay groups in mitigation planning than if lay groups are not included.
- H7: Scientists who experience science communication training will see listening to audiences and planning one's communication as more responsible and more ethical than not listening to audiences and not planning one's communication.

The A in CAUSE: Lack of Awareness

A second challenge to communicating climate change is that its causes, consequences, and communication may all be difficult to detect and decode. By "detect" we mean difficult to sense with the five senses or difficult to respond to with empathy. The phenomenon, climate change, is difficult to detect because it is a "slow-onset hazard," not an acute one (Beamish, 2002; Wilkins & Patterson, 1990). Acute hazards, or those that happen quickly, such as plane crashes, terrorist attacks, and wildfires, typically garner more attention than do slow-onset phenomena (Fischhoff et al., 1978; Loewenstein et al., 2001). Unlike singular weather events occurring over minutes or months, climate refers to the average weather conditions for an area over a period of time such as a season (Le Treut et al., 2007; NASA, n.d.). The gradual experience of climate, as opposed to weather, contributes to climate change being less detectable than an acute event, and it also means the causes of climate change may be hard to visualize or feel. For example, extra heat-trapping gases pumped into the atmosphere by humans are one of several sources of climate variability (Intergovernmental Panel on Climate Change, 2014). The release of one of these gases, carbon dioxide, is increased through processes such as deforestation, transportation, and heating/cooling of buildings (Forster et al., 2007). If carbon dioxide emissions were visible to humans as a dark purple or red – perhaps dark purple for carbon dioxide released through automobile exhaust and red for the same gas emitted through exhalation – they might be more easily detected. The effects of extra carbon dioxide in the atmosphere are also not felt immediately, so it can be hard to feel or visualize the connection between, for example, increasing airline use (an important emitter of heat-trapping gases) and many harmful effects, such as an increasing number of high-heat, high-humidity days in the US (Luber & McGeehin, 2008). Communication designed to illustrate links among emissions, temperature, regional health, and environmental harms sometimes uses iconic images such as polar bears or glaciers. But while these images capture attention and make climate change seem important (see Graber, 1976, on "condensation" symbols), animals and objects associated with remote areas of the world also serve to remove viewers both psychologically and geographically from the problem, and may leave audiences feeling helpless (O'Neill & Nicholson-Cole, 2009; O'Neill & Smith, 2014).

Steps to Gain Awareness

Since the causes and consequences of climate change may be hard to feel or visualize, steps for enhancing awareness of these phenomena should make them more detectable. Evidence-based steps for enhancing detection include: (a) describing impacts of climate change in regions *familiar to lay stakeholders and in time frames they find familiar*; (b) finding ways to make the abstraction, climate change, a phenomenon *lay stakeholders can experience* through visual, audible, tactile, and emotionally resonant materials such as photo essays and stories; (c) statistics rendered in visually or aurally compelling ways; and (d) ensuring that communication outreach is "detectable" and "decode-able" by sharing it through experiences, relationships, and products that employ familiar contexts, channels, languages, and symbols.

DISCUSS ALREADY OCCURRING, LOCAL CHANGE

First, because hazards perceived as remote in time or location tend to be underestimated, some climate science communicators discuss impacts that *have already occurred in regions close to their audiences*. A TV meteorologist in the US Southeast says: "[One] of the things that I talk about in [my] blog [is that] this [change in precipitation patterns from gentle rains that benefit crops to droughts and extreme downpours hat do not] is not a computer projection. *This is based on observation* [italics inserted]. This was collected from the Global Precipitation Climatology Project. And it is covering a period of time from 1979 to 2007" (Rowan et al., 2018, P6, T50).

Similarly, a TV meteorologist in Alaska encourages viewers to send her photos documenting environmental changes they have observed, such as animals washing up on beaches in recent years that viewers do not recall seeing in their childhood or photos of sea ice and glaciers that were considerably larger in viewers' youth. She shares these photos at community presentations (Rowan et al., 2018, P7, p. 12).

A number of scholars have established the effectiveness of connecting visuals to viewers' locales (Leiserowitz, 2006; Lorenzoni, Nicholson-Cole, & Whitmarsh, 2007; Lowe et al., 2006; Munro, 2012). Some have studied this step explicitly as it relates to communicating climate science (Bangay & Blum, 2010; Lotz-Sisitka, 2010). The everyday experience of local places contributes to framing concerns, perceptions, and responses (Bélanger, 2003). Importantly, too, while scientists find it harder to establish clear links between climate change and regional impacts than to show these links at a global scale (Intergovernmental Panel on Climate Change, 2014), evidence shows regional links can be established. Mote et al. (2005) document declining mountain snowpack in western North America, a trend that threatens wildlife, forests, and water supplies. Thousands of Europeans died during the heatwave of 2003, a phenomenon whose effects were probably exacerbated by climate change (Robine et al., 2008). Another likely impact of climate change is the increasing evidence of disease and death in the world's coral reefs. Reefs serve as habitats for marine life and as attractions to tourists, divers, and fishers. According to a 2017 study by the Nature Conservancy, "coral reefs are worth $36 billion annually to tourism industries in key tropical regions such as Florida, Hawaii, the Queensland coast in Australia, and the coast of Kenya on the Indian Ocean" (Mooney, 2017, p. A16).

PROVIDE VICARIOUS EXPERIENCES

A second approach for enhancing awareness of climate change is to make the impacts of climate change available to the senses and emotions, with photos and evidence-based stories. This step is essential since *people do not address risks they do not feel* (Loewenstein et al., 2001; Slovic et al., 2004; Weber, 2006). In 2010, the International League of Conservation Photographers mounted what they call a Rapid Assessment Visual Expedition (RAVE) of the Chesapeake Bay. Drawing upon professional conservation photographers, they conducted RAVEs across the globe to bring attention to specific environmental issues (Hansen & Machin, 2016). The goal, according to Schwarz (2013), is to illustrate problems as quickly as possible and disseminate photos to media, encouraging coverage. In another series of projects, photographer Subhankar Banerjee documented conditions in the Arctic National Wildlife Refuge. His photos counter uninformed notions that there is "nothing" in the Arctic and that the Arctic is untouched by contemporary industrial life. Instead, they make explicit the impact of climate change on Arctic animals as well as the impact of pollution, which now creates a distinctive haze even in the Arctic. His and others' photos of the Arctic have played an essential role in debate over drilling for oil and gas (Banerjee, 2012). Photography has the power to assist stakeholders in seeing the impacts of climate change. Sheppard (2005), for example, documents the power of "before" and "after" landscape photos, essential tools for communicating climate change.

USE EVIDENCE-BASED STORIES

Compelling stories, informed by careful science, can transform abstractions into attention-getting, emotionally engaging, and evidence-informed experiences. Consider Public Radio International's story about a small marine organism, a mussel, and its experience with a warming Earth:

> "As humans, we have this really biased view of the world. Well over 95 percent of the organisms on Earth, they're completely dependent on the ambient environment for their temperature," says Northeastern University marine biologist Brian Helmuth.
>
> Think about a mussel that's stuck to a rock in a tidal area for most of its life. It can't move to find shade when it's hot out. It can't control its own body temperature.

> When the tide is low and the sun is out, its dark shell absorbs heat just like asphalt on a summer afternoon.
>
> "You are sitting there in the blazing sun, you're not going to be able to move," Helmuth says...
>
> Mussels can literally start to cook on the rocks if they get too hot. (Beeler, 2017)

This story's impact may come from the way the journalist Carolyn Beeler uses specifics to foster empathy for this small animal. She describes the way a mussel's "dark shell absorbs heat just like asphalt." Additionally, Beeler and Brian Helmuth, the scientist interviewed, use specifics to convey just how "stuck" mussels are, as compared to humans, who are less likely to be confined to a single harsh environment for their entire lives.

Research has shown that vivid, emotion-evoking specifics make stories especially memorable (Heath & Heath, 2007; see also Zillmann, 2006, on exemplification). Heath and Heath (2007) use the mnemonic "SUCCES" to help communicators remember that more memorable stories meet certain criteria. They are **s**imple, **u**nexpected, **c**oncrete, **c**redible, **e**motional **s**tories. Some of these qualities are also those that journalists use to judge what counts as news. That is, events likely to be viewed as news are novel, proximate, or local events, often marked by conflict or prominent individuals who have impact on audiences (Kennamer, 1988), Thus, to draw attention to important information, and encourage processing (i.e., thinking, at some level), communication should include simple, unexpected, concrete, emotional stories – when evidence warrants such treatment. One caution, however, is that vivid, emotion-evoking but irrelevant details can distract audiences from the principal message. Indeed, "seductive details" harm learning (Chang & Choi, 2014; Harp & Mayer, 1998).

USE COMPELLING GRAPHIC DESIGN TO CONVEY STATISTICAL INFORMATION

Lazard and Atkinson (2015) write that "infographics, short for 'information graphics' are visual displays designed to communicate information that range from anything as simple as a pleasing arrangement of figures to stylized illustrations to complex interactive data animations" (p. 7; see Lankow, Ritchie, & Crooks, 2012; Lester, 2013). Lazard and Atkinson (2015) studied environmental infographics through the lens of the Elaboration Likelihood Model (Petty & Cacioppo, 1986). Petty and Cacioppo distinguish "central processing," or thinking a lot about an argument, from "peripheral processing," which refers to superficial, quick, heuristic cognition of the sort one does when choosing food on a menu because of a momentary glance at the food's photo, rather than thinking more extensively about the food's similarity to past meals, likely nutritional value, cost, and so forth (Petty & Cacioppo, 1986, p. 128). Lazard and Atkinson found that in many studies, researchers assume that visual material is peripherally processed and textual material is more apt to be centrally processed. To test this idea, they studied two pro-environmental infographics, one concerning recycling and another on genetically modified food. Contrary to prior assumptions, these found infographics were processed "centrally"; that is, the infographics in this study led to viewers "elaborating" or making connections between prior knowledge and the knowledge they learned from these infographics. This study and other studies of the effectiveness of infographics suggest that effective graphic design may encourage lay stakeholders to become "aware" of information more so than if such information is presented in less compelling visual formats, and that this awareness can lead to more careful processing. Infographics that make climate change science accessible and vivid for lay stakeholders are available on a host of sites, such as those generated by universities, governments, and commercial interests. The online site Pinterest, for example, offers climate change infographics: https://www.pinterest.com/worldresources/infographics-climate-change-energy.

SHARE CLIMATE SCIENCE IN FAMILIAR CONTEXTS, CHANNELS

Channel use in the current era is often diverse, with people simultaneously watching television ads, using their mobile phones to seek additional information about ad content, and posting on social media to share what they learned (Couldry, Livingstone, & Markham, 2016). This means that to assess the impact of content offered through one channel or context, the ideal approach would be to explore all ways in which several specified populations of stakeholders receive content across several channels. Further, big data analyses of the *volume* of content traveling on either social or traditional media can be measured and linked to risk data such as regional mean temperatures or increases in regional diseases (Fellenor et al., 2017).

Hypotheses on Gaining Awareness

To explore ways in which to enhance the accessibility and detectability of climate change materials for designated stakeholders, the following hypotheses could be tested:

H1: People who report experiencing climate change in informal contexts, such as taking photos and comparing contemporary ones to those taken in childhood, will be more aware of climate change than those who are exposed to similarly contrasting images encountered in school or work settings.

H2: Stories of climate change's impacts will create greater awareness of climate change and concern about its harm if these stories concern regional or local environments than if these stories concern animals and environments perceived as remote.

H3: Stories told through multiple media, such as text, infographics, and video, will be more likely to be recalled by lay stakeholders than stories told in a single medium.

H4: Experiences where lay stakeholders are active (e.g., taking photos themselves) will increase awareness of plants, animals, and people affected by the harms of climate change more than experiences where lay stakeholders are relatively passive (looking at photos).

The U in CAUSE: Deepening Understanding

A third challenge to communicating climate change is its complexity. That is, even if lay stakeholders have heard the terms "climate change" and "global warming," they may not be able to explain fully to themselves or others what these terms mean and why the current rate of climate change is harmful (Bostrom et al., 1994; Ranney et al., 2012). One reason that climate change and its impacts are difficult to explain is that these phenomena are studied by numerous branches of science. They include chemistry, physics, biology, meteorology, oceanography, marine science, atmospheric sciences, earth sciences, forestry, economics, and many fields of medicine. Additionally, the challenges of managing and communicating climate science are informed by several branches of engineering, decision science, psychology, sociology, risk communication, and science communication. Further, the causes of climate change in the current era and its effects may not be apparent to lay stakeholders. Bostrom et al. (1994) conducted in-depth "mental models" interviews with lay stakeholders where participants talk aloud to describe their sense of some phenomenon. Analysis of these interviews showed that stakeholders have a number of misconceptions about key terms and the mechanisms of climate change. For example, some thought the greenhouse effect was bad, rather than (what it is), a necessary phenomenon for life to exist. For them it referenced reasons for a hot, sticky climate. Additionally, they confused stratospheric ozone depletion with climate change and weather with climate. Further, their notions of mitigation measures were confused. They discussed steps for controlling general pollution when asked about how to reduce climate change, rather than steps for reducing the excess heat-trapping gases that increase atmospheric temperatures; these lay stakeholders could not visualize how extra heat-trapping gases lead to harmful effects such as increases in pollen production and respiratory disease (Shea et al., 2008; Ziska & Beggs, 2012).

Still another challenge is stakeholders' difficulties envisioning why or how greenhouse gases are able to *transmit* visible light when it travels from the Sun to the Earth, but, when this light bounces back from the Earth as infrared radiation (IR) or heat, greenhouse gases such as carbon dioxide *trap* or absorb most of it. Raney et al. (2012) have shown that the chemistry and physics of these mechanisms are not well understood.

Therefore, to deepen understanding of climate change, it is useful to consider two sorts of barriers to understanding the science explaining the current era's rapid increase in average global temperature. The first barriers are cognitive or intellectual; the second, emotional and relational.

Steps to Deepen Understanding: Address Cognitive Sources of Confusion

There are predicable sources of confusion when people learn any complex topic. Four common sources are: (a) extensive use of unfamiliar terms; (b) confusion about the essential meaning of key terms; (c) difficulties visualizing complex structures and processes; and (d) lay theories that make intuitive sense but are inconsistent with established science (Hassol, 2008; Mayer, 2005; Mayer & Moreno, 2003; Merrill & Tennyson, 1977; Rowan, 1988, 1990, 1991, 1999, 2003, 2010). There are evidence-based steps for addressing each confusion.

AVOID OR REPLACE CLUSTERS OF UNFAMILIAR TERMS

Hassol (2008) has found that some terms helpful to climate scientists do little to deepen stakeholders' understanding of climate change. According to Hassol (2008), one should say the amount of heat-trapping gases in the atmosphere has increased since the Industrial Revolution because of "human activities", rather than "anthropogenic sources." Another term that may confuse is "contributes." Hassol finds that "contribute" is interpreted by some to mean "contributes very little"; therefore, "cause" may be clearer. Next, Hassol recommends avoiding "uncertainty" and using instead "range."

CLARIFY THE ESSENTIAL MEANING OF KEY TERMS

Research also shows that lay stakeholders are assisted in understanding complexities not by avoiding or replacing a key term, but *rather by explanation of the term and its essential, as opposed to associated, meanings.* Merrill and Tennyson (1977) summarize research that identifies four steps for clarifying the essential meaning of a key term. These steps describe an especially thorough form of definition, which Rowan (1988, 1999, 2003, 2010) calls "*elucidating explanation*," because this discursive form clarifies what is essential to a term's meaning and what is not. The four steps in an elucidating explanation are: (a) note what the term does *not* mean; (b) say what it *does* mean; that is, define the term by its essential meaning; (c) give a *range of examples* illustrating the term's use, not just a single example to avoid having the term's use under- or over-generalized; and (d) if needed, offer a false example or incorrect instance of the term's use and explain why it is incorrect. For instance, the US National Oceanic and Atmospheric Administration's website offers an elucidating explanation of "weather" versus "climate" on its website. It says that weather refers to atmospheric conditions of short duration, such as moments, days, or months. In contrast, climate refers to average weather conditions in certain regions over longer periods of time (NASA, n.d.). This elucidating explanation effectively gives the essential meanings of weather and climate, but it may be even more effective for lay stakeholders if it were augmented with a range of differing examples, such as noting that while weather may change in a matter of hours, climate refers to the *average atmospheric conditions* that make living in Alaska different from living in Alabama or living in Bermuda different from living in Boston. A concluding statement might note that climate is easier to predict than weather because climate refers to averages and trends rather than single data points such as the temperature or rainfall in the next hour in some single location.

HELP LEARNERS VISUALIZE THE ESSENTIAL COMPONENTS AND MECHANISMS OF COMPLEX STRUCTURES AND PROCESSES

There are several types of textual and graphic tactics that assist audiences in visualizing complex structures and processes. These tactics are needed by those explaining climate change because the processes that allow the Earth to have an atmosphere, conditions that make life on Earth possible, as well as those that cause *extra* heat-trapping gases, which are harmful to life, are not easy to discern. Here we discuss three types of text and graphic material that can address this challenge: (a) textual and graphic cues such as titles, headings, previews, italics, white space, and summaries; (b) narratives, which have predictable structures (problem, complication, resolution) that assist comprehension; and (c) analogies. Research has shown that passages having these features are better understood and more able to facilitate novel application of scientific material than are identical passages and materials that lack these features (Mayer, 2005; Mayer & Moreno, 2003). Rowan (1988. 2003) calls any text or graphic that assists audiences in visualizing complex processes or structures a *quasi-scientific explanation.*

Text and graphic cues

Numerous scholars have shown that *text and graphic cues such as titles, headings, white space, italics, previews, and summaries* make important contributions to comprehension (e.g. Ausubel, 2000; Bromage & Mayer, 1981; Loman & Mayer, 1983; Maes, van Geel, & Cozijn, 2005; Mayer, 2005; Mayer & Moreno, 2003). In a classic study, Loman and Mayer (1983) devised two versions of a printed passage explaining "red tides," a phenomenon where warm, calm ocean waters lead to proliferation of dinoflagellates, microscopic animals that consume much of the oxygen in ocean waters and sometimes produce toxins harmful to plants, animals, and humans. A dinoflagellate bloom turns waters red, hence the name "red tides." Red tides, or harmful algal blooms, as scientists prefer to call them, may be more frequent in a world where the Earth's average temperature is increasing (Moore et al., 2008; National Ocean Service, n.d.). Loman and Mayer found that when college students were randomly assigned to read the *Mystery of the red tides* without a title and headings, they were less able to comprehend the passage's key points and suggest scientifically correct ways of reducing red tides. In contrast, those who read the passage with a title, headings, and a preview had better comprehension and could offer novel and accurate – if sometimes unfeasible – ways of addressing red tides, such as dropping ice into the warm waters. Such proposed solutions indicated that the students who read the structurally cued passage had understood the environmental conditions leading to red tides.

Narratives

As noted in the "A in CAUSE" discussion, in addition to creating awareness by engaging emotions, *narratives can help learners master complexities by calling attention to the key components of complex structures and processes.* In the story of the mussel getting baked in the hot sun in part because of climate change, this account cuts through many complexities involved in explaining climate change. The story does not delve into the intricacies of climate change such as, for example, the role of clouds or the complex ways in which various factors that humans do not control – such as the tilt of the Earth on its axis, the role of water vapor, the most ubiquitous heat-trapping or greenhouse gas, and numerous other factors – affect climate. These complexities are explained at varying levels of depth in, for example, the IPCC report (Pachauri et al., 2014), and websites of governmental science agencies and professional science associations. The simple narrative of the mussel, however, assists learners in visualizing *one* way in which climate change causes harm. As the story notes, "95 percent of the organisms on Earth [are] completely dependent on the ambient environment for their temperature" and human-caused climate change is, as the story says, "baking" some of these creatures.

The story, like all narratives, eases comprehension because its structure is simple. It states a problem: many animals are stationary and the Earth is getting warmer. A complication: some animals are in dark-colored shells that absorb heat, exacerbating the heat they experience. And it leaves open the "resolution": what will humans do to address this problem?

Analogies

A third, especially powerful tactic to help learners visualize complex phenomena, structures, and processes is that of analogies. Several lines of research have established the effectiveness of analogy as a way of linking established, familiar knowledge to new knowledge and supporting learners' problem-solving abilities (Ausubel, 2000; Bromage & Mayer, 1981; Mayer, 2005; Mayer & Moreno, 2003; Walsh-Thomas, 2016). Explanations of climate change science for lay stakeholders frequently employ analogies. Often they begin with accounts of the greenhouse effect, an analogy used to explain a key reason why life on Earth is possible. For example, the website for the University Corporation for Atmospheric Research (UCAR), a nonprofit consortium of more than 100 North American colleges and universities, discusses "greenhouse gases" and the "greenhouse effect" this way:

> Greenhouse gases and the greenhouse effect play an important role in Earth's climate. Without greenhouse gases, our planet would be a frozen ball of ice. In recent years, however, excess emissions of carbon dioxide and other greenhouse gases from human activities (mostly burning fossil fuels) have begun to warm Earth's climate at a problematic rate. (UCAR Center for Science Education, n.d.)

The "greenhouse" analogy is embedded in the term "greenhouse gases." The greenhouse effect refers to the fact that the structure of three-atom gases such as carbon dioxide causes them to *transmit* visible light from the Sun, just as the glass roof of a greenhouse does, but, when that light travels to the Earth and bounces off it, as infrared heat or radiation, these gases *trap* rather than transmitting this heat, causing the inside of the greenhouse to remain warm. Walsh-Thomas (2016) found that an effective way of explaining humanly caused climate change was to first explain the greenhouse effect and then compare the extra greenhouse or heat-trapping gases emitted from human activities such as burning fossil fuels to an extra blanket on someone sleeping. The greenhouse effect is like a sleeper who sleeps with a sufficient, single blanket that traps his body heat, keeping him warm. However, on planet Earth, when extra heat-trapping gases are emitted through activities such as driving gasoline-powered vehicles, we increase the amount of carbon dioxide, one of the heat-trapping gases, in the atmosphere, which – like an extra blanket on a sleeper – traps heat and increases the Earth's average temperature.

To deepen understanding further, it would be helpful to explain more fully *why* some gases trap heat, or IR, and others, such as oxygen and nitrogen, do not. Should one use an elucidating explanation or a quasi-scientific explanation? Consider this definition of greenhouse or heat-trapping gases on the website Chemistry in context:

> *Question*: What is a greenhouse gas, effectively?
> *Answer*: Any molecule that can absorb photons of IR radiation can behave as a greenhouse gas. (Chemistry in context, n.d.)

The answer in this text defines a greenhouse gas, but it does so in a circular way and by introducing terms that may be unfamiliar – such as photon and IR radiation. Would this response assist comprehension? Would a more thorough elucidating explanation be more effective, one that alerted the reader to the essential features of greenhouse gases as *heat-trapping gases*, that is a molecular structure that allows these gases to absorb photons of heat or IR as opposed to the structure of other molecules, such as oxygen that *cannot*? And would an animation be helpful, an animation that illustrated the ways in which carbon dioxide molecules "transmit" visible light and *trap* much of the IR emitted by the Earth? Is a combination of elucidating explanations (extended definitions) and quasi-scientific explanations (verbal or visual efforts to assist visualization) more likely to enhance learning? These are questions that can be tested empirically. There are numerous websites providing explanatory text and animations explaining the chemistry of what counts as a greenhouse or heat-trapping gas. For example, the UCAR website uses an animation to assist learners in visualizing how the three-atom structure of the carbon dioxide molecule allows it to trap heat reflected from the Earth (https://scied.ucar.edu/carbon-dioxide-absorbs-and-re-emits-infrared-radiation). In contrast, the two-atom structure of oxygen and nitrogen does not prevent heat from escaping into space.

ADDRESS LAY THEORIES

The fourth obstacle to comprehending complexities is that some ideas are difficult to understand not because of a confusing term or hard-to-visualize structure or processes, but rather because the ideas themselves are hard to believe. That is, people often have powerful lay notions inconsistent with established science. Research in physics education identifies lay theories as obstacles to comprehension (e.g. Duit & Treagust, 2004; Garnett, Garnett, & Hackling, 1995; Hewson & Hewson, 1984). These scholars study text features that assist learners in recognizing that they have a lay theory, questioning that notion, and considering orthodox scientific notions that account for the phenomena lay theories have been used to explain. Consider, for example, the established scientific notion that it is possible for human beings to affect the climate of planet Earth. This notion sometimes seems implausible to some lay stakeholders. They reason, understandably but erroneously, that planet Earth is quite large compared to the size and abilities of individual humans and that humans seem insignificant compared with other factors such as the tilt of the Earth on its axis, volcanoes, water vapor, and other phenomena that affect climate but do not detract from the impact of burning fossil fuels on the Earth's average temperature. Another erroneous lay notion is that living in a rural setting reduces one's carbon footprint more effectively than would city living. While there are many factors affecting one's "carbon footprint," or use of heat-trapping gases, often urban living is more sustainable than is rural living because of the physics of scalability (West, 2017).

To address counter-intuitive ideas and assist learners in questioning lay theories, scholars have identified four effective steps, which Rowan (e.g. Rowan, 1990, 1994b, 2003; Rowan et al., 2009) describes as *transformative explanations* because they are designed to cause dissatisfaction with lay notions and consideration of more accepted orthodox science. The features of effective transformative explanation often mirror the steps that science writers use in the lead paragraphs of feature stories, where their goal is to surprise and intrigue readers with fresh understandings of familiar phenomena. Consider the opening paragraphs of a book review:

> A dog owner weighs twice as much as her German shepherd. Does she eat twice as much? Does a big city need twice as many gas stations as one half its size? Our first instinct is to say yes, but, alas, we are wrong. On a per-gram basis, a human requires about 25% less food than her dog, and the larger city needs only 85% more gas stations…
>
> As Geoffrey West explains in *Scale*, the reason behind these intriguing phenomena is a universal law known as allometry – the finding that as organisms, cities, and companies grow, many of their characteristics scale nonlinearly…
>
> [West] observes that complex systems – from cells to cities – require networks to ensure that every component has access to … resources. These networks have evolved to optimally transport resources, minimizing, for example, the energy hearts exert to transport blood or the time we spend traveling from work to home. (Barabasi, 2017, p. 138).

Barabasi's review of West (2017) enacts several key steps in transformative explanation. First, it creates puzzlement or dissatisfaction with the lay theory by introducing familiar phenomena that the lay notion does not explain: that is, the examples concerning the dog's and the owner's diet and the number of gas stations large cities need. Second, it helps the lay reader recognize that she holds a lay theory by pointing out "our first instincts" are to assume need for resources grows linearly with the size of an organism or a city. Third, Barabasi briefly explains allometric scaling, a notion first discovered in ecology, which says that something other than sheer size affects the resources complex systems need, and that additional factor is network optimization. The fourth step, explaining the orthodox theory, or fully explaining network optimization and the mathematics underlying it, is not fully offered in this book review, but the reviewer continues to intrigue by noting more surprising findings – such as that the time it takes to commute to and from a large city to home may increase, but not double, the time needed to commute to and from a less large one.

Transformative explanations are powerful tools for explaining. One challenge, however, is that their use assumes an audience is emotionally ready and interested in learning. That may well be the case in a classroom or work setting, where those participating accept their roles as teachers and learners. But these conditions do not always exist. In some contexts, emotions or social barriers hamper science learning.

Deepen Understanding by Addressing Emotional and Social Barriers

The second set of barriers to deepening understanding of climate change are emotional and social. Research in formal science education, the sort occurring in school or work settings, explores these barriers (e.g. Van den Bossche et al., 2006), as does research in informal science education contexts where people choose to learn science for recreation or personal interest, such as hiking, fishing, watching television, or leisure reading (NRC, 2009).

MAKE SCIENCE EXCITING, BUT NOT TOO EXCITING

Research suggests that the optimal emotional context for learning is a state of excitement, but not excessive excitement. For example, research shows that science news stories, especially ones evoking a sense of awe or offering a fresh perspective on phenomena once deemed ordinary, are among the news stories people most frequently share (Tierney, 2010). Perhaps a sense of awe encouraged people to share research revealing the "rollercoaster" strategy bar-headed geese use to manage the incredible feat of maintaining altitude as they fly through the Himalayans (Bishop et al., 2015). In small group settings at science museums and in after-school programs, attendees often find hands-on activities or field trips emotionally engaging. A key, however, is that the activity is not unduly exciting. A certain degree of emotional engagement makes learning more likely, whereas over-excitement decreases learning (National Research Council, 2009).

ENCOURAGE PEERS TO EXPLAIN SCIENCE TO ONE ANOTHER

Research on learning in collaborative teams describes the social conditions that encourage learning of both scientific concepts and the scientific method. People learn scientific concepts best when encouraged to make observations and investigate them while interacting with peers in a process cast as discovery, rather than as passive or rote learning (National Research Council, 2009; Van den Bossche et al., 2011). For example, Reef-Stout and Medvedev (2017) created a multimedia exhibit entitled "Fashion and Sustainability." Hands-on activities, visuals, and videos encouraged attendees to explore problems that exist in the fashion industry. Through comparison of open-ended pre- and post-surveys, the researchers learned that there was high concept recognition and understanding, as well as very little difference in knowledge acquired between students currently enrolled on fashion courses at a local university and those with no fashion schooling, attending the exhibit. For example, before attending the exhibit, when asked to explain social sustainability, many attendees mentioned sweatshops, but very few knew what that term meant. After visiting the exhibit, all attendees could explain sweatshops in more detail, and many were able to make connections between sustainability and problems in fashion sustainability, even offering solutions to identified problems.

Adults may be most apt to explain science to one another when involved in citizen science projects, multi-disciplinary research, study groups, or deliberative meetings (e.g. Akerlof et al., 2016; Fishkin & Luskin, 2005). More work should be done to explore the emotional and relational conditions that support peer-to-peer explaining of scientific methods and concepts in such contexts. Research in group communication, collaboration, and peer assessment may be illuminating (e.g. Järvenoja & Järvelä, 2009; Olaniran, 1994; Shimazoe & Aldrich, 2010; Tracy & Dimock, 2004; Van den Bossche et al., 2011).

ACQUAINT AUDIENCES WITH SCIENCE AS A HUMAN ENDEAVOR

Science can be perceived erroneously as facts that appear in textbooks but are unconnected with real, fallible people who make mistakes, but also have social practices such as peer review and professional associations to improve their work. According to research in informal science education, lay stakeholders sometimes feel detached from scientists. A study by Steinke et al. (2007) explored the influence of media on middle-school-aged children's perceptions of scientists. Steinke and her associates asked children to draw a picture of a scientist and list the source of their ideas. Stereotypes of scientists were heavily present, with the most frequent ones being "wearing a lab coat" (66.8%), "wearing glasses" (56.9%), and "being male" (56.9%). Most students (40%) stated that they got their ideas from movies and films. The students who drew "less stereotypical" pictures of scientists often reported knowing someone who is a scientist.

Another approach to teach the fallibility of science, as well as its potential for excitement, is to foster science learning that is active, not passive – where learners are encouraged to use scientific tools, touch equipment, ask questions, and offer solutions. The Cell Lab Exhibition at the Science Museum of Minnesota allows participants to use a variety of scientific tools, such as microscopes, test tubes, UV detectors, etc., throughout their exploration of the exhibit (Science Museum of Minnesota, n.d.). For example, Guichard (1995) studied the effects on learning of an interactive exhibit on the form and function of the human skeleton. Visitors would pedal a bike next to a wall of glass that would reflect back that person's skeleton in movement. Out of 93 children, aged 6 to 7, who experienced the exhibit, 96% could draw a skeleton's silhouette correctly, compared to the 3% who never visited the exhibit. Further, 92% of the children remembered how to draw the skeleton and how joints functioned eight months later without additional guidance.

In summary, there are intellectual, emotional, and social barriers to deepening understanding both of scientific concepts relevant to climate change and the scientific method. Addressing these barriers can enhance understanding, the U in CAUSE. This discussion suggests several hypotheses.

Hypotheses Concerning How to Deepen Understanding of Climate Change

H1: Exposure to text or visuals having the features of elucidating explanation will be associated with more accurate understanding of climate science concepts than will exposure to definitions of the same concepts.

H2: Exposure to text or visuals having the features of a quasi-scientific explanation will be associated with more accurate understanding of climate change processes than will exposure to a passage lacking the features of a quasi-scientific explanation.

H3: Exposure to text or visuals having the features of a transformative explanation will be associated with more accurate understanding of the inadequacies of lay theories relevant to understanding climate change science than will exposure to accounts lacking the four features of transformative explanations.

H4: Social conditions that promote peer-to-peer explanations of climate science concepts will be associated with more accurate understanding of climate science concepts than will conditions that lead to listening to or watching presentations about climate science without opportunities for peer-to-peer explanations.

H5: Active, hands-on learning – where scientific equipment is used or plants and animals touched carefully – will be associated with more accurate understanding of climate change science concepts and the scientific method than will conditions where participants read about these concepts and methods.

The S in CAUSE: Support for Decision-Making

Assuming that the first three challenges identified by CAUSE have been addressed, the next challenge involves supporting decision-making, the S in CAUSE. In this analysis, we discuss four obstacles to deciding that climate change is real, harmful, and happening now (Climate Reality Project, 2017) and deciding upon steps for its management. They are: (a) concern about social sanction or criticism from others; (b) doubt about the probability and severity of harm resulting from climate change; (c) disagreement about the costs, benefits, and workability of proposed actions; and (d) doubts individuals have about their own capacity to enact proposed solutions.

Concern about social sanction

The first barrier to decision-making about management of climate change is concern with social sanction, embarrassment, or loss of "face." Identity-protective cognition (Kahan, 2012, 2015; Kahan, Jenkins-Smith, & Braman, 2011; Kahan et al., 2007, 2012) posits that cultural worldviews interact with risk perception such that individuals selectively credit and dismiss hazards such as climate change. That is, Kahan and associates argue that there is little public disagreement about what science knows about climate change: when discussing climate change, people aren't reasoning to gain knowledge as much as to maintain an affiliation with those with whom they share notions of an ideal life. In a series of studies, Kahan and associates provide evidence that individuals and groups form and maintain beliefs on climate change in ways that reinforce their cultural identity. When the choice presents a conflict between what one knows and who one is, Kahan and colleagues argue cultural identity usually proves more compelling. Kahan's evidence for this pattern is that many who deny the existence of climate change – or doubt its harmfulness – can describe some findings of climate science if asked. But if asked if they "believe in" climate science, a question that seems to ask about loyalties, not knowledge, they say that they do not (Kahan, 2015). His theory describes the thinking processes of both those who do not agree that climate change is a serious problem requiring action now and those who do. That is, those who agree with climate change science are also influenced by desired group identities.

Cultural identity and social affiliation are potent influences that have been used effectively by those resisting acting on climate change. Historically, those who deny the legitimacy of climate science have linked climate change issues to prominent social discourses, garnering public support and delaying policy action (Roper, Ganesh, & Zorn, 2016). For example, some commentators recently have questioned the patriotism of those who believe climate change deserves attention (Samenow, 2014). In polling, the issue of climate change is a concern for many in the US, but it is less of a concern than are jobs or the economy (e.g. Fox News Poll, 2017).

Doubts about the likelihood and severity of harm

Second, in the US, some question the likelihood and severity of the harm climate change will cause them and their region. As a result, stakeholders may underestimate their vulnerability to climate change. Even those Americans who accept the reality of global warming tend to see it as a distant threat spatially and temporally (Leiserowitz, 2005; Lorenzoni et al., 2006). A May 2017 report found that Americans think climate change will primarily impact future generations (71%), people in developing countries (62%), and non-human species (71%). Only 58% of Americans thought that climate change will harm people in the US, their family (47%), or themselves (43%) (Leiserowitz et al., 2017). In this light, the benefits of acting on climate change today, which involves weaning the economy from fossil fuels, can be viewed as sacrificing resources that raise the living conditions of millions. Further, when groups and individuals are psychologically vested in the fossil fuel economy as a component of industrial capitalism, perceptions of the imminence and dangers of climate change may seem less important than factors such as jobs or economic wellbeing (Taber & Lodge, 2006; Van der Linden et al., 2017).

Concerns about benefits, costs, workability

Third, decisions about the management of climate change are influenced by concerns about benefits, costs, and the workability or effectiveness of solutions. Over a decade ago, the Stern report (Stern, 2006) concluded that the benefits of strong and early action to address climate change far outweigh the economic costs of not acting. Research has continued to make this argument, noting that changes in global heat-trapping gas emissions should have occurred by 2020 to avoid severe climate change-associated impacts (Figueres et al., 2017). But many remain unfamiliar with the range of direct and indirect harms to human health from climate change (Luber et al., 2014) and the benefits of reducing heat-trapping gases (Frumkin & McMichael, 2008; Patz, 2016).

Doubts about effectiveness of solutions and one's own abilities

The fourth barrier to decision-making about climate change emanates from self-doubt. Research shows that dissatisfaction with solutions can stem from doubts about the extent to which stakeholders perceive themselves as being able to enact proposed solutions (Witte, 1994). According to Witte's (1994) extended parallel process model, efficacy plays a large role in acceptance of and acting upon the solutions to a hazard. There are two essential types of efficacy needed to increase support for climate change management: response efficacy and self-efficacy. Response efficacy is the perceived effectiveness of a proposed solution at averting a threat. Self-efficacy is belief that one has the ability to perform the recommended action (Witte, 1994). For instance, one can reduce energy consumption by changing household lightbulbs to compact fluorescents (Gardner & Stern, 2008). However, given the enormity of the climate change problem, some people perceive this small action as doing little to influence climate change (Slocum, 2004); that is, they perceive the response efficacy of this step to be unimpressive. If satisfaction with the effectiveness of these steps is low, backing for them will be limited.

Steps for Supporting Stakeholders' Decision-Making

TO AVOID CAUSING CONCERN ABOUT SOCIAL SANCTION, LOCATE UNIFYING FRAMINGS OF THE PROBLEM

If support for decisions about climate change is inhibited by communication that causes stakeholders to feel that outsiders are forcing agendas on them, or that they are being forced to choose sides on an issue inconsistent with deeply held values, then communicators should shift from focusing on differences to similarities in lived experience and goals (Postmes, 2015). Communities can be cast as "Virginians" or "Floridians," collective identities that unite rather than divide. Communicators might also develop opportunities for people to understand that their members are already experiencing climate change, and begin to develop norms that acknowledge the collective "new normal." For example, homeowners who experience sunny-day flooding may increase their efforts to reduce heat-trapping emissions by planting more trees, or incentivizing development away from flood-prone areas. Importantly, in doing so, these steps model behaviors others can emulate so climate change becomes a shared challenge (Clark, 1984).

Still another approach is to cast "green behaviors" as symbolic of one's identity (Berger & Heath, 2007; Griskevicius, Tybur, & Van den Bergh, 2010; Lee, 2008; Loock et al., 2011; Ottman, Stafford, & Hartman, 2006). Studies have shown that peer perception, in addition to concern for the environment, influences the adoption of green behaviors (Griskevicius, Tybur, & Van den Bergh, 2010; Lee, 2008; Loock et al., 2011). People enact behaviors that reinforce who they want to be and how they want to be seen. For example, buying a Toyota Prius was a symbolic behavior – it reinforced individuals' desire to be more environmentally conscious and made a statement to others about their identity (Griskevicius, Tybur, & Van den Bergh, 2010; Maynard, 2007). To encourage people to adopt green behaviors, such as reducing water consumption or buying green products, the behavior needs to be marketed in a way that moves people to believe that action is part of their individual identity and is something that will make them positively perceived by others. This approach is used to encourage people to take pride in a threatened animal or plant species important in their region. Rather than outlawing use of the animal or plant, researchers recommend a "pride of place" effort that encourages communities to view the threatened animal, plant, or physical entity as something about which to take pride (Gupta et al., 2014).

TO ADDRESS DOUBT ABOUT THE PROBABILITY AND SEVERITY OF CLIMATE CHANGE'S REGIONAL HARM, FOCUS ON LOCAL IMPACTS

Climate change has traditionally been framed as an analytical, temporally and spatially distant risk that constitutes future loss for society. In contrast to the delivery of information through the deficit model of communication, highlighting a community's shared experience can also reframe climate change as a present and proximal threat. Unfortunately, many localities can now point out climate change impacts, whether an extreme weather event, a vector-borne disease outbreak, or damage to local infrastructure from sea-level rise or wildfire. In this context it may be possible to de-link identity from political ideology by making it more relevant to local people and places. Researchers have identified public perceptions of local vulnerability to climate change as an important explanation for existing sub-national action to address climate change (Rabe, 2004; Selin & VanDeveer, 2009). The Climate Matters program is one successful effort to localize climate change (Placky et al., 2016; Sanford & Placky, 2015; Zhao et al., 2014), facilitating a more nuanced understanding of personal vulnerability. Zhao et al. (2014) found that a series of news features on the CBS-affiliate in Columbia, South Carolina, increased knowledge among viewers of what climate change is and how it is harming their region through increasing numbers of high-heat, high-temperature days and contributing to changes in rainfall, which may harm crops. Those who watched other network news programs were less knowledgeable than the CBS viewers about climate change's regional impacts.

ADDRESS DISAGREEMENT ABOUT COSTS, BENEFITS, AND WORKABILITY OF PROPOSED ACTIONS, BY SUPPORTING PUBLIC DISCUSSION OF MITIGATION EFFORTS

When it is emphasized that members of the public were involved in policy development, acceptance of the policy is higher (Arvai, 2003; Hillier, 1998; Syme, Macpherson, & Seligman, 1991). Studies, such as those by Arvai (2003), have shown that even if an individual was not directly involved in the decision-making process, he or she will still have higher satisfaction with policies where polices are viewed as involving a community than with policies perceived as imposed because collective or community decisions are perceived to have more legitimacy.

In other words, even if individuals disagree with a step or policy, they are more likely to accept it because they feel that the process for its adoption was "fair, reasonable, and amenable to allowing all interested parties an opportunity to voice their feelings and concerns" (Arvai, 2003, p. 286). Additionally, inviting lay stakeholders to be involved in the planning process for climate change adaptation strategies, as seen in case studies on sea-level rise in the UK (Few, Brown, & Tompkins, 2007) and agricultural adaptation in Italy (Bojovic et al., 2015), may inform local leaders about stakeholders' views.

ADDRESS DISAGREEMENT ABOUT COSTS AND BENEFITS, BY DESCRIBING BENEFITS GAINED FROM ACTING

Research indicates that messages appealing to the benefits of acting can galvanize audiences. For example, Bain et al. (2016) found that for participants across 24 countries, messages about two potential co-benefits of addressing climate change – development (economic and scientific advancement) and benevolence (a more moral and caring community) – were more motivating than the belief that climate change is important. Other messages about co-benefits of climate change highlight the fact that limiting greenhouse gas emissions can reduce traffic congestion, improve air quality, and enhance energy options (Beg et al., 2002). Focusing on the benefits gained from acting can help draw attention away from disagreement about a policy and increase satisfaction with its implementation.

PROMOTE A SENSE OF AGENCY OR SELF-EFFICACY, AND OFFER A RANGE OF SOLUTIONS FOR CONSIDERATION, NOT A SINGLE SOLUTION

A study analyzing hard (government controls), soft (incentive-based or changes in default options), and voluntary (no regulation – free choice) policies by Attari et al. (2009) explored which of these approaches people preferred for limiting the purchase of SUVs and trucks and increasing green energy (wind and solar). The authors found that people prefer voluntary and soft policies because voluntary options preserve personal freedom and choice. If individuals are provided with multiple solutions, there may be a greater likelihood that many will be satisfied with at least one of the steps to manage climate change's impacts (response efficacy). Further, options provide individuals with the opportunity to select actions that match their available resources (self-efficacy). This multiple-solution method was used in California to address increasingly frequent and intense droughts. During a drought in California, Congresswoman Anna Eshoo released a statement on the need for conserving water that provided options (Eshoo, 2014). They included washing clothes and dishes only when one has a full load, installing low-flow shower heads, cleaning driveways with a broom instead of a hose, landscaping with drought-tolerant plants (xeriscaping), and watering yards when temperatures are cooler, such as during evening and early morning hours, to reduce evaporation and amount of water needed. Eshoo's premise was that if everyone in California could take a few of these steps, this effort would result in mass water conservation.

This strategy of multiple solutions should address concerns both about self-efficacy and response efficacy or the effectiveness of proposed solutions. Those who do not have the funds to install low-water-flow technology or xeriscape their yards may be capable of limiting the number of dishwasher loads they run. This same method can also be applied to reducing individual carbon footprints, or the amount of carbon personally generated. Most people are probably aware of recommendations to carpool or install energy-efficient appliances, but other options can include keeping car tires properly inflated, programing one's thermostat at a moderate temperature, or consuming more chicken than beef (Carbon offsets to alleviate poverty, n.d.). When people are provided multiple options, rather than told that they must accept a single recommendation, it may be easier for them to find options that they believe will effectively address the problem and work for them.

Hypotheses on Supporting Decision-Making

H1: People are more likely to feel satisfied with the reality of and response options regarding climate change if there is consensus on discrete sub-issues such as the costs and benefits of the proposed actions or concern about the effectiveness of the proposed steps.
H2: People are more likely to feel satisfied with the reality of and response options regarding climate change if they feel their point of view is respected.
H3: People are more likely to feel satisfied with the reality of and response options regarding climate change if they can talk about their views without fear of social sanction.
H4: People are more likely to feel satisfied with the reality of and response options regarding climate change if they are exposed to examples of how climate change is affecting others in their community.
H5: People are more likely to feel satisfied with the reality of and response options regarding climate change if they feel a sense of personal and collective efficacy regarding the workability of a recommended action.
H6: People are more likely to feel satisfied with the reality of and response options regarding climate change if they feel a sense of ownership and agency in the decision-making process.
H7: People are more likely to feel satisfied with the reality of and response options regarding climate change if there is a mix of voluntary options as well as mandates.

The E in CAUSE: Motivate Enactment

Even when people endorse solutions, belief in the rightness of certain actions does not translate automatically to enduring behavioral change. The E in CAUSE refers to analyses of factors undermining collective and personal efficacy and evidence-based steps for motivating enactment. Therefore, to support enduring behavioral changes, communication strategies must work on at least two interrelated levels: individual and societal.

At the individual level, climate change advocates often exhort lay stakeholders to change their personal behavior. Examples include advice about changing transportation (Maibach, Steg, & Anable, 2009) or food choices (Hunter & Röös, 2016). However, while individual, voluntary actions are necessary, they will be insufficient on their own to meaningfully address climate change. Social and structural impediments to behavior change include, for example, the fact that most transportation and food systems rely on cheap fossil fuels (Ockwell, Whitmarsh, & O'Neill, 2009). Further, existing research and practice does not yet give good guidance about how to communicate about and connect high-level scientific and policy debates with local discourses about climate change impacts and responses (Moser, 2014).

This is not to dismiss the need for and the value of individual action – the core of societal or community action. Yet changing individual behaviors is challenging. The more integrated a behavior is in daily life, the harder it is to change it (Booth-Butterfield, 2003). Embedded behaviors are often intertwined with other behaviors, are influenced internally by personality, image concerns, perceptions of behavior, and self-efficacy, and are reinforced externally by an individual's social circle, society, and physical environment (Booth-Butterfield, 2003). Further, because the causes of climate change are heavily engrained in consumer purchases and lifestyles, these habits are difficult to change. According to the behavioral perspective model (BPM), decisions and behaviors are guided ultimately by consequences and are influenced by the openness of the decision-making environment and past experiences or "learning history" (Foxall et al., 2006). The consequences (cost) and reinforcements (benefits) of a behavior are both utilitarian and informational. Utilitarian factors of decision-making are inherently ones of functional purpose such as time, money, quality, value, and practicality (Foxall et al., 2006), and they generate feelings of "pleasure and satisfaction" (Foxall, 1992, p. 191). Informational factors are social and guided by the reactions and feedback of peers. This feedback involves the "correctness and appropriateness" of a decision or behavior and includes potential "ramifications of status, prestige, and social acceptance" that a particular decision or behavior may bring (Foxall, 1992, p. 191). Fossil fuel use is deeply woven into daily life, making even the smallest change in behavior difficult.

Additionally, communication about the desired behavioral change can be difficult because the proposed action is often seen as worthwhile but too difficult, expensive, or time-consuming, and too insignificant to make a difference (Rowan, 1991, p. 323). Recall, too, that unsolicited advice from friends and family is not appreciated (MacGeorge et al., 2004). For example, choosing to take public transit is often suggested as an action individuals can take to reduce carbon emissions. Driving a car, however, is a highly embedded behavior. Driving a personal car assists with travel to work, grocery shopping, traveling for leisure, transporting children to appointments, and so forth, making it hard to introduce another more time-consuming transportation option. Further, driving a personal car is a set of behaviors supported by various factors – such as the belief that public transit is insufficient, owning a car is a statement of status, and driving creates feelings of independence and freedom (Foxall et al., 2006; Heath & Gifford, 2002; Steg, 2005). Social factors such as lack of access to public transportation, having many friends, family, and co-workers who drive, and believing that driving is part of one's identity all support choices to drive. A study on climate change and barriers to taking mitigation action (Semenza, Ploubidis, & George, 2011) found that not knowing how to change behavior, lack of money and time, and belief that their personal changes would make no difference were reasons individuals in Houston, Texas, and Portland, Oregon, reported as obstacles to changing behavior, even though they believed in the value of the change.

Steps for Motivating Enactment

This analysis suggests that enduring behavioral change is more likely when it is socially supported at many levels. Strategic, evidence-based steps for providing such support have been identified.

CREATE A SENSE OF COMMUNITY

Discursive and participatory learning processes have been suggested as a means to overcome these enactment challenges by helping individuals and communities develop awareness, agency, and association through action and reflection (Ballard, 2005). Groups, for example, have formed to support food production and transportation systems that reduce the use of packaging and food transportation costs. Food cooperatives and "community-supported agriculture" are groups that make arrangements with local farmers to pre-buy healthful food and have it delivered to specific locations, bypassing the need for grocery stores and increasing consumers' abilities to consume food grown in the ways they wish it to be produced. Membership in such groups creates iterative action, reflection, and learning that may cause the previously unquestioned to be questioned. It's not just the discursive processes that create positive behavior change, but the "forms of knowledge represented in this questioning process" (Hobson, 2003, p. 105). Ballard (2005) describes a pilot project during which two previously self-described skeptics became advocates for acting on climate change.

A sense of agency is essential to combating the impression that climate change is too large a problem to take on. Even when people agree that change is warranted, they struggle because change is stressful (Prochaska & DiClemente, 1982, 1983). Ballard (2005) suggests that agency is primarily acquired by working in groups with like-minded others, communicating personal experiences and building shared commitment. Ballard (2005) also suggests that association with others can not only sustain energy but bring a variety of perspectives to decision-making.

EMPHASIZE SOCIAL NORMS IN PROMOTING DESIRED BEHAVIOR

Intention can be influenced by social norms – particularly descriptive norms, or what others do or what is considered "normal." People use descriptive norms when deciding what adaptive measures to take because these norms give evidence that the desired action is effective. Norms are also used as "informative-processing shortcuts in choosing how to behave in a given situation" (Heath & Gifford, 2002). In Heath and Gifford's study, descriptive norms were significant predictors of using the bus among university students in Canada.

FIND WAYS TO MAKE BEHAVIOR EASY AND SIMPLE

To encourage greater levels of enactment, local governmental bodies, non-profits, and other groups working to encourage climate change mitigation behaviors can identify steps that are specific, easy, and popular. Examples of making climate mitigation actions easier include programming thermostats to turn off and on at certain times or utilizing phone apps to find ecofriendly products when shopping (i.e. GoodGuide) or to conserve water (i.e. Dropcountr). Actions can also be hard to remember, especially when new to a routine. Using prompts as visual reminders can make it easier for an individual to remember a new action. Examples include signage with pictures on compost bins indicating which items to compost or recycle or signage reminding drivers not to idle automobile engines when parked or waiting at schools, train stations, and airports (McKenzie-Mohr, 2011). To establish norms, people need to feel they should be doing something other people are already doing. McKenzie-Mohr (2011) explains how norm-emphasizing messages should be visible near where the desired action would occur. Examples of encouraging climate change mitigation behavior through norms include utility companies providing customers with feedback on their use compared to other energy or water saving by homes in their neighborhood, or displaying in the entrance to a business the percentage of people who get to work by carpooling or using public transit (McKenzie-Mohr, 2011).

Hypotheses on Motivating Enactment

H1: People will be more likely to take action on climate change if recommended steps are well delineated and made attainable.

H2: People will be more likely to act to build resilience at the community and individual level if they are frequently reminded to enact these behaviors at predictable times of the year (e.g. "King" or exceptionally high tides during hurricane season).

H3: Individuals will be more likely to take resilience actions if they view themselves as members of organizations that are supportive, than if they do not see themselves as supported in this manner.

H4: People are more likely to undertake actions if climate change impacts and actions are placed in a localized context.

H5: People are more likely to undertake actions if they are supported in developing awareness, agency, and association.

H6: People are more likely to undertake actions if benefits are emphasized to offset the perception of loss (e.g., of lifestyle options).

H7: People are more likely to undertake actions if there is an iterative process of action and reflection – at the individual and community level – in responding to climate change.

H8: People are more likely to undertake actions if there are prompts to act, such as visual reminders of the action(s) to be taken.

Conclusion

Communicating climate change is challenging in many ways. Progress is unlikely if the effort is cast solely as the responsibility of a few professional groups and solely as one-way communication where the scientific community transmits its knowledge to lay stakeholders. As this chapter's discussion of the deficit model of science communication shows, it is easy to fall back on a paternalistic view that only the scientifically informed are able to manage complex problems. A more nuanced view of science communication, one encouraged by the CAUSE model of strategic science communication, asks all parties to reflect on their own goals and concerns and become knowledgeable about the goals and concerns of others. It also provides specific analyses of likely obstacles and practical, strategically guided and evidence-based steps for addressing these obstacles with specific communication objectives and strategies.

The CAUSE model has limitations. While it is backed by extensive studies, the model's practical application, in its entirety, has not been tested. That is, there are no studies saying campaigns generated with this model are especially effective. Another weakness is that it taps an array of theories which may not be compatible with one another. A strength, however, is that it was developed from an analysis of communication itself, not from analyses of attitudes and behaviors that may or may not involve communication. Additionally, its specificity with regard to identifying communication goals and strategic and evidence-guided steps for achieving them alerts communicators and researchers to the importance of considering, for example, effective methods of explaining complexities, a step that is often under-explored in theories that cast all communication as persuasion and a feature which may be especially important in communicating about climate change.

More work should be done to assess the effectiveness of CAUSE in increasing scientists' sense of their challenges, goals, and options when sharing their research with lay stakeholders. As Dudo and Besley (2016) found, there is still relatively little research on scientists' knowledge of specific groups of stakeholders' concerns, and more could be done to enhance "science communication capacity building," as the NASEM (2017) report describes it. For instance, involving faculty and students in local planning commission meetings concerning energy use and infrastructure could be informative and helpful. Promoting efforts such as the "Student Environmental Action Showcase" or having students assist local government agencies in promoting energy conservation may help as well. In the US, students in communication are often given projects to deepen their understanding of social challenges. Assisting scientists, communities, non-profit organizations, and governmental bodies in tackling the regional impacts of climate change could engage students and professionals in learning more about one another and about climate change.

References

Akerlof, K. L., Rowan, K. E., La Porte, T., Batten, B. K., Ernst, H., & Sklarew, D. M. (2016). Risky business: Engaging the public on sea level rise and inundation. *Environmental Science & Policy*, 66, 314–323.

Anderson, A. A., Myers, T. A., Maibach, E. W., Cullen, H., Gandy, J., Witte, J., … Leiserowitz, A. (2013). If they like you, they learn from you: How a brief weathercaster-delivered climate education segment is moderated by viewer evaluations of the weathercaster. *Weather, Climate, and Society*, 5(4), 367–377.

Anderson, D. (2016). *Economic impact of recreational trout fishing in the driftless area*. Madison, WI: Northstar Consulting.

Arvai, J. L. (2003). Using risk communication to disclose the outcome of a participatory decision-making process: Effects on the perceived acceptability of risk-policy decisions. *Risk Analysis*, 23(2), 281–289.

Attari, S. Z., Schoen, M., Davidson, C. I., DeKay, M. L., de Bruin, W. B., Dawes, R., & Small, M. J. (2009). Preferences for change: Do individuals prefer voluntary actions, soft regulations, or hard regulations to decrease fossil fuel consumption? *Ecological Economics*, 68(6), 1701–1710.

Audubon (2017). About the great backyard bird count. http://www.audubon.org/content/about-great-backyard-bird-count

Ausubel, D. P. (2000). Preview of assimilation theory of meaningful learning and retention. In D. P. Ausubel (Ed.), *The acquisition and retention of knowledge: A cognitive view* (pp. 1–18). Dordrecht, Netherlands: Springer.

Bailey, E., Bronnenkant, K., Kelley, J., & Hein, G. E. (1998). Visitor behavior at a constructivist exhibition: Evaluating *Investigate!* at Boston's Museum of Science. In C. Dufresne-Tassé (Ed.), *Évaluation et education muséal: Nouvelles tendances* (pp. 9–68). Quebec, Canada: International Council of Museums, Committee for Education and Cultural Education.

Bain, P. G., Milfont, T. L., Kashima, Y., Bilewicz, M., Doron, G., Garðarsdóttir, R. B., ... Saviolidis, N. M. (2016). Co-benefits of addressing climate change can motivate action around the world. *Nature Climate Change*, 6(2), 154–157.

Ballard, D. (2005). Using learning processes to promote change for sustainable development. *Action Research*, 3(2), 135–156.

Banerjee, S. (Ed.). (2012). *Arctic voices: Resistance at the tipping point.* New York: Seven Stories Press.

Bangay, C., & Blum, N. (2010). Education responses to climate change and quality: Two parts of the same agenda? *International Journal of Educational Development*, 30(4), 359–368.

Barabasi, A. L. (2017). The elegant law that governs us all. *Science*, 357(6347), 138.

Bauer, M. W., Allum, N., & Miller, S. (2007). What can we learn from 25 years of PUS survey research? Liberating and expanding the agenda. *Public Understanding of Science*, 16(1), 79–95.

Beamish, T. D. (2002). *Silent spill: The organization of an industrial crisis.* MA: MIT Press.

Beeler, C. (2017). To understand climate change, look at it from a mussel's perspective. In Public Radio International's The World. https://www.pri.org/stories/2017-04-25/understand-climate-change-look-it-mussels-perspective

Beg, N., Morlot, J. C., Davidson, O., Afrane-Okesse, Y., Tyani, L., Denton, F., ... Parikh, K. (2002). Linkages between climate change and sustainable development. *Climate Policy*, 2(2–3), 129–144.

Bélanger, P. (2003). Learning environments and environmental education. *New Directions for Adult and Continuing Education, 2003*, 99, 79–88.

Berger, J., & Heath, C. (2007). Where consumers diverge from others: Identity signaling and product domains. *Journal of Consumer Research*, 34(2), 121–134.

Besley, J. C. (2010). Public engagement and the impact of fairness perceptions on decision favorability and acceptance. *Science Communication*, 32(2), 256–280.

Besley, J. C. (2015). What do scientists think about the public and does it matter to their online engagement? *Science and Public Policy*, 42(2), 201–214.

Besley, J. C., Dudo, A., & Storksdieck, M. (2015). Scientists' views about communication training. *Journal of Research in Science Teaching*, 52(2), 199–220.

Bishop, C. M., Spivey, R. J., Hawkes, L. A., Batbayar, N., Chua, B., Frappell, P. B., ... Butler, P. J. (2015). The roller coaster flight strategy of bar-headed geese conserves energy during Himalayan migrations. *Science*, 347(6219), 250–254.

Bitzer, L. (1968). The rhetorical situation. *Philosophy and Rhetoric*, 1(1), 1–14.

Bojovic, D., Bonzanigo, L., Giupponi, C., & Maziotis, A. (2015). Online participation in climate change adaptation: A case study of agricultural adaptation measures in Northern Italy. *Journal of Environmental Management*, 157, 8–19.

Booth-Butterfield, M. (2003). Embedded health behaviors from adolescence to adulthood: The impact of tobacco. *Health Communication*, 15(2), 171–184.

Bostrom, A., Morgan, M. G., Fischhoff, B., & Read, D. (1994). What do people know about global climate change? 1. Mental models. *Risk Analysis*, 14(6), 959–970.

Botan, C. H. (2018). Strategic communication theory and practice: The cocreational model. New York: Wiley.

Botan, C. H., & Hazleton, V. (2010). *Public relations theory II*. New York: Routledge.

Botan, C. H., & Taylor, M. (2004). Public relations: State of the field. *Journal of Communication*, 54(4), 645–661.

Bradbury, J., Ray, I., Peterson, T., Wade, S., Wong-Parodi, G., & Feldpausch, A. (2009). The role of social factors in shaping public perceptions of CCS: Results of multi-state focus group interviews in the US. *Energy Procedia*, 1(1), 4665–4672.

Bradbury, J. A. (1989). The policy implications of differing concepts of risk. *Science, Technology, & Human Values*, 14(4), 380–399.

Bromage, B. K., & Mayer, R. E. (1981). Relationship between what is remembered and creative problem-solving performance in science learning. *Journal of Educational Psychology*, 73(4), 451.

Bucchi, M. (2008). Of deficits, deviations and dialogues: Theories of public communication of science. In M. Bucchi & B. Trench (Eds.), *Handbook of public communication of science and technology* (pp. 57–76). London: Routledge.

Burke, M., Hsiang, S. M., & Miguel, E. (2015). Global non-linear effect of temperature on economic production. *Nature*, 527(7577), 235–239.

Carbon offsets to alleviate poverty. (n.d.). https://cotap.org

Chang, Y., & Choi, S. (2014). Effects of seductive details evidenced by gaze duration. *Neurobiology of Learning and Memory*, 109, 131–138.

Chemistry in context. (n.d.). Chemistry in context 3.4 flashcards. Retrieved from https://quizlet.com/29647213/chemistry-in-context-34-flash-cards

Clark, R. A. (1984). *Persuasive messages*. New York: HarperCollins.

Climate Reality Project. (2017). Retrieved from https://www.climaterealityproject.org/blog/use-research-backed-message-talk-about-climate-change-and-health-anyone

Couldry, N., Livingstone, S., & Markham, T. (2016). *Media consumption and public engagement*. London: Palgrave MacMillan.

Dudo, A., & Besley, J. C. (2016). Scientists' prioritization of communication objectives for public engagement. *PloS One*, 11(2), e0148867.

Duit, R., & Treagust, D. F. (2004). Conceptual change: A powerful framework for improving science teaching and learning. *The RoutledgeFalmer Reader in Science Education*, 25(6), 56.

Eshoo, A. G. (2014). 14 ways to conserve water during the California drought. Retrieved from http://eshoo.house.gov/news-stories/e-newsletters/14-ways-to-conserve-water-during-the-california-drought

Fellenor, J., Barnett, J., Potter, C., Urquhart, J., Mumford, J. D., & Quine, C. P. (2017). The social amplification of risk on Twitter: The case of ash dieback disease in the United Kingdom. *Journal of Risk Research* 21(10), 1163–1183.

Few, R., Brown, K., & Tompkins, E. L. (2007). Public participation and climate change adaptation: Avoiding the illusion of inclusion. *Climate Policy*, 7(1), 46–59.

Ficke, A. D., Myrick, C. A., & Hansen, L. J. (2007). Potential impacts of global climate change on freshwater fisheries. *Reviews in Fish Biology and Fisheries*, 17(4), 581–613.

Figueres, C., Schellnhuber, H. J., Whiteman, G., Rockström, J., Hobley, A., & Rahmstorf, S. (2017). Three years to safeguard our climate. *Nature News*, 546(7660), 593.

Fiorino, D. J. (1989). Technical and democratic values in risk analysis. *Risk Analysis*, 9(3), 293–299.

Fischhoff, B., Slovic, P., Lichtenstein, S., Read, S., & Combs, B. (1978). How safe is safe enough? A psychometric study of attitudes towards technological risks and benefits. *Policy Sciences*, 9(2), 127–152.

Fishkin, J. S., & Luskin, R. C. (2005). Experimenting with a democratic ideal: Deliberative polling and public opinion. *Acta Politica*, 40(3), 284–298.

Fiske, S. T., & Dupree, C. (2014). Gaining trust as well as respect in communicating to motivated audiences about science topics. *Proceedings of the National Academy of Sciences*, 111(Suppl. 4), 13593–13597.

Forster, P., Ramaswamy, V., Artaxo, P., Berntsen, T., Betts, R., Fahey, D. W., & Nganga, J. (2007). Changes in atmospheric constituents and in radiative forcing. In *Climate change 2007. The physical science basis*. Geneva: World Meteorological Organization and the United Nations Environment Program.

Fox News Poll. (2017). Fox News Poll, questions 11 to 19 [asking how concerned respondents were about issues including climate change]. Retrieved from http://www.foxnews.com/politics/interactive/2017/05/25/fox-news-poll-may-25-2017.html

Foxall, G. R. (1992). The behavioral perspective model of purchase and consumption: From consumer theory to marketing practice. *Journal of the Academy of Marketing Science*, 20(2), 189–198.

Foxall, G. R., Oliveira-Castro, J. M., James, V. K., Yani-de-Soriano, M. M., & Sigurdsson, V. (2006). Consumer behavior analysis and social marketing: The case of environmental conservation. *Behavior and Social Issues*, 15(1), 101–124.

Frumkin, H., & McMichael, A. J. (2008). Climate change and public health. *American Journal of Preventive Medicine*, 35(5), 403–410.

Gardner, G. T., & Stern, P. C. (2008). The short list: The most effective actions US households can take to curb climate change. *Environment: Science and Policy for Sustainable Development*, 50(5), 12–25.

Garnett, P. J., Garnett, P. J., & Hackling, M. W. (1995). Students' alternative conceptions in chemistry: A review of research and implications for teaching and learning. *Studies in Science Education*, 255(1995), 69–95.

Graber, D. A. (1976). *Verbal behavior and politics*. Urbana-Champaign, IL: University of Illinois.

Griskevicius, V., Tybur, J. M., & Van den Bergh, B. (2010). Going green to be seen: Status, reputation, and conspicuous conservation. *Journal of Personality and Social Psychology*, 98(3), 392.

Guichard, J. (1995). Designing tools to develop the conception of learners. *International Journal of Science Education*, 17(2), 243–253.

Gupta, N., Sivakumar, K., Mathur, V. B., & Chadwick, M. A. (2014). The "tiger of Indian rivers": Stakeholders' perspectives on the golden mahseer as a flagship fish species. *Area*, 46(4), 389–397.

Hansen, A., & Machin, D. (Eds.). (2016). *Visual environmental communication*. New York: Routledge.

Harp, S. F., & Mayer, R. E. (1998). How seductive details do their damage: A theory of cognitive interest in science learning. *Journal of Educational Psychology*, 90(3), 414.

Hassol, S. J. (2008). Improving how scientists communicate about climate change. *Eos Transactions American Geophysical Union*, 89(11), 106–107.

Heath, C., & Heath, D. (2007). *Made to stick: Why some ideas survive and others die*. New York: Random House.

Heath, Y., & Gifford, R. (2002). Extending the theory of planned behavior: Predicting the use of public transportation. *Journal of Applied Social Psychology*, 32(10), 2154–2189.

Hewson, P. W., & Hewson, M. G. (1984). The role of conceptual conflict in conceptual change and the design of science instruction. *Instructional Science*, 13(1), 1–13.

Hillier, J. (1998). Beyond confused noise: Ideas toward communicative procedural justice. *Journal of Planning Education and Research*, 18(1), 14–24.

Hobson, K. (2003). Thinking habits into action: The role of knowledge and process in questioning household consumption practices. *Local Environment*, 8(1), 95–112.

Holgate, S. J., & Woodworth, P. L. (2004). Evidence for enhanced coastal sea level rise during the 1990s. *Geophysical Research Letters*, 31(7), L07305.

Hunter, E., & Röös, E. (2016). Fear of climate change consequences and predictors of intentions to alter meat consumption. *Food Policy*, 62, 151–160.

Intergovernmental Panel on Climate Change. (2014). *Climate change 2014–Impacts, adaptation and vulnerability: Regional aspects*. Cambridge. Cambridge University Press.

Janiszewski, C., & Meyvis, T. (2001). Effects of brand logo complexity, repetition, and spacing on processing fluency and judgment. *Journal of Consumer Research*, 28(1), 18–32.

Järvenoja, H., & Järvelä, S. (2009). Emotion control in collaborative learning situations: Do students regulate emotions evoked by social challenges? *British Journal of Educational Psychology*, 79(3), 463–481.

Kahan, D. (2012). Why we are poles apart on climate change. *Nature News*, 488(7411), 255.

Kahan, D. M. (2015). Climate-science communication and the measurement problem. *Political Psychology*, 36(S1), 1–43.

Kahan, D. M., Braman, D., Gastil, J., Slovic, P., & Mertz, C. K. (2007). Culture and identity-protective cognition: Explaining the white-male effect in risk perception. *Journal of Empirical Legal Studies*, 4(3), 465–505.

Kahan, D. M., Jenkins-Smith, H., & Braman, D. (2011). Cultural cognition of scientific consensus. *Journal of Risk Research*, 14(2), 147–174.
Kahan, D. M., Peters, E., Wittlin, M., Slovic, P., Ouellette, L. L., Braman, D., & Mandel, G. (2012). The polarizing impact of science literacy and numeracy on perceived climate change risks. *Nature Climate Change*, 2(10), 732–735.
Kennamer, J. D. (1988). News values and the vividness of information. *Written Communication*, 5(1), 108–123.
Kent, M. L., & Taylor, M. (2002). Toward a dialogic theory of public relations. *Public Relations Review*, 28(1), 21–37.
Kinneavy, J. (1969). The basic aims of discourse. *College Composition and Communication*, 20(5), 297–304.
Kinneavy, J. L. (1971). *A theory of discourse*. New York: Norton.
Lankow, J., Ritchie, J., & Crooks, R. (2012). *Infographics: The power of visual storytelling*. New York: Wiley.
Lazard, A., & Atkinson, L. (2015). Putting environmental infographics center stage: The role of visuals at the elaboration likelihood model's critical point of persuasion. *Science Communication*, 37(1), 6–33.
Le Treut, H., Somerville, R., Cubasch, U., Ding, Y., Mauritzen, C., Mokssit, A., ... Prather, M. (2007). Historical overview of climate change. In S. Solomon, D. Qin, M. Manning, Z., M. Marquis, K. B., M. Tignor, & H. L. Miller (Eds.), *Climate change 2007: Fourth assessment report of the intergovernmental panel on climate change*. Cambridge: University Press.
Lee, K. (2008). Opportunities for green marketing: Young consumers. *Marketing Intelligence & Planning*, 26(6), 573–586.
Lehr, R. L., Guild, W., Thomas, D. L., & Swezey, B. G. (2003). *Listening to customers: How deliberative polling helped build 1,000 MW of new renewable energy projects in Texas*. Report No. NREL/TP-620-33177Golden, CO: National Renewable Energy Laboratory.
Leiserowitz, A. A. (2005). American risk perceptions: Is climate change dangerous? *Risk Analysis*, 25(6), 1433–1442.
Leiserowitz, A. (2006). Climate change risk perception and policy preferences: The role of affect, imagery, and values. *Climatic Change*, 77(1), 45–72.
Leiserowitz, A., Maibach, E., Roser-Renouf, C., Feinberg, G., & Howe, P. (2012). *Climate change in the American mind: Americans' global warming beliefs and attitudes in September, 2012*. New Haven, CT: Yale Project on Climate Change Communication.
Leiserowitz, A., Maibach, E., Roser-Renouf, C., & Hmielowski, J. D. (2011). *Politics & global warming: Democrats, Republicans, Independents, and the Tea Party*. New Haven, CT: Yale Project on Climate Change Communication.
Leiserowitz, A., Maibach, E., Roser-Renouf, C., Rosenthal, S., Cutler, M., & Kotcher, J. (2017). *Climate change in the American mind*. New Haven, CT: Yale Program on Climate Change Communication.
Leiserowitz, A., Maibach, E. W., Rosenthal, S., Kotcher, J., Bergquist, P., Ballew, M., Goldberg, M., & Gustafson, A. (2019). Climate change in the American mind: April 2019. Yale University and George Mason University. New Haven, CT: Yale Program on Climate Change Communication, 2019, Available at SSRN: https://ssrn.com/abstract=3532010
Lester, P. M. (2013). *Visual communication*. Boston, MA: Cengage Learning.
Loewenstein, G. F., Weber, E. U., Hsee, C. K., & Welch, N. (2001). Risk as feelings. *Psychological Bulletin*, 127(2), 267.
Loman, N. L., & Mayer, R. E. (1983). Signaling techniques that increase the understandability of expository prose. *Journal of Educational Psychology*, 75(3), 402.
Loock, C.-M., Landwehr, J. R., Staake, T., Fleisch, E., & Herrmann, A. (2011). I am green: The role of effort and image on green identity signaling. Paper presented to the European Marketing Academy, Brussels https://www.alexandria.unisg.ch/85487
Lorenzoni, I., Leiserowitz, A., de Franca Doria, M., Poortinga, W., & Pidgeon, N. F. (2006). Cross-national comparisons of image associations with "global warming" and "climate change" among laypeople in the United States of America and Great Britain. *Journal of Risk Research*, 9(03), 265–281.

Lorenzoni, I., Nicholson-Cole, S., & Whitmarsh, L. (2007). Barriers perceived to engaging with climate change among the UK public and their policy implications. *Global Environmental Change*, 17(3), 445–459.
Lotz-Sisitka, H. (2010). Changing social imaginaries, multiplicities and "one sole world": Reading Scandinavian environmental and sustainability education research papers with Badiou and Taylor at hand. *Environmental Education Research*, 16(1), 133–142.
Lowe, T., Brown, K., Dessai, S., de França Doria, M., Haynes, K., & Vincent, K. (2006). Does tomorrow ever come? Disaster narrative and public perceptions of climate change. *Public Understanding of Science*, 15(4), 435–457.
Luber, G., Knowlton, K., Balbus, J., Frumkin, H., Hayden, M., Hess, J., McGeehin, M., & Ziska, L. (2014). Human health, climate change impacts in the United States: The Third National Climate Assessment. In J. M. Melillo, T. C. Richmond, & G. W. Yohe (Eds.), *U.S. Global change research program* (pp. 220–256). doi: 10.7930/J0PN93H5
Luber, G., & McGeehin, M. (2008). Climate change and extreme heat events. *American Journal of Preventive Medicine*, 35(5), 429–435.
MacGeorge, E. L., Feng, B., Butler, G. L., & Budarz, S. K. (2004). Understanding advice in supportive interactions. *Human Communication Research*, 30(1), 42–70.
Maes, A., van Geel, A., & Cozijn, R. (2005). Signposts on the digital highway: The effect of semantic and pragmatic hyperlink previews. *Interacting with Computers*, 18(2), 265–282.
Maibach, E. W., Leiserowitz, A., Roser-Renouf, C., & Mertz, C. K. (2011). Identifying like-minded audiences for global warming public engagement campaigns: An audience segmentation analysis and tool development. *PloS One*, 6(3), e17571.
Maibach, E. W., Steg, L., & Anable, J. (2009). Promoting physical activity and reducing climate change: Opportunities to replace short car trips with active transportation. *Preventive Medicine*, 49(4), 326–327.
Martiello, M. A., & Giacchi, M. V. (2010). High temperatures and health outcomes: A review of the literature. *Scandinavian Journal of Social Medicine*, 38(8), 826–837.
Mayer, R. E. (2005). *The Cambridge handbook of multimedia learning*. Cambridge: Cambridge University Press.
Mayer, R. E., & Moreno, R. (2003). Nine ways to reduce cognitive load in multimedia learning. *Educational Psychologist*, 38(1), 43–52.
Maynard, M. (2007, July 4). Say "hybrid" and many people will hear "prius." The New York Times. Retrieved from https://www.nytimes.com/2007/07/04/business/04hybrid.html
McKenzie-Mohr, D. (2011). *Fostering sustainable behavior: An introduction to community-based social marketing*. Gabriola Island, BC [Canada]: New Society Publishers.
Merrill, M. D., & Tennyson, R. D. (1977). *Concept teaching: An instructional design guide*. Englewood Cliffs, NJ: Educational Technology.
Mooney, C. (2017, June 25). The race to save Florida's devastated coral reef rom global warming. The Washington Post. Retrieved from https://www.washingtonpost.com/graphics/2017/business/environment/florida-reef/?utm_term=.411fe15cdd57
Moore, S. K., Trainer, V. L., Mantua, N. J., Parker, M. S., Laws, E. A., Backer, L. C., & Fleming, L. E. (2008). Impacts of climate variability and future climate change on harmful algal blooms and human health. *Environmental Health*, 7(2), S4.
Moser, S. C. (2014). Communicating adaptation to climate change: The art and science of public engagement when climate change comes home. *Wiley Interdisciplinary Reviews: Climate Change*, 5(3), 337–358.
Moser, S. C., & Dilling, L. (2011). Communicating climate change: Closing the science-action gap. In J. S. Dryzek, R. B. Norgaard, & D. Schlosberg (Eds.), *The Oxford handbook of climate change and society* (pp. 161–174)). Oxford: University Press.
Mote, P. W., Hamlet, A. F., Clark, M. P., & Lettenmaier, D. P. (2005). Declining mountain snowpack in western North America. *Bulletin of the American Meteorological Society*, 86(1), 39–49.
Munro, T. (2012). Visualizing climate change through photography: Outdoor educators examine climate change within their personal contexts. Unpublished doctoral dissertation, University of Alberta.
Myhre, G., Shindell, D., Bréon, F. M., Collins, W., Fuglestvedt, J., Huang, J., ... Nakajima, T. (2013). Anthropogenic and natural radiative forcing. *Climate Change*, 423, 658–740.

NASA. (n.d.). What's the difference between weather and climate? Retrieved from https://www.nasa.gov/mission_pages/noaa-n/climate/climate_weather.html

National Academies of Sciences, Engineering, and Medicine. (2017). *Communicating science effectively: A research agenda*. Washington, D.C. National Academies Press.

National Ocean Service (n.d.). What is a red tide? Retrieved from https://oceanservice.noaa.gov/facts/redtide.html

National Research Council. (2009). *Learning science in informal environments: People, places, and pursuits*. Washington, D.C.: National Academies Press.

National Research Council. (2011). *Advancing the science of climate change*. Washington, D.C.: National Academies Press.

O'Keefe, D. J. (2002). *Persuasion: Theory and research*, Vol. 2. Thousand Oaks, CA: Sage.

O'Neill, S., & Nicholson-Cole, S. (2009). "Fear won't do it" Promoting positive engagement with climate change through visual and iconic representations. *Science Communication*, 30(3), 355–379.

O'Neill, S. J., & Smith, N. (2014). Climate change and visual imagery. *Wiley Interdisciplinary Reviews: Climate Change*, 5(1), 73–87.

Ockwell, D., Whitmarsh, L., & O'Neill, S. (2009). Reorienting climate change communication for effective mitigation: Forcing people to be green or fostering grass-roots engagement? *Science Communication*, 30(3), 305–327.

Olaniran, B. A. (1994). Group performance in computer-mediated and face-to-face communication media. *Management Communication Quarterly*, 7(3), 256–281.

Ottman, J. A., Stafford, E. R., & Hartman, C. L. (2006). Avoiding green marketing myopia: Ways to improve consumer appeal for environmentally preferable products. *Environment: Science and Policy for Sustainable Development*, 48(5), 22–36.

Pachauri, R. K., Allen, M. R., Barros, V. R., Broome, J., Cramer, W., Christ, R., … van Ypserle, J.-P. (2014). *Climate change 2014: Synthesis report. Contribution of working groups I, II and III to the fifth assessment report of the Intergovernmental Panel on Climate Change*. Geneva: IPCC.

Patz, J. A. (2016). Solving the global climate crisis: The greatest health opportunity of our times? *Public Health Reviews*, 37, 30.

Pedestrian & Bicycle Information Center. (n.d.). Retrieved from http://www.pedbikeinfo.org/data/factsheet_crash.cfm

Petty, R. E., & Cacioppo, J. T. (1986). The elaboration likelihood model of persuasion. *Advances in Experimental Social Psychology*, 19, 123–205.

Pidgeon, N., & Fischhoff, B. (2011). The role of social and decision sciences in communicating uncertain climate risks. *Nature Climate Change*, 1(1), 35–41.

Pielke, R. A., Jr. (2007). *The honest broker: Making sense of science in policy and politics*. New York: Cambridge University Press.

Placky, B. W., Maibach, E., Witte, J., Ward, B., Seitter, K., Gardiner, N., … Cullen, H. (2016). Climate matters: A comprehensive educational resource program for broadcast meteorologists. *Bulletin of the American Meteorological Society*, 97(5), 709–712.

Poff, N. L., Brinson, M. M., & Day, J. W. (2002). *Aquatic ecosystems and global climate change*. Arlington, VA: Pew Center on Global Climate Change.

Porter, J. R., Xie, L., Challinor, A. J., Cochrane, K., Howden, S., MarkIqbal, M. M., … Ziska, L. (2014). Food security and food production systems. In C. B. Field et al. (Eds.), *Climate change 2014: Impacts, adaptation, and vulnerability. Part A: Global and sectoral aspects* (pp. 485–533)). New York: Cambridge University Press.

Postmes, T. (2015). Psychology: Climate change and group dynamics. *Nature Climate Change*, 5(3), 195–196.

Prochaska, J. O., & DiClemente, C. C. (1982). Transtheoretical therapy: Toward a more integrative model of change. *Psychotherapy: Theory, Research & Practice*, 19(3), 276–288.

Prochaska, J. O., & DiClemente, C. C. (1983). Stages and processes of self-change of smoking: Toward an integrative model of change. *Journal of Consulting and Clinical Psychology*, 51(3), 390–395.

Rabe, B. G. (2004). *Statehouse and greenhouse: The emerging politics of American climate change policy*. Washington, D.C.: Brookings Institution Press.

Ranney, M., Clark, D., Reinholz, D., & Cohen, S. (2012). Changing global warming beliefs with scientific information: Knowledge, attitudes, and RTMD (Reinforced Theistic Manifest Destiny theory). In *Proceedings of the Cognitive Science Society* Vol. 34.

Reef-Stout, B. E., & Medvedev, K. (2017). Multimedia exhibition teaches undergraduate students about sustainable fashion. In L. Filho, W. Brandli, L. Castro, & L. Newman (Eds.), *Handbook of theory and practice of sustainable development in higher education* (Vol. 4, pp. 83–101). Washington, D.C.: Springer.

Robine, J.-M., Cheung, S. L. K., Le Roy, S., Van Oyen, H., Griffiths, C., Michel, J.-P., & Herrmann, F. R. (2008). Death toll exceeded 70,000 in Europe during the summer of 2003. *Comptes Rendus Biologies*, 331(2), 171–178.

Rogers, E. M. (2003). *Diffusion of innovations*. New York: Free Press.

Roper, J., Ganesh, S., & Zorn, T. E. (2016). Doubt, delay, and discourse: Skeptics' strategies to politicize climate change. *Science Communication*, 38(6), 776–799.

Rowan, K. E. (1988). A contemporary theory of explanatory writing. *Written Communication*, 5(1), 23–56.

Rowan, K. E. (1990). Cognitive correlates of explanatory writing skill: An analysis of individual differences. *Written Communication*, 7(3), 316–341.

Rowan, K. E. (1991). Goals, obstacles, and strategies in risk communication: A problem-solving approach to improving communication about risks. *Journal of Applied Communication Research*, 19(4), 300–329.

Rowan, K. E. (1994a). The technical and democratic approaches to risk situations: Their appeal, limitations, and rhetorical alternative. *Argumentation*, 8(4), 391–409.

Rowan, K. E. (1994b). Why rules for risk communication are not enough: A problem-solving approach to risk communication. *Risk Analysis*, 14(3), 365–374.

Rowan, K. E. (1999). Effective explanation of uncertain and complex science. In S. Friedman, S. Dunwoody, & C. L. Rogers (Eds.), *Communicating uncertainty: Media coverage of new and controversial science* (pp. 210–224). Mahwah, NJ: Erlbaum.

Rowan, K. E. (2003). Informing and explaining skills: Theory and research on informative communication. In J. O. Greene & B. R. Burleson (Eds.), *The handbook of communication and social interaction skills* (pp. 403–438). Mahwah, NJ: Erlbaum.

Rowan, K. E. (2010). Risk communication: An overview. In S. H. Priest (Ed.), *Encyclopedia of science and technology communication* (pp. 652–658). Thousand Oaks, CA: Sage.

Rowan, K. E., Botan, C. H., Kreps, G. L., Samoilenko, S., & Farnsworth, K. (2009). Risk communication education for local emergency managers: Using the CAUSE model for research, education, and outreach. In R. L. Heath & H. D. O'Hair (Eds.), *Handbook of risk and crisis communication* (pp. 168–191). New York: Routledge.

Rowan, K. E., Kotcher, J., Walsh-Thomas, J., Baldwin, P., Trowbridge, J., Thaker, J. T., Witte, J., Klinger, B. A., Cohen, L., Tresch, C., & Maibach, E. W. (2018). Best practices of "innovator" TV meteorologists who act as climate change educators. In D. O'Hair (Ed.), *Risk and health communication in an evolving media environment*. London: Routledge.

Saad, L., & Jones, J. M. (2016). US concern about global warming at eight-year high. Gallup Politics. http://news.gallup.com/poll/190010/concern-global-warming-eight-year-high.aspx

Sackler Colloquia Home. (n.d.). Retrieved from http://www.nasonline.org/programs/sackler-colloquia/?referrer=https://www.google.com

Samenow, J. (2014). Pat Sajak: "Global warming alarmists are unpatriotic racists." Retrieved from https://www.washingtonpost.com/news/capital-weather-gang/wp/2014/05/20/pat-sajak-global-warming-alarmists-are-unpatriotic-racists/?utm_term=.3e91aa7889eb

Sanford, T. J., & Placky, B. W. (2015). Climate matters: Increasing climate literacy through broadcast meteorologists. Abstract for the fall meeting of the American Geophysical Union. Retrieved from http://adsabs.harvard.edu/abs/2015AGUFMED32A.07S

Sauer, J. R., & Butcher, G. S. (2014). The role of citizen science in bird conservation: The Christmas bird count and breeding bird survey. *All Bird Bulletin*, Fall, 3–6.

Schlaepfer, D. R., Bradford, J. B., Lauenroth, W. K., Munson, S. M., Tietjen, B., Hall, S. A., … Lkhagva, A. (2017). Climate change reduces extent of temperate drylands and intensifies drought in deep soils. *Nature Communications*, 8, 14196.

Schwarz, E. A. G. (2013). Visualizing the Chesapeake Bay watershed debate. *Environmental Communication: A Journal of Nature and Culture*, 7(2), 169–190.

Science Museum of Minnesota. (n.d.). Cell lab. Retrieved from https://www.smm.org/educators/standards/cell-lab

Selin, H., & VanDeveer, S. D. (2009). Climate leadership in northeast North America. In H. Selin & S. D. VanDeveer (Eds.), *Changing climates in North American politics: Institutions, policymaking, and multilevel governance* (pp. 111–136). Cambridge, MA: MIT Press.

Semenza, J. C., Ploubidis, G. B., & George, L. A. (2011). Climate change and climate variability: Personal motivation for adaptation and mitigation. *Environmental Health*, 10, 46.

Shannon, C. E., & Weaver, W. (1949). *The mathematical theory of information*. Urbana, IL: University of Illinois.

Shea, K. M., Truckner, R. T., Weber, R. W., & Peden, D. B. (2008). Climate change and allergic disease. *Journal of Allergy and Clinical Immunology*, 122(3), 443–453.

Sheppard, S. R. (2005). Landscape visualization and climate change: The potential for influencing perceptions and behaviour. *Environmental Science & Policy*, 8(6), 637–654.

Shimazoe, J., & Aldrich, H. (2010). Group work can be gratifying: Understanding and overcoming resistance to cooperative learning. *College Teaching*, 58(2), 52–57.

Silvertown, J. (2009). A new dawn for citizen science. *Trends in Ecology & Evolution*, 24(9), 467–471.

Slocum, R. (2004). Polar bears and energy-efficient lightbulbs: Strategies to bring climate change home. *Environment and Planning D: Society and Space*, 22(3), 413–438.

Slovic, P., Finucane, M. L., Peters, E., & MacGregor, D. G. (2004). Risk as analysis and risk as feelings: Some thoughts about affect, reason, risk, and rationality. *Risk Analysis*, 24(2), 311–322.

Slovic, P., Fischhoff, B., & Lichtenstein, S. (1985). Characterizing perceived risk. In R. W. Kates, C. Hohenemser, & J. X. Kasperson (Eds.), *Perilous progress: Managing the hazards of technology* (pp. 91–125). Boulder, CO: Westview.

Smith, K. R., Woodward, A., Campbell-Lendrum, D., Chadee, D. D., Honda, Y., Liu, Q., ... Sauerborn, R. (2014). Human health: Impacts, adaptation, and co-benefits. In C. B. Field et al. (Eds.), *Climate change 2014: Impacts, adaptation and vulnerability. Part A: Global and sectoral aspects* (pp. 709–754). New York: Cambridge University Press.

Steg, L. (2005). Car use: Lust and must. Instrumental, symbolic and affective motives for car use. *Transportation Research Part A: Policy and Practice*, 39(2), 147–162.

Steinke, J., Lapinski, M. K., Crocker, N., Zietsman-Thomas, A., Williams, Y., Evergreen, S. H., & Kuchibhotla, S. (2007). Assessing media influences on middle school-aged children's perceptions of women in science using the Draw-A-Scientist Test (DAST). *Science Communication*, 29(1), 35–64.

Stern, N. (2006). What is the economics of climate change? *World Economics*, 7(2), 1–10.

Sturgis, P., & Allum, N. (2004). Science in society: Re-evaluating the deficit model of public attitudes. *Public Understanding of Science*, 13(1), 55–74.

Syme, G. J., Macpherson, D. K., & Seligman, C. (1991). Factors motivating community participation in regional water-allocation planning: A test of an expectancy-value model. *Environment and Planning A*, 23(12), 1779–1795.

Taber, C. S., & Lodge, M. (2006). Motivated skepticism in the evaluation of political beliefs. *American Journal of Political Science*, 50(3), 755–769.

Tierney, J. (2010, February 8). People share news online that inspires awe, researchers find. The New York Times. Retrieved from https://www.nytimes.com/2010/02/09/science/09tier.html

Tracy, K., & Dimock, A. (2004). Meetings: Discursive sites for building and fragmenting community. *Annals of the International Communication Association*, 28(1), 127–165.

Trench, B. (2008). Towards an analytical framework of science communication models. In D. Cheng, M. Claessens, T. Gascoigne, J. Metcalfe, B. Schiele, & S. Shi (Eds.), *Communicating science in social contexts*pp. 119–135. Dordrecht: Springer.

UCAR Center for Science Education. (n.d.). The greenhouse effect. Retrieved from https://scied.ucar.edu/longcontent/greenhouse-effect

Van den Bossche, P., Gijselaers, W. H., Segers, M., & Kirschner, P. A. (2006). Social and cognitive factors driving teamwork in collaborative learning environments: Team learning beliefs and behaviors. *Small Group Research*, 37(5), 490–521.

Van den Bossche, P., Gijselaers, W., Segers, M., Woltjer, G., & Kirschner, P. (2011). Team learning: Building shared mental models. *Instructional Science*, 39(3), 283–311.

Van der Linden, S., Leiserowitz, A., Rosenthal, S., & Maibach, E. (2017). Inoculating the public against misinformation about climate change. *Global Challenges*, 1(2), 1600008.

Walsh-Thomas, J. M. (2016). An evaluation of metaphors in climate change discourse. Unpublished doctoral dissertation, George Mason University.

Weber, E. U. (2006). Experience-based and description-based perceptions of long-term risk: Why global warming does not scare us (yet). *Climatic Change*, 77(1), 103–120.

West, G. (2017). *Scale: The universal laws of growth, innovation, sustainability, and the pace of life in organisms, cities, economies, and companies*. New York: Penguin.

Wilkins, L., & Patterson, P. (1990). Risky business: Covering slow-onset hazards as rapidly developing news. *Political Communication*, 7(1), 11–23.

Witte, K. (1994). Fear control and danger control: A test of the extended parallel process model (EPPM). *Communication Monographs*, 61(2), 113–134.

Wong, P. P., Losada, I. J., Gattuso, J.-P., Hinkel, J., Khattabi, A., McInnes, K. L., ... Salenger, A. (2014). Coastal systems and low-lying areas. *Climate Change*, 2104, 361–409.

Zhao, X., Maibach, E., Gandy, J., Witte, J., Cullen, H., Klinger, B. A., Rowan, K., Witte, J., & Pyle, A. (2014). Climate change education through TV weathercasts: Results of a field experiment. *Bulletin of the American Meteorological Society*, 95(1), 117–130.

Zillmann, D. (2006). Exemplification effects in the promotion of safety and health. *Journal of Communication*, 56(uppl. 1), pp. S221–S237.

Ziska, L. H., & Beggs, P. J. (2012). Anthropogenic climate change and allergen exposure: The role of plant biology. *Journal of Allergy and Clinical Immunology*, 129(1), 27–32.

17

Organizations and Participation of Environmental Publics

A Cocreational Perspective Case Study

Janey G. Trowbridge

Environmentally focused initiatives take place in an era of increased involvement of publics in the decision-making process, often required by legislation at the local, state, national, and international levels. Political activism and public distrust of government institutions are prominent contemporary features. These initiatives have witnessed increased multi-level governmental collaboration across borders and competition in ever-changing economic, political, sociocultural, climatic, and geographical environments. Rapid improvements in public access to electronic communication technologies and the need to effectively communicate complex scientific developments have also characterized these initiatives.

The US–Canadian International Joint Commission (IJC)'s high-profile International Lake Ontario-St. Lawrence River (LOSLR) Study from 2000 to 2016 was no exception. The initiative involved hundreds of government representatives, scientific experts, and members of the public from both countries. The purpose of this chapter is to explore the application of an emerging strategic communication (SC) paradigm, cocreation, to the LOSLR Study. Such an analysis can shed light on some of the limitations of cocreation on large-scale environmental public participation (EPP) initiatives, but also some of the ways that cocreation can potentially improve the ways those initiatives are executed.

In the context of environmental decisions, "public participation is when everyday people who are not representing the government or a private interest are able to know what decisions are being made about collective life, and, ideally, to have an opportunity to shape those decisions in meaningful ways" (Pezzullo & Cox, 2018, p. 286).

One implication of this definition is that communication between organizations and environmental publics is critical. Thus an EPP initiative can potentially involve SC as defined by Botan (2018): "The use of information flowing into the organization (research) to plan and carry out communication campaigns addressing the relationship between an organization and its publics. SC is research based and publics-centered rather than organization or message centered" (p. 8). Botan's (2018) definition of cocreation is also used in this chapter: "Where publics add the campaign's content to the meanings they started with and arrive at new meanings which can be different from, or even opposed to, the meanings the sender or practitioner hoped for" (p. 51). Even the importance of scientific and medical information is only really determined when publics cocreate their own meanings from it and act upon them.

As for the organization of this chapter, the first section explores various levels of public involvement in EPP initiatives, linking them to different types of goals and communication

The Handbook of Strategic Communication, First Edition. Edited by Carl H. Botan.

processes, especially the cocreation approach. This section serves as an analytical framework for the next section, which describes the various phases of the 16-year-long IJC's LOSLR Study. The third section focuses on the challenges of applying a cocreational approach to that case, while the fourth section presents recommendations for addressing these challenges. Finally the conclusion looks at broader implications of analyzing EPP initiatives using such an approach.

Overview of Environmental Public Participation and Communication Processes

This section sets forth a preliminary framework of EPP for analyzing the LOSLR Study case. Though not ideal in terms of following a progression toward a cocreational model, the International Association for Public Participation (iap2)'s 2018 Spectrum of Public Participation does combine goals for different levels of involvement and examples of communication tactics. Moving along the iap2's spectrum from left to right implies a greater degree of public impact on decision-making, that is, from inform, consult, involve, to collaborate and empower.

Low Levels of Public Involvement

The lowest level, ***inform***, refers to providing "the public with objective, balanced information to assist them in understanding the problem, alternatives, opportunities and/or solutions" (International Association for Public Participation, 2018). Examples of communication tactics in this context include one-way organization-to-publics communication tactics, such as print-based fact sheets, websites, or public informational sessions. The goal of involving publics in these cases would be strictly instrumental, such as minimal compliance with a legal requirement. Though it represents the lowest level of involvement and is not strategic, keeping publics informed is a basic building block for all other forms of involvement.

The second lowest level is ***consult***, in which organizations "obtain publics' feedback on analysis, alternatives and/or decisions" (International Association for Public Participation, 2018). Examples of communication tactics include public hearings, meetings, or surveys. This communication approach is two-way because it does promise that the organization will "keep you [the publics] informed, listen to, and acknowledge concerns and aspirations and provide feedback on how feedback influenced decisions" (International Association for Public Participation, 2018). However, the communicative relationship between the organization and the publics is asymmetrical and the public participation goals are still largely instrumental.

Higher Levels of EPP Involvement

Situated in the middle of the public involvement spectrum is ***involve***, which means "to work directly with the public throughout the process to ensure that public concerns and aspirations are consistently understood and considered" (International Association for Public Participation, 2018). Examples include periodic workshops involving organizations and representatives of publics and deliberate polling of publics, providing for real-time give and take. But these meetings are likely to be mostly presentations by leaders rather than being symmetrical. Unlike the previous two levels, this level promises to "provide feedback on how public input influenced decisions" (International Association for Public Participation, 2018); however, the organization's goals still predominate.

Collaborate, to the right of the middle of the continuum, means "to partner with the public in each aspect of the decision including the development of alternatives, and the identification of preferred action" (International Association for Public Participation, 2018). Communication tactics include the use of intensive workshops lasting years or even months, public interest advisory groups (PIAG), and consensus building. Like involve, collaborate implies two-way communication with the organization as the final decision-maker. The organization only promises to "look to you [the publics] for advice and innovation in formulating solutions and incorporate your advice and recommendations into the decision to the maximum amount possible" (International Association for Public Participation, 2018).

At the other end of the spectrum, *empower* promises "to place final decision making in the hands of the public" and for the organization to be the implementer (International Association for Public Participation, 2018). This approach implies that the organization gives agency to the publics. In contrast, in a cocreational approach the organization accepts the fact that all along publics have had the power to generate new meanings and interpretations of data collected in their interactions. Moreover, publics have the power to act on the decisions they make.

The next section describes the LOSLR case study in terms of the public involvement levels, goals, and communication tactics.

LOSLR Case Study

Begun in 2000, the LOSLR Study's original purpose was to review the management of water levels and flows at the Moses-Saunders Dam, affecting over 12 million people in New York State, Ontario Province, and Quebec Province (International Lake Ontario-St. Lawrence [LOSLR] Study Board, 2006). The St. Lawrence River-Lake Ontario Plan of Study Team (1999) stated that direct involvement of those affected by the results of the LOLSR Study's actions was critical to successful adjustments resulting from the water management review. The assumption was that participation in the study would lead to a common understanding on how to better regulate the LOSLR basin system. From a cocreational perspective it was unclear which of the parties – the managing organization (IJC), other government agencies, or multiple publics – would determine when a common understanding was reached. The entire initiative can be broken down roughly into three phases, each of which involved the publics, affected governments, and scientific experts to varying degrees and used different communication approaches and tactics.

Phase I (2000–2005)

The first phase is an example of intense involvement over time of over 200 members of publics in the US and Canada, as well as government officials and scientific experts – by far the largest engagement of publics in the IJC's history. The study's structure consisted of (1) the Study Board, which guided the study; (2) nine Technical Work Groups (TWGs) representing key interest groups; and (3) the PIAG, which served as a liaison between the Study Board and the general public (International Lake Ontario-St. Lawrence River (LOSR) Study Board, 2006).

The Study Board used a number of tools to attempt to create a common understanding of the scientific dimension of the study, including a computer-based shared vision model, information sessions, and webinars. The PIAG's public relations function published a quarterly newsletter and organized town council meetings. Nevertheless, at the end of the 5-year period of funding the Study Board presented a set of options instead of an agreed-upon plan (International Lake Ontario-St. Lawrence River Study Board, 2006), while some PIAG members issued a minority opinion (Minority Report of the Lake Ontario-St. Lawrence River Study to the International Joint Commission, 2007), indicating differences in meanings and interpretations of how to address the management of LOSLR basin water levels and flows. Thus, it could be considered an example of collaboration, but was not an example of empowerment or cocreation because of constraints on the Study Board's power and persistent tensions between multiple publics, both of which will be discussed in the Challenges section.

Phase II (2006–2008)

The IJC decided to take matters into its own hands and develop a compromise plan internally on the foundation of the three interest-based options presented by the LOSLR Study Board. Draft plans were coordinated on a quarterly basis with governments and interest groups and presented for public comment through information and question-and-answer sessions. But a number of members of the public, government representatives, and scientific experts perceived that the IJC had developed the new 2007 plan behind closed doors. The level of involvement could be characterized as consult (a low level), and the communication approach as two-way asymmetrical. The IJC was pressured to withdraw that plan in 2008.

Phase III (2007–2016)

In light of the failure of the 2007 plan, the IJC decided to engage senior governmental officials from the affected jurisdictions (Canada, US, New York, Ontario, and Quebec) in the third phase. The commission formed an informal working group with the goal of creating yet another plan. It also developed and implemented a sophisticated plan for communicating with the affected publics, including hiring a public relations firm, as well as conducting web-based and face-to-face information and comment sessions in multiple locations.

However, final decision-making was out of the hands of the IJC and its publics. New York State also effectively relinquished their decision-making power by not taking a position on the 2014 plan. In compliance with a 1999 letter to the US secretary of state and the Canadian foreign minister, the IJC sent the draft plan to the federal governments for concurrence. First, Canada accepted the 2014 plan. Subsequently, in an example of inter-agency negotiation of meaning, a US Government Executive Branch agency took the lead and agreed to an increase in water levels in the proposed regulation plan. The agency decided that while the increase was not absolutely critical to its own interests, it was important to another government agency.

Thus, after more than a decade of sometimes contentious cross-border collaboration between publics, experts, and multiple government organizations, the IJC enacted the 2014 plan in December 2016, during the waning days of the Obama administration. The new plan attempted to balance the interests of all key publics affected by the study's results, while formally incorporating the interests of the environment and recreational boating (see International Joint Commission, n.d.a). The communication process during this final phase could be considered as involvement of the publics and collaboration between senior representatives and the IJC with a two-way symmetrical form of communication predominating, and finally collaboration between the two federal agencies.

Nevertheless, some publics in New York State continued to oppose the IJC plan (McKinley, 2016). Following the approval of the plan in 2016, a dry summer delayed the IJC's release of water levels at the Moses-Saunders Dam. In spring 2017, an unusually warm winter resulted in severe flooding of parts of southern Lake Ontario (Rojas, 2017). Some residents and their local and state representatives, including the New York State governor, called for the IJC to rescind the 2014 plan (Figura, 2017). However, some of the leaders who had strongly opposed the 2014 plan agreed that the IJC had acted appropriately in light of the 100-year flood, while other officials and residents blamed the IJC (Rojas, 2017) – effectively putting a damper on efforts to cocreate new meaning.

The first two sections of this chapter provided context by discussing levels of public involvement in EPP initiatives, their relationship to various communication processes, and illustrating these processes in the LOSR Study case. As shown, a truly cocreational approach was rarely put into practice. The next section analyzes the internal communication challenges of implementing that approach in EPP initiatives such as LOSLR. External challenges such as droughts, floods, and political and economic changes – largely beyond the control of the organizations and their publics – will not be addressed in any detail in this chapter.

Challenges of Using a Cocreational Approach

In a cocreational approach the relationship of central importance is that of the shared creation of meaning between groups and organizations. Obstacles to using this approach were revealed in several different types of relationships, as shown in the interviews conducted in 2011 for this author's dissertation and in this author's unpublished analysis of the 2014 plan's public comments (see International Joint Commission, n.d.a). These included: (1) communicative relationships between the IJC and its publics before and during the study; (2) communicative relationships between diverse publics before and during the study; (3) communicative relationships between the IJC and the LOSLR Study Board; and (4) communicative relationships between LOSLR Study scientific experts and publics.

Communicative Relationships Between IJC and Publics

This subsection explores relationships between the IJC and its publics prior to the LOSLR Study and during the study, focusing on the politicization and differential access to communication resources.

Relationships Prior to the Study

According to Botan (2018), "the primary determinant of what a public will think and do after a campaign is what they thought and did before the campaign" (p. 49). The LOSLR Study was no exception. From the IJC's perspective some publics, especially those historically affected by flooding and drought, lacked understanding of the agency's limited capabilities. Operations at the Moses-Saunders Dam can only affect water levels and flows to a small extent compared to Mother Nature's effects. One could also argue that the IJC had not succeeded in effectively communicating those limitations to its publics, but it is difficult for an international government agency to explain the way things work when people's lives are directly affected at the local level.

Politicization of the Study

In addition, during the LOSLR Study the IJC saw itself as promoting the broader interests of the LOSLR basin, whereas some interest groups, such as coastal property and business owners and local and state governments, voiced shorter-term economic and political concerns. In other words, the IJC and these groups had two separate meanings in mind about the role of the IJC in relation to the control of water levels, as opposed to one cocreated meaning. Some publics, moreover, viewed the IJC with distrust because it was an international government agency and not a locally based organization.

The IJC tried to keep the LOSLR Study as objective and scientifically based as possible and thus free from the politicization that affects so many EPP initiatives. In the first two phases, the IJC presumably had decision-making power and the power of access to scientific and legal expertise to come up with a new regulation plan for the LOSLR basin. However, it did not adequately anticipate and prepare for the intensity of certain publics' opposition to its efforts and the politicization of the project at various government levels, especially in New York State. In the US, the power shifted from the IJC to New York State because of the political sensitivity of the issue and ultimately to the US and Canadian federal governments.

Diverse Communication Resources

At least in the first two phases of the study, the IJC appeared to have less effective SC resources than did some of its publics. As an international organization, the IJC is at a disadvantage because it has no grassroots constituencies. In response to the 2007 plan, various activist interest groups had mounted sophisticated campaigns, using the media and their ties to local communities to oppose other interest groups and the IJC.

On the positive side, the IJC's US and Canadian public information officers did have an important seat at the IJC senior management table, as well as more flexibility in developing and implementing SC campaigns than their counterparts in national government bureaucracies. Furthermore, in the third phase the IJC learned lessons from the first two phases and came much closer to cocreating new meanings with its publics through more effective communicative exchange of scientific meaning in face-to-face meetings and in the development of its website.

Communicative Relationships Among Diverse Publics

Relationships among diverse publics also represented an obstacle to using a cocreational approach in the LOSLR Study. Competing interests were evident, shaped by differing priorities and values between, for example, environmentalists (who traditionally supported greater water level fluctuations) and coastal property owners (who advocated less fluctuation to protect their land). Interest groups were represented on the Study Board, the PIAG, or the TWGs, and efforts were made to arrive at a common understanding in Phase 1 (from 2000 to 2005) through electronic, print-based, and face-to-face communication. Some IJC staff and PIAG members noted that progress was achieved during this period. However, in some cases positive developments were short-lived. When some interest group representatives communicated about the Study Board's work to their constituencies, those representatives inevitably reverted to their own parochial agendas.

In addition, environmental and riparian (coastal residents) activist groups separately exerted political pressure through various communication mechanisms on New York State and the IJC, so that the study's work was effectively stalled at various points in its 16-year duration. As noted, even though the 2014 plan was approved, opponents continue to communicate their opposition in the local, regional, and statewide media.

Communicative Relationships Between the IJC and the LOSLR Study Board

Three aspects of the IJC's communicative relationship with the LOSLR Study Board also represented obstacles to using a cocreational approach. They included confusing directives, the imperceptible shift in study goals, and finding the right participants for the Study Board, PIAG, and TWGs.

Confusing Directives

The LOSLR Study Board comprised scientific experts and representatives of the IJC's publics, supposed to be more or less independent of the IJC. Nevertheless, in the eyes of some Study

Board members, the IJC issued confusing directives from time to time and did not give clear guidance about compliance of the Study Board's work with the 1909 Boundary Waters Treaty creating the IJC. This situation made it difficult for the board members to move ahead with the task of cocreating meaning.

As noted previously, at the end of the 5-year study period, the Study Board issued three options instead of a single plan for managing LOSLR water levels. The IJC felt that it needed to step in and manage the process. Thus, in Phase II the IJC effectively closed out the option of a collaborative or cocreational approach; the result was the failed 2007 plan.

Shift in Study Goals

Another obstacle to using a cocreational approach was lack of communication about the almost imperceptible shift in the LOSLR Study's goals. Originally in 2000 the Study Board was directed to "review operations at Moses-Saunders Dam *taking into account the impact of regulation on affected interests*" (International Lake Ontario-St. Lawrence River Study Board, 2006, p. i) (italics added by the author). The Study Board was also directed to "develop an improved understanding of the system among all concerned and provide all relevant technical and other information needed for review" (International Lake Ontario-St. Lawrence River Study Board, 2006, p. i). As noted previously, this goal could potentially have been cocreational depending on who (the managing organization or the publics or the experts) determined when that understanding of the system was reached.

Over time, the Study Board's goal changed imperceptibly from the original goal in the 2000 directive to the following goal in the Study Board's 2006 Final Report: "To come up with a *plan* that would best serve the range of affected interests in the LOLSR basis and which would be *widely accepted by all interests*, and address climatic conditions" (p. 7) (italics added by the author). The original goal did not call for a plan nor did it expect the study to be widely accepted by all interests – only that these interests would be taken into account. This shift in the study's goals was never consciously acknowledged between 1999 and 2007, and thus was never clearly conveyed. This miscommunication among the IJC, the Study Board, and other representatives of publics engaged in the study resulted in some publics' unrealistic expectations of what the study could achieve.

The study's original goal was to be reached within five years and within a $20 million budget. Some study participants felt that there was not enough time or money to achieve the original goal of reviewing and coming to an improved understanding of the LOSLR system operations, and then eventually reaching the board's more ambitious goal of trying to satisfy all parties to the EPP initiative. However, according to several IJC staff and PIAG members, some participants were unlikely to ever give up their own interests in favor of integrating a common understanding, interpretation, and goal – in other words, being disposed to engage in a cocreational approach.

Finding the Right Participants

A related issue was finding the right people to play key roles on the Study Board and the PIAG. In Phase I the IJC and the Study Board selected interest group representatives to serve as liaisons between the general public and the study based primarily on their visibility within various interest groups. Some of the opinion leaders had risen to leadership positions because of a history of promoting their own agendas; it was unlikely that they would be good candidates for adopting a broader perspective and actively engaging in cocreating new meanings. Furthermore, the study struggled to engage the participation of a broad range of publics who would be at least indirectly affected by the study's results.

Communicative Relationships Between Scientists and Publics

Another challenge to a cocreational approach was the complexity and uncertainty of water management science and the fact that some publics were more directly affected by changing water levels than others in the LOSLR basin. As noted, the LOSLR Study Board attempted to facilitate dialogue between volunteer PIAG members and scientific experts using a variety of cutting-edge technologies and face-to-face communication. At the same time, some experts admitted their difficulties in communicating scientific information in a way that publics could integrate with their own experiences. In particular, one Study Board scientific expert noted the difficulty of explaining to publics the critical role of uncertainty in science.

The Study Board experts also had to contend with a general trend toward public distrust of scientific expertise (cf. Dietz & Stern, 2008). Moreover, in comparison to some of the PIAG and other community opinion leaders, the IJC staff and scientific experts were often viewed in a negative light as representatives of an external governmental organization (the IJC). They had to respond to some community opinion leaders' at times inaccurate sound bites, with their own sound bites encapsulating very complex technical information.

A cocreational approach was also made difficult because measurements of environmental impacts in the LOSLR basin were communicated in ratios, while measurements of economic impacts on coastal residents and business owners were communicated using dollar values. According to one scientific expert, these values were of concern to varying degrees to different publics, but it was like comparing apples to oranges. Unfortunately, at that time, these two different ways of measuring key impacts – economic and environmental – were the only ones available.

This section explored four interrelated communicative relationships in the LOSLR Study case as barriers to using a cocreational approach. The next section sets forth recommendations for addressing some of those challenges.

Recommendations for Using a Cocreational Approach

EPP initiatives seeking to create shared meaning among multiple government organizations and multiple affected interest groups, institutions, and individuals should take into account factors prior to, continually during a strategic initiative, and following the initiative. These recommendations include many actions that the IJC has taken, as well as lessons learned for improvement.

Prior to Undertaking an EPP Strategic Initiative

The successful use of a cocreational approach in an EPP project requires that the managing organization be willing to work toward shared outcomes by adapting its policies and practices to the needs and values of its diverse publics. It also involves the implementation of at least three practices prior to undertaking the initiative. First, a thorough unbiased analysis of the history of communicative relationships between the managing organization and key publics and other interested organizations and their members should be conducted prior to undertaking an EPP initiative (and of course during the effort). It should also take into account the power dynamics, motivations, financial and human resources, and SC capabilities of all key participating groups. This analysis should take place in addition to examining whether the benefits of the proposed project, such as environmental and economic, outweigh the costs of undertaking the project or the costs of not doing anything at all. As Dietz and Stern (2008) pointed out, these challenges may not be easy to capture in an initial diagnostic assessment.

"It is crucial, nevertheless, to take a careful and nonjudgmental look at whether the process offers sufficient incentives for good-faith participation by all interest groups" (p. 212).

Second, if the initiative is undertaken and a cocreational approach is used, the managing organization should systematically build relationships with publics, government organizations, the media, especially with those with whom it has a history of mismanaged communication relationships that have established negative expectations. Examples include educational programs and face-to-face meetings, which were conducted during the LOSLR Study, but perhaps they should have taken place earlier in the process.

Third, if a cocreational approach is used, the managing organization should consider modifying the goals of an EPP undertaking so that they are achievable. The modified LOSLR Study goals of deciding on a new plan for water levels and flows in the LOSLR basin may have been too ambitious and exclusively instrumental for a cocreational model to succeed within the initially anticipated timeframe and budget. Perhaps the original goal of reviewing the LOSLR basin system through the cocreation of new and shared meanings between the IJC, affected government agencies, scientists, and publics, through the development of improved relations could have been more easily achieved.

During the EPP Strategic Initiative

This case demonstrates the challenges of simultaneously engaging affected publics, agency staff, technical experts, and elected government representatives across borders in cocreating meaning. First, the managing organization should involve senior leadership of affected organizations from the beginning of an EPP initiative. As noted, the IJC created the working group in Phase III, but the study process could possibly have moved along more rapidly with the effective management of communication processes to secure the support of senior government officials in the earliest phase.

Second, managing organizations should take advantage of information technologies to facilitate faster and wider exchanges of information. New technologies have enabled more democratic and inclusive participation and they do increase the opportunities for shared creation of meaning – by putting people in touch – and for more give-and-take (Botan & Hazleton, 2006). In Phase III, the IJC did attempt to convene publics simultaneously from different regions of the LOSLR basin and encourage participants to understand each other and take a broader perspective through conducting webinars, which were translated into English and French. The IJC also worked with a professional public relations firm to effectively communicate technical information in a publics-centered way, about the urgency of acting in a concerted way to shape environmental and economic improvements affecting them, and to serve mutual values and interests (see International Joint Commission, n.d.b).

Third, managing organizations – or publics, if appropriate – should select representatives for a public interest advisory board based not only on their technical expertise and visibility within the community, but also on their ability to promote the broad-based interests of an issue. They should be able to energetically pursue the cocreation of new meanings in their relationships with scientific experts and organizational representatives. Based on these meanings, the representatives should continue the process of cocreating new meanings with their own publics. Similarly, scientific experts should be selected based not only on their technical expertise but also on their ability to communicate complex scientific information and cocreate meaning with the publics' representatives.

Fourth, as noted, the managing organization should be willing to work toward shared outcomes by adapting its policies and practices to the needs and values of its diverse publics. For example, in collaboration with its publics, the IJC attempted to realize a balanced approach to water levels and flow management with the 2014 plan. It sought to create more natural water levels in the lake and river, favored by environmental interests, while continuing to provide the basin community – such as coastal property owners – with substantial but changed benefits in relation to the current plan (see International Joint Commission, n.d.b).

Finally, if feasible financially, legally, and politically, a cocreational approach may have to be supplemented with, for example, financial or other incentives or compensation for losses, in order for participants to engage in creative dialogue and cocreate new meaning. In the case of the 2014 plan, some elected representatives in the US federal, state, and local governments, as well as some non-elected public opinion leaders, pressed the IJC hard for compensation for losses due to flooding and erosion, even though the damages could not be attributed directly to the IJC's actions or proposals. But the IJC and the US federal and New York State governments were either unable or unwilling to provide compensation. As noted in the previous section, the availability of incentives for good faith participation should be assessed prior to undertaking an EPP initiative.

The process of cocreating meaning does not end with the conclusion of an agreement. As illustrated in the LOSLR Study case, not only is there substantial technical follow-up in implementing the 2014 plan, but there has also been political fallout from the agreement in light of unforeseen weather conditions. The latter has required ongoing cultivation of relationships with publics, government officials, and the media, and the continuous cocreation of new meanings.

Conclusion

Using a cocreational perspective as an analytical framework exposes the challenges and opportunities of international government-run projects involving publics. Development of new meanings, understandings, interpretation, and integration of complex scientific issues with competing political and economic interests may exhaust human, financial, and material resources. Moreover, there may not be sufficient time to achieve an initiative's goals without doing harm (in the LOSLR Study case, potential damage to the environment and to economic interests, and hence to the short- and long-term interests of people living in the watershed).

Thus, the managing organization or organizations invested with final decision-making authority need to have patience and persistence in allowing for the cocreation of meaning between the organizations, publics, technical experts, and government officials. At the same time, as illustrated in the IJC case, decision-making entities should be flexible and ready to act, taking advantage of collaborative involvement (if not cocreation of meaning) between most parties to a controversy. The managing organizations should also be prepared to cultivate relationships before, during, and after the conclusion of an initiative, and to manage the consequences of relationships with publics who are uncommitted to – or who want to back out of – an EPP agreement.

To paraphrase Taylor and Botan (2006), the application of a cocreational perspective to an EPP strategic initiative has the potential to contribute to our understanding of more than just specialized practices in this domain, and in this case of two democratic, affluent nations which share the longest peaceful border in the world. It also has the potential to help us understand the complexities of interpersonal, organizational, national, and international relationships that influence our daily lives.

References

Botan, C. H. (2018). *Strategic communication theory and practice: The cocreational model.* Hoboken, NJ: Wiley Blackwell.

Botan, C. H., & Hazelton, V. (2006). *Public relations theory II.* Mahwah, NJ: Lawrence Erlbaum.

Dietz, T., & Stern, P. (Eds.). (2008). *Public participation in environmental assessment and decision-making.* Washington, D.C.: The National Academies Press.

Figura, D. (2017 June 13). Cuomo visits 2 flood-damaged Lake Ontario communities; rails again at Plan 2014. Retrieved from upstatenewyork.com/weather/2017/06_cuomo_visits_lake_ontario_communities_rails_again_at_plan_2014

International Association for Public Participation. (2018). 3 pillars of public participation. Retrieved from http://iap2.org/page/pillars

International Joint Commission. n.d.a Lake Ontario-St. Lawrence River Plan 2014. Retrieved from https://ijc.org/sites/default/files/IJC_LOSR_EN_Web.pdf

International Joint Commission. n.d.b Lake Ontario St. Lawrence River: A new path forward. Retrieved from https://loslr.ijc.org/en/solution/balanced_approach.php

International Lake Ontario-St. Lawrence River Study Board. (2006). *Options for managing Lake Ontario and St. Lawrence River water levels and flows: Final report* Buffalo, NY: International Joint Commission. Retrieved from https://losl.org/PDF/report-main-e.pdf

McKinley, J. (2016, December 10). Fiercely debated water level plan is adopted for Lake Ontario. *The New York Times* (p. A21).

Minority Report of the Lake Ontario-St. Lawrence River Study to the International Joint Commission. (2007, March). Retrieved from https://unitedshorelineontario.ca/wp-content/uploads/2018/04/Minority-Report-March-2007.pdf

Pezzullo, P. C., & Cox, R. (2018). *Environmental communication and the public sphere* (5th edn). Los Angeles, CA: Sage.

Rojas, R. (2017, June 19). While officials point fingers, a lake spills into backyards. The New York Times (p. A15).

St. Lawrence River-Lake Ontario Plan of Study Team (1999). Plan of study for criteria review in the orders of approval for regulation of Lake Ontario-St. Lawrence River levels and flows. Retrieved from https://legacyfiles.ijc.org/tinymce/uploaded/LOSLR/LOSL-POS-Sept-99.pdf

Taylor, M., & Botan, C. (2006). Global public relations: Application of a cocreational approach. In M. DiStaso (Ed.), *9th International Public Relations Research Conference: Changing Roles and Functions in Public Relations Conference* (pp. 484–491). Miami, FL: University of Miami and Institute of Public Relations.

18

Strategic Communication in Religious and Belief Communities

Lessons from Holocaust Re-education

Denise Edwards-Neff

Azusa Pacific University

Nongovernmental and nonprofit organizations are the most rapidly growing types of organizations in the world (Hall, 2005), and include many types of organizations, such as religious and belief communities. Although it is difficult to approximate data on nongovernmental organizations (NGOs) worldwide due to lack of reliable data, the frequency with which new organizations develop, and varying incorporation statuses by country, it is estimated that there are more than 10 million NGOs throughout the world, according to nonprofitaction.org (Ferguson, 2018). In the US, religious and belief communities have had the largest proportional increase in both revenue and expenses in recent years, growing from $12.3 billion in revenue in 2005 to $19.6 billion in 2015 after adjusting for inflation, a change of 59.3% (McKeever, 2018).

An NGO (also known as a non-business entity) is an organization with the purpose of something other than making a profit; instead, it operates to serve a public or group interest and often is dedicated to furthering a particular social cause or advocating for a particular point of view. Variously referred to as nonprofit, voluntary, NGOs, and collectively as the third sector, they encompass a broad array of organizations including foundations, labor unions, professional associations, sports and recreation clubs, art and cultural associations, private schools, research institutes, hospitals, charities, humanitarian assistance and relief organizations, advocacy groups, foundations, charitable trusts, religious congregations, and faith-based organizations (Tice, Salamon, & List, 2001). Some provide traditional charitable, educational, and religious services; indeed, some charitable, educational, and religious organizations (such as the Roman Catholic Church) are thousands of years old (Hall, 2005). They vary enormously in scope and scale, ranging from informal grassroots organizations with no assets and no employees through to multibillion-dollar foundations, universities, religious bodies, and health care centers complete with thousands of employees or members.

The Johns Hopkins Comparative Nonprofit Sector Project, with a team of social scientists from over 35 countries, developed a structural-operational definition of the nonprofit sector that encompasses all entities, including religious and belief communities, that are:

1. organizations (i.e. institutionalized to some extent);
2. private (i.e. institutionally separate from government);
3. non-profit-distributing (i.e. not returning profits generated to their owners or directors);

The Handbook of Strategic Communication, First Edition. Edited by Carl H. Botan.

4. self-governing (i.e. able to control their own activities); and
5. voluntary (i.e. non-compulsory and involving some meaningful degree of voluntary participation) (Tice, Salamon, & List, 2001).

Tracing the history of NGOs, and religious and belief communities in particular, illumines the various ideas and types of institutions that make up today's nonprofit domain, how they have evolved over time, and how social causes and movements have relied on strategic communication (SC) to serve the public interest, advocate for causes, and maintain the viability of these NGOs.

This chapter focuses specifically on religious and belief communities. There are three types of faith-based nonprofit organizations: (1) congregations; (2) international and national networks, which include religions and their denominations, their social service arms (e.g. Catholic Charities, Lutheran Social Services), and networks of related organizations (e.g. YMCA, YWCA); and (3) freestanding religious organizations, which are incorporated separately from congregations and national networks (The Urban Institute, 2001). Some religious and belief communities are "bounded," that is, members of the group share "fixed geographic and/or ideological boundaries that limit their engagement with outsiders" (Golan & Campbell, 2015, p. 468). Religious-Zionist and ultra-Orthodox communities in Israel, and Amish communities in the US, are examples of rigidly bounded religious and belief communities.

In the next sections, I will: (1) describe the characteristics and functions of religious and belief communities, and of NGOs more broadly; (2) discuss theoretical frameworks and techniques in activism, framing, and digital media research relevant to religious and belief communities; and (3) apply these frameworks and techniques through a discussion of the Lithuanian Jewish Community (LJC)'s SC directed at ensuring that the Holocaust is accurately remembered and commemorated in Lithuania and internationally.

Characteristics of Religious and Belief Communities, and NGOs

Religious and belief communities exist, as do other nonprofit and for-profit organizations, through the process of communication. SC can be considered broadly to include all "strategic uses of communication within and by organizations" (Botan, 2018, p. 6); it may also be defined more narrowly as research-based and "planned campaigns that grow out of first understanding what publics think and want" (p. 6). Another approach to SC focuses on how the organization presents and promotes itself through the intentional activities of its leaders, employees, and communication practitioners (Hallahan et al., 2007).

Religious and belief communities, like other nonprofit organizations, use SC for a variety of purposes (e.g. to serve their publics, advocate for causes, manage relationships with their publics, maintain their viability, and crisis and reputation management). All religious and belief communities rely on their supporters' participation and funding support, and employ SC in these efforts. These types of communicative functions of NGOs are consistent with the description of SC offered by Hallahan et al. (2007) as the purposeful use of communication by organizations, causes, and social movements to achieve their goals, specifically in advocacy, development, and training in the public debate about issues.

Nonprofit organizations perform major functions in national and community life, and rely on SC to perform these functions identified by Salamon (2012), applied below specifically to religious and belief communities.

1. *Service function*. Religious and belief communities are service providers, delivering wellbeing programs, religious education, self-help services, entertainment and religious ceremonies, development and support of local community organizations. For example, local congregations and national denominations serve their members and attendees by holding a wide variety of events throughout the week, month, and year.
2. *Advocacy function*. Religious and belief communities contribute to social life by identifying unaddressed problems and bringing them to public attention, by speaking out about human rights and giving voice to a wide assortment of social, political, environmental, ethnic, and community interests and concerns. Faith-based issues organizations advocate for public policy legislation and election outcomes that are consistent with their members' beliefs, and apply pressure to government, corporate, and community organizations when their actions are in conflict with their beliefs. Many social movements are operated in and through religious and belief communities, such as anti-slavery, women's rights, civil rights, temperance, environmental, anti-war, gay rights, and conservative movements, across a wide spectrum of belief positions.
3. *Expressive function*. Artistic, religious, cultural, ethnic, social, and recreational issues and concerns find expression through religious and belief communities, which enrich human existence and contribute to a vibrant social and cultural life. For example, the Mormon Tabernacle and Brooklyn Tabernacle choirs are considered to be of the highest musical quality.
4. *Community-building function*. Religious and belief communities are also important in building social capital, or bonds of trust and reciprocity that allow societies to function. By establishing connections among individuals, involvement in associations teaches norms of cooperation that carry over into political and economic life. For example, local places of worship and their members are often the greatest contributors to community service organizations – such as Habitat for Humanity – which serve under-represented or disadvantaged populations.
5. *Value guardian function*. Religious and belief communities embody, and help to nurture and sustain, values that are crucial to the global, national, regional, state, and other communities to which members belong, and the values to which they subscribe. Faith-based organizations reinforce the notion that people can take initiatives not simply to promote their own wellbeing, but also to advance the wellbeing of others.

In addition to these functions of nonprofits in national and community life, Golan, Arceneaux, and Soule (2019) explore the function of public diplomacy, or governments', corporations', and NGOs' "attempts to build and maintain positive relationships with foreign citizens for the purpose of securing support for foreign policy objectives" (p. 97). They argue that global religious organizations and their leaders, such as the Catholic Church and Pope Francis, also perform important roles as transnational actors in international engagement between nations and foreign publics – what they have termed *religious diplomacy*. Diplomatic actors such as the Pope attempt to build relationships with foreign audiences through messages intended to build trust between the leader and the recipient(s) for strategic purposes – in the case of the Catholic Church, to rebuild its trust with a global audience (see also Kampf, 2016).

As Hallahan et al. (2007) note, the emphasis in SC is on the purposive nature of communication, and how the organization functions as a social actor to advance its mission. Relevant research in NGOs, specifically religious and belief communities, addresses a broad range of theoretical frameworks and models, including activism, agenda setting, framing, organization–public relationship, and dialogue that are foundational in the study of religious and belief communities and to the example of the LJC, which will be discussed later in the chapter.

Theoretical Frameworks and Techniques in Religious and Belief Communities' Strategic Communication

Religious and Belief Communities

Religious and belief communities, like other nonprofits or NGOs, use SC for a variety of purposes. This section discusses some of the theoretical frameworks and techniques religious and belief communities rely on to educate and engage constituents to effect change in public perception and public policy, specifically activism, framing, and social and digital media.

Activism

One of the most studied areas of SC in NGOs is activism, which can be found in political science (e.g. interest and interest groups), communication (e.g. social movement), media (e.g. framing), and public relations (e.g. issues management) theory and research. Activism is a process by which an organized group of people (as are religious and belief communities, by definition) exert pressure on organizations or other institutions (such as government bodies) to change policies, practices, or conditions that they find problematic. This section discusses the two goals of activist organizations, and strategies and techniques that they may use in working to achieve their goals.

MAINTAIN THE ORGANIZATION

One goal of activism is to maintain the organization established to pursue the activists' purpose(s), or, more broadly, to sustain the movement. The principal purpose here is to secure ongoing support for the goals of the religious and belief community in the form of followers, volunteers, and monetary donations and goods. These goals reflect the dual publics for which the organization must account. On the one hand, there are those organizations, legislators, regulators, or other publics that might get involved in advocacy and join with the religious organization in helping it achieve its goals and resolve issues. On the other hand, there are organizations (e.g. corporations and government) which religious and belief communities are pressuring for change and/or opposing. The point is that religious and belief communities have their own publics with varying levels of awareness and involvement in the community's activities. These organizations must maintain membership, thrive in what might be described as a competitive marketplace of ideas and issues, and adjust to changes in their environments. The concepts of issues, identity, and legitimacy are each important to understanding the maintenance function (Smith & Ferguson, 2018). Activist organizations that can frame an issue and promote it through the lifecycle of an issue often attract new members and other resources. Those members see the organization as a vehicle through which they can effect change (Smith, 1997). Indeed, one component of an organization's attempts to establish its ethos is to cite examples of its competency or success, often promoted as victories in issue advocacy (Hoffman & Ford, 2010). However, as an issue moves toward dormancy, many organizations struggle to remain viable. An organization that appears to be a legitimate advocate, and is addressing a popular or current issue with a plan that seems to be effective, has an easier time attracting donations (Smith & Ferguson, 2018). One communication strategy to maintain the vitality of an organization is to link its primary issue to another issue that is rising in popularity, an evolution that also influences the activist organization's identity. For example, the Christian Coalition (CC) broadened its issue base in advance of the 1994 congressional mid-term elections to include health care and the economy, in hopes of attracting new supporters; this issues expansion beyond moral issues such as abortion and marriage was problematic to some CC members, yet did promote alliance with other faith groups (Ferguson, 1999).

While SC directed at this second activist goal has been accomplished primarily through internal publications aimed toward members, followers, or interested recruits, the success of external strategies also impacts the ability of an organization to maintain itself. Studies have indicated that internal documents establish and reflect activist organizations' (read religious and belief communities') values, and serve as manifestos for action. In today's digital and social media environment, many more communication channels are available to NGOs as they work to achieve their goals.

RECTIFY CONDITIONS

According to Smith and Ferguson (2001), the primary goal of activist organizations is to rectify conditions in three ways: (1) to either elicit or resist change on the part of a target organization or, more broadly, an industry or field; (2) to seek public policy or regulatory changes that would, in turn, effect change in institutional or public behavior; or, most broadly, (3) to change social norms. As issues advocates, they must draw attention to the problem, position themselves as legitimate advocates, and successfully argue for their recommended resolutions to the problem. In pursuing the first goal of solving problematic conditions, activist organizations generally attempt to either confront organizations (e.g. corporations) directly or seek regulation from the government or administrative agencies.

Activist organizations employ a wide variety of strategies and techniques to gain attention and recruit and mobilize supporters to pressure governments and organizations for change. A number of studies have examined how activists use public relations and SC to achieve their goals (Smith & Ferguson, 2010). These studies have primarily looked at strategies, or the general approach to communicating to achieve a goal, and tactics, or the specific tools used in public relations, such as press releases, newsletters, and digital (especially websites) and social media (Ferguson & Smith, 2012; Knight & Greenberg, 2002; Smith & Ferguson, 2013; Taylor, Kent, & White, 2001; Yang & Taylor, 2010; Zoch et al., 2008). Several of the studies in this area seek to refine the typologies of techniques used by activists and by institutions and government in responding to activism. Previous studies grouped activist techniques by their function, such as informational activities (meant to educate publics about issues), or legalistic activities, which seek solutions to issues through the courts or legislative/regulatory venues (Jackson, 1982). Jackson identified five general categories of tactics:

1. informational activities, including interviews and other media relations techniques;
2. symbolic activities, including boycotts;
3. organizing activities, such as distributing leaflets, networking, and holding meetings;
4. legalistic activities, such as petitions, lawsuits, filing legislation, testimony at hearings, or prodding regulatory and administrative agencies; and
5. civil disobedience, such as sit-ins, blocking traffic, or trespassing. (p. 215)

Activist organizations rely on the media as they work to stimulate the agenda-setting process by formulating issues, seek the legitimation of issues, and attempt to capture the attention of the media and key public opinion leaders (Crable & Vibbert, 1985; Ferguson, 1999). Because organizations and government must pay increased attention to these pressure groups and their ability to influence public opinion, proactive media relations and effective SC through social and digital media become increasingly vital aspects of activists' public relations strategy (Ferguson, 1999; Grunig, 1989; Sriramesh, 1992).

Framing

Due to NGOs' dependency on media coverage in their SC efforts to gain issues and financial support, framing theory has been a prominent area of study in activism. Framing is considered to be a second level of agenda-setting theory (McCombs & Shaw, 1972). Agenda-setting theory has often been explained simply as the notion that the news media may not tell people *what* to think, but what to think *about*; that is, the more media coverage an individual or issue receives, the more salient it will be in the minds of news consumers (McCombs, 2004). The first level simply examines the perceived importance (or salience) of an issue in relation to its coverage in the media. The second level (McCombs et al., 1997) – framing – takes the issues highlighted in the first level and focuses on specific attributes or dimensions of the issue being examined. The process through which the news media choose particular elements of a story or issue to emphasize is at the center of framing research, which probes the way media emphasize elements of an issue to promote specific problem definitions, causal attributions, moral evaluations, or treatment recommendations (Bowe, Fahmy, & Wanta, 2013; Entman, 1993).

An understanding of framing can provide insight into how and why religious and belief communities, and all NGOs, strategically create their messages for news media and communication outlets (including the organization's website) for other publics, and can reveal the ways in which news media and other sharers of their messages reshape these messages and impact public perceptions of the activist organization. Bowe, Fahmy, and Wanta (2013) examined the substantive (cognitive) and affective (evaluative) attributes of the religion of Islam in the coverage of 18 US newspapers and compared those attributes with the results of a Gallup Center for Muslim Studies poll to determine whether a relationship exists between the coverage of Islam and public perception, as framing suggests. They found that the attributes related to Islam were overwhelmingly covered in negative terms. However, the media coverage appeared to have little influence on public opinion and attitudes, suggesting that the relationship between media framing and effects is "complicated" and may be "mediated by other perceptual phenomena" (p. 639).

FRAMES OF RELIGIOUS AND BELIEF COMMUNITIES

Through the dissemination of purposively (strategically) designed messages, or packages made up of individual frames (Gamson & Modigliani, 1989), religious and belief communities and their leaders seek to present themselves in a desirable context, build relationships with audiences, and repair damage to their reputations (Golan, Arceneaux, & Soule, 2019). These frames are conceived and employed strategically. For example, after the 2012 American presidential election, the US Conference – the United States Conference of Catholic Bishops (USCCB) – announced that the religious body was moving forward with the canonization of Dorothy Day, the co-founder of the Catholic Worker movement. The timing of the announcement was also significant. O'Keefe (2013) argued that, faced with the rhetorical problem of persuading Catholics to adhere to doctrine without being perceived as arguing, the timing of the USCCB's decision – when "bishops' political influence is waning, their moral authority is compromised, and they are in the midst of an unpopular campaign to discipline women religious, particularly nuns involved in social justice" (p. 1) – and its framing were strategic. In a separate study, Golan, Arceneaux, and Soule (2019) concluded that in his major speeches since his election in 2013 as leader of a sovereign state (the Holy See) and the leader of the Catholic faith, Pope Francis used similar message framing and three consistent themes to engage foreign publics throughout the world: universal identity and values, shared responsibility, and calls to action. In his public messages, or "strategic narratives" (Golan, Arceneaux, & Soule, 2019, p. 100), the Pope attempted to connect the identity of the audience to that of himself and the Vatican in order to promote the idea of a universal identity and shared values, emphasizing that "we" must work together to solve the world's problems, and called on foreign audiences to pursue peace and take collective action. A rhetorical analysis of the CC's messages during the 1994 congressional midterm election campaign to members of the faith-based issues organization found that messages to members and potential allies featured narratives that incorporated values and facts for strategic purposes to highlight the "moral crisis facing current society," and the "continued and increasing negative impact on families unless citizens joined together to oppose anti-family policies and worked to bring America back to traditional values" (Ferguson, 1999, p. 240).

As religious and belief communities engage in strategies and techniques of activist organizations to achieve their two goals and work to stimulate the agenda-setting process by framing issues and positions, seek the legitimation of issues, and attempt to capture the attention of the media and key public opinion leaders, effective SC through social and digital media becomes increasingly vital. The ways in which organizations strategically create their messages on digital and social platforms can reveal the ways in which news media and other sharers of their messages reshape these messages and impact public perceptions of the activist organization.

Social and Digital Media

WEBSITES AND EMAIL

Especially relevant to this study is how religious and belief communities use their web-based technology. In an analysis of social movement networks, Diani (2000) concluded that web-based communication is especially important for activist organizations that need to mobilize and secure resources from a dispersed and fairly unorganized membership body. However, Taylor, Kent, and White (2001) examined the mediated communication of 100 nonprofit organizations and the use of their websites to build relationships with publics, and found that, overall, these activist groups failed to take full advantage of their websites' dialogic capacities to achieve their policy goals. Specifically, the nonprofits failed to fully utilize the principles of dialogic loops, ease of interface, conservation of visitors, generation of return visits, and providing information relevant to a variety of publics.

Religious and belief communities' websites can be managed to achieve strategic purposes, even in bounded communities. Golan and Campbell (2015) examined how webmasters of orthodox Jewish communities in Israel strategically managed their websites to accommodate the communities' assumed publics and fit communal goals and needs. Webmasters employed three unique strategies: control (shunning outer evils); layering (facing inner diversity); and guiding (charting community lines). They concluded that webmasters in these types of communities must "fully understand their readership and then plan and manage strategically in order to avoid disrespectful language and problematic rhetoric," while carefully addressing "the emergence of new technologies and new types of knowledge that can be disseminated through the Internet" (p. 481).

Websites are an important resource for religious and belief communities, and in all nonprofit organizations, to communicate dialogically and strategically as an ethical and practical means for providing information to publics, building relationships, and as a means for mobilizing resources necessary to become successful in achieving their goals (Sommerfeldt, Kent, & Taylor, 2012). Effective dialogic websites require content, strategic thinking, integration into existing and future campaigns, the guidance of a skilled communicator capable of understanding how to appeal to multiple publics, creation of a navigational interface that visitors will find compelling, and efforts to provide content that visitors want to see, recommend Sommerfeldt, Kent, and Taylor (2012). Although websites present religious and belief communities with many strategic opportunities (e.g. providing volunteer communication, inviting new members, sharing information, and generating public responsiveness) and their interactive nature offers a unique medium in terms of gathering information, monitoring public opinion, and participating in direct dialogue, many NGOs' websites fall short in accessing their full potential. In their study of 13 activist organizations, Sommerfeldt, Kent, and Taylor (2012) found that websites are viewed as passive communication tools that must be supplemented with traditional public relations practices, they cater to existing and highly involved publics, and website communication is perceived to be most effective when tied to issue-specific events and issue currency.

Use of the internet has been found to be effective in building relationships with like-minded social actors and extending activists' existing networks (Taylor, Kent, & White, 2001; Xie & Ho, 2008). NGOs were early adopters of low-cost communication technology, which is not surprising given the limited resources with which most NGOs work and their need to communicate their messages to a variety of audiences. Internet activism by religious and belief organizations is sustained through a variety of communication tools and distribution outlets, and this ongoing attention shapes public thinking. Recent studies focus specifically on how activist organizations marshal digital and social media to spread their messages and rally supporters. For example, the American Family Association (AFA) capitalized on internet technology's ability to instantaneously and inexpensively communicate with members and followers of the organization when it mobilized thousands of people to pressure organizations to stop advertising on television programs that promote lifestyles and values that are in opposition to the AFA, and to boycott organizations that offered benefits to same-sex couples and donated money to homosexual organizations and events (see American Family Association, n.d.). The AFA developed the boycottford.com website, posting numerous documents "exposing and indicting Ford's pro-homosexual agenda" and links to websites that provide Ford's "gay-themed advertisements" (Coombs & Holladay, 2007, p. 72). Word of the boycottford.com website spread virally, and more than 700 websites had links to the AFA website within three days. This mobilization blitz was effective: within one week Ford dealers met with the AFA, and soon after the AFA suspended its boycott.

Nonprofit research in technology encompasses examining how NGOs are using a variety of digital and social media platforms, including their website, video documentaries, YouTube, Facebook, and microblogs such as Twitter and Weibo. A survey of representatives from 75 transnational NGOs based in the US found that the two most important communicative functions to an NGO are promoting the organization's image and fundraising, and that their websites were considered the most important new media tool, followed by blogs, videocasts, podcasts, and wikis (Seo, Kim, & Yang, 2009).

SOCIAL MEDIA PLATFORMS

Current research increasingly addresses how social media or social networking sites (SNSs) have engendered new opportunities for NGOs in terms of transparency, dissemination of information, and involvement with stakeholders. Generating deep engagement with stakeholders has been regarded as the most prominent potential application of SNSs for religious and belief communities, as well as other NGOs, because this engagement can further facilitate collective action in the community or lead to greater social impact. Researchers have investigated the use of Web 2.0, specifically SNSs and their use by NGOs as a tool for interaction and engagement. Prior research has found that the two major organizational functions for Web 2.0 are information sharing and dialogic relationship building (see e.g. Lovejoy & Saxton, 2012). Social networking aids in the communication between an NGO and its public, and in communication with stakeholders, volunteers, and mass media to form and strengthen relationships, build trust and organize constituents. The two-way dialogic components of social media provide an excellent opportunity to create organization–public relationships by allowing two-way communication with publics.

In the next section, a case study of the LJC's SC allows for a discussion of the principles and techniques of activism, framing, and digital media in the SC used by religious and belief communities and NGOs in general. A brief overview of the history of Lithuanian Jews is provided, followed by a discussion of the LJC and an analysis of the organization's SC directed toward achieving its goals.

The Lithuanian Jewish Community: Using Strategic Communication for Identity Building and Holocaust Re-education

The History of Lithuanian Jews

The Lithuanian government's framing of the Holocaust has emphasized crimes by Soviet regimes and Lithuanian victims of the Soviet occupation, often failing to acknowledge the scale of the Holocaust in Lithuania and the role of Lithuanians in the mass shootings within the country's borders (Ben-David, 2010; Clark, 2006; Lefkovits, 2009; Liphshiz, 2016a,b). Before World War II, Lithuania was home to a large and influential Jewish community, comprising 7% of the country's total population – more than 200,000 people. During the Holocaust, more than 95% of Lithuanian Jews were killed. Today, fewer than 5,000 Jews remain in Lithuania.

The Jewish remnant and supporters have opposed this framing by the Lithuanian government, and have organized to correct this perceived rewriting of history and neglect of the record of the Jewish tragedy in their country, to publicly recognize Lithuanian heroes who rescued their Jewish neighbors, and to educate younger generations and the international community and engage them on this issue. The LJC is one of the foremost Jewish organizations, which operates a comprehensive website and blog, and utilizes public relations strategies and techniques that are characterized by issues organizations and activist groups to inform, engage, and mobilize supporters.

Grunig (1992) defined an activist organization as "a group of two or more individuals who organize in order to influence another public or publics through action that may include education, compromise, persuasion, pressure tactics or force" (p. 504). The LJC exemplifies an activist organization, organized around a common goal and attempting to influence public policy, organizational action, or social norms and values in order to reach that goal (Berry, 1984; Smith & Ferguson, 2001, 2010). LJC, as an activist religious and belief community, strategically uses communication and public relations strategies and techniques to achieve those goals: to rectify problematic conditions through education, engagement, and pressure on the Lithuanian government, and to maintain support for the LJC and recognition of the importance of the LJC.

The focus in this case study is on the first purpose: historically, activism in Lithuania has had the goal of securing and maintaining independence; activism by Lithuanian Jews, which is the subject of the analysis below, has been directed at seeking justice for the Holocaust massacre of their people, advocating for the punishment of war criminals, correcting the historical record of Lithuania's role in the murders, rebuilding the Jewish community and culture in Lithuania, and educating Lithuania's future generations and the world community. This case study will examine the LJC's strategic use of framing narratives on their website. The analysis demonstrates how religious and belief communities strategically communicate via their websites to build relationships (Taylor, Kent, & White, 2001), the framing techniques they use in website messages (Golan, Arceneaux, & Soule, 2019; Zoch et al., 2008), and how their use of the internet reflects their social, political, and relational environment (Yang & Taylor, 2010).

Lithuanian Jewish Community's Framing and Website Strategies and Techniques

The LJC's website messages related to the Lithuanian government on the issue of Lithuania's involvement in the Holocaust are analyzed. In addition, the LJC's activism directed toward the organization's mission of communicating what the Jewish community perceives as an accurate history of the Lithuanian government's involvement in the Holocaust, and methods of educating and engaging people, is examined. LJC website content and updated posts (at http://www.lzb.lt/en) during 2015–2016 comprise the sample of messages analyzed.

Website messages were examined for themes or frames that emerged, both within and across texts (Golan, Arceneaux, & Soule, 2019; Weberling, 2012). According to Gamson and Modigliani (1989), as discussed earlier, a frame can be viewed as a "central organizing idea or story line that provides meaning" (p. 143) to the events related to a story or issue. Frames were recognized when there was significant recurrence and repetition (Golan, Arceneaux, & Soule, 2019); once recognized, diagnostic, prognostic, and motivational framing tasks were identified (Snow & Benford, 1988; Zoch et al., 2008).

Because the goal or "mission of activist organizations is to solve some problem or issue, it follows that action by the organization and its publics is contingent not only on identification of the problem, but also identification of those who have caused or contributed to the problem and thus can be blamed" (Zoch et al., 2008, p. 351). Snow and Benford (1988) call this "diagnostic framing." Activist organizations must also generate support for their positions and goals by "articulating a proposed solution to the problem and the strategies for carrying out a plan of action" (Zoch et al., 2008, p. 351). Snow and Benford (1988) refer to this articulation of a proposed solution as "prognostic framing." Finally, activist organizations' messages contain "motivational framing" to encourage action by "individuals who … agree with [the organization's] views and aims" through a "call to arms" (Snow & Benford, 1988, p. 199).

Lithuania Jewish Community

The LJC is the umbrella organization of Lithuanian Jewry. It unites 27 different Jewish organizations, operating from headquarters in Vilnius. According to the European Jewish Congress website, the LJC "lives in harmony" with the Lithuanian majority and with other ethnic and religious minorities in the country, and "stands up proudly for Jewish rights and interests and has made much progress in many areas in close partnership with Lithuanian colleagues who champion tolerance and dialogue" (The Jewish Community of Lithuania, n.d.).

The LJC operates a comprehensive website and blog, and utilizes public relations strategies and techniques that are characterized by issues organizations and activist groups to inform, engage, and mobilize supporters. Visitors to the LJC website (http://www.lzb.lt/en) find a website that provides relevant up-to-date news and public policy developments, photos and articles about the history of Jews in Lithuania and the massacre of the community during the Holocaust, commemorations of deceased Jewish members and historical events, news of current events and issues that are relevant to the Jewish community, and ways to get involved in the Jewish community. Membership and language (English, Russian, Lithuanian) option links are provided on the top right. The banner flashes photos with news headlines and brief descriptions of upcoming events and news items. On the main menu, from left to right under the banner images, are these labels: News; About us; Learning, History, Culture; Programmes; Social center; Bagel Shop; Heritage. Tabs beneath the main menu identify these links: Religion, Announcements, Greetings, Grateful, Condolences.

Through thematic analysis of the LJC website, four frames emerged that perform the diagnostic, prognostic, and motivational tasks identified by Snow and Benford (1988). Some articles contained more than one frame, and some articles accomplished more than one framing task.

The Four Frames

1. Nazis, the former Soviet Union, and the Lithuanian government must take responsibility for the deportation and murder of more than 95% of Lithuanian Jews (diagnostic framing).

2. The rights of Lithuanian Jews, especially the citizenship of deportees, must be ensured (prognostic framing task).
3. The Jewish community in Lithuania's proud heritage and Holocaust must be commemorated, and future generations of Lithuanians and the global community must be educated to correct history and prevent future occurrence (prognostic and motivational framing tasks).
4. Participation in the LJC to ensure that the Jewish community in Lithuania flourishes (motivational framing task).

FRAME 1: NAZIS, THE FORMER SOVIET UNION, AND THE LITHUANIAN GOVERNMENT MUST TAKE RESPONSIBILITY FOR THE DEPORTATION AND MURDER OF MORE THAN 95% OF LITHUANIAN JEWS

The LJC website contains many articles that assign responsibility and blame to Nazi, Soviet, and Lithuanian perpetrators of violence against Lithuanian Jews. According to one article, the founders of the Provisional Government of Lithuania, "Kowtowing to the Nazis," announced when Nazis invaded Germany in 1941 that Jews were "personae non gratae and turned them over to the Nazis and their [Lithuanian] collaborators" (LJC, 2016a). An LJC website story (LJC, 2015a) about an April 2015 Holocaust education conference quoted a prominent professor and Holocaust historian:

> The summer of 1941 was the very bloodiest page in the history of Lithuania. We shouldn't call it "the tragedy of the Lithuanian Jews", but must call it instead the mass crime of the destruction of the Jews of Lithuania. A crime in which participated not hundreds, but thousands of Lithuanians ... [and] included representatives of all the social strata. The participation of local collaborators and anti-Semites in the mass murder of the Jews during World War II aided Berlin's task to a remarkable degree.

A June 6, 2016, story reprinted from the Baltic News Service reviewed an event to discuss "Questions and Answers after 75 years: Numbers of Perpetrators of Jewish Genocide" that was organized by the parliamentary group For Historic Memory and Justice and the alumni society of Vilnius University's History Faculty in partnership with the International Commission for the Investigation of Crimes Committed by Nazi and Soviet Regimes in Lithuania. Algis Gurevicius, the director of the Jewish Culture and Information Center, "stressed the risk of the entire Lithuanian nation being dubbed as shooters of Jews if the country does not conduct a probe of the perpetrators of the Jewish genocide" (LJC, 2016b). The Nazis annihilated about 90% of Lithuania's pre-war Jewish community of over 200,000 during World War II, often assisted by local Lithuanian collaborators, said Gurevicius. Alfredas Ruksenas, a specialist of the Genocide and Resistance Research Center of Lithuania, said that the rough number of Lithuanians involved in the shooting of Jews may be around 6,000 people. In a story reviewing the June 12, 2016, event in Los Angeles to commemorate the 75th anniversary of the Soviet mass deportation, Latvian consul Dr. Juris Bunkis was quoted as saying:

> Historians attribute the efficiency of these murderers to the massive collaboration in the genocide by Baltic locals who eagerly participated in the rounding up and murdering of hundreds of thousands of innocent people ... Yet some like Jonas Noreika in Lithuania are considered heroes today and have had buildings and streets named after them! (LJC, 2016c)

A summary of a conference held at the Lithuanian parliament in June 2016 relayed a speaker's warning that "[a]voiding the subject of the Holocaust and research in this field, Lithuania is in danger of becoming a nation of Jew-killers in the eyes of the world" (LJC, 2016d). Conference attendees said that it was difficult "to calculate who took part in mass murder operations, for example, some people's names are duplicated because they participated at different locations," and to decide "who should be included as perpetrators: should they only include people who fired weapons, or also those who transported the victims to the mass murder sites or otherwise aided the process" (LJC, 2016d). At the close of dozens of articles on the LJC website is this boilerplate: "During World War II, the Nazis and their Lithuanian collaborators killed over 90 percent of Lithuania's pre-war Jewish population of more than 200,000" (see e.g. LJC, 2015b).

Frame 2: The Rights of Lithuanian Jews, Especially Citizenship of Deportees, Must Be Ensured

One of the most heavily covered issues on the LJC website is the advocacy efforts directed toward the June 2016 passage of the amendments to Lithuania's citizenship law to ensure the rights to citizenship of Jews who left Lithuania between the two world wars and to their descendants. One article cites the Commission for the Evaluation of the Crimes of the Nazi and Soviet Occupation Regimes in Lithuania's statistic that "Soviets deported more Jews to Siberia as a percentage and in larger scope than Lithuanians (about 1 percent of members of the LJC were deported, whereas about 0.5 percent of ethnic Lithuanians)," and that it was incomprehensible that "Litvaks who emigrated in the interwar period shouldn't be granted in principle Lithuanian citizenship." Yet, the Migration Department, since November 2015 "has rejected almost every request for restoration of Lithuanian citizenship by people who left Lithuanian between 1920 and 1939 and their descendants" (LJC, 2016a).

Writing to members of the LJC and to Litvaks living abroad in May 2016, a week before the passage of the constitutional amendment on citizenship, LJC chairwoman Faina Kukliansky charged:

> After the extermination of the Jews in Lithuania … to prevent the Lithuanian Jewish Community from welcoming into our ranks Litvaks who are citizens of another state and who want to become Lithuanian citizens – this is a stupid and short-sighted political decision. (Kukliansky, 2016)

She called on the interior minister to "immediately make a decision, because people have been waiting for three to four years." During the same month the website featured a story recapping Kukliansky's participation on a panel on a Lithuanian radio program on the topic of citizenship. She argued: "Lithuanian Jews – Litvaks – are not just people who have achieved great things in the world, they contributed greatly to the strengthening of the Lithuanian state as well. They sought Lithuanian independence and they fought in the battles for independence" (Kukliansky, 2016). The article noted that the debate over citizenship for Lithuanian Jews evolves around arguments on whether the Lithuanian law on citizenship makes some sort of distinction between those who left on their own volition and who therefore "withdrew," and "those forced to leave by the Nazi or Soviet regime" (Kukliansky, 2016).

Another May 2016 website article reported that [a]s the Lithuanian Migration Department and the courts "issue rejections on applications for Lithuanian citizenship by Litvaks, parliamentarians are preparing to amend the Lithuanian law on citizenship, even though, they say, the current law provides for granting citizenship to the aforementioned people" (LJC, 2016e). An article two days later reported that "[l]awsuits by Litvaks living in Israel and South Africa regarding Lithuanian citizenship have come to the attention of the Lithuanian parliament" (LJC, 2016f) and that two parliamentary committees planned to make inquiries into why Lithuanian Jews who had left the country were getting negative responses to their applications for citizenship. According to a May 9, 2016, LJC website article, about 1,000 requests from Litvaks from Israel, South Africa, the US, and other countries for Lithuanian citizenship had been granted; about 200 requests were denied. When the Baltic News Service reported parliament's decision to amend the citizenship law on June 23, LJC chairwoman Faina Kukliansky was quoted: "I very much welcome the change in the law, and I am certain the Lithuanian state has lost nothing at all, and on the contrary, has received much more, a good name and living potential" (LJC, 2016g).

FRAME 3: JEWISH HERITAGE AND HOLOCAUST MUST BE COMMEMORATED AND PEOPLE EDUCATED TO CORRECT HISTORY AND PREVENT FUTURE OCCURRENCE

Articles and announcements about events educating and commemorating Lithuanian Jewish history, Lithuanian Jews (e.g. interwar Lithuanian President and chess enthusiast Kazys Grinius), and "Jew savers" numbered in the dozens, and Holocaust events (e.g. deportations from Lithuania in June 1941) during 2015–2016. In September 2015 a story was reprinted from the Baltic News Service about a ceremony awarding "47 people with Life Saving Crosses for saving Jews from the Nazis during WWII" (LJC, 2015b), which included LJC leader Faina Kukliansky's description of them as heroes. The next day, on the National Memorial Day for the Genocide Victims of the Lithuanian Jews marking the liquidation of the Vilnius Ghetto, 800 Lithuanians were to be recognized as "Righteous Among the Nations for saving Jews" (LJC, 2015b). Photos and a June 2016 article (LJC, 2016h) reported that efforts to "commemorate and clean up Jewish cemeteries and memorial sites continues in Kaunas," showing photos of new information boards and signs. Condolences of recent deaths were accompanied by photos and stories about their service to Lithuania and loyalty to the Jewish community and noted statues, monuments, and events honoring them.

Another September 2015 story printed the program for a commemoration marking the 90th anniversary of the founding of Yivo and the Lithuanian Day of Holocaust Remembrance. The week-long conference-commemoration included a presentation of the scarf donated by a Kaunas ghetto and Stutthoff concentration camp survivor, the reading of another prisoner's diary, prayer, multiple musical concerts, a documentary film screening, a tour of "Jewish Vilna," and a conference dedicated to the 90th anniversary of the founding of the YIVO institute for Jewish research, and commemoration of Holocaust victims at Ponar. An article earlier that year, on June 27, marked the 74th anniversary commemoration of

> one of the iconic events of the Lithuanian Holocaust, the infamous Lietūkis Garage Massacre of 27 June 1941 … carried out by local Lithuanian "patriots" wearing the white armbands of the Lithuanian Activist Front (LAF) butchered dozens of Jewish passers by at a garage on Kaunas's Vytautas Avenue, using a variety of execution methods, including clubbing to death with crowbars, and particularly, forcing water from high-pressure hoses into bodily orifices of the victims until they burst. A growing crowd, including women holding up their young children to get the best views, cheered them on. (LJC, 2015c)

The liberation from Nazi concentration camps was commemorated (e.g. the 70th anniversary of the liberation of Auschwitz).

Many articles combined the functions of commemoration and education. An October 2015 article recapped the Svencionys Jewish Community's commemoration of Holocaust victims, when 8,000 Jews were murdered in the surrounding forest. The article quoted LJC chairwoman Faina Kukliansky, explaining the importance of the commemoration of Jewish victims and remembering those responsible:

> We should remember not just the names of those who were murdered, but the names of those who murdered as well. This is necessary not just for condemnation or revenge, because those who are some still alive are very old, while others have passed on and stand in the court of the Almighty. I think it is necessary for all of us, their inheritors, so that our neighbors might know by whose

> hand the most horrific crime of the 20th century was committed. Because only when everyone whose hands were sullied with the blood of innocent victims is named and condemned, even if only in our thoughts, only then can we start to hope Lithuania might rid itself of its shameful title as a "nation of Jew-shooters." (LJC, 2015d)

A June 2016 article reported a meeting between Deputy Lithuanian Foreign Minister Mantvydas Bekešius and LJC chairwoman Faina Kukliansky during which they discussed "protection of Jewish heritage and the renovation and upkeep of the old Jewish cemetery in Molėtai and Holocaust mass graves by the regional administration" (LJC, 2016i). They also spoke about the need to honor rescuers of Jews, increased public sensitivity to Jewish issues, and the organization of a March of Memory in August. Chairwoman Kukliansky's speech at the Lithuanian Parliament at Commemoration of the Day of Mourning and Hope and the Day of Occupation Genocide was quoted in another June 2016 article, combining commemoration and education about the lives of Lithuanian Jews as the nation was being invaded by Nazis in 1941, which described a rich, vibrant Jewish culture:

> On the eve of the first Soviet occupation the majority of Lithuanian Jews were involved in different cultural, social and political organizations and associations ... there were 16 Jewish daily newspapers, 30 weeklies and 13 non-periodical publications as well as 20 collections of literature being published in Lithuania before World War II ... Of the total number of enterprises seized in 1940, 83% belonged to Jews and provided a living to a large portion of the Lithuanian population. (LJC, 2016j)

Kukliansky concluded with a reference to the current Litvak citizenship issue: "It is a great shame the figure of the Jewish deportee has all but been forgotten in Lithuanian society today, or is ignored, with deportation being understood as solely the tragedy of the Lithuania people" (LJC, 2016j).

FRAME 4: PARTICIPATION IN THE LJC TO ENSURE THAT THE JEWISH COMMUNITY IN LITHUANIA FLOURISHES

The fourth frame emphasizes the broad LJC and invites Jews and LJC supporters to join in events, and combines with the function of commemoration and Frame 3 in many articles. For example, in June 2016 an article quoted LJC's Kukliansky: "The centennial of the restoration of statehood is a holiday for the Lithuanian Jewish Community. We are so glad to have our homeland which we love" (LJC, 2016k). The author said that Kukliansky confirmed that Lithuanian Jews will take an active part in the centennial celebrations, including plans to hold a 5th World Litvak Congress, publish a calendar, and commemorate appropriately Lithuanian Jewish history and culture in Lithuanian towns and cities "where Jews who helped put Lithuania on the map lived, worked and created" (LJC, 2016k). Commemoration, education, and religious events are promoted in advance, and website readers are encouraged to attend. The website's "Social center" posts invite LJC members to concerts, summer camps, conferences, the eve of Shavuot ceremony, and offer birthday greetings, tell readers of new Bagel Shop news and free matzo, and provide photos and stories about members and recent events. In her letter reviewing 2015 LJC accomplishments, chairwoman Kukliansky concluded with a call to increase the community:

> I am pleased that the number of Vilnius residents joining the Community is quickly growing. Although we have always said that all Jews living in Vilnius are members of the Community, today we see them becoming true members and paying membership fees, which have been greatly reduced. And non-Jews are also taking part in the Community's work, and just as we ask for tolerance for others, we strive to be tolerant people ourselves ... The Community is hoping for more participation by the youth because we are not just elderly people. Taking a more active part means

each individual may contribute according to their desire, talent and ability. If an individual wants to preserve his or her Jewish identity and those of his or her children and grandchildren, we welcome any and all such initiatives. (Kukliansky, 2015)

Conclusion

This chapter addressed SC in religious and belief communities, with an analysis of the LJC's website messages; it sought to integrate and apply some of the earlier lines of inquiry and findings related to SC in nonprofit organizations (i.e. NGOs), activism, framing, and use of digital and social media. The LJC engages in communication strategies and techniques found in earlier studies of activist organizations, however, this is one of the few examinations of an ethnic-religious community.

Analysis of the website demonstrates how messages perform functions, in this case informational and legislative (Jackson, 1982), commemorative and relationship building, and reveals that key strategies and tactics included the LJC's and chairwoman Kukliansky's advocacy for citizenship of Litvak deportees, commemorating dates and events of significance to Lithuanian Jews, and publicizing events and engaging members of the community in many other ways. The LJC's website is directed toward utilizing principles of dialogic loops, ease of interface, conservation of visitors, generation of return visits, and providing information relevant to a variety of publics (Taylor, Kent, & White, 2001). Consistent with Sommerfeldt, Kent, and Taylor (2012), the LJC communicates dialogically and strategically as an ethical and practical means for providing information to publics, building relationships, and as a means for mobilizing resources necessary to become successful in achieving organizational goals. Effective, dialogic websites require content, strategic thinking, integration into existing and future campaigns, the guidance of a skilled communicator capable of understanding how to appeal to multiple publics, creation of a navigational interface that visitors will find compelling, and efforts to provide content that visitors want to see, recommend Sommerfeldt, Kent, and Taylor (2012), and the examples above evidence that LJC website content demonstrates these principles.

In these ways, this study continues the exploration of how religious and belief communities, as one type of activist organization and NGO, strategically use websites to build relationships (Taylor, Kent, & White, 2001), and the framing techniques they use in website messages (Zoch et al., 2008). The analysis and Kukliansky's quotes demonstrate the organization's emphasis on continuing to grow the LJC.

Framing theory research suggests that how a message is presented can make a major difference in how it is received (Zoch et al., 2008). Examination of LJC website messages revealed the use of four frames: (1) Nazis, the former Soviet Union, and the Lithuanian government must take responsibility for the deportation and murder of more than 95% of Lithuanian Jews; (2) the rights of Lithuanian Jews, especially citizenship of deportees, must be ensured; (3) The Jewish community in Lithuania's proud heritage and Holocaust must be commemorated, and future generations of Lithuanians and the global community must be educated to correct history and prevent future occurrence; and (4) participation in the LJC to ensure that the Jewish community in Lithuania flourishes. These frames reflect the conditions identified that need to be rectified, or the first purpose of activist organizations (Smith & Ferguson, 2001).

A number of authors (Gamson & Modigliani, 1989; Snow & Benford, 1988) have suggested core framing tasks as potentially important factors in the successful framing of messages. Zoch et al. (2008) argued that such tasks and devices would be especially critical to the framing of messages that are not only designed to describe a problem but also motivate adherents to take action to achieve a solution. Examination of LJC website messages confirmed the strategic use of diagnostic, prognostic, and motivational framing tasks, and found that messages contained multiple framing tasks.

Finally, this analysis highlights how activist religious and belief communities' use of the internet reflects their social, political, and relational environment (Yang & Taylor, 2010). The LJC's activist communication cannot be examined without taking into account the pre-Holocaust history of the nation, the Jewish community, including Soviet occupation and the geopolitical environment; the Holocaust era extermination of more than 90% of Lithuanian Jews and deportation of thousands more, and the role of the Nazis and Lithuanian government; and the post-war developments and rebuilding of the LJC and global understanding.

The LJC, like other religious and belief communities, and nonprofits or NGOs, use SC for a variety of purposes (e.g. to serve their publics, advocate for causes, manage relationships with their publics, and maintain their viability). The examination of the LJC's SC directed at ensuring that the Holocaust is accurately remembered and commemorated in Lithuania and internationally, and to build community for Lithuanian Jews, also illuminated how religious and belief communities, as with other NGOs, use SC when engaging in activism to change policies, practices, or conditions that they find problematic.

References

American Family Association. (n.d.). Who we are: Our mission. Retrieved from https://www.afa.net/who-we-are/our-mission

Ben-David, R. (2010, August 6). Digging up the future. The Jerusalem Post. Retrieved from http://www.lexisnexis.com.lib.pepperdine.edu/hottopics/lnacademic

Berry, J. M. (1984). *The interest group society.* Boston, MA: Little Brown.

Botan, C. (2018). *Strategic communication theory and practice: The co-creational model.* Hoboken, NJ: Wiley-Blackwell.

Bowe, B. J., Fahmy, S., & Wanta, W. (2013). Missing religion: Second level agenda setting and Islam in American Newspapers. *The International Communication Gazette*, 75(7), 636–652.

Clark, T. (2006). Nationalism in Post-Soviet Lithuania. In L. W. Barrington (Ed.), *After independence: Making and protecting the nation in postcolonial and postcommunist states* (pp. 162–186). Ann Arbor, MI: University of Michigan Press.

Coombs, W. T., & Holladay, S. J. (2007). *It's not just PR: Public relations in society.* Madden, MA: Blackwell.

Crable, R. E., & Vibbert, S. L. (1985). Managing issues and influencing public policy. *Public Relations Review*, 11, 3–16.

Diani, M. (2000) Social movement networks virtual and real. *Information, Communication & Society*, 3(3), 386–401.

Entman, R. M. (1993). Framing: Toward clarification of a fractured paradigm. *Journal of Communication*, 43(4), 51–58.

Ferguson, D. P. (1999). Rhetorical public relations and issues management strategies of social movement organizations: The communication of values and policy preferences. Published dissertation, Purdue University.

Ferguson, D. P. (2018). Nonprofit organizations. In R. L. Heath & W. Johansen (Eds.), *International encyclopedia of strategic communication* (pp. 1–13). Malden, MA: Wiley-Blackwell.

Ferguson, D. P., & Smith, M. F. (2012). No frackin'way: Activism in the Marcellus Shale region. *Business Research Yearbook*, 18(1), 497–504.

Gamson, W. A., & Modigliani, A. (1989). Media discourse and public opinion on nuclear power: A constructivist approach. *American Journal of Sociology*, 95(1), 1–37.

Golan, G. J., Arceneaux, P. C., & Soule, M. (2019). The Catholic Church as a public policy actor: An analysis of the Pope's strategic narrative and international engagement. *The Journal of International Communication*, 25, 95–115.

Golan, O., & Campbell, H. A. (2015). Strategic management of religious websites: The case of Israel's orthodox communities. *Journal of Computer-Mediated Communication*, 20, 467–486.

Grunig, J. E. (1989). Sierra Club study shows who become activists. *Public Relations Review*, 25(3), 3–24.

Grunig, L. (1992). Activism: How it limits the effectiveness of organizations and how excellent public relations departments respond. In J. Grunig (Ed.), *Excellence in public relations and communication management* (pp. 503–530). Hillsdale, NJ: Erlbaum.

Hall, P. (2005). Historical perspectives on nonprofit organizations in the United States. In R. Herman (Ed.), *The Jossey-Bass handbook of nonprofit management and leadership* (2nd edn) (pp. 3–38). San Francisco, CA: Jossey-Bass.

Hallahan, K., Holtzhausen, D., van Ruler, B., & Krishnamurthy, S. (2007). Defining strategic communication. *International Journal of Strategic Communication*, 1(1), 3–35.

Hoffman, M. F., & Ford, D. J. (2010). *Organizational rhetoric: Situations and strategies.* Thousand Oaks, CA: Sage.

Jackson, P. (1982). Tactics of confrontation. In J. S. Nagelschmid (Ed.), *The public affairs handbook* (pp. 211–220). New York: AMACOM.

Kampf, Z. (2016). Rhetorical bypasses: Connecting with the hearts and minds of people in the opponent's side. *Journal of Multicultural Discourses*, 11(2), 149–163.

Knight, G., & Greenberg, J. (2002). Promotionalism and subpolitics: Nike and its labor critics. *Management Communication Quarterly*, 15(4), 541–570.

Kukliansky, F. (2015). Lithuanian Jewish Community chairwoman takes stock of accomplishments over patyear. Retrievedfromhttps://www.lzb.lt/en/2015/12/29/lithuanian-jewish-community-chairwoman-takes-stock-of-accomplishments-over-past-year

Kukliansky, F. (2016). What should be done with the law on dual citizenship of several years standing?. Retrievedfromhttps://www.lzb.lt/en/2016/05/24/what-should-be-done-with-the-law-on-dual-citizenship-of-several-years-standing

Lefkovits, E. (2009, June 30). Baltic states assailed for "Holocaust obfuscation". The Jerusalem Post. Retrieved from http://www.lexisnexis.com.lib.pepperdine.edu/hottopics/lnacademic

Liphshiz, C. (2016a, February 21). Is Lithuania ready to own up to its Holocaust past? The Times of Israel. Retrieved from https://www.timesofisrael.com/is-lithuania-ready-to-own-up-to-its-holocaust-past

Liphshiz, C. (2016b, February 17). New book prompts soul-searching in Lithuania about Holocast-era complicity. *Jewish Telegraphic Agency* Retrieved from http://www.jta.org/2016/02/17/news-opinion/world/new-book-prompts-soul-searching-in-lithuania-about-holocaust-era-complicity

LJC(2015a). Criticism leveled at Lithuaniana government and society of Vilnius Holocaust conferenceRetrievedfromhttps://www.lzb.lt/en/2015/04/24/criticism-leveled-at-lithuanian-government-and-society-at-vilnius-holocaust-conference

LJC(2015b). Jew savers awarded in Lithuania. Retrieved from https://www.lzb.lt/en/2015/09/22/jew-savers-awarded-in-lithuania

LJC(2015c). The June 2015 memorial for the Lietukis Garage massacre in Kaunas, Lithuania. Retrieved from https://www.lzb.lt/en/2015/07/02/the-june-2015-memorial-for-the-lietukis-garage-massacre-in-kaunas-lithuania

LJC(2015d). When will Lithuania improve its Holocaust reputation? Retrieved from https://www.lzb.lt/en/2015/10/14/when-will-lithuania-improve-its-holocaust-reputation

LJC(2016a). Darius Udrys: What does Lithuania owe its Jews? Retrieved from https://www.lzb.lt/en/2016/05/30/darius-udrys-what-does-lithuania-owe-its-jews

LJC(2016b). Lithuanian historian: Guards of massacre sites should also be listed as murderers. Retrieved from https://owl.purdue.edu/owl/research_and_citation/apa_style/apa_formatting_and_style_guide/reference_list_electronic_sources.html

LJC(2016c). Latvian consul speaks frankly about Holocaust. Retrieved from https://www.lzb.lt/en/2016/06/15/latvian-consul-speaks-frankly-about-holocaust

LJC(2016d). List of Lithuanian Holocaust perpetrators could run to 6,000. Retrieved from https://www.lzb.lt/en/2016/06/06/list-of-lithuanian-holocaust-perpetrators-could-run-to-6000

LJC(2016e). Plans to amend Lithuanian citizenship laws for Litvaks. Retrieved from https://www.lzb.lt/en/2016/05/12/plans-to-amend-lithuanian-citizenship-law-for-litvaks

LJC(2016f). Lithuanian parliament to investigate why Litvaks aren't getting citizenship. Retrieved from https://www.lzb.lt/en/category/history-and

LJC(2016g). Lithuanian parliament passes amendment to ensure citizenship for Litvaks. Retrieved from https://www.lzb.lt/en/2016/08/01/lithuanian-parliament-passes-amendment-to-ensure-citizenship-for-litvaks

LJC(2016h). Work to commemorate and clean up Jewish cemeteries and memorial sites continues in Kaunas. Retrieved from https://www.lzb.lt/en/2016/05/26/work-to-commemorate-and-clean-up-jewish-cemeteries-and-memorial-sites-continues-in-kaunas

LJC(2016i). Deputy Lithuanian Foreign Minister and LJC Chairwoman visit Moletai. Retrieved from https://www.lzb.lt/en/2016/06/14/deputy-lithuanian-foreign-minister-and-ljc-chairwoman-visit-moletai

LJC. (2016j). Chairwoman Faina Kukliansky's speech at the Lithuanian Parliament at commemoration of the Day of Mourning and Hope and the Day of Occupation and Genocide. Retrieved from https://www.lzb.lt/en/2016/06/14/chairwoman-faina-kuklianskys-speech-at-the-lithuanian-parliament-at-commemoration-of-the-day-of-mourning-and-hope-and-the-day-of-occupation-and-genocide

LJC(2016k). Discussion of Litvak heritage protection at Lithuanian government. Retrieved from https://www.lzb.lt/en/2016/06/23/discussion-of-litvak-heritage-protection-at-lithuanian-government

Lovejoy, K., & Saxton, G. D. (2012). Information, community, and action: How nonprofit organizations use social media. *Journal of Computer-Mediated Communication*, 17(3), 337–353.

McCombs, M. E. (2004). *Setting the agenda: The mass media and public opinion*. Cambridge: Polity Press.

McCombs, M. E., & Shaw, D. (1972). The agenda-setting function of mass media. *Public Opinion Quarterly*, 36, 176–187.

McCombs, M. E., Llamas, J. P., Lopez-Escobar, E., & Rey, F. (1997). Candidate images in Spanish elections: Second-level agenda-setting effects. *Journalism and Mass Communication Quarterly*, 74(4), 703–717.

McKeever, B. (2018). The nonprofit sector brief 2018: Public charities, giving, and volunteering. Retrievedfromhttps://nccs.urban.org/publication/nonprofit-sector-brief-2018#the-nonprofit-sector-in-brief-2018-public-charites-giving-and-volunteering

O'Keefe, M. (2013). Sainthood as rebuke: The U.S. Conference of Catholic Bishops' strategic canonization of Dorothy Day. *Journal of Contemporary Rhetoric*, 3(1/2), 1–16.

Salamon, L. M. (2012). *The state of nonprofit America* (2nd edn). Washington, D.C.: Brookings Institution Press.

Seo, H., Kim, J. Y., & Yang, S. (2009). Global activism and new media: A study of transnational NGO's online public relations. *Public Relations Review*, 35(2), 123–126.

Smith, M. F. (1997). Public relations from the 'bottom-up': Toward a more inclusive view of public relations. Paper presented at the National Communication Association Annual Convention, Chicago, IL.

Smith, M. F., & Ferguson, D. P. (2001). Activism. In R. L. Heath (Ed.), *Handbook of public relations* (pp. 291–300). Thousand Oaks, CA: Sage.

Smith, M. F., & Ferguson, D. P. (2010). Activism 2.0. In R. Heath (Ed.), *The SAGE handbook of public relations* (pp. 395–408). Thousand Oaks, CA: Sage.

Smith, M. F., & Ferguson, D. P. (2013). "Fracking democracy": Issue management and locus of policy decision-making in the Marcellus Shale gas drilling debate. *Public Relations Review*, 39(4), 377–386.

Smith, M. F., & Ferguson, D. P. (2018). Organizing for advocacy: Activist organizational rhetoric. In O. Ihlen & R. L. Heath (Eds.), *Handbook of organizational rhetoric and communication: Foundations of dialogue, discourse, narrative, and engagement* (pp. 439–452). Malden, MA: Wiley-Blackwell.

Snow, D. A., & Benford, R. D. (1988). Ideology, frame resonance, and participant mobilization. In B. Klandermans, H. Kriesi, & S. Tarrow (Eds.), *International social movement research* (pp. 197–217). Greenwich, CT: JAI Press.

Sommerfeldt, E. J., Kent, M. L., & Taylor, M. (2012). Activist practitioner perspectives of website public relations: Why aren't activist websites fulfilling the dialogic promise? *Public Relations Review*, 38, 303–312.

Sriramesh, K. (1992). The impact of societal culture on public relations: An ethnographic study of South Indian organizations npublished doctoral dissertation, University of Maryland, College Park, MD.

Taylor, M., Kent, M. L., & White, W. J. (2001). How activist organizations are using the internet to build relationships. *Public Relations Review*, 27(3), 263–284.

The Jewish Community of Lithuania. (n.d.). European Jewish Congress. Retrieved from http://www.eurojewcong.org/communities/lithuania.html

The Urban Institute. (2001). Faith-based organizations in community development. Report prepared for the U.S. Department of Housing and Urban Development, Office of Policy Development and Research. Retrieved from https://www.huduser.gov/portal/publications/faithbased.pdf

Tice, H. S., Salamon, L. M., & List, R. A. (2001). *Finding a sacred bard: Portraying the global nonprofit sector in official statistics.* John Hopkins Center for Civil Society Studies. Retrieved from http://ccss.jhu.edu/wp-content/uploads/downloads/2011/09/CCSS_WP19_2001.pdf

Weberling, B. (2012). Framing breast cancer: Building an agenda through online advocacy and fundraising. *Public Relations Review*, 38, 108–115.

Xie, L., & Ho, P. (2008). Urban environmentalism and activists' networks in China: The cases of Xiangfan and Shanghai. *Conservation & Society*, 6, 141–153.

Yang, A., & Taylor, M. (2010). Relationship-building by Chinese ENGOs' websites: Education, not activation. *Public Relations Review*, 36, 342–351.

Zoch, L. M., Collins, E. L., Sisco, H. F., & Supa, D. H. (2008). Empowering the activist: Using framing devices on activist organizations' web sites. *Public Relations Review*, 34(4), 351–358.

19

Gender in US Strategic Communication Research and Practice
Confronting the Master Narratives

[1]Linda Aldoory, [2]Elizabeth L. Toth, and Liang Ma[2]
[1]University of Maryland [2]Texas Christian University

This chapter was motivated by the dearth of literature in strategic communication (SC) on the multiplicative and discursive ways that power and gender guide research and practice in the field. We argue that a multi-faceted perspective should be enacted to understand how gender is constituted and how power is enacted. One way that social and organizational norms are created is through master narratives, which are constructed and reaffirmed and become hegemonic and difficult to untangle. These narratives result in dualistic gender expectations that play out in the communication profession and with professionals. Assumptions, then, about gender are learned via the enactment of the narratives. These implicit narratives mark reward, invisibility, and judgment for workers in the field of SC and prevent workers from looking at other explanations for what may seem "natural" gender distinctions and roles. This chapter will illuminate some key master narratives affecting gender in SC.

First, we highlight the conceptualizations used for SC and gender. Then, we lay the theoretical groundwork that informed our perspective on gender and power and define some key terms. The theories reveal how certain entrenched cultural power norms influence current research and practice in SC. We then propose a feminist framework based on a socioecological model that shows how different levels of influence mark gender for the field. We conclude by suggesting a multi-layered way of considering gender for the field and we dive into a case example of how to use the framework to analyze power and gender in SC. The definitions, theory, and framework are applied to a case concerning Abercrombie & Fitch. Rather than focusing on "how to" do gender or how to break out of gender discrimination for any one public, we hope to elevate the conversation to that of constitutive gender constructions at the institutional level and professional level. To do so, we offer what may be viewed as controversial narratives that are implicitly defining what is accepted in practice and research.

Conceptualization Basics: Strategic Communication and Publics

Authors argue that SC is a "trans-boundary" concept (Falkneimer & Heide, 2014) that aptly describes organizational deliberative communication processes. Strategic communication scholars argue that communication is at the core of how organizations structure, adapt, and adjust to information/messages received from the environment (Hallahan et al., 2007;

The Handbook of Strategic Communication, First Edition. Edited by Carl H. Botan.

Werder, 2015). Authors use the term "constitutive" to mean that communication represents the shared meanings and interpretation of messages between actors that creates organizations, relationships, and structures.

There are about as many definitions for SC as there are researchers attempting to define it. Botan in this volume defines SC as the use of information flowing into the organization (or research) about the relationship it shares with publics to plan and carry out a communication campaign addressing that relationship. Strategic communication is publics-centered rather than organization or message-centered.

In their introduction to a new journal focused on SC research, Hallahan et al. (2007) called SC: "the purposeful use of communication by an organization to fulfill its mission" and assume that people will engage in "deliberative communication practice on behalf of organizations, causes and social movements" (p. 3). Lie and Servaes (2015) recently stated that "strategic communication deals with the organizational planning of communication and relates to persuasive communication, marketing, and public relations. Strategic communication is planned communication with a strategic, intentional goal" (p. 245). Holtzhausen and Zerfass (2013, 2015) defined SC as the practice of deliberate and purposive communication that a communication agent enacts in the public sphere on behalf of a communicative entity to reach set goals. "The ultimate aim of strategic communication is to maintain a healthy reputation for the communication entity in the public sphere" (Holtzhausen & Zerfass, 2015, p. 6). The term "strategy" is defined by Botan in this volume as "the campaign-level decision-making involving maneuvering and arranging resources and arguments to carry out organizational grand strategy."

The concept of *publics* is distinct from *audience* in that it defines a group of individuals who interpret communication in similar ways (Botan, 2018, p. 58). According to Botan: "… publics act as conscious groups making choices – some rational, some not so rational, but choices nevertheless" (p. 74). It is because of these shared understandings that publics can express their will through language use, thus exerting power on relationships because they are organized. Botan theorizes that publics are not "fixed" but change constantly, agreeing on meanings or adapting to changes in meanings. He contrasts this view with those who communicate from past experience or from cross-sectional measures on needs or attitudes. These frameworks take instead an instrumental view. Publics constantly make meanings that are dynamic rather than static in nature.

Botan (2018) focuses on two key elements of SC theory: that communication is constitutive and that meanings are shaped (cocreated) through interactions between organizations and their publics. He proposed a model depicting the cocreation in overlapping components: the inflow of meanings of publics about their relationship with the organization; the organization's use of a public's meanings to plan how to respond; and an organization's responses (campaigns) as interpreted by publics and new meanings cocreated by publics, leading to changes in the relationship (p. 48). Botan states that for this strategic process to be successful, the communication must reflect shared language and culture (p. 51).

For the purposes of this chapter, we view SC as constitutive, discursively constructing relationships between organizations and publics. The definition of a public is an interpretive community engaged in an ongoing process of developing a shared understanding of its relationship with an organization and its behaviors (Botan, 2018). The relationship and the discourse can differ substantially between organizations and publics, as it is based on perceptions and co-constructions of meaning.

Theoretical Foundations

Below are brief summaries of the broad theoretical frameworks that informed this chapter and the multi-perspective framework developed for gender in SC.

Gender and Feminist Theory

Jackson (2006) stated that gender is the distinction between the binary categories of women and men/male and female, and the characteristics and identities embodied through membership of them (p. 106). Gender is not biologically created but rather socially and culturally constructed. Participation in gendered realities is enacted implicitly and perhaps without intent, but nonetheless continues to re-inscribe frames for what is acceptable and unacceptable beliefs and behaviors for categories of gender.

Feminist theory examines the impact of gender, focusing on power and its role in the marginalization of people, thoughts, professions, and institutions, based on their gendered realities. Definitions of power here center on the domination and control of one group of people over another (Yoder & Kahn, 1992). Power can be analyzed at different levels, from individual to ideology, and it is examined differently depending on the definition of feminism. Different definitions of feminism guide theory – from liberal feminist theory that is based on the proposition of formal equality between males and females supporting equality and opportunity and access for women (Chegwe, 2014), to radical feminist theory that attempts to rewrite history and politicize the present, in order to topple masculinist systems governing society, media, and organizations (Nachescu, 2009). Acker (1990, 2006) was one of a handful of scholars to apply feminist theory to how organizations privilege masculinity and men over women. In 1994, the scholarly journal *Gender, Work and Organization* was created to debate and analyze "gender relations, the organization of gender, and the gendering of organizations" (journal mission statement, found at http://onlinelibrary.wiley.com/journal/10.1111/%28ISSN%291468-0432/homepage/ProductInformation.html).

In communication research specifically, feminist theory became a more active area of study in the late 1970s with the creation of the journal *Women's Studies in Communication*. By the early 1990s, a core group of scholars in public relations and organizational communication illuminated the influence of power on women and gender in organizations and SC and paved the way for research and practice that addressed different spheres of power and influence: the individual, professional, and organizational spheres (Buzzanell, 1994; Grunig, 1988; Hon, 1995; Rakow, 1989; Toth, 1988; Toth & Cline, 1989, 1991). Since then, a body of knowledge has emerged that examines gender as a socially constructed and discursively constituted meaning maker (see, for example, Aldoory, 2005, 2009; Aldoory & Toth, 2000; Ashcroft, 2014; McDonald, 2015; Pompper, 2005, 2012; Toth & Aldoory, 2001). Recently, some authors have interrogated feminization and feminine values for SC (Pompper & Jung, 2013). As Pompper and Jung (2013) argued, organizations value masculinity over femininity, thus when professions such as public relations become female dominated this still constrains gender role expectations and harms both men and women working in the field.

Critical Race Theory

Critical race theory (CRT) has its origins in social movements, education, and legal rights, and has been used to help critique the social nature of race and the inherent whiteness of organizations and society. Critical race scholars have revealed "harmful fictions" that "mask institutions' subversion of race equality, ensure White privilege, and normalize or naturalize racism in American society" (Pompper, 2005, p. 144). There are some main tenets of CRT. First, racism is a permanent component of American life. Second, whiteness is a property that is used as a commodity. Third, story telling, used to validate racial norms, is not truth and can be addressed through counter-narratives. Fourth, the goals of Blacks will be achieved when they are consistent with the needs of Whites. Fifth, basic liberal notions of color blindness and neutrality are to be critiqued. Finally, race is critiqued along its intersections with other identities and differences (Capper, 2015; Horsford, 2010).

Importantly, CRT has been used as both an epistemological lens and a methodological tool to help analyze the experiences of historically under-represented populations (Ledesma & Calderón, 2015). One focus of CRT as a methodology is its reliance on story telling, and counter-stories to retell history, politics, education, and communication from the neglected and missing contexts of Black lives. However, some authors have cautioned against the simple use of story telling without a critical lens that ensures the main point is disseminated (Ledesma & Calderón, 2015). Outcomes from using CRT are to be action as well as analysis and critique.

While not as prolific as gender scholarship, there has been some scholarly discourse in communication that has examined CRT (Anguiano & Castaneda, 2014) and applied it to organizations (Pompper, 2005). In this chapter, we consider CRT as an epistemological lens by which to intersect feminist theory and queer theory in understanding the importance of counter-narratives about gender and power in SC. This means we look at how CRT can help define our knowledge about SC.

Queer Theory

Queer theory and feminist theory are similar in their examinations of power and oppression on the basis of social oppression. They also both interrogate gender and sexuality as vectors that create social norms. Below we define queer theory and describe how it helps understand a cultural system that impacts SC. According to Yep, Lovaas, and Elia (2003), "Queer theory is one of the most significant intellectual movements of the last two decades" (p. 2). Queer theory directs attention to the socially constructed normativity and privilege provided heterosexuality (Chevrette, 2013; McDonald, 2015). Queer theory presumes that a system of sexuality structures and organizes everyday life, and that system is heteronormative (Jackson, 2006). In other words, scholarship and practice "affirms the normalization of hegemonic heterosexuality as invisible, natural, given, and taken for granted" (Yep, Lovaas, & Elia, 2003, p. 2). Hegemonic defines how certain assumptions become normalized to the point where people do not even see the assumption as a guide for behavior and thoughts. Normalization of marriage, sex, and gender is a primary instrument of power and control as it marginalizes people who identify as LGBTQ (McDonald, 2015). Theorists do not merely focus on examining the oppression of homosexual individuals, but also critique institutional practices and discourse for how they construct sexual identity (Chevrette, 2013; McDonald, 2015). As Gamson (2003) explained, theorists look at how "homosexual," "gay," and "lesbian" became categories: "how those categories are defined, by whom and through what processes, what boundaries they set on what we can know, on how and whom we desire, and so on" (p. 386). Queer theory approaches sexual identities as multiple, unstable, and fluid social constructions (Gamson, 2003; Yep, Lovaas, & Elia, 2003).

Examining heterosexuality as a cultural system aligns with presuppositions of feminist theories that examine power and its role in subjugating certain voices. Jackson (2006) argued that heterosexuality is a key site of intersection between gender and sexuality. However, some critics have lambasted the feminist focus on women as a fixed sexual category (Chevrette, 2013). Similarly, while much of queer theory includes gender within its analytical lens, some theorists have excluded gender, assuming that it was only for the feminist domain of theorizing. Chevrette noted that an absence of gender analysis as part of queer theory re-inscribes white gay male identities and erases gendered and radicalized differences (p. 172).

Authors in communication have been developing and debating queer theory for only about a decade. However, Yep, Lovaas, and Elia (2003) characterized the work in communication as having a longer history but with "long period(s) of silence and scholarly inactivity" (p. 2). As Chevrette (2013) argued, queer theory and communication studies have grown alongside one another but only recently become more integrated, in particular, in rhetoric, media, and performance studies. Tindall and Waters (2013) edited a volume of work in LGBTQ issues in theory and research. The authors addressed practitioner concerns, industry context, and campaigns. However, McDonald (2015) argued that queer theory still remains underexplored (p. 321).

Master Narratives Guiding Strategic Communication

The integrated theoretical groundwork we developed motivated a look at certain master narratives governing professional practice and scholarly research in SC. These discursive narratives reveal how gender and power are defined and enacted, by individuals, by organizations, and by the society in which they work. The three main narratives described below are largely the same ones found in many other fields, such as public relations, education, and management, where they act as powerful motivators for behaviors in the workplace. They provide a profession a "seemingly real story to tell" and produce identities for individuals in that story (Trethewey, 2001, p. 187). Subsequently, gendered ideology thrives off these master narratives playing out in US SC, and prepares women and men to enact certain performances that are gendered.

Narrative for Individual Behavior: Individualism and Autonomy

One master narrative is that individuals, regardless of gender, have the power or agency and autonomy to make change and define success in SC. However, communication and experience are "always structured by discourses of power" beyond the individual (Trethewey, 2001, p. 189). Because of this master narrative, professionals struggle to adopt certain attitudes and behaviors. For example, many women search for ways to manage "like a man." There are gendered expectations for men and women about "moving up" and "out" of "dead-end" service jobs in communication. Importantly, the assertive, ambitious woman is made responsible for her own personal and professional success (Trethewey, 2001).

Narrative for Organizational Practice: Diversity and Equality

The rhetoric of equality has overtaken organizational life. However, the equality narrative allows for a cloak of tolerance and tokenism in place of true equity, rather than promoting difference and allowing non-dominant perspectives to be part of institutional value and decision-making. Parker (2002) argued, "Race and gender conflicts are inevitable as non-dominant culture interests and experiences are suppressed, devalued, and muted through organizational discourses that privilege dominant culture interests and experiences" (p. 252), such as the calls for diversity and quality.

The relationship management paradigm, although valuable in its practical contribution to organizations that wish to better their relationships with some publics, still has not clearly addressed the constitutive process of SC because of the "lack of focus on communication in the relationship building process" (deBussy, 2013, p. 294). We argue that the constitutive lens of communication might expose the meanings behind diversity and equity in relationships, thus allowing for further dialogue and co-construction of the value of equity and difference in relationships.

Narrative for Strategic Communication Outcomes: Reputation Repair

"Reputation repair" plays out by researchers and practitioners looking at the deficits or gaps in plans, processes, expertise, or knowledge of organizations, organizational systems, and employees. According to Coombs (2015), reputation repair "seeks to reduce the negative effects a crisis has on the organization's reputation and related assets" (p. 142). The focus on reputation and repairing what can go wrong normalizes a "fix-it" perspective. Under this narrative, employees are scrutinized for their potential for error or for filling gaps in knowledge and skill, and are valued only so much as their ability to alleviate a potential crisis and maintain organizational reputation. The skill level for employees becomes narrowed, as does the range of training and backgrounds that organizations view as relevant for ameliorating crisis.

While perhaps not obvious on the surface, there are latent gender and power meanings within this accepted approach to SC for organizations. The norms of "fixing it" and one-way communication essentially required to repair a reputation are stereotypically associated masculine traits that are positively reinforced in professional and organizational settings. Deficits – lack of power, strength – do not meet the potential to fix a problem facing the organization. There were no published studies found from the last 10 years that interrogated the meanings of gender within the crisis communication context.

This is a significant gap in moving forward with dialogue on how the different parts of SC practice and theory reinforce ongoing assumptions about what is masculine and good and what is feminine and bad, in terms of reputation, strength, and power for an organization. By revising expectations of success (read reputation repair) and the process by which to get to that success, we add our analysis of what is the good gender and which is the better gender for SC in organizations.

(Re)conceiving the Framework for Strategic Communication

Taking the theoretical groundwork laid out above, along with the awareness of master narratives guiding SC, we (re)conceive the framework for SC. The new framework derives from a socioecological model that visualizes where influences occur on gender and power within a body of professional discourse. The socioecological model suggests that multiple layers of influence impact an individual's rendering of meaning and communication (see Figure 19.1). This multiple-level perspective considers how societal norms, organizational behavior, and individual identities reconstitute and get reconstituted by gender and power. The levels of influence include ideology, which plays out at the societal level, through media and through social norms; institutional, which includes organizational culture, policy, and practices; professional, which embeds both routines and practices as well as discursive practices governed by professional associations; and individual, where factors such as identity, cognition, self-efficacy, and job satisfaction come into play and affect personal behaviors. Each level of the model affects the level embedded within it, and all levels should be considered in SC practice and research.

The socioecological model considers how gender is discursively constituted at different layers of influence, and produces counter-narratives in order to re-vision what gender and power could be in SC. The levels of influence are fluid when it comes to discursive practice and interact to produce the narratives that implicitly guide communication and gender. Thus, by creating counter-narratives that embed the different levels of influence, we hope to re-vision the field in ways that can be discursively shared. Below are three holistic, critical, and intersectional narratives that encounter the different levels illustrated by a socioecological approach to SC.

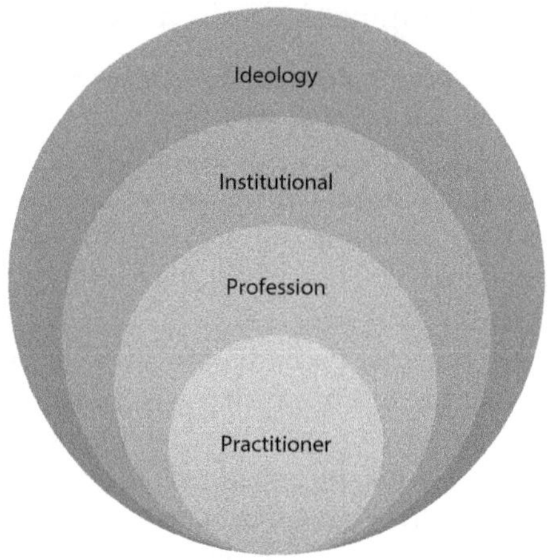

Figure 19.1 Socioecological model used for analyzing gender in strategic communication.

Identity and Community

Identity here can be defined as the qualities of a person, group, or entity that helps define it and what others perceive it to be. This can be applied to the identity of a person, organization, or profession. Identity in public relations can be connected to an individual or a community of practitioners. The narrative of individuality should be redefined with a community imperative. Community can be interpreted in multiple ways and include the community of stakeholders for an organization, community of scholars, communities of practice, and the larger, societal community. In SC, the profession must consider crafting a new identity for itself and in support of practitioners to successfully integrate multiple gender identities at work. Authors who write about public relations typically call it a pre-profession because it lacks such criteria as autonomy, a code of ethics, a body of knowledge, and licensing of its practitioners. However, personal efforts and associations have still to achieve the support of the majority of those who practice public relations, or the interest of government in regulating the practice. Although associations have created voluntary codes of ethics for their members to acknowledge, these codes have yet to be challenged as problematic in how they reinforce beliefs about gender and labor (Rakow & Nastaisa, 2008).

Regarding societal community, that which is feminine and masculine is reinforced through social discourse, media, and other tools that present ideological norms. This resonates with Botan's definition of publics that emerge and establish identities through discourses. People shape their cultures through the activity of discourse, creating a meaning system that ascribes gender characteristics and their resulting power in human interactions. Both men and women experience gendered constraints because their identities are constantly questioned through all communicating acts (Aldoory et al., 2009). For example, Aldoory et al. (2009) identified what it is to be masculine – individualism, rationality, competition, work in the public sphere, and suppression of the private sphere – and ascribed less-valued characteristics to the feminine – cooperation, community, and work in the private sphere. Through the use of language, signs, and objects, marketers, advertisers, and SC practitioners should become more aware that they reinforce masculine or feminine meanings through these characteristics, especially through the use of stereotypes and gendered expectations.

Equity and Organizational Accommodation

While the body of research in SC has already forged ground in addressing equity, it needs to continue to uncover differential practices and theory that prevent equity. This can be done through hearing the voices of under-represented employees and organizational publics. Scholars need to share their findings with organizations and communicators in order for the research to translate into practical value for communication in context. Parker (2002) interviewed 15 African American women executives to explore their communicative strategies for negotiating workplace interactions. Parker found that "the different, and sometimes seemingly conflicting, communication strategies enacted by these African American women executives can be understood as attempts to 'un-fix' these meanings. Aspects of the formal structure, such as meetings and cross-functional networks, became sites for negotiating informal power relationships in which the women asserted their identity as Black women, as executive leaders, and as legitimate members of the organization" (p. 266). Anzaldua (2002) described the need for influence to come from outside as well as from within: you are aware of the changeability of racial, gender, sexual, and other categories rendering the conventional labelings obsolete. Though these markings are outworn and inaccurate, those in power continue using them to single out and negate those who are "different" because of color, language, notions of reality, or other diversity. You know that the new paradigm must come from outside as well as within the system (p. 541).

Organizations are gendered and raced to the extent that power relations are patterned through taken-for-granted, often hidden, assumptions about gender and race that are embedded in organizational discourses and that privilege the experiences and interests of the dominant racial and gender group (White, middle-class men) (Parker, 2002, p. 252).

Institutions can take several steps to recreate their gender identity to be open and to have multiple meanings. Organizations must become advocates for multiplicative gender enactment in order to stay competitive in the changing labor market. They could become advocates by offering incentives to managers for changing culture and acceptance of differing gender enactments, such as health and retirement benefits for all partnerships and families; a larger conversation about their collective responsibility to multiple genders and how it could play out successfully in mission and vision of the organization; and re-trainings around gender identity and gender roles for supervisors.

Professional Development and Community Outcomes

The outcomes from SC should include not only success by organizational standards, but also success in terms of professional and community success. Professionals in communication resist master narratives by *crafting new identities for themselves and for the profession.* Trethewey (2001) studied aging women in the workforce and found that some women who resisted the master narrative of decline did so through crafting new identities. For example, some women created new selves based on their unpaid work and outside hobbies; for others, they found ways to integrate other parts of themselves into their work identities. Similarly, Parker's (2002) participants attempted to communicate in ways that were counter to the "identity" norms for senior leadership. This identity work, however, will not address the ultimate concerns of gender discrimination unless "a full accounting of the politics … is addressed by individuals, organizations, and the larger culture" (Trethewey, 2001, p. 213).

Professional associations such as the Public Relations Society of America have work–life committees that educate members about salary inequities based on gender, how discriminatory practices limit advancement, and model policies on family leave. Strategic communicators also have opportunities to increase organizational contributions to their communities because they often create employee volunteer programs and oversee charitable giving.

Case Example

Strategic communication would be strengthened by its actors acknowledging the multiplicative and discursive ways that gender and power influence decision-making. We encourage theorists to examine the gendered social constructions of publics and organizations as efforts are made to build relationships through communication campaigns. We identified such gendered master narratives as individualism and autonomy, communication equality, crisis and reputation repair, and offer counter-narratives that allow for broader understandings of gender and power. We now turn to a case example to illustrate how discourse and power is at work to define gender and power.

Confronting the Master Narratives of Abercrombie & Fitch

Gendered comments made in 2006 by Abercrombie & Fitch (A&F) CEO Mike Jeffries resurfaced in a 2013 *Business Insider* story (Lutz, 2013), causing national controversy and losses to the fashion retailer in reputation, sales, and stock prices. Jeffries had said:

> In every school there are the cool and popular kids, and then there are the not-so-cool kids. Candidly, we go after the cool kids. We go after the attractive all-American kid with a great attitude and a lot of friends. A lot of people don't belong [in our clothes], and they can't belong. Are we exclusionary? Absolutely. Those companies that are in trouble are trying to target everybody: young, old, fat, skinny. But then you become totally vanilla. You don't alienate anybody, but you don't excite anybody, either. (Denizet-Lewis, 2006)

This statement was coupled with A&F's strategy to not carry women's clothing above a size 10 while 14 is the average American women's size (Jarvis, 2013). Yet the company offered over-size male clothes to appeal to strong male athletes (Lutz, 2013).

Jeffries' comments brought condemnation from all sides. Celebrities Ellen DeGeneres and Kirstie Alley criticized the company's marketing strategy (Adams, 2013). Protester and former Abercrombie & Fitch customer, Cali Lindstrom, told ABC News: "Its body discrimination and its bullying and it encouraging bullying" (Jarvis, 2013). Blogger and activist Jes M. Baker posed in a series of mock Abercrombie & Fitch ads, smartly titled "Attractive & Fat" together with a male model (Adams, 2013). The images present a counter-narrative in SC that publics can use to challenge the gender and body expectations posed by Abercrombie & Fitch. Baker addressed Jeffries in an open letter: "I challenge the separation of attractive and fat, and I assert that they are compatible regardless of what you believe" (Adams, 2013) (see Figure 19.2 for an example of Baker's ad series).

Twelve days into the controversy, Abercrombie & Fitch issued on Facebook an official statement from CEO Jeffries (from Temin, 2013):

> I want to address some of my comments that have been circulating from a 2006 interview. While I believe this 7-year-old, resurrected quote has been taken out of context, I sincerely regret that my choice of words was interpreted in a manner that has caused offense. A&F is an aspirational brand that, like most specialty brands, targets its marketing at a particular segment of customers. However, we care about the broader communities in which we operate and are strongly committed to diversity and inclusion. We hire good people who share these values. We are completely opposed to any discrimination, bullying, derogatory characteristics or other anti-social behavior based on race, gender, body type or other individual characteristics.

His words were not well accepted. His apology is about how publics misinterpreted his meaning, and not about how sorry he is for the content of his message. *The Huffington Post* reported

Figure 19.2 "Attractive & Fat" by Jes M. Baker.

that consumer perception among 18 to 34-year-olds plummeted after CEO Jeffries' comments resurfaced (Bradford, 2013). Reuters reported that A&F revealed "another double digit drop in quarterly same store sales" following the CEO's post (Cavale, 2013).

Abercrombie & Fitch was definitely not a controversy-free company prior to the *Business Insider* story. On the one hand, "the brand is arguably more blatantly in-your-face about sex and body image than other brands marketed to teenagers" (McGregor, 2013), but the teens who had loved Abercrombie & Fitch were the retailer's primary targeted consumers (Thrasher, 2013).

In likely response to the backlash to Jeffries' comments, in November 2013 Abercrombie & Fitch redirected its branding strategy, announcing that it would carry larger-size women's clothes in 2014 (Cavale, 2013; Guo, 2013). However, controversies over the company's image strategy continue as A&F's Jeffries retired in December 2014 (Lutz & Peterson, 2014).

Analysis of the Case

Abercrombie & Fitch had been known for its strategic brand decisions for many years with limited controversy for its consumers, teenagers, who until 2013 had supported CEO Jeffries' narrative of his company's decision to use "exclusion" and the stereotype of "coolness" to sell its clothing to "all-American kids with great attitudes and a lot of friends," thus limiting its fashion to small sizes for women and extra-large sizes for athletic men. These themes had worked very successfully from an SC perspective. They are also illustrative of the master narratives of gender at work and also how invisible and "natural" gender distinctions and roles can be. A&F had, up until the Jeffries comments (not inflammatory in 2006, but were in 2013), reinforced successfully societal beliefs that women should be thin to be attractive. The "in-your-face sexualized body-image ads" were greeted positively by A&F's customers.

That Jeffries rebutted the controversy by claiming that he'd been quoted out of context continued to reinforce his position of power. His apology is slow to appear, allowing for the narrative to get away from him by his most important publics – his consumers – but also the traditional and social media. When the apology came, it was in keeping with societal expectations that organizations must express care and concern for diversity and inclusion, citing the typical list of anti-discrimination topics: “opposition to derogatory characteristics based on race, gender, body type or other individual characteristics.” However, from a feminist framework, Jeffries’ language continued to reinforce socially acceptable beliefs without addressing the objections of his publics, which had changed their interpretation over time to A&F’s strategy to celebrate “thinness,” and the all-American stereotype.

Effective SC would suggest that to operate in the public sphere an organization’s messages must be publics-centered, requiring that it be in constant adaptation as social values change. In response to the *Business Insider* rehashing of 7-year-old comments, A&F seemed blindsided by an activist public that no longer accepted earlier gender stereotypes. Secondary reports from the A&F case suggest that an organizational adjustment to the public sphere was made – women could find larger-sized A&F fashions. However, the quelling of this image controversy was apparently not enough to avoid Jeffries having to resign as CEO.

Conclusion

This chapter potentially brings up more questions than answers, and that is one of our goals: to critique the absence of gender dialogue in SC and to offer space to reconstitute the discursive constructions of gender and power in the field. This chapter seeks to reveal the broader concerns in efforts to achieve organizational, professional, and individual goals. Strategic communication as an organizational communication function accepts a public sphere as part of its theorizing, but has to become more complicated by gender, race, and LGBTQ issues that constrain and fuel work practices and scholarship.

After posing a socioecological model of influence, we challenged the current discursive norms with counter-narratives to consider, share, and construct in SC. Much more research needs to be done, though, in particular on historically under-represented groups and how they experience gender at work. We need to also include men in our conversations, as gender, race, and queer theory include men’s constraining roles and implicit tactics of power. Eventually, we hope that practice and research will take into account the dual role of SC practitioners to both create and transform the social and institutional systems that guide professional and individual beliefs and practices, and contribute to a multiplicity of meanings in SC.

Discussion Questions

1. How have you observed that organizations communicate that they value masculinity over femininity?
2. How, through advertisements, can you identify the usage of master narratives based on social norms to depict gender, race, and sexuality?
3. In addition to the A&F case, can you give examples of how publics have influenced organizations to change their communication about gender, race, or sexual orientation?

Links

Abercrombie & Fitch website: http://www.abercrombie.com/shop/us
Business Insider: www.businessinsider.com
The Militant Baker: http://www.themilitantbaker.com

References

Acker, J. (1990). Hierarchies, jobs, bodies: A theory of gendered organizations. *Gender & Society*, 4 139–158.

Acker, J. (2006). Inequality regimes: Gender, class, and race in organizations. *Gender & Society*, 20 441–464.

Adams, R. (2013, May 20). 'Fat' Abercrombie ads are a brilliant response to CEO Mike Jeffries. *Huffington Post.* Retrieved from http://www.huffingtonpost.com/2013/05/20/fat-abercrombie-ads-photos_n_3308199.html

Aldoory, L. (2005). A (re)conceived feminist paradigm for public relations: A case for substantial improvement. *Journal of Communication*, 55(3), 668–684.

Aldoory, L. (2009). Feminist criticism in public relations: How gender can impact public relations texts and contexts. In R. L. Heath, E. L. Toth, & D. Waymer (Eds.), *Rhetorical and critical approaches to public relations II* (pp. 110–123). New York: Routledge.

Aldoory, L., & Toth, E. L. (2000). The complexities of feminism in communication scholarship today *Communication Yearbook*, 24 345–361.

Aldoory, L., Reber, B. H., Berger, B. K., & Toth, E. L. (2009). Provocations in public relations: A study of gendered ideologies of power-influence in practice *Journalism and Mass Communication Quarterly*, 85, 735–750.

Anguiano, C., & Castaneda, M. (2014). Forging a path: Past and present scope of critical race theory and Latina/o critical race theory in communication studies. *Review of Communication*, 14(2), 107–124.

Anzaldua, G. E. (2002). Now let us shift… the path of conocimiento… inner work, public acts. In G. E. Anzaldua & A. Keating (Eds.), *This bridge we call home: Radical visions for transformation* (pp. 540–578). New York: Routledge.

Ashcroft, K. L. (2014). Feminist theory. In L. L. Putnam & D. K. Mumby (Eds.), *The SAGE handbook of organizational communication: Advances in theory, research, and methods* (pp. 127–150). Thousand Oaks, CA: Sage.

Botan, C. H. (2018). *Strategic communication theory and practice: The cocreational model* Hoboken, NJ. Wiley-Blackwell.

Bradford, H. (2013, May 16). Abercrombie & Fitch's reputation takes a hit after CEO's 'fat' comments re-surface. *Huffington Post.* Retrieved from http://www.huffingtonpost.com/2013/05/16/abercrombie-reputation-ceo-comments_n_3288836.html

Buzzanell, P. M. (1994). Gaining a voice: Feminist organizational communication theorizing. *Management Communication Quarterly*, 7(4), 339–383.

Capper, C. A. (2015). The 20th-year anniversary of critical race theory in education: Implications for leading to eliminate racism. *Educational Administration Quarterly*, 51 791–833.

Cavale, S. (2013, November 6). Abercrombie & Fitch offer larger sizes by spring. *Reuters.* Retrieved from http://www.reuters.com/article/abercrombie-analystday-idUSL3N0IR4TW20131106.

Chegwe, E. (2014). A gender critique of liberal feminism and its impact on Nigerian law *International Journal of Discrimination and the Law*, 14 66–78.

Chevrette, R. (2013). Outing heteronormativity in interpersonal and family communication: Feminist applications of queer theory "Beyond the Sexy Streets." *Communication Theory*, 23 170–190.

Coombs, W. T. (2015). The value of communication during a crisis: Insights from strategic communication research. *Business Horizons*, 58 141–148.

deBussy, N. M. (2013). Refurnishing the Grunig edifice: Strategic public relations management, strategic communication and organizational leadership. In K. Sriramesh, A. Zerfass, & J.-N. Kim (Eds.), *Public relations and communication management* (pp. 79–92). New York: Routledge.

Denizet-Lewis, B. (2006, January 4). *The man behind Abercrombie & Fitch.* Retrieved from http://www.salon.com/2006/01/24/jeffries

Falkneimer, J., & Heide, M. (2014). From public relations to strategic communication in Sweden *Nordicom Review*, 35, 123–138.

Gamson, J. (2003). Reflections on queer theory and communication. *Journal of Homosexuality*, 45 385–389.

Grunig, L. A. (1988). A research agenda for women in public relations. *Public Relations Review*, 14(3), 48–57.

Guo, J. (2013, November 20). Abercrombie & Fitch to offer plus-sizes. *CNN Money*. Retrieved from http://money.cnn.com/2013/11/20/investing/abercrombie-fitch-plus-sizes/index.html.
Hallahan, K., Holtzhausen, D., van Ruler, B., Verčič, D., & Sriramesh, K. (2007). Defining strategic communication. *International Journal of Strategic Communication*, 1(1), 3–35.
Holtzhausen, D. R., & Zerfass, A. (2013). Strategic communication: Pillars and perspectives of an alternative paradigm. In A. Zerfass, L. Rademacher, & S. Wehmeier (Eds.), *Organisationskommunikation und public relations. Forschungsparadigmen und neue perspektiven* (pp. 73–94). Wiesbaden: Springer VS. [Reprinted in K. Sriramesh, A. Zerfass, & J-N. Kim (Eds.). (2013). *Public relations and communication management. Current trends and emerging topics* (pp. 283–302). New York: Routledge.
Holtzhausen, D. R., & Zerfass, A. (2015). Strategic communication: Opportunities and challenges of the research area. In D. Holtzhausen & A. Zerfass (Eds.), *Routledge handbook of strategic communication* (pp. 3–17). New York: Routledge.
Hon, L. C. (1995). Toward a feminist theory of public relations *Journal of Public Relations Research*, 7 27–88.
Horsford, S. D. (2010). Mixed feelings about mixed schools: Superintendents on the complex legacy of school desegregation *Educational Administration Quarterly*, 46 287–321.
Jackson, S. (2006). Gender, sexuality and heterosexuality: The complexity (and limits) of heteronormativity *Feminist Theory*, 7 105–121.
Jarvis, R. (2013, May 15). Abercrombie & Fitch faces protests, backlash for not selling larger sizes. *ABC News*. Retrieved from http://abcnews.go.com/blogs/entertainment/2013/05/abercrombie-fitch-faces-protests-backlash-for-not-selling-larger-sizes
Ledesma, M. C., & Calderón, D. (2015). Critical race theory in education: A review of past literature and a look to the future *Qualitative Inquiry*, 21, 206–222.
Lie, R., & Servaes, J. (2015). Disciplines in the field of communication for development and social change *Communication Theory*, 25, 244–258.
Lutz, A. (2013, May 3). Abercrombie & Fitch refuses to make clothes for large women. *Business Insider*. Retrieved from http://www.businessinsider.com/abercrombie-wants-thin-customers-2013-5
Lutz, A., & Peterson, H. (2014, December 3). Abercrombie & Fitch is running out of options. *Business Insider*. Retrieved from http://www.businessinsider.com/abercrombie-and-fitch-earnings-2014-12
McDonald, J. (2015). Organizational communication meets queer theory: Theorizing relations of "difference" differently *Communication Theory*, 25 310–329.
McGregor, J. (2013, May 22). Abercrombie & Fitch's big, bad brand mistake. *Washington Post*. Retrieved from https://www.washingtonpost.com/news/on-leadership/wp/2013/05/22/abercrombie-fitchs-big-bad-brand-mistake
Nachescu, V. (2009). Radical feminism and the nation *Journal for the Study of Radicalism*, 3 29–59.
Parker, P. S. (2002). Negotiating identity in raced and gendered workplace interactions: The use of strategic communication by African American women senior executives within dominant culture organizations *Communication Quarterly*, 50 251–268.
Pompper, D. (2005). "Difference" in public relations research: A case for introducing critical race theory *Journal of Public Relations Research*, 17 139–169.
Pompper, D. (2012). On social capital and diversity in a feminized industry: Further developing a theory of internal public relations *Journal of Public Relations Research*, 24 86–103.
Pompper, D., & Jung, T. (2013). "Outnumbered yet still on top, but for how long?" Theorizing about men working in the feminized field of public relations *Public Relations Review*, 39 497–506.
Rakow, L. F. (1989). Information and power: Toward a critical theory of information campaigns. In C. T. Salmon (Ed.), *Information campaigns: Balancing social values and social change* (pp. 164–184). Newbury Park, CA: Sage.
Rakow, L., & Nastaisa, D. I. (2008). On feminist theory of public relations: An example from Dorothy Smith. In O. Ihlen, B. Van Ruler, & M. Fredricksson (Eds.), *Public relations and social theory: Key figures and concepts* (pp. 252–277). New York: Routledge.
Temin, D. (2013, May 17). When is an apology not an apology? New lessons from Abercrombie & Fitch. *Forbes News*. Retrieved from http://www.forbes.com/sites/daviatemin/2013/05/17/when-is-an-apology-not-an-apology-new-lessons-from-abercrombie-fitch.

Thrasher, M. (2013, July 10). How consumers fell in and out of love with Abercrombie & Fitch. *Business Insider*. Retrieved from http://www.businessinsider.com/the-rise-and-fall-of-abercrombie-and-fitch-2013-7

Tindall, N. T. J., & Waters, R. D. (2013). *Coming out of the closet: Exploring LGBT issues in strategic communication with theory and research* New York: Peter Lang.

Toth, E. L. (1988). Making peace with gender issues in public relations. *Public Relations Review*, 14(3), 36–47.

Toth, E. L., & Aldoory, L. (2001). *The gender challenge to media*. Cresskill, NJ: Hampton Press.

Toth, E. L., & Cline, C. G. (1989). *Beyond the velvet ghetto*. San Francisco, CA: IABC Research Foundation.

Toth, E. L., & Cline, C. G. (1991). Public relations practitioner attitudes toward gender issues: A benchmark study *Public Relations Review*, 17 161–174.

Trethewey, A. (2001). Reproducing and resisting the master narrative of decline: Midlife professional women's experiences of aging *Management Communication Quarterly*, 15 183–226.

Werder, K. P. (2015). The integration of domains: Multidisciplinary approaches to strategic communication campaigns. *International Journal of Strategic Communication*, 9(2), 79–86.

Yep, G. A., Lovaas, K. E., & Elia, J. P. (2003). Introduction: Queering communication: Starting the conversation. In G. A. Yep, K. E. Lovaas, & J. P. Ella (Eds.), *Queer theory and communication: From disciplining queers to queering the discipline(s)* (pp. 1–10). New York: Routledge.

Yoder, J. D., & Kahn, A. S. (1992). Toward a feminist understanding of women and power *Psychology of Women Quarterly*, 16 381–388.

PART VI

Strategic Communication and Health

20

Strategic Communication Campaigns in Health

Satveer Kaur-Gill and Mohan J. Dutta
National University of Singapore
Mohan J. Dutta
Massey University

Introduction

That communication strategically, developing communication based on a plan, improves the quality of health outcomes shapes the scholarship and practice of health communication. Identifying problems of health to be examined, developing and implementing research designs, and incorporating the emerging lessons from research into practices of communicating health (Atkin & Rice, 2013; Dutta, 2005). Historically, the literature on communication campaigns has formed a key area in health communication scholarship, with an emphasis on the strategic use of communication (Atkin & Wallack, 1990). Strategy in this sense refers to the process of planning, driven by objectives and formative research carried out on key publics, and culminating in an evaluation framework that guides the evidence to be generated for theory building (see Botan, this volume). In the health communication literature, this is a key point; the evaluation of campaigns generates the empirical evidence, which in turn, shapes the theorizing informing future strategy (Dutta, 2005). Strategy, referring to the process of planning, is closely intertwined with implementation or, what is referred to as tactics. In the messy world of carrying out health campaigns, the academic language separating strategy from tactics makes little sense. I offer the term "strategic implementation" as a way to capture the iterative, intertwined, and embedded relationship between strategy and tactics in the context of campaigns. The scholarship of health communication campaigns is driven by the evidence generated from strategic implementation (Dutta, 2005) and, in turn, shapes the framework of health communication campaigns (Atkin & Rice, 2013). At the heart of the development of health communication strategy is the systematic gathering of data on the various aspects of campaigns, which constitutes the body of knowledge on communication campaigns and is built into the ongoing development of campaigns. In this chapter, we will review the literature on strategic health communication campaigns, draw out the key lessons that have emerged from the literature, and point to future directions for strategic communication (SC) scholarship in health.

In doing so, the chapter will first offer an overview of the framework of health communication campaign processes, depicting the ways in which these processes incorporate elements of strategy. It will then identify the key elements of the strategic framework, drawing attention to the ways in which these elements are incorporated into the campaign design process. Of

The Handbook of Strategic Communication, First Edition. Edited by Carl H. Botan.

particular interest to effective health communication strategy is the role of formative research as a tool for understanding the characteristics of the audience and working with these characteristics to create effective health communication campaigns. We will also attend to the increasing importance of community-based processes in health communication, foregrounding the ways in which these processes shape the formulation of health communication strategy.

Campaign Processes

Strategy is key to the very definition of health communication campaigns, incorporated into the concept of effectiveness that defines health campaigns (Atkin & Rice, 2013; Dutta, 2005). Campaigns are planned communication efforts that are directed at producing behavior change in a target audience within a specified timeframe. Integral then to the definition of campaigns is the concept of planning. Campaigns emerge with specified objectives, tied to outcomes that they are set to achieve within the specified timeframe. These outcomes are tied to the evaluation framework of health campaigns, with campaigns being evaluated on the basis of the objectives they set out to achieve. The process incorporated into the health communication frameworks depicts the strategic elements of health communication, drawing on and forming the bases for health communication scholarship that examine different aspects of communication strategy.

Health Campaign Process

The health campaign process is linear, setting objectives, gathering information about audience, setting the strategic framework, and implementing the tactics. The concept of strategy is intertwined with the treatment of communication as episodic, outlining a set of steps in a sequential order in order to reach effectiveness. The skeleton of the campaign process is built on the understanding of communication as uni-directional, emerging from the sender and generating behavior change in the recipient, with the strategic plan establishing a pre-determined framework for objectives. The various strategic elements of communication then are tied to configuring the most effective ways of reaching out to the audience to produce change. What defines the concept of health communication campaigns is therefore the effectiveness of communication, its ability to induce change in the recipient along the lines desired by the sender of the message. In the following section, we discuss the strategic elements of the health communication campaign.

Strategic Elements

In this section, we summarize the key areas from the literature on the overarching nature of the strategic elements in health communication campaigns. Health communication campaigns are dominantly molded within a specific paradigm of thinking on how to modify health behaviors toward intended positive health outcomes. However, campaigns have also come to communicate unintended effects (Cho & Salmon, 2007), indicating a need to discuss health communication campaign processes and outcomes in shaping health discourses in both positive and negative ways. Cho and Salmon (2007) define health campaigns as social actions. Understanding health communication campaigns from the point of view of social actions attends to the ways in which imbalances in power constitute the differentials in attention various stakeholders in society compete for (Dutta, 2005). These include the evaluation of the outcomes by these social actions (Cho & Salmon, 2007; Guttman, 1997; Salmon, 1989). When thinking about campaigns from the perspective of power imbalances, the identification of these imbalances can be understood from how the source, message, and appeal affect message transmission and its unintended outcomes. In order to address these shortcomings and suggest new directions, we first begin by discussing campaign elements before moving on to a critique of the strategic processes.

The design of campaigns is definitionally tied to the strategic employment of communication activities (Rice & Atkins, 2012; Rogers & Storey, 1987; Snyder, 2007; Sood et al., 2014). Communication activities are organized in a manner that it is targeted for a well-defined population within an organized timeframe, for the purposes of accomplishing a specific and measurable goal (Snyder, 2007). Fundamentally, the process of campaign formulation is typically designed with intentioned decisions to influence health behavioral outcomes through a formulation of communication activities that are specific, strategic, and intentional (Rogers & Storey, 1987; Sood et al., 2014). The literature suggests that campaigns that were notably successful had ascribed to the strategic processes of campaign development (Briscoe & Aboud, 2012). Yet, the effect sizes of campaigns continue to be debated (Noar, 2006).

Aboud and Singla (2012) and Briscoe and Aboud (2012), in discussing health communication campaigns in developing countries, indicate the need for further examination of the strategic process to offer greater insight into behavior change theories and how to target for specific and tailored audiences. The authors also discuss the way behavior has been operationalized to locate elements of opinions and attitudes as determinants of behavior, providing a critique that such an operationalization fails to include other factors that are non-cognitive. These include how environmental factors limit behaviors, as well as the role of social structures. Furthermore, the authors express the value of evidence of campaign successes as key to understanding best practices in the development of health communication campaigns.

Currently, the literature discusses approximately 27 principles that contribute to good campaigns (Becker et al., 1992). Noar and Head (2011) discuss the limitations of strategic campaigns when campaign planners cherry-pick a few of these principles, as opposed to working through all of the principles in an integrated way. According to Noar and Head (2011), this is a limitation of current campaigns focusing on certain principles over others, such as an overemphasis on theory, message appeal, or channel. Moving forward, health communication campaigns must also consider the contemporary trends of campaigns that include marketing principles and new media use as key considerations (Noar & Head, 2011). Despite mass media having the ability to create awareness among large groups of target audiences (Haider & Kreps, 2004), new media channels provide opportunities to disseminate messages in different ways. These include personalization and impersonalizaton of messages (Sundstrom, 2016). The ability of new media to reach audiences interpersonally can have an important influence on the persuasiveness of behavior change campaigns (Rogers, 2003). These shifts toward new media introduce new dimensions for strategy.

The literature on the strategic elements shapes the effectiveness of campaign design. The scholarship on communication strategy attends to the characteristics of each of the elements that leads to effectiveness. The communication elements are studied as isolated parts of the overall campaign, with the communication mix resulting from the systematic consideration of the different elements of communication. Much of the scholarship of campaign elements uses an experimental design to study the persuasive effects of a specific element. When designing campaigns, the knowledge regarding each component of communication is therefore included in an overall plan that would generate the desired results for the campaign planner.

Role of Formative Research #1

The campaign process begins with formative research, research that delves into the nature of the campaign issue/behavior, as well as the key characteristics of the audience. Of significance here are the characteristics of the audience that are considered most relevant in the campaign planning process. A clearly formulated framework for formative research gathers audience data, systematically organizes audience data, and then incorporates audience data into shaping effective communication strategy. Worth noting here is the vital role of research in shaping the campaign process, as a driver of the strategic planning framework. With the incorporation of relevant and key audience knowledge, campaign planners are able to develop strategies that are effective and efficient in producing change in the target audience.

Role of the Community #2

The community is the site of the intervention, the space where the health communication campaign is carried out. As will be noted later in this chapter, the earliest forms of health communication campaigns were carried out on the concept of the community, with key individuals in the community acting as agents of change. Categorized as opinion leaders in the campaign process, these key individuals disseminated the health message to the wider community and served as catalysts of the change process. The work of health communication strategy therefore was one of identifying the key characteristics of the community that can – as aggregates – serve the design of communication.

Message and Channel #3

Messages can be thought of from two perspectives. (1) The designing of the message itself to persuade target audiences to participate in health-related behaviors. (2) The mechanisms of dissemination to reach targeted audiences that constitute the message design. Rice and Atkin (2001) suggest that health campaigns are more effective if messages are advancing new behaviors as opposed to modifying them. Furthermore, campaigns that shared novel health information that had not become common knowledge in the public domain were found to have stronger persuasive effect (Robinson et al., 2014; Snyder & Hamilton, 2002). Snyder (2007) discussed a health communication campaign focusing on new mothers, or mothers-to-be, promoting the benefits of breastfeeding. The campaign consistently introduced a new language in the discourse on breastfeeding in its message design. This was understood as the key aspect of the campaign's success in terms of effectiveness. Similarly, enforcement messages (Rice & Atkin, 2001) that touch on the law – such as seatbelt campaigns – were found to be especially effective in terms of effect size. Other aspects of message design include source and appeal, which are discussed in the following subsections.

The delivery of messages across channels requires close examination of the intended audiences of the message. In thinking about message delivery, channels have often been discussed from the perspective of reach and exposure (Schooler et al., 1998). Researchers studying health campaigns discuss channels as having the ability to reach the widest targeted audience possible (Evans et al., 2009). According to the campaign's literature, in order to be effective, health communication campaigns must target channels in multiple ways. Channels include those relating to traditional mass media and social media. A study by Robinson et al. (2014) categorizes channels as traditional mass media – such as television, radio, and newspaper – and social media, referring to examples such as Twitter and Facebook. Furthering this breakdown, the authors coin the term "small media" as channels relating to fliers, posters, and brochures, and interactions in group settings such as workshops and forums. Channels of interpersonal interactions would include hotline counseling services. All of these potential channels must be carefully calibrated for maximum exposure to targeted audiences for strategic message dissemination. Dutta's (2004) study, however, argues that channels should be utilized depending on the motivations of the audience's health information-seeking behaviors. Therefore, channels that are typically consumed by active information seekers are channels that require one to participate actively in the message content in order to acquire health information (Atkin & Wallack, 1990). Such active information channels are fairly limited in their capacity to influence passive health audiences.

In other studies, the strategies for channel use were highlighted. The Stanford Community Studies on reducing cardiovascular disease in the US have been studied extensively in the health communication campaigns literature (Snyder et al., 2004) for their integrated and multidimensional approach to channel use. The Stanford Community Studies were noted for successfully utilizing various media components in message dissemination. Multiple channel use is aimed at achieving an extensive amount of exposure to campaign messages proposed by campaign researchers as critical in measuring campaign effectiveness (Baker & Rogers, 1993; Flora et al., 1997).

The literature discusses what channels are effective in reaching audiences in relation to health communication campaigns. The mass media are often cited as important channels for the dissemination of campaigns of health communication because of their effectiveness in behavioral change outcomes temporally (Randolph & Viswanath, 2004). Scholars investigating campaign effectiveness in the context of the US found that the effectiveness of health communication campaigns saw an approximately 7% shift in behavioral change from mass media campaign exposure (Snyder & Hamilton, 2002).

In more recent discussions in the literature, other channel forms are highlighted. Stephens et al. (2004) posit the value of community as a medium for sharing health campaign messages as communities have the greatest reach to target communities. These include infrastructures of communication that reach community members – such as community newsletters and social support networks. Other trends include the advent of technology, such as new media and social media, as necessary channels today when thinking about message dissemination and delivery to targeted audiences.

Source #4

The source of a message is known to be one of the key elements of message persuasiveness (Kim, 2017; Slater & Rouner, 1996). Sources of messages have had implications for message perception by targeted audiences (Kim, 2017). It is understood in the literature that the greater the source credibility, the more likely the reception of the message, with a corresponding shift in favorable attitudes toward campaign messages (Smith, De Houwer, & Nosek, 2013). How credible the source is, is related to attitudinal perceptions regarding health-related issues (Case et al., 2018). Key research on sources and campaigns reveals that in the discussion of source credibility, the trustworthiness and expertise of the source matter. Trustworthiness relating to advice, information, or argument, and expertise referring to a source's ability in terms of skill, knowledge, and the content of information, provide increased attention paid to the message (Case et al., 2018; Pornpitakpan, 2004).

Slater and Rouner (1996) – in a seminal piece on source attributes and message effectiveness – discussed extensively the relationship between source credibility and message effectiveness. To break it down, source attributes have multiple references to credibility – such as bias, identification, and expertise – that influence and impact the way messages are received by audiences in campaigns (Slater & Rouner, 1996). These factors impact message perception, because it is assumed that the target audiences are adopting "different processing strategies that result in the subsequent message arguments' being more readily accepted or rejected" (Slater & Rouner, 1996, p. 975). A source that is viewed as having greater similarity to the targeted audience has been found to encourage message acceptance rather than reactance (Zhang & Sapp, 2013). Kim's (2017) study on the indirect effects of source information on anti-smoking messages highlighted insights into the ways in which sources were construed from the perspective of "trustworthiness, intentions, and affiliations" (p. 654), with important implications for the persuasiveness of messages.

A dominant way of conceptualizing what sources may look like in campaign development has been the adoption of the elaboration likelihood model (ELM) as a theoretical framework for deducing message development (Petty & Cacioppo, 1986). Where the message is likely to appeal because of one's motivation to learn, factual sources of information that are rich in informative elements would be considered to be more effective. On the contrary, less involvement would require techniques such as heuristics or strategic cues because the individual is processing information peripherally. These types of messages might use sources that are "issue-irrelevant message cues" (Flynn et al., 2011, p. 977), where the message development can be focused on "the attractiveness of the source, the presence of an 'expert' opinion, or the quantity of information presented" (Weber, Westcott-Baker, & Anderson, 2013, p. 308).

In more recent research, Niederdeppe, Shapiro, and Hye (2014), in studying obesity-related policies, located the value of narrative as a persuasion technique for health communication campaigns. They offer insights into how narrative techniques have the potential to impact and influence policy. Thus, the study indicates that sources can also be conceptualized from the standpoint of narratives, with narrative use as a persuasion technique when designing sources for messages.

Sources in messages are used to facilitate the process of persuasion on shifting behavioral outcomes, a key goal of health communication campaigns. Atkin and Rice (2013) highlight the role of sources in shifting a target audience's position by carefully selecting the type of source for the message. A few ways to think of sources could include the similarity and dissimilarity of a source with an intended target audience, the credibility of sources, as well as the level of engagement in a message that contributes to internalizing of a message. In thinking from a community-centered health communication campaign, the similarity of a source to community groups can include community residents who are most identifiable by community members that are the targets of health communication campaign messages (Morgan, Miller, & Arasaratnam, 2002; O'Toole et al., 2003). The engagement of community members will be discussed further later in the chapter.

Appeal #5

Another aspect of the campaign element entails thinking about how messages are designed with specific appeals, a strategy used to change people's behaviors based on how the content of the message is delivered (Carey & Sarma, 2016). These appeals can include emotions, fear, and threats, a few common forms discussed in the communications campaigns literature. The fear appeal is a strategy studied since 1953, and was derived based on practical thinking about how greater fear invoked in a message would more likely cause individuals to be receptive to the campaign message (Carey & Sarma, 2016). Fear appeals can be broken down into three key variables that include fear, perceived threat, and perceived efficacy, where fear refers to the emotive state and threat refers to the cognitive aspects of the materialization of fear (Witte & Allen, 2000). These variables come to interact with each other intricately (Witte & Allen, 2000).

Based on key understandings regarding the emotive response of fear, Wong and Cappella (2009) argue that fear appeals persuade targeted audiences to avoid destructive health behaviors. This is done through messaging that typically constitutes graphic and gory content (Witte & Allen, 2000). This leads individuals to take up self-protective behaviors (Wong & Cappella, 2009). The literature in this area continues to reflect dissimilar views. Researchers such as Lewis, Watson, and White (2013) suggest that messages which focus on threat or fear can elicit emotions that were not intended by the campaign message, with adverse implications.

More recent research reveals that in creating fear through messages that adopt the fear appeal, other emotions – including anger, surprise, or irritation – may also follow. However, it remains unclear how these various responses interact with one another and affect the persuasion outcomes (Cho & Salmon, 2006; Dillard et al., 1996). Other unintended outcomes of fear appeals include stigmatizing individuals who partake in specific health behaviors. Thainiyom and Elder (2017) studied how emotional appeals used in campaigns to prevent HIV unintendedly caused audiences to have stigmatized perceptions and behaviors regarding the disease. These stigmatizing attitudes and behaviors were suggested to be an outcome of using fear appeals, as opposed to other forms of appeal that instead focused on information or on hope-centered messages. As summarized by the authors, studying appeals can be critical to not just ensure behavior change, but also commit to strategies of communication that do not create further harm to victims of health conditions (Thainiyom & Elder, 2017). Cho and Salmon's (2006) research indicates that in order to minimize the unintended outcomes of fear appeals, behavioral change must be conceptualized from the perspective of stages, where the effects of fear appeals must relate to the targeted audience's own stage of development toward behavioral change. The use of fear appeals continues to be an important strategy adopted in public health communication campaigns for persuading target audiences to shift health behaviors. It is understood as an important element in motivating individuals to their goal state, so long as audience efficacy is high in relation to the management of their protective health behaviors (Peters, Ruiter, & Kok, 2013).

Understanding the strategic elements of health communication campaigns entails thinking about campaigns from a perspective of how behaviors are impacted by communication campaigns. A key aspect of the strategic process has been a focus on the individualized response to campaigns, specifically looking at the ways in which behavioral outcomes are measured at the individual level. In reference to the discussion on source, message, and appeal, the strategic processes involved in the selection and curation of campaign messages are ultimately tied to changing norms, knowledge, attitudes, and beliefs at the level of the individual as the key aspect of the campaign, resulting in an individualistically focused campaign process. Despite little agreement on campaign success, a broad consensus on the relatively modest impact campaigns have had on behavioral outcomes is acknowledged (Noar & Head, 2011). Studies indicate an average 8% expected change in positive health behaviors in health communication campaigns (Snyder et al., 2004). Dutta (2005) postulates that the small effect sizes of campaigns may be attributed to the focus on individualized conceptualization of health behaviors in campaigns. Now that we have discussed the key strategic elements of health communication campaigns, we will turn to the innovations and new directions in campaign scholarship.

Innovations and New Directions in Campaign Scholarship

The literature on health communication campaigns is situated amid large-scale transformations in the wider context of health. The emergence of new and innovative communication technologies, the role of communities in shaping health communication campaigns, critical approaches to health campaigns, and culture-centered approaches to health campaigns capture some of the contemporary directions in the literature.

Technology-Based Interventions

Acknowledging the role of technology as an efficient and effective channel for the dissemination of health messages, technology-based strategic health communication campaigns address the ways in which new communication technologies can drive campaign strategy (Noar, 2006). Of particular importance is the interactive nature of new communication technologies, which enable message tailoring. Integral to the framework of message tailoring is the interaction of the communication, with the message received by the audience tied to her/his most salient characteristics. Based on the characteristics of the target audience, health messages are strategically presented as responsive to the particular characteristics that have been identified. Key then to the framework of message tailoring is the identification of specific characteristics in the target audience that would serve as the basis of effective tailoring. Whereas many interventions use stages of behavior change as the basis of message tailoring, reaching an audience member with a message that is suited to her/his position in the process of change, other interventions use psychographic, personality, and demographic characteristics to build tailoring. Key in the tailoring framework is the acknowledgment of individual-level differences in shaping the communication mix. Interactivity enables communication practitioners to experiment with the various elements of communication and how they are weaved into a campaign. Moreover, campaigns incorporating digital health records and large databases can build in messages as reminders responding to particular characteristics that are captured in the database.

Community-Based Interventions

The community is increasingly acknowledged as a vital player in the design and development of health communication interventions (O'Toole et al., 2003). The earliest health communication interventions were often situated at the community level, targeting entire communities with campaigns. The history of health communication within the development communication framework attends to the community-based nature of health campaigns. The community is conceptualized as a tool for disseminating health messages. Community-based participation contributes to effective dissemination through the deployment of community peer leaders and health workers embedded in the community. The earliest forms of diffusion of innovation campaigns in health identified opinion leaders in the community, who served as instruments for diffusing the message in the community.

Internationalizing Health Campaigns

Although the roots of the health communication literature have been international, with much of the early development communication literature in health emerging from field studies conducted in the Global South, the knowledge produced internationally has mostly been absent from hegemonic health communication structures in the US, spaces where campaign knowledge is generated and reproduced (Dutta, 2005). Increasingly, the discipline has internationalized, with the presence of scholars from international contexts conducting important work on the effective strategies and tactics underlying health communication campaigns. Reflecting global trends in concerns about health and communication and the patterns of international expertise, areas such as technology-based health interventions and communication around epidemics have seen the emergence of scholarship that is international and that shifts the locus of knowledge production. However, there are two points to be noted about these shifts in the production of knowledge of strategic health campaigns. First, the shift reproduces and replicates US/Euro-centric patterns and claims to knowledge, with new international contexts offering new sites for testing and extending US-centric knowledge. Second, the shift, although a reflection of internationalization, obfuscates the North–South inequalities in the production of knowledge, with voices from the Global South erased from the sites of knowledge production regarding strategic health communication campaigns. The hegemonic framework of SC is reproduced through the incorporation of international contexts.

Critical Approaches to Campaigns

Critical approaches to health communication campaigns interrogate the overarching logics of campaigns, constituted within hegemonic structures of global health (Dutta, 2005). Interrogating the power inequalities in the distribution of opportunities for communication, critical approaches note the ways in which communication in health campaigns is shaped by the agendas of dominant actors. Attention is paid to the strategies of incorporation and co-optation within the hegemonic structures that perpetuate the dominant logics, operating within the neocolonial and capitalist interests of global power. The voices of the subaltern margins are erased as campaigns target subaltern bodies as target audiences of interventions.

Culture-Centered Interventions

Culture-centered interventions seek to invert the inequalities in the distribution of communication, seeking to build infrastructures for communication at the margins that are owned by communities at the margins (Dutta, 2008). The work of building these communication infrastructures is situated in resistance to dominant structures that erase subaltern voice, often co-opting such voice in the form of formative research that guides expert-driven campaign strategy (Dutta, 2011). Conceptualizing communication inequalities as the inequalities in distribution of opportunities for voice, the culture-centered approach (CCA) seeks to invert these inequalities through partnerships with communities at the margins (Dutta, 2011). The CCA foregrounds the meaning-making capacities of communities, recognizing the decision-making capacity of communities at the margins as strategic communicators. The power of communication is therefore shifted into the hands of communities at the margins, seeking to develop communication solutions emerging from communities at the margins and targeting to bring about change in the structural inequalities in the dominant structures. Culture-centered campaigns therefore emerge as campaigns for health as a human right, identifying the structural challenges to health and seeking to transform these structural challenges (Dutta et al., 2019). As opposed to seeking behavior change, culture-centered campaigns seek structural transformation by co-creating democratic spaces for community participation anchored in socialist imaginaries (Dutta et al., 2019). The goals of such campaigns are to bring about revolutionary transformations in how health and wellbeing are organized through collaborations with marginalized communities, activists, movements, and political parties based on the principles of grassroots democracy.

Conclusion

In conclusion, the body of scholarship on strategic health communication campaigns offers robust evidence on the various elements of communication and their effectiveness. The literature points toward some key findings that form the basis of planned social change communication in the arena of health, guided by strategy. The transformations in the technology landscape and in the international nature of health communication as a field have contributed to some broad changes and shifts in the conversations of health campaigns. These conversations offer new anchors to taking forward the challenges of SC.

References

Aboud, F. E., & Singla, D. R. (2012). Challenges to changing health behaviours in developing countries: a critical overview. *Social Science & Medicine*, 75(4), 589–594.

Atkin, C. K., & Rice, R. E. (2013). Theory and principles of public communication campaigns. In R. E. Rice & C. K. Atkin (Eds.), *Public communication campaigns* (pp. 3–19). Thousand Oaks, CA: Sage.

Atkin, C. K., & Wallack, L. M. (1990). *Mass communication and public health: Complexities and conflicts.* Newbury Park, CA: Sage.

Baker, T. E., & Rogers, E. M. (Eds). (1993). Organizational aspects of health communication. *campaigns*: What works? Thousand Oaks, CA: Sage.

Becker, H. K., Agopian, M. W., & Yeh, S. (1992). Impact evaluation of Drug Abuse Resistance Education (DARE). *Journal of Drug Education*, 22(4), 283–291.

Briscoe, C., & Aboud, F. (2012). Behaviour change communication targeting four health behaviours in developing countries: A review of change techniques. *Social Science & Medicine*, 75(4), 612–621.

Carey, R. N., & Sarma, K. M. (2016). Threat appeals in health communication: Messages that elicit fear and enhance perceived efficacy positively impact on young male drivers. *BMC Public Health*, 16(1), 645. doi:10.1186/s12889-016-3227-2

Case, K. R., Lazard, A. J., Mackert, M. S., & Perry, C. L. (2018). Source credibility and E-cigarette attitudes: Implications for tobacco communication. *Health Communication*, 33(9), 1059–1067.

Cho, H., & Salmon, C. T. (2006). Fear appeals for individuals in different stages of change: Intended and unintended effects and implications on public health campaigns. *Health Communication*, 20(1), 91–99.

Cho, H., & Salmon, C. T. (2007). Unintended effects of health communication campaigns. *Journal of Communication*, 57(2), 293–317.

Dillard, J. P., Plotnick, C. A., Godbold, L. C., Freimuth, V. S., & Edgar, T. (1996). The multiple affective outcomes of AIDS PSAs: Fear appeals do more than scare people. *Communication Research*, 23(1), 44–72.

Dutta, M. J. (2004). Primary sources of health information: Comparisons in the domain of health attitudes, health cognitions, and health behaviors. *Health Communication*, 16(3), 273–288.

Dutta, M. J. (2005). Theory and practice in health communication campaigns: A critical interrogation. *Health Communication*, 18(2), 103–122.

Dutta, M. J. (2008). *Communicating health: A culture-centered approach*. New York: Polity Press.

Dutta, M. J. (2011). *Communicating social change: Structure, culture, agency*. London: Taylor & Francis.

Dutta, M. J., Pandi, A. R., Mahtani, R., Falnikar, A., Thaker, J., Pitaloka, D., Dutta, U.(2019). Critical health communication method as embodied practice of resistance: Culturally centering structural transformation through struggle for voice. *Frontiers in Communication*, 4(67). doi:10.3389/fcomm.2019.00067

Evans, W. D., Uhrig, J., Davis, K., & McCormack, L. (2009). Efficacy methods to evaluate health communication and marketing campaigns. *Journal of Health Communication*, 14(4), 315–330.

Flora, J. A., Saphir, M. N., Schooler, C., & Rimal, R. (1997). Toward a framework for intervention channels: Reach, involvement, and impact. *Annals of Epidemiology*, 7, S104–S112.

Flynn, B. S., Worden, J. K., Bunn, J. Y., Connolly, S. W., & Dorwaldt, A. L. (2011). Evaluation of smoking prevention television messages based on the elaboration likelihood model. *Health Education Research*, 26(6), 976–987.

Guttman, N. (1997). Ethical dilemmas in health campaigns. *Health Communication*, 9(2), 155–190.

Haider, M., & Kreps, G. L. (2004). Forty years of diffusion of innovations: Utility and value in public health. *Journal of Health Communication*, 9, 3–11.

Kim, H. (2017). The indirect effect of source information on psychological reactance against antismoking messages through perceived bias. *Health Communication*, 32(5), 650–656.

Lewis, I., Watson, B., & White, K. M. (2013). Extending the explanatory utility of the EPPM beyond fear-based persuasion. *Health Communication*, 28(1), 84–98.

Morgan, S. E., Miller, J., & Arasaratnam, L. A. (2002). Signing cards, saving lives: An evaluation of the worksite organ donation promotion project. *Communication Monographs*, 69(3), 253–273.

Niederdeppe, J., Shapiro, M. A., Kim, H. K., Bartolo, D., & Porticella, N. (2014). Narrative persuasion, causality, complex integration, and support for obesity policy. *Health Communication*, 29(5), 431–444.

Noar, S. M. (2006). A 10-year retrospective of research in health mass media campaigns: Where do we go from here? *Journal of Health Communication*, 11, 21–42.

Noar, S. M., & Head, K. J. (2011). Trends in the research and practice of health communication campaigns: Research and practice of health communication campaigns. *Sociology Compass*, 5(6), 426–438.

O'Toole, T. P., Aaron, K. F., Chin, M. H., Horowitz, C., & Tyson, F. (2003). Community-based participatory research: Opportunities, challenges, and the need for a common language. *Journal of General Internal Medicine*, 18, 592–594.

Peters, G. J. Y., Ruiter, R. A. C., & Kok, G. (2013). Threatening communication: A critical re-analysis and a revised meta-analytic test of fear appeal theory. *Health Psychology Review*, 7(S1), S8–S31.

Petty, R. E., & Cacioppo, J. T. (1986). *Communication and persuasion: Central and peripheral routes to attitude change*. Springer Science & Business Media.
Pornpitakpan, C. (2004). The effect of celebrity endorsers' perceived credibility on product purchase intention: The case of Singaporeans. *Journal of International Consumer Marketing*, 16(2), 55–74.
Randolph, W., & Viswanath, K. (2004). Lessons learned from public health mass media campaigns: Marketing health in a crowded media world. *Annual Review of Public Health*, 25(1), 419–437.
Rice, R. E., & Atkin, C. K. (2001). *Public communication campaigns* (3rd edn). Thousand Oaks, CA: Sage.
Rice, R. E., & Atkin, C. K. (Eds.). (2012). *Public communication campaigns*. SAGE publications.
Robinson, M. N., Tansil, K. A., Elder, R. W., Soler, R. E., Labre, M. P., Mercer, S. L., ... & Community Preventive Services Task Force. (2014). Mass media health communication campaigns combined with health-related product distribution: a community guide systematic review. *American Journal of Preventive Medicine*, 47(3), 360–371.
Rogers, E. M. (2003). *Diffusion of innovations* (5th edn). New York: Free Press.
Rogers, E. M. (2004). A prospective and retrospective look at the diffusion model. *Journal of Health Communication*, 9, 13–19. doi:10.1080/10810730490271449
Rogers, E. M., & Storey, D. (1987). Communication campaigns. In C. Berger & S. (Eds.), Handbook of communication sciences (pp. 817–846). Newbury Park: Sage.
Salmon, C. T. (1989). *Information campaigns: Balancing social values and social change*. Sage Publications, Inc.
Schooler, C., Chaffee, S. H., Flora, J. A., & Roser, C. (1998). Health campaign channels: "tradeoffs among reach, specificity, and impact". *Human Communication Research*, 24(3), 410.
Slater, M. D., & Rouner, D. (1996). How message evaluation and source attributes may influence credibility assessment and belief change. *Journalism & Mass Communication Quarterly*, 73(4), 974–991.
Smith, C. T., De Houwer, J., & Nosek, B. A. (2013). Consider the source: Persuasion of implicit evaluations is moderated by source credibility. *Personality and Social Psychology Bulletin*, 39(2), 193–205.
Snyder, L. B. (2007). Meta-analyses of mediated health campaigns. Mass media effects research: Advances through meta-analysis, 327–344.
Snyder, L., & Hamilton, M. (2002). A meta-analysis of US health campaign effects on behavior: Emphasize enforcement, exposure, and new information, and beware the secular trend. In R. C. Hornik (Ed.), *Public health communication: Evidence for behavior change* (pp. 357–383). Mahwah, NJ: Lawrence Erlbaum Associates.
Snyder, L. B., Hamilton, M. A., Mitchell, E. W., Kiwanuka-tondo, J., Fleming-Milici, F., & Proctor, D. (2004). A meta-analysis of the effect of mediated health communication campaigns on behavior change in the United States. *Journal of Health Communication*, 9(1), 71–96.
Sood, S., Shefner-Rogers, C., & Skinner, J. (2014). Health communication campaigns in developing countries. *Journal of Creative Communications*, 9(1), 67–84.
Stephens, K. K., Rimal, R. N., & Flora, J. A. (2004). Expanding the reach of health campaigns: Community organizations as meta-channels for the dissemination of health information. *Journal of Health Communication*, 9(S1), 97–111.
Sundstrom, B. (2016). Mothers "Google it up": Extending communication channel behavior in diffusion of innovations theory. *Health Communication*, 31(1), 91. doi:10.1080/10410236.2014.936339
Thainiyom, P., & Elder, K. (2017). Emotional appeals in HIV prevention campaigns: Unintended stigma effects. *American Journal of Health Behavior*, 41(4), 390–400.
Weber, R., Westcott-Baker, A., & Anderson, G. (2013). A multilevel analysis of antimarijuana public service announcement effectiveness. *Communication Monographs*, 80(3), 302–330.
Witte, K., & Allen, M. (2000). A meta-analysis of fear appeals: Implications for effective public health campaigns. *Health Education & Behavior*, 27(5), 591–615.
Wong, N. C. H., & Cappella, J. N. (2009). Antismoking threat and efficacy appeals: Effects on smoking cessation intentions for smokers with low and high readiness to quit. *Journal of Applied Communication Research*, 37(1), 1–20.
Zhang, Q., & Sapp, D. (2013). Psychological reactance and resistance intention in the classroom: Effects of perceived request politeness and legitimacy, relationship distance, and teacher credibility. *Communication Education*, 62, 1–25.

21

Cocreating in the Wonderland
Communication and Patient-Oriented Healthcare in Russia

Alexandra Endaltseva, Nelli Bachurina, and Maria Mordvinova

L'École des hautes études en sciences sociales (EHESS), National Research University Higher School of Economics (HSE)

> *Alice thought she had never seen such a curious croquet ground in her life; it was all ridges and furrows; the balls were live hedgehogs, the mallets live flamingoes, and the soldiers had to double themselves up and to stand on their hands and feet, to make the arches.*
>
> (Lewis Carroll, *Alice's Adventures in Wonderland*)

In the era of post-truth and healthcare 2.0, when lay experts have equal credibility as medical professionals and when the internet challenges the techniques of seeking and gaining health information, healthcare systems are in need of change. The key to the path of systemic change lies in un-knowing not only the ways health issues have been communicated, but also the very process of the production of meanings of health. In Russia, neglecting the critical assessment of communication strategies in healthcare (or, as the direct translation suggests, *health protection*) might well result in the field looking like the famous croquet game in *Alice's Adventures in Wonderland*. Reconciling the strategies of each "hedgehog" and each "flamingo" through a careful consideration of constantly fluctuating goals might be a much-needed shift to cocreation in Russian health communication.

In this chapter we discuss the messy meaning-making strategies (and their interactions) which characterize Russian health communication today. We open our discussion by situating the game field that produces the meaning of health in contemporary Russia. In this opening, we introduce the key health communicators (pharmaceuticals, governmental or regulatory actors, the institutional medical sector, health professionals, and patient nongovernmental organizations [NGOs] and communities) and how they share the field. We then introduce the Russian national strategy of patient-oriented health protection and the contradictory meanings that each sector of communicators attaches to it. We elaborate on the mismatch in communication of patient-oriented health protection, discussing the successes and failures of health communication practices in different sectors. We analyze how the government, activists, institutions, business, and medical professionals communicate their meanings, the place of other communicators in campaign planning and execution, and how flexible and interactive the practices of each communicator sector are. We conclude with propositions on how the road toward patient-oriented health protection can be built in Russia.

The Handbook of Strategic Communication, First Edition. Edited by Carl H. Botan.

"A Very Difficult Game Indeed": Situating the Communication Game Field

After being established as a new country in the 1990s, the Russian Federation went through a number of systemic reforms. These reforms have been applied to different parts of civil society, including the healthcare sector, where there was a shift from the strategies of the Soviet Semashko public healthcare model toward mixed insurance-based healthcare provision. The problem was how to reconcile this new healthcare provision model with the constitutional right to free healthcare and with the established sociocultural image of medical professionals as public servants. The shift toward insurance-based healthcare provision has been implemented top-down, along with the other shock economic policies. It was not properly prepared or explained. The officials were blindly following neoliberal models taken from Western developed countries. Finally, the entire process was implemented with scarce material resources and an economic crisis affecting virtually every sphere of life for Russian citizens. All in all, the health reforms that accompanied the formation and maturation of a new country have not been integrated well into the public meaning of good care and health protection. The governmental failure to communicate reforms and to involve the public in the integration of new healthcare models into everyday realities (ideally, however, the entire process of reforming would include the public) still affects how different actors act and react within the field of *health protection*. This process manifests as dangerous self-treatment, distrust in the quality of care, medical staff that juggle public and private clinical work, and patient NGOs that start serving as mediators between patients, the government, and the business sector. And although the state is now reaching out to the patient community to cocreate the new strategies and tactics in healthcare communication, the field is still too fragmented and immersed in the shadows of past reforms.

Russian film director Andrei Khlebnikov, in his film *Arrythmia*, has captured how the tragic legacy of chaotic structural changes is playing out on intrapersonal, interpersonal, organizational, and societal levels. In *Arrythmia*, doctors and paramedics are underpaid and question their values and commitments in light of the absence of a proper reward for their work. Hospitals are underequipped and have little knowledge capacity to properly implement the models imposed on them by governmental officials. Managerial decisions are detached from the ambiguity of on-the-ground medical work and, finally, the idea of "healthcare modernization" appears as a ground-shaking force in this precious system. The major systemic conflict, which results in personal tragedies for the people who do the work, in Khlebnikov's reading is the conflict in the meaning of *health protection*. Health professionals act in the interest of ensuring the fastest improvement for a given patient; nonmedical health management – in the interest of maintaining a manageable healthcare system amid the sociopolitical chaos. Or, shall we say, the major conflict is strategic communication (SC) responsibilities articulated by no party in this story. Khlebnikov's depiction is quite representative of the state of health communication in Russia today. The "croquet ground" might be "curious" yet the game is still being played. The sections that follow will expand on how exactly the game is being played and what looks to be working or not for the participants.

Finally, as an important caveat in situating the Russian healthcare game field we want to emphasize that there are considerable income and cultural gaps among the different regions in Russia. The high heterogeneity of the field limits the generalizations that we propose in this chapter. The practices and processes of health protection and health communication differ immensely in each region. While Moscow hospitals may provide their patients with state-of-the-art diagnostic machinery for free with state insurance, some small Siberian towns may have a shortage of syringes and may solicit bribes to ensure that anesthesia works. Therefore, all systemic processes in Russian healthcare must be regarded through the lens of the high variability of their translations on the ground.

Players on the "Croquet Ground"

The "croquet ground" of Russian healthcare described above is being created and recreated by different players, their practices, and often conflicting commitments and strategies. We call these actors *communicators.* The meanings of health protection that each communicator includes within their practices are often contradictory. Institutional budget optimization tactics, for example, are not compatible with the medical staff's commitment to attend to the patient's needs. Nevertheless, they coexist within the same game field and, hence, their tactics are blended with the tactics of the other communicators. In this respect, the actions of each communicator (neoliberal reforms, patient-oriented care, public accountability, opening of new markets) are cocreated with the meanings that other communicators introduce into the field. And in some cases, as in the case of patient organizations or in some cases clinical trials, the strategies themselves are co-created because otherwise it would be impossible to act.

Zvonareva et al. (2017) present an example of such cocreation in their study of patients' enrollment in clinical trials. In transition times, the common strategy of medical institutions in precarious situations has been to take matters into their own hands. What that has meant in most cases is looking for windows of opportunity within the strategies of other communicators. Medical institutions were "pleading to officials for support, requesting aid and assistance grants from the international community, participating in international research projects and, finally, joining commercial clinical trials [...] Russia quickly earned a reputation as a location where eligible and often treatment-naïve patients could be easily identified and quickly enrolled due to a highly centralized healthcare system" (p. 7).

Using the momentum provided by such a reputation, medical institutions joined clinical trials in the pursuit of their own interests (which included improving the material base, better communication with patients). Although collaborative work between the medical professionals and the pharmaceutical industry is often perceived negatively, in this case medical professionals were able to use recruitment for clinical trials for the provision of care, communication and follow up, going beyond the top-down imposed neoliberal treatment protocol. Patients also used participation in the trials to their benefit. According to Zvonareva et al. (2017), the patients who participated in trials have gained by learning new techniques to measure their pulse, having a regular medication regime, establishing close relationships with care providers, and gaining a sense of belonging to the research team. "One common strategy Russian CVD patients reportedly use is to try to be admitted to a hospital as often as possible in order to gain access to physicians and receive their attention," which was problematic (Zvonareva et al., 2017, p. 16).

In a similar manner, the Russian Union of Patients, a public organization uniting independent patient organizations and communities, emerged in 2010 as a strategic grassroots union advocating patients' interests. The strategy of uniting different patient organizations developed in anticipation of the election year of 2008. At this time, the ruling party was building its arguments around the issues successfully resolved in the first presidential term, and health was one of them. The leaders of the most prominent patient organizations gained momentum and started to form relationships with those in power by exchanging favorable constituencies for providing Russian chronic patients with the governmental coverage of treatment and civil rights protection. In a similar manner as building on governmental strategies, patient organizations sought support from the pharmaceutical companies, brought together experts from the professional medical ethics committee, and formed public advisories to the Ministry of Healthcare. Thus, the Russian Union of Patients became a junction for the different strategies and the key communicator of the new "patient-oriented model of health protection."[1]

The idea of a patient-oriented model of health protection has gradually appeared as the economic conditions in the country stabilized and as health information became more available within and beyond national borders. The national healthcare strategy, the mass media, and the marketing slogans all across the country showcase that the key communicators (from the government to the patient organizations) have come to an agreement that orientation toward the patient must be the basis for communication in the field. However, the meaning of patient-centeredness is still under construction. For some communicators it is patient = client; for some, patient = partner; for others the patient is a consumer, subordinate, etc. The following section will elaborate on how different communicators construct the meaning of patient-centered healthcare, and how these meanings relate to each other and to the communicators' strategies.

Practices that Work, Practices That Fail: Cocreating Patient-Oriented Health Protection

According to a survey conducted by the Russian Public Opinion Research Center in October 2017, 52% of Russians were dissatisfied with the quality of healthcare, 37% were satisfied, and only 9% of responders could characterize the state of the Russian healthcare system as being of high quality (Ehffektivnost Rossijskogo Zdravoohraneniya i Sistema OMS [Efficiency of the Russian healthcare and government-funded insurance policy], 2017). The decision-makers started to realize that in order to satisfy the needs and meet the requirements of Russian citizens, the entire healthcare system needs to be reorganized. Satisfying healthcare needs meant not only an improvement in the quality of life in the country, but also securing a loyal constituency. Such a reorganization strategy has been given the name of the ***national strategy of patient-oriented health protection***. The Russian healthcare "croquet ground," however, does not have an agreement on how this reorganization should proceed: each sector – medical professionals, government decision-makers, patient groups, and pharmaceuticals – is struggling with incorporating the ambiguous national strategy into their daily practices. Importantly, the discussion of what patient-oriented health protection means in practice for different actors started to happen only after the strategy had been declared at the official round tables, in strategic documents, and in the mass media. So now each sector unavoidably negotiates their established and new practices with the other sectors, building on the strategies and practices of different communicators. Therefore, rather than talking about the national strategy of patient-oriented health protection, we offer a notion of the patchwork of meanings of patient-oriented health protection which forms the health communication field.

Government Communication Practices

As the Russian healthcare system is highly regulated by the government (e.g. as regards advertising, doctors' choice of national generics over international originals, and the closed information policy), communicating legislative decisions plays an important role in making patient-oriented care a reality. One can hardly speak seriously of strategic actions until:

> patient-centered care can be elevated above a philosophical and historic point of debate by legislation that regulates healthcare and consumer rights, and that makes non-compliance with said legislation punishable by law. This is the only way to bring patient-based care to the forefront of the Russian healthcare system; to make it an official and integral part of the government-provided healthcare plan; and to ensure the advancement and promotion of patient-based care throughout the Russian community. (Pavlovskykh & Shardin, 2015)

Ironically, the announced governmental strategy of patient-oriented health protection coexists with a health optimization plan, where one of the requirements is for the medical professionals to spend no more than 15 minutes with one patient. These 15 minutes include not only dealing with the patient's needs, but also filling out the documentation, which is still being done manually by the health professionals.

Another major bump on the road to being patient-oriented is the strong ideological component embedded in government health communication. In governmental rhetoric, healthcare is not only a constitutionally protected sphere of life, but also the basis for ideology-building and reinforcement. For instance, techniques which allow Russian patient organizations to advocate the coverage of expensive treatments for rare diseases, or the improvement of life for disabled people, often come down to persuading decision-makers to have a loyal constituency among chronic patients or to keep public discontent from manifesting on the streets. However, government officials resist the cocreational view, introducing public health campaigns in a top-down manner without perceiving communication campaigns as having a direct effect on the realization of government plans. The reasons for this resistance are both the historical image of the government as the protector of health and the most credible expert, and the lack of informational transparency or clarity (and, therefore, critical assessment) of how health-related macro decisions are made. For example, the government-run online campaign which claims that donating blood is beneficial for the donor prompts many Russians to eagerly donate, which they do often without questioning whether alternative sources of information support this claim (Hrebtovskaya, 2017).

The Constitution of the USSR stated that the health of its citizens was one of the country's most precious resources. In the practices of health protection in the USSR, great emphasis was placed on protection. Many Russians to this day are eager to leave health-related systemic decisions to governmental protectors. Historically, Russians have been proud that the state is responsible for the health of its citizens. This responsibility is manifest, for example, in a requirement for all working people to undergo obligatory health checks each year (this practice is still present among most state employers, although more as a ritual of meaningless paper signing). It also includes provision of free care, the introduction of disease prevention education in the workplace, and support for disability communities.

Now, however, the long-established ideal that each person's healthcare is a government responsibility is being replaced by the sense of personal responsibility (without systematic communication interventions), creating discontent and poorly informed self-treatment among middle-aged and older Russian citizens. The authority of the Russian government in healthcare regulation is nevertheless supported by the majority of Russian citizens, which is why the government has an almost sacred status when it comes to translating the morality of health-related professions and imposing standards of quality in healthcare. Therefore, in order to make patient-oriented health protection meaningful beyond the legislative papers and rhetorical tactics, government decision-makers have to carefully consider how citizens cocreate the meanings of health and health protection. It is also important to consider the conflict of meanings that different practices of "heath protection" bring about. Careful consideration of whether the practices of different communicators coincide with the actual governmental strategy is the "moving soldier arch" on the field of Russian healthcare and a path toward SC.

Activist Communication Practices

In the 1980s, Russian health protection experienced a shift in its protector posture from the responsible state to an abstract idea associated with no distinct actor. The reason for that was the fall of the USSR and the economic crisis which accompanied this fall. The state was left with an elaborate infrastructure of public health institutions, staff were trained on the moral idea of care, and patients expected to receive care. Yet the state had no resources, either financial or intellectual, to manage this residue in the new realities.

This shift of posture prompted chronically ill patients and their relatives to unite and form patient communities. Yan Vlasov, the president of the Russian Multiple Sclerosis Society and the co-chair of the Russian Union of Patients, mentions that at that time both medical professionals and proactive chronic patients realized that the only protector in the constantly changing environment was the joint activist effort. This realization led to the formation of organizations of chronic patients' NGOs which consisted of patients, their relatives, and proactive doctors, and which advocated treatment provision and constitutional patient rights. As it is phrased on the Russian Union of Patients' website, the formation of patient organizations as a key communicator happened because in Russia "the salvation of the drowning is in the hands of the drowning."[2] With the increasing availability of information and community development via the internet, these patient organizations started to gain in membership and knowledge resources (outreach to immobile patients or patients in remote areas, reading medical journals, organizing webinars, etc.). Nevertheless, Russian sociologists indicate that patient organizations are one of the least researched areas of Russian society (Krashennikova, 2009; Masyuk, 2015; Shirokova, 2011). The reasons are claimed to be lack of unity or lack of a single patient movement, but these are not the only reasons.

Russian patient organizations are composed of chronic patients, their relatives, and sometimes doctors. They do not receive financial support from the state, other than through very scarce and highly competitive government grants. Due to recent government regulations, they are losing support from the pharmaceutical companies which previously provided them with resources (such as space or supplies for community events) and knowledge (training in internet use, financial matters, or legal literacy, etc.). They self-manage their online resources and self-organize rehabilitation and educational campaigns, such as patient schools. And they keep all this quiet. In other words, in order to stay vital and do the work, patient organizations use targeted, personalized communication tactics, tailored to each stakeholder. They provide officials with loyalty and absence of public escalation; they provide the mass media with speakers, expert opinions, and in-community research. For medical professionals they provide collaborating patients, and for institutions they offer constructive criticism and scandal mitigation. Finally, they provide pharmaceuticals with educated clients adhering to the treatment routine. With these practices, patient organizations cocreate their strategy with a multitude of other communicators, balancing the needs and resources and finding the middle ground that serves each party. Unlike it is perceived in the government enactment of patient-oriented health protection strategy, patient organizations do not reduce their agency to that determined by the government. They actively coconstruct the meanings of patient-oriented health protection and communicate their strategies based on their embodied experience and within the meaning windows that other communicators bring to the field.

Such an approach to SC has made patient organizations the leading actors in building patient-oriented health protection in Russia, and the communicators who showcase the best practice of cocreation in SC. Such cocreational SC has allowed patient organizations to introduce the idea of patient-centeredness into the agendas of the other health sectors. As Yuri Zhulyov, the co-chair of the Russian Union of Patients, mentioned in his address to the participants of the All-Russian Congress of Patients in 2017, today patient organizations have become mediators between the government, business, and the patient community.

Institutional Communication Practices

Patient advocacy organizations and patient communities, including the League for Healthcare Consumer Rights Protection and the Russian Union of Patients, have been and still are at the forefront of making patient-oriented health protection a national priority and a personal right in Russia. However, the meanings of health, care, and health protection that the patients and other concerned publics act on are often not considered by the institutions that provide care, creating a discrepancy between announced and perceived expertise.

Yuri Zhulyov, the co-founder of the Russian Union of Patients, mentioned at the All-Russian Patients' Congress that patient-oriented health protection provides patients with rights as well as responsibilities to be knowledgeable about their condition. The materials of the annual forum for healthcare providers – "Competition in Healthcare" – meanwhile claim that while plenty of clinics in Russia's capital city of Moscow have been practicing patient-oriented health protection for 5 years, the other Russian regions still do not have cases to build on (Konkurenciya sistem vzglyadov i podhodov [Competition of systems of opinions and approaches], 2018). The relation between these two meanings suggests that healthcare providers understand patient-oriented health protection as the patient = client framework, not taking seriously the patient = partner framework communicated by the patient organizations. It also suggests that care providers see the practice of patient-oriented care as a one-way street, leaving patients with no agency – despite the fact that patients already create their own meanings. The roadblocks to the institutional communication of patient-oriented health protection, therefore, are not only the regional income inequalities in the country, but also the policies and practices of the healthcare providers themselves.

The increasing presence of patient-oriented care rhetoric in the media and health authority documents has prompted the professional medical sector to re-evaluate their practices in a search to cocreate their communication with these meanings. Medical institutions translate the meaning of patient-oriented care as a complex and varied approach to healthcare, individually tailored to each patient. Russian medical experts believe that patient-centered care cannot function without evidence-based medicine, which incorporates the latest scientific studies and tests into the care practices, helping patients to make informed decisions about their treatments.

The annual Russian forum "Competition in Healthcare" is the communication channel for progressive clinics to share their best practices of operating under the paradigm of patient-centered care and evidence-based medicine. The Moscow-based private clinic "Rassvet" is considered to be one of the best examples of the development of the Russian healthcare system. Rassvet claims to provide evidence-based medical care to patients who may have been misled by corrupt competitors who misinterpret the meaning of evidence-based medicine for their own gain. Meanwhile, the cost for a standard first-time consultation with a specialist in Rassvet is 4,000 rubles (as a reference, the average monthly salary in a town near Moscow would be around 15,000 rubles).

The state-run healthcare organizations (which provide free care with state insurance), in contrast, see patient-oriented health protection as represented by the patient's responsibility to form their own opinion and choose their own healthcare plans and providers. Unfortunately, patients can sometimes be misinformed by doctors who promote their expertise on social media. They are called *insta-doctors* (physicians with an Instagram account) who claim that only a professional doctor (emphasis on "doctor") should make medical decisions. One such *insta-doctor* convinced patients that advocates of evidence-based medicine were misleading them with fancy rhetoric and confusing medical facts. According to this doctor, doctors were simply trying to impress their patients, when really the patients do not need to be informed about the details of their diagnosis and treatment if they have a competent doctor (Minisiyarov, 2018). Therefore, the lack of agreement on the meaning of patient-oriented health protection created dangerous marketing tactics, feeding on distrust in the healthcare system and the tendency of patients to search the internet for health information.

At the same time, not all patients are ready to accept an evidence-based approach to medical care, especially when no explanatory communication campaign is being implemented, either by the government or by the healthcare providers. Kovaleva (2018) cites one patient's opinion as not believing "in all this evidence-based mambo-jumbo." For the healthcare professionals this is the equivalent of saying that a person does not believe in the multiplication table. Thus, health institutions are faced with the challenge of planning and implementing their communication strategy, cocreating both with the national strategy of patient-oriented health protection and conflicting meaning of health, existing among their publics. These conflicting meanings result in dangerous self-treatments, income-based health discrimination (not every patient can afford Rassvet and not every clinic has the same communication budget as Rassvet), distrust, and other negative effects.

The private clinics see patient-oriented health protection as promotion of evidence-based medicine, which requires financial investment, while emphasizing that the government run institutions leave patients with choices they are not informed enough to make. At the same time, there is a prejudice about the public–private healthcare dichotomy in the minds of the majority of older Russian citizens. The Soviet-era belief that government-funded healthcare is moral and good, while private medical practice is run by greed and deceit, is still resonating in the perceptions of Russian citizens. According to data from the Fund of Public Opinion, 52% of Russians believe that high-quality medical care is available for free (research from Fund of Public Opinion, 2019). Since the majority of Russians get medical services from government-funded clinics, their perception of the quality of medical care as stated above is based on their experience (Ruvinskiy, 2019). Larisa Rakitina, an expert doctor for one insurance company, noticed that patients of government-funded and private clinics are different. Patients of government-funded clinics are mostly low-income, pensioners, and state employees, whose mindset strongly resists the idea that medical care needs payment (Rakitina, 2014). This explains the prejudices that private medicine is corrupt or that government-funded medicine is moral. Nevertheless, private health institutions use such splits in meanings and prejudices to their advantage, to communicate the message that they provide higher-quality care and are more patient-oriented.

A survey conducted by the Russian Public Opinion Research Center in April 2017 showed that 40% of Russian citizens would prefer a combination of the two healthcare systems, where they would receive a private-class service through a government-funded insurance policy. The same survey indicated that 80% of consumers were satisfied with the quality of service they received in private clinics. The number of customers who were willing to pay extra to get better care kept increasing over the years (Ehffektivnost Rossijskogo Zdravoohraneniya i Sistema OMS [Efficiency of the Russian healthcare and government-funded insurance policy], 2017). Therefore, private healthcare institutions have created strategic messages of a patient = client (educated client) paradigm alongside the existing and historically situated meanings of good care.

Some government-funded clinics are also building on the patient = client paradigm communicated by private clinics, creating the meaning of the best practices in patient-oriented health protection. One of these clinics is the S. S. Yudin Hospital. Its Dean of Medicine reports on the multitude of "puzzle pieces that make up patient-centered care" as follows:

> Hospital administrative staff no longer have office hours, meaning that patients can approach any of the leading doctors or the Dean of Medicine at any time. The reception area is arranged in an open-space format, which contradicts the Soviet organization-centered approach, where the

> patients were made to physically and symbolically bow down to the powerful, superior doctors. Recreational areas are equipped with comfortable chairs and water coolers. The hospital security personnel are dressed in nondescript uniforms, making them seem less intimidating. (cited in Plisenkova, 2017)

This report showcases consideration of the overall experience of visiting a clinic in creating the communication strategy. Therefore, the design and user-friendliness of the clinic's website, the customer service of the clinic's reception, etc. become tactical tools in communicating and practicing patient-oriented healthcare in a co-creational way.

Business Communication Practices

During the Soviet era, the Russian pharmaceutical market was locally based, with a minor influx from the COMECON market (The Council for Mutual Economic Assistance). During market liberalization, Russia was flooded with foreign pharmaceutical goods. Private pharmaceutical companies, such as Protech, SIA, Biotech, and Genesis, made a massive push to get registered on the Russian market. The reasons varied: Russia had become a fruitful place for clinical trials (as already mentioned) and, at the same time, the demand for drugs was higher than ever due to the economic crisis and the crisis of in-house production. The trade laws, however, were still under-developed, causing plenty of fraud cases as well as a discrepancy between the market offers and the ability of the public hospitals (committed to free healthcare) to provide patients with expensive foreign drugs. Interestingly, this discrepancy gave a push to the emergence of public NGOs of chronic patients. According to the president of the Russian Multiple Sclerosis Society, it was when neurologists were prohibited by their institutions from prescribing expensive German treatments in the 1980s and 1990s (due to lack of resources) that the patients and their doctors started to mobilize and advocate for health.

Since then the volume of pharmaceutical products on offer has been maximized. By 2005, 76% of the pharmaceutical market was made up of generic products that were very different from the original trademark. The patient community has expressed concerns about compliance policies, clinical testing of generics, and the import substitution strategy imposed by the government on the pharmaceutical industry in the past few years. Also, due to the lack of transparency in the pharmaceutical market, differentiating between generic and original medications is still difficult, both for patients and their care providers, with the result that decision-making is left to marketing staff.

In the communication plan of the pharmaceutical companies, the patients are barely considered (unless they are chronic patients belonging to a patient organization). Under the current Russian law, prescription medication can only be advertised within the professional medical environment, such as at pharmaceutical conferences and in medical journals. Since prescription medication comprises over half of the whole market, advertising and marketing agencies tailor their campaigns mostly to healthcare providers, pharmacists, and expert patients. Non-prescription medications are less government-controlled, yet patients are still largely influenced by the doctors' and pharmacists' recommendations. Therefore, a patient-oriented approach in pharma communications has yet to be established: patients remain ill-informed and the validity of doctors' opinions is almost never questioned.

The danger of regarding patient-oriented health protection as a marketing trick can be demonstrated by the case of the Invitro diagnostic campaign. Invitro, one of Russia's leading medical companies that specializes in high-end diagnostics and various forms of treatment, used targeted marketing via text messaging, inviting their clients to get tested for sexually transmitted diseases. These messages used slogans such as "Nearly half of all men and a third of all women aged 16 to 40 have a sexually transmitted disease"; "Make sure your health isn't threatened by one of these highly contagious viruses" (Reklama ne Dolzhna Ubezhdat Cheloveka v Nalichii Zabolevaniya [Advertising should not convince a person in the presence of a disease], 2018). With such a campaign, Invitro undercut the patients' right to elicit meaning from their medical history, and the campaign was disrespectful to the public.

Building Relationships with Patients

According to the ADV Group, 12% of the Russian advertising market is composed of pharmaceutical advertising, while 23% of TV advertising budgets are spent on pharmaceuticals. In fact, pharmaceutical companies spend more on TV marketing than any other industry (Milosh, 2018). In Russia, advertisers reach their audiences mostly through TV commercials, and the competition in the pharmaceutical market is quite high. The main advertising technique is to show a person in pain taking medication which leads to instant relief. Lately, pharmaceutical companies have started to try new, edgy advertising tactics, some of which are not compatible with the idea of patient orientation. A good example is an advertising campaign for the anti-inflammatory medication Tantum Verde Forte, which aired on federal TV channels from December 2016 until May 2017. The advert featured popular Russian rapper Timati, who performed a song about the healing effects of this medication. The goal was to have the rapper reach out to the audience "while speaking their language" (Druzhinin, 2016). One could suppose that the advertising agency attempted to build their campaign on the meanings that resonate with young people, who were previously ignored by the marketing campaigns. However, the advertisers did not consider that young people communicate via social media and do not watch TV. The mostly middle-aged and older TV audiences, meanwhile, expressed their disdain for this advertising campaign. According to Alla Bogdanova, the head of marketing at Angelini Pharma Russ, the goal of the advertising campaign was "to stand out among the sea of identical commercials, to inform the consumers on the benefits of this medication, and to make an impact on the new target audience" (Druzhinin, 2016). The advertising agency which produced these commercials used a so-called company-based approach: "The idea came from the client – they needed a strong, masculine figure to showcase their product as the most effective in soothing a sore throat." Ekaterina Mikhno confirmed that this advertising campaign was not based on market research: "When we meet our potential clients – in this case a pharmaceutical company – we offer them a creative way of reaching their goals, and then we equip them with the necessary tools to do so" (Shirokova, 2012). Therefore, as SC is always based on the relationship between the organization and its public (as shown by research), this campaign cannot be an example of SC.

This example showcases how the failure to incorporate a "patient-oriented" campaign based on collecting strategic information and cocreation with the target audience results in the failure of both advertising agencies and the pharmaceutical "client." Advertising agencies that count on their clients (pharmaceutical companies) for revenue seem not to contradict their clients' wishes, even if a certain creative approach might hurt their clients' brand. This communication ill-practice appears to be a disruptive force in the shaky process of creating a collective meaning of patient-oriented health protection.

Building Relationships with Pharmacists

Due to the advertising regulations in Russia, pharmaceutical companies can hardly ever reach consumers directly. Meanwhile, the level of trust between pharmacists and consumers is a staggering 70–80%, which means that consumers trust pharmacies to make decisions on choosing the appropriate medication. Face-to-face interactions between pharmacists and consumers, therefore, present an important communication channel for the pharmaceutical business. Petrova, Sokolova, and Kononova (2006) point out the moral dilemma in such a situation: while answering the question "What cough medication would you suggest?," a pharmacist can either recommend a cheap medication (Bromgeksin or Mukaltin, for an average price of 30 rubles) or a more expensive alternative with the same active components (Lazolvan or ACC, for an average price of 300 rubles). Pharmacists base their advice on professional integrity and competency, the correlation between the price of the product and its quality, the corporate ***modus operandi*** (if there is a bonus from selling more), etc. When pharmacists are driven by empathy, politeness, excellent listening skills, proactiveness, and concern for the patient's situation, they establish meaningful long-term relationships with their customers, changing the strategy "sell more" to the strategy "sell well."

The promotion and distribution of pharmaceutical products from manufacturers to healthcare providers remain veiled in secrecy to Russian patients. For the most part, this process is mediated by the pharmaceutical representative, a medical care professional (usually a certified doctor or pharmacist) who informs healthcare providers about the latest medications and convinces them to recommend them to consumers. This job appeared in Russia with the arrival of foreign pharmaceutical companies in the Russian market. According to the fall 2017 research "The practicing physician's review" conducted by Ipsos research company, 51% of doctors view pharmaceutical sales representatives as the main source of current information, while 48% of doctors rely on medical journals (Na Osnovanii Dannyh Sindikativnogo Isledovaniya "Prindex Monitoring Naznachenij LP Vrachami" [On the data based on longitudinal research "Prindex monitoring prescriptions of physicians"], 2017). Therefore, pharmaceutical sales representatives play a key role in transmitting accurate information, especially on prescription medications, to care providers and pharmacies.

The latest trend, however, shows that pharmacies are starting to break free from the influence of pharmaceutical representatives and their employers, "Big Pharma." The pharmacists are instead encouraged to use trustworthy online resources and to be equally, if not more, informed on the medications as the sales representatives. Sensing that their grip on the market is slipping, "Big Pharma" is heavily invested in building relationships with pharmacists, mostly by means of research. Olga Chernichenko, the director of the department of research on the pharmaceutical market for GFK Russia, has elicited responses from pharmacists who described pharmaceutical brands as "villains," "best friends," "strangers," "colleagues," "old pals," etc. in order to advance the companies' relationships with the pharmacists. For instance, the pharmacists stated that for a brand to turn from a "stranger" into a friend, their medications must be well known to the consumers and must be well stocked at the pharmacy. Also, if the "colleague" brand wants to become an "old pal," they need to provide a detailed catalog of their products, organize educational seminars, etc. If a "stranger" brand wants to become an "acquaintance," they only need to organize regular visits and provide pharmacists with informational materials. But if a "colleague" brand wants to become an "old pal," they need to invest in business lunches and decorate the pharmacy with posters, stands, and other promotional materials (Sovremennye Podhody k Prodvizheniyu Brendov [Modern approaches to brand promotion], 2014).

Thus, we see that the shift to patient-oriented health protection is also changing the relationship dynamic between the different communicators. This dynamic can be characterized by strategic information gathering and further campaign planning sensitive to the meanings and attitudes of other actors.

Building Relationships with Health Professionals and Institutions

While the pharmaceutical sales representatives are the most common communication mediators between the business and the care providers, the latest government regulations have changed the way this mediation is practiced. Federal law #323-FZ "On the basics of healthcare in Russian Federation" states that pharmaceutical sales reps can no longer meet with doctors in their offices. Doctors are prohibited from accepting gifts from the sales reps (previously a common practice); doctors cannot partake in any entertainment or educational (conference) activities paid for by the pharmaceutical companies; doctors cannot accept and redistribute samples of medications; and doctors cannot sign contracts promoting certain medications to patients.

As a result of these regulations, pharmaceutical sales reps are finding new ways to communicate with healthcare providers. These new methods are implemented mainly online: specialized private forums, social media, Skype, emails, video chats, video conferences, e-detailing, etc. The most popular channels are the pharmaceutical companies' websites, as well as e-mailing and e-detailing (Kak Farmacevticheskie Kompanii Prodvigayut Lekarstva v Usloviyah Ogranichenij [How do pharmaceutical companies promote medications in the context of limitations], 2015). Users, registered as care providers or pharmacists, can access specialized websites explaining medications and related conditions. Such websites as *ivrach.com*, *evrika.ru*, *mirvracha.ru*, *Doctor at work*, for example, implement complicated registration procedures to make sure that only trained doctors are granted access to these resources (sometimes exceptions can be made for medical students and nurses). The patients, meanwhile, are left out of these discussions. Consumer protection and patient advocates pinpoint this issue as critical to compliance with professional and legal standards, and imperative for building patient-oriented health protection.

Professional Communication Practices

Patient-oriented health protection refers to the paradigm of healthcare development as well as to the treatment approach. Patient-oriented care focuses on the patient as an individual with unique and specific physical, psychological, and social characteristics which inform short-term and long-term treatment plans (Pavlovskykh & Shardin, 2015). Doctor–patient communication lies at the heart of such an approach to care.

In Russia, doctor–patient communication is still predicated upon the doctor's sole authority and expertise in the field of medicine. Apart from very rare individual cases of chronically ill patients or patients attending expensive private clinics such as Rassvet, patients have no say in their own treatment plan. However, the doctor's sacred status as an expert in biomedicine is now threatened by the availability of informatization among internet-literate citizens, as well as by strong patient communities. Patients tend to use internet forums and social media groups to inform themselves about their symptoms, diagnosis, and available medications and treatments. Meanwhile, old-fashioned medical professionals are strongly opposed to this wealth of information being available to patients and would prefer for medical information to be available only to those capable of fully understanding it. Patients who have "done their research" are a threat to the authority of medical experts in their opinion.

Those who introduce patient-centered care in their practice are more respectful and more responsive to their patients. These doctors view their patients as well-informed peers who make the final choices about their own health. Yet many Russian doctors (mostly employees of the public hospitals outside of Moscow) practice a so-called veterinarian approach to their patients – a snobbish attitude of doctors who refuse to divulge any additional information to patients, who are barely allowed to utter a word during their doctor's monologue (cited in Orlova, 2015). As a result, the patient becomes silently, or sometimes publicly, disgruntled with the doctor, expressing their frustration through social media, medical review sites, and so-called patient terrorism (harassing doctors by calls and personal visits). According to Sonkina-Dorman, the doctor–patient dynamic is such that patients often feel mistreated, belittled, and offended, while doctors believe that they treat their patients well (cited in Orlova, 2015). Here we would like to remind the reader of the irony of health optimization regulation, where doctors have only 15 minutes for an individual consultation.

However, apart from miscommunication among practitioners, the Ministry of Healthcare, and patients, where each party is left discontented, there are more constructive cases of assessing doctor–patient communication in the line of patient-oriented health protection. There follows an example of a doctor–patient interaction, which the doctor viewed as a success and the patient viewed as a failure. Sergey Butyj, a pediatrician at a private Moscow clinic, wrote in his Telegram account about a communication error he experienced with one of his patients; an incident "which made me reconsider the importance of effective, high quality communication with my patients" (Butryj, 2018). Dr. Butyj was able to diagnose a chronic disorder in his 6-month-old patient, previously missed by other doctors. Dr. Butyj felt pride in his professional accomplishment, yet this was overshadowed by a poorly managed interaction with the patient's mother. The issue was that during the consultation, Dr. Butyj's phone was ringing off the hook. To him, that meant he was a sought-after specialist, yet his patient's mother did not see it that way. Later she posted a negative review on social media, accusing Dr. Butyj of being distracted, curt, and interrupting her. Therefore, a remarkable medical achievement – a complex diagnosis of a disorder that other doctors had missed – was overshadowed by poor doctor–patient communication.

Such communication examples are being actively discussed within the professional community. One incident demonstrating the value of explaining the quality of care to the patient was recounted at the 2018 Annual Forum for healthcare providers "Competition in Healthcare." The National Research Institute of Epidemiology (Center of Molecular Diagnostics) withheld a patient's test results for a few days in order to run additional tests to further investigate the patient's condition. In the end, they found atypical blood cells that would have been missed during the routine blood test. The patient, however, filed a complaint about the delay in getting her test results and received a refund from the institute. This communication error was corrected by the doctor that referred her to this institute in the first place: he reached out to the patient and explained the situation, emphasizing how she had received high-quality care at no personal expense, while the institute had had to cover additional costs of multiple tests. After the issue was resolved, the patient wrote a thank you letter to the institute (Konkurenciya sistem vzglyadov i podhodov [Competition of systems of opinions and approaches], 2018). At the same forum, Dr. Yaroslav Ashikhmin shared how a patient was satisfied with the service even though the prescribed treatment did not work (Konkurenciya sistem vzglyadov i podhodov [Competition of systems of opinions and approaches], 2018). In this case, the overall experience of visiting the clinic was more important than the diagnosis and prescribed treatment.

The issue is that medical universities do not provide proper training in doctor–patient interaction, since the tradition of teaching communication skills in the Russian higher education system is practically non-existent.

> No one ever taught us how to establish relationships with patients; how to show them that we are on their side; that we're on the same team. We aren't trained to deliver bad news, to deal with overwhelming emotions, to properly express sympathy (which we feel more often than you'd think), says Sergey Butryj, a paediatrician. (Butryj, 2018)

The professional community has a long way to go as regards SC. Currently, the first steps being taken are short-term courses on doctor–patient communication. An example of such first steps is "Soobshchenie," a school specifically designed to lead the way in training for the practice of patient-oriented care.

The Roadmap Toward Patient-Oriented Health Protection

Today, the Russian healthcare system is facing numerous challenges: a low level of trust among citizens, fierce market competition, increasing informatization of the healthcare industry, and changes in the financing of healthcare. For decades, Russian patients were relegated to the role of mere spectators of the healthcare regime imposed by the government, while medical experts and government officials executed the role of decision-makers. With the advocacy efforts from patient NGOs, with the healthcare crisis concerning resources and facility capacity, and with the availability of information on the internet, the practices of health communication are shifting toward a cocreational paradigm (although not among all communicators). This shift has been reflected in a change in doctor–patient communication and cooperation, leading to an increase in the overall quality of healthcare. It has also produced a new type of patient: knowledgeable, actively seeking health information, and ready to be included in the treatment design and even in building health-related agendas at the national level. Within such changes in communication practices, patient organizations play an imperative role as the main communicators and practitioners of cocreational SC practices to facilitate the development of patient-oriented health protection.

The advancement of digital technologies also plays a key role in shifting the paradigm toward patient-oriented health protection. Patients are more apt to be an active public and make informed decisions regarding their healthcare when current and reliable medical information is available online. For example, patient organizations hold expert patient forums that not only provide treatment-related information but also explain the administrative procedures of the health protection field. However, the caveat to use of the internet is that the "searcher" must have the digital and information literacy to be able to make a good search request and make a good judgment on the trustworthiness of the sources.

The introduction of government-regulated telemedicine in 2018 has become a new step on the communication road toward patient-oriented health protection. The federal law "On the use of telecommunication in medicine" (entered into force on January 1, 2018) states that Russian citizens have the right to receive distanced medical consultations as well as to have their condition monitored by a healthcare provider who cannot see them in person. However, this law stipulates that first-time consultations must be carried out in person and that a diagnosis and a form of treatment must be established during face-to-face interaction. Although coming with its own controversies which lie beyond the scope of this chapter, this law incorporates into the conversation the interests of patients living in remote areas and patients with restricted mobility.

Finally, an important step on the road toward patient-oriented health protection is using careful market research instead of "creative advertising campaigns" in pharmaceutical companies' SC agendas. Technological advancement has given an opportunity for this research to be detailed and tailored to the companies' needs: chatbots improve consumer satisfaction; telemedicine includes neglected populations and makes virtual clinics, such as Doc+, Doctor at work, and Pediatrician 24/7, a reality; and Big Data and powerful data processing programs open up new questions and new interpretations. Yet these advances have to be filtered and refined through the ethical codes and knowledge accumulated within the Russian patient organizations in order to move from being fragmented tools to use for SC concerning patient-oriented health protection.

Notes

1 Here we use "patient-oriented" (direct translation from Russian) and "patient-centered" (established notion) as synonyms, although we acknowledge the differences between these two notions. Likewise, in the text we sometimes substitute Russian "health protection" with "healthcare", yet with the emphasis on "protection" not "care" as the key objective.

2 Russian phraseological expression.

References

Butryj, S. (2018, March 25). Re: Eshche odin post o navykah obshcheniya [One more post about communication skills]. [Web log message]. https://t.me/DrButriy/1017

Donorov vypustil socialnyj rolik o donorstve krovi [Foundation of donors has produced social ad about blood donation]. (2018, 7 July). Retrieved from https://www.asi.org.ru/report/2018/08/07/fonddonorovvy

Druzhinin, A. (2016, November 9). Est li v Rossijskoj farme mesto rreativu [Is there a place for creativity in the Russian pharmaceutical industry?]. Retrieved from https://www.sostav.ru/publication/est-li-v-rossijskoj-farme-mesto-kreativu-24466.html

Ehffektivnost rossijskogo zdravoohraneniya i sistema OMS [Efficiency of the Russian healthcare and government-funded insurance policy]. (2017, November 17). Retrieved from https://wciom.ru/index.php?id=236&uid=116534

Hrebtovskaya, A. (2017). Vospriyatie donorami oplachivaemoj sistemy donorstva krovi v sovremennoj Rossii: Rabota ili blagotvoritelnost [Perception of paid system of blood donation in contemporary Russia: The job or charity?]. (Bachelor thesis, Higher School of Economics, Russia). Retrieved from https://www.hse.ru/edu/vkr/206736019

Kak farmacevticheskie kompanii prodvigayut lekarstva v usloviyah ogranichenij [How do pharmaceutical companies promote medications in the context of limitations]. (2015, March 18). Retrieved from https://www.cossa.ru/149/99037

Konkurenciya sistem vzglyadov i podhodov [Competition of systems of opinions and approaches] (2018). *Proceedings of the Annual Forum for Healthcare Providers "Competition in Healthcare"*. Retrieved from https://youtu.be/zpZ318u6j_Q

Kovaleva, K. (2018, November 7). Re: Pro dokazatelnuyu medicinu. [About evidence-based medicine]. [Web log message]. Retrieved from https://www.instagram.com/p/Bp3_63fjI-3/?utm_source=ig_share_sheet&igshid=1n53h8j8iut0l

Krashennikova, Y. A. (2009). Rol NKO v upravlenii sistemoy zdravookhraneniya i perspektivi razvitiya patzienskogo dvizshenya v Rossii. [Role of NPO in management of healthcare system and perspectives of patient movement in Russia]. *Zhurnal Issledovanij Social'noj Politiki*, 7(4), 519–534.

Masyuk, S. (2015). Deyatel' nost' pacientskih organizacij v sisteme zdravoohraneniya rossijskoj federacii. [Activity of patient organizations in the health system of the Russian Federation]. *Vestnik Universiteta*, 6, 44–49.

Milosh, I. (2018, September 10). Farma uderzhivaet liderstvo na TV. [The pharmaceutical industry leads in TV advertising]. Retrieved from https://www.sostav.ru/publication/farma-uderzhivaet-liderstvo-na-tv-33228.html

Minisiyarov. (2018, December 6). Re: Dokazatelnyj vrach. *[Evidence-based physician]. [Web log message]*. Retrieved from https://www.instagram.com/p/BrDqqwgjr0Y/?utm_source=ig_share_sheet&igshid=12nx8wqze0tbo

Na osnovanii dannyh sindikativnogo isledovaniya "Prindex monitoring naznachenij LP vrachami" [On the data based on longitudinal research "Prindex monitoring prescriptions of physicians"]. (2017, April 12). Retrieved from https://www.ipsos.com/ipsos-comcon/ru-ru/formula-recepta

Orlova, A. (2015, March 19). Kak ponyat i prinyat pacienta: Shest sovetov ustalomu vrachu. intervyu s pediatrom i specialistom po medicinskoj ehtike Annoj Sonkinoj-Dorman. [How to understand and accept a patient: Six suggestions for tired physicians. Interview with paediatrician and specialist in

medical ethics, Anna Sonkina-Dorman]. Retrieved from https://www.miloserdie.ru/article/kak-ponyat-i-prinyat-pacienta-shest-sovetov-ustalomu-vrachu-2
Pavlovskykh, A. Y., & Shardin, S. A. (2015). Pacientoorientirovannost kak osnovnaya paradigma razvitiya sovremennogo otechestvennogo zdravoohraneniya. [Patient-centered care as the main paradigm of the modern Russian healthcare]. *Vrach-aspirant*, 70(3.2), 309–315.
Petrova, S. B., Sokolova, N. N., & Kononova, S. V. (2006). Ehffektivnost marketingovy tekhnologij na farmacevticheskom rynke [Efficiency of marketing technologies on pharmaceutical market]. *Remedium*, 5, 28–31.
Plisenkova, O. (2017, November 22). Denis Procenko: Pacientoorientirovannost process beskonechnyj [Denis Protsenko: "Patient-centered care is a never-ending process"]. Retrieved from http://www.niioz.ru/events/gkbu-protsenko-interviyu
Rakitina, L. (2014, October 2). Gosudarstvennye versus chastnye. [Governmental versus private]. Retrieved from https://www.katrenstyle.ru/articles/journal/medicine/spotlight/gosudarstvennyie_vs_chastnyie
Reklama ne dolzhna ubezhdat cheloveka v nalichii zabolevaniya [Advertising should not convince a person in the presence of a disease]. (2018, February 12). Retrieved from https://m.medsovet.info/news/7863
Ruvinskiy, V. (2019, May 27). Pacient platit dvazhdy. [Patient pays twice]. Retrieved from https://www.vedomosti.ru/opinion/articles/2019/05/26/802480-patsient-platit
Shirokova, I. (2012). Ehvolyuciya PR uslug na rossijskom farmrynke. [Evolution of public relations in the pharmaceutical market]. *Remedium*, 10, 20–27.
Shirokova, Y. A. (2011). Pacientskoe dvizhenie v Rossii. [Patient movement in Russia]. *Remedium*, 3, 20–27.
Sovremennye podhody k prodvizheniyu brendov. [Modern approaches to brand promotion] (2014, August 12). Retrieved from http://www.remedium.ru/state/detail.php?ID=62730
Zvonareva, O., Engel, N., Kutishenko, N., & Horstman, K. (2017). (Re)configuring research value: International commercial clinical trials in the Russian Federation. *BioSocieties*, 12(3), 392–414.

22

Bridging Tobacco Control Advocacy and Strategic Communication Scholarship

Tackling the Tobacco Industry's Extrinsic Corporate Social Responsibility with Strategic Networking

Jungmi Jun, Chang-Won Choi, and Joonkyoung Kim
University of South Carolina

Introduction

Tobacco kills more than 8 million people each year worldwide, including deaths attributed to second-hand smoke exposure according to the World Health Organization (WHO, 2019). For comparison, the number of confirmed deaths associated with the harrowing pandemic of novel coronavirus COVID-19 was about 350,000 globally in the half year from its first outbreak (WHO, 2020). The cumulative death toll from tobacco use was 100 million during the 20th century and is estimated to reach 1 billion this century (Jha, 2011). Nonetheless, tobacco companies have continued to develop various types of novel tobacco products, such as electronic cigarettes (e-cigarettes) and heated tobacco products, and have successfully recruited new tobacco user groups including youth, kids, young adults, and international consumers (Arnott, 2018; US Department of Health and Human Services, 2016).

To reach the young and global consumers as well as to take advantage of poor tobacco marketing regulations, social media has become a critical venue for the tobacco industry to promote novel tobacco products and interfere in tobacco control. Various social media activities by big tobacco companies and manufacturers/retailers of novel tobacco products have been discovered, including but not limited to youth/kids-aimed marketing, circulation of misinformation using bots, and sponsorship of vape influencers, which all connect to young people's perceptions, trials, and continuous use of novel tobacco products (Kwon & Park, 2020; Villanti et al., 2016; Yang et al., 2019). Of those, this chapter focuses on the tobacco industry's corporate social responsibility (CSR) and pseudo-activism. We propose these areas can be where tobacco control advocacy and strategic communication (SC) scholarship collaborate to counteract the tobacco industry's marketing strategies.

Communication scholars have long been studying activism as well as activist organizations' communication strategies. For instance, dialogic communication (Kent & Taylor, 1998) has been a popular framework to diagnose activist organizations' relationship building via digital and social media, and recent studies employ social network approaches to examine activist organizations' SC and public engagement (Saffer et al., 2019; Yang, 2013). In addition, CSR is one of the most researched topics in the field. Yet, these and other communication theories have rarely been applied to support tobacco control organizations' advocacy communication and strategic relationship building with their stakeholders.

The Handbook of Strategic Communication, First Edition. Edited by Carl H. Botan.

Given the context, this chapter aims to explore potential connections between tobacco control advocacy and the scholarship of SC. First, we introduce tobacco control initiatives at the national and international level and recent challenges to tobacco control advocacy. Second, we provide a brief overview of the tobacco industry's various SC and social media activities to promote novel tobacco products and interfere in tobacco control. Third, we discuss the industry's CSR programs and pseudo-activism based on a review of academic research papers and the World Health Organization's 2008 report: *Tobacco industry interference with tobacco control*. Fourth, we discuss the issue of limited attention paid to tobacco control advocacy in SC scholarship and suggest the potential for research in the field to guide tobacco control advocacy organizations' social media advocacy. In particular, we review dialogic communication (Kent & Taylor, 1998), the village network approach (Saffer et al., 2019), and several studies in CSR, and discuss the implications for tobacco control advocacy organizations.

Tobacco Control Worldwide and in the US

Global Tobacco Control Initiatives

Tobacco kills more than 8 million people each year; more than 7 million of these deaths are the result of direct tobacco use, while around 1.2 million are the result of second-hand smoking (WHO, 2019). In response to the global tobacco epidemic, the World Health Organization Framework Convention on Tobacco Control (WHO-FCTC), the first international treaty, was ratified and entered into force in February 2005. As of 2018, 181 countries have ratified, accepted, or approved this multilateral treaty (Navas-Acien, 2018). Countries that ratify the treaty signal intent to develop regulatory strategies with regard to including – but not limited to – pricing/taxation to reduce demand, regulation of the content of tobacco products, packaging and labeling, prohibition of tobacco advertising/promotions, protection of the public from second-hand smoking, and education/communication (WHO, 2005).

Tobacco Control Regulations in the US

In the US, the Family Smoking Prevention and Tobacco Control Act (Tobacco Control Act) became law on June 22, 2009. It grants the Food and Drug Administration (FDA) the authority to regulate the manufacture, distribution, and marketing of tobacco products to protect public health (Public Law 111–31). Although the prevalence of conventional cigarette smoking has declined over the past few decades, tobacco use remains the single largest preventable cause of death and disease in the country. There have been 480,000 deaths annually, or one of every five deaths caused by tobacco use in recent years (CDC, 2017). In addition, smoking-related illness in the US costs more than $300 billion a year, including nearly $170 billion in direct medical care for adults and $156 billion in lost productivity. As of 2017, it is estimated that 14%, or 34.3 million US adults are current cigarette smokers and 75% of them smoke every day (CDC, 2019).

Tobacco Control Advocacy and New Challenges

Along with the regulatory efforts, tobacco control is also an activism movement supported by social activists, public health advocates, health/tobacco scientists, educators, health care providers, and others who work to control the spread of tobacco use (Derry & Waikar, 2008). Many of these tobacco control activists work collectively, and these organizations are supported by state or federal funding or by large nonprofits, such as the American Cancer Society, the American Lung Association, the Legacy Foundation, or major cancer research centers (Derry & Waikar, 2008). As of September 2019, there are approximately 50 national member organizations of the Tobacco Partners Coalition and a number of small/local nonprofit organizations advocating tobacco cessation and prevention programs (AARC, 2019). Table 22.1 presents a list of tobacco control advocacy organizations obtained by the snowballing method based on the list of tobacco control organizations available on the Tobacco Portal (https://tobacco.publichealth.gsu.edu/). Many tobacco control advocacy organizations have dedicated communication/media staff, whose role is to ensure the public presence and voice of tobacco control objectives (Wakefield et al., 2012).

Tobacco control advocacy has been successful in gaining legitimacy from the public and policymakers that tobacco is exceptionally harmful, and thus should be regulated as such. Tobacco control advocacy groups have achieved this legitimacy by emphasizing the lethality and addictiveness of tobacco and arguing that it kills a high proportion of its users, as well as second-hand users, and that it should be regulated with strong and extensive enforcements much more than other legal products. Indeed, tobacco has become the only legal consumer good that has a binding international treaty dedicated to its control and prevention, enacted by the WHO-FCTC (Arnott, 2018).

Table 22.1 Tobacco control advocacy organizations.

Organization	*Website*
American Cancer Society	https://www.cancer.org/cancer/cancer-causes/tobacco-and-cancer.html https://www.fightcancer.org/what-we-do/tobacco-control
American Heart Association	https://www.heart.org/en/healthy-living/healthy-lifestyle/quit-smoking-tobacco
American Lung Association	https://www.lung.org/our-initiatives/tobacco/reports-resources/sotc
Smoke-Free Kids	http://www.jeffreywigand.com/smokefreekids.php
Tobacco Control Network	http://tobaccocontrolnetwork.org
Americans for Nonsmokers' Rights	nonsmokersrights.org
UCSF Center for Tobacco Control Research and Education	https://tobacco.ucsf.edu
World Health Organization Tobacco Free Initiative	https://www.who.int/tobacco/en
Smokefree.org	https://smokefree.gov
Americans for Nonsmoker's Rights Foundation	https://no-smoke.org
Truth Initiative	https://truthinitiative.org
Campaign for Tobacco-Free Kids	https://www.tobaccofreekids.org
Action on Smoking and Health	https://ash.org
Protecting local control	protectlocalcontrol.org
Smokefree Casinos CASINOS	smokefreecasinos.org
Smokefree Music Cities	smokefreemusiccities.org
Tidatabase (Tobacco Institute Database)	http://tidatabase.org
Toolkit for implementing smoke-free laws	http://goingsmokefree.org

(*Continued*)

Table 22.1 (Continued)

Organization	*Website*
Stanford Research into the Impact of Tobacco Advertising	http://tobacco.stanford.edu/tobacco_main/index.php
Kids Live Smokefree	http://www.kidslivesmokefree.org
Tobacco Portal	https://tobacco.publichealth.gsu.edu
TheTruth.com	https://www.thetruth.com
Tobacco Free Air	http://www.tobaccofreeair.org
Tobacco Free Funds	https://tobaccofreefunds.org
Tobacco Free Nurses	https://tobaccofreenurses.org
STOP	https://exposetobacco.org
Kick Butts Day	https://www.kickbuttsday.org
Taking Down Tobacco	https://www.takingdowntobacco.org
Tobacco Control Laws	https://www.tobaccocontrollaws.org
Tobacco Control Grants	https://tobaccocontrolgrants.org
Campaign for Tobacco-Free Kids (Digital Advocacy Center)	https://digitaladvocacycenter.com
Knock Tobacco Out of the Park	https://tobaccofreebaseball.org
Tobacco Free Retailers	https://shoptobaccofree.org
American Academy of Pediatrics Julius B. Richmond Center of Excellence	https://www.aap.org/en-us/advocacy-and-policy/aap-health-initiatives/Richmond-Center/Pages/default.aspx
Bloomberg Initiative to Reduce Tobacco Use	https://www.bloomberg.org/program/public-health/tobacco-control
Tobacco Technical Assistance Consortium (TTAC)	http://tacenters.emory.edu/focus_areas/tobacco/index.html
Association of State and Territorial Health Officials (ASTHO)	http://www.astho.org/Programs/Prevention/Tobacco
Robert Wood Johnson Foundation: Tobacco	https://www.rwjf.org/en/library/collections/tobacco-control.html
National Networks for Tobacco Control Prevention	NA
Tobacco Control Legal Consortium	NA
World Lung Foundation	NA
The Legacy Foundation	NA
Healthy Children	https://www.healthychildren.org/english/our-mission/pages/default.aspx
Your Lung Health	http://www.yourlunghealth.org
American Nonsmokers' Rights Foundation	https://no-smoke.org
Smoke-Free World	https://www.smokefreeworld.org/our-vision
Tobacco Free	https://tobaccofree.org
Notobacco (belongs to Tobacco Free)	http://www.notobacco.org

(*Continued*)

Table 22.1 (Continued)

Organization	*Website*
Change Lab Solution	https://www.changelabsolutions.org/tobacco-prevention
Smoke Free Movies	http://smokefreemovies.ucsf.edu
Maryland's Tobacco Resource Center	https://mdquit.org/prevention/community-based-programs
ClearWay Minnesota	http://clearwaymn.org
KidsHealth	https://kidshealth.org
CounterTobacco.org	https://countertobacco.org/partners
Public Health and Tobacco Policy Center	https://tobaccopolicycenter.org
Public Health Law Center	https://www.publichealthlawcenter.org/about
The QuitDoc Foundation	https://www.quitdoc.com
Tobacco Free Allegheny	http://tobaccofreeallegheny.org
Association for Nonsmokers-Minnesota	http://www.ansrmn.org
Breathe California Sacramento Region	http://sacbreathe.org
Global Advisors on Smokefree Policy	https://www.njgasp.org
Arizona Smoke-Free Living	http://www.azsmokefreeliving.org/about-us-2
NYC Smoke-Free	http://nycsmokefree.org/about-us
The Southeastern Pennsylvania Tobacco Control Project	https://www.sepatobaccofree.org/about
Arizonans Concerned About Smoking	http://arizonansconcernedaboutsmoking.com/ACAS_Mission.html
The Virginia Smoke Free Association	https://virginiasmokefree.org

Emerging Tobacco Products and Challenges to Tobacco Control Advocacy

However, the emergence of new tobacco products, including but not limited to e-cigarettes and various vape products, hookah, smokeless tobacco, and heated tobacco products, poses significant challenges to tobacco control advocacy. First, there is a lack of scientific consensus on the harm of new tobacco products and their effects on smoking cessation/reduction, even among members of tobacco control communities, such as health scientists, health care providers and educators, and tobacco control advocates. This hinders collaborative advocacy for control of new tobacco products (Fairchild & Bayer, 2015; Farsalinos, 2018). Second, the public's misperceptions are so prevalent that there is a false belief that new tobacco products are safer alternatives to conventional cigarettes, often harmless, and effective smoking cessation aids, which results from the industry's harm-reduction claims (Jun, Kim, & Wu, 2019; Tan, Lee, & Bigman, 2016). This public misperception challenges the legitimacy of tobacco control advocacy organizations' opposition to new tobacco products and demand for stringent regulation of these products. Third, the lack of scientific consensus and the public's acceptance of new tobacco products delays government's restriction of these products. For instance, the FDA did not expand their regulatory authority to prohibit minor access and regulate retail sales of new/alternative tobacco products, including e-cigarettes, hookah tobacco, and cigars until May 2016 (FDA, 2016), a decade after the introduction of e-cigarettes to the US market. Yet, the FDA has no jurisdiction on where e-cigarettes can be used or taxed, setting a higher minimum age, or licensing retailers at the state level (Cox, Barry, & Glantz, 2016), and state regulations on e-cigarettes and other novel tobacco products are still being developed (Tremblay et al., 2015).

Decreasing Trust in Tobacco Control

Several research findings suggest there has been a decrease in public trust in tobacco control and related organizations. The FDA, a US federal agency, is in charge of tobacco control and implements communication and public education campaigns, as well as disseminating tobacco safety information. Therefore, the agency is expected to serve as a reliable and accurate source of tobacco information (Kowitt et al., 2017). However, the US public's trust in the FDA is low. In a 2015 survey by the Pew Research Center, only 51% of American adults reported that they trust the FDA, while the rate was higher for the Centers for Disease Control and Prevention (CDC) (71%; Pew Research Center, 2015). In a more recent survey, a higher rate of adults (62.5%) or adolescents (78.8%) demonstrated trust in the FDA, but the rates were still lower than those for the CDC (adults = 94.3%) or adolescents (81.9%; Kowitt et al., 2017). Additionally, the public's trust in government health agencies as a source of e-cigarette information (e.g. FDA, CDC) was lower than other sources, such as health care providers and health organizations (Alcalá & Shimoga, 2019).

Meanwhile, the tobacco industry has successfully recruited new tobacco user groups including young adults, youth, kids, and international consumers, and subsequently increased market share, achieving significant corporate growth in profits in the past decade (Arnott, 2018; US Department of Health and Human Services, 2016). The tobacco industry appeared undisturbed even during the global COVID-19 pandemic. According to British American Tobacco (BAT), consumers continued to purchase tobacco products, even in the hardest-impacted areas. The BAT Chief Executive Officer stated: "we don't see any change in patterns of consumption of cigarettes because of Covid-19... It is a daily purchase, so consumers continue to go to shop... where tobacco shops are still open" (TobaccoReporter, 2020). His statement was also supported by financial analysts, who recommended tobacco stocks as a good buy and "immune" to the coronavirus crisis in the market (Sun, 2020; Williams, 2020).

In taking advantage of poor tobacco marketing regulations on social/digital media platforms as compared to traditional media and inconclusive health effects of novel tobacco products, the tobacco industry uses various communication strategies to interfere in tobacco control efforts and promote novel tobacco products (Noel, Rees, & Connolly, 2011; Yamin, Bitton, & Bates, 2010). We suggest that understanding of the tobacco industry's communication strategies will guide tobacco control advocacy organizations to identify new stakeholder groups to build networks as well as to counteract the tobacco industry's underlying motives of CSR and other communication activities. Given that, we discuss the tobacco industry's recent SC on social media with particular attention to CSR and pseudo-activism.

Tobacco Industry's Strategic Communication and Social Media

Advertising and Circulation of Misinformation on Social Media

Over $2 million is spent each year on e-cigarette advertising in the US and Canada alone (Richardson, Ganz, & Vallone, 2015), and this is reflected in the growth in commercial presence of e-cigarettes on traditional media, points of sale, and social media in recent years (Clark et al., 2016). Twitter is used as a marketing tool for manufacturers and retailers of novel tobacco products. More than 90% of e-cigarette-related tweets are commercial, and these commercial tweets are largely driven by a small group of highly active accounts; 94% of them include links to websites, many of which sell or promote e-cigarettes and other vape products. Approximately 10% of tweets mention smoking cessation, and 34% of commercial tweets include mentions of prices or discounts (Huang et al., 2014).

Research has found that millions of vaping-related tweets exist, and 77% originated from bots (vs. 22% humans) that are suspected to relate to major e-cigarette companies or retailers. These bots are programed not only to sell vape products, but also to exchange smoking cessation for vaping, to advocate vaping (e.g. "fight against the big tobacco"), and to spread misinformation. With the overwhelming quantity and programed message framing strategies, bots lead online conversations around e-cigarettes and tobacco products (Public Good Projects, 2019). In particular, Basáñez et al. (2018) found that at least one in eight vape tweets include healthy food-related labels (e.g. natural, vitamin, vegan, organic), and nearly 30% of tweets describe e-cigarettes as harmless. Although a smaller number of studies are available, a Twitter analysis of other novel tobacco products – such as smokeless tobacco, heated tobacco products, and hookah – indicates similar patterns (Jo et al., 2016; Lienemann et al., 2017). In addition, the dominance of advertising/marketing content and misinformation regarding novel tobacco products appears on other social media platforms, such as Instagram, Reddit, and Pinterest (Chu et al., 2017; Guidry et al., 2016; Kreitzberg et al., 2019).

YouTube is the most popular video-sharing site as well as the second most used social media platform for information/content search worldwide, with 5 billion video views per day. YouTube offers unique opportunities for the tobacco industry to promote novel tobacco products. Big tobacco companies and manufacturers/retailers of novel tobacco products create their own channels and sponsor influential tobacco reviewers' channels. YouTube videos are widely used to promote various novel tobacco products, including e-cigarettes, hookah, smokeless tobacco, cigars/little cigars, and heated tobacco (Kong et al., 2019). For instance, vape pens have been placed in popular music videos on YouTube, and these music videos have been viewed over 1.4 billion times in 24 months (Allem et al., 2019). Not surprisingly, tobacco content on YouTube is predominantly pro-tobacco, including various marketing claims, visual/audio effects, and persuasive appeals (e.g. humor, credibility, parasocial relationships) that are professionally developed by tobacco retailers or by creators who are associated with the tobacco industry (Bromberg, Augustson, & Backinger, 2012; Forsyth & Malone, 2010; Freeman & Chapman, 2007; Luo et al., 2014; Sears et al., 2017).

Vape/Tobacco Influencers

There are a number of social influencers who promote novel tobacco products or connect young people to tobacco manufacturers/retailers. For instance, there are thousands of vape influencers on Instagram, and some of them have more than a million followers. Instagram has banned paid vape influencers, and JUUL closed their Instagram and Facebook accounts after pressure from the FDA in 2018. Despite these measures to counter pro-vape posts, of nearly 250,000 Instagram posts featuring vaping-related hashtags (think #ejuice or #vape), #TheRealCost hashtag (the FDA's youth tobacco prevention campaign) was used only about 50 times per month. Hashtags that mention vaping in a positive way were used about 10,000 times more frequently (Vassey et al., 2020).

On YouTube, there are also countless vape/tobacco influencers. YouTube celebrities operate one or more channels and post videos of themselves (vlogging) on a subject matter in which they view themselves as an expert. They often have a large number of subscribers and thus possess the potential to reach and market products to many young viewers. Some of them are vape enthusiasts, who describe themselves as experts on e-cigarettes and other novel tobacco products. They professionally review novel tobacco products, provide instructions on how to use and maintain such products, and entertain their viewers with vaping tricks (Kong et al., 2019). A concerning finding is that they describe and promote themselves as resources and guides to quit smoking, as well as advocates to fight against big tobacco companies and the government's regulation of novel tobacco products, and protect vapers' health and rights.

Impact on Youth/Kids

One of the biggest concerns about the tobacco industry's aggressive use of social media and the popularity of tobacco/vape influencers is their impact on young people. Research has found that a quarter of JUUL Twitter followers are minors (Chu et al., 2018), and youth/kids have easy access to pro-tobacco content on YouTube (Forsyth & Malone, 2010; Freeman & Chapman, 2007). YouTube reaches more youth than any single cable television network (McKay, 2018). One-third of parents reported allowing their child (age 11 or younger) to watch YouTube videos regularly (Pew Research Center, 2018). Youth and kids can easily access tobacco content on YouTube. For instance, only 1% of e-cigarette-related and 3% of heated tobacco product-related videos on YouTube had an age restriction (Huang, Kornfield, & Emery, 2016). The creators of tobacco videos rarely disclose warnings to prevent minors' access to their content, and the effect of the YouTube Parental Control on filtering tobacco content is unknown. Prior studies found that commercial internet filters failed to prevent minors' access to tobacco content online (Primack et al., 2012).

The Master Settlement Agreement (MSA) banned marketing targeting youth (Hamilton, 2002), yet the ban has not been sufficiently applied to the marketing of novel tobacco products, particularly on social media. Numerous studies have found e-cigarette companies' social media messages incorporating marketing aimed at youth (Dai, Deem, & Hao, 2017; Duke et al., 2014; Laestadius et al., 2019; Phua, Jin, & Hahm, 2018); this includes the use of celebrities and cartoon characters (Kirkpatrick et al., 2017), images of attractive people, desirable lifestyle images, and popular trends (Phua, Jin, & Hahm, 2018), which are prohibited by the MSA. The FDA authorized sales of heated tobacco, including Phillip Morris International's IQOS device and Marlboro Heatsticks on April 30, 2019 (FDA, 2019a) after continuous assurance by Phillip Morris International (PMI) that the company would warn young people away from the product (Kirkham, 2019). However, Reuters discovered PMI's global social media campaign using young online personalities to promote IQOS, including a 21-year-old woman in Russia (Hickman, 2019; Kirkham, 2019). Research has demonstrated that youth's exposure to social media marketing reduces the perceived harm of novel tobacco products and increases trial intent (Kwon & Park, 2020; Villanti et al., 2016; Yang et al., 2019).

During the completion of this chapter, the FDA raised the federal minimum age of sale of tobacco products, including e-cigarettes, from 18 to 21 years (FDA, 2019c) and finalized their enforcement policy on unauthorized flavored cartridge-based e-cigarettes that appeal to children, including fruit and mint (FDA, 2020). The agency also proposed new tobacco health warnings and requires such warnings to appear directly in advertisements on social media and smartphones (FDA, 2019b), and sent warning letters to flavored e-liquid firms to review their disclosures of the health risks of nicotine for social media content (FTC, 2019). Yet, the impacts of these regulatory acts on tobacco prevalence among young people are unknown. According to the 2019 National Youth Tobacco Survey, more than 5 million youth in the US reported current usage of e-cigarettes; 27.5% of high-school students and 10.5% of middle-school students are current vapers (FDA, 2019d).

Tobacco's Corporate Social Responsibility and Pseudo-activism

In 2008, the World Health Organization released a report entitled "*Tobacco industry interference with tobacco control.*" According to this report, effective tobacco control is antithetical to the economic interests of the tobacco industry, associated industries, and their shareholders or government owners. The primary goals of tobacco control are to prevent tobacco-caused disease and death and to reduce exposure to second-hand smoke. Tobacco control objectives – prevention of initiation, promotion of cessation, and prohibition of tobacco use in public – stand in direct opposition to the commercial wellbeing of the tobacco industry. Thus, when tobacco control succeeds, the tobacco industry fails. Therefore, the tobacco industry seeks to ensure that effective tobacco control policies fail, to maximize their profits (p. 1).

The tobacco industry thwarts tobacco control efforts with multiple tactics, such as intelligence gathering, political funding, lobbying, funding research and educational institutions, litigation, and smuggling (as detailed in Table 22.2). Among these, we focus on CSR, as it reflects the tobacco industry's attempts to build and maintain stronger relationships with various stakeholders. In recent years, the tobacco industry has shifted its core frames to include a large component of responsibility, primarily in response to growing public skepticism about the industry's intentions; a reflection of tobacco control's success in influencing the public. Social media serves as a platform for the tobacco industry to openly publish their CSR agenda (Watts, Hefler, & Freeman, 2019). The tobacco industry has embraced and used digital and social media to purposefully oppose, weaken, and resist tobacco control efforts.

Research found that all four global tobacco companies consistently and regularly tweeted about the positive impact of their companies on society and the environment. Such tweets were coded under CSR and made up 29.1% of PMI's tweets, 20.9% of JTI's tweets, 18.4% of Imperial's tweets, and 18.4% of BAT's tweets. These social media strategies highlight that the tobacco industry is continuing to heavily promote CSR activities to shape their public identity and interfere in tobacco control policies in the public domain. In addition, PMI operates multiple YouTube channels and BAT also has a channel, called "A Better Tomorrow." A majority of these channel videos promote companies' CSR. PMI also operates a communication campaign: "Smoke Free Future UK." The company promotes their novel tobacco products, such as IQOS, as smoking cessation aids on their website and YouTube channel, which is typical stealth marketing. Nonetheless, their YouTube channel describes itself as a resource for information on giving up smoking cigarettes and categorizes the channel as "nonprofit and activism." The tobacco industry's CSR violates WHO-FCTC Article 5.3 – *Tobacco industry interference by effectively promoting tobacco companies as socially responsible companies.* Regardless, the tobacco industry, especially global tobacco companies, has continued the use of CSR. We summarize the tobacco industry's CSR extrinsic motives, strategies/tactics, and target audiences or stakeholder groups.

Extrinsic Motives

The CSR literature suggests that there are two types of CSR motives: intrinsic and extrinsic (Ham & Kim, 2019). Intrinsic motives are based on the company's genuine concern for the social issues and potential benefits of the public, while extrinsic motives are based on the company's attempts to increase its profits or other business returns. The tobacco industry's extrinsic motives for their CSR include (1) image or reputation, (2) employee morale, and (3) stock value management (Hirschhorn, 2004). For instance, Coombs (2017) reviewed the CSR-related documents of BAT and identified that the company recognizes CSR as a means of enhancing reputation and improving financial success. Also, CSR activities were often described as *reputation case* for favorable environment operation and employee reinforcement. CSR was a means of enhancing reputation, leading to business success. In the words of a BAT executive,

Table 22.2 Tobacco industry's strategies to interfere in tobacco control.

Strategies	*Goal*
Intelligence gathering	To monitor opponents and social trends in order to anticipate future challenges
Public relations	To mold public opinion, using the media to promote positions favorable to the industry
Political funding	To use campaign contributions to win votes and legislative favors from politicians
Lobbying	To make deals and influence political processes
Consultancy	To recruit supposedly independent experts who are critical of tobacco control measures
Funding research, including universities	To create doubt about the evidence on the health effects of tobacco use
Smokers' rights groups	To create an impression of spontaneous, grassroots public support
Creating alliances and front groups	To mobilize farmers, retailers, advertising agencies, the hospitality industry, grassroots, and anti-tax groups with a view to influencing legislation
Intimidation	To use legal and economic power as a means of harassing and frightening opponents who support tobacco control
Philanthropy	To buy friends and social respectability from arts, sports, humanitarian, and cultural groups
Corporate social responsibility	To promote voluntary measures as an effective way to address tobacco control and create an illusion of being a "changed" company and to establish partnerships with health interests
Youth smoking prevention and retailer education programs	To appear to be on the side of efforts to prevent children from smoking and to depict smoking as an adult choice
Litigation	To challenge laws and intimidate tobacco industry opponents
Smuggling	To undermine tobacco excise tax policies and marketing and trade restrictions and thereby increase profits
International treaties and other international instruments	To use trade agreements to force entry into closed markets and to challenge the legality of proposed tobacco control legislation
Joint manufacturing and licensing agreements and voluntary policy agreements with governments	To form joint ventures with state monopolies and subsequently pressure governments to privatize monopolies
Pre-emption	To overrule local or state government by removing its power to act

Note: Adopted from the 2018 WHO report: *Tobacco industry interference with tobacco control* (pp. 12–13).

CSR can provide important "air cover" to distract governments and the community from the industry's core business. The self-regulating CSR movement is designed to replace government-mandated regulation (Lee & Bialous, 2006). Similarly, Hirschhorn reviewed the other global tobacco company, PMI's CSR documents and found that they justify the use of CSR to maintain its responsibility to its principal stakeholders, the investors. The justifiable terms of PMI, however, contradict those of public health (Hirschhorn, 2004).

Tactics and Target Stakeholder Groups

McDaniel, Cadman, and Malone (2016) reviewed CSR information on global tobacco companies' websites and identified four CSR focus areas that were universally mentioned: youth smoking prevention programs, voluntary marketing standards, acknowledgment of smoking's health harms, and management of the tobacco supply chain. With the youth smoking prevention program, three additional types of CSR activities and target stakeholder groups are discussed below.

Addressing Environmental/Social Issues in Partnership with NGOs

Watts, Hefler, and Freeman (2019) have reviewed publicly available internal documents of global tobacco companies and revealed that the tobacco industry has focused on improving their corporate image for almost two decades. CSR has been a significant component of the industry's overall marketing strategy. In particular, they approached pro-environmental or pro-social nongovernmental organizations (NGOs) to build strategic relationships to use their reputation and social networks as a gateway to reach media and policymakers.

For instance, BAT sought a partnership with a well-respected global NGO, Earthwatch Europe, to gain a global ally that could provide entry into the NGO community. They attempted to increase their presence in the developing nations, as well as to shape public policy, influence media coverage, and mobilize the public on social, economic, and environmental issues that affected the company by working with Earthwatch Europe. Earthwatch Europe promoted the partnership with BAT to other NGOs and policymakers during debates on the ethics of working with a tobacco company. This extended BAT's reputation and helped the company gain entry into influential circles (McDaniel & Malone, 2012).

The tobacco industry was involved in sustainable development projects in South Asian countries, such as the Philippines, Malaysia and Vietnam. In particular, BAT used the La Mesa Dam Watershed Project to build a connection with the Philippines government. Also, BAT supported tree plantation and forest protection projects in Malaysia and Vietnam. It is ironic that the industry is responsible for deforestation, because one of the main materials used in cigarette production is paper – from the cartons to the cigarette wrapper – and much of it is not recycled, including the plastic outer wraps (Kin, Lian, & Yoon, 2010).

Ethical or sustainable management of the tobacco supply chain has been promoted as a CSR focus on global tobacco companies' websites (McDaniel, Cadman, & Malone, 2016). In Malawi, global tobacco companies are using anti-child-labor activism projects to enhance corporate reputation and distract public attention from profits obtained through low wages and cheap tobacco (Otanez, 2006).

Sponsorship for Arts/Education Communities and Journalists

The tobacco industry carries out sponsorship indirectly through foundations. Scholarships and art awards have been distributed in Indonesia, Malaysia, Thailand, and the Philippines. In Malaysia, for example, the children of tobacco farmers were given US$140 each. Tobacco companies have also sponsored message boards, the construction of basketball courts, or provided meals in schools. Academic researchers and health professionals have been approached with tobacco funding. PMI offered research funds to Bicol University in 2007, but this was blocked by the Department of Health, Philippines (Kin, Lian, & Yoon, 2010). Additionally, the tobacco industry has provided sponsorship for a number of arts, dance, music, culture, film, religious, and other festivals. They have also sponsored annual awards for journalists and journalist/opinion leaders' social events (Tandilittin & Luetge, 2015).

Youth Smoking Prevention Campaign

Multinational tobacco companies have promoted youth smoking prevention as part of their CSR since the early 1980s. Interestingly, in the US, the tobacco industry has promoted at least four types of youth smoking prevention programs which targeted parents (e.g. the Tobacco Institute's "Helping Youth Decide," 1984), youths (e.g. RJR's "Right Decisions, Right Now," 1991), and retailers (e.g. Philip Morris USA's "Action Against Access," 1995), and programs providing funding to youth organizations (e.g. 4-H's "Health Rocks").

In Latin America, tobacco companies have partnered with third-party allies, most notably nonprofit educational organizations and education and health ministries. Even though there is no evidence that these programs reduce smoking among youths, they have met the industry's goal of portraying the companies as concerned corporate citizens and undermining tobacco control interventions.

In 2001, Japan Tobacco International (JTI), BAT, and PMI launched a television advertising campaign on the MTV European network for 18 weeks, "featuring young, hip and active people who don't smoke." The message of the campaign was, "You can be 'cool' and not smoke." Encouraged by the campaign's good publicity, PMI and JTI ran a new campaign on MTV in 2002 in 80 countries in Europe, Asia, Australia, and Latin America (Sebrié & Glantz, 2007), as well as in Asian countries including Thailand, Malaysia, and the Philippines. BAT and PMI sponsored youth smoking prevention campaigns. Studies have shown that these campaigns, sponsored by the tobacco industry, are not effective in encouraging youth smoking cessation, but the campaigns worked successfully for the tobacco industry to stop governments from enacting strict legislation that curbs the industry's promotions (Kin, Lian, & Yoon, 2010).

Strategic Relationship Building with Women

McDaniel and Malone (2009) analyzed tobacco company documents and how the industry has strategically built relationships with American women and women's groups since the late 1970s. PMI aimed to "establish mutually beneficial relationships with leaders and members of major women's organizations" in 1978, and the company made the first donation to the National Organization of Women (NOW) Conference. In subsequent years, PMI and other tobacco companies funded a variety of women's political and professional organizations. Additionally, tobacco companies have bought memberships or seats/tables at events in women's organizations, such as the New York Women's Agenda and the American Association of University Women. The recognition from women's organizations was seen as a significant achievement for female executives in tobacco companies. In 2000, PMI targeted "active moms" – socially or politically active mothers who have an influential voice in their White, African American, and Hispanic communities – for their corporate image campaign, "Philip Morris in the 21st Century."

In short, the tobacco industry has approached or built relationships with diverse stakeholder groups including youth and their parents, women, journalists, educators/researchers, governments, arts communities, and NGOs through diverse communication activities on social media, including CSR, despite its violation of WHO-FCTC Article 5.3. We propose that understanding of CSR strategies and their impacts in the field of SC can help tobacco control advocacy to monitor and tackle the tobacco industry's CSR. In addition, the network and relationship-building approaches in SC and its subfield, public relations, can offer an opportunity for tobacco control advocacy organizations to enhance organization–public relationships. In particular, we review dialogic communication (Kent & Taylor, 1998) and the village network approach (Saffer et al., 2019) and their practical implications for tobacco control advocacy organizations' SC to overcome recent challenges.

Tobacco Control Advocacy Communication

Communication scholars have studied activism (Coombs & Holladay, 2012a,b; Heath & Vasquez, 2001) as well as activist organizations' rhetoric or issues framing (Reber & Berger, 2005; Sommerfeldt, 2011) and the impacts of their networks and communication strategies (Jahng, Hong, & Park, 2014; Uysal & Yang, 2013). For instance, dialogic communication (Kent & Taylor, 1998) has been a popular framework to diagnose activist organizations' relationship building via digital and social media, and recent studies employ social network approaches to examine activist organizations' SC and public engagement (Saffer et al., 2019; Yang, 2013). CSR is one of the most researched areas in the field of SC, and there is rich understanding of effective as well as not so effective CSR strategies, which can provide insights on how tobacco control advocacy organizations can surveil and disrupt the tobacco industry's CSR. In addition, SC researchers have critiqued CSR with extrinsic motives and deceptive lobbying practices that undermine and fake grassroots movements (Lock, Seele, & Heath, 2016).

However, these theories and SC research have rarely been applied to explain tobacco control as an activism movement or to support tobacco control advocacy organizations' SC or relationship building with their stakeholders. As of September 2019, no research on tobacco control advocacy or tobacco control activist groups has been published in peer reviewed academic journals in SC or its subfield, public relations. Only one relevant study has been published in the *Journal of Public Relations Research*, where Stokes and Rubin (2010) examined the public relations battle between a grassroots anti-smoking advocacy group and PMI. There has been more research on the tobacco industry's public relations, including tobacco companies' image restoration (King, 2006), global communication practice (Pratt, 2011), or CSR (Du Plessis & Grobler, 2014; Kim & Choi, 2012, p. 201), and these studies have been published in two public relations journals, although it should be noted that SC scholars' publication platforms are not limited to these journals only. Given the importance of organization–public relationships, issue management, and SC for tobacco control advocacy organizations and their critical role in public health activism, it is surprising that little research is available on these organizations or tobacco control advocacy in the field of SC.

Prior research outside of the SC literature, such as health communication and public health, has focused on tobacco control advocacy organizations' media advocacy and risk communication. In particular, media coverage and frames have been proposed as critical means for influencing public health policies, and the volume of news coverage and the issue frames have been associated with tobacco control advocacy organizations' media advocacy efforts (Wallack & Dorfman, 1996). Tobacco control advocacy organizations influence media content and contribute to an increase in tobacco coverage by generating events that are deemed newsworthy, such as programs, policies, legal cases, and research findings (Chapman, 2007; Niederdeppe, Farrelly, & Wenter, 2007). News stories from individuals or organizations, press releases, and press conferences are key sources of health/medical news, as revealed in surveys with health or medical science journalists (Viswanath et al., 2008), and more than a fifth of tobacco-related newspaper articles mentioned a tobacco control advocacy group (Wakefield et al., 2012).

While we agree that media advocacy is a critical means for tobacco control advocacy and an area that should continue to be researched, we propose that at least two communication theories, dialogic communication (Kent & Taylor, 1998) and the village network approach, can also assist tobacco control advocacy organizations' social media advocacy, as well as surveillance, and counteracts the tobacco industry's extrinsic CSR. Social media has become an integral advocacy communication tool for tobacco control advocacy organizations to monitor the tobacco industry's activities, implement communication campaigns, raise petitions, promote collaboration with partner organizations, and extend the supporter base (Hefler,

Freeman, & Chapman, 2013). The two models can guide tobacco control advocacy organizations' interactive use of information technology, including social media and strategic networking with fellow advocacy organizations.

Dialogic Communication and Interactive Use of Information Technology

Following the arrival of the internet, Kent and Taylor (1998) proposed that when organizations wish to engage in dialogues – genuine and cooperative communication with their stakeholders to build mutually satisfying relationships – the interactive communication technology can facilitate dialogic communication and be used as a tool for relationship building. They presented five principles that organizations can use to achieve dialogic communication and mutually beneficial relationships. Taylor, Kent, and White (2001) published the first study that applied the principles of dialogic communication to a sample of activist websites. In this study, they provided a 32-item questionnaire to measure the degree to which principles of dialogic communication were represented on the websites. Dialogic communication and its five principles have been applied to explain and support organizations' communication and relationship management strategies via web, digital, or social media. Since Kent and Taylor's proposition in 1998, at least 35 peer-reviewed academic studies have applied the theory to analyze nonprofit or advocacy organizations (Wirtz & Zimbres, 2018).

In responding to the development and changes in digital and social media platforms, the measures have been revised. Table 22.3 displays a summary of the five principles (Kent & Taylor, 1998) and measures that can be used to analyze tobacco control and other advocacy organizations' websites as well as social media (i.e. Facebook and Twitter), adopted from the latest research in dialogic communication (e.g. Erwin & Dias, 2016; Wirtz & Zimbres, 2018).

Wirtz and Zimbres (2018) conducted a systematic review of 79 studies applying dialogic communication and suggested several practical implications for organizations' communication technology use. We connect their implications to tobacco control advocacy organizations' interactive use of communication technologies. Tobacco control advocacy organizations may design their websites so they are easy to navigate and update the content regularly. It would be beneficial to operate online forums or Q&A/F&Q areas to discuss issues surrounding emerging tobacco products, extension or strong government regulations for tobacco control, and the tobacco industry's extrinsic motives. Additionally, tobacco control advocacy groups may host real-time online meetings or webinars to generate initial and return visits. Online newsrooms should be operated and useful information for journalists should be provided. In particular, the tobacco industry's CSR, youth target marketing, and other violations of the international treaty, national and global cases, and monitoring results may influence news valence toward the tobacco industry and public discourses.

The Village Approach and Collaborative Advocacy

According to Saffer et al. (2019), with a number of political and social issues consuming the public's attention, advocacy organizations are challenged with sustaining the public's engagement. For instance, evidence shows that tobacco control advocates were less likely to be represented as sources in news items related to the tobacco industry's CSR, when compared to tobacco company spokespersons and beneficiaries of CSR initiatives. However, when tobacco control advocates were cited in news articles, positive slants toward tobacco industry CSR were less likely to appear (McDaniel, Lown, & Malone, 2018); this implies there is a need for tobacco control advocates to increase their presence in the media, as well as the potential to influence the valence of tobacco news.

Table 22.3 Dialogic communication and measures for websites, Facebook, and Twitter.

	Measures		
Principles[*]	Websites[1]	Facebook[2]	Twitter[3]
The dialogic loop A feedback loop that allows the public to pose questions to organizations and for organizations to respond publicly to questions and concerns	• Newsletter sign-up • Facebook logo/link • Twitter logo/link • YouTube logo/link • Development staff email hyperlinks • Generic email hyperlinks • Facebook site with comments posted • Opportunity for moderated discussions • Customizable fundraising pages • Ability/invitation to share information from website • Links to personalized appeals on third-party sites (e.g. other tobacco control advocacy groups) • User/audience surveys	• Links to organization homepage • Use of applications • Ease of donations • Join now option • Offers of regular information through email • Profile sharing • Content sharing • Number of advertisements on a site	• Responding to a question in comments • Posing a question in comments

Usefulness of information
Organizations should provide content that is useful for website visitors (e.g. contact information, organizational background and history); information should not only serve the interests of organizations but the interests of the public
	• General information about giving
	• Director's message
	• Message from an organization leader other than current director
	• Multiple links to specific donor/giving info web pages
	• Annual report
	• Organization's form
	• Mission statement
	• Organizational goals
	• Current news
	• Patient feature stories
	• Research study/studies info
	• Board of directors list
	• Case for support (why give?)
	• How contributions are utilized
	• Ways to give
	• How to donate:
	  • Stocks
	  • Property
	  • In-kind donations
	  • Matching gifts
	  • Memorials and honorariums
	  • Planned giving
	  • Endowments
	• Specific gift designations/programs/projects
	• Giving clubs/levels
	• Center-hosted special events
	• Information on how to host special event for center
		• Links to news releases
		• Media room
		• Speeches
		• Policies
		• Video and audio
		• Industry news
		• Links to annual reports
		• Links to a careers' webpage
		• Weblinks to organizational social networking sites or a company's blog
		• Contact information
		• Links to an online media room
		• On Twitter profile:Mission
		• Information and photo of the profile manager

(*Continued*)

Table 22.3 (*Continued*)

	Measures		
*Principles**	Websites[1]	Facebook[2]	Twitter[3]

Generation of return visits
Generating return visits should go beyond simply regular updates of website content; interactive strategies, such as online forums and public questions and answer sessions, should be used
	• Current news: fundraising page
	• Volunteer opportunities
	• Calendar of events
	• Blogs:
	  • Staff
	  • Patients
	  • Board
	  • Supporters
	  • Directors
	• FAQs
			• Links to pages on the organization's site where visitors can request additional information
			• Links to a page on the organization's website describing company events
			• Links to newsworthy information about the organization
			• Links to news items about the organization in the trade or mainstream media
			• Links to discussion forums and FAQs on the organization website

Ease of interface Websites should be organized logically and information should be easy to find; "content should take precedence over aesthetic considerations"	• Sitemap • Search box • Choice of high- or low-resolution graphics • Menu link(s) to center fundraising information from home page • Menu link(s) to online giving from home page • Link(s) on home page to center fundraising info • Links on home page to online giving • Graphic link(s) on home page to center fundraising info • Graphic link(s) on home page to online giving • Text box link(s) on home page to center fundraising info • Text box link(s) on home page online giving • Link(s) on home page to parent organization giving related content		N/A

Conservation of visitors Visitors to websites should be valued and organizations must recognize that a link to another website may result in a visitor never returning; advertising on an organizational website should be avoided or minimized, as dialogic communication should be the goal rather than marketing or advertising	• Link(s) to external websites • Online giving links directed to parent org/foundation • Center default designation for online giving when redirected • Inclusion of list of giving designations not related to cancer center	• Facebook link • YouTube link • Blog link • Links to a page featuring a description of an organization • Last tweet appearing on the first page of the profile • Recent update within the last 24 hours
Organization engagement Organization comments in dialogic spaces	• Wall • Discussion boards	

*Adapted from Kent and Taylor (1998, pp. 326–331).
[1]Adopted from (Wirtz & Zimbres, 2018).
[2]Adopted from (Bortree & Seltzer, 2009).
[3]Adopted from (Rybalko & Seltzer, 2010).

Saffer et al. (2019) suggest that one way advocacy organizations can capture the public's limited attention is by engaging with them on social media as well-connected actors. This village approach considers how advocacy groups' connections to other advocacy groups, and their public, create subgroups or "villages" within a network. Advocacy groups often address social or political issues through collaborative networks. Their collaborative networks represent a powerful approach to solve pressing issues, hold powerful social actors accountable, and strengthen civil society. Thus, it is reasonable to expect that advocacy groups, as a village inside a larger network, can garner the public's attention on certain issues.

Tobacco control advocacy organizations can develop collaborative networks with advocacy groups in other fields, such as the environment, climate change, gender equity, labor, gun control, and more. This collaborative network can be used to closely monitor the tobacco industry's approaches to other advocacy groups in the network and controversial industry marketing and communication activities, and demand for government regulations on communication activities. For instance, gun control advocacy groups may experience the same challenges because of CSR and other SC activities and stakeholder relationship building by the National Rifle Association (NRA). In fact, the NRA's CSR programs and target segments described in their webpages (NRA, 2019) are similar to the tobacco industry's CSR tactics. Tobacco control and other advocacy organizations, who share similar challenges from the corporation, may have a better opportunity to obtain public attention and influence government regulations by forming collaborative networks and acting collectively through social media. In Costa Rica, Red National Anti-Tobacco Network (RENATA), with the assistance of international health groups, submitted formal comments and succeeded in convincing the Health Ministry to expand advertising restrictions by banning CSR programs by the tobacco industry (Crosbie, Sosa, & Glantz, 2017).

The collaborative networks can also identify the extrinsic motives of CSR and enhance public understanding of such motives. Research found that consumers are able to identify the extrinsic motives of CSR and when they do so (e.g. a company's self-interest in increasing profits or restoring damaged images after a crisis), CSR with extrinsic motives has a negative impact on the company's CSR effectiveness (Ham & Kim, 2019). Tobacco control advocacy organizations and other advocacy groups can partner to identify common extrinsic motives of CSR across controversial industries and convey such motives to the public via social and digital media. For instance, Dorfman et al. (2012) argue that the tobacco industry's and soda company's CSR or public education campaigns emphasize consumers' personal responsibility, instead of the corporate, by highlighting the importance of consumers' health behavior and decision-making instead of the companies' roles in creating an unhealthy environment. Similarly, in its "Balanced Living" message on Live Positively, Coca-Cola suggests that the company is responsible only for providing labels with calorific information to consumers, and that their health is ultimately up to the consumer. PepsiCo UK's Change4Life campaign likewise insists that "active parents make active kids" – suggesting drinking soda is an informed decision and managing a healthy and active lifestyle is entirely up to kids and their parents.

In conclusion, novel tobacco products and the tobacco industry's social/digital media activities pose significant challenges to tobacco control advocacy. Tobacco control advocacy organizations need to re-examine and extend their network with key stakeholders, especially young people, adjust to constant changes in tobacco/health science and policies, thrive in the social/digital media battles against the tobacco industry, and gain the public's legitimacy for advocating control of new tobacco products. In doing so, traditional communication methods of anti-smoking campaigns relying on fear and one-way public education will not be effective. According to the cocreational model (Botan, 2017), stakeholders are cocreators of organizations' messages, strategies, tactics, and identities. Scholars in the field of SC are proposing and testing tools that can guide organizations to create shared meanings with stakeholders on social media (Heath, 2013), and strategic networking and collaboration among advocacy groups that can lead to bolstering the power of advocacy (Saffer et al., 2019). These approaches and tools may assist tobacco control advocacy groups in identifying active stakeholders, connecting and listening to stakeholders, identifying sharable or shared meanings, creating messages/strategies based on the shared meanings, dissemination of messages, and monitoring of stakeholders' responses to cocreated messages/strategies on social media. We hope to see more collaboration between tobacco control advocacy and SC scholarship, and the two fields' contribution to prevent and control the number one killer of global populations.

References

AARC. (2019). Tobacco coalition. Retrieved from http://www.aarc.org/advocacy/aarc-coalitions/tobacco-partners

Alcalá, H. E., & Shimoga, S. V. (2019). It is about trust: Trust in sources of tobacco health information, perceptions of harm, and use of e-cigarettes. *Nicotine & Tobacco Research*. https://doi.org/10.1093/ntr/ntz004.

Allem, J. P., Escobedo, P., Cruz, T. B., & Unger, J. B. (2019). Vape pen product placement in popular music videos. *Addictive Behaviors*, *93*, 263–264.

Arnott, D. (2018). The impact diverging public opinion on cannabis and tobacco regulation has on constructive engagement between advocates. *Addiction*, *113*(4), 605–606.

Basáñez, T., Majmundar, A., Cruz, T. B., & Unger, J. B. (2018). Vaping associated with healthy food words: A content analysis of Twitter. *Addictive Behaviors Reports*, *8*, 147–153.

Bortree, D. S., & Seltzer, T. (2009). Dialogic strategies and outcomes: An analysis of environmental advocacy groups' Facebook profiles. *Public Relations Review*, *35*(3), 317–319.

Botan, C. H. (2017). *Strategic communication theory and practice: The cocreational model*. Hoboken, NJ: Wiley-Blackwell.

Bromberg, J. E., Augustson, E. M., & Backinger, C. L. (2012). Portrayal of smokeless tobacco in YouTube videos. *Nicotine & Tobacco Research*, *14*(4), 455–462.

CDC. (2017). Tobacco-related mortality. Retrieved from https://www.cdc.gov/tobacco/data_statistics/fact_sheets/health_effects/tobacco_related_mortality/index.htm

CDC. (2019). Burden of tobacco use in the U.S. Retrieved from https://www.cdc.gov/tobacco/campaign/tips/resources/data/cigarette-smoking-in-united-states.html

Chapman, S. (2007). *Public health advocacy and tobacco control: Making smoking history*. Oxford: Blackwell.

Chu, K.-H., Allem, J.-P., Cruz, T. B., & Unger, J. B. (2017). Vaping on Instagram: Cloud chasing, hand checks and product placement. *Tobacco Control*, *26*(5), 575–578.

Chu, K.-H., Colditz, J. B., Primack, B. A., Shensa, A., Allem, J.-P., Miller, E., Unger, J. B., & Cruz, T. B. (2018). JUUL: Spreading online and offline. *Journal of Adolescent Health*, *63*(5), 582–586.

Clark, E., Jones, C., Williams, J., Kurti, A., Norotsky, M., Danforth, C., & Dodds, P. (2016). Vaporous marketing: Uncovering pervasive electronic cigarette advertisements on Twitter. *PLoS ONE*, *11*(7), 1–14.

Coombs, T. (2017). Origin stories in CSR: Genesis of CSR at British American Tobacco. *Corporate Communications: An International Journal*, *22*(2), 178–191.

Coombs, W. T., & Holladay, S. J. (2012a). Privileging an activist vs. a corporate view of public relations history in the U.S. *Public Relations Review*, *38*(3), 347–353.

Coombs, W. T., & Holladay, S. J. (2012b). Fringe public relations: How activism moves critical PR toward the mainstream. *Public Relations Review*, *38*(5), 880–887.

Cox, E., Barry, R. A., & Glantz, S. (2016). E-cigarette policymaking by local and state governments – 2009–2014. *The Milbank Quarterly*, *94*(3), 520–596.

Crosbie, E., Sosa, P., & Glantz, S. A. (2017). The importance of continued engagement during the implementation phase of tobacco control policies in a middle-income country: The case of Costa Rica. *Tobacco Control*, *26*(1), 60–68.

Dai, H., Deem, M. J., & Hao, J. (2017). Geographic variations in electronic cigarette advertisements on Twitter in the United States. *International Journal of Public Health*, *62*(4), 479–487.

Derry, R., & Waikar, S. V. (2008). Frames and filters: Strategic distrust as a legitimation tool in the 50-year battle between public health activists and big tobacco. *Business & Society*, *47*(1), 102–139.

Dorfman, L., Cheyne, A., Friedman, L. C., Wadud, A., & Gottlieb, M. (2012). Soda and tobacco industry corporate social responsibility campaigns: How do they compare? *PLoS Medicine*, *9*(6), e1001241.

Du Plessis, N., & Grobler, A. F. (2014). Achieving sustainability through strategically driven CSR in the South African retail sector. *Public Relations Review*, *40*(2), 267–277.

Duke, J. C., Lee, Y. O., Kim, A. E., Watson, K. A., Arnold, K. Y., Nonnemaker, J. M., & Porter, L. (2014). Exposure to electronic cigarette television advertisements among youth and young adults. *Pediatrics*, *134*(1), e29–36.

Erwin, C. O., & Dias, A. M. (2016). The utilization of websites for fundraising by NCI-designated cancer centers: Examining the capacity for dialogic communication with prospective donors. *Health Marketing Quarterly*, *33*(4), 369–385.

Fairchild, A. L., & Bayer, R. (2015). Smoke and fire over e-cigarettes. *Science*, *347*(6220), 375–376.

Farsalinos, K. (2018). Electronic cigarettes: An aid in smoking cessation, or a new health hazard? *Therapeutic Advances in Respiratory Disease*, *12*. https://doi.org/10.1177/1753465817744960.

FDA. (2016). FDA takes significant steps to protect Americans from dangers of tobacco through new regulation. Retrieved from https://www.fda.gov/news-events/press-announcements/fda-takes-significant-steps-protect-americans-dangers-tobacco-through-new-regulation

FDA. (2019a). FDA permits sale of IQOS tobacco heating system through premarket tobacco product application pathway. Retrieved from http://www.fda.gov/news-events/press-announcements/fda-permits-sale-iqos-tobacco-heating-system-through-premarket-tobacco-product-application-pathway

FDA. (2019b). Federal register – tobacco products; required warnings for cigarette packages and advertisements. Retrieved from https://www.federalregister.gov/documents/2019/08/16/2019-17481/tobacco-products-required-warnings-for-cigarette-packages-and-advertisements

FDA. (2019c). Selling tobacco products in retail stores. Retrieved from https://www.fda.gov/tobacco-products/retail-sales-tobacco-products/selling-tobacco-products-retail-stores

FDA. (2019d). Youth tobacco use: Results from the national youth tobacco survey. Retrieved from http://www.fda.gov/tobacco-products/youth-and-tobacco/youth-tobacco-use-results-national-youth-tobacco-survey

FDA. (2020). FDA finalizes enforcement policy on unauthorized flavored cartridge-based e-cigarettes that appeal to children, including fruit and mint. Retrieved from http://www.fda.gov/news-events/press-announcements/fda-finalizes-enforcement-policy-unauthorized-flavored-cartridge-based-e-cigarettes-appeal-children

Forsyth, S. R., & Malone, R. E. (2010). "I'll be your cigarette – Light me up and get on with it": Examining smoking imagery on YouTube. *Nicotine & Tobacco Research*, *12*(8), 810–816.

Freeman, B., & Chapman, S. (2007). Is "YouTube" telling or selling you something? Tobacco content on the YouTube video-sharing website. *Tobacco Control*, *16*(3), 207–210.

FTC. (2019). FTC and FDA send warning letters to companies selling flavored e-liquids about social media endorsements without health warnings. Retrieved from https://www.ftc.gov/news-events/press-releases/2019/06/ftc-fda-send-warning-letters-companies-selling-flavored-e-liquids

Guidry, J., Jin, Y., Haddad, L., Zhang, Y., & Smith, J. (2016). How health risks are pinpointed (or not) on social media: The portrayal of waterpipe smoking on Pinterest. *Health Communication*, *31*(6), 659–667.

Ham, C.-D., & Kim, J. (2019). The role of CSR in crises: Integration of situational crisis communication theory and the persuasion knowledge model. *Journal of Business Ethics*, *158*(2), 353–372.

Hamilton. (2002). *Settling States and Participating Manufacturers, Master Settlement Agreement*. www.naag.org/tobac/cigmsa.rtf

Heath, R. L. (Ed.). (2013). *The handbook of public relations*. Thousand Oaks, CA: Sage.

Heath, R. L., & Vasquez, G. (Eds.). (2001). *Handbook of public relations*. Thousand Oaks, CA: Sage.

Hefler, M., Freeman, B., & Chapman, S. (2013). Tobacco control advocacy in the age of social media: Using Facebook, Twitter and change. *Tobacco Control*, *22*(3), 210–214.

Hickman, A. (2019). Philip Morris suspends IQOS influencer campaigns. Retrieved from https://www.campaignlive.com/article/philip-morris-suspends-iqos-influencer-campaigns/1584446

Hirschhorn, N. (2004). Corporate social responsibility and the tobacco industry: Hope or hype? *Tobacco Control, 13*(4), 447–453.

Huang, J., Kornfield, R., & Emery, S. L. (2016). 100 million views of electronic cigarette YouTube videos and counting: Quantification, content evaluation, and engagement levels of videos. *Journal of Medical Internet Research, 18*(3), e67.

Huang, J., Kornfield, R., Szczypka, G., & Emery, S. L. (2014). A cross-sectional examination of marketing of electronic cigarettes on Twitter. *Tobacco Control, 23*(S3), iii26–iii30.

Jahng, M. R., Hong, S., & Park, E. H. (2014). How radical is radical? Understanding the role of activists' communication strategies on the formation of public attitude and evaluation. *Public Relations Review, 40*(1), 119–121.

Jha, P. (2011). Avoidable deaths from smoking: A global perspective. *Public Health Reviews, 33*(2), 569–600.

Jo, C. L., Kornfield, R., Kim, Y., Emery, S., & Ribisl, K. M. (2016). Price-related promotions for tobacco products on Twitter. *Tobacco Control, 25*(4), 476–479.

Jun, J., Kim, S.-H., & Wu, L. (2019). Tobacco risk information and comparative risk assessment of e-cigarettes vs. cigarettes: Application of the reinforcing spirals model. *Journal of Health Communication, 24*(4), 422–431.

Kent, M. L., & Taylor, M. (1998). Building dialogic relationships through the world wide web. *Public Relations Review, 24*(3), 321–334.

Kim, Y. S., & Choi, Y. (2012). College students' perception of Philip Morris's tobacco-related smoking prevention and tobacco-unrelated social responsibility. *Journal of Public Relations Research, 24*(2), 184–199.

Kin, F., Lian, T. Y., & Yoon, Y. C. (2010). How the tobacco industry circumvented ban on tobacco advertising, promotion and sponsorship: Observations from selected ASEAN countries. *Asian Journal of WTO & International Health Law & Policy, 5*(2), 449–465.

King, G. (2006). Image restoration: An examination of the response strategies used by Brown and Williamson after allegations of wrongdoing. *Public Relations Review, 32*(2), 131.

Kirkham, C. (2019, May 11). Philip Morris suspends social media campaign. Reuters. https://www.reuters.com/article/us-philipmorris-ecigs-instagram-exclusiv-idUSKCN1SH02K

Kirkpatrick, M. G., Cruz, T. B., Goldenson, N. I., Allem, J.-P., Chu, K.-H., Pentz, M. A., & Unger, J. B. (2017). Electronic cigarette retailers use Pokémon Go to market products. *Tobacco Control, 26*(e2), e145–e147.

Kong, G., LaVallee, H., Rams, A., Ramamurthi, D., & Krishnan-Sarin, S. (2019). Promotion of vape tricks on YouTube: Content analysis. *Journal of Medical Internet Research, 21*(6), e12709.

Kowitt, S. D., Schmidt, A. M., Hannan, A., & Goldstein, A. O. (2017). Awareness and trust of the FDA and CDC: Results from a national sample of US adults and adolescents. *PLoS ONE, 12*(5), e0177546.

Kreitzberg, D. S., Murthy, D., Loukas, A., & Pasch, K. E. (2019). Heat not burn tobacco promotion on Instagram. *Addictive Behaviors, 91*, 112–118.

Kwon, M., & Park, E. (2020). Perceptions and sentiments about electronic cigarettes on social media platforms: Systematic review. *JMIR Public Health and Surveillance, 6*(1), e13673.

Laestadius, L. I., Wahl, M. M., Pokhrel, P., & Cho, Y. I. (2019). From apple to werewolf: A content analysis of marketing for e-liquids on Instagram. *Addictive Behaviors, 91*, 119–127.

Lee, K., & Bialous, S. A. (2006). Corporate social responsibility: Serious cause for concern. *Tobacco Control, 15*(6), 419.

Lienemann, B. A., Unger, J. B., Cruz, T. B., & Chu, K.-H. (2017). Methods for coding tobacco-related Twitter data: A systematic review. *Journal of Medical Internet Research, 19*(3), e91.

Lock, I., Seele, P., & Heath, R. L. (2016). Where grass has no roots: The concept of 'shared strategic communication' as an answer to unethical astroturf lobbying. *International Journal of Strategic Communication, 10*(2), 87–100.

Luo, C., Zheng, X., Zeng, D. D., & Leischow, S. (2014). Portrayal of electronic cigarettes on YouTube. *BMC Public Health, 14*, 1028.

McDaniel, P. A., Cadman, B., & Malone, R. E. (2016). Shared vision, shared vulnerability: A content analysis of corporate social responsibility information on tobacco industry websites. *Preventive Medicine, 89*, 337–344.

McDaniel, P. A., Lown, E. A., & Malone, R. E. (2018). US media coverage of tobacco industry corporate social responsibility initiatives. *Journal of Community Health, 43*(1), 117–127.

McDaniel, P. A., & Malone, R. E. (2009). Creating the "desired mindset": Philip Morris's efforts to improve its corporate image among women. *Women & Health, 49*(5), 441–474.

McDaniel, P. A., & Malone, R. E. (2012). British American Tobacco's partnership with Earthwatch Europe and its implications for public health. *Global Public Health, 7*(1), 14–28.

McKay, B. (2018). The future of media buying: YouTube versus traditional TV. Retrieved from https://www.forbes.com/sites/forbesagencycouncil/2018/01/16/the-future-of-media-buying-youtube-versus-traditional-tv

Navas-Acien, A. (2018). Global tobacco use: Old and new products. *Annals of the American Thoracic Society, 15*(S2), S69–S75.

Niederdeppe, J., Farrelly, M. C., & Wenter, D. (2007). Media advocacy, tobacco control policy change and teen smoking in Florida. *Tobacco Control, 16*(1), 47–52.

Noel, J. K., Rees, V. W., & Connolly, G. N. (2011). Electronic cigarettes: A new "tobacco" industry? *Tobacco Control, 20*(1), 81.

NRA. (2019). NRA Explore. Retrieved from https://explore.nra.org

Otanez, M. G. (2006). Eliminating child labour in Malawi: A British American Tobacco corporate responsibility project to sidestep tobacco labour exploitation. *Tobacco Control, 15*(3), 224–230.

Pew Research Center. (2015). Beyond distrust: How Americans view their government. Retrieved from https://www.people-press.org/2015/11/23/beyond-distrust-how-americans-view-their-government

Pew Research Center. (2018). Many turn to YouTube for children's content, news, how-to lessons. Retrieved from https://www.pewresearch.org/internet/2018/11/07/many-turn-to-youtube-for-childrens-content-news-how-to-lessons

Phua, J., Jin, S. V., & Hahm, J. M. (2018). Celebrity-endorsed e-cigarette brand Instagram advertisements: Effects on young adults' attitudes towards e-cigarettes and smoking intentions. *Journal of Health Psychology, 23*(4), 550–560.

Pratt, C. B. (2011). China's tobacco industry's communication practices: Paradoxes and proposals for public policymaking. *Public Relations Review, 37*(3), 318–320.

Primack, B. A., Rice, K. R., Shensa, A., Carroll, M. V., DePenna, E. J., Nakkash, R., & Barnett, T. E. (2012). U.S. hookah tobacco smoking establishments advertised on the internet. *American Journal of Preventive Medicine, 42*(2), 150–156.

Public Good Projects. (2019). Over half of tweets about ecigs might come from bots. Retrieved from https://thenicholsonfoundation.org/sites/default/files/PGP-TNFBot_Detection_Report.pdf

Reber, B. H., & Berger, B. K. (2005). Framing analysis of activist rhetoric: How the Sierra Club succeeds or fails at creating salient messages. *Public Relations Review, 31*(2), 185–195.

Richardson, A., Ganz, O., & Vallone, D. (2015). Tobacco on the web: Surveillance and characterisation of online tobacco and e-cigarette advertising. *Tobacco Control, 24*(4), 341–347.

Rybalko, S., & Seltzer, T. (2010). Dialogic communication in 140 characters or less: How Fortune 500 companies engage stakeholders using Twitter. *Public Relations Review, 36*(4), 336–341.

Saffer, A. J., Yang, A., Morehouse, J., & Qu, Y. (2019). It takes a village: A social network approach to NGOs' international public engagement. *American Behavioral Scientist, 63*(12), 1708–1727.

Sears, C. G., Walker, K. L., Hart, J. L., Lee, A. S., Siu, A., & Smith, C. (2017). Clean, cheap, convenient: Promotion of electronic cigarettes on YouTube. *Tobacco Prevention & Cessation, 3*. https://doi.org/10.18332/tpc/69393.

Sebrié, E. M., & Glantz, S. A. (2007). Attempts to undermine tobacco control: Tobacco industry "Youth Smoking Prevention" programs to undermine meaningful tobacco control in Latin America. *American Journal of Public Health, 97*(8), 1357–1367.

Sommerfeldt, E. (2011). Activist e-mail action alerts and identification: Rhetorical relationship building strategies in collective action. *Public Relations Review, 37*(1), 87–89.

Stokes, A. Q., & Rubin, D. (2010). Activism and the limits of symmetry: The public relations battle between Colorado GASP and Philip Morris. *Journal of Public Relations Research, 22*(1), 26–48.

Sun, L. (2020). These 3 dividend stocks are immune to the coronavirus crisis | The Motley Fool. Retrieved from https://www.fool.com/investing/2020/02/19/these-3-dividend-stocks-are-immune-to-the-coronavi.aspx

Tan, A. S. L., Lee, C., & Bigman, C. A. (2016). Comparison of beliefs about e-cigarettes' harms and benefits among never users and ever users of e-cigarettes. *Drug and Alcohol Dependence, 158*, 67–75.

Tandilittin, H., & Luetge, C. (2015). CSR activity of tobacco companies in Indonesia: Is it a genuine social responsibility? *Online Journal of Health Ethics, 11*. https://doi.org/10.18785/ojhe.1101.03.

Taylor, M., Kent, M. L., & White, W. J. (2001). How activist organizations are using the Internet to build relationships. *Public Relations Review, 27*(3), 263–284.

TobaccoReporter. (2020). BAT unaffected by virus outbreak. Retrieved from https://tobaccoreporter.com/2020/03/19/bat-unaffected-by-outbreak

Tremblay, M.-C., Pluye, P., Gore, G., Granikov, V., Filion, K. B., & Eisenberg, M. J. (2015). Regulation profiles of e-cigarettes in the United States: A critical review with qualitative synthesis. *BMC Medicine, 13*. https://doi.org/10.1186/s12916-015-0370-z.

U.S. Department of Health and Human Services. (2016). E-cigarette use among youth and young adults: A report of the surgeon general – Executive summary. Retrieved from https://e-cigarettes.surgeongeneral.gov/documents/2016_SGR_Exec_Summ_508.pdf

Uysal, N., & Yang, A. (2013). The power of activist networks in the mass self-communication era: A triangulation study of the impact of WikiLeaks on the stock value of Bank of America. *Public Relations Review, 39*(5), 459–469.

Vassey, J., Metayer, C., Kennedy, C. J., & Whitehead, T. P. (2020). #Vape: Measuring e-cigarette influence on Instagram with deep learning and text analysis. *Frontiers in Communication, 4*. https://doi.org/10.3389/fcomm.2019.00075.

Villanti, A. C., Rath, J. M., Williams, V. F., Pearson, J. L., Richardson, A., Abrams, D. B., Niaura, R. S., & Vallone, D. M. (2016). Impact of exposure to electronic cigarette advertising on susceptibility and trial of electronic cigarettes and cigarettes in US young adults: A randomized controlled trial. *Nicotine & Tobacco Research, 18*(5), 1331–1339.

Viswanath, K., Blake, K., Meissner, H., Saiontz, N., Mull, C., Freeman, C. et al. (2008). Occupational practices and the making of health news: A national survey of U.S. health and medical science journalists. *Journal of Health Communication, 13*(8), 759–777.

Wakefield, M. A., Brennan, E., Durkin, S. J., McLeod, K., & Smith, K. C. (2012). Making news: The appearance of tobacco control organizations in newspaper coverage of tobacco control issues. *American Journal of Health Promotion, 26*(3), 166–171.

Wallack, L., & Dorfman, L. (1996). Media advocacy: A strategy for advancing policy and promoting health. *Health Education Quarterly, 23*(3), 293–317.

Watts, C., Hefler, M., & Freeman, B. (2019). 'We have a rich heritage and, we believe, a bright future': How transnational tobacco companies are using Twitter to oppose policy and shape their public identity. *Tobacco Control, 28*(2), 227–232.

WHO. (2005). WHO framework convention on tobacco control. Retrieved from https://www.who.int/fctc/text_download/en

WHO. (2019). Tobacco; key facts. Retrieved from https://www.who.int/news-room/fact-sheets/detail/tobacco

WHO. (2020). Coronavirus disease (COVID-19) pandemic. Retrieved from https://www.who.int/emergencies/diseases/novel-coronavirus-2019

Williams. (2020). Coronavirus income stocks: 7 high-yield dividend stocks to buy right now | Nasdaq. Retrieved from https://www.nasdaq.com/articles/coronavirus-income-stocks%3A-7-high-yield-dividend-stocks-to-buy-right-now-2020-03-23

Wirtz, J. G., & Zimbres, T. M. (2018). A systematic analysis of research applying 'principles of dialogic communication' to organizational websites, blogs, and social media: Implications for theory and practice. *Journal of Public Relations Research, 30*(1–2), 5–34.

Yamin, C. K., Bitton, A., & Bates, D. W. (2010). E-cigarettes: A rapidly growing internet phenomenon. *Annals of Internal Medicine, 153*(9), 607–609.

Yang, A. (2013). When transnational civil network meets local context: An exploratory hyperlink network analysis of Northern/Southern NGOs' virtual network in China. *Journal of International and Intercultural Communication, 6*(1), 40–60.

Yang, Q., Liu, J., Lochbuehler, K., & Hornik, R. (2019). Does seeking e-cigarette information lead to vaping? Evidence from a national longitudinal survey of youth and young adults. *Health Communication, 34*(3), 298–305.

23

Research and Evaluation in Strategic Communication

Yi Grace Ji, Zifei Fay Chen, Zongchao Cathy Li, and Don W. Stacks

Boston University & University of San Francisco & San Jose State University & University of Miami

Introduction

This chapter introduces the reader to the concept of strategic communication (SC) research. It differentiates between research as the gathering of information (data, whether numeric, alphabetical, observational, and so forth) and how that information is evaluated and interpreted in order to make decisions regarding the progress of a communication campaign.

Research is an important part of SC and good research is what makes the communication process strategic. So, what is research? The *Dictionary of public relations measurement and research* defines research as "the systematic effort before (formative, aka strategic research) or during and/or after (summative or evaluative research) a communication activity aimed at discovering and collecting the facts or opinion pertaining to an identified issue, need, or question" (Stacks & Bowen, 2013, p. 26). This definition stresses the importance of having an identified issue and incorporating research in all stages of a SC or program.

Research may be formal or informal (Stacks & Bowen, 2013). *Formal research* uses either quantitative or qualitative methodology to gather, analyze, and evaluate data systematically, that is, the data are collected, reviewed, analyzed via appropriate tools (statistics or logic), and then evaluated and interpreted. *Informal research* typically uses qualitative methods to observe people, events, or objects of interest as they occur without additional analyses. Quantitative and qualitative methods are different approaches to data collection, assessment, and outcome. Each approach has its own advantages and disadvantages – quantitative methods help predict and generalize outcomes, and qualitative methods help provide more in-depth description and understanding of a particular subject (Stacks, 2017). To have a better understanding of both approaches, we will briefly cover some specific methods in this chapter.

No matter which approach is taken, good research for SC should be *planned*, *deliberate*, and *executed*. First of all, research should be planned well ahead. Not only does research need well-defined goals and objectives, but it also needs a plan for how the findings will be used (Michaelson & Macleod, 2007). Second, research should be deliberate. Best practices in SC research entail rigorous research design and detailed supporting documentation (Michaelson & Macleod, 2007; Michaelson & Stacks, 2017). Last, but not least, research needs to be executed and the organization should prepare to take action based on the findings. In other words, research is a continuous effort that follows an "end-to-end" process (Michaelson &

The Handbook of Strategic Communication, First Edition. Edited by Carl H. Botan.

Stacks, 2017). Eventually, research results should be used to help achieve an organization's long-term goals and objectives. If the decision-makers are unwilling to take action based on the research findings, then creating a research program and conducting research will be of little value to the organization, however well-planned and rigorous the design (Michaelson & Macleod, 2007). Only when a research program is planned, deliberate, and executed can it make the communication program truly strategic, thereby helping to achieve the organization's goals and objectives.

Why Do Research?

SC essentially serves as a communication management function, as a way to produce the best results of impact on outcomes both on "hard" data (e.g. sales volume, revenue, donation) and "soft" data (reputation, relationship, credibility, trust – outcomes that require social psychological interpretations that are not directly observable). Research not only renders SC professionals the ability to establish baseline, benchmarks, and evaluate outcomes, but also provides a way to demonstrate the value of SC to organizations. For example, in the corporate context, we need to demonstrate the value of SC efforts not only on the non-financial outcomes, but also the financial outcomes.

Goals and Objectives

To demonstrate the value of SC, one needs to provide *evidence* that the *outcomes* of a SC program meet stated and measurable objectives and can advance the organization's goals. Therefore, research needs to start with setting goals and measurable objectives. A goal is the general outcome expected at the end of the campaign. A goal gives direction and is usually long-term based. Objectives, on the other hand, are very specific. While goals may reflect the SC campaign or program in general, objectives can be defined in terms of outputs, outtakes, and outcomes (Stacks, 2017). It has been argued that any SC objective should be *measurable*, not only by simple counts, but also by more sophisticated forms of *analysis* (Broom & Dozier, 1990; Michaelson & Stacks, 2017; Stacks & Michaelson, 2010).

Objectives should be stated with some specific results in mind. Stating objectives can be considered as following the roadmap for getting from problem to solution (Stacks, 2017). While the goal statement provides general directions, the objectives tell us specifically *how* to achieve the goal and set up expected outcomes. There are three basic types of objectives in SC campaigns that focus on three levels of outcomes: informational objectives, motivational objectives, and behavioral objectives (see Figure 23.1). Note that they are in order of the type of data required to meet the objective. If the information is not received, can there be predicted motivation? If the motivational objectives are not met, even though the information objectives were met, there may be problems still in the informational state of the campaign. Thus, the feedback looks between motivational and informational objectives. Finally, where the "rubber meets the road" are the results as wanted – has the campaign been a success? Are these three related to outputs, outtakes, and outcomes in some way?

Informational objectives specify what the audience should know during and after the campaign (Stacks, 2017). A common mistake in many SC programs is to assume that the audience has the necessary information to behave in the way desired. To avoid this error, the first campaign effort should be to educate the target audience with accurate information and make sure the information is received and understood as expected when that information has been presented.

Knowing about the campaign does not necessarily translate into action. In many instances, knowledge is insufficient to produce actions. Thus, we need to specify *motivational objectives.* Motivational objectives assess whether the information is having an effect and whether the

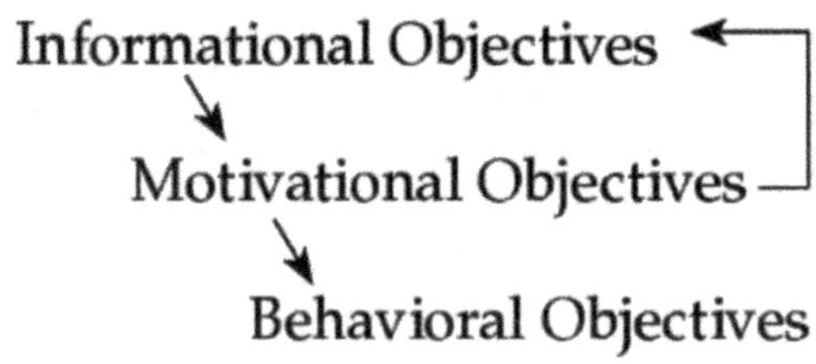

Figure 23.1 Outcome levels in strategic communication campaigns.

strategies and tactics are likely to affect further behaviors. Motivational objectives test the cognitive, emotional, and connotative (i.e. behavioral intent) responses. Once defined, the motivational objectives can be tracked over the course of a campaign. When audience motivation is found to be lacking, efforts should be redirected at providing necessary information and reasons for action.

Finally, *behavioral objectives* assess what we expect at the end of the campaign and how well they correlate with other outcomes and the return on investment (ROI). Behavioral objectives are of the greatest importance to the client – they are often what "count" and define the success or failure of a campaign.

The concept of research as a process can be seen in what Michaelson and Stacks (2017) described as the BASIC© model to understanding the communication lifecycle (see Figure 23.2). This five-part model closely aligns with the three communication objectives and reinforces the "end-to-end" research process. Awareness and knowledge are a function of the informational objective. Relevance and action initiation are a function of the motivational objective. Creating advocacy – creating a third-party endorsement of the campaign or program messaging (Stacks, 2017) – is a function of the behavioral objective, but should be taken one step further: to actually induce some overt behavior based on that advocacy with peer others. Thus, the process continues in a cycle much like Maslow's "Hierarchy of Needs" (1943, 1954), which notes that once self-actualization is achieved, the process begins over again, only at a higher plane of awareness. As should be clear by now, the BASIC© model is process-oriented. That is, the model allows the researcher to choose and validate his or her starting point in the campaign. It also provides a way to establish whether the campaign objectives need to be revised based on where the audience is on the given problem or opportunity.

Research in the Strategic Communication Campaign or Program

Goals and objectives need to be considered in the SC campaign being implemented. Thus, another way of understanding the relationship between goals and objectives is to interoperate them along a SC campaign timeline. A SC campaign encompasses three phases – development, refinement, and evaluation (Stacks, 2017). Research needs to be incorporated in all three phases.

The *developmental phase* can also be understood as the pre-campaign stage. This is the phase where goals and objectives are set prior to the implementation of the campaign. Both secondary and primary research can be used to help specify both broad and detailed objectives. Secondary research, such as the use of historical records, industry reports, and government reports, can be utilized to help obtain background information for better environmental scanning. The information, obtained through secondary research, in turn helps create appropriate research instruments for primary research if needed. Such instruments can be survey questionnaires, focus groups, or interview protocols (Stacks, 2017). Research conducted during the

Figure 23.2 The BASIC model (Michaelson & Stacks, 2017).

developmental phase is essential to establishing campaign baselines against which final evaluations can be made (Michaelson, Wright, & Stacks, 2012) and sets a minimal standard for campaign "success." Rigorous research conducted prior to the implementation of the campaign can help professionals set benchmarks throughout the campaign to evaluate and re-evaluate whether the goals and objectives are achieved.

The *refinement phase* – or second phase – happens when the campaign is actually activated. What is assumed for this stage is that the campaign lifespan is systematically evaluated. Research, in this regard, helps provide phased *benchmarks* to measure the effectiveness of a given campaign on certain stages. The benchmarks, in turn, serve as feedback to help evaluate whether strategic or tactic adjustments are needed. We need to be aware that campaigns are not implemented in a competitive vacuum. In reality, few campaigns go exactly as targeted and scheduled because internal and external factors may bring counter-forces after a campaign kicks off (Michaelson, Wright, & Stacks, 2012). Research allows us to constantly monitor the progress of the campaign using phased benchmarks and conduct refinements when needed, thereby demonstrating systematic progress toward goals and objectives.

The *evaluation phase* occurs toward the end of the campaign, before it is completed. In this phase, research is used to evaluate the effectiveness of the campaign and assess whether it will be a success. This is done by projecting the final behavioral outcomes – purchasing, voting, attending, and so forth – through sophisticated statistical analyses. Additionally, evaluation traces the various goals and objectives set and refined, as well as the baselines and benchmarks established throughout the entire campaign process. The SC campaign outcomes also need to be tied back to the business outcomes to establish the effectiveness in generating return on expectations (ROE) and ROI. Finally, the impact of the campaign needs to be evaluated by correlating other functional outcomes to the communication outcomes (Stacks, 2017). In a corporate campaign dealing with absenteeism, for instance, reduction in employee absenteeism on the product line would be compared against company objectives toward product quality, time to manufacture, and other functional metrics, all of which indicate whether a company's business goals have been met.

To measure the impact of a SC campaign, Michaelson et al. (2012) created the "Excellence Model" for campaign evaluation. After defining excellence in a potentially measurable way based on previous studies conducted by excellence scholars in the field of public relations (e.g. Dozier, Grunig, & Grunig, 1995; Grunig & Grunig, 2006; Grunig, Grunig, & Dozier, 2002, 2006) and industry researchers (e.g. Edelman, 2016; Weiner, 2006), a model known as the "Excellence Pyramid" (see Figure 23.3) was proposed.

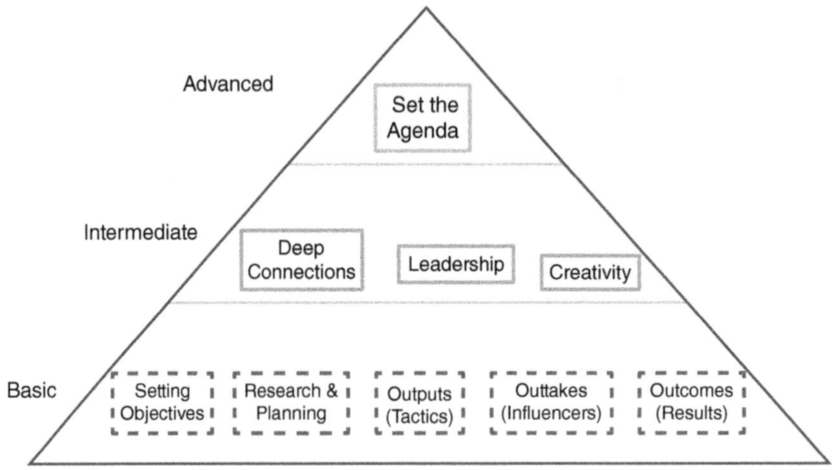

Figure 23.3 The Excellence Pyramid (Michaelson, Wright, & Stacks, 2012).

The Excellence Pyramid consists of three different levels. The basic level contains five components: setting objectives, research and planning, outputs, outtakes, and outcomes/results (Michaelson, Wright, & Stacks, 2012, p. 14). This level can be measured by the presence of each component using nominal-level measurement such as 1 and 0. The intermediate level consists of three factors: deep connections with target audiences, global leadership support and engagement, and creativity and innovation that yields a unique approach to the problem, product, brand, or issue (Michaelson, Wright, & Stacks, 2012, p. 18). Finally, in the advanced level, the campaign can set the agenda to extend the impact to a larger degree through advocacy. The intermediate and advanced level can be measured through scaling forms using interval-level data (Michaelson, Wright, & Stacks, 2012). The "Excellence Model" can be used for the evaluation phase of a SC campaign and can provide quantifiable evidence on that evaluation (Michaelson, Wright, & Stacks, 2012). Three cases can be found in two volumes of international campaign research focusing on two excellent campaigns (Chen et al., 2017; Stacks, Wright, & Bowen, 2014) and one failed campaign (Bowen, Stacks, & Wright, 2017).

Once the campaign has been planned – strategic objectives set – researchers create ways to measure the results of the campaign against baseline and planned benchmarks. These measurements must demonstrate that they are both reliable and valid indicators of what they purport to measure. For instance, hard data such as finances, votes, and the like are fairly easy to measure – they are counted. Soft data, such as reputation, trust, and credibility, are perceptive variables and exist in some form of attitudes, beliefs, and values and must be "created" as "scalar data" (see Michaelson & Stacks, 2017; Stacks, 2017).

Standardized Approaches to Strategic Research in Communication

Up to this point we have provided an overview of SC research. This section goes into the "nuts and bolts" of data generation and argues that there are specific standards of practice that must be met (see Michaelson & Stacks, 2017 for a complete discussion of the need for and demonstration of standards). Here we introduce how data are created and validated.

Now that we have understood the importance of quantifying and standardizing public relations programs and campaigns, we turn to measuring variables related to SC campaigns/programs in a standardized manner. It is necessary to recognize the critical role data play in SC.

A communication program will not be *strategic* unless it is grounded in the inputs from data generated through research. Only with data, can professionals (1) set up baseline and benchmarks in a SC campaign to evaluate against objectives and goals; (2) assess whether strategies and tactics have been carried out effectively; and (3) adjust the campaign road map accordingly to turn latent audiences to aware audiences, and to ultimately change their behaviors, becoming active. In this process, it is crucial for professionals to keep track of whether each objective is successfully checked off the list.

Output, Outtake, and Outcome

As noted earlier, objectives can be further classified into *outputs*, *outtakes*, and *outcomes*, each defined as key performance indicators (KPIs) or variables to be evaluated throughout the campaign. *Outputs* are results generated by a SC program or campaign that may be received and processed by members of a target audience, and may have a cognitive impact on outtakes (Stacks & Bowen, 2013, p. 21). In practice, outputs are tactical, which could include brochures, press releases, a press conference, website, or other messages (Stacks, 2017). Thus, when quantifying outputs, they can be measured as categorical data, such as (1) if a company has released a message through major media outlets (yes or no), or (2) continuous data such as the number of different media outlets that have been adopted. *Outtakes* are perceptions of influencers or target audiences that the outputs have been created to change or maintain (Stacks, 2017). In a communication campaign, outtakes can be used to measure what audiences have understood and/or heeded and/or responded to (Stacks & Bowen, 2013, p. 21). *Outputs* can also serve as mediating variables between outtakes and outcomes. *Outcomes* are the final effects and consequences of a communication campaign, which are defined as quantifiable changes taking place in informational, attitudinal, and ultimately behavioral levels (Stacks, 2017; Stacks & Bowen, 2013, p. 21).

Reflecting outputs, outtakes, and outcomes, data can provide professionals insights on how a SC campaign is progressing. While it is important to acknowledge the role of data in research, it is also critical to be aware that data do not mean anything unless we assign meanings to them. When assigned meanings, data can be analyzed using statistical procedures to provide results and drive managerial insights. So how can data be assessed? This has to do with *measurement*. The following section introduces the concept of measurement, different levels of measurement, and pragmatic adoption of valid and reliable measurement in SC research to assess and track the process and results of the campaign.

What Is Measurement?

Measurement is the process by which we observe things seen and unseen and assign numbers to categories. It is important to understand that measurement *levels* determine how precise we will be in explaining what we have observed and which analytical tool (statistical analysis) would be most appropriate for results reporting, analysis, and interpretation. In some instances, our measurement requires "hard" data, which are found in the economic or natural sciences – such as gross national product, miles per hour. However, most of the variables that interest SC professionals are "untouchable," "soft," or "non-financial" variables, such as attitudes, beliefs, and values. To measure these variables, we need to state how we measure what we observe and the measurement we adopt must be as precise as possible.

Measurement Levels

As discussed earlier, how we measure observations determines data analysis and results interpretation. In general, measurements can be made at four levels: nominal, ordinal, interval, and ratio. They can be further summarized into two distinctive classes – categorical or continuous. *Categorical* measures include *nominal* and *ordinal* data, which place our observations into classes (Stacks, 2017) such as car brands (e.g. Mercedes, BMW, Jeep). *Continuous* measures include interval and ratio data. They are more complex and assume that observations are equidistant apart (Stacks, 2017), such as inches, miles, degrees of temperature, and income. Categorical observations are simple to make but difficult to interpret. Continuous observations are more difficult to make but are easier to explain. Furthermore, continuous observations may be collapsed downward from ratio to interval, to ordinal, and to nominal. However, this process cannot be reversed. Finally, continuous observations, when summed and described, offer more information than categorical observations. More details will be discussed later in the data section.

What Are Data?

All data are analyzed through a data structure. For instance, variables are defined and then acquired through different methodologies. Each data source (e.g. the respondent or source where the data is being collected) is input into the analysis as a line of individual responses or observations that are called *data sets*. More recently, Stacks (2017) has differentiated between three basic data sets used in SC research. A data set is a group of data based on variables and observations made on those variables. Today, "big data" attracts a lot of attention; however, big data has been around since the credit card. Big data sets are huge – they have thousands of observations and hundreds or more variables, often collected in real time through the internet or packaged in data warehouses. Additionally, big data sets are unstructured – that is, they allow variables to create new variables based on additional data. Typically, most big data sets are used for segmentation and priority research. Large data sets differ in that, although they may be as large as big data sets, the variables and observations are structured – they do not change unless the researcher operationally redefines them through specific database commands. Large data are used to set and analyze an audience's normative data. Finally, small data sets are typically determined by the number of variables being studied. While large data set norms, we use small data to test to see if the relations between variables actually exist and, if so, what the relationships between them are. Good SC research uses all three types of data sets.

Following the process of quantifying observations, researchers should be able to come to the data collection stage of a quantitative research project. According to Stacks and Bowen (2013), data can be viewed in two ways. First, as a part of research methodology – "the observations or measurements taken when evaluating a public relations campaign or program" (p. 8). Second, from a statistical approach – presented as the frequencies, means, and percentages used to assess a campaign or program (Stacks, 2017). In the language of data, an individual observation is a datum; while a set of observations are data. The following introduces the concept and measurement of data.

Determined by four types of measurements, in general data can be classified into two levels: categorical and continuous. These data levels dictate the analytical tools used to evaluate similarities and differences in the variables being observed. Each of them can be further divided into two other subgroups, four in total: nominal, ordinal, interval, and ratio. *Nominal* data, as the most basic type of data, simply distinguish between the units being counted. *Ordinal* data not only distinguish, but also rank the units based on some criteria, such as larger or smaller. For example, income variable can be measured by both nominal and ordinal data. Categorizing people's income into "yes" or "no" yields nominal-level data; while categorizing participants' annual income into low income, middle income, and high income results in ordinal-level data. In contrast, continuous data are placed on a continuum, not in categories. More sophisticated than ordinal-level data, when data are defined as *interval*, the assumption is that the individual data points or units are equidistantly distributed. That is, the distance between 1 and 2 is one unit and the distance between 1 and 5 is four units. When data are defined as *ratio*, the interval assumption is extended to include an ***absolute zero point***. It is also important to note that data "reduction" occurs only in a top-down fashion: we can "downgrade" the data level from ratio to interval to ordinal to nominal, but the data level cannot be "upgraded" in the opposite fashion. To elaborate, we can redefine the income measure from dollars (ratio) to more subjective units: low, medium, high (ordinal) or yes and no (nominal).

It is important to understand that the way the data are initially defined (i.e. nominal, ordinal, interval, ratio) determines the statistical analysis procedures. Although we continue to use the terms categorical and continuous when describing how data are analyzed, statistical theory redefines them according to how they are distributed (Stacks, 2017). In statistics-speak, continuous data are referred to as ***parametric*** data. Because parametric data are at least interval in nature, they have a tendency to group together, to have a common mean from which they vary individually. Parametric data fall under the hypothesized normal curve. The distribution of parametric data can be described or reported in two ways – *central tendency* (commonly reported by mean, medium, and mode) and *dispersion* (commonly reported by range, variance, and standard deviation). When statisticians refer to categorical data, they use the term *nonparametric*. Counts, frequency, and percentage are usually used to describe categorical data. The distinction of how to collect and report categorical and continuous data becomes even more important when inferential statistics are needed for hypothesis testing, or when the campaign cannot afford anything less than minimal error (the minimal error standard for years has been no more than 5% error, allowing for 95% confidence in the results).

Once the data have been gathered, the first thing that must be done is to establish the reliability and validity of the data. While there are published standards for establishing reliability, validity is a more nuanced concept. As we will note in the next section, validity can be established in four ways, while reliability can be established through statistical analyses.

Reliability and Validity

One of the critical features of quantitative research methodology is the ability to state the reliability. Quite simply, a measure can have a demonstrated reliability and still not be a valid measure. Consider a watch that is 5 minutes early at all times. Is it reliable? Yes! It is measuring precisely the same way each time you look at it. Is it valid? No! It is not measuring the *real* time, it is 5 minutes earlier than the actual time (Michaelson & Stacks, 2017; Stacks, 2017).

Reliability is an estimate of how much error you have in your measures (Stacks, 2017). As such, reliability can be estimated through statistical tests, such as coefficient alpha for continuous data and the KR-20 test for categorical data. Each provides you with estimates of how reliable your measure is. The standard for acceptable reliability is a coefficient above 0.80, which is considered good. Some research that is exploratory in nature may accept a coefficient of 0.70, but the standard is at least 0.80 (which still yields 36% variability in measurement; a coefficient of 0.90, which is "excellent," still yields 19% variability in measure).[1] The higher the reliability, the less the measurement variance, and we can say the measure is reliably measuring what we sought to measure.

However, the problem is that reliability, a necessary condition for measurement, does not mean the measurement is valid. The *Dictionary of public relations measurement and research* defines "validity" as whether a measure is actually measuring what you defined it to measure (Stacks & Bowen, 2013, p. 26). Validity is closely related to the question of definition. In other words, how we operationalize variable impacts on the measure's validity. There are four types of validity, each a little more rigorous in turn: face validity, content validity, construct validity, and criterion validity.

Face validity occurs when you operationally define the measurement by just saying it is measuring what you say it measures (Stacks & Bowen, 2013, p. 12). Suppose you are creating a measure of social media usage. Based on your secondary research of contemporary social media studies, you create a series of statements that you believe measure social media use. At this stage, your personal research and understanding of the problem gives your measure face validity (Stacks, 2017; Wrench, Thomas-Maddox, & Richmond, 2008).

Content validity provides more rigorous testing of a measure's validity, providing a second level of impartial judgment (Stacks, 2017). Content validity is "based on other researchers or experts evaluations of the measurement items contained in a measure" (Stacks & Bowen, 2013, p. 6) and occurs when you ask others who have studied the area to review your measure. For example, content validity can be achieved as such: in your social media usage measurement construction research, you can reach out to a number of other social media researchers and ask them as a panel to review your measure. After review, you may revise the measure or find that the panel agrees with your definitions and facts.

The third type of validity, *construct validity*, is "a statistically tested form of measurement validity that seeks to establish the dimensionality of a measure" (Stacks & Bowen, 2013, p. 6).[2] It is obtained through an analysis of how the measure is actually used. That is, you derive construct validity through observation or statistical testing. Most attitudinal measurement scales are composed of a number of statements that people can react to. These scales usually have more than one underlying conceptual construct being measured. Relational outcome measures, for example, can be broken into different dimensions, such as commitment, satisfaction, control mutuality, and trust – which are subgroup measures of four different aspects of organization–public relational outcomes (Hon & Grunig, 1999), and the measure's validity is established through several rounds of item reductions, with pretests and a statistical procedure called factor analysis.

Finally, *criterion-related validity*, which "compares one measure against others known to have specific relationships with what is being measured" (Stacks & Bowen, 2013, p. 8), is established when your measure is shown to be related to other established measures, or if it successfully predicts behavior. For instance, knowing that social media has relationships with age, education, and computer skills, you can perform a pretest to see if your measure correlates well with the other measures.

Once the data have been tested for reliability and validity, usually through pretesting the measures during the developmental stage or by obtaining measures with published reliability coefficients and tested for validity, the next stage is to collect data first at the baseline to establish where you are at the beginning of the campaign, during the refinement stage and against planned benchmarks, and finally, against which you will measure for campaign progress and ultimate success through your specified behavioral goals and objectives. Different research methods are used to collect data, usually driven by the kinds of questions that data are being used to answer. We turn now to how that data will be acquired.

Research Methods

Research Methods Classification

Secondary research is generally the first step in any research program. It is how researchers access the data that distinguishes it from primary research. Secondary research systematically examines or re-analyzes data already used by others to draw conclusions. The results and the process of conducting secondary research helps SC professionals to establish baselines and benchmarks at an early stage of a campaign to set up attainable objectives and goals. Through secondary research, it becomes clearer for researchers to define research questions and objectives and to choose an appropriate measurement system with further research activities.

Compared with secondary research, primary research takes a variety of methods, which can be classified into two categories – *qualitative research* and *quantitative research.*

Qualitative Research

Qualitative research is "research that seeks in-depth understanding of particular cases and issues, rather than generalizable statistical information, through probing, open-ended methods" (Stacks & Bowen, 2013, p. 25). The most used qualitative research methods in SC include *in-depth interviews, focus groups*, and *participant observation.*

In-depth interviews are conducted on a one-to-one basis. It is probably the most "controlled" method compared with the other two qualitative methods (Stacks & Michaelson, 2010). In-depth interviews are most effective when the research objectives are to answer questions of definition, value, and policy (Stacks, 2017). They also offer rich information to answer "why" and "how" questions.

Focus groups can be deemed to conduct a simultaneous interview with a group of people. The size of the group usually ranges from 8 to 12, though in reality it will vary due to the specific research topic and participants' availability. The focus group is a moderated group discussion, in which a moderator asks questions and then probes for richer answers in a group dynamic. In SC practices, the best value in conducting a focus group is to have a group of stakeholders with a common background exchange and discuss their opinions on a research object, such as attitude toward a product, service, or a company's image.

Compared with in-depth interviews and focus groups, researchers have the least amount of "control" while conducting the participant observation method. While unobtrusively studying participants' daily activities, researchers usually immerse themselves, either actively or by pure observing, in the life of an organization or community to observe and record interactions, and then analyze those qualitative data. Participant observation is most appropriate to understand how organizations or individuals behave and communicate in naturalist settings (Stacks & Michaelson, 2010).

In essence, qualitative research investigates a small group of stakeholders or audience understandings, opinions, and reactions to an issue of interest. While it demonstrates the sophistication and depth of information, it lacks the power of generalizability due to the limited sample size, data level, and how that data was gathered.

Quantitative Research

One of the most distinguished features of quantitative research is that it deals with numeric data. This kind of research produces generalizable findings in objective ways with sufficiently large samples (Stacks & Bowen, 2013). *Content analysis*, *survey*, and even *experiment* are quantitative methods adopted in SC.

As a transition between qualitative and quantitative research, content analysis grants SC researchers the power to look at qualitative data in a quantitative way. Based on a predetermined categorization system, researchers can break down a rich stream of qualitative data into countable categories and then systematically count and analyze the numbers generated (Stacks, 2017). Content analysis can be conducted on two levels based on content types, namely *manifest content* and *latent content* (Stacks, 2017; Stacks & Michaelson, 2010). When dealing with manifest content – what we actually see and count – conducting a content analysis can be simply counting the number of times an organization is covered in a media outlet and collecting specific financial figures. However, latent content is more qualitative and embedded with deeper meanings, thus it is more difficult to be counted and measured (Stacks, 2017).

A survey is one of the most frequently used research methods in SC research. It is a method of gathering information about participants' attitudes and beliefs. By adopting surveys, researchers aim to gauge how stakeholders or the general public perceive an issue or an event, an organization, or a person in a relatively controlled fashion (Stacks, 2017). The questions used in a survey are usually adopted from established scales, which have been tested to be valid and reliable. Overall, there are four types of survey: telephone, mail, person-to-person, and internet. Each of them has pros and cons in terms of time and financial cost.

An experiment is the only way that researchers can define *causality* – whether something actually causes a change in something else with time order. In experimental terminologies, an *independent variable* is the factor that effects a change in a *dependent variable*, which is measured as the outcome (Stacks, 2017). In SC research, experiment can help us better understand SC's impacts on organizational decision and ROI. For instance, in crisis management, a number of case studies suggest that the change in compression time leads to the variety of strategies carried out by companies, however, this prediction cannot be validated without conducting a controlled experiment (Stacks, 2017).

Research, Evaluation, and Measurement in the Digital Era

Beyond traditional research methods, more innovative ways of collecting and analyzing data are emerging with new formats of data and communication generated by individuals and organizations in the digital age.

As a group of online applications, social media provide platforms for users to create and exchange user-generated content (Kaplan & Haenlein, 2010). Although the specific functions vary for specific social media channels/tools, they all share five common characteristics (Voit, n.d.):

- Participation
- Openness
- Conversation
- Communities
- Connectedness

These characteristics not only enable individuals to connect with one another and share content (Boyd & Ellison, 2007; Raacke & Bonds-Raacke, 2008), but also provide organizations great opportunities to communicate and engage with their stakeholders for different organizational and relationship cultivation purposes.

The participatory nature of social media has led to its prevalent adoption by both individuals and organizations and has changed tremendously the way people communicate with and about organizations. Now, stakeholders are provided with these platforms to directly and instantly voice their opinions toward companies, products, and services. As the continual feedback loop shortens the distance of time and space between sender and receiver, social media has further allowed organizations and stakeholders to jointly co-manage relationships and to reach mutually beneficial agreements and goals from a cocreational perspective (Botan & Taylor, 2004; Heath, 2014). This interconnectedness has made social media impact on stakeholder decision-making more profound and salient. Stakeholders, such as employees, customers, and regulators, now have direct lines for their electronic word-of-mouth (eWOM) communication and are also influenced by opinions from sources other than the companies or products themselves (DiStaso & McCorkindale, 2013).

Social media has brought abundant opportunities for research, evaluation, and measurement. Although the emergence of social media has provided SC researchers and professionals powerful tools to observe, record, and measure SC efforts with *real-time monitoring*, a major question remains unanswered: do the SC activities on social media have any real impact on organizational ROI?

In addition to the traditional methods discussed previously, organizations are adopting new methods such social listening/monitoring and log data analysis with social media data (such as "favorites," "followers," and "retweets" on Twitter, "likes," "shares," and "comments" on Facebook, and examining conversational sentiment (e.g. positive, neutral, or negative) and using them as campaign benchmarks and KPIs for success. Although only limited empirical evidence suggests such causal relationships, these numbers are not only being used to measure SC outcomes such as engagement and relationships, but are also modeled with financial indicators to suggest future ROI. In fact, identifying and demonstrating the effects of social media-based SC programs on the "bottom line" has been one of the greatest challenges for our profession in this digital era. For SC to gain a seat at the dominant coalition table, it is important to demonstrate our value through quantified non-financial and financial impact (Ji et al., 2017; Li & Stacks, 2015).

Another challenge brought about by social media is data collection and analysis. Research is only as good as the variables employed. Social media offer extremely rich and powerful behavioral data. Depending on the research questions, data can be collected using web-based analytical services through the application programming interface (API; Weller et al., 2013) and then analyzed to test for differences, relationships, and more sophisticated trend predictions. As discussed earlier, the collection and analysis of "big data" remains challenging, but it should not stop us from grasping new techniques that are able to render us substantially richer information to evaluate public opinions, track behaviors, and predict trends. Researchers have been aware of researcher-effect and measurement-effect as byproducts of self-reported data generated from traditional research methods, such as survey and lab experiments (e.g. Liu, 2006; Neuman et al., 2014; Parks, 2014). The wide adoption of social media provides researchers "rich" data both in volume and variety to test and develop communication theories (Mahrt & Scharkow, 2013; Neuman et al., 2014).

However, it is important to note that the use of social media user panels for data collection hinders an accurate understanding of what has been found due to a lack of participant random selection (Michaelson & Stacks, 2017; Stacks, 2017). Therefore, best practices of social media analytics must take "a more social psychological approach and tie sender and receiver perceptions of credibility, confidence, relationship, reputation, and trust" (Li & Stacks, 2016).

Notes

1 Variability is determined by squaring the coefficient and subtracting it from 1 ($1 - r^2$). Thus, 0.80^2 is 0.64; 1 – 0.64 = 0.36).

2 There is the possibility of something being theoretically valid, but typically these measures are found in hard data research. Einstein's famous $e = mc^2$ is an example. Some variables are clearly theoretical; they have been conceptualized but not operationalized. For the purposes of SC, measurement should be validated statistically as the construct level.

References

Botan, C. H., & Taylor, M. (2004). Public relations: State of the field. *Journal of Communication*, *54*(4), 645–659.

Bowen, S. A., Stacks, D. W., & Wright, D. K. (2017). Volkswagen emission scandal: An example of bad public relations on a global scale and the "defeat device" that defeated a reputation. In J. V. Turk & J. Valin (Eds.), *Public relations case studies from around the world* (2nd edn, pp. 3–21). New York: Peter Lang.

Boyd, D. M., & Ellison, N. B. (2007). Social network sites: Definition, history, and scholarship. *Journal of Computer-Mediated Communication, 13*(1), 210–230.

Broom, G. M., & Dozier, D. M. (1990). *Using research in public relations: Applications for program.*

Chen, Z., Stacks, D. W., Ji, Y., & Yook, B. R. (2017). Cargill's Indonesian Palm Oil Sustainability Program. In J. V. Turk & J. Valin (Eds.), *Public relations case studies from around the world* (2nd edn). New York: Peter Lang Publishing.

DiStaso, M. W., & McCorkindale, T. M. (2013). A benchmark analysis of the strategic use of social media for Fortune's most admired U.S. companies on Facebook, Twitter, and YouTube. *Public Relations Journal, 7*(1), 1–33.

Dozier, D. M., Grunig, L. A., & Grunig, J. E. (1995). *Manager's guide to excellence in public relations and communication management.* Mahwah, NJ: Lawrence Erlbaum Associates.

Edelman. (2016). 2016 Edelman Trust Barometer: Executive summary. Retrieved from http://www.edelman.com/insights/intellectual-property/2016-edelman-trust-barometer/executive-summary

Grunig, J. E., & Grunig, L. A. (2006). Characteristics of excellent communication. In T. A. Gillis (Ed.), *The IABC handbook of organizational communication* (pp. 3–18). San Francisco, CA: Jossey-Bass.

Grunig, J. E., Grunig, L. A., & Dozier, D. M. (2006). The excellence theory. In C. H. Botan & V. Hazleton (Eds.), *Public relations theory II* (pp. 21–55). Mahwah, NJ: Lawrence Erlbaum Associates.

Grunig, L. A., Grunig, J. E., & Dozier, D. M. (2002). *Excellent public relations and effective organizations: A study of communication management in three countries.* Mahwah, NJ: Lawrence Erlbaum Associates.

Heath, R. L. (2014, May). Public relations' role in engagement: Functions, voices, and narratives. Paper presented at *Engagement as Strategy, Theory and Practice.* International Communication Association (ICA) pre-Conference, Seattle, WA.

Hon, L. C., & Grunig, J. E. (1999). *Guidelines for measuring relationships in public relations.* Gainesville, FL: Institute for Public Relations.

Ji, Y., Chen, Z., Li, C., & Stacks, D. W. (2017). What's ROI got to do with it? In S. Duhe (Eds.), *New media and public relations* (3rd edn, pp. 76–85). New York: Peter Lang.

Kaplan, A. M., & Haenlein, M. (2010). Users of the world, unite! The challenges and opportunities of social media. *Business Horizons, 53*(1), 59–68.

Li, C., & Stacks, D. W. (2015). *Measuring the impact of social media on business profit & success: A Fortune 500 perspective.* New York: Peter Lang.

Li, Z., & Stacks, D. W. (2016). A great leap: Bridging a new media era of organization–public relationships. In K. Vaidya (Ed.), *Public relations and social media for the curious: Why study public relations and social media.* Retrieved from: http://works.bepress.com/zongchao-li/7

Liu, Y. (2006). Word of mouth for movies: Its dynamics and impact on box office revenue. *Journal of Marketing, 70*(3), 74–89.

Mahrt, M., & Scharkow, M. (2013). The value of big data in digital media research. *Journal of Broadcasting & Electronic Media, 57*(1), 20.

Maslow, A. H. (1943). A theory of human motivation. *Psychological Review, 50*(4), 370–396.

Maslow, A. H. (1954). *Motivation and personality.* New York: Harper & Row.

Michaelson, D., & Macleod, S. (2007). The application of "best practices" in public relations measurement and evaluation systems. *Public Relations Journal, 1*, 1–14.

Michaelson, D., & Stacks, D. W. (2017). *A professional and practitioner's guide to public relations research, measurement, and evaluation* (3rd edn). New York: Business Expert Press.

Michaelson, D., Wright, D. K., & Stacks, D. W. (2012). Evaluating efficacy in public relations/corporate communication programming: Towards establishing standards of campaign performance. *Public Relations Journal,* 6(5). Retrieved from http://www.instituteforpr.org/wp-content/uploads/Michaelson-Wright-Stacks-PR-Journal-2012-Vol-6-No-5.pdf

Neuman, W. R., Guggenheim, L., Jang, S. M., & Bae, S. Y. (2014). The dynamics of public attention: Agenda-setting theory meets big data. *Journal of Communication, 64*(2), 193–214.

Parks, M. R. (2014). Big data in communication research: Its contents and discontents. *Journal of Communication, 64*(2), 355–360.

Raacke, J., & Bonds-Raacke, J. (2008). MySpace and Facebook: Applying the uses and gratifications theory to exploring friend-networking sites. *Cyberpsychology and Behavior, 11*(2), 169–174.

Stacks, D. W. (2017). *Primer of public relations research* (3rd edn). New York: Guilford Press.

Stacks, D. W., & Bowen, S. A. (Eds.). (2013). *Dictionary of public relations measurement and research* (3rd edn). Gainesville, FL: Institute for Public Relations.

Stacks, D. W., & Michaelson, D. (2010). *A practitioner's guide to public relations research, measurement, and evaluation.* New York: Business Expert Press.

Stacks, D. W., Wright, D. K., & Bowen, S. A. (2014). IBM's Smart Planet Initiative: Building a more intelligent world. In J. Turk, J. Valin, & J. Paluszek (Eds.), *Public relations cases from around the world* (pp. 1–22). New York: Peter Lang.

Voit, L. (n.d.) Participation, openness, conversation, community, connectedness... Yes that's what social media is all about! Retrieved from http://www.leskovarlm.com/participation-openness-conversation-community-connectedness-yes-thats-what-social-media-is-all-about

Weiner, M. (2006). *Unleashing the power of PR: A contrarian's guide to marketing and communication.* San Francisco, CA: IABC.

Weller, K., Bruns, A., Burgess, J. E., Mahrt, M., & Puschmann, C. (Eds.). (2013). *Twitter and society.* New York: Peter Lang.

Wrench, J. S., Thomas-Maddox, C., & Richmond, V. P. (2008). *Quantitative research methods for communication: A hands-on approach (4th edn).* New York: Oxford University Press.

Index

action plan for national tobacco control program 2015–2018, 55
Affordable Care Act (ACA), 147–148
communication struggles after ACA becoming law, 148–149
president (*See also* Obama, Barack; president (US))
communication advantages and limitations, 149–150
marketing and new media, 150
Tea Party movement, 148
agenda-setting theory, 278–279
air force strategic communication, 116–117
All-Russian Congress of Patients, 325
American Association for the Advancement of Science, 232
American Association of University Women, 347
American Family Association (AFA), 280
Analysis on the Provincial Organization of Central Administration (1966) report, 47
anti-mining movement, 19–20
anti-tobacco campaign:
passive smoking, 54–55
smoke-free air zone campaign, 54
smoking is regret, 55
"your life, your choice" slogan, 55
Arctic National Wildlife Refuge, 236
Arrythmia, 321
audience-centered model, 228

BASIC model, 362, 363*f*
behavioral perspective model (BPM), 249
belief communities. *See* religious and belief communities
Bell-Boeing CV-22 and the Mosque, 131–132
Between Two Ferns, 149, 151, 160
big data, 366, 371
biosecurity, 194
Board of Animal Health (BOAH), 195, 198, 199, 201, 204
British American Tobacco (BAT), 341
business:
civil society, 170
communication practices in health, 328–329
Business Start Up Center Monrovia, 167

Camp Fire in Northern California (2018), 211
CAUSE model:
A in CAUSE: lack of awareness
hypotheses on gaining awareness, 238
steps to gain awareness, 235–238
C in CAUSE: lack of confidence in communicators, 230–231
hypotheses on earning confidence, 234
steps for earning confidence, 232–234

The Handbook of Strategic Communication, First Edition. Edited by Carl H. Botan.

E in CAUSE: motivate enactment, 249–250
hypotheses, 251
steps for motivation, 250–251
fundamental goals or aims, 229–230
imperfection, 230
limitations, 252
persuasion, 230
reference discourse, 230
rhetorical or communication situations, 230
risk communication, 229
self-expressive discourse, 230
S in CAUSE: support for decision-making
benefits, costs, workability, 246
effectiveness of solutions and one's own abilities, doubts about, 246
hypotheses, 249
likelihood and severity of harm, 246
social sanction, 245
stakeholders' decision-making, steps for supporting, 246–248
theoretical context, 229–231
U in CAUSE: deepening understanding
by addressing emotional and social barriers, 243–244
analogies, 241–243
hypotheses concerning to climate change, 244–245
mental models, 238
narratives, 240–241
steps: address cognitive sources of confusion, 239–240
text and graphic cues, 240
Central Government Organization Research Project (CGORP) report (1963), 47
Central Intelligence Agency, 139
Chairman of the Joint Chief of Staff (CJCS):
SC definition by, 116
channels, 238
character assassination (CA), 76, 86–87
cocreation
as foundation of subversive internet campaigns, 81–82
model of SC, 79
perspective, 78–79
subversive campaigns as cocreational practice, 79–80
Kompromat
dual nature of, 82–83
wild card of Navalny's campaigns, as, 84–85
Rybkagate case, 85
sociocultural paradigm, 77–78
Chief of Staff of the Air Force (CSAF), 116
civil society, 165–166
described, 167–168
Ebola crisis in Liberia
civil society groups, 167
communication network, 166–167
community radio stations, 167
media, 166
FFST, 174–175
historic roots, 168
interactants in, 168
participants, 169–170
business community, 170
government officials, 170
individuals, 169
international organizations (INGOs), 169
media, 170
NGOs, 169
non-profit organizations (NPOs), 169
societal institutions, 169
political process, treated as, 168
SC role in, 170–171
contested issues, 171
openness to arguments, 171
relationships or linkages, 171
statements and counter statements, systems for acting on, 172
trusted communication channels, 171
social capital and, 173–174
trust, and, 172–173
classical dialogic theory, 34
climate change communication:
audience-centered model, 228
democratic model, 229
dialogic model, 228–229
economic impacts, 226
science communication (*See* science communication)
climate matters program, 247
cocreational approach:
CA (*See* character assassination (CA))
challenges of using, 266–269
counterterrorism (*See* counterterrorism)
diverse publics, communicative relationships among, 267
health organizations, 70–71
IJC and LOSLR Study Board
confusing directives, 267–268
right participants, finding, 268
shift in study goals, 268
IJC and publics
diverse communication resources, 267
politicization of study, 266–267
relationships prior to study, 266
Norwegian road tunnels (*See* Norwegian road tunnels)
recommendations for using
during EPP strategic initiative, 270–271
EPP strategic initiative, prior to undertaking an, 269–270
scientists and publics, 269
SMCC model (*See* social-mediated crisis communication (SMCC))

cocreational communication (Turkey):
  BİMER, 52–53
  CIMER, 53
  citizens, 50–53
  communication campaign for prevention of use of tobacco and tobacco products, 54–55
    Action Plan for National Tobacco Control Program 2015–2018, 55
    anti-tobacco campaign, 54–55
    non-prohibitive and integrative approach, 55
  e-Government Gateway, 52
  Ethics Committee for Civil Servants, 51–52
  JDP, 49
  Ministry of the Interior Open Door Project, 53
  Ombudsman Institution, 52
  professionalization of public relations campaigns in public administration, 54–55
  Right to Information Act, 51
  TIBA, 49–50
cocreational model:
  background, 9
  core role of communication, 25–26
  definition of SC, 24–25
  molecule metaphor, 10–12
  publics at center, 26–27
  scholarship, 9–10
cocreational molecule, 10–12
cocreational scholarship, 9–10
communication:
  CA (*See* character assassination (CA))
  cocreational perspective on Norwegian road tunnels, 104
  evacuation, facilitating, 105
communitas, 175
communities, 19
  extractive industries defined, 22
  gender, 298
community-based interventions, 316
community competence, 218
construct validity, 368
consultas comunitarias, 26
content validity, 368
co-orientation, 104–105
corporate social responsibility (CSR), 344
  extrinsic motives, 344–345
  tactics and target stakeholder groups
    arts/education communities and journalists, sponsorship for, 346
    environmental/social issues in partnership with NGOs, 346
    women, 347
    youth smoking prevention campaign, 347
corporate social responsibility (CSR) programs, 20–21
counterterrorism, 91–92
  START (*See* Study of Terrorism and Responses to Terrorism (START))
  US war on terror, 93–95
  war metaphor, 92–93
crisis communication, 61–62
  channel obsession, 188–189, 191
  diffused publics, 64
  digital age, 187
  digital communication, 189–190
  digital platforms, 181–182
  early crisis communication articles, 182
  enabling publics, 64
  functional publics, 64
  goal defined, 62
  guidance, 190
  image repair theory, 63
  image restoration strategies, 184*t*
  infectious disease outbreaks (IDOs), 67–68
  initial practitioner writings, 182–183
  normative publics, 64
  organization, 191
  from organization-focused to publics-based approaches to, 63–64
  primary publics, 64, 65
  private-facing aspects
    monitoring, 186
    organizational and operational crises, 187
  public defined, 63
  reputation, 191
  rhetoric influences emerging crisis communication theory, 183–184
  secondary publics, 64
  situational crisis communication theory, 63
  SMCC (*See* social-mediated crisis communication (SMCC))
  social media crisis, 187
  speed, 187–188
  stakeholders, 191
  strategic communication and, 62
  theory and cognition, 184
  Twitter, 189
criterion-related validity, 368
critical race theory (CRT), 294–295
culture-centered approach (CCA), 317
culture-centered interventions, 317
culture change, communicating:
  DADT, 123–124
  DoD and its services, 122–123
  homosexuals, 123–124
  LGBT community, 123
  sexual orientation, 122–123

de facto measures *(medidas de hecho)*, 22
defense acquisition process, 133, 133*f*
Defense Advanced Research Projects Agency, 138
defense industry:

Bell-Boeing CV-22 and the Mosque, 131–132
Central Intelligence Agency, 139
ethical considerations, 143
grand strategy (*See* grand strategy)
key publics
concentric circles, 136, 137*f*
Congress role, 137–138
domestic influencers and media, 140–142
external publics, 136
international and adjacent markets, 142
military services and other government agencies, 138–140
US government clients, 139, 140*f*
US government officials, 140
Lockheed Martin F-35 Joint Strike Fighter, criticism on, 130–131
SC and business
contributing to business outcomes, 132–133
defense acquisition process, 133
market-shaping, 133–134
SC role in, 135–136
Defense Intelligence Agency, 139
democratic dialogue, 104
democratic model, 229
dependent variable, 370
development communication, 23
dialogic communication, 24
activist organizations' relationship, 336, 348
cocreational definitions and, 67
tobacco control, 349, 350–353*t*
dialogic model, 228–229
dialogic strategic communication, 17–18
dialogic theory, 34
dialogue. *See also* rhetoric and dialogue
described, 32
dialogic theory, 34
features of, 34–35
interpersonal communication features, 34
principles, 33–34
dialogue committees *(mesas de diálogo)*, 20
digital communication:
crisis communication, 181, 187, 189–190
digital media:
religious and belief communities, 279–280
disasters. *See also* natural disasters
defined, 208
emergency management (*See* emergency management)
management, 212
vs. natural disasters, 209–211
SC in management of, 216–217
doctor–patient communication, 331–333
"Don't Ask, Don't Tell" (DADT), 123–124

Ebola, 211
Liberia, 166–167
outbreak crisis and social media, 68–71
case analysis, 69
case overview, 68–69
cocreational assessment, 70–71
health organizations, 68–69
Instagram, 69
Twitter, 69
e-Government Gateway, 52
elaboration likelihood model (ELM), 237, 313
electronic cigarettes (e-cigarettes), 340–343
emergency management:
communication functions
activities across five stages of crisis, 213, 214–215*t*
cognition, 216
crisis communication, 213, 215, 215*t*
dynamic inter-organizational system, 216
three Cs, 215
coordination, 212
emergency planning *vs.*, 213
FEMA, definition by, 211
mitigation phase, 212
phases of, 211–212, 212*f*
preparedness phase, 212
recovery phase, 212
Red Cross, 212
resilience, 217–218
response phase, 212
United States, in, 212
volunteer civilian groups, 212
emergency planning:
emergency management *vs.*, 213
emergency preparedness, 208
emergent self-organization, 208
environmental public participation (EPP), 262–263
cocreational approach
challenges of using, 266–269
recommendations for using, 269–271
communication processes and, 263–264
higher levels of involvement
collaborate, 264
empower, 264
involve, 263
low levels of involvement
consult, 263
inform, 263
equality narrative, 296
Esquipulas Accords, 18
evidence-based stories, 236–237
excellence model, 363–364
excellence pyramid, 363, 364*f*
explanatory timeline model, 105–107, 106*f*

Facebook, 26, 102, 150, 151, 201, 280, 300

dialogic communication and measures, 350–353*t*
health campaigns, 312
research in SC, 371
face validity, 368
Family Smoking Prevention and Tobacco Control Act (Tobacco Control Act), 337
F/A-18 Super Hornet fighter jet, 138
feminist theory, 294
F-35 Joint Strike Fighter. *See* Lockheed Martin F-35 Joint Strike Fighter
floods, 210, 211
focus groups, 369
food and drug administration (FDA), 337, 341–343
fully functioning society theory (FFST), 40, 174–175
Fund of Public Opinion data, 327
Future Years Defense Program, 121

Gary Hart scandal (1987), 77
gender in US:
Abercrombie & Fitch, confronting master narratives of, 300–302
case example, 300–302
(re)conceiving framework for SC
equity and organizational accommodation, 299
identity, 298
professional development and community outcomes, 299
societal community, 298
socioecological model, 297, 298*f*
CRT, 294–295
gender and feminist theory, 294
master narratives guiding SC
diversity and equality, 296
individualism and autonomy, 296
reputation repair, 297
queer theory, 295–296
SC and publics, 292–293
generalized trust, 173
geopolitical strategic communication, 118–120
global precipitation climatology project, 235
global tobacco control initiatives, 337
global warming, 231
Goldwater-Nichols Department of Defense Reorganization Act (1986), 116
government communication practices:
Russian health, 323–324
government officials, 20, 83, 84, 116, 234
military, 123
as partners in civil society, 170
US, 140
grand strategy, 8
cocreational, 135
collaborative or partnership, 135
defined, 114
integrated, 135
intransigent, 134
military, 115–116
resistant, 134
grayzone conflict, 125–126
green behaviors, 247
greenhouse effect, 241
greenhouse gases, 241
Guatemala, 18–19
conflicts, 18–19
socioenvironmental conflict, 19–23, 27–28
strategic communication (SC)
cocreational definition, 24–25
for conflict management, 20–21
core role, 25–26
dialogue and participation, 23–27
failure of, 21–23
publics at the center, 26–27
Headquarters Air Force Space Command Public Affairs (AFSPC/PA), 121
health campaigns, 309–310
process
appeal, 314–315
community, role of, 312
formative research, role of, 311–312
message and channel, 312–313
source of message, 313–314
strategic elements, 310–311
scholarship, innovations and new directions in
community-based interventions, 316
critical approaches to campaigns, 316–317
culture-centered interventions, 317
internationalizing health campaigns, 316
technology-based interventions, 315–316
health communication, 10
health crisis communication, 67–68
health organizations:
cocreational assessment of Ebola crisis communication by, 70–71, 70*t*
heattrapping gases, 241–242
heterosexuality, 295
highly pathogen avian influenza (HPAI):
described, 195
IDEA model, explanation through
actions, 203–204
distribution, 200–201
explanation, 201–203
internalization, 198–200, 204
Iowa, 205
Minnesota, 205
United States, 195

House Armed Services Committee, Subcommittee on Strategic Forces (HASC-SF), 121, 122
human behavior:
described, 103
in fire emergencies, 105–107
explanatory timeline model, 105–107, 106*f*
RSET model, 105, 106*f*
human-generated disasters:
biosecurity, 194
crisis communication as strategic action, 195–196
action-based message, 197
deliberate communication practice, 195–196
IDEA model, 197
productive bias toward action, 196–197
emergency preparation and response, 194–195
HPAI crisis explanation through IDEA model, 198–204
productive bias toward action
action as emergent, 196
emergent action as participative communication, 196–197
strategic turn, 196
Hurricane Maria in Puerto Rico, 211
hybrid warfare, 125

identity defined, 298
image repair strategies (IRT), 183, 184
image repair theory, 63
image restoration strategies, 184*t*
independent variable, 370
in-depth interviews, 369
Indiana:
HPAI crisis (*See* highly pathogen avian influenza (HPAI))
Indiana Department of Homeland Security (DHS), 195
Indiana's State Poultry Association, 200
Indian Ocean tsunami (2004), 211
individualism, 296
infectious disease outbreaks (IDOs), 67
Ebola (*See* Ebola)
infographics, 237
information, 37
crisis, 67, 70–72, 182
defined, 7
Ebola crisis, 70, 71
strategic, 7
initial practitioner writings, 182–183
insta-doctors, 326–327
Instagram, 69
instrumental communication in public administration in Turkey (1980s and 1990s), 47–48
market policies, 48
press and public relations offices, 48
Prime Ministry Public Relations Department, 48–49
television, 49
internalization, distribution, explanation, and action (IDEA) model, 197
action, 205
disease recognition and reporting, 203
line of separation, 203–204
preparedness, 204
distribution, 200
conference calls, 201
door-to-door visit, 201, 205
traditional media, 201
explanation, 201–202
capitalizing on previous experience, 202
human risk, 202–203
HPAI crisis explanation
actions, 203–204
distribution, 200–201
explanation, 201–203
internalization, 198–200
internalization, 204
collaboration, 198–199
local focus, 199
targeted messaging, 199–200
International Lake Ontario-St. Lawrence (LOSLR) case study:
IJC and LOSLR Study Board, 267–268
phase I (2000–2005), 264–265
phase II (2006–2008), 265
phase III (2007–2016), 265–266
International League of Conservation Photographers, 236
international organizations (INGOs), 169, 176
interval data, 366–367
Iowa:
HPAI outbreaks, 195, 199, 200, 202, 204, 205
irregular warfare (IW) defined, 125

Japan Tobacco International (JTI), 347
Joint Functional Component Command for Space Public Affairs (JFCC Space/PA), 121
Journal of Public Relations Research, 348
Justice and Development Party (JDP), 49

Kompromat of Russian politics:
dual nature, 82–83
Russia defined, 83
wild card of Navalny's campaigns, as, 84–85

language, 36
League for Healthcare Consumer Rights Protection (Russia), 326
Liberia:
- Ebola crisis in, 166–167

Lithuanian Jewish Community (LJC):
- framing and website strategies and techniques, 281–282
  - activist organizations, 282
  - diagnostic framing, 282
  - four frames, 282–287
  - motivational framing, 282
  - prognostic framing, 282
  - website messages, 281–282
- history of Lithuanian Jews, 281
- website messages, 281–282, 287

Lockheed Martin F-35 Joint Strike Fighter, 130, 138
- stakeholder criticism, 131

marketing communication, 9
market-shaping:
- time-phasing, 134
- US Air Force Long Range Strike Bomber (LRS-B) competition, 133–134

master settlement agreement (MSA), 343
Mayan communities, 19, 22, 25–27
mean world syndrome, 31
media.*See also* social media
- advocacy, 348–349
- civil society, 170
- defense industry, 140–142

mega-crises, 211
mental models, 238
military, 113–114
- air force strategic communication, 116–117
- approach to SC, 114–115
- grand strategy defined, 114
- grayzone conflict, 125–126
- hybrid warfare, 125
- information inflow, 114
- information outflow, 114
- irregular warfare (IW), 125
- SC
  - case studies, 118–125
  - culture change, 122–125
  - defined, 114, 116
  - geopolitical, 118–120
  - space, for, 120–122
- strategy defined, 114
- terrorism, 125–126
- VEO threat, 125

Mining Law, 19
Ministry of the Interior Open Door Project, 53
Minnesota:
- HPAI outbreaks, 195, 199, 200, 202, 204, 205

modern dialogic theory, 34
monkey business, 77

National Academies of Science, Engineering, and Medicine (NASEM), 228, 252
National Academy of Science 2009, 228
National Dialogue System, 21
National Incident Management System (NIMS), 209, 212
National Organization of Women (NOW) Conference, 347
National Reconnaissance Office, 139
National Women's Commission of Liberia, 167
national youth tobacco survey (2019), 343
natural disasters, 219. *See also* disasters
- described, 208
- disaster defined, 208
- disasters *vs.*, 209–211
  - FEMA, disaster events identified as natural by, 210–211, 210*t*
  - human activities, 210
  - mega-crises, 211
  - US Geological Survey, 210
- emergency management (*See* emergency management)
- emergency preparedness, 208
- emergent self-organization, 208
- impacts, 218
- NIMS, 209
- post-traumatic growth, 218
- resilience, 217–218
- SC, 216
- values, 218
- WHO definition of, 209

Navalny's subversive campaigns, 84–85
New York Women's Agenda, 347
nominal data, 366
nongovernmental organizations (NGOs):
- civil society, 169
- environmental/social issues in partnership with, 346
- religious and belief communities, 273–274

nonparametric data, 367
non-profit organizations (NPOs), 169
North Atlantic Treaty Organization (NATO), 118–120
Norwegian Public Roads Administration (NPRA), 102, 103, 105, 108
Norwegian road tunnels, 102–103
- cocreational perspective on communication, 104
- co-orientation, 104–105
- evacuation, 102–103, 105
- functional perspective, 105
- human behavior in fire emergencies, 105–107
- risk communication, 103–104
- socially necessary information, 107–108
- worry and willingness to evacuate, 107

Obama, Barack, 147–151. *See also* president (US)
- ACA and public opinion, 152–155
- counter-narratives regarding Obama's character, 152

democrats *vs.* republicans, 154*t*
marketing of presidential character, 155–160
public opinion
ACA, regarding, 156*t*
and presidential approval, 153*t*
president Obama's character, regarding, 156–158*t*
uncertain about Obama's religion, 159*t*
Obamacare, 148–150, 160, 161
Office of the Secretary of Defense Public Affairs (OSD/PA), 121
one-size-fits-all approach, 228
Operation Desert Storm, 120
opinion leader, 54, 55, 170, 268, 269, 312, 316
climate change science, 233
public, 168, 271, 277, 279
ordinal data, 366

panic, 108
parametric data, 367
particularized trust, 172–173
patient-oriented health protection, 333
patients, 329
patient terrorism, 332
Peace Accords, 18
peace as viable option, 35–37
pharmacists, 329–330
Phillip Morris International (PMI), 343–348
Philosophy of right, 168
Presidency of the Republic of Turkey Directorate of Communications and Presidency Communications Center (CIMER), 53
president (US). *See also* Obama, Barack
communication advantages and limitations, 149–150
counter-narratives regarding Obama's character, 152
framing presidential character marketing and new media, 150
Presidential Dialogue Commission, 21
Prime Ministry Communications Center (BİMER), 52–53
Prison notebooks, 168
procreational molecule, 10
professional communication practices, 331–333
pseudo-activism, 344–347
public defined, 63
public interest advisory groups (PIAG), 264, 267–269
public relations in public administration in Turkey (1960s and 1970s):
Family Planning Campaign, 46
General Directorate for Family Planning, 46
SPT, 46
Public Relations Society of America, 299
publics:
diffused, 64
enabling, 64
functional, 64
normative, 64
primary, 64
secondary, 64

qualitative research, 369
quantitative research, 369–370
queer theory, 295–296

rapid assessment visual expedition (RAVE), 236
Rassvet, 326
ratio data, 367
Red Cross, 212
Red National Anti-Tobacco Network (RENATA), 354
Red-Tapism Program, 46
reference discourse, 230
relationship skills, 38
reliability, 367
religious and belief communities:
activism
organization maintenance, 276–277
rectify conditions, 277
advocacy function, 275
characteristics and NGOs, 274–275
community-building function, 275
expressive function, 275
framing theory, 277–279, 287
NGOs, 273–274
service function, 275
social and digital media
SNSs, 280
websites and email, 279–280
theoretical frameworks and techniques
activism, 276–277
framing theory, 277–279
social and digital media, 279–280
value guardian function, 275
Reorganization of Administration-Principles and Recommendations report (1971), 47
reputation repair, 297
research in SC:
BASIC model, 362, 363*f*
behavioral objectives, 362
campaign or program
developmental phase, 362–363
evaluation phase, 363
excellence model, 363–364
excellence pyramid, 363, 364*f*
refinement phase, 363
causality, 370
data
big data, 366
large data sets, 366
nonparametric, 367
parametric, 367
defined, 360
deliberate, 360
digital era, evaluation, and measurement in, 370–371
executed, 360

formal, 360
informal, 360
informational objectives, 361
motivational objectives, 361–362
objective types in SC campaigns, 361–362, 362*f*
planned, 360
qualitative, 369
quantitative, 369–370
secondary, 368–369
standardized approaches, 364–365
data, 366–367
measurement levels, 365–366
outputs, outtakes, and outcomes, 365
reliability, 367
validity, 367–368
resilience, 217–218
characteristics, 217
community, 217–218
response efficacy, 246
rhetorical theory, 33–34
rhetoric and dialogue. *See also* dialogue
described, 32
peace as viable option, 35–37
principles, 32–35
strategy *(strate-gia)*, 35–37
Right to Information Act, 51
risk communication, 103–104
analytical system, 104
democratic dialogue, 104
experiential system, 104
government agencies and experts, 103
RSET model, 105, 106*f*
Russia:
defined, 83
health communication (*See* Russian health communication)
Kompromat of Russian politics, 82–85
Navalny's subversive campaigns, 84–85
Rybkagate case, 85
Russian health communication, 320
activist practices, 324–325
business practices, 328–329
cocreating patient-oriented health protection, 323
communicators, 322
Competition in Healthcare, 326
croquet ground, 322–323
game field, 321
government practices, 323–324
health professionals and institutions, building relationships with, 331
institutional practices, 326–328
patient organizations, 325
patient-oriented health protection, 333–334
patient-oriented model, 322–323
patients, building relationships with, 329
pharmacists, building relationships with, 329–330
professional practices, 331–333
Rassvet, 326
Russian Multiple Sclerosis Society, 328
Russian patient organizations, 325
Russian Public Opinion Research Center, 327
Russian Union of Patients, 322, 325, 326
Rybkagate case, 85

science communication, 226–227
CAUSE model (*See* CAUSE model)
deficit model of, 227–228
disadvantages of deficit and technical models, 227–228
one-size-fits-all approach, 228
technical model, 227
secondary research, 368–369
Secretary of the Air Force (SecAF), 116
Secretary of the Air Force Public Affairs (SAF/PA), 121
self-efficacy, 246
sense-making, 105
situational crisis communication theory (SCCT), 63, 181
account acceptance, and, 185–186
crises types, 184
described, 184
ethical base response, and, 185
prescriptive recommendations from, 185*t*
stealing thunder concept, 186
social actors, 78
social capital, 169–171
civil society and, 173–174
social media, 150
advertising and circulation of misinformation
e-cigarettes, 341–342
vaping-related tweets, 342
YouTube, 342
advocacy, 348–349
channel obsession, 188–189
communicating infectious disease outbreak crises on, 67–68
crisis, 187
Ebola outbreak crisis and, 68–71
Obama, 150
religious and belief communities, 279–280
research in SC, 370–371
subversive campaigns, 80
vape/tobacco influencers (*See* vape/tobacco influencers)
social-mediated crisis communication (SMCC), 190
cocreational approach to, 66–67
model, 61, 64–65

primary publics, types of, 65
social networking sites (SNSs), 280
social sanction, 245
societal community, 298
societal institutions, 169
sociocultural paradigm:
CA, 77–78
space:
SC for, 120–122
Spanish flu, 210–211
stakeholders:
climate change science, 233–235
crisis communication, 191
Lockheed Martin F-35 Joint Strike Fighter, criticism on, 131
Stanford Community Studies, 312–313
State Planning Organization (SPT), 46
stealing thunder concept, 186
steering process, 50
strategic communication (SC):
CA (*See* character assassination (CA))
characteristics, 7
cocreational definition, 24–25
cocreational model, 79
concepts and terms, 6–9
core role of, 25–26
counterterrorism (*See* counterterrorism)
crisis communication research and, 62
defense industry (*See* defense industry)
defined, 7, 135, 293
in disaster management, 216–217
disasters (*See* disasters)
gender in US(*See* gender in US)
Guatemala (*See* Guatemala)
health (*See* health campaigns)
HPAI crisis (*See* highly pathogen avian influenza (HPAI))
information, 7
military (*See* military)
natural disasters (*See* natural disasters)
relationship between grand strategy, strategy, and tactics, 8–9
religious and belief communities, in (*See* religious and belief communities)
research (*See* research in SC)
strategy and tactics, 8
tobacco control (*See* tobacco control)
Turkish public sector (*See* Turkish public sector)
Strategic communication theory and practice, 99
strategic information, 7
strategy defined, 114
strengths, weaknesses, opportunities, and threats (SWOT) analysis model, 117
student environmental action showcase, 252
Study of Terrorism and Responses to Terrorism (START), 92, 96–97
described, 97
educational hub on terrorism, as, 98
mission *vs.* vision statement, 98
questions about terrorism, 98
subversive campaigns:
anti-ethos rhetoric, 79–80
digital, 80
SC, 80
social media, 80
strategic attacker, 80
subversive internet campaigns:
activist and social movement campaigns, 81
activist stakeholders, 82
smartphones and mobile applications, 82

Tea Party movement, 148
technology-based interventions, 315–316
telemedicine, 333
terrorism, 91–92, 125–126
defined, 95
framing, 95–96
social and economic capital disparity, 96
"The Battle Above" report, 121
The Long Now (TLN), 38
collective action, 38
FFST, 40
long-view projects, 39
principles of, 39–40
relationship skills, 38
strategic communication activities, 39–40
The theory of communicative action, 168
TLN.*See* The Long Now (TLN)
tobacco control, 336–337
advocacy (*See* tobacco control advocacy)
corporate social responsibility and pseudo-activism, 344–347
global tobacco control initiatives, 337
regulations in US, 337tobacco industry (*See* tobacco industry)
trust, decrease in, 341
tobacco control advocacy:
communication, 348–355
dialogic communication, 349, 350–353*t*
information technology, interactive use of, 349
media advocacy, 348–349
village approach and collaborative advocacy, 349, 354–355
emerging tobacco products and challenges, 340–341
and new challenges, 337–340
organizations, 338–340*t*
village approach and collaborative advocacy, 349, 354–355
Tobacco Control Framework Convention, 54–55
tobacco industry:
SC and social media

advertising and misinformation circulation, 341–342
vape/tobacco influencers, 342–343
strategies to interfere in tobacco control, 345*t*
transformative explanations, 243
trust:
civil society and, 172–173
generalized, 173
particularized, 172–173
tsunami (2004), 211
Turkish Industry and Business Association (TIBA), 49–50
Turkish public sector:
cocreational communication (from 2000s till today), 49–55
instrumental communication (1980s to 1990s), 47–49
public relations (1960s and 1970s), 45–47
Twitter, 69, 70, 150
crisis communication, 189
dialogic communication and measures, 350–353*t*
health campaigns, 312
research in SC, 371

United States (US):
emergency management, 212
gender (*See* gender in US)
HPAI crisis, 195
military (*See* military)
START (*See* Study of Terrorism and Responses to Terrorism (START))
war on terror, 93–95
United States Conference of Catholic Bishops (USCCB), 278
United States Department of Agriculture (USDA), 195, 199, 201, 204
University Corporation for Atmospheric Research (UCAR), 241, 242
US Department of Agriculture Veterinary Services (USDA-VS), 195
US Department of Defense (DoD), 113, 115, 116, 119, 121–124
US Department of Homeland Security (DHS), 96–97
US Federal Emergency Management Agency (FEMA):
disaster events identified as natural by, 210–211, 210*t*
four phases of emergency management, 212*f*
US National Defense Strategy (NDS), 115–117, 119
US National Security Space Strategy, 121
US National Security Strategy (NSS), 115, 116
US Strategic Command Public Affairs (USSTRATCOM/PA), 121

vape/tobacco influencers:
youth/kids, impact on, 343
YouTube, 342–343
violent extremist organization (VEO) strategy, 125
volunteer civilian groups, 212

Warsaw Pact, 120
White House Twitter, 150
women, 347
Women's Studies in Communication, 294
World Health Organization (WHO):
Ebola outbreak crisis, 68–71
emergency management, 212
natural disasters defined by, 209
World Health Organization Framework Convention on Tobacco Control (WHO-FCTC), 337, 338, 344, 347

YMCA, 167
youth smoking prevention campaign, 347
YouTube, 85, 134, 149, 150, 151, 280, 342–344